The Orthodox Church

The Orthodox Church

An Introduction to its History, Doctrine, and Spiritual Culture

JOHN ANTHONY McGUCKIN

© 2008 by John Anthony McGuckin

BLACKWELL PUBLISHING
350 Main Street, Malden, MA 02148-5020, USA
9600 Garsington Road, Oxford OX4 2DQ, UK

The right of John Anthony McGuckin to be identified as the author of this work has been asserted in accordance with the UK Copyright, Designs, and Patents Act 1988.

First published 2008 by Blackwell Publishing Ltd

1   2008

Library of Congress Cataloging-in-Publication Data

McGuckin, John Anthony.
   The Orthodox Church : an introduction to its history, doctrine, and spiritual culture / John Anthony McGuckin.
      p. cm.
   Includes bibliographical references and index.
   ISBN 978-1-4051-5066-8 (hardcover : alk. paper) 1. Orthodox Eastern Church. I. Title.

BX320.3.M34 2008
281.9—dc22

                                    2007049377

A catalogue record for this title is available from the British Library.

Set in 10/12pt Minion
by SPi Publisher Services, Pondicherry, India
Printed and bound in Singapore
by Utopia Press Pte Ltd

The publisher's policy is to use permanent paper from mills that operate a sustainable forestry policy, and which has been manufactured from pulp processed using acid-free and elementary chlorine-free practices. Furthermore, the publisher ensures that the text paper and cover board used have met acceptable environmental accreditation standards.

For further information on
Blackwell Publishing, visit our website at
www.blackwellpublishing.com

For Bill and Maria Spears
two extraordinary patrons of Orthodox theology in the New World

Contents

Preface

In the course of my own winding, pilgrim's, road to Orthodoxy it was the tangible sense of beauty that served as a constant allure. It was the radiant kindness of a few luminous souls, several of them bishops and priests, that made flesh for me what I had been searching for, not so much the zealotry that many were eager to offer me as their witness to the truth. Years later I came across a saying of St Symeon the New Theologian to the effect that a candle can only be lit from the flame of another living candle, and it struck me as exactly apposite. When Truth is a living person, we can no longer try to make it synonymous with mere accuracy. What is at stake is more a question of authenticity. Orthodoxy is often approached by those outside it as a system of doctrines. But it is far more than this, and this is why a book of systematic theology does not quite capture the reality. Orthodoxy is the living mystery of Christ's presence in the world: a resurrectional power of life. It cannot be understood, except by being fully lived out; just as Christ himself cannot be pinned down, analysed, digested, or dismissed, by the clever of this world, whom he seems often to baffle deliberately.[1] His message is alive in the world today as much as when he first preached it. The Orthodox Church is, essentially, his community of disciples trying to grow into his image and likeness, by their mystical assimilation to the Master who abides among them.

This book is an attempt to explain that mystery of church in a variety of approaches: theological, historical, liturgical, spiritual, political, and moral. The union of all these avenues is difficult to effect intellectually, but is much easier to accomplish organically. Indeed it is clear that the Christian life itself, in its deepest and most authentic manifestations, is exactly a matter of this synthesis: this 'coming together' or 'coming home' that is sought after as the life of virtue that brings peace to the soul and the mind. The Fathers of the Church tended to refer to the Christian faith as 'our philosophy', which exactly caught the aspect of Christianity as a fundamental lifestyle; a way of being, as much as a way of thinking. This book, then, has been designed to assist Orthodox to a renewed appreciation of their faith, at once 'ever ancient and ever new', as well as to introduce it in a way that could be of benefit to readers who are not overly familiar with Orthodox life and practice. The book's imagined readership is a double one: English-speaking readers who have come to Orthodoxy by the grace of God and wish to learn more of their own tradition; and those who have an ecumenical interest in the

Orthodox Church, and wish to question it about a range of concerns. I hope this volume will serve as a useful dialogue partner on the pilgrimage trails of each of its readers.

The book is deeply concerned with theological doctrine, but not to the exclusion of other important matters. There are some very good treatises of Orthodox theology available.[2] A common denominator among them is that they are all heavily based on the Scriptures and the Fathers,[3] and I hope that this study will also pass that litmus test. It has been arranged in three chief divisions: the historical context of the church in its long pilgrimage (chapter 1), the theological task proper, namely the doctrine of God (chapters 2 and 3), and finally the several aspects of the economy of salvation; that is, the impact of God's Kingdom in the world, and among the communion of the saints (chapters 4 through 7).

I am grateful to the Henry Luce III Foundation of America for its generous award of the Luce Fellowship in 2006 which allowed me the space to complete such a large project. I am also indebted to a number of readers, all of them skilled commentators in Orthodox theology and ecclesiastical affairs, and friends of long standing, whose advice, disagreements, and encouragement have helped me make this better than it was. Orthodox faith is one and harmonious. It is my trust that this book conforms to that unity of the faith. Such was my constant intention. Orthodox culture, however, is, like any family: subject to many discussions, and often loud disagreements, over the interpretation of many things. My brothers and sisters who have dialogued with me are examples of how such a conversation can be conducted in love and mutual respect, for the greater clarification of the truth. It is a rare charism in a loud and aggressively superficial world.

Fr. John A. McGuckin
Feast of St Basil the Great
New York, 2007

Notes

1 Matt. 11.25.
2 Beginning with the two most outstanding patristic exemplars: St Gregory of Nazianzus' *Five Theological Orations*, and St John of Damascus' *Orthodox Faith*, both of which are accessible online. In terms of modern literature one can think of Staniloae (1998, 2005), Popovitch (1997), Pomazansky (1997), Tsirpanlis (1991), Lossky (1978), and Yannaras (1991) as six easily accessible examples in differing tonalities, and with varying depths of profundity.

3 A word that designates the early generations of saints and theologians (often bishops) who defended the Orthodox faith and articulated its inner spirit.

Illustrations

Abbreviations

LXX   Septuagint
OCA   Orthodox Church in America
PG   *Cursus Completus Patrologiae Graecae*, ed. J. P. Migne, 162 vols. Paris: Garnier, 1857–66
PL   *Cursus Completus Patrologiae Latinae*, ed. J. P. Migne, 222 vols. Paris: Garnier, 1844–64
ROCOR   Russian Orthodox Church Outside of Russia
SCOBA   Standing Conference of Orthodox Bishops in America

Note on Sources

Patristic Writings

Throughout this book there are extensive references to patristic writers and texts from the early Christian centuries. Readers will find a guide to the authors, the contents of major treatises, and the availability of the best editions and translations in J. A. McGuckin, *The A–Z of Patristic Theology* (London: Student Christian Movement, 2005), and J. Quasten, *Patrology*, vols. 1–3 (Antwerp: Spectrum, 1972–5).

Psalm Numbering

Orthodoxy follows the psalm numbering of the Septuagint (Greek) Bible, whereas the Western world, by and large, follows the numbering of the Hebrew Bible. Roman Catholicism used to follow the Septuagintal system, but (except in liturgical altar-books) has now largely gone over to the Hebrew numeration. The table of equivalence is as follows:

Greek Septuagint	Hebrew
1–8	1–8
9	9–10
10–112	11–113
113	114–15
114–15	116
116–45	117–46
146–7	147
148–50	148–50

For most of the psalms, then, the LXX numbering will be one psalm behind the Hebrew. The LXX also frequently begins the verse numbering with the psalm title (if it is more than a few words long), which in the Hebrew is not counted as part of the verses. In such cases verse 1 in the Hebrew numbering system will be verse 2 in the LXX.

Introduction
Strange Encounters

The Orthodox (generally) do not regard themselves as exotic. If they have come to Orthodoxy from other forms of Western Christian tradition, or from secular atheism, they often are tempted to regard themselves as exotic for a while, but it soon wears off. Apparently, however, many external observers do still retain that perspective, and it can often tempt the Orthodox to live up to it by 'posing' as exotic: a dangerous state of affairs which postcolonial theory has put its finger on already as 'subalternism', or that state where a small group with a residual minority consciousness tries to live up to expectations foisted on it by the dominant hegemonic powers of the age.[1] The Christian Orthodox, as they have been encountered relatively rarely, 'in the flesh', in the ordinary experience of most Western Christians, are certainly a 'strange encounter'. The root presuppositions, and the basic style of worship and attitude that are so familiar in many forms of Western Christian practice, seem different here. If the Orthodox feature in the public eye of the media at all, it is usually with a view to the 'strange' rituals of a church that has a very ancient liturgical style, and often uses languages that outsiders do not remotely understand.

The temptation to categorize the Eastern Orthodox as romantically exotic is a powerful one, and is often a fate wished on them by those who hold them in kind regard and who value many of the things Orthodoxy represents in Christian history, such as faithfulness to tradition, endurance under suffering, and reverence in worship. Those who are less enamoured of Orthodoxy look at it from the perspective of their own philosophies, ideologies, and orthodoxies, and sometimes censure it as reactionary, exclusive, patriarchal, rigid in its doctrines and liturgy. Rarely, however, do either its critics who dislike it, or its non-Orthodox friends who cherish it,[2] have much awareness of the wider context of what an Orthodox articulation of the church and society would be on its own terms. This book tries to set out such a vision. It is offered as a sustained essay in Orthodox history, theology, and culture, and offered as much to the Orthodox reader who wishes to enter into a discussion of his or her own tradition as it is to a general reader who might simply wish to gain a deeper understanding of where the Orthodox came from, and what they claim to represent.

But running throughout all the sections of this book is the message that 'exotic, the Orthodox Church is not'; rather, it is a full-blooded community of the faithful who have their feet planted firmly in the earth, and their eyes raised joyfully to heaven. In its own understanding it is simply the catholic heart of the Christian witness; not peripheral but at the very core of the Christian endurance throughout history. Notions of 'Eastern' or 'Western' Christianity have often been far too heavily overdone in the past. Is Russia the 'East' any more? Is Greece, any longer, a journey too far for a 'Western' traveller? Those terms 'Western Christianity' and 'Eastern Christianity' have been retained in these pages as convenient shorthand for distinguishing Orthodox forms of thought from the more familiar Roman Catholic and Protestant worlds of discourse that have so massively dominated English-language Christian literature to date. But the present author is always lost for words (a rare state of affairs) whenever anyone asks him to speak as an 'Eastern Christian'. Being an Irish, English-born, Romanian Orthodox priest teaching and ministering in America may not be a very common position; but it is surely not an unusual state of affairs any more to have an ethnic and cultural weave of many different colours in our histories, minds, and hearts in this era of the global village. This book is an attempt to present Orthodoxy in such a way that English-speaking readers may be able to gain a sense of an ancient theological tradition that does not see itself as 'strange' or 'closed off' or as 'having nothing to say to postmodernity', but one that has only relatively recently been released from a long nightmare of oppression, and which will, in the immediate future, be a voice that will be raised again in the counsels of world Christianity.

Because of the nature of this book as a 'learned introduction', sometimes I have had to cover immense ground very quickly. This leads to a species of didactic writing that is necessary if one wishes to draw up an honest guide to the terrain, but is a difficult medium to make shine. If one stops too long and discusses the depth and detail of history, it would become something wholly other than an introduction. This aspect of the book, what we could call the mode of the 'Grand Levantine Tour', is nonetheless important for what it reveals about our general presuppositions about things. How obsessively, it seems, all available church history has been written out of the Reformation experience. Orthodoxy did not know there had been a Reformation until the late seventeenth century. It is still true to say that it sees more or less nothing through the lens of that experience. Its view of the history of the church still tends to be dominated by older constructs: who was it that was oppressing us yesterday, and what was it about this time? I am not saying that this is a good thing, necessarily. The aftermath of extensive persecutions (and Orthodoxy has suffered considerably and relentlessly in the course of the last five centuries, most especially in the last one) often marks the survivors with deep traumas that need generations of sunlight to heal. I am saying only that it makes for a very different perspective on what really matters in telling a history of the church: endurance, community, and shared story.

Another thing that one learns very quickly about English-language books on Orthodoxy (not that the bookstores are overloaded with them, one has to say) is that they are relatively recent, and almost inevitably written by non-Orthodox scholars. There are only four written by cradle Orthodox that I can think of immediately: those of Meyendorff, Bulgakov, Zankov, and Zernov, all Russians coming out of the diaspora scattered as a result of the Soviet revolution. They try to offer a general introduction, mainly aimed at non-Orthodox who want a broadly based guide to the Orthodox world. In the geographical and social context from which they originate, that means they were written chiefly to imaginary audiences from the Anglican (Episcopalian) or

Roman Catholic worlds, and were often concerned to present Orthodox ideas 'in terms of their differences' from post-Reformation contexts. In contrast, I have here been more concerned to speak simply as an Orthodox, and not worry too much about how other traditions have approached things, knowing that the bookstores are indeed groaning with their articulations on their own terms. His Grace Bishop Kallistos Ware's popular book on Orthodoxy set a new bar when it first appeared in 1963. Written primarily to explain Orthodoxy to the outside, it has since become a cherished vade mecum for almost all English-speaking Orthodox, who have often had great difficulty accessing balanced and cultured discussions of their faith and history.

Nevertheless, the majority of scholarly 'Introductions to Orthodoxy' in the English language have not been written by Orthodox at all, but by learned Roman Catholic clergy. Invariably these demonstrate two warring principles in the breast of their authors: the first a deep respect for the Eastern Church and its venerable customs and catholic spirituality; the second a progressive impatience with the Orthodox, mounting at times to a barely concealed desire to castigate them for their indifference to the advances of the early stirrings of Catholic ecumenism. Here, I am speaking especially of the first forty years of the twentieth century, before matters changed dramatically after the Second Vatican Council. Some of these books remain as valuable sources, but they are now showing their age, and their biases.

This introduction, therefore, tries to do something different; something, I hope, that is new and valuable, in so far as that is possible in what sets out to be a faithful iteration of what it is to be Orthodox. This approach to the subject is heavily invested in theological investigations. It is biblical and patristic in tonality (how could it not be if it were to be Orthodox?), but it is not solely an essay in the history of theology but always an attempt to see how the living word of the evangelists, apostles, and Fathers can speak to the present moment, in and through the experience of the Orthodox. It is a theology written from the perspective of how Christianity functions as a way of life, as a progressive seduction into beauty and simplicity.

Christian Orthodoxy, as it once more emerges into a public role in eastern Europe, and grows deeper roots in western Europe, Oceania, and America, is faced with many problems, not few of which derive from the lack of functioning theological schools for many generations past. In the context of a severe purge of leaders of intellectual acuity over the past generation, the Orthodox Church today is offered many temptations to take refuge in an authoritarianism learned from decades of hostile oppression, or to pose as the subaltern 'other' to the alleged norms of Roman Catholicism or Protestantism. I believe that both are ill-fitting responses: the first counteracts the Orthodox Church's potential role as a paradigmatic model for new freedoms and traditions of constructive, and open-ended engagement with a post-Christian society; the other betrays the Orthodox Church's spirit of catholic universality by the adoption of alien agendas, and subalternisms of various types, or the ill-advised encouragement of dangerous new nationalisms and ethnic phyletisms.

Then who is it that this book addresses? Well, in the first place: you who have this text in your hands, and have been brought to it not accidentally (for the Orthodox do not believe in such a notion) but by the gracious providence of the Lord of Wisdom who delights in discussion, learning, and mutual enlightenment. My 'proposed readership' is a pastoral audience of English-speaking Orthodox, and those Christian men and women of good will who are interested in understanding more of Orthodoxy, and in entering into fruitful dialogue with it, in an age of relativities and secularism that have weakened a divided Christendom. The potential vocation of Orthodoxy to facilitate mutual dialogue between the divided churches of the West is a motive that has not been far from my mind.

Throughout its long history, and especially so in times when it was free and had assets, and could design its own programmes of outreach, Orthodoxy has always been a church that has valued communion, communication, freedom, and developmental initiatives to reshape the Gospel *kerygma* in terms accessible to contemporary culture. This deeply evangelical sensitivity has consistently renewed Orthodoxy after long seasons of political and economic decline or social reversals. In the present era, when I hope the Orthodox churches are emerging from recent nightmares into a 'New Spring', this book may help to enable the wonderful conversations that could result for the glory of the Lord and the extension of his blessed Kingdom among us.

Notes

1 For more see McGuckin 2005c.
2 And how much Orthodoxy in western Europe has been supported by the gracious help of the Anglican Church is an untold story.

Chapter 1

The Pilgrimage of the Orthodox through History

A BRIEF HISTORY OF THE ORTHODOX FROM THE APOSTOLIC ERA TO THE MIDDLE AGES

Perspectives of history

It is a basic premise of Orthodox theology that the history of Orthodoxy is synonymous with the history of the church. Historians may puzzle over that, thinking of all the concerns, developments, and controversies that constitute church history that seem to have no bearing on the history of the Orthodox (the Avignon Papacy, the Inquisition, the Reformation, the Oxford Movement, the ordination of women, to name only a few), but Orthodox generally regard the church world-wide up to the Middle Ages as 'their church', with divisions and separations only becoming a chronic and permanent state of affairs as the high medieval West introduced more and more patterns of behaviour that were in conflict with the ancient procedures, and doctrines, established in patristic times. The Orthodox, at large, see the Latin church of the first millennium to be substantially in harmony with the Orthodox tradition, so that there was one church only in its validly distinct Eastern and Western forms. Accordingly, the Orthodox to this day in countries such as England, Italy, or France honour the ancient saints of the local churches there as entirely Orthodox. The Orthodox, when they find Anglican or Catholic churches in Europe that contain the relics of the ancient saints, will usually make a point of going to venerate them (sometimes having some confusion when they find the holy reliquaries of fathers and martyrs set up in glass museum-cases in sacristies rather than upon the altars).

Ordinary readers may also find this understanding of the church's history a strange perspective because in so many of the commonly available church histories that one reads, the Orthodox Church hardly features. If it does make an appearance, for the period of the first 500 years, it mysteriously tails off into invisibility as the story of the rise of the medieval West is undertaken, something that tends to push away all else to the side. Most English-language church histories, if they were properly labelled, should admit that they are largely the history of the Western Church as it developed after the great shock wave of the Reformation. Because of this, Reformation apologetics still heavily condition the way the story of the church is told. Until the latter part of

5

the twentieth century the same attitude of neglect (and often scorn) attached itself to secular history of the eastern Roman empire. Byzantine studies, though now enjoying a revival, were traditionally looked down upon. Historians such as Gibbon and others following him had caricatured the history of the Greek Christian East as a long and dismal chronicle of barbarism and autocracy.

Both from the Roman Catholic viewpoint and from Protestant perspectives, Eastern Orthodox history was not something to linger over. For Roman Catholicism the Greek Orthodox (and all other Orthodox churches in communion with them) were stubborn schismatics who had always resisted the eirenic advances of Rome, and had thrown off Roman order and clarity. To Protestant critics the Orthodox were often seen as stranger versions of all that they hated in medieval Catholicism: relic veneration, icons, devotion to the saints and the Virgin Mary, sacraments, and priesthood. Each side of the Western Reformation divide saw the Orthodox through a distorting lens of its own concerns. From the viewpoint of the Orthodox, both forms of Western Christianity, Catholic and Reformed, seemed very much alike: two similar but variant forms of development of the same premises with the same styles of theologizing and closely related patterns of worship. Studies of the Orthodox Church by external commentators tended to resonate with those aspects of Orthodoxy that 'conformed' to their Western Catholic, or Protestant, expectations, depending on the ecclesial starting point, and allegiance, of the various authors.

This relative neglect, however, was not simply due to the vagaries of the European press. History had something to do with it too. As the story of the Western Church grew to the 'interesting point' of its early medieval ascendancy (the time princes of the church started to become real power-brokers in Western politics), so the history of the Christian East started a long twilight time, pressed and harried by the relentless westward advance of Islam. The Byzantine and Slavic Christian worlds, along with their own histories and perspectives on the Christian Church, simply did not fit the common picture, and so were easily ignored or fitted into the more dominant Western archetypes of historiography. Nevertheless, it is still something of a shock for Orthodox readers to find, in many religious education books in western European schools, phrases describing the Orthodox Church as a schismatic branch of Christendom that broke off union with the pope in the medieval period. Such a view may be part and parcel of a particular Roman ideology of church history, but it is, obviously, not a perspective that is acceptable to the Orthodox, either in terms of theology of the church, or in terms of simple accuracy in the historical record.

Orthodoxy does not give up the title 'catholic'. It regards itself as the catholic church (the marks of the church are to be one, holy, catholic, and apostolic) and catholicity in this sense demands that any Orthodox church cannot be Greek, Russian, Romanian, American, or English in its fundamental 'character', but on the contrary is fundamentally catholic and universal in its being and its spiritual ethos. Its national characteristics are legitimate variations of its catholicity, but must not obscure it. Orthodoxy in some parts began to call itself 'Greek Catholic'[1] in reaction to the way in which 'Roman Catholic' started to appear as a designation of the larger part of the Western Church; but these terms are not ancient, and not part of the original deposit of Christianity. Instead they show signs of the 'denominational' mentality that had grown up as part of post-Reformation apologetics in western Europe. When they speak of themselves the Orthodox never evoke denominationalism as a legitimate mark of church identity. For the Orthodox 'denominationalism' is the heart of ecclesiological heresy, and rises only out of the ruin of ecclesial order.

For many centuries the lack of regard for Orthodox history in the West did not much matter. The universities and schools of the Orthodox had been progressively reduced to rubble all over the Eastern world, where centres of the ancient Christian ascendancy such as Damascus, Alexandria, or Constantinople were overwhelmed by Islamic armies, and where oppressive rulers restricted Christian rights in a severe and often bloody manner. The few books of Orthodox-focused history that were still produced in the remaining free territories of the Orthodox world such as Russia were, as far as Protestant and Catholic European readers were concerned, in 'obscure languages' that never made it into translation. It is only when Orthodox accounts began to appear in European languages in modern times that the clash of values became apparent more widely to the Western churches.

So much for history as an ideological battle ground for apologetics. What would it be for the Orthodox to tell the tale of the rise of Christianity from their perspective? It is a hopeless expectation to imagine such a short chapter as this could ever hope to do justice to the complexity of the Christian story. The only merit of this rapid survey will be to signal some of the 'turning points' that the Orthodox think are seminal. It may be surprising to Western readers to see how many of the familiar episodes of their own history are not part of that story, and what a difference to the overall topography that might make in reimagining Christian origins.

Earliest Christian foundations

When the Orthodox think about the Church, they instinctively understand that it is the living communion which contains the angelic orders, as well as the prophets and saints before the historical advent of the Lord who were liberated to become the heavenly church as a grace of the Resurrection,[2] and also the countless generations who have gone before us, and those which may possibly come after us. Thus, when we speak of the 'beginning' of the church in this chapter, it is taken to mean the earthly church after the Incarnation. Orthodox Christianity begins at several sacred 'moments' within history, that have been prepared by the great pre-history of the scriptural revelation, and are rooted in the great plan of God's creation ordinance.[3] Within that nexus of moments, however, there are certain key events that constitute the beginning of the Church historically speaking. Orthodoxy would place the first great epiphany in the Incarnation of the Holy Word. The icon of the Nativity of the Saviour features, prominently, the arrival of the Magi as symbols of the enlightened nations. More narrowly, the earthly church is said to have been brought together with Jesus' commissioning of his apostles and, ultimately, with their consecration as his witnesses to the world at the great experience of Pentecost.[4] It is the pentecostal descent of the Spirit that leads the apostles into the fullness of the truth of Jesus, and energizes their mission to evangelize others and draw them consciously into a life-giving relation with God, through his Christ. The pentecostal Spirit energizes the 'Great Commission' to evangelize the world,[5] a grace that itself is part of the Resurrection life poured out over history, to sanctify it. The church, from that time onwards, has had the duty of preserving fidelity to the Lord's Gospel commission, and it has always been propagated in the same 'pneumatic' way: namely, by the charismatic grace of the Lord passing through generations, embodied in the pentecostal proclamation of the Gospels and the celebration of the sacramental mysteries, under the care of the apostles and their successors.

Orthodoxy regards the episcopal ranks, the senior order of priesthood in the church, as the chief example of the successors to the original apostolic order. All those, however, who share the vitality of the faith with others, especially those who lead others deeper into the experience of Jesus, are seen to be endowed with an apostolic charism in a missionary sense. Some great saints of the past, such as Thekla the Megalomartyr, Nina of Georgia, or Vladimir of Kiev, are called apostles figuratively in the Orthodox liturgical tradition, because of the great effect they have had in evangelizing nations and regions. Even on a lesser scale, parents and grandparents who transmit the faith with loving care to their children serve in the apostolic role as propagators of the faith, under God. This 'lesser' role is the standard way whole generations of believers are born, passing from their natural birth to a new spiritual consecration as disciples in a baptismal experience mediated to them by their parents, who have treasured the faith and wish to hand it down their family. Of course, because it is a charism, passing on the faith cannot be guaranteed, or mechanically presumed, even across a family that has been steeped in the life of the church for centuries past. All men and women must make their choice freely, and personally, each in their own lifetime. The gift cannot be presumed (though it will always be offered), and faith only shines in true brightness when it is freely affirmed and voluntarily embraced. It is the basic task of the church to ensure that in each generation the call of the Gospel can be heard clearly, and purely, and that the church communion itself is an accurate, living, and gracious icon of Christ, acting to attract men and women to the Lord of Love.

The apostles served the Lord while he lived, and after his resurrection, so church traditions recount, travelled far and wide preaching the Good News that he had entrusted to them. The form of the apostolic *kerygma* is impressed at several instances on the scriptural record. Acts 2.14–40 gives a stylized example of the shape of one of the earliest apostolic *kerygmata*, and it was with sermons and appeals such as this that the first missionaries of the church made their way through the ancient agoras, synagogues, and odea of the Graeco-Roman world in late antiquity. In the generation after them the apostolic preachers, and the itinerant prophets we hear about in ancient texts such as the *Didache*, left behind churches, that is, communities of committed believers, which they had established by their kerygmatic proclamation, and already before the end of the second century we have records of how those earliest communities began to organize themselves for the times ahead, when they would be without the authorities of the great leaders of the first generation. The pastoral epistles of the New Testament give an account of how the communities were settling down, and learning to regulate themselves and organize their patterns of worship.

One major factor in this the earliest period of the apostolic and immediate post-apostolic generation was the organization of worship. The Christian *cultus* centred around the celebration of Jesus' salvific life and death and resurrection, as the fulfilment of the scriptural hope (the 'Old Testament' as they soon began to call the ancient prophetic narratives) and as the promise of new life in the present moment. The Eucharist served to gather Christians together regularly for the shared 'recounting' of the Lord's saving death and resurrection that was epitomized by the eucharistic meal.

In the course of the Eucharist, the concept of the New Testament as a body of apostolic writings that served to explain and orientate the prophetic writings first arose.[6] The canon is merely the formalized recognition of what was, and ought to be, read in the course of worship. Along with the formal readings of sacred texts, the role of the eucharistic president expanded significantly. These, the earliest bishops, were heirs of the apostles, not least because they continued the prophetic office in the church of 'interpreting' and explaining the Scriptures, how they related to Jesus and to contemporary life, to their congregations. It would be several centuries before the task of preaching extended also to the bench of presbyters. At first the 'breaking of the word of God' to the people was quintessentially an episcopal function, and thus it synopsized their status as heirs of the apostles.

The first Christian communities often began as offshoots, or minority groups, attached to the Jewish synagogues in the Mediterranean world, but tensions rising with the majority groups following from the exalted praise the Christians gave to Jesus as Son and Wisdom of God, led soon enough to regular schisms among the Judaeo-Christian settlements, and already by the time of the Gospel of John (which reflects the tension in its text[7]), that is, towards the end of the first century, Christians were finding themselves increasingly 'separate' and learning to affirm their distinct identity with a growing sense of wonder and expectation. This separation into a distinctly organized existence was accompanied by much apologetical conflict. The records of the New Testament and the earliest Christian writings are charged with the sense of conflict between the nascent Christian movement and groups variously described, but which we might sum up as: Judaism, the many varieties of pagan cult, and the more frightening encounters with mob violence and official state sanctions against illicit religions in the empire. By the time that the wider world realized the separate existence of the Christians, now distinct from the Jews, who had enjoyed the status of a protected religion under the Roman system, punitive measures were being taken against them. This particularly began to happen at the end of the second century and into the fourth. We now look back on this early period of the church as the 'age of persecutions', often forgetting that even today an estimated 175,000 Christians are assassinated each year for their faith (greater numbers than ever suffered in the past).[8]

By the mid second century, therefore, the churches across the Mediterranean world were 'growing up'. They had a good degree of unity, provided by their common faith in Jesus and their shared interest in attaching themselves to the great teachers of the first generations. It is for this reason that the canon of the New Testament had more or less already established itself as 'good practice' for worshipping Christian communities far and wide, long before it had ever attracted to itself a theory of why it should be adopted. The Gospels were given pride of place, and, despite their differences of perspective, each of the four canonical texts shows a substantial reliance on the structure of the ancient apostolic preaching: the kerygmatic proclamation that Jesus' life and saving death were the liberating forces that had redeemed the world under God. For this reason the Orthodox regarded the New Testament as the quintessential record of the apostolic tradition. To this day the concept 'apostolic faith' means primarily an accordance with the apostolic doctrine of the sacred Scriptures. The details of each and every apostle, and his historical ministry, might not be available to the record of ecclesiastical history, just as everything that Jesus himself said and did is not recorded. What matters is that in the New Testament texts we have a substantive and faithful account of the 'song of the apostles' that they raised in honour of Jesus: interpreting him to the generations that would follow, and doing so with careful regard to allow the Master himself to speak as much as, if not more than, themselves. In all Orthodox thought, the apostolic tradition gives pride of place to John, Paul, and Peter's doctrine, but sees all the apostolic utterance as collectively synopsized in the canon of New Testament writings, whether or not these were actually written by the hand of an apostle or transmitted through a disciple of an apostle.

The idea of the canon of the New Testament has been a notion over which recent generations of scholars have fought, arguing that it does not fully represent the diversity of the early Christian experience as lived throughout the first 300 years. Of course it does not. It was meant to represent the apostolic tradition that was to be held on to as authentic and faithful to Jesus as he was portrayed through the first apostolic preaching, and to rule out of consideration among the mainstream churches that burgeoning library of texts, and weltering array of religious speculations, that were being produced by other thinkers (history tends to sum them up as Gnostics or the like). Many of these heterodox texts depicted a Jesus who was not fully embodied (ancient religious philosophers tended to regard embodiment as equivalent to defilement, and so several teachers thought that by projecting a docetic, non-corporeal, Jesus they were defending his honour). The acknowledgement of a universally recognized canon of Scripture was a decisive reaction to close out books that did not fit into the 'diverse harmony' that is represented by the church's present canon of New Testament writings. All of the canonical Scriptures represent different perspectives, but together they make a many-veined harmony of voice that fills out and rounds off the earliest picture of the experience of Jesus in the church. Certain doctrines and claims about Jesus, however, clash with this harmony, and many (in the past, just as today) are incompatible with it. It is obvious that the canon is not a 'representative cross-section' of all the voices that could be heard in the ancient communities. It is the pure distillation of what was offered by the Spirit-led, as the essence of the apostolic tradition. The tradition, and the sum total of voices, are not the same at all. Orthodoxy is interested in the former, not in being an archival record of things antiquarian.

It was the early generation of bishops in the larger churches – generally men who were educated in the wider perspective of how other Mediterranean churches were conducting themselves – that first began to call for some system of common governance: to preserve doctrinal orthodoxy and rule out extreme heterodox movements. The bishops of Antioch, Alexandria, and Rome feature prominently in this part of the story. Important bishops, such as St Ignatius, Dionysios, or Pope Clement, have left behind them a body of literature that is afforded great respect in the Orthodox tradition, as giving evidence of some of the earliest post-apostolic models of governance. The writings of St Ignatius the God-Bearer (of Antioch), dating to approximately AD 107, show that already the principle of the single presiding episcopate is spreading through the churches as the preferred model for good order. Ignatius speaks of the bishop as the icon of Christ governing the church. 'No one is permitted', Ignatius writes, 'to do anything that concerns the church, without the bishop.' Ignatius describes the bishop as the focal point of unity, because around him the church is enabled to gather eucharistically: and Christ himself is the unity of the communion.[9]

What Christians did in these great and early churches, which were the capital cities of the Roman empire of the time, determined what other communities wanted to do as well. Good practice was always a dominating factor in how the wider community of churches in the ancient world emulated, and learned from, one another. Eventually this system of common awareness and respect became enshrined in the important principle of mutual episcopal recognition. Bishops who were ordained were acknowledged by 'letters of peace' as they introduced themselves to neighbouring bishops and gave an account of their standard of Christian teaching. By the late second century it is clear that the bishops had also begun to organize the churches by reliance on province-wide meetings of bishops. These meetings, known as synods (a Greek word meaning 'coming together'), were arranged to discuss common affairs and decide on common policy in the face of perceived threats to Christian coherence. It is in one of the very earliest of synods in Asia Minor that the enthusiast movement of Montanism was first censured as a threat to church order. So it was by practical methods achieving results of elevating the best practice, and local bishops ensuring heterodox texts were ruled out from local church worship, that by the end of the second century a system of guarding orthodoxy was practically elaborated. Its chief elements were threefold: the upholding of a canon of Scripture to serve as an authoritative paradigm of the apostolic teaching; the putting forward of the senior priests (the bishops) as the successors of the apostles, and affording them the authority to govern the churches according to this apostolic standard; the setting up of a system of synods of bishops (at first province-wide, then growing in a wider international remit) to ensure common teaching and harmonious traditions among all the local churches.[10]

Early episcopal theologians such as St Irenaeus reflected on the problems occurring in the local community with heterodox groups who were producing a veritable outpouring of 'alternative' Gospel literature. These, the so-called apocryphal Gospels, were refused admittance to the worship services of the early Orthodox communities. When one reads examples of these texts today, alongside the sober and inspiring message of the canonical Gospels, the Orthodox do not regard the early bishops as having been 'oppressors' at all, but saviours of the purity of the faith. The apocryphal Gospels, in the main, are trivializations of the solemnity of the apostolic teaching, or they lead it out into elitist metaphysical speculations that have little bearing on Jesus and his heavenly message that was so deeply rooted in the soil of reality. This clash with speculative heterodoxy marks the last pages of the New Testament record[11] just as much as it does the writings of the second-century Fathers. Irenaeus, and other theologians of this early period, articulated more details as time went on about how to recognize and protect the system of Orthodoxy and avoid heterodox opinions that falsified the authentic Gospel. In addition to the canon of the Scripture, the concept of apostolic succession of the bishops, and the concept of synodical harmony, Irenaeus also pointed to the manner in which practices of worship enshrined the true belief of the people. This process was described in the Latin text of Irenaeus as the principle of the Regula Fidei (Rule of Faith). What it soon came to be summed up by was the manner in which candidates for baptism presented their 'confession of faith' before the sacrament. The confession was generally taught to them by the local bishop, and so this 'Creed' was an active summation of the whole belief of that church. Creeds, and the theological attitudes manifested by the practice of the rituals of prayer and worship (the hymns, the liturgical prayers, and details of the sacramental rites) all accumulated, in Irenaeus' view, to presenting a veritable dossier of authentic Christianity that was not dependent on the intelligentsia to articulate it. It was a lived

11

theology of the whole church, not a theoretical religion for the highly educated. From ancient times to the present day, therefore, Orthodoxy has held to that principle, and it is the people as a whole in the Orthodox Church who hold to the tradition of belief they have received from earlier times. Orthodoxy is much less susceptible than are many Western churches to the theological writings of contemporary theologians among it. The wider church, the ordinary faithful as well as monks and bishops, expect modern theologians to conform their doctrine to the writings of the apostles and Fathers, and to the liturgical tradition they themselves received at baptism. An Orthodox theologian who departs from fundamentals of the Rule of Faith is, *de facto*, no longer an Orthodox theologian at all.

The development of ecclesiastical centres

The patterns laid out in the New Testament literature and the earliest of the patristic writings were records of the church in its infancy. They are informative, even determinative of some things, but not prescriptively unalterable as methods of church governance. Orthodoxy does not agree with, and strongly resists the reductionism of, some forms of Protestantism that argue that unless something is to be found in the explicit writings of the New Testament it cannot be a constitutive part of authentic church life. Orthodox understanding of Christian tradition is much wider and deeper than this. By the third century the great spread of Christianity around the Mediterranean basin, and in the vast heartland of Asia Minor, led to pressing needs to organize the local churches on more formal models. From this period many forms of governance that are still used today in churches were elaborated in Christian public life.[12] At this stage the great capital cities, such as Rome, Alexandria, and Antioch, began to serve as models of emulation for Christian communities world-wide. Later in the fourth century we can see this process of 'great centre imitation' working clearly as liturgical ideas that were first tried out in Jerusalem, Antioch, Constantinople, or Rome (focal points for pilgrim interest) made their way all over wider Christendom. In the great capital cities of Roman late antiquity the bishops of these large centres were assisted by a cohort of elders, and the pattern of establishing a single presiding bishop with a larger circle of presbyters became a standard mode of governance. Deacons were, historically, always seen as the helpers of the bishops, and remained an order more attached to the episcopate than the presbyterate. By the later third century when the very size of the Christian communities led to the need to establish several churches in each diocese[13] (it had been an old ideal to have one church, one bishop, and one eucharistic celebration, for each town before that), it was the presbyters who went out to form separate churches. These were still under the presidency of the presiding diocesan bishop (the Orthodox now speak about a 'ruling' bishop), but the pattern that would endure was coming into force: an episcopal cathedral church,[14] and a variety of parish churches served by presbyters, with the possible assistance of a smaller number of deacons and deaconesses.

The imperial authorities at this time were frequently hostile to the church, and often the bishops became the target for focused attack. Many of the ancient martyrs were victims of persecutions from this period in the third and early fourth centuries. It is also clear, however, from the more extensive writings that the early bishops began to leave behind them, that 'good order' in doctrine and practice was something that was powerfully moving them. In the third century the system of international correspondence between bishops is developed extensively. The great churches tended to keep an eye on the smaller and more provincial communities, ensuring that Christian life developed in a harmonious commonality (allowing for cultural differences in many regions) and that serious doctrinal divergences, or liturgical differences, were smoothed out as best as possible. The Asia Minor churches which observed Pascha on the fourteenth of the month of Nisan (an equivalent to April) regardless of the day of the week on which it fell, were publicly censured from Pope Victor's Rome for not observing the common tradition of observing Pascha on a Sunday (as an all-night Saturday vigil).[15] There were many differences, of course, and some scholars have compared the church of this period to a 'quarrelsome kind of union', but by virtue of the authority of larger sees, the appeal to good practice, and the use of synodical meetings of bishops, the older ideas established in the preceding centuries were faithfully developed in the new circumstances of the growing church. Episcopal governance was, at this period, a very strong force for ensuring the concept of ecclesial 'communion'. On the wider front this was done by each local bishop keeping an eye on neighbouring bishops' teachings and conduct, and, on the local scene, by the bishop keeping a close eye on the good order of the diocesan eucharistic celebrations, where faith was lived and taught on a weekly basis. At the end of the third century, monasticism also began to make a strong appearance in the church.

The monastic life had a real flowering in the early fourth century, in both Syria and Egypt, before spreading to Rome, Constantinople, Armenia, and Cappadocia, and eventually all over the Christian world. The early monks, known also as 'zealots' or 'ascetes' (athletes) were dedicated to the living out of Christian values in an uncompromising way. They too became zealous defenders of the tradition of theology they held up as the ancestral faith. At times the monks' stubbornness was problematical for the Orthodox bishops, as for example when they attached themselves to dissident positions (such as the anti-Chalcedonian ascetics in Egypt, or Palestine), but generally they were so popularly venerated as defenders of the faith against encroachments by imperial compromisers that by the end of the fifth century almost all the bishops were selected exclusively from the ranks of monastics. It is a practice which Orthodoxy adheres to even in the present, though the very early bishops in the Scriptures were meant to be married before they could be chosen,[16] and some of the great Fathers (such as Gregory of Nyssa) were married men. From the later fourth century, the Orthodox Church developed as a single structure with double pillars of support: the diocesan level of churches administered from the cathedral church and bishop's chancery, and also the ringing of monasteries constituting the ascetical life of a province. At the best times of the church's life, the two systems have been in close harmony, one refreshing the other.

The fourth century is often seen as a sea-change for the affairs of the church. With the vision of the Emperor Constantine (now revered by Orthodoxy as Constantine Among the Saints and Equal to the Apostles) in the prelude to his battle[17] with the pagan Emperor Maxentius for control of the western empire, Constantine was convinced that the God of the Christians had enabled his rise to power. He was, accordingly, a defender and patron of the Christian movement (also enjoying its support for his administration) and eventually was baptized on his deathbed by Bishop Eusebios of Nicomedia. For the church, emerging from generations of bloody persecution, his patronage seemed like a dream come true. Soon local bishops were given administrative powers within the empire, and to them was handed over the role of local judgement of matters concerning Christians. Many of the provincial bishops became virtually synonymous with Roman imperial administration (other than that regarding tax returns and military defence), as they were frequently the most educated people of the region. By the end of the fifth century a working relationship had been established, that the church would recognize the 'God-loving Christian emperor' as having a sacred right to rule, and the emperor would guard the peace of the church. The ritual of the anointing of the Christian emperors[18] underlined their sacramental office, and envisaged it as something along the lines of a New David, set over the New Israel.

The relation between the Christian imperium and church affairs was described in the patristic writings (not without perennial struggle breaking out in times of stress and conflict) as ideally being a 'symphony' of relations of powers. The political affairs of the empire were God-blessed, as long as they followed the Gospel dictates; but the spheres of religion and politics were separate.[19] The emperor could look over the good order of the churches, but he was not to intervene in matters of doctrine or conduct, which were part of the sacred tradition of the church, and were to be supervised by the priesthood. Often this ideal 'symphonic balance' was tipped too far one way (usually by imperial pressure on the church) but generally it worked throughout the long ages of the Byzantine empire (up until the mid fifteenth century). Monastics were always at the front of dissent from imperialist over-control. Many examples of this abound in church history, such as the manner in which the emperor's policy of iconoclasm was rejected by popular dissent, or the way in which the Paleologan state's attempts to impose unity with Rome were decisively rejected.

After the fall of Byzantium to Islam, the imperial model of governance of the state was exported to Russia, where the tsars saw themselves as continuing the office as church protectors. Even where it was resisted, as in the medieval West, where separate nationalist dreams were always more alluring than the concept of a trans-national imperium of the Christians, it was often followed in default.

The age of the Fathers

The final victory of the Emperor Constantine, and his assumption of sole monarchical control over the Roman empire in 323, coincided with his decision to bring healing and order back into the affairs of a Christian East that had been so disrupted by the brunt of the fourth-century persecutions. He paid the church compensation for much of the property it had lost, gave several buildings for its use (the Lateran basilica in Rome for example), and commanded several new churches to be built (such as Bethlehem, the old St Peter's basilica, and the church of the Anastasis, or Holy Sepulchre). He also commanded the bishops of the Eastern Church to come together and end the dissensions that had compromised their unity. This they did, at his own palace at Nicaea in Asia Minor in the year 325. This large synod of bishops was to become a great moment in church history, featuring as the first of the ecumenical (world-wide) synods that the church has looked back on as being of monumental importance in settling universal matters of the Orthodox faith. There are now seven ecumenical councils which the Orthodox regard as the supreme legislative assembly of the church on earth. Roman Catholicism continued the process of holding universal councils (the last being Vatican II in the 1960s) but the Orthodox have only regarded the first seven as authentically ecumenical, when all the ancient 'popes'[20] were represented. The decisions of an ecumenical council are seen by the Orthodox as having the authoritative blessing of the Holy Spirit, affirming the judgement of all the assembled bishops as to substantial matters of faith and discipline. This is why the vote of the bishops at ecumenical councils was not taken as a 'majority' prospectus. If a matter of faith was at stake, it was presumed that all the assembled bishops, as vessels of the Spirit who had been formed in the Orthodox faith, would be able to 'recognize' it without difficulty, not search for it laboriously among a welter of possibilities. The apostolic teaching was (and is) taken with utmost seriousness: 'We have the mind of Christ.'[21] If a bishop dissented from the unanimous vote of an ecumenical council, therefore, or resisted it once it had been proclaimed, he was inevitably regarded as resisting the Spirit, and was always deposed from his office as bishop by the vote of the assembly.

The decrees of the Council of Nicaea strongly proclaimed the divinity of the Word of God, and laid the foundations of the doctrine of the Trinity. Nicaea, and the creed of faith it issued, has always been regarded by the Orthodox as the foundation stone of theological truth after the Scriptures, and an example of how the Orthodox tradition (almost in every generation) has to recognize the challenges that present themselves (Arianism in the time of Nicaea) and defend the truth in harmony with the received tradition of the past. This ministry of harmonious consensus in faith, and vigorous defence of truth, still remains the quintessential role of the Orthodox bishop. In this period of the church the writings of numerous episcopal theologians became widely accepted as authoritative, either because they formed part of the significant context of an ecumenical council (such as the writings of SS Athanasios, or Gregory the Theologian, or Cyril of Alexandria) or because their spiritual wisdom carried a large weight and reputation with it (such as the writings of the monastic saints and ascetics[22]).

The pastoral works of such theologians as Basil of Caesarea, or the historical works of such writers as Eusebios of Caesarea, or the liturgical instructions of Cyril of Jerusalem, all accumulated to form a very rich and extensive body of literature on exegesis, doctrine, liturgy, and spirituality, which is still read to this day in the Orthodox communion. These writers, especially those of unquestioned authority and ancient status, are given the title of the 'Fathers of the Church'. The phrase primarily signified the ancient office of bishop-theologian. There were 'Mothers of the Church' too (*Ammas*): such great saints and teachers as Macrina of Cappadocia, Olympias of Constantinople, Melania of Rome, Syncletica the Ascetic, and many others. They did not have an ordained role as teacher, as the Fathers who were bishops did, (though some of them were deaconesses) but the stature of their lives and the quality of their ascetic witness has given them a pre-eminent status as early Christian women theologians. Orthodoxy affords deep respect to the writings of the Fathers and Mothers, as an example of the Spirit-filled (*pneumatophoroi*) who can teach the church the authentic message of the Spirit of God in any given age or era. For this reason Orthodoxy does not restrict the age of the Fathers and Mothers to a dead past. Those who are Spirit-bearers in the present age are also the authentic theologians of God, even though not all of them may have the duty of public teaching in the church, and many of them may not have academic qualifications. The writings of each Father

15

Figure 1 St Cyril of Alexandria, fifth-century archbishop and major patristic theologian. The icon is in the style of Athonite wall frescoes of the eighteenth century, its vigorous rendering suggesting the energy and sense of elan that Cyril himself brought to his church life in the defence of Orthodoxy against Nestorianism. As one of the traditional 'liturgical doctors' of Orthodoxy (saints who traditionally composed eucharistic liturgies), Cyril's icon often features in the apse of churches in the company of the other doctors. Each bears a phrase from the liturgy typically associated with their work. Here, St Cyril carries a scroll relating to his defence of the Theotokos (Mother of God) title as this was enshrined in an exclamation of the Eastern liturgy after the consecration. It reads: 'We remember especially our all holy, most blessed Mother of God and ever-Virgin Mary.'
Modern icon by Eileen McGuckin

individually considered, however, are not afforded any level of infallibility. It is how the patristic writings merge with the harmony of the great tradition that affords them their apostolic quality of truth. Some of the individual Fathers were great men of faith, but raised theories and ideas that the church, in relation to its wider tradition, rejected and discountenanced. Orthodoxy venerates St Augustine, for example, but regards much of his work as seriously flawed, and as a source of much disunity that would follow after him, between the respective Latin and Orthodox readings of the church's tradition on important issues. Origen of Alexandria is a writer whose biblical exegesis, and much of his thought, has inspired generations of saints, but whose 'overall system' was severely censured by the Orthodox ecumenical tradition, and he has been denied patristic status accordingly.

In the fourth and fifth centuries there were so many great writers, defending the tradition and establishing the tenor of the conciliar teachings, that it has ever afterwards been regarded as 'the Golden Age of the Fathers'. For the fourth century, SS Athanasios, Gregory the Theologian, Basil of Caesarea, Gregory of Nyssa, Ambrose of Milan, John Chrysostom, and Ephrem the Syrian stand out as the great defenders of the Nicene faith. For the fifth century there were such giants as Cyril of Alexandria, Pope Leo I, and St Augustine. There has hardly been a century since, in all the long annals of Orthodoxy, where great spiritual teachers and theologians have not appeared. The whole Orthodox tradition is marked by these luminaries: writers of patristic status reaching out of the classical ages of the church and into the medieval period and beyond. Notable among them are St Maximos the Confessor, St John of Damascus, St Symeon the New Theologian, St Gregory Palamas, and St Gregory of Sinai. In every instance their teaching has formed a seamless union with the quality of their lives. In doctrine the saint-theologians of Orthodoxy are faithful to the apostolic tradition, and in their life they represent the charism of the Spirit-filled. Without both characteristics visibly present, Orthodoxy does not afford such high recognition to any teacher; when both are present it recognizes them as manifesting the 'mind of Christ'. It is an enduring ecumenical sadness that their lives and works are so little known in Western Christianity.

Creeds and councils

After Nicaea in 325, there was a series of great councils that received ecumenical status in retrospect. A council can often be called together, intending to be of ecumenical significance, but may be rejected by the general sentiment of the faithful over the course of time. In such cases the Orthodox regard those councils as never having had the spiritual charism to assume the role of authoritatively binding the church at large and, as such, not deserving the title 'ecumenical'. One clear example of that failure was the attempt at church reunion initiated by the Byzantine emperors in the fifteenth century. The Council of Florence (1438–9) is regarded by the Latin Church as having ecumenical significance; but when the Orthodox delegates returned home to Byzantium the general sentiment of the people rejected their proclamation of union with Rome, and so this council is not listed as authentic in the annals of Orthodoxy. What is at issue here is the very important concept of the conscience of the church at large; what is known in the West as *sensus fidelium*. There is no doubt that it is the Council of Nicaea and its credal exposition of Orthodox faith that holds pride of place in Orthodoxy.[23] The council declared for the full and coequal deity of the Word of God, personally incarnate in the Lord Jesus. It stood against the arch-heretic Arius, who had argued that Jesus was a creature, and the Word of God merely an elevated angelic being, not possessed of deity except in a nominal way. Nicene faith is the affirmation that, in Christ, God himself came to save us. It is the pillar that holds up the roof of the holy Orthodox tradition. St Alexander of Alexandria and his deacon (then successor) St Athanasios of Alexandria, along with Bishop Hosius of Cordoba were the Orthodox (Greek and Latin) leaders of the Nicene cause. The council's extensive canons also set out patterns of church governance in terms of the arrangement of sees,[24] provincial meetings of synods, and the precedence to be held in matters of appeal by the larger capital sees.

The Council of Nicaea ending in 325 did not bring peace to the church for a long time. The entire generation after it was filled with synods and counter-synods, where the Arians continued to fight long and hard against the Nicene theologians. It was a bitter period of international Christian division and disunity, but one in which the leading Orthodox Fathers never ceased to argue single-mindedly for the preservation of the faith defined by the Orthodox Fathers of Nicaea. In doing this they resisted every attempt at political 'compromise', a path that was advocated by the sons of Constantine who then occupied the imperial throne.

Nicaea was followed by the second ecumenical council, which took place at Constantinople in 381, and which served as a 'capstone' to the council of 325. It brought an end to a long period of Arian ascendancy, coinciding with the death of the last emperor (Valens) who had protected and advanced Arian theologians in the court. With the removal of state patronage the Arian movement soon lost ground (though some have called it a perennial Christian heresy). The Council of Constantinople declared the full deity of the Holy Spirit, and thus set out a more explicit theology of the Holy Trinity. Its doctrine is enshrined in the Creed which is today recited at all Orthodox eucharistic liturgies. This Creed is often called the 'Nicene', but it is in fact the Constantinopolitan. They are synonymous in all respects, except that the clauses on the Holy Spirit are more extensive in the latter. The Spirit of God is divine, the Creed teaches, and his worship alongside the Father and the Son, which has always been part of the ancient faith of Christians, demonstrates this truth sufficiently.

The third ecumenical council was gathered at Ephesus in 431 under the presidency of St Cyril of Alexandria.[25] It taught the necessity of recognizing the inner unity of Christ the Lord, despite the recognition of his two natures (divine and human). The Divine Word of God was not mediated to the world through a man called Jesus of Nazareth. On the contrary, Jesus was the Eternal Word of God, now made manifest incarnated within history. The Incarnation is the great and life-giving paradox of the Word made flesh. To fix this in the common imagination in the simplest way possible, the conciliar Fathers at Ephesus insisted that the Blessed Virgin Mary should rightly be celebrated and called the 'Mother of God' (Theotokos). Their opponents, who in various forms wished to create some form of 'baffle' so as to avoid the implication of the immediate immanency of God within the flesh, argued that Mary should only be called the 'Mother of Jesus'. The Christology of the council, with its profound sense of joy that Jesus is none other, and no less, than God made flesh among us, has always been at the heart of Orthodox thought and spirituality ever since.

The fourth and fifth ecumenical councils were more precise elaborations of the Christology set out at the third, making a clearer exposition of its terms. The fourth was held at Chalcedon (a suburb of Constantinople) in 451, the fifth at the capital itself in 553. Both meetings were held in the cause of unity because of extensive arguments over the person and work of the Saviour. In the aftermath of the Council of Chalcedon, which declared the rightfulness of asserting two natures (divine and human) inhabited by the single divine person (hypostasis) of the Word, and Lord, Jesus, the Divine Son of God, several sections of the Eastern Church left the unity of the Greek and Latin communion of the church. These communities endure to this day and are commonly known as the Non-Chalcedonian Orthodox. Among them are the Coptic, Ethiopian, Armenian, and Assyrian churches. Their tradition of life and spirituality is both immensely venerable and very close to the Orthodox, but because of the theological divisions, and the difference in admitting the decrees of the councils after Ephesus 431, they do not share in the eucharistic communion of the Orthodox.[26]

The sixth ecumenical council was held in Constantinople in 681. Its immediate cause was another Christological heresy of the period, teaching that Christ only had one will, and that a divine one. In each instance of Christological dissent, the conciliar Fathers from Ephesus 431 to Constantinople (III) 681 doctrinally insisted that Christ was at one and the same moment fully and authentically human, and wholly divine: God from God, and man among us. All attempts to fudge the issue of Jesus' person, or to blur the impact of his real humanity in the cause of diminishing it in the face of his deity, were consistently rejected by the Orthodox councils of the church. In 692 another synod was held in Constantinople, and is now known as the Quinisext Council. It was designed to serve as reformist synod, tightening the discipline of the church with extensive canons, or rules, for good behaviour. It added these canons retrospectively to the fifth and sixth ecumenical councils, but did not want to stand independently apart from them, and so has been 'included in' the numbering of seven councils.

The latest, seventh ecumenical council was held at Nicaea in 787, to teach the importance for correct faith of the veneration of icons. Many non-Orthodox have regarded this as a decline in the significance of the matter dealt with by the general councils, but the Orthodox tradition has insisted that the discernible trend in parts of the wider Christian experience, to turn away from imagery and concreteness in the spiritual life, or to resist the principle of God's encounter with his people through sacramental material forms, is a perennial heresy that weakens the true spiritual life. Those in the medieval Greek Church who argued that images and icons and relics ought to be destroyed violently, on the pretext that they separated believers from Christ rather than drawing people nearer to the Lord in devotion and piety, were resisted by the conciliar Fathers. Their iconoclasm was exposed as a form of Platonism, or abstract spiritualism that resisted the path of incarnation that God took towards his people. Many Orthodox thinkers have since argued that iconoclasm, in the many forms in which it still exists within Western Christianity (the rejection of a full range of sacraments, or a distaste for the veneration of the saints, or a refusal to honour the icons of the Lord, the Virgin, or the saints) signals a serious matter of theological divergence, a different conception of what the communion of Christ is, and is not something that is peripheral or an incidental difference in the faith.

The whole teaching of the seven ecumenical councils is a very significant, and substantial part of the Orthodox tradition of faith. Orthodoxy clings to the Bible, the writings of the Fathers, and the decrees and creeds of the councils as some of its foundational and most important articulations of Christian truth. It regards the doctrine of the seven councils as an organic whole; a coherent mindset that is in harmony with the scriptural revelation, and with the living springs of spiritual life today. The harmony of the councils is one example (and a major one at that) of the harmony of the Orthodox tradition as a whole. Orthodox saints who have taught after the age of the councils, such as St Photios (810–95) or the Hesychast Fathers such as St Gregory of Sinai or St Gregory Palamas, in the fourteenth century, have been very careful to guide all of their writing and reflection on the apostolic standards of the Scriptures, the patristic consensus, and the conciliar tradition. In this way they have secured their Orthodoxy in line with that of the saints from times past. It remains a mark of authentic Orthodox theologization.

St Photios, known as 'the Great' in Orthodox tradition, is an important theologian who stands as a bridge between the ancient and medieval ages of the church. In the course of a council, held at Constantinople in 867 when he was patriarch of the capital city, Photios' arguments against papal supremacy (the first time the Orthodox world had faced up to the issue, although it had long been uneasy about the development) and the untraditional nature of the Latin *Filioque* theology,[27] resulted in the synodical condemnation of the pope. The ultimate alienation of the Byzantine and Roman churches has often been posited as happening in 1054, but the work of Photios marked the first time (there had been many prior incidental divisions and would be several others after) that the Eastern and Western churches officially and instinctively drew apart on profoundly significant theological issues, especially those related to the manner in which papal authority was felt by the Easterners to have changed the ancient pattern of the Christian ecumene.[28] The rift that yawned open at that time between the Latins and the Orthodox, on the understanding of the Trinity, was not a separate 'doctrinal' matter distinct from the ecclesiological tensions then in evidence; rather it was something, Photios argued, that was part of a general tendency of the medieval West, the ongoing alteration of the ancient tradition in the name of 'development'. His treatise *On the Holy Spirit* became a foundational study for later Eastern Orthodox theology, and one that for centuries to come focused the mind of the Byzantine world on why it held Latin Catholicism in suspicion, both in terms of ecclesiastical organization and in relation to its understanding of Christian doctrine.

East and West: the parting of ways

After the last council in 787, the political affairs of the Byzantine empire went into a long decline, largely because of the pressure of the advance of Islam in the form of the Seljuk and Ottoman Turks. The emperor's role in the gathering together of the synodical bishops, and his supervision of the proclamation of their decrees as part of Christian law for the Eastern churches, was progressively hindered by the political reality that saw more and more parts of the ancient Christian lands now under the control of Islamic rulers, the caliphs, and then the sultans. The weakened position of the Eastern Christians was exacerbated even more as a result of the Crusades. From the late eleventh century onwards western armies, inspired by the appeal of the pope for Christian soldiers to liberate the holy sites in Palestine, were regarded as a mixed blessing by the Christian emperors in Constantinople. Only forty years before the beginning of the First Crusade there had been a particularly bitter 'falling out' between the Papacy and the Constantinopolitan patriarchate. Pope Leo IX had, with the emperor's support, sent legates, among them Cardinal Humbertus, to resolve the several differences between the Latin and Greek churches that were currently causing friction. The list of problems included the *Filioque* clause, and the extent to which the pope was entitled to a jurisdiction of power over churches outside his immediate territory, but also included the sense of the widening gap that had grown up between Greek and Latin liturgical life and spiritual customs.

Far from being resolved, the argument between Humbertus and patriarch Michael Caerularios flared to new heights. It ended with the cardinal leaving a decree of excommunication against the patriarch on the altar of Hagia Sophia, in July 1054, and the Holy Synod of Constantinople, in return, excommunicating the papal legates. This was not an exchange of excommunications between the churches in any sense, but it had the effect of being a public severance of unity, and it is often cited as a significant 'moment' in the story of what was to become the long separation of the Orthodox and Latin catholic churches. Increasingly from that time onwards, the Papacy regarded the Greeks as having become 'schismatic' by having refused the rights of papal jurisdiction, and the Orthodox regarded the Western Church as having lapsed into heresy for elevating the Papacy to such extraordinary heights, while tampering with the ancient deposit of the faith in such matters as adding the *Filioque* to the Creed, and using unleavened bread in the Eucharist. Mutual respect, by the high Middle Ages, was at a low ebb. By 1190, the sense among the Orthodox that the long alienation had actually become a schism becomes apparent in the great Orthodox canonist Theodore Balsamon, the patriarch of Antioch, who wrote:

> For many years now, the western church has been divided in spiritual communion from the other four patriarchates and has become alien to the Orthodox...so no Latin should be given communion unless he first declares that he will abstain from the doctrines and customs that separate him from us, and that he will be subject to the canons of the church in union with the Orthodox.[29]

The sense of separation, even at this late date, however, was such that it could be 'repaired' by a simple statement of assent. Today there is a sense that things have gone further astray; and a simple individual statement of faith is not generally felt to be sufficient remedy to initiate intercommunion.

The worst fears of the Byzantines, in regard to the crusading movement, however, were realized in 1204, during the infamous Fourth Crusade, when the crusading fleet turned aside from their goal of Jerusalem, and settled into several days of looting after their involvement in the toppling of the incumbent Byzantine emperor. The behaviour of the Crusaders, who looted the Orthodox churches of their relics,[30] suggested to the Orthodox observers that not only were the Latins more hostile to them than their Islamic foes, but they clearly had little respect for them as fellow Christians. The invading force desecrated the altars and monasteries of the Byzantine capital, and even though the behaviour of the Crusaders was censured by the pope, it left an abiding sense among the Greeks that Latin Christianity had changed, substantively, had adopted a new attitude to fundamental matters of religion that, to them, now appeared alien and hostile to the churches of the East. From the time of the Fourth Crusade onwards there is clearly a sharp frost in the air in relation to all issues of Orthodox dialogue with the Western Church. There is in addition a pervasive sense (still discernible among many Orthodox in eastern Europe to whom one might talk to this day) that the hostility of the Western Church, and its designs against Orthodoxy, were part of the reason why the Orthodox Church fell so heavily before the might of the Ottoman armies in 1453.

From that time onwards, most of the Orthodox world was to know subjection for centuries to come. It carried on its Christian life, for the most part, under sufferance of non-Christian powers. From this time to the nineteenth century the Orthodox Church lists a massive list of neo-martyrs and confessors among its ranks. There were attempts to broker reunion, and these were especially led by the Byzantine emperors of the day who were desperate to secure the political support of the Western Christian states (and thus needing the pope's blessing) as Islam advanced more and more aggressively against the East-Roman Christian empire. The first reunion council was that of Lyons in 1274. The Orthodox delegates then present agreed (though in as vague a way as they could) to recognize papal claims to supremacy, and also to recite the Creed with the *Filioque* added. Their 'acceptance' of these ideas led to their wholesale repudiation among the Orthodox at large. The emperor's sister is reputed to have replied to the news of Lyons with the words: 'Better my brother's empire should perish, than the unity of the Orthodox faith.'[31] When the empire was once more in critical need of military aid, Emperor John VIII made a passage to the west, and personally attended the unionist Council of Ferrara-Florence (1438–9). The discussions at Florence were much more substantial than anything that had occurred since the time of the patriarch Photios in the ninth century.

The Orthodox delegates at Florence all signed the Act of Union, with the exception of Markos Eugenikos, the archbishop of Ephesus, who has since gained the title of 'Pillar of Orthodoxy'. But the terms of the union were never accepted by the Orthodox back in the home countries, and remained a policy adopted by a tiny minority of court clerics in the capital city. John, and his successor Emperor Constantine IX, the last of the Byzantine emperors, tried to act as if it were an accomplished fact, but it was indicative that the imperial court did not even proclaim publicly that the Act of Union had been signed until 1452, one year before the city's conquest. Many of the Orthodox signatories revoked their names as soon as they left Florence. In the West, by contrast the decree of union was widely announced as a 'return of the schismatic Greeks', and the subsequent evidence of the ineffectiveness of the union was equally widely interpreted as a sign of Orthodox perfidy. At this time, and having little hope that any promised military assistance would ever be forthcoming anyway, the Constantinopolitan Grand Duke Loukas Notaras is reported to have said: 'I would rather see the Muslim turban in the heart of the city, than to see the Latin mitre here.'[32] The political end came quickly for the eastern Roman empire. The forces of Mehmet II, Ottoman sultan, attacked the capital on 7 April 1453, and despite a courageous defence of the Great Walls, broke through on 29 May. At dawn on that day, the last Christian Eucharist was celebrated in the great cathedral of Hagia Sophia. Faced with the prospect of death or enslavement, Latins and Greek Orthodox alike stood together to receive the holy gifts.

In the same period that Constantinople suffered her long decline, Russia rose to political eminence and, along with other eastern European states that retained some degree of free action (such as Wallachia and Moldovia, the precursors of modern Romania), they gave princely help to the wider Orthodox world, and acted as the patrons of Orthodoxy. One of the greatest casualties of the long decline was the great diminution of the schools of the Orthodox at the very time the Renaissance was starting to take effect with the boom of knowledge and literacy in the West. Orthodoxy still suffers from the destruction of its schools to the present, and only in the late twentieth century did the signs change, promising a revival, and good new things for the future, as theological studies once more flourish in Russia and eastern Europe after decades of suppression.

The Slavic mission

When Byzantium was at its zenith, it expanded its sphere of influence by a vast system of federation and alliances with outlying states and peoples.[33] To be adopted by the emperor or to be married into the imperial family was a way in which a political web of treaty and interdependence was extended far and wide as a form of kinship relation of princes all looking to the Byzantine emperor as the centre. This inevitably involved the transmission of Christianity itself into the new regions with which Byzantium came into contact. With the exportation of books and literacy came Christianization of eastern European tribes, and their incorporation into the federation of the Christian imperium. One mission that would have a far-reaching effect was the evangelization of the pagan Slavs, who lay to the north and north-west of the Byzantine borders: the tribes of the Moravians, the Bulgars, Serbs, and Rus, all precursors of great Christian nations to come. Patriarch Photios of Constantinople inspired the Slavic mission and blessed two Greeks from Thessalonica to organize it: Constantine (826–69) and his brother Methodios (c.815–85). They are more commonly known as SS Cyril and Methodios.[34] As children they had already encountered Slavic tribes around their city and had gained familiarity with their language. Inventing a script, based upon Greek letters but with extra sound-signs added, Cyril and Methodios prepared extensive translations of church service books and Gospel translations into this dialect. It would have a vast transmission as 'Church Slavonic' and is still the common ecclesiastical language of Russia, Bulgaria, and Serbia.

When the two brothers left Constantinople they disseminated the literature, the language, and the spiritual culture of Orthodoxy wherever they went. Their mission was hampered by a conflict with the German missionaries who were also at work Latinizing Moravia and Bulgaria. Issues of divergence between the two Christian traditions soon led to acrimony, and the brothers appealed to the Papacy to limit the range of the hostile German preachers, and to allow them to use their vernacular method of spreading the Gospel. Pope Hadrian II gave them his support, but Cyril died in Rome, and when Methodios returned he found papal support actually counted for little on the missionary field. His work was hindered at every turn by German ecclesiastics in Moravia, and after his death his followers were expelled. However, the dramatic failure of the Byzantine-Slav mission in Moravia was not the case elsewhere. The work took root in Bulgaria, Serbia, and among the Rus, the ancestors of Russia. At the very end of the reign of Tsar Simeon (893–927) Bulgaria was recognized as an autonomous patriarchal church, the first national Christian church of the Slavs. Serbia became progressively Christianized in the later ninth century. The multi-patterned picture of the rise of Slavic Christian Orthodoxy is told below, under the rubric of the later 'organization' of the Orthodox churches.

Whether or not the general view of the 'fall' of the Christian East as partly caused, or at least hastened, by the abandonment of the Christian West is correct, it became a deep part of how the Orthodox in the late Middle Ages and into the present had the story of their decline recounted to them. But, as they declined, the Western Church grew in power and status, until the extraordinary events of the multiple scissions among it that are known to us today in the West as the Reformation. Orthodoxy was not able to repair the breach with the West before that extensive fragmentation happened. Even in the present day, its dialogues with Western Christianity are haunted by the suspicion that Western Christians have 'ulterior motives', and even now the relations between the patriarchate of Moscow and the Roman Papacy have been troubled by this ongoing issue, in the form of why the Vatican, after the end of communist control, restored an independent catholic hierarchy within the territory of Russia, at the same time as the pope called for restoration of communion between Western Catholicism and Orthodoxy. Issues that are for many Western Christians things long forgotten, or mere dim memories, are often to the fore of the collective memory and sense of identity of the Orthodox, most of them rooted in a church history which European textbooks still tend to neglect as too obscure for general issue. It will take a long time and much mutual honesty before dialogue can really flower into mutual understanding and reconciliation. The relations of the Orthodox with the Roman Catholic and Protestant worlds, in the meantime, are often badly served by the rhetoric and ceremonial of an ecumenics that sometimes tries to dispense with the laborious task of hearing one another clearly.

THE ORGANIZATION OF THE ORTHODOX CHURCHES FROM MEDIEVAL TO MODERN TIMES

The extension of the Orthodox Church

In the course of the twentieth century Christianity, demographically speaking, became the most extensive and universal religion known to human history.[35] At the beginning of the third millennium there were a total of 2,000 million Christians on earth – one-third of the entire world's population. Among that number the Orthodox are present as 210 million souls bearing witness to the history of the Church, its active present, its anticipated future. One of the important aspects of that witness is the complete unanimity in the faith of all of the Orthodox believers, and their common allegiance to the self-same spiritual ethos of their theological tradition. It is this unanimous bonding and spiritual unity which constitutes their very identity as those who possess the *phronema Christou* (mind of Christ), and share the ancient faith of the apostles and martyrs, who handed it on to them authoritatively and charismatically.

The term 'Orthodox' originally came into popular usage in the Eastern Christian world as a descriptor of the church communities in the sixth century, to distinguish those who accepted the decrees of the Council of Chalcedon (451) from those who refused them.[36] It grew up as a party term, therefore, meant to distinguish the Byzantine Christians (and the Latins along with them) from those dissenting from the Christological settlement of Chalcedon. In subsequent times the anti-Chalcedonian churches of the East have also adopted the epithet, applying it in its wider patristic sense of 'true to the correct opinion' or 'proper in faith'. Thus most of the churches of the East have the word 'Orthodox' in their descriptive title. In the sense of the normal understanding of the 'Orthodox Church', however, the word can be taken here in its original intent, to signify those churches that are in communion with one another because they share the same faith, in which is included the acceptance of the decrees of the Council of Chalcedon, within the totality of the seven ecumenical councils from the first Council of Nicaea in 325 to the second of the same name in 787. The churches which rejected Chalcedon, were historically separated from the communion of the Roman and Byzantine churches from the end of the fifth century onwards and, accordingly, were also not part of the settlement of any of the three subsequently recognized ecumenical councils following Chalcedon (Constantinople II in 553, Constantinople III in 681, and Nicaea II in 787).

The liturgical and spiritual life of these other separated churches of the East[37] is very close to that of the Orthodox Church. The ethos and style of thinking, the attitude to prayer and sacraments, the overall 'ecclesiastical mentality' is also immensely close, since the separation took place at a time so early in the patristic age. By the grace of God a union may once more be a thing that can be accomplished, if more ways can be opened up for a renewal of mutual love and respect. Historically so much of the division was the result of political tensions and nationalist rivalry, and misunderstood intellectual initiatives. In the present century, where the political environment is so different, and the chances for a truer and deeper mutual understanding are so much better, the ecumenical 'dialogue of love' between Orthodoxy and the non-Chalcedonian Eastern churches may indeed be coming to a new era of hope and fruitfulness, based on a deeper understanding that the *Mia physis*[38] of St Cyril of Alexandria's early theology (which the non-Chalcedonians prioritize) is not intrinsically opposed at all, to the Christology of 'one hypostasis and two natures' presented by the Chalcedonian Fathers, who were also prioritizing (and nuancing) St Cyril.[39] Formerly designated the 'Monophysite' churches, and now more eirenically the 'Miaphysite' or non-Chalcedonian Eastern churches,[40] these are the Syrian,[41] Armenian, Coptic, Ethiopic, and Malabar Indian churches. There is also the so-called 'Nestorian' Church of Syria, which is more properly known as the Assyrian Church. This took a line of resistance quite different to the anti-Chalcedonian Miaphysites, and stressed the distinction of the natures of the Incarnate Lord in a way that held Cyril of Alexandria to be anathema (thus also rejecting the legitimacy of the generally accepted Council of Ephesus in 431).

In addition to this, there is also a local presence of the hierarchs in the communion of the Orthodox Church in most of these Eastern countries (Orthodox clergy of the patriarchate of Alexandria in Egypt, for example, along with the Coptic hierarchy; Syrian Orthodox clergy of the patriarchate of Antioch in Syria along with the Syrian anti-Chalcedonians, and so on). In many places there are also representative clergy in communion with Rome. In Jerusalem, for example, there is now the Orthodox patriarch, and a 'Latin' patriarch. In Syria there have been at one time seven senior ecclesiastics all designated as 'patriarchs of Antioch'. In most cases, if not all, the churches all have the word 'Orthodox' in their title. The simplest clarifying issue, in the view of the Byzantine Orthodox tradition, and the one followed in this book is that the term 'Orthodox Church' refers to those churches in communion with one another who accept the statement of faith as established by the seven ecumenical

25

councils, as the sum total of the great councils. The patriarchs whom we recognize, and there can only be one in each instance in accordance with the strictest principles of Orthodox ecclesiology,[42] are those senior members of the hierarchy who lead the Orthodox communities of those places. This will not reduce or resolve the confusion Western Christians will have, on encountering representatives of the different Eastern communions, but it should serve to explain that, for Orthodoxy, there is no confusion at all. Belonging and self-identity are, as always, determined by the issue of communion. The church, in essence, is a reality, indeed an ontology, of communion. Outside of the family of the communion, there is no Orthodox Church, because Orthodoxy is the communion.

The members of this historic community of the Orthodox faithful are still today in communion with one another, joined by the strongest of spiritual bonds in oneness of faith and practice, though distinguished by legitimate distinctions of national characteristic and organization. This Orthodox Church in the present world order knows much about national character (perhaps too much, for such 'new' things as national spirit sometimes militate against the ancient and God-given concept of the universal union of catholicity) but still the use of different national titles for Orthodoxy (such as the Greek Orthodox Church, or the Russian Orthodox Church, or the Romanian, Serbian, and so on) simply means the Orthodox Church as it concretely exists in Russia, Greece, Romania, or any of the other countries. The Orthodox canons[43] have, from antiquity, recognized the principle of the organizational division of the church on the basis of territorial separateness, that is the operative civic divisions. It is this dynamic principle of conformity to political realities, without capitulating to them, that has allowed Orthodoxy to develop and reorganize for so many centuries, whether under political rulers who favoured the Church or persecuted it.

This principle of the division of church jurisdiction by civic boundaries must not, however, be equated with division by ethnic border (with which it can be mistakenly identified). The Church of Christ unites races, it does not divide them or celebrate the mere fact of racial distinction.[44] The notion that each race or nation (modern conceptions overlaid superficially onto the bedrock of the apostolic faith) 'ought to be' a separate church, distinct to itself, has rightly been recognized as a heretical tendency of the modern era, and condemned as such by the patriarchate of Constantinople in 1872, who named it 'phyletism'.[45] It is proper for a nation to be a church organized on its own autonomous basis; it is not appropriate to argue that the church should be organized along tribal lines, towards which many aspects of modern 'nationalism' now run (especially in the diaspora).

This disease of phyletism has nevertheless gained a hold on some parts of the contemporary Orthodox mentality, encouraged by secular attitudes of governments in times past and present. It can be particularly seen in the desires of ancient churches located within the territorial comprehensiveness of a modern nation, to sustain 'missions' in other countries where the Orthodox have now been established for many centuries. Such is the situation applying to many parts of America and Oceania where the Orthodox are split up into many different 'jurisdictions', giving allegiance to bishops appointed by various 'home synods' as if they were temporary missions in colonial provinces. Such a situation (certainly as the initial reality of mission dwindles away across generations of establishment) is wholly against the spirit of Orthodox ecclesiology, and must one day be settled with the establishment of new autocephalous churches in those new continents.

This is not at issue, substantively, among the Orthodox. The only question of argument is how long is it suitable for a church to be established and rooted in a new land before it can take on its own identity canonically speaking. There is also the related question of who has the authority to initiate this and organize it. This is perhaps already long overdue in Australia and America. But movement towards the declaration of a real national presence of the Orthodox in a new church will require, of course, the eirenical co-operation of the existing major patriarchates, especially Constantinople and Russia, so that it can be canonically effected. In the meantime the 'on-the-ground' situation of the Orthodox Church in places such as America and Oceania presents to the observer (and to the faithful who look that far) a bewildering diversity of 'jurisdictions' that most of the laity walk through as if they were annoying jungle creepers, but which actually prevent the hierarchy and clergy of those countries from organizing their mission for the best allocation of church resources. The days are now long past when the 'Eastern' Church existed only in a geographical 'orient'. There are now far more Greeks spread across the world than there are in the Greek homelands, and the situation has been like this for several generations.

Just as it would be ridiculous to go on indefinitely imagining that the American Irish after 150 years were still Irish citizens who simply happened accidentally to be living a long way from home, so it is with the Greek diaspora situation. The same truth applies to those of Slavic origin who have also entered the New World and become absorbed into it, with their children no longer speaking any of the original languages. The issue of multi-jurisdictions of Orthodox in the same country, envisaged on a permanent basis as a normal form of ecclesiastical life is, needless to say, an aberration. But it cannot be resolved until there is the will to face the issue, the inspiration to assume a common identity as Orthodox in a new world environment, and the sense of catholicity that overcomes residual nationalisms that do not form a true perspective on the mind of the church.

Some believe that western Europe should also be declared no longer a 'mission' for the Orthodox who happen to live there, but this is a different situation, for this 'territory' is historically that of the ancient Roman patriarchate, and to establish a national Orthodox Church there would be a serious matter hindering the return to unity. In the other cases the canons of the ancient councils (especially Chalcedon 451) already directed that 'new worlds' would fall initially under the care of the ecumenical patriarchate (implying that it would arrange their admission into the communion of churches). Western Europe, however, is not 'New World', and most of the Orthodox churches are there, deliberately without erecting a parallel hierarchy to that existing from ancient times. This silence, and inaction, in relation to the establishment of a canonical fully 'local' church,[46] is a very basic form of expression of the spirit of Eastern ecclesiology. It is also an important, if implicit, statement of ecumenical eirenicity to the ancient churches of the West who pre-exist there. Christian proselytism in Russia or other parts of Orthodox eastern Europe, from Protestant sects, for example, is regarded there as a sign that an 'ecclesial mentality' has been lost among them. But the establishment of churches subject to bishops of the Roman patriarchate within Russia or other Orthodox countries (the so-called 'Uniate' problem) is at the root of much contemporary strife. It has currently turned away the face of the local Orthodox hierarchies from the otherwise laudatory ecumenical initiatives of the Roman patriarchate, as the desire to affirm a right to intervene in eastern Europe

27

is taken as a sure 'give-away' of deeper principles of Roman ecclesiology which are regarded by the Orthodox as objectionable – not least the principle of jurisdictional superiority as it is expressed in the Roman Catholic theology of the Papacy.

The Orthodox Church at present consists of the four ancient patriarchates which remain in communion, out of the five ancient, patristic, exemplars of the pentarchy of patriarchates[47] that once established the largest-scale (what we would now call the 'international') form of the canonical structure of early Christianity: Constantinople, Alexandria, Antioch, and Jerusalem. To these four patriarchates are now added the other churches that have been formed as the Church of Christ expanded in the world, and new nations and peoples were added to the family of Christ in the course of history, or as older parts of the whole reached a stage of legitimate self-determination and organized themselves more independently from the ancient centres of the empire. They can be briefly listed: first, those that were once part (or allies) of the ancient Byzantine empire but emerged into separate nationhood as that vast system began to fragment; Bulgaria, Ukraine, Russia, Serbia, Georgia, Romania, Greece, Poland, Hungary, Albania, Latvia, Moldavia, and Macedonia. Secondly, those also that were historically never part of the eastern Roman empire but came into their Christian maturity at a later date: Finland, Slovakia and the Czech Republic, Estonia, China, Japan, sub-Saharan Africa,[48] Australia, America, and many parts of western Europe (as missions and exarchates).

Some of these newer churches have subsequently, and more recently, been lifted to the designation of 'patriarchates' signifying their large extent, historical importance, and general venerability. There is a precedence operating in the Orthodox under-standing of the 'order' of the churches, but it is not one that can be understood in the sense of a jurisdictional order, such as a hierarchical line of authority that runs down, in the manner of army authority working in a simple linear fashion, or suchlike. Orthodox ecclesiology is adamant on one central point: that each local church under its single bishop is the full and entire Church of Christ. Each Orthodox bishop is, therefore, coequal with all his other brother bishops throughout the world. There may be a 'ranking of honour' in the sense that a metropolitan of a city (an archbishop, for example) has a supervisory role over a number of the other bishops of his local province, or in the way that a patriarch has a significant degree of precedence in the synod of all the bishops of his country, and sometimes (in accordance with the canons) in relation to appeals sent to him from other parts of the church over which he has the right to adjudicate;[49] but all of this does not contravene the more fundamental principle that each bishop in his own diocese is entirely equal in apostolic status to all other bishops in the world.[50]

For this reason Orthodoxy has no pope, among its patriarchs.[51] The outside world, especially the media, may simplify their reports of Orthodox organization, so as to describe the patriarch of Constantinople as the 'Leader of the Orthodox World', but in fact this is an erroneous representation of the inner life of the church. The patriarch of Constantinople is certainly 'first among equals' among all Orthodox bishops; but the issue of who leads the church, who speaks for it, can not be answered in this simplistic linear sense of monarchical governance (except to point to Christ, the undying Lord of his church in heaven as well as on earth). In terms of authority within the church polity, however, the patriarch of Constantinople has a prestigious office, and often 'speaks for' Orthodox interests on a broad world platform. But the patriarch of Moscow is the senior hierarch of the single largest Orthodox Church in the world. For generations past his office has been stifled, and censored. Today it is learning to speak out again in freedom. Its future will be immensely significant, for world-wide Christianity just as it once was before the disaster of the Soviet oppression of the early twentieth century overwhelmed it. But who leads the church? No single earthly voice, but Christ, and Christ's inspired people in their various offices and duties (bishops, priest, deacons, ascetics, married couples, prophets, martyrs among them). Who speaks for it? Christ and his saints (in the Gospels and Scriptures) as well as the whole body of the faithful, formed in his mind, in all their historic embodiment (including the utterances of the faithful from the past, epitomized in the symbolical sources, and those who may come from the future too). Bishops, among all these inspired offices which are represented across the great body of the faithful, have the special and particular office of teaching and guiding the flock; but this teaching charism does not exhaust, let alone supersede, that charism as it exists in many other places too: the multiform teaching ministry of parents, grandparents, catechism and school teachers, saints and martyrs, who all sing the song of Christ's glory through and across the generations, and pass on the charge and flame of faith like the flickering of a lighted candle from soul to soul, and from heart to heart; the only way Christ's love can be communicated truly.

This is not, in any sense, a 'confusion of order' among the Orthodox, though it may seem to be such to those catholic Christians of the West who are used to a more linear and bureaucratic way of organizing the exercise of power within the church; or to those who from their different Protestant traditions have exalted the principle of individual apprehension of the truth to a degree that Orthodoxy does not accept. Nor is it a hopelessly romantic way of understanding church order and discipline. Because Orthodoxy, for all it has a broadly diffused and essentially charismatic understanding of the mystery of authority within the church, is not thereby rendered 'paralysed' in the concrete historical instance. The authority of bishops is seen, and accepted, as the focused voice of the Lord's authority in his earthly Church. It is a great power that is cared for, and balanced, within the system of synodical oversight. But even so, Orthodoxy will never say that the bishop is the 'only' source of authority within Christ's Church.

Accordingly it is not the bishops or the priests who alone are the 'voice' of the church. (Certainly not the theologian or the historian among us acting as some 'super-consciousness'.) None of the clergy can claim to be the conscience of the church either, or at least if they do so, they of necessity make such an extraordinary claim in the light of speaking out the faith prophetically in times of stress, in the awareness that they are in harmony with the whole body of the faithful from time immemorial – not that their personal or official authority entitles them to make such statements as a matter of course. Orthodoxy, then, is deeply collegial in character as regards its understanding of authority and principles of guidance. The hierarchy plays an immensely important part, but even in doing so its members are not 'set apart' from the whole consciousness, the *sobornost*, of the Church of Christ, whose sacred tradition forms and governs each member in a direct and concrete way. The clergy are never, simply, 'the church'. The whole body, what the blessed Augustine designated as the *totus Christus* (Christ in all his fullness, complete with his mystical body), alone claims that dignity.

Synopsis of the organization of the Orthodox churches

The jurisdictional organization of the Orthodox Church, then, flows out of the principle of the local churches gathered under their bishops, arranged in larger metropolitan provincial synods, and this as eventually culminating in the expression of the ancient pentarchy of patriarchates which were felt to express an 'international' sense of different Christian cultures in harmony with the whole. The ancient pentarchy was: Rome, Constantinople, Alexandria, Antioch, and Jerusalem. To the latter four of this number, which remain in Orthodox communion, there are now included several other autocephalous Orthodox[52] churches, and other autonomous Orthodox churches which are still attached to their supervisory 'sponsor churches' by closer organizational ties. These autonomous churches are an extension of the 'international character' of world Orthodoxy that prevailed in antiquity within the pentarchy of patriarchates that constituted the Christian Roman empire. The pattern is now as follows:

The four ancient patriarchates
Constantinople
Alexandria
Antioch
Jerusalem

The eleven autocephalous churches[53]
Cyprus (431)
Sinai[54] (1575)
Russia (1589)
Greece (1850)
Bulgaria (1870)
Serbia (1879)
Romania (1885)
Georgia (1919)
Poland (1924)
Albania (1937)
the Czech lands and Slovakia (1951)

The Orthodox Church in America is 'in process' of belonging to this group (in the sense that it is still in the process of gaining world-wide Orthodox recognition). It assumed autocephalous ecclesiastical status in 1970 with the blessing of the patriarchate of Moscow. The autonomy has not been acknowledged by the patriarchate of Constantinople.

The three autonomous churches
Finland (1923; patriarchate of Constantinople)
Japan (1970; patriarchate of Moscow)
China (1957; patriarchate of Moscow)
(See also Estonia and Ukraine, below)

30

Various 'diaspora' churches

The so-called diaspora churches are the Orthodox of different ethnic groupings who for historical reasons, such as immigration or trade over past generations, have been removed from their original homelands and now reside in what were formerly seen as 'Western' countries. Orthodoxy is now deeply rooted in most parts of western Europe and America, as the old geographical simplicities have increasingly been blurred by global mobility. There are, for example, incomparably more Orthodox belonging to the patriarchate of Constantinople living in North America than there are in the old heartlands of Thrace, Asia Minor, or Greece. There are more Orthodox living in Britain today than there are Baptists.

The old religious maps are changing. Diaspora churches began as a pastoral concern for mission. They were set up by the authority of the home synods of the various churches (above) who had faithful resident in foreign parts, and their organization was complex or simple, extensive or merely local, depending on the size of the original immigrant communities in different language groups.[55] As time went on, throughout the late nineteenth century to the present, the long-term nature of these communities tended to 'establish' them in ways that had not originally been foreseen. Moreover, the political problems of eastern Europe (particularly as they affected the countries which fell under the Soviet yoke) led to significant problems of unity and coherence both within these communities (which resisted the communist yoke from the vantage point of their freedom) and in terms of their relation to the home synod. In most cases the fundamental issue of an extension of the home synod's authority for a mission in a foreign country did not come into dispute. In most of the instances, Orthodox 'presences' were simply being set up within the historically defined territory of the ancient Western patriarchate, where a national Orthodox hierarchy had never been in existence, and for which there was no intention to newly constitute a resident one (which would be an act of proselytizing that disregarded all the rights of the Western Church).

But there was a problem that was destined to grow in the new millennium, and that was in relation to countries which could not be regarded as once having been constituent parts of the Western Church (Oceania, America, Asia, for example). There the Orthodox could claim the right to establish the national church of the country on the basis of the canon of the Council of Chalcedon attributing care of newly discovered lands to the patriarch of Constantinople. This question we can discuss shortly. Although the planting of the church historically tends to follow national trade missions, in the main, and the Chalcedonian canon is not entirely relevant to the actual global situation, nevertheless the question of long resident Orthodox 'mission' communities in Oceania, Asia, and America becomes acute when it is obvious to all that the original 'mission' has now grown into the status of a new potentially indigenous Orthodox church. Today this does not apply, in practice, except perhaps in relation to Oceania and North America, instances we shall also discuss.

The ancient patriarchates

1 The patriarchate of Constantinople

The patriarch of Constantinople[56] now has a primacy of honour within Orthodoxy. There is enduring historical controversy among scholars (as was the case in ancient church history too) over whether the twenty-eighth canon of the Council of Chalcedon (451) which gave it primacy, intended to make it first after Rome, that is 'second' in rank and precedence, which was more or less the import of the third canon of Constantinople I (381), or whether it was meant to make it into the new first see of Christendom, the 'next' of that rank, succeeding to the privileges of the old first see which itself had enjoyed its erstwhile primacy by virtue of being the former capital of the empire.[57] The wording and intention of the Chalcedonian canon remain the subject of historical exegesis, as it is not simply the case that Constantinople is made 'second in rank after Rome' as most Western church writers have presumed. The range of privileges granted to it as court of appeal, especially in canon 9 of the same Council of Chalcedon, far exceeded those which Old Rome had commanded up to that time. The issue of canon 28 would be a constant friction in East–West church relations afterwards, until the Great Schism of the eleventh century made it, practically speaking, irrelevant. It continues to have controversial status as to its exact sense of application in contemporary church law, not merely with regard to ecumenical relations between Orthodoxy and Roman Catholicism, but also internally (especially in a lively tension between the patriarchates of Constantinople and Moscow) as to the extent of canon 28's applicability in terms of executive 'superintendence'.

The patriarch, known as His All-Holiness the archbishop of Constantinople, the New Rome, and ecumenical patriarch, is now still resident in Istanbul, the ancient Constantinople. This capital of 'New Rome' was founded by Constantine the Great in the early fourth century to be the military and political centre of the Roman empire. From this time onwards, and it remained the case until the ninth century, the fortunes of the older Western capital at Rome went into serious decline. Even late into the fourth century, however, Constantinople's ecclesiastical significance was very modest, reflecting its origins (as the colonial port of Byzantium) as a subordinate part of the diocese of Thrace (now Bulgaria). Byzantium had been a thoroughly insignificant city before Constantine's re-foundation, and the new capital took some time to establish itself as a powerful magnet of ecclesiastical affairs, just as it did to establish itself as the veritable centre of all political power in the Roman world. The rise to pre-eminence was rapid enough when it did happen, of course. And by the late fourth and early fifth centuries the bishops of Constantinople had become in effect archbishops by gathering together a whole ecclesiastical territory that looked to them for supervision and guidance. The institution of the home synod was encouraged by the archbishop of Constantinople. Because so many bishops came to the capital so regularly, to pursue political and other business there, they were invited to share in the deliberations of the local church. The home synod still functions in a more limited way as the governing body of patriarchal affairs. It is now made up of the ecclesiastical eparchies which are still immediately subject to the patriarch (Derkos, Chalcedon, Prinkipo, and Imbros), along with other titular archbishops who, as senior hierarchs, govern the diaspora churches as exarchs on behalf of the patriarch.

This ever-increasing and effective functioning as an international clearing house in the heart of the capital set Constantinople on a path of collision with the more ancient patriarchates, particularly Rome, Alexandria, and Antioch. Their grumbling and friction mark the pages of almost every ecclesiastical argument of antiquity. Rome, by the universal agreement of all until the time of the Council of Chalcedon, was regarded as the primary court of appeal for the Christian world. Even though the city had lost much of its effective political power after the fourth century, it was still afforded the 'right' to be considered as the last ecclesiastical court of appeal. This right was effectively undercut in practice by the simple reason that travel in antiquity was immensely difficult, so only the most critical of any issues from the Eastern, Greek-speaking, churches would ever be heard as an appeal in Rome anyway. To complicate matters, language difficulties also stood in the way, and this too was reflected in the ancient canons of the church. For most practical affairs, then, the see of Alexandria at first held the precedence in the Eastern Church, mirroring what Rome did in practical terms for all the Western churches, where it was the sole patriarchal and apostolic see. The rise to political pre-eminence of Constantinople changed this system of ecclesiastical governance. Constantinople's expansion not only 'put out' Alexandria; it also began to overshadow the patriarchate of Antioch and the Syrian hierarchs, whose territory it was very close to. There were moments of tension between Constantinople and Antioch, also reflected in the decisions of the early councils, but many of the most important of the early Constantinopolitan archbishops were drawn from the ambit of the Syrians and Cappadocians who adjoined that region.

The second ecumenical council, which took place at Constantinople in 381, and the Council of Chalcedon in 451, gave the precedence of Constantinople greater clarity and force. It has always been seen as a matter of 'normalcy' among the Orthodox that a city's ecclesiastical importance should reflect its role in the structure of the civic governance.[58] By this period the position of the imperial capital was unarguably central in church affairs just as it was in political affairs, and from this time on the patriarchate of Constantinople was established as the centre of precedence among the Eastern churches. The Roman patriarchate continued to resist the implication that a see's precedence should be tied to its geopolitical importance.[59] Nevertheless the canonical position of the patriarchate of Constantinople was universally accepted in the East, and Rome itself came to admit it, long before the time of the Great Schism of the Middle Ages. After the rise of Arab power in the seventh century, the once great Christian communities of Antioch and Alexandria fell into disastrous decline, which further elevated the prestige and importance of Constantinople as a Christian nucleus. The decree of the sultan set the patriarch of Constantinople as the political superior of the other patriarchs for the first time ever. This immense temptation to follow the path to political domination over the other churches was largely resisted. The potential of the patriarchate under Islamic power to lord it over the other sees was also under-mined by a certain degree of corruption of the Phanar, which closeness to the seat of the sultanate brought with it; for in the late fifteenth and throughout the sixteenth and seventeenth centuries the patriarchate was massively unsettled by the extent of bribery the sultans encouraged for elevation to that sacred office.

After the first cabal of Greek merchants from Trebizond offered the sultan a bribe of 1,000 florins to depose the incumbent patriarch Mark II (1466–7) and replace him with a candidate of their own choice, the sultan's eyes were opened to the possibilities. By 1572 the standard 'investiture fee' for the patriarch was the substantial 'gift' of 2,000 florins, and an annual payment of 4,000 more, gathered from taxation of the Christian 'Rum' people who were placed under the patriarch's supreme charge throughout the Ottoman empire. There were always more than enough Christian factions lining up to pay the highest premium to ensure the election of their candidate after that point. Accordingly the tenure of the patriarchs under Turkish rule was usually very short. Sometimes the same candidate acceded to the office, was deposed, and re-elected to it five or six times (each time paying the necessary fees). Between the sixteenth century and the early part of the twentieth century 159 patriarchs held office. Of this number the Turks drove out of office 105. Several were forced to abdicate, and six were judicially assassinated. The cadre of Greeks who sailed this stormy sea, trying to keep the prestige of the patriarchate intact and effective (sometimes using it for unworthy ambitions), tended to live in what was then the wealthy suburb called the Phanar; and were thus known as Phanariots. Many of the higher offices of the church were subsequently put into their hands when a new patriarch acceded, and this in turn led to the Phanariot Greek clergy becoming a kind of colonial superior race directing churches in distant lands, using the mandate of the sultan and the decree of the patriarch to justify it. They in turn, as local archbishops, levied taxes on their new people. As a result the Turkish 'yoke' cast a long pall over Orthodox relations with the patriarchate. The British historian Kidd acerbically described the situation in the following terms:

> Thus the patriarchate, degraded by simony and made the sport of intrigue by its own people, has come to be regarded by many of the Orthodox as an agent of the Turkish government, and identified with its oppression. But the patriarchate has also come to be identified by such of the Orthodox as are non-Greek, with the cause of Hellenic nationalism. . . . A widespread hostility has thus pursued the Phanariot clergy among the non-Greek Orthodox; and the revolts which the Phanar puts down to Phyletism[60] have issued in the enforced recognition of national churches, as a refuge from Phanariot oppression.[61]

His view explains why some of the newer national Orthodox churches sprang into being after the collapse of the power of the sultanate in the nineteenth century, although it does not give the whole picture: how in most instances this return to independence was a return to more venerable ecclesiastical situations that had pre-dated the Turkish yoke. One other note, we might add (as Kidd himself does later), is a necessary reference to the way that the patriarchate and the Greek Orthodox world also shone with the glory of new martyrdoms throughout this dreadful period. Hostile critics of the Orthodox scene have sometimes been too ready to cry 'collaboration' and 'simoniacal conformism' when they have seen Orthodoxy under the foot of either Turkish or Soviet oppressions. But they have generally done so from the comfort and safety of their armchairs, and the financial security of ecclesiastical establishment. But the blood that has been spilled in the Orthodox Church over the last three centuries is incomparably greater than the amount of the blood of the martyrs that was shed in the first three centuries of what we now call the period of the 'Great Persecutions'.[62] It is all too often forgotten, and martyrdom is sometimes all too easily draped with the clothes of romanticism, by those who do not have to bear its impact. But the effects on a martyred church are truly felt for generations, even centuries, after. The appalling suffering often leaves generations of traumatic reactions in its aftermath.

One continuing effect is the relative paucity of establishments of higher learning in the Orthodox world at large. Another is the way in which communities learn to be suspicious and mutually distrustful of one another in dark times, and need to unlearn these pathologies that were once understandable, but never blessed. For Orthodoxy across the world, the dark ages are now passing. What was done, in all its splendour, and in all its defects, in those hard times, now leads into a new dawn. In this new day it is our general hope that the patriarchates of Constantinople, Moscow, Romania (and the other great centres) will shine ever more brightly, in new-found freedoms, and so in a deepening spirit of collegiality with all the other Orthodox churches. But, as in the aftermath of every sustained time of oppression, the church's most pressing task is for internal reconciliation. It is always the destiny and vocation of the church to be the sign and sacrament of unity in the world. Its own fragmentation, whether as a result of human passions or the wickedness of external oppressors and the wide trail of misery this leaves behind it, can never deflect it from its overwhelming task of unity and reconciliation. This is a command which Christ himself has laid upon it. He never said that reconciliation would be easy. He simply commanded his church to 'be one'.[63] The primary impetus for such union is the evangelical love of the Lord himself. His path is difficult, for Christ's love is sacrificial, and (hardest for human hearts of all things) profoundly humble and merciful.

The end of political coherence within the sprawling Ottoman empire, which was becoming more and more obvious at the end of the nineteenth century, certainly witnessed the breaking up of the immediate jurisdictional sphere of Constantinople. Russia had already detached from its orbit in the fifteenth century following the controversy concomitant on the Council of Florence. It declared itself a new patriarchate in 1589. Greece (while remaining in the closest of all ties of affection and loyalty to the patriarchate) declared its independence from the Phanar organizationally in 1850, Bulgaria in 1870, Serbia in 1879, and Romania in 1885. Georgia and Ukraine did the same in regard to the Moscow patriarchate, which had formerly supervised them, in 1919 but these would be brought back under control through the enforced Sovietization of their nations later, and would again seek independence when those powers of political control were once more loosened from the Russian centre.

In the tenth century, however, when it was in its glory, Constantinople had supervisory rank over no fewer than 624 dioceses. In its heyday its ecclesiastical territory of influence embraced all the Balkans, all Thrace, all of Russia from the White Sea to the Caucasus, and the whole of Asia Minor. Today, five and a half centuries after the fall of the city to the power of Islam, it is in a state of very sad decline 'on the ground', though it remains a brightly shining beacon and example to Orthodox world over, by virtue of its spiritual fidelity and the enduring ecclesiastical role of the patriarch as *primus inter pares*.[64] Many of the patriarchs of Constantinople, throughout its long history, have been Christian leaders of the highest calibre, and the historical record of the throne is (overall) a vastly prestigious one. It continues this office in straitened circumstances, under difficult political and religious constraints. Today there are hardly any resident Greeks left of the thousands of Greeks, Armenians, and other Christian nationals who once made Istanbul a truly universal and cosmopolitan centre of world affairs.

Since the bitter Graeco-Turkish war of 1922 the massive exchange of populations that took place meant that Asia Minor was more or less denuded of its Greek inhabitants[65] for the first time in recorded history. Turkish law only permits the residence of Greeks in Istanbul itself, but after 1922 it became more and more impossible for most Christian families to feel secure, and so the mass exodus began. Current Turkish law forbids nuns or priests to wear clerical dress in public (with the single exception of the patriarch), and there is much popular hostility to the idea of a Greek Christian leader living in the heart of this Islamic city. On 6 September

1955 a large anti-Greek riot, sparked by the Cyprus problem, led to the burning or sacking of sixty out of the eighty Orthodox churches remaining in Istanbul, and most of the surviving Christian community lost heart at that point. Damage to Christian property was then estimated at more than £50 million. The Turkish government subsequently paid £4 million in compensation. With deportations and voluntary emigration following, the resident Greek population continued over the remainder of the latter half of the twentieth century to dwindle to demographic insignificance.

Those entering the Phanar today are swept with electronic searching devices to discourage hidden weapons, or the leaving of bombs in church (incidents which are, alas, not imaginary). The Orthodox theological school of Halki, on one of the adjoining islands of the city, founded in 1844, was once a centre of the advancement of the clergy. In the middle of the century it had begun to acquire an international reputation among the Orthodox churches as a centre of learning. In 1971 the Turkish government forcibly suppressed the admission of new students, on the grounds of preventing 'propaganda and anti-Turkish sentiment' (a reference to the Cyprus crisis) and despite many efforts since to reopen it, its enforced closure remains a stain on that government's record of religious toleration. The modern post-war patriarchs Athenagoras, Dimitrios, and Bartholomew have brought great dignity and honour to their office, enduring these difficulties, and by their personal gifts restoring an internationally luminous reputation to their throne, far beyond the formal extent of Orthodox circles. Relations with the Turkish secular powers have tended to improve, and the prospect of Turkey's entrance into the European community of nations has also acted as a spur to better relations between the Phanar and its political overlords. The Treaty of Lausanne (1923) formally governs relations between the Phanar and the Turkish state. It currently requires the patriarch always to be a Turkish citizen. It also restricts his role to 'only spiritual' matters, preventing him from being involved in politics.

The present territorial extent of Constantinople's ecclesiastical jurisdiction is comprised by Turkey, the ancient parts of Thrace that are not in present-day Bulgaria, Crete, some Greek islands in the Aegean,[66] the monasteries of Mount Athos, all Greeks of the diaspora (large numbers in Europe, America, and Oceania), and a jurisdictional oversight over the Church of Finland (since 1923), and some parts of the Russian diaspora communities who have sought the Phanar's guidance for historical reasons related to the Russian Revolution. The total number of faithful directly belonging to the jurisdiction of the patriarchate is today in the region of 7 million. The vast majority of them are in the diaspora. The category of the diaspora at first initiated as a mission to Greeks who came to the West has now been extended, in some places over many generations, to cover the very large Greek Christian communities of America and Australia, and also the smaller exarchate of Great Britain and Ireland, which can no longer be considered missionary territories. Much more than half the lay members of the patriarchate, for example, now reside in North America, and many of the Greek Orthodox there are so thoroughly Americanized that some of them have forgotten their ancestral language. The Phanar continues to exercise jurisdictional oversight over several Slavonic rite dioceses in 'exile', Russian, Ukrainian, Polish, and Albanian, which put themselves under the patriarchal protection in the difficult times following the large flight westwards from communist oppression in the early part of the twentieth century. The question of the continuing need for 'exile' is a current point of inter-Orthodox tension.

The monasteries of Mount Athos

The famous Athonite monasteries fall directly under the administration of the patriarch of Constantinople for all religious matters. The twenty ruling houses, and other smaller dependencies, exist under special protocol as an autonomous region within the sovereignty of the Greek state.

Mount Athos, on the Halkidiki peninsula in Greece, is a remarkable survival of Byzantine religious life, over a thousand years old, a jewel of Orthodox monasticism, which once could boast of several such 'holy mountains', whole areas of wilderness that been colonized by hermits and cenobitic ascetics. After the fall of Constantinople in 1453, Athos was able to negotiate its own continuance by paying taxes to its new Islamic masters, and by fighting off as best it could the regular depredations of Mediterranean pirates. Its increasing impoverishment and obscurity took it far away from its former glory in the times of the Byzantine empire when it was a veritable centre of intellectual scholarship and political influence (one of the great centres of imperial patronage and influence), but this also managed to ensure its survival. It is not only a great living museum of Byzantine heritage[67] whose architectural and natural beauties are world-renowned,[68] but it still continues with its most important function in the Orthodox world: the quiet living out of the monastic life. Athos in its heyday had an estimated monastic population of 40,000. By 1913 the years of decline had taken their toll. Its population then was just under 8,000. In a few years the large flow of Russian monks and pilgrims to the holy mountain would dry up. By 1954 the population of resident monks had fallen to 3,000. The decline seemed irreversible in the mid twentieth century. In 1969 there were only 1,350 monks, and in 1971, not more than 1,145. Since the 1980s there have been signs of a dramatic reversing of the tide, and the present state of the holy mountain is one of promising material and intellectual revival, though on certain issues (such as the patriarchate of Constantinople's involvement in the ecumenical movement) they take a very negative and hostile stand.

Athos is a renowned centre for the strict observance of the monastic Typikon, and also for the advanced eremitical life of its solitaries and small groups of hermits. Its excellence in liturgical style, and matters of church music is well known across the Orthodox world. Many of its elders are household names among the Orthodox of Greece, and many Orthodox from all over the world regularly make a pilgrimage to the holy mountain to visit the different monasteries and to consult the spiritual fathers on a variety of matters. Some of the Athonite elders have also had a wider impact, with monks having trained there and then coming out to other countries to reinvigorate the monastic life. One example is the patriarchal monastery of St John the Forerunner, at Tolleshunt Knights in Essex, England, which was founded by Archimandrite Sophrony, the spiritual disciple of St Silouan of Athos. At the present moment there are twenty 'ruling' monasteries comprising Mount Athos, and these also have smaller dependencies, known as *sketes* (isolated houses where small communities live together) or *kellia* (even smaller cottages and chapels, and sometimes comprised of remote hermitages with an isolated monk living the solitary life). In former times, its intellectual life set a standard for the world. For centuries after the fall of Byzantium, however, its intellectual life dwindled, and the monks were more often drawn from the peasant classes.

37

The administrative centre of the mountain is at Karyes, and representatives of the ruling monasteries take turns to sit on the central council, presided over by the representative of the Great Lavra monastery, the first-ranking foundation on the mountain. The current administrative protocol largely follows the Typikon drawn up by the Constantinopolitan patriarch Gabriel IV in 1783. The Greek government administers the holy mountain under a protocol which allows it an autonomous governance. The readmission of Slav and east European ascetics (once the Russian, Romanian, Bulgarian, and Serbian monks had an extensive presence on the holy mountain, and the patronage of the Romanian princes sustained Athos in difficult times) is still heavily restricted. Only when this situation is remedied will Athos be able once again to be a true centre of Orthodox monasticism, a role which it aspires to. The patriarch has had the right to supervise all the monasteries of Athos since the time of Emperor Alexios Comnenos (1081–1118). The bishop of Ierissos is appointed as his representative to the holy mountain.

The monks, while following his spiritual leadership, are generally less ready to follow the ecumenical example, or the openness, which the ecumenical throne offers the wider world. Recent legal, emotional, and physical struggles on the mountain between exclusivist rigorists and those who advocated a more open attitude, (televized world-wide as monks fought with each other and pulled one another's beards) did little to give wider society an edifying image of how the solitary life can assuage the passions. The pressure of tourism (motivated both by religious and secular curiosity) has in recent times threatened to overwhelm the tiny colony, which has rightly acted to preserve its fundamental *raison d'être*, which is the serious pursuit of the ascetic contemplative life. Athos' role in the future of Orthodoxy will be secured more fully only when it rises to the challenges posed by the changed conditions of the modern world, and when it renews its intellectual life to the extent that it can take a powerful lead in Orthodox dogmatic and pastoral theology once more, as it did in times past. It also needs to make statements about the faith, and the condition of the churches which are not solely seen to be motivated by antiquarianism and fearful hostility to the world. When these conditions can be met, Athos may once again be a lighthouse to the whole Orthodox world. Its life of faithful prayer and worship, nevertheless, continues, quietly sustaining a world in the blessings of God, unknown to the multitudes outside who are busy in their own affairs.

2 The patriarchate of Alexandria

Second after Constantinople in the order of precedence of the Orthodox world is the patriarch of Alexandria. This church was once the glory of the Christian world. The city was founded by the Ptolemies around the tomb of Alexander, in whose honour it was built. After the fall of the last of the Ptolemies, Cleopatra, it became one of the richest and most important of the Roman imperial provinces. From two centuries before the time of Christ the city was active as the real centre of world Judaism, and several of the later parts of the Old Testament were written here, as well as the massively influential Greek translation of the scriptures known as the Septuagint (LXX) which has always been the bible used in the services of the Greek Christians. In the third century the famous Alexandrian Academy, with the Museion that attempted to gather together all the greatest literature of the world, served as an inspiration to the Christian school located there that had among its earliest and brightest luminaries the theologians Clement, Origen,[69] Heraclas, and Dionysios. In the fourth century the Church of Alexandria was racked by the Arian crisis. Arius was one of its city priests who defied his bishop, Alexander, to teach the doctrine of the temporal origination (and creaturely status) of the Divine Logos. St Athanasios, Alexander's deacon in attendance at the Council of Nicaea, who became his successor and one of the church's greatest defenders of the Nicene faith, stands out as one of the most significant theologians in the history of Christianity. The same can be said of St Cyril, the fifth-century archbishop of Alexandria, the intellectual disciple of Athanasios who brought his work to a perfection in Christology.[70]

At the time of Cyril in the mid fifth century, Alexandria was probably the most important city in the Christian world. Its intellectual and cultural record were outstanding. It was the patriarchate that nurtured the phenomenal rise to glory of the early desert monasteries that gave to the church so many saints. But after that point its fortunes as a church have suffered constant decline. The first major setback was the Christological controversy of the later fifth century. After the death of Cyril of Alexandria in 444 the synodical settlement he had agreed to (under Constantinopolitan guidance) with the Church of Antioch, was set aside by his successor Dioscorus. This precipitated a reopening of the Christological crisis that had been thought to have been resolved at the Council of Ephesus in 431. As a result the Council of Chalcedon in 451 censured Dioscorus for his actions and deposed him from office. At that juncture the entire Egyptian episcopate disconnected itself from affairs on the grounds that it was 'headless' and could not take further part. The discontent caused by this, as well as the continuing protests in Egypt against the settlement of the Council of Chalcedon, led to a period of many generations when pro-Chalcedonian and anti-Chalcedonian bishops revolved on the episcopal throne of the Alexandrian Church; deeply dividing it, and weakening its cohesion and prestige.

The second great fissure happened in the seventh century when Islamic armies under the caliph conquered Jerusalem, then Alexandria in 639, and severed them from Byzantine imperial control. From that time onwards the Christian life of the city moved further and further away from the Byzantine orbit. Opposition to the decrees of the Council of Chalcedon eventually caused the radical separation of the Christians of Egypt into the Melkites[71] and the Copts.[72] The political impotence of the Byzantine rulers in Islamic Egypt meant that neither by compulsive means nor by cultural or intellectual influence could the schism be effectively addressed, or healed. It was, in fact, one of the first great schisms to scar Christianity in such a long-lasting manner, and no one at the time probably ever felt that it would endure so extensively. That it did (and of course because of the political isolation imposed on it by the Islamic conquest) is one of the reasons the once great patriarchate of Alexandria fell into a long and deep-seated decline.

The Orthodox patriarchs of Alexandria, in times past, used to spend many years of exile in Constantinople. The majority of the local Christians having become adherents of the anti-Chalcedonian settlement, the appointment of the patriarch came to be largely a matter of election from among the select cadre of senior Phanariot clergy, not any longer from the indigenous clergy of the province. By the

39

end of the thirteenth century the specifically Alexandrian Christian Orthodox culture, and its liturgical practices, were more or less entirely supplanted by Byzantine norms, and Alexandrian Orthodoxy (once so fiercely independent of the imperial capital) became an outpost of Constantinople. Today this is still the case, and the patriarch and almost all of the serving Orthodox clergy are Greek, introducing the peculiar modern position of the division of the Orthodox from the Copts, in Egypt, along ethnic lines, whereas in the past the genius of Alexandria in the culture of the Byzantine empire, had made a distinct and powerful synthesis of the Egyptian and Greek cultures, at least among the Christians.

The patriarch himself is known as His All Holiness the Ecumenical Judge, the Pope and Patriarch of the Great City of Alexandria, of Libya, the Pentapolis, Ethiopia, all Egypt and all Africa. From antiquity he had precedence over Egypt, Libya, Arabia and Nubia (Sudan). Now all of the African continent falls under his jurisdiction with the exception of the tiny church at Sinai. In the seventeenth and eighteenth centuries the patriarch removed his residence to Cairo, but the chancery subsequently returned to Alexandria, where the monastery of St Sabas became the residence.[73] While there are approximately 5.5 million Copts there are fewer than 15,000 Orthodox Christians in the whole of Egypt (four times that number at the turn of the twentieth century), and perhaps 300,000 in the rest of Africa. Alexandria, like Constantinople itself, was a truly cosmopolitan city at the end of the nineteenth century. The active Greek population in both places served as its leaven. Since then there has been a constant leaching away of Greeks and the other Christian merchant classes. Nasser's process of Arabization only served to hasten the end of Alexandria's ancient identity as a 'city of the world', though the decline in Christian fortunes has served to draw the Orthodox communities closer to the Copts than was the case in times prior to the mid twentieth century. There were, however, a growing number of African Orthodox missions in the course of the latter part of the last century, and in sub-Saharan Africa parish life is now taking root in a small but lively growth of indigenous Orthodox faithful and clergy, especially centred around Uganda and Kenya.[74] This infant church has been taken under the Alexandrian patriarch's Omophorion and has excited much interest and enthusiasm in other parts of the Orthodox world, where missionary activity had for so long seemed to have lain dormant.

3   The patriarchate of Antioch

Antioch shares with Alexandria a glorious Christian past, but the advances of Islam from the seventh century onwards left its Christian civilization in a state of slow suffocation. Several of its greatest theologians have left their mark on the patristic tradition: writers such as Mar Theodore the Interpreter (of Mopsuestia), and St John Chrysostom, Mar John of Antioch, and numerous ascetics and saints. The cultural and theological sphere of influence exercised by the Syrian Church in its time of glory was much greater than the (very large) extent of its ancient territories. The Syrian ritual gave the substructure to the Byzantine liturgical rite, for example. It was also the Syrians who perfected the art of setting poetic synopses of Scripture to sung melodies. The church's greatest poets, such as Ephrem and Romanos the Melodist, were Syrians who taught this theological style to Byzantium and prepared the way for the glories of the medieval Orthodox liturgical chant. The Syrian Church generously organized missions to Ethiopia, Persia, India, and China. Its presence in China was historically covered up by the deliberate burning of Syriac Christian literature by the later Renaissance missionaries who claimed the origination of Christianity in that continent. It influenced the whole of ancient Cappadocia in its time, men such as the Great Basil and Gregory the Theologian were mentored by Syrian hierarchs such as Meletios, or Paul of Samosata, the great defenders of the Nicene faith at the time of the second council, that of Constantinople in 381.

In its time of glory, the Christian orators of Syria spoke and wrote the finest Greek in the Roman world. The schools of Antioch were renowned for the purity of their Greek eloquence. Writers such as Gregory the Theologian and John Chrysostom have left behind a memorial of work that reaches to the standards of the greatest of all Greek rhetoric. Gregory, for example, has been favourably compared to Demosthenes himself. John gained his epithet 'Golden Mouth' because of the limpid quality of his Greek; but he was a Syrian by birth. This outpost of pure Greek culture on the banks of the Orontes was a bubble that broke before the advance of Islam, and since the seventh century the flourishing of Christianity in the Antiochene patriarchate has given way to a long and slow twilight. As the patriarchate of Constantinople flourished in the ambit of the Byzantine empire, so Antioch declined in prestige and influence.

The first major land mass to go was Asia Minor, which was assigned to the purview of Constantinople in the early fifth century. Then the Church of Cyprus successfully asserted its independence from Antioch between 431 and 488. The vast territory of Persia asserted its independence in 424, after which point it refused its assent to the Council of Ephesus of 431 and fell away from communion with the Orthodox. Its continuing energy, for many centuries afterwards, drew away the allegiance of many Assyrian Christians from the patriarchate of Antioch. The continuing prevalence of the Miaphysite resistance to the Council of Chalcedon after the sixth century also drew away many other Syrians from the communion of the patriarch. Jerusalem became a separate patriarchate in 451 and took with it the territory of Palestine. In later times the scattered state of the Christian communities and their appalling vulnerability to the forces of an increasingly hostile Islamic majority led to large numbers of the Syrian Christian communities fleeing for protection to the arms of a strong and missionary active Rome.[75] The result is that there are now large communities of the so-called Uniates.[76] At the beginning of the twentieth century there were no fewer than seven distinct Uniate communities in the Syrian Church all representing another historic fragmentation of the ancient patriarchate of Antioch, and seven senior clergy all claiming the right to be, and be designated as, the Antiochene 'patriarch'.[77]

The Orthodox recognize only one patriarch, who is in communion with the other ancient patriarchates of the Orthodox Church, and resides at Damascus.[78] The remaining jurisdictional territory for the Orthodox patriarch is Syria, and the Asiatic Roman provinces of Cilicia, Mesopotamia, and Isauria. Most of his faithful today are Arabic-speaking Christians. From 1724 to 1899 the Orthodox patriarch of Antioch was always a Phanariot Greek. Since that time Arabs have occupied the office. Today there are just over a million Syriac-speaking Christians in the world and half a million Arabic speakers, who belong to the Antiochene patriarchate. The Orthodox patriarch's flock currently consists of fewer than half a million faithful, centred largely in Syria, the Lebanon, and Iraq, with the rest, a considerable diaspora, largely in America. The patriarch's title is His Blessedness the Patriarch of Antioch the City of God, of Cilicia, Iberia, Syria, Arabia and All the East.[79]

In America, the hierarchs of the Antiochene patriarchate have proved to be immensely creative and open to the new situations presented by life in the New World. The Antiochene Orthodox there have a large degree of autonomy afforded to them by the patriarch, and are particularly ready to engage in evangelical mission. As well as being important pillars of support for their suffering church in the homelands, they have sponsored several highly valuable translations of the liturgical texts and prayer books in English, and in recent times have encouraged numbers of evangelical Christians who have made their way into the Orthodox Church, both in America and England, and established them within their jurisdictional care.

4   The patriarchate of Jerusalem

The patriarchate of Jerusalem ranks fourth in the precedence of honour of the Orthodox churches. Even in antiquity Jerusalem was never a large church with a significant sphere of political influence. In the third century it was politically in the saddest state of decline, and ecclesiastically was the minor partner of Caesarea Maritima, itself the seat of a most important Christian university school.[80] Jerusalem had a different kind of symbolic influence, and importance, however, chiefly as the site of the holy places where the Lord taught, and suffered, and rose again. In its most important patristic phase it was the centre of an internationally influential liturgical revival, that followed after Constantine's building of the church of the Anastasis (Resurrection)[81] and other places of pilgrimage. The story of Helena's discovery of the True Cross in Jerusalem, was added to by several other major discoveries of the relics of New Testament saints such as John the Forerunner or Stephen the Protomartyr, stories that electrified Christian Constantinople and led to a massive movement of the building of pilgrimage churches in the Holy Land. From the late fourth to the sixth centuries Roman Palestine, with Jerusalem at its centre, was renowned throughout the Christian world as a thriving church based around pilgrim traffic.

Pilgrimage continued throughout ancient times. Its moment of glory came at the time of the Council of Chalcedon when the city's bishop, Juvenal, managed to secure from the conciliar fathers the admission of its right to be regarded as the primary see of Palestine (by virtue of its ancient status and contemporary importance), and they also gave to it then the status and title of a patriarchate (though without extending its territorial jurisdiction). The bloody wars of the Crusades often suggest to observers that passage to the holy places was cut off by the Islamic occupation of the holy city after the seventh century, but in fact there were many times when the Byzantine emperors regained control of the land routes, and even when they did not have the military upper hand, they easily negotiated pilgrim access by means of treaty. So it was that until the massive disruptions of the first three Crusades, the church in what was formerly Roman Palestine, centred round Jerusalem, continued as a fairly lively nexus of pilgrim sites, sustained by the city church and by numerous monasteries in the desert regions of Judaea and modern Jordan, reaching down to Gaza and Sinai. The fame of these Judaean monasteries rivalled that of the earlier settlements of Christian Egypt, which by this stage had themselves fallen into a degree of obscurity following barbarian devastations of the desert settlements. In the fifth century the instability of the churches, following in the aftermath of the Council of Chalcedon 451, was acutely felt in Jerusalem.

The seventh century, however, was definitely to throw a curtain over any further expansion of the patriarchate, as it soon found itself thereafter in the unenviable position of a city that was not only sacred to the Jews, but had also become a holy site for the new politically ascendant religion of Islam. Even so, with a few exceptions[82] the Christian holy places were allowed to operate in reduced numbers for most of the time. Pilgrimage has always been one of the *raisons d'être* for the patriarchate of Jerusalem therefore, and continues to be so. But in saying this it is extremely important not to overlook the profound significance of the increasingly dwindling local population of about 35,000 Arab Christians who have been suffering politically for so long, in a form of silent martyrdom. These have long felt themselves pinned between a rock and a hard place.

On the one side was the old Ottoman government, representing the massive Islamic majority of the region (successively replaced by the British Administration, and then by the state of Israel) which had little intrinsic care for resident Christian Arabs (to put it euphemistically), and on the other side was the higher Orthodox clergy who occupied all the offices of the patriarchate, and were almost entirely Phanariot Greeks. The church of the Anastasis, with the patriarch at its centre, continues to be governed by the Brotherhood of the Holy Cross, which still makes up a powerful and focused Greek clerical community. The monks are known as Hagiotaphites (brothers of the holy tomb), and the patriarch is *ex officio* the head of its affairs. His title is His Beatitude the Patriarch of the Holy City of Jerusalem and of All the Promised Land. All bishops of the local synod (two eparchies at Akka (Ptolemais), and Nazareth, and several other titular archbishops such as Mount Thabor, Jordan, and Kerak) whose complement does not exceed eighteen, must be members of the Brotherhood. The senior hierarchs are all predominantly occupied with the administration of one of the chief shrines of the Holy Land.

The local faithful are almost entirely Arabs (the resident Greek Christians number in the low hundreds) with predominantly Arabic parish priests. The latter are mostly married, and the celibates among them are rarely admitted to the higher offices of the church so that the synod of the Jerusalem patriarchate will never lose its Greek operative majority. Since 1958 there has been a new constitution partly influenced by the Hashemite kingdom of Jordan, that gave the Christian Arabs more voice. Since then (from 1960) there has been a reluctant admission that there should always be a small number of Arab bishops in the local synod. Meanwhile, in the midst of all this, the local Christian population shrinks day by day, as a result of some assimilation, but largely the desire of local Arab Christians to emigrate to an easier life elsewhere.[83] There are currently about 156,000 Orthodox faithful belonging to the jurisdiction of the Jerusalem patriarchate, living in the Palestinian territories, Israel, and Jordan. Throughout the twentieth century there have been regular occasions of disruption and unrest in the patriarchate's affairs. Most recently the incumbent patriarch was deposed on the grounds of uncanonical collaboration with Israeli governmental interests in buying out Christian land in Jerusalem. At the time of writing he remains in Jerusalem refusing to admit the legitimacy of his rejection by his own synod, with the Israeli government refusing to admit the legitimacy of his canonically elected successor. As a result all the legal and administrative activities of the patriarchate are in a limbo of paralysis.

The structure of the governance of the patriarchate cries out for a root-and-branch reconsideration, not only because of the tension between the Greek leaders (with their power vested in the Brotherhood of the Holy Cross) and the local Arab Christians, but also because of the role Jerusalem should (or could) play in the whole Christian world. The Brotherhood's record of administrative care and charitable works is historically impressive, but its desire to retain intact the church and its properties as the last glimmer of a once prestigious outpost of Byzantine Hellenism is one that hardly corresponds with contemporary reality, and one which is party to threatening the very Christian heritage it so earnestly seeks to protect. The terrible strains that mark this patriarchate have largely been caused by the historically chaotic government of its affairs over many ages past, as presided over by the Ottomans, with massive interventions (and subventions) by the Latins, the tsars, and then the British, who let loose a whirlwind before they stepped back from it.

Today, under the suffocating policies of a beleaguered and increasingly paranoid state apparatus, and the ever-present pressures to 'buy out' and segregate land in Israel, the outlook for Christian affairs in general in the Holy Land is very bleak indeed. If the ancient patriarchate of Jerusalem sinks back into being simply a colonial outpost of Greek monks it will be a tragedy for all of Christianity, not simply for the Orthodox world. Its small size, and the manner in which (like Alexandria) it is so intimately linked to the ecclesiastical life of the Church of Greece and the patriarch of Constantinople, point the way towards where the call for *ressourciement* might fruitfully come. But the ideas and inspiration for change surely can be provided not only by the monks of the church, but also by the suffering Arab Christians whose Gospel path has been profoundly ascetic on their own terms, and has earned them a right to the admiration and empathy of the Christian ecumene. It is also not beyond imagination to think that in future years a modest revival of the once massive amount of pilgrimage to Jerusalem that came from the Slavic Orthodox lands (now once more liberated from their own oppressions) might revive and regenerate the Christian holy places, and bring a sense of profound relief to their beleaguered local communities, who are now pressed very threateningly between the Scylla and Charybdis of nationalist Arabic Islam and militant Zionism.

The Orthodox Church of Cyprus

The Church of Cyprus has been autonomous from ancient times, headed by its own archbishop and local synod. Even though it was founded by the apostle Barnabas in the first century, it was at first organized as a smaller dependency of the Antiochene patriarchate, to which it was geographically proximate. During a long period in the late fourth century when the incumbents of the local Roman capital at Antioch were Arians, or of dubious theological persuasion, Cyprus withdrew its allegiance of communion, defending (in the process) the Orthodox Nicene cause. One way it showed this separation was by refusing to allow the hierarchs of the Antiochene patriarchate to have a say in the election and consecration of its archbishop. It petitioned for its independence from that patriarchate at the seventh session of the Council of Ephesus in July 431.

At that time Patriarch John of Antioch was protesting at the irregularity of their independence continuing any longer, since the Arian crisis was long past, and he

44

asked for the reimposition of Antiochene control over the island, as had been agreed in the earlier canons of the church. The conciliar fathers gathered at the Council of Ephesus nevertheless sympathetically heard the appeal of the Church of Cyprus,[84] and decreed that its independence could continue, having endured for sufficiently long time as to become a *de facto* reality. This independence was again confirmed under the Emperor Zeno, by a synod of the Constantinopolitan patriarchate in the later fifth century. Since that time the autocephalous status of the Cypriot Church has been accepted in all the Orthodox world. The long medieval period of Latin domination was a hard one for the Orthodox of Cyprus, and during the 'Reunion' of Florence, it showed the Cypriots that the Latin overlords continued to despise the Byzantine Church, despite the alleged proclamation of ecclesiastical union, and sought always to eradicate it if they could in favour of Latin rite and practice. The even longer shadow of the Ottomans was also a time of suffocation. At the time of the Greek War of Independence the Turks assassinated the Cypriot archbishop (Cyprianos) and all his synod. Only in 1878, with the British occupation of the island, did the church enter a period of peace and (relative) political stability, although the British (between 1930 and 1947) interfered greatly in the election of the hierarchs, in order to put a brake on the move to 'self-annexation' to Greece. In 1960 Cyprus' independence was effected as a sovereign republic, with Archbishop Makarios becoming the first head of state. The movement (which he himself tempered throughout his life) to effect *henosis* (union with Greece) asserted itself powerfully in his old age, despite his counsel, and in its aftermath Turkey invaded the island illegally claiming justification from the need to protect its nationals. From that time onwards the situation has not been resolved. The northern territories remain under Turkish occupation, and have been heavily colonized by Turkish immigration.

The archbishop of Cyprus is known as His Beatitude, and still exercises the (once very refined and exalted) privilege given to him by the emperor, to sign all his documents in scarlet ink, and to wear vestments of silk and purple. He himself is the archbishop of Constantia (Famagusta) and is resident at Nicosia. He has suffragan eparchs whose sees are at Paphos, Larnaka, and Kyrenia. Together they comprise the Holy Synod. There are currently 552,000 faithful in this church, representing almost the entire Christian population, and three-quarters of the entire population, of Cyprus. There are also numerous Cypriots in the diaspora, especially England, which for many years exercised a protectorate over the island. The Greek Cypriot Orthodox of the diaspora, however, belong to the oversight of the patriarch of Constantinople, although many of the parishes in the patriarchate's British exarchate are comprised entirely of Orthodox who are of Cypriot origin, with clergy who are also mainly Cypriot. The Church of Cyprus has eleven active monasteries, some dating back to Byzantine times, and renowned throughout the Greek-speaking Orthodox world as pilgrimage centres, such as the Kykko monastery in the Troodos mountains. There are also a total of sixty-seven other monasteries, many of which contain historically important frescoes, which are either currently unused or presently in ruins, and which date back to many different periods of the island's rich and venerable Christian history. Its resourceful and generous people have in recent times been blessed with an abundance of priests who, in turn, have often volunteered for missionary work in Orthodox communities overseas.

45

The Church of Sinai

The monastery of St Catherine's at Sinai is one of the most venerable monasteries in the Orthodox world. It is located dramatically at the foot of Mount Sinai, in Egypt, and from ancient times it was a major pilgrim site for Christians. It is mentioned in the *Voyages of Egeria,* a travelogue from the late fourth century. Today it is unique among all Orthodox monasteries for having a small Fatimid mosque within its grounds (now unused). The local Bedouin attached to the monastery (especially the Jelabiya tribe[85]) themselves worship in their own mosque not far away from Jebel Musa.[86] By the late fifth century the desert monasteries of Egypt were suffering massive depredations from tribal raiders, as the Byzantine hold on the territories was increasingly relaxed. Mount Sinai itself was threatened on several occasions with complete extinction as a Christian settlement, but the Emperor Justinian, with an eye to the venerability of the site, as well as its strategic advantage as a military post, massively fortified the buildings in the sixth century, and stationed a garrison there, settling several villages of Christians nearby for the service of the monks and the garrison (those who remain as the tiny lay membership of this church often claim to be the descendants of those settlers, though the majority of the Bedouin are now Islamic). The architecture today is still largely from this period, with some medieval and modern additions. It is now one of the last surviving monasteries of a once flourishing circle of Greek-speaking ascetic sites across the Middle East. The archbishop of Sinai also presides over the two churches of Pharan and Raithu (by the Red Sea shore) which were once monasteries of great repute.

Sinai is justifiably a world heritage centre, a veritable jewel box of ancient and wonderful things in terms of art, manuscripts, and relics; but the monks who still live there point also, with a deep sense of satisfaction, to something they hold as even more precious than their treasures, namely their fidelity to the ascetical evangelical life after so many unbroken centuries of witness in the wilderness, which is the *raison d'être* of Sinai as an Orthodox holy place.[87] From the beginning, the monks of Sinai kept up livelier relations with the Jerusalem patriarchate than with Alexandria, and eventually this was reflected in the ecclesiastical organization, for Sinai became a monastery under the care of the Jerusalem Church. At the height of its flourishing it had Metochia, or dependent monasteries and estates, in Egypt, Palestine, Syria, Crete, Cyprus, and Constantinople, which supported it and ensured its effective independence during the long years when it had to buy the patronage of its Islamic overlords. It was also extensively patronized by the voivodes of Wallachia (later Romania) and the tsars of Russia.

All these important supports eventually eroded, but not before Sinai had more or less asserted its importance and its claims for autonomous governance over and against the patriarchate of Jerusalem, which itself had fallen on hard times. Its independence (against the initial grumbling of Jerusalem) was affirmed by Constantinople in 1575, and again confirmed in 1782. Today the monks of the community (only a few dozen are still resident there) elect one of their own number as the abbot and also as the prospective archbishop of Sinai. The patriarch of Jerusalem always has the right to perform the consecration (which fact – along with its peculiar smallness – limits its complete claim to autocephaly). After that point, however, the archbishop, with his synaxis, entirely governs the affairs of the monastery-church. It is the smallest independent church of the entire Orthodox world: a unique and special instance, poised between autocephalous and autonomous condition.

The Russian Orthodox Church (patriarchate of Moscow)

The Russian Orthodox Church, which holds rank as fifth in the precedence of honour among the patriarchal churches, is a complete contrast to this, with 27,942 parishes, and 80,451,000 faithful. There are wider estimates than this which speak of the world total of Russian Orthodox (meaning those who would regard themselves of the Slavic Orthodox tradition) approaching 160 million, but this takes in Russia, Belorussia, Ukraine, Moldova, and the Baltic as well as the central Asian countries and the diaspora. Even in its smaller, national configuration, the Russian Orthodox is a massive church, and indisputably one of the most important voices in contemporary global Orthodoxy. This the case not only because of its size, but more so because of its profoundly Christian culture, with its rich historical manifestations for almost a thousand years past, as well as the immense depth of its variegated spiritual tradition, not to mention the recent experience of martyrdom that its members have shared along with many of the eastern European lands that fell under the Soviet communist oppression.

The Russians hold up 988 as the date of the foundation of their church. At this time Prince Vladimir was baptized (at Chersonesus) and commanded the turning of his people, the Rus, to the Gospel. Mass baptisms were held in the then capital of the land, Kiev (now in the Ukraine). It had from the beginning the closest relations with the patriarchate of Constantinople, and the whole liturgical and spiritual culture of Russian Orthodoxy was fostered by Constantinopolitan missionaries for many generations. The rise of the people of ancient Rus to nationhood went hand in hand with the emergence of the Muscovite princes as the most powerful ruling families in the vast land. The capital transferred with the princes from Kiev to Moscow (many other Russian cities, of course – Vladimir, Novgorod, and Kazan among them – played an important part in the foundation of the Christian culture) and after the overcoming of internal disunity, as well as external threats from the Golden Horde, Russia was well aware of its political and military might, and had a developed national consciousness by the late sixteenth century. In 1453 the Byzantine emperors themselves fell to the might of the Crescent. Christian Byzantium was a political reality no more, and the affairs of the Christians passed, in the Greek-speaking East, to the condition of subjugated slaves under the administration of the Constantinopolitan patriarch acting as agent of the sultans.

The Russian tsar (whose government had progressed hand in hand with the metro-politan archbishops of Moscow who were largely drawn from the aristocracy and always had a primary concern in the affairs of state) then declared that he and his own people had entered a stage of new destiny for the Russian and Christian peoples. Two Romes had fallen, was the famous utterance of the monk Philotheos,[88] a third had now arisen. The grand dukes of Moscow had entered into their heritage as the successors to the Caesars. The new 'tsars'[89] would continue the duties (with the concomitant privileges over the world-wide church) of the former Byzantine emperors, as the last defenders of Christianity. Russia saw its recent overthrowing of Tartar power as a providential sign that God had intended it to remain free for the protection and supervision of all Christendom, now that the Byzantine empire had come to so disastrous a conclusion.

Its ecclesiastical independence went quickly hand in hand. Up until the fifteenth century the patriarch of Constantinople had always appointed the senior hierarch of the Russian Church, the metropolitan of Moscow. With his synod he then ruled with a large degree of autonomy. In 1441 the metropolitan of Moscow was Isidore, a Greek who was closely related to the policies of the church in Constantinople. As a legate at the Council of Florence he strongly supported the concept of the reunion with Rome, which the Byzantine emperor desperately desired (under the sad illusion that it would secure Western military help to stave off the Ottomans). After the Council of Florence was over, Isidore returned to Russia, and attempted to convince the grand duke to introduce the unionist policy. But as was the case with the faithful in Constantinople, there was a widespread reaction against the Union of Florence, and the grand duke imprisoned Isidore. He was eventually allowed to escape, and made his way into exile in Italy. The emperor at Constantinople, however, was still insisting on the policy of union which Florence represented, and so for a time the Russian synod broke off communion and did not proceed with the election of a new metropolitan, refusing to accept any nomination that the imperial city would be likely to send it.

In 1448 the Russian synod decided to go ahead with its own consecration of a metropolitan without Constantinople's involvement. After the fall of the imperial city in 1453, and the subsequent installation of Gennadios Scholarios as the new patriarch, the former imperial church abandoned the unionist policy, and communion between it and Russia was restored. But from that time onwards the Russian synod elected and consecrated its own senior hierarch, and had effectively established autocephaly. In 1589, with the consent of the patriarchate in Constantinople, the metropolitan of Moscow was given the status of patriarch, and the right to have the precedence of honour after Jerusalem (above that of the patriarchate of Serbia which had pre-dated its own rise to patriarchal status, but not higher than any of the ancient patriarchates, which was a blow to its aspirations to take over the governance of global Orthodox affairs under the tsar's political patronage).

Relations between the Moscow patriarchs and the tsars were always extremely close. Between 1613 and 1633 Philaret was patriarch and his son, Michael, ruled as the first in the dynastic line of the Romanov tsars, a line that would last until the twentieth century, with the abdication of Nicholas II. In Peter the Great's time, however, Patriarch Adrian resisted many of the reformist and Europeanizing strategies of the tsar, and as a result, following Adrian's death in 1700, Peter abolished the office of patriarch, restoring the Russian Church to a synodical form of government. The 'Holy Governing Synod' was constituted so as to have complete and total authority over the life of the Church. This was established under the guidance of the tsar (functioning as the supposed heir of the Byzantine emperors), and led by the metropolitans of Petersburg, Moscow, and Kiev, along with six other hierarchs (who were nominees of the tsar and removable at his will), the imperial and military chaplains, and the lay procurator. Its membership of twelve was later reduced to six. The lay procurator was the real power behind this synod which had, in fact, degenerated to the level of a civil service committee, wholly under the thumb of the monarchy. Throughout Russia the bishops and local clergy had to act not only as pastors but as state officials representing various state departments.

Peter's overall aim was to modernize and secularize Russia. His church policy was dictated by the simple aim of bringing the church into complete submission to the royal power, a travesty of the imperial Byzantine model, which Russia had symbolically adopted though without much comprehension of its deeper roots and historical actualities. His policy needed more and more repressive force to effect it, and this turned many of the Orthodox against it. The monks were looked to as the real defenders of the people. In the eighteenth century there was a strong revival of monastic spirituality in Russia, and a growth of the influence of the *starets*, the leading monastic elder of the region, who served as a focal point for a wide geographical area, offering counsel and prophetic leadership. SS Paisy Velichovsky (d. 1794) and Tikhon of Zadonsk (d. 1783) were outstanding figures of this time.

Peter's successors Catherine the Great (d. 1796), Nicholas I (d. 1855), and Alexander III (d. 1894) were all highly active in continuing Peter's policy of ensuring the church never moved far away from the side of the monarchy. After the assassination of Tsar Alexander II in 1881, the monarchy became deeply suspicious of its people and set up a massively extended secret service that had a similar effect on the church to that it had on all ranks of society. Everyone had a sense that someone was looking over their shoulder, ready to pen a report. It was a suspicion that had solid grounds. In church affairs, at the end of the nineteenth century, the Machiavellian figure of Constantine Pobiedonostsev seemed to sum up the spirit of the time. He was the lay procurator of the Holy Governing Synod, and his rule was founded upon a vast network of intelligence about the lives and behaviours of the clergy of every level. Described by Norman Douglas, the novelist, as: 'A silent bloodless all powerful creature, a Torquemada', his rule lasted into the reign of Nicholas II, last of the Romanovs, who, in 1905, voided his office, permitting a new constitution, guaranteeing general religious freedom outside the state's prescriptive intervention. This lifting of the oppressive weight of oversight led, even within the Orthodox mainstream, to an excitement and a new ferment that began to hope for some more deeply considered reforms. Plans were set in hand for a large national synod, but political events in the next decade would overwhelm Russia in ways it could never imagine.

After Nicholas II's abdication in March 1917, the formal relation of church and state in Russia was also voided, and the long years of difficulty began. During the provisional government, in August 1917, a Russian church council was convoked, which restored the patriarchate. While it was in session the Bolsheviks were shelling the walls of the Kremlin. Tikhon Belavin, archbishop of Moscow, was the first incumbent of the restored patriarchate, but after his death in 1925 no one was allowed to hold the office until 1944, when Stalin began to make some concessions to the church in return for its co-operation in building national unity in the war. Tikhon was a man of deep spirituality and is now widely revered as a saint both in and outside Russia. In his first year as patriarch he spoke out boldly against the 'godlessness' of the Bolsheviks. When they assumed power they played a waiting game with him while they set about wrecking the Orthodox Church around him.

The church *sobor* of 1917 had established a synod of twelve bishops along with an assembly of fifteen clergy and laymen, to serve along with the patriarch in the governance of the Russian Church. The communist powers quickly disrupted this

Figure 2 Image of St Tikhon, an energetic missionary bishop who came from America to be the first patriarch of Moscow after the restoration of the Russian patriarchate in the early decades of the twentieth century. Unfortunately the end of the heavy tsarist oversight of Russian church affairs was soon followed by the long nightmare of communist oppression, and Tikhon himself suffered much at the hands of Lenin and Stalin. It is widely suspected that his alleged natural death may have been one of the many 'secret murders' ordered by Stalin. The decades of state persecution and suppression following Tikhon's death caused much disruption in the national and international organization of Russian Orthodoxy.
Photograph: © TopFoto

and isolated Tikhon. In 1922 he was imprisoned in a monastery while moves were made to initiate the systematic breaking up of the ecclesiastical organization. The government launched its massive programme of confiscating church goods (icons and chalices and so on) under the heading of 'relief for the poor', the victims of the state-induced famine of 1921–2. Simultaneously it sponsored the formation of the 'Higher Church Administration' (HCA) which, using pro-communist clergy, declared that Tikhon had resigned his office and thenceforth the patriarchate was abolished, leaving the HCA as the supreme governing body of the Russian Church. Agathangel, the archbishop of Yaroslavl, who had been nominated by Tikhon as one of those who might lead the church if he himself was liquidated by the communists, immediately denounced the HCA and was exiled to Siberia. Metropolitan Benjamin of Petrograd then courageously took up the challenge and excommunicated the cleric Vvedensky who was then spokesman for the HCA. In return the HCA decreed that all Russian bishops and priests who did not recognize its authority were immediately to be considered deposed from office. There followed a Bolshevik purge on them, and there were widespread arrests that had the general effect of dampening down opposition. Benjamin of Petrograd and three other leading bishops were shot by the security police, and all the chief hierarchs who supported the patriarchate were sent into exile. Large numbers of the lower clergy started to accede to the governance of the HCA, which began a series of 'reforms' of church life in the spirit of 'proletarian openness'.

The HCA quickly began to fragment into separate movements: the Living Church, the Union of the Old Apostolic Church, the Union of Church Rebirth, and so on, all of which have come to be collectively known as 'The Living Church Movement'. In 1923 it met in a council and declared itself to be a 'genuine proletarian and revolutionary force', and designated itself as the Church of Renewal, declaring all other ecclesiastical groups to be forthwith abolished. But just as quickly its fortunes waned. The Bolsheviks' interest ebbed away. They had turned their attentions back on Tikhon. Just what pressures they applied to him in his time of incarceration are not known, but it is certain that they did not simply offer him tea and polite chat. In 1923 he issued a statement expressing regret for 'mistakes' which the church had made, and especially for acts of disloyalty to the revolutionary government. He promised renewed loyalty to the regime. The reason the Bolsheviks wanted this statement so much was to offset the rapid moves of the Russian bishops outside the boundaries of the country (most of whom were monarchists and formed a network of resistance in Europe and America) to organize the Russian Orthodox Church Outside of Russia (ROCOR) in defiance of the Bolshevik subversions.

The ROCOR hierarchs had faith in Tikhon, who had actually encouraged them early on to make their move for independence. Now, in 1923, he was set free to resume his governance of the internal affairs of the Russian Church, the HCA was abandoned (and, losing its political force for terrorizing its opponents, quickly lost ground), but the cost was to rein in the ROCOR bishops who comprised the Karlovtzy synod. Their subsequent history is discussed later in terms of the Russian diaspora. Suffice it to say here that, as time went on after Tikhon's release, the bishops in exile progressively lost confidence in the hierarchy of the church in the homeland, and gave little credence to their claim to be able to speak freely, or act honestly for the greater benefit of Russian Orthodoxy, while all the time being under the eye (and the fist) of such totalitarian atheists who were bent on manipulating them. Tikhon died in 1925. He has been thought by many to have been liquidated as one of Stalin's many clandestine political murders. Of the three potential 'successors' he had nominated before his incarceration (a strategy he conceived in the early 1920s on the grounds that he might not always have freedom to act) only one hierarch was still alive at that time, Sergius Starogrodsky, the metropolitan of Nizhni-Novgorod. He raised few expectations among any of the bishops, and enjoyed no confidence among the exiles comprising the Karlovtzy synod. As a result the synod and the Russian mother church parted ways acerbically.

After an educational period of imprisonment in 1927 Sergius was himself a broken man, ever after very anxious to affirm that all was well in the Russian Church, and persuade all who would listen how benevolent the government was. He was rewarded in 1943 with Stalin's permission to restore the patriarchate, to which he was duly elected. He died only six months afterwards in May 1944. The majority of the Orthodox churches outside Russia acknowledged the legitimacy of the leadership of Sergius, and his successor Alexis Simansky, the former metropolitan of Leningrad. But from this time onwards elements in the ROCOR began to argue the point that a synod which is not free cannot issue canonically binding results. Accordingly the division between the Russian Orthodox in the country, under the Soviet regime, and those outside the country grew more and more tendentious as the twentieth century progressed.

The communist yoke caused great damage to the church. In 1900 there were 56 million faithful, amounting to 75 per cent of the population. By 1970 this number had fallen to 39 million, representing 29 per cent of the population (though there were many more crypto-Orthodox than this figure suggests). In 1914 Russia had 550 monasteries for men and 474 monasteries for women. Most of them were state-subsidized or had powerful endowments to undergird their life and work. There were, at that time, 21,000 monks and 74,000 nuns. The greatest monasteries were those of 'The Caves' (Pechersky Lavra) at Kiev on the banks of the Dnieper, founded by SS Antony and Theodosius between 1032 and 1062; the Trinity Monastery (Troitsky) near Moscow (Sergeyev Posad) founded by St Sergius of Radonezh; and the Alexander Nevsky monastery, founded at St Petersburg in 1724. There were numerous others whose spiritual and intellectual life was remarkable: the Donskoy monastery at Moscow, the Simonov, Novospassky, St George's at Novgorod, Novodievichy, the Ascension monastery at Tver, Solovky in the White Sea (which as a Gulag would be the place of martyrdom for so many under Stalin), Sarov (which gave the world the shining saint Seraphim), Rostov, Yaroslav, Uglich, Valaam (in Finland), the Optina hermitages, and the Pochaevskaya Lavra in Volhynia (Poland). The destruc-tion of the monastic life was among the first achievements of the Bolsheviks. Its rebuilding will bring with it an immense reflowering of the spiritual power of the Russian Church.

Under communism all expression of Christian freedom was dangerous. All formal evangelistic and catechetical work was forbidden to the church. Even so the religious life of Russian Orthodoxy was irrepressible. Even in the dark times of communist persecution the Orthodox attendance at the divine liturgy was far higher than European church attendance. The Bolshevik government rapidly passed anti-religious legislation even before it had secured a totalitarian grasp on the state. It confiscated all private and all ecclesiastical property in December 1917, and in January 1918 withdrew any state subsidy for ecclesiastical institutions, separating church and state, and out-lawing any form of religious instruction of the state's citizens. Between 1917 and 1923, when the Bolshevik zeal was hot, twenty-eight Russian bishops and 1,400 priests were executed. After the revolution, the newly elected pope, Pius XI, made powerful intercessions on behalf of suffering Russia, at the International Conference of Genoa, but the British imperial representative, David Lloyd George, strongly opposed him, and carried the day for no 'interference' in Russian religious affairs; a policy adhered to on wider fronts that would also abandon the last tsar and his family to a bloody death after England shamefully refused them asylum.

Thousands of the leading clergy and laity of Russia were sent to labour camps, and many of them never returned. Churches were turned into museums or cinemas; the sacred relics, ikons, and vestments were burned or defaced. If anything could gain a price, it was sold off. The Western churches slowly began to gain a taste in iconic art by its appearance on the markets there at bargain-basement prices. The sacrilege and suffering behind the phenomenon took longer to reach a more universal consciousness. In 1926 the law explicitly forbade the continuing exercise of communal monastic life in the fewer than half the monasteries which had somehow managed to carry on in spite of the persecutions, a measure that accelerated the monastic decline, but still could not quench monasticism completely. The measures against the church were conducted by the 'League of Militant Atheism' with cells in every village. In 1927 the Council of People's Commissars tried to initiate a Five Year Plan, whose aim was to 'eradicate the very concept of God from the minds of the people, and to leave not a single house of prayer standing in the whole territory of the USSR'.

By God's grace their anti-religious measures proved as effective as their economic policies; shambolic, ignorant, but none the less damaging for that. By the mid 1930s the stories of the persecution against the Russian Church were becoming more widely known in Europe and America (in fact this persecution has been the greatest in extent, savagery, and duration of the whole history of the church) and there was a certain slowing down of the sufferings. In 1936 a new Russian constitution reaffirmed the 'freedom for the conduct of religious worship', though it left intact the law of 1929 that forbade the churches to conduct any catechesis or sponsor any social or charitable efforts. The penalization of clergy was relaxed at this time, subject to Stalin's express caveat: 'As long as they are not hostile to Soviet power.' It was a let-out that afforded him much room for manoeuvre in the unimaginably vast programme of the annihilation of so many luminous lives over which he sat enthroned throughout his wretched life.

Later in 1937 the state once more desired to show its hand, and twenty bishops were arrested on charges of espionage, sabotage, or fascism. The clergy were forbidden to minister in state hospitals, and churches that showed much vitality were closed on the grounds of non-payment of taxes. Stalin decided to allow the Orthodox Church more breathing space in 1944 when he was desperately gathering every resource he could to fight the German armies. In 1954 under Khrushchev, it was thought that a certain level of thaw might be setting in, in relation to the church. A decree was issued admitting certain 'mistakes' had been made in relation to the over-zealous suppression of religious freedom (a very euphemistic gloss on the astounding amount of martyrdoms the communists had inflicted). After that point the anti-religious propaganda was conducted on the less bloody level of innuendo, career restrictions, and bigoted propaganda in the press. The campaign of denunciation of 'parasitic' clergy led to an actual stepping up of state hostility towards the church. Gangs of hooligans were organized to disrupt church services (often containing many hundreds of worshippers each Sunday, much to the frustration of the authorities who could generally command little love for themselves or their programmes).

The eight seminaries that had been allowed to reopen after Stalin's thaw, beginning in 1945, began to be closed once more. By 1966 only three were operating. Similarly, of the eighty monasteries functioning in 1947 (such a small fraction of those which flourished under the tsars) only sixteen remained open in the entire country by 1971, rising to eighteen in 1980. Many monks and nuns were once again brutally treated, and numbers were sent to imprisonment in Gulags and mental hospitals for their allegiance to Christ; giving a new twist, full of pathos, to the ancient witness (the word,

53

of course, means 'martyrdom') of the 'fool for Christ' (Iurodivy), and the deep Russian tradition of the 'passion-bearers'.[90] At the end of Stalin's political career (1924–53) the number of functioning priests in Russia could be counted only in hundreds. As Vera Bouteneff has expressed it: 'The scale of this martyrdom is unprecedented in the history of the Christian church.'[91] The whole Soviet persecution is estimated to have killed 600 bishops, 40,000 priests, and 120,000 monks and nuns.

Between 1960 and 1963 many of the village parish churches (which had a more flourishing attendance than the city churches and were generally felt by the people to be less scrutinized by the authorities) began to be targeted, and large numbers were abruptly closed. In 1947 there were an estimated 22,000 churches serving the liturgy on Sundays; by the late 1970s fewer than 7,000 remained open. Today, in the restructuring of Russian society in the aftermath of its long night of communism the Orthodox Church is in a relatively favoured position. It is widely looked to in Russian society as a sign of hope for the making of a new future, with a deeper cultural and historical memory than the banalities of the old regime. There is much restructuring going on in the wider society, as well as in the church itself, and a general spirit of good will has affirmed itself between the hierarchy and the new political leaders from Gorbachev's time onwards. Churches are being restored and rebuilt, the numbers of the faithful are again increasing, and the Russian Church is busily repairing decades of profound structural and psychological damage. The 80 million who have currently affirmed themselves as Orthodox believers, represent 54 per cent of the nation's population.

Today there are 219 functioning monasteries of men and 240 of women, all busy with renewal. The Russian synod has 193 bishops and 142 dioceses, 26,540 priests, and 3,301 deacons. The educational establishment now is starting to flourish again with five theological academies, and twenty-one seminaries, as well as two Orthodox universities and a Theological Institute. The central Moscow diocese comprises 298 parishes, 182 metochias, and sixty-eight monastery churches. Thirty-three churches are still being requested to be returned to ecclesiastical use, and ninety churches and chapels are in process of construction. There are 820 priests and 297 deacons. In addition the monastic priests comprise 400 clergy and there are 125 monastic deacons. There are thirty-seven senior and thirty-eight junior seminaries functioning. After generations of trauma the Russian patriarchate is now for the first time coming to terms with the need to re-establish unity and trust among its scattered diaspora. How it approaches that task will be something that the Orthodox world watches with careful attention. It will require immense tact and sensitivity, on both sides: that of a mother church reasserting its vast reservoirs of energy and new hope for the future; and that of the scattered communities who once looked with dismay on a hierarchy under the thumb of atheistic tyrants, and which sometimes seemed both supine and neo-imperialist in its attitudes to other churches that themselves had fallen under the Soviet yoke. The rapprochement may be a thorny one in the immediate future; but it is one that is undeniably important. It is an exercise in what the church represents at its very core and essence: the power and possibility of reconciliation. It is more likely to succeed if the temptations to neo-imperialism and self-assertive authority are set aside (on both sides) in favour of the gentle spirit of the humble Christ, who knew that his role was 'to serve and not to be served'.[92]

The wider Russian heritage

1   The Ukrainian Orthodox

The Ukraine now has a total of 3,100 Orthodox parishes, with 27,400,000 faithful, representing more than half the entire country. There are eighty-seven functioning monasteries of men, and eighty-one of women. Many Ukrainian Orthodox are also found in the diaspora, especially America and Britain, as a result of the large displacements of the Second World War and the communist oppression. Ukraine declared its political independence from the Soviet Union in 1991, but still has profound links socially and economically with that great power. These continue to mark, and to a certain extent problematize, its current ecclesial experience. Ukraine, so long a part of the Russian patriarchate, was once the originating mission ground for the foundation of the Russian Church. The recorded history of Christianity in Ukraine stretches back over a thousand years, when Kiev, still the Ukrainian capital, was also the historic capital of the whole Rus people, and the initiating point of the country's evangelization. Church traditions describe also how the apostle Andrew came up to Crimea through the Black Sea and preached the Gospel in the city of Chersonesus (Sevastopol). Afterwards, it is told, he sailed up the river Dnieper, prophesying that a great city would one day flourish on its banks. The baptism of Vladimir the prince of the Rus, at Chersonesus in 988, is taken as the official beginning of Christianity among the Slavs. The indigenous Slav gods were proscribed by the prince, and the new religion took root and flourished under the care of Byzantine missionaries and advisers.

A metropolitan archbishop was appointed at Kiev by the patriarch of Constantinople, to lead and organize the church throughout the region. Byzantium profoundly supported, and deeply influenced, the development of the church of the Rus,[93] and Vladimir's son, Prince Yaroslav, developed the first Slavic law-code, built many churches, and arranged for the translation of Byzantine religious texts into Church Slavonic, the language which had been founded as the medium of the evangelization. Yaroslav began the great cathedral of Sancta Sophia[94] which is still the glory of the city of Kiev. By the eleventh century the Slavic Church was strongly established, and monasticism had also taken root in a way that would deeply mark the nature of Slavic Orthodoxy with a distinctive ascetic spirit of its own.[95] Pechersky Lavra, built over and into the banks of the river Dnieper at Kiev, was a major centre of Slavic ascetical and mystical life. It has been recently reopened as an active monastery, and the catacombs under it, holding the tombs of many saints and teachers, are once again becoming a site of pilgrimage.

During the twelfth and thirteenth centuries, however, the Mongol invasions of the land profoundly disrupted the political stability of the region, and Kiev was overshadowed, as the rise to dominance of the princes of Moscow began. Ukraine eventually fell under the power of the grand duchy of Lithuania. In 1299 the metropolitan of Kiev moved north to settle in Moscow and claimed the title of 'Metropolitan of Kiev and All Rus', which caused a large degree of protest in the church at the time, much of it fomented by the Lithuanian rulers of Ukraine. These agitated for a separate metropolitan to come back to reside in Kiev. In 1448 the hierarchy split, in a movement which we have already recounted, and the Moscow metropolitanate leading the largest section of the bishops, declared its independence from Constantinople, initiating the birth of the autonomous Russian Orthodox Church.

One hundred and fifty years later, in 1589, the metropolitanate of Moscow was reorganized as an independent patriarchate, with its seat at Moscow. Present-day Ukraine has since then been part of that ecclesiastical world focused around Moscow. The power of the tsars made that a natural political as well as ecclesiastical state of affairs. But the centre always started to give in times when the political force of Moscow was disrupted. The Russian Revolution of 1917 was one such instance, and the Second World War another. Only recently has the heavy hand of the communist autocrats started to lift, allowing Ukraine to make its progress, somewhat slowly, towards genuine democratic government.[96] The long Soviet political oppression, and its frequently bitter treatment of the Ukrainian people, has left extensive hostility there towards the very idea of lingering Russian control, and some of the same spirit has unfortunately leached in some quarters into the ecclesiastical relations with Moscow. Ukraine has been much marked in recent times by its desire to form a wholly new basis of the historic relationship with the adjacent Russian empire that so over-shadows it. The declaration of political independence in 1991 was one mark of that. But the continuing massive dependence of the state of Ukraine on Russian oil and gas is another side of the same problem.

Since the break-up of the Soviet Union there has been considerable ecclesial unrest in Ukraine, which now has some of the Orthodox there looking back to its founda-tional role in the history of the country's Christianity, and wishing to press for church autocephaly to match the political independence, or radical autonomy under the presidency of Constantinople. Currently two ecclesiastical divisions upset the harmony of the Orthodox experience in this region, leading to the condition of no less than two claimant 'patriarchs of Kiev' and a considerable struggle for legitimate 'possession' of church properties.

The Ukrainian Orthodox Church

The Ukrainian Orthodox Church is the continuing hierarchy who are faithful to the presidency of the Moscow patriarchate, and under the leadership of the metropolitan of Kiev and all Ukraine they lead the majority of the Orthodox faithful in the country. This is the ecclesiastical *status quo ante* 1991. After the declaration of independence, the new political rulers of the country withdrew their financial and political support, pressing for the hierarchs to declare ecclesiastical independence from Moscow. The Ukrainian Orthodox Church was the resultant majority body after its claim for autocephalous status in 1921 (acknowledged by the Phanar in 1924) was dissolved in the years after the Second World War, and Ukraine came back politically under the control of the Moscow Soviet empire, and was ecclesiastically reabsorbed into the jurisdiction of the Moscow patriarchate. Ukraine's independence in the last years of the twentieth century reopened the question of national self-determination. The metropolitan of Kiev and his synod now have considerable autonomy from the patriarchate of Moscow, and have not wished to declare a revival of the autocephalous status. Smaller dissident groups have, however, but they have not received the support of either Moscow or the Kievan metropolitanate. They are described below.

The Ukrainian autocephalous Church

The Ukrainian autocephalous Orthodox Church is a division from the Ukrainian Orthodox Church of the Moscow patriarchate, and is a group with a history related to the problems following the Russian Revolution. It possesses approximately 1,200 parishes. It is the heir of a church which originally came into being from a synod of the Ukrainian hierarchs in 1921 which declared their church's independence from Muscovite control, following on the communist takeover in Russia. It was dismissed as uncanonical by the Moscow patriarchate, but in 1924 it received an acknowledgement of its autocephalous status from the Phanar under Patriarch Gregory VII. Even so, politically the country came under the ever more powerful sway of the communist regime emanating from Moscow. In 1942 the German army occupied Ukraine and cut off the power of the Soviet government.

The independent Ukrainian churches were encouraged by the German authorities at that time, who saw in their desire to break free from years of Soviet domination a bridgehead into the destabilization of Soviet power. After the collapse of the Nazis, the independent Ukrainian churches were regarded with great suspicion by the Soviet powers and were repressed. The communist government then only acknowledged the legitimacy of Orthodox churches in the canonical jurisdiction of Moscow, and most of the clergy assented to the reunion. Many dissenting Ukrainian clergy at this time emigrated to the west. There are now large diasporas in America and Canada, and parts of Europe. Those in America and Canada subsequently separated from all Ukrainian control and declared themselves independent. In the late 1980s the Ukrainian state once more gave its acknowledgement, and some limited support, to the church in the home country and encouraged its renewed claims to independence. It is presently mainly based in the western Galician province of the Ukraine. In 1993 it decided to declare its autocephalous status once more, but it has not been able to attract the majority of the Orthodox clergy of the country, who have stayed in the jurisdiction of the Moscow patriarchate. The senior hierarch of this body also claims the title of Patriarch of Kiev and All Ukraine, but neither the status of independence nor the title is acknowledged by a wide range of the other Orthodox churches.

The Kievan patriarchal Church

In 1992 a small separate group of the hierarchs of the Ukrainian Orthodox Church also declared independence from Russian influence and jurisdiction (following on from the political independence of Ukraine) and declared the reconstitution of the independent Kievan Church with its own patriarchate. Its first leader, Filaret of Kiev and All Ukraine, was excommunicated by the Moscow patriarchal synod. It is not recognized among the Orthodox at large, though it argues that it is the rightfully independent Orthodox Church in Ukraine. Its senior hierarch also claims the title of Patriarch of Kiev and All Ukraine.

The Ukrainian Orthodox diaspora

Several parishes of the Ukrainian Orthodox in the western diaspora, in aversion to the communist oppression of their church during the Soviet period, put themselves under the protective Omophorion of the patriarch of Constantinople. These Orthodox also remain in the wider communion, but the ecclesiastical arrangement reflected the times when the diaspora could not trust a hierarchy that was widely believed to be controlled by Soviet communist masters. This situation is increasingly non-relevant. In America and Canada there were once large diaspora congregations of the Ukrainian autocephalous Church (above). These have recently declared their own independence.

2   Belorussia

Belorussia has been an independent republic since 1991. Ecclesiastically its history derives from its existence as part of ancient Kievan Rus, from which centre Christianity was first delivered to the Slavs. Its has in times past belonged to the patriarchates of Constantinople and Moscow. In the late nineteenth century the Muscovite tsars applied a heavy programme of Russification to the area, forbidding the very use of Belorussian language and any nationalist expression of indigenous culture. In 1922 the Belorussian hierarchs attempted a move towards autonomy, but it was resisted by the patriarch of Moscow and suppressed by the Bolshevik government, which took in Belorussia as an integral part of the Soviet Union. It thereafter experienced the usual suffocation of its church life, and suffered greatly during the Second World War. There has been some strong feeling for independence ecclesiastically, after the political division occurred in recent times, but the patriarchate of Moscow granted the Belorussian Church a large degree of autonomy in 1990, raising it to the status of an exarchate. Most of its church life naturally looks to Moscow for its direction, and most sermons are preached in the Russian language (not Belorussian). Today there are about 5 million faithful in this church, which is part of the patriarchate of Moscow.

3   Moldova[97]

Between the tenth and twelfth centuries Moldavia was part of Kievan Rus. But in more recent times the largest number of the population were ethnic Romanians. Before the power of the Soviet Union absorbed what is now known as Moldova, the majority of the Orthodox there looked to the Romanian church as their natural home. As an integral part of the Soviet Union, the patriarchate of Moscow has had, and continues to have, jurisdictional charge over it. The Soviet communist authorities attempted by every means to suffocate Christianity in the region, but unsuccessfully, even though most churches and monasteries in the land were destroyed or put to secular use. After the collapse of Russian communism there were the usual deep stirrings of a desire to dissociate from the very shadow of Moscow. In the light of their newly found political independence many of the lower clergy wished to return to a union with the patriarchate of Romania, but this was strongly contested, and a considerable schism occurred as a result, which is still in process of being healed. Moldova is a heavily agricultural economy, and had been bled dry by the communist system. Today it is struggling to emerge from generations of poverty and neglect, and the ecclesial divisions are hindering its progress. The Moldovan Orthodox, in their beautiful land, amount to a total of 850 parishes with eleven monasteries, and about 2 million faithful.

4   The Baltic Lands

The Baltic states were formerly small satellites of the Soviet Union. The political break-up of the empire in the 1990s caused considerable ecclesiastical instability as parts of the church in this area sought release from Moscow, to mirror their new-found political freedom.

The Lithuanian Orthodox are a very small minority of 114,000 faithful from the national Christian total of 3.25 million, the majority of whom are Roman Catholics.

The Latvian Orthodox have been in the sphere of Russian influence since the early eighteenth century when Peter the Great annexed the land. Most recently, after fifty years of Soviet oppression, the country regained its independence in 1991. The Orthodox in the land number just under half a million faithful, and represent about one-third of the Christians of the nation (Catholics and Protestants being equally divided to make up the other two-thirds).

The Estonian Orthodox make up about half of the total of the Christians in this nation, numbering as they do just under a quarter of a million faithful. The other half is predominantly Protestant. Among the Orthodox there are 100 parishes, attached to the Estonian Apostolic Orthodox Church. It is jurisdictionally under the care of the ecumenical patriarchate, though the patriarchate of Moscow claims that ecclesiastically it should be what it was in the days before the break-up of the Soviet empire: one of the dioceses of the Russian Orthodox Church (the diocese of Tallinin and Estonia). The considerable ecclesiastical friction precipitated by the flight from Moscow of the Estonian Orthodox brought about a short-lived state of mutual excommunication, in 1996, between the patriarchates of Moscow and Constantinople. Recently the patriarchate of Constantinople has endorsed the Estonian Church's claim for autonomous status, which Moscow continues to reject.

5 Hungary

There are a very small number of Hungarian Orthodox, largely of Serbian and Romanian origin. The country is otherwise largely Catholic with a sizeable Protestant minority. The Orthodox amount to 1 per cent of the country, totalling 90,00 faithful. In 1925 the Serbian patriarch announced that he was taking the jurisdiction of these faithful into his own care, establishing a bishop in Budapest. The Hungarian government of the day then encouraged the priest Stephen Nemetz to resist this, and having been ordained as a bishop in Syria he led a movement of secession. It was ended when Hungary fell under communist control in 1946, and the Orthodox of the country were placed under the administration of the patriarchate of Moscow.

6 The Russian diaspora

There is also the Russian diaspora to consider. This will be treated in more detail subsequently, after the cases of the greater various autocephalous and autonomous churches have been set out completely. But for clarity's sake it will be useful simply to give the barest outlines here (while we are considering the Russian heritage) in relation to the four major divisions which now constitute the very large Russian Orthodox diaspora in the world outside Russia.

Moscow patriarchal parishes abroad

In the first place, the Moscow patriarchate has several exarchates and missions in various countries; many of them operative from long before the revolution. There was a resident Russian bishop in New York in the time of the tsars, for example, and another well-known example is the (British) diocese of Sourouzh, headed for many years by the much-loved metropolitan, Antony Bloom. These parishes continue to be directly responsible to the Moscow patriarchate in all respects.

The Russian Church outside Russia

After the revolution many of the Russian hierarchs fled the country, and those who were already living abroad, serving the needs of Russians in different countries, set up a governing synod independent of communist control and infiltration. This was known as the Karlovtzy synod. Sometimes this part of the Russian Church is known as the Synod, or Synodal Church, and more properly as the Synod of the Russian Orthodox Church in Exile, or the Russian Orthodox Church Outside of Russia (ROCOR). In the latter years of the twentieth century there were extensive discussions under way for what promised to be the eventual return of the hierarchs and faithful of this jurisdiction to full canonical union with the Moscow patriarchate. In the autumn of 2006, after earlier eirenic approaches to the ROCOR by the Moscow patriarchate, the bishops of the Synod announced the decision for restitution of canonical union with the patriarchate. They have retained an autonomous governance of their parishes under the terms of the reunion; but the reconciliation, which was formally celebrated in 2007, is an important and positive event, welcomed by the whole Orthodox Church, and signalling a new era of harmony for the Russian diaspora.

The Russian archdiocese of western Europe

There is also another part of the Russian Church abroad known as the Russian archdiocese of western Europe. Again growing up as part of the great fragmentation that affected the Russian Church after its devastating oppression by Soviet communism, several bishops and many parishes of the Russians who had fled for safety to western Europe placed themselves under the patronage of the patriarch of Constantinople, who now takes under his Omophorion these parts of the heritage of Russian Orthodoxy.

The Russian Metropolia of America (the Orthodox Church in America)

Before 1970 this church, of Russian origins, was known as the Metropolia. In 1970 the patriarchate of Moscow granted autocephaly to it, acknowledging the large degree of autonomy it had exercised in the years after the revolution. It is now a large and important body of the Orthodox in the New World with important seminaries and presses. After 1970 it changed its name from the Russian Orthodox Greek Catholic Church in America, to the Orthodox Church in America (OCA). It is no longer solely of Russian character, but has not, since its birth in 1970, grown into the position of being the undisputed 'national' church of the Orthodox in America. The Greek Orthodox archdiocese of North America remains under the Omophorion of the patriarchate of Constantinople, and the OCA now stands (in effect) as one more 'jurisdiction' in the welter of the jurisdictions of Orthodox that comprise the melting-pot of the United States. It is governed by its own metropolitan, based in Washington, and its own synod. It enjoys full communion with the patriarchate of Moscow and the wider Orthodox world, but not all the Orthodox churches apart from Russia recognize its autocephalous status. It is discussed in more detail under its own heading below.

The Orthodox Church of Greece

The Greek Orthodox Church is the concept most west Europeans immediately think of in reference to Orthodoxy as a whole, and it sometimes comes as a surprise to them to discover how relatively small the actual local church of the Greeks is, and how recently it came into its independence among the Orthodox family of churches. The Greek Church of course, is the heir to an immensely proud and ancient heritage. It is quite amazing to sit in the church at Corinth, for example, or in the several beautiful churches in the region of the Acropolis in Athens, and see the fruits before one's very eyes of the preaching ministry of the apostle Paul. The impact of the Greek people on the formation of Christianity is inestimable, and inestimably beautiful too. One often takes it for granted. But even a slight reflection can restore the insight. The Lord himself lived and taught and spoke entirely in a Semitic medium, using Aramaic as the language of his teachings. Even so, within less than one generation after the historical ministry of the Lord, the entirety of the New Testament was conceived and written in the medium of Greek. The very name of the Lord was transmitted, not in its Aramaic form (Yeshu), but in its Greek translation, Jesus, and everything of formative significance for the first four centuries of Christianity (and indeed for long afterwards) was delivered in the medium of Greek: Gospels, epistles, creeds, liturgies, and councils.

The Greek Orthodox are the guardians of the whole theology of the early church. These pillars of the faith have been preserved by them in an undying heritage which makes the Greek people outstanding in the annals of Christianity. Even the great Church of Rome, the capital and bastion of the Western empire, prayed and worshipped in the medium of Greek for the first four centuries of its life, and has among its earliest popes many who were Greeks. The missions of the Greeks to the wider world have brought the light of the Gospel to all nations, either directly or by not so remote a mediation. The Greek evangelization of the Slavs was a work of immense import, and the history of so many of the other, newer, national Orthodox churches shows that it was to Constantinople, the home of the Greek Christian empire, that almost all Eastern Orthodox faithful once looked. As the Russian theologian Father Georges Florovsky once remarked: 'We are, all of us, Greeks.'

The present Orthodox Church of Greece was formerly part of the patriarchate of Constantinople. It sought its separate national identity, as a jurisdictionally free church, largely because of the continuing Ottoman domination of the Phanar in the time of the Greek struggle for independence. Even now as an autocephalous church, it is immensely closely bonded to the patriarchate, which it supports, and the patriarch is one of the most revered figures in the wider Greek world and the extended consciousness of Hellas, which of course reaches far beyond the present national boundaries of the Greek state. Its continuing level of relationship with the patriarchate gives the best witness possible that autocephaly in church government is not a rupture of the deeper reality of church communion, but merely one of its mature manifestations.

Even at the height of the Byzantine empire, Greek culture was not primarily located in what is now known as the heartland of the Greek nation. The real centres were twofold: Constantinople and Thessaloniki. Athens and its environs were very provincial places indeed during the long Byzantine period. In the medieval era many Slavs migrated south into the Greek homelands, and Frankish knights held dominance over the Orthodox faithful until the tide of the Ottomans finally engulfed them in the aftermath of the fall of Constantinople. The Byzantine aristocrats held out a few years longer in isolated pockets, but soon all the Greek lands were under Turkish Islamic rule. At the beginning of the nineteenth century the sprawling Ottoman administration was noticeably weakening, and aspirations for freedom gripped the Greek peoples, even though the fight against the power of so great an oppressor seemed suicidal. In 1821 the Greeks in the homeland raised the new national flag with the blessing of Metropolitan Germanos of Patras, and declared their political independence. So the Greek War for Independence began. Immediately relations with the Phanar were suspended. The Ottoman government regarded Patriarch Gregory V as responsible for the good behaviour of all subject Christian peoples throughout the empire and, having seized him in full vestments, immediately after the paschal liturgy, hanged him from the main gate of his palace at the Phanar (which remains closed to this day in respect to his memory). The revolutionary government declared at the time that 'Greece is autonomous and independent; and her church is autocephalous.' This state of affairs was regularized by the constitution agreed between the church and the state in 1833, when Greece became an independent kingdom whose sovereignty was recognized and assured by the Christian powers. The new charter was submitted to the patriarch of Constantinople for his comment and approval, and the autocephalous status of the Greek Church was eventually recognized in 1850.

Originally the Greek Church covered the extent of the kingdom of the Hellenes, the Peloponnesos, and continental Greece (until the disastrous war of 1921 with the enforced exchange of populations when the Greeks were expelled from Asia Minor). The Ionian Greek islands were added to it in 1864, as they too achieved independence, and in 1881 the territory of Thessaly. Today these are called the Ancient Regions (Palaiai Chorai) and amount to thirty-seven dioceses. After the further collapse of Turkish power in 1912–13, Macedonia, Epirus, and the Aegean islands were also included in the Greek Church. Their adoption into the autocephaly was not acknowledged by the Phanar until 1928. These are now called the New Regions (Neai Chorai) and amount to thirty-three dioceses. Several parts of the modern Greek state developed along a different line ecclesiastically, and have retained a direct jurisdictional relationship with Constantinople: namely the monastic republic of Mount Athos (near Thessaloniki), the islands of the Dodecanese, the patriarchal exarchate of Patmos, and the semi-autonomous Church of Crete. Today the Greek Orthodox Church is the only example of Orthodoxy which is state-supported. There are presently a total of 36,00 parishes and just under 10 million faithful.

The patriarchal Church of Bulgaria

Christianity came to ancient Roman Thrace in the second century, and was established in a secure way despite the regular waves of invaders (Goths, Huns, Slavs, Bulgars, Avars) from the fourth century onwards. These were generally assimilated to Roman ways. In the time of the Byzantine empire present-day Bulgaria was an important part (Thrace) of the patriarchate of Constantinople, but also contained territories (Illyria) that had once formed part of the Roman patriarchate. Ecclesiastically Bulgaria's church history has long been marked by the grinding friction between the two great patriarchal sees as to who should have jurisdiction over it. This was, in no small measure, one of the disaffections that led to the increasingly bitter alienation of the two great sees at the end of the first millennium. By the seventh century the lands comprising present-day Bulgaria were settled by new immigrants from the east, the Turanian nomads, who were tribal offshoots of the Avars and Huns. Byzantium sent missionaries from the south-east, and Rome sent missionaries from the north-west.

The Turanian Bulgars set up their Khanate (princely state) in successful opposition to the Byzantine emperors and were later caught up in the evangelizing mission of SS Cyril and Methodios. In light of this, the Bulgarians adopted the Slavonic language after the early ninth century, and since then have been counted among the Slavic peoples. In 865 Khan Boris I wished to adopt Christianity, and strengthen alliances with Byzantium. After his baptism by the Greeks, he approached St Photios, the patriarch of Constantinople, asking him outright to set up an independent hierarchy in Bulgaria. This the patriarch was not ready to accede to so quickly, and so the khan took advantage of the strained relations between Constantinople and Rome and approached Pope Nicholas I with the same request. The pope sent two bishops to examine the situation, but the khan broke off relations with Adrian II, Nicholas' successor, and returned with his suit to Constantinople. For centuries afterwards the 'Bulgarian question' became something like an ecclesiastico-political football. In 889 Khan Boris left the throne in favour of the monastic life. His son, Prince Simeon, who was also a monk, was highly energetic in making Slavonic the language of the new church. It was Simeon who led the Bulgarian hierarchy, despite Constantinople's opposition, to declare their ecclesiastical independence. They then led the Serbs, to their west, into the Orthodox fold and encouraged their own path to autocephaly.

Bulgaria's burgeoning independence was severely nipped in the bud by the military and political renaissance experienced by the Byzantine empire in the time of Basil II (the 'Bulgar-Slayer'!) who violently brought the country, and its church, back into the obedient fold of the Christian Romans in 1018. After that time the church, centred on Ohrid, was increasingly Hellenized, but retained a large degree of autonomy until 1767 when, by order of the sultans, it was suppressed, and the Bulgarian Church was fully subjected to the immediate jurisdiction of Constantinople. Eastern Bulgaria reasserted its independence from the Byzantines in 1186 and thereafter had its church life centred on Trnovo. The patriarchate was re-established in 1235. It was overrun by the Ottoman Turks in 1396, and also lost its ecclesiastical autonomy in 1767. After this absorption of all the Bulgarians by Constantinople a rigorous Hellenization was enforced among them; the liturgical language of Slavonic was suppressed in favour of mandatory Greek, and Phanariot Greeks monopolized all the senior clerical positions.

Relaxation of the Turkish yoke led to the Bulgarian petition to the sultan in 1856 for measures of independence for their church, and some Bulgarian bishops were then appointed as a concession by the Phanar, but the course was set for independence from Constantinople and from the sultan too. The sultan proved more amenable than the patriarchate to hearing the requests, made with increasing insistence from 1860 onwards. In 1870 the declaration of ecclesiastical independence was acknowledged by a Firman of the Sublime Porte, against the wishes of the patriarchate, and the Bulgarian Church declared its autonomy under an exarch and a local synod. The patriarch of Constantinople promptly held a synod of his own in 1872, to which he invited the (Greek) patriarchs of Alexandria and Antioch, and excommunicated the Bulgarian hierarchy, rejecting their petition for autonomy on the grounds that the concept of a 'national church' was contrary to the spirit of ecclesial oneness and led to the heresy of 'phyletism'.[98] The Bulgarian Church ignored this, and though their separation was at first classed as schismatic by the Greek churches, the Slavic churches came to acknowledge it, especially after the successful Bulgarian revolt which, with the assistance of the Russians, forced the Ottomans to give the country a large measure of independence.

The other European nations, fearing Russian control of the region, considerably undermined this, and shored up the Turkish administration of Bulgaria. It was not until 1908 that the Bulgarian people effected their full independence. In both the world wars they allied with the losing side, and lost much territory and political prestige as a result. Seventy-three years after their declaration of independence, in 1945, the exarch of the Bulgarian Church approached the Phanar once more and reconciliation was effected, with Constantinople acknowledging the autocephaly.

The year before this, Bulgaria had fallen under communist control, and most of those involved could see the dark clouds on the horizon. Within three years the exarch, Metropolitan Stephen of Sofia, was forcibly retired from office, and the communist authorities pursued a policy comparable to that in Romania: simultaneously seeking the rights of the Bulgarians (even ecclesiastically) while at the same time suffocating their own people (especially religiously). The communist government established a new 'constitution' for the church in 1950, among whose provisions was the declaration of the Bulgarian Orthodox Church to have the status of a patriarchate, based at Sofia. This was effected in 1953. Constantinople at first objected to the procedure, but acknowledged the new status quo in 1961.

The communist yoke was immensely stifling in Bulgaria. Monastic life was particularly hard hit. The higumen of the ancient monastery of Rila, one of the most important centres of church life in the country, was quickly targeted and arrested in 1945, dying in prison. The buildings were turned into a meteorological station. The hierarchy declared the church's loyalty to the state authorities in 1953 and as a result were given back many church properties, even receiving some (very poor) state subsidy. There was a slight thaw in the 1970s, but church attendance had dwindled to a trickle, and the task of rebuilding a vibrant Christian life now faces a church with relatively few young clergy. In the years before the Second World War the Orthodox Church represented the faith of 85 per cent of the country (though church attendance was not particularly high). A census in 1962 estimated that Orthodoxy then represented only 27 per cent of the population. A church census conducted in 1970 set the figure of believers at more than 5 million, 65 per cent of the country. The church is currently constituted of about 6 million faithful (71 per cent of the nation) worshipping in 4,200 parishes. After the fall of communism in 1991 there was a series of bitter divisions in the Bulgarian Church, with priests and faithful protesting loudly about the conformism of the existing hierarchs, and demanding their dismissal. The crisis was only partly resolved when the government and representatives of the patriarchate of Constantinople came to Sofia to join with the patriarch and his synod in the celebration of the divine liturgy, as an act of public endorsement. Relations among the Bulgarian Orthodox themselves, as well as the repair of the church's much devastated infrastructure and educational programme, remain a pressing part of the long rebuild required after the communist gloom.

There is a Bulgarian diaspora in America whose hierarchs retain the closest links with the Bulgarian synod. The Bulgarian monastery of St George, on Mount Athos, is (like all Athonite monasteries) under the jurisdiction of the patriarch of Constantinople.

The patriarchal Church of Serbia

The Serbs are a Slav nation originating from the Carpathian region. In the sixth and seventh centuries, with the active encouragement of the Byzantine emperor, Heraclios (d. 641), they established themselves in the regions of southern Dalmatia, Herzegovina, and Serbia, and acted as a frontier guard for Byzantium. An early mission from Rome did not gain much fruit, but a mission from Constantinople later in the ninth century was more long-lasting, and Christianity in Serbia looked to Constantinople for its guidance. The foundations of the modern state and nation of Serbia were laid between 1159 and 1195 by Stephen I Nemanya. It was his son, Stephen II, who was crowned as the first Serbian king, and who established the first metropolitan see for his Orthodox people in 1219. He appointed his own brother, St Sava, as metropolitan archbishop, and Patriarch Manuel of Constantinople consecrated him to the office, at Nicaea, where he was in residence because of the Latin occupation of Byzantium. St Sava had already founded the Serbian monastery of Hilandar, on Mount Athos (1197), and in his own country he efficiently organized the infrastructure of the churches, crowning his brother as king in 1221 with a golden crown supplied for the occasion by Pope Honorius III.[99]

In 1346 the synod of Uskub, in the time of King Stephen III, declared the Serbian Church to be autocephalous, and the archbishop of Ipek (Pec) was given the title patriarch. Its time of early glory was to be short-lived, however, for the military disaster of Kossovo in 1389, followed by another at Smederevo in 1459, marked the subjugation of the country to the power of the expanding Turks. The Serbian Church followed the pattern witnessed in all provinces subordinated to the Ottoman power, and was made a direct jurisdiction of the Phanar. The patriarchate of Ipek was abolished and the archbishop subjected to the Greek archbishops of Ohrid. In 1557 it had another era of independence. A Serbian grand vizier, Mohammed Sokolovich, who had converted to Islam to serve the sultan, appointed his natural brother, a Christian monk, to be patriarch once more. The independence lasted until 1767 when the sultan ordered the independent churches of the empire to revert to the immediate jurisdiction of the patriarch of Constantinople.

During the early years of the nineteenth century independence once more became a possibility given the weakened state of the Ottoman empire. After the treaty of Adrianople the church adopted autonomous status in 1832, with a metropolitan see at Belgrade. After Serbian political independence was fully secured in 1879, the church declared itself for autocephalous status. At the end of the First World War the Balkan borders were redrawn again, bringing together the Serbs, Croats, and Slovenes into Yugoslavia. At this time four smaller autonomous Orthodox churches were joined together: Karlovtzy in southern Hungary, Montenegro, Czernovits, and Bosnia-Herzegovina. The reunion, accomplished finally in 1920, was announced at the same time as the restoration of the patriarchate at Pec. The senior hierarch, based at Belgrade, is called His Holiness the Archbishop of Ipek, Metropolitan of Belgrade

65

and Karlovtzy, and Patriarch of All Serbia. The autocephaly and elevation to patriarchal status were acknowledged formally by the patriarchate at Constantinople in 1922.

After the Second World War Serbia fell under communist control, but life under Tito was freer than was the case elsewhere in eastern Europe. Under Tito's regime, monasticism, which was already in a weakened state in Yugoslavia, fell into a poor condition. Women's houses seemed to do better than those of men, and several of the vacant monasteries were taken over by nuns at this time. The largest women' s community is at Ljubostinja. In 1939 there were 166 active monasteries with a total of only 540 monks. The medieval Serbian monasteries are world-famous sites: Krushedol (1512), Studenica (1190), Milacevo (1230), Gracanica (1320). Because of their association with Serbian national history, several of them became targets in the bitter civil war that followed the break-up of Yugoslavia after the collapse of communism, when Christian–Islamic divides shattered the national synthesis. Throughout the communist period church attendance was very low, although there have been signs of revival since. Today there are about 7.5 million Serbian Orthodox faithful worshipping in 3,100 parishes. Of these, 12,000 Orthodox are in the Republic of Slovenia (overwhelmingly Catholic for the rest). There are also Serbian diaspora parishes in America, Australia, and England, closely related to the patriarchate. The liturgical language of the church is Slavonic.

The Macedonian Orthodox Church, with a small synod of six bishops and 1,260,000 Orthodox faithful in the country, encouraged by the communist government, broke away from its union within the Serbian Orthodox Church in 1967 and declared its autocephalous status. This has not been recognized either by Serbia or by any other of the Orthodox churches.

The patriarchal Church of Romania

The Romanian Orthodox Church is the heir to the Christianity of the ancient Roman province of Dacia. It was an imperial province established by the Emperor Trajan for his veterans, in the second century. The Romanian language and culture, to this day, are marked by a deep basis in Latin, of course with many later Slavic elements added, making it, arguably, the only Latin Orthodox culture in the world. There are archaeological remains of proto-Christian churches, especially in the Black Sea region. Recently proto-Christian martyr shrines have been discovered, all of which gives testimony to the great antiquity of Christianity in these lands. Church tradition looks to the planting of the Gospel here by the missionary efforts of the apostle Andrew around the Black Sea shores. By the third century Christians were so strong in the region that they attracted the attention of the Emperor Diocletian, and many were victims of the Great Persecution which he initiated at the dawn of the fourth century. One of the Romanian Church's great patristic theologians was John Cassian, who travelled throughout the ancient church, settling in the west after years spent among the Egyptian ascetics. He became a foundational figure in ascetical theology: having an equally marked influence on the Eastern as well as the Western monastic culture.

The Romanian Church's Latin basis has always remained part of the special character of Romanian Orthodoxy, whose geographical position is, as it were, still a bridge point between the Latin and Greek ecclesiastical worlds. The mission of Cyril and Methodios and their establishment of the Slavic liturgy which became the dominant culture of the newly emergent eastern European churches such as Bulgaria and Russia were important elements in decisively bonding Romania to the eastern ecclesiastical world. And this orientation was not fundamentally shifted despite Dominican missionary activity from the west in the fourteenth century and extensive pressure from the Catholic Austro-Hungarian empire from the seventeenth century onwards. For a long time in its early existence the Bulgarian Church exercised a strong influence over Christianity in the region.

In the tenth century the territory was organized into Wallachia, which became an independent princely state in 1290. Its voivodes, the princely rulers, would become great patrons of international Orthodoxy both before and after the fall of Byzantium. A second state, Moldavia, was established to the north in 1363. Both territories had their own metropolitan archbishops. Daniel, the metropolitan of Moldavia in the fifteenth century, was one of the Orthodox hierarchs at the Council of Florence, who signed the *Tomos* (official decree) of Union. But it was rejected by his faithful at home, and both he and his successor were forced into exile in Rome. The establishment of the province of Transylvania, to the west, followed in 1526. At the same period the Turkish armies were extending outwards to increase their hold over Europe. During this time of expansion and settlement of the Orthodox, against a backdrop of bitter military struggles against the invading Turks, magnificent monasteries were established. Several of them have functioned uninterruptedly, and many more are now undergoing extensive renewal.[100] Under the Turkish domination, the leaders of the Romanian Orthodox hierarchy were Phanariot Greek clergy appointed from Constantinople, and the political rulers of the country were also appointed from the Phanar, under the supervision of the sultans.

After Transylvania's capture by the Austrian and Habsburg armies in 1688 there was extensive proselytism conducted, under the aegis of the Jesuit order, and in 1698 a great number of the local Orthodox churches seceded to Roman communion as 'Uniate' or Greek Catholic communities. By 1733 the Transylvanian clergy numbered 2,294 Greek Catholic priests compared to 458 Orthodox. The nineteenth century witnessed the great national struggle for independence from Turkish control to the east, and for the reclamation of control over Transylvania to the west. The rule of Phanariots, under the supervision of the Sublime Porte, came to an end in 1829 when the treaty of Adrianople conceded autonomous political status to Wallachia and Moldavia. In 1856, at the congress of Paris, Moldavia and Wallachia reasserted their ecclesiastical autonomy.

In 1862 the Romanian Church signalled its desire to end the long period of Phanariot domination by the replacement of Greek liturgical usage with the Romanian language, which had already been used in the country regions of Transylvania, to encourage the local congregations to know and value their faith in the face of the appearance of Calvinism in those areas. The whole Romanian Church has worshipped in this elegant romance language ever since, and a distinctive form of liturgical music has also evolved alongside the classical Byzantine musical styles. In 1864 the country won its complete formal independence under the rule of Prince Alexander Cuza. In 1865 the Romanian hierarchy declared the church to be autocephalous, with the primate being the Wallachian metropolitan, with his see at Bucharest, and the metropolitan of Moldavia second in honour. In 1881 Charles von Hohenzollern-Sigmaringen was crowned king of Romania (the monarchy lasted until the Second World War), and four years afterwards, in 1885, the *de facto* situation of Romanian ecclesiastical autocephaly was eventually recognized by the patriarch of Constantinople, Joachim IV.

After the collapse of the Austro-Hungarian empire in the wake of the First World War the 'greater Romanian territories' were once more reorganized, bringing together three separate church groups: Transylvania, Bukovina, and Bessarabia. The negotiation of union took six years, from 1918 to 1924, and culminated in the declaration of the Romanian Church as a patriarchate in 1925, which was immediately recognized by the patriarchate of Constantinople and the other Orthodox churches. The patriarch is known as His Beatitude the Patriarch of Romania, Locum-Tenens of Caesarea in Cappadocia, Metropolitan of Ungaro-Wallachia and Archbishop of Bucharest. The first patriarch was Miron Cristea, who has since been followed by a succession of skilled and energetic leaders. After the end of the Second World War Romania fell under heavy Soviet control. During the communist regime, the Greek Catholic communities were suppressed and ordered to rejoin the Orthodox. Since the post-Ceausescu liberation many of them have wished to return to Roman communion, though many parishes have also expressed the desire to remain Orthodox. There was some lively tension over the rightful attribution of church properties which is now being resolved in a collaborative inter-church dialogue.

During the communist years following the Second World War, the condition of the Romanian Orthodox Church was among the best in all the zone of Soviet satellites, though it was far from happy. Soon after the communist takeover, 200 priests were imprisoned, and six bishops were forcibly retired. Patriarch Justinian (1948–77) often annoyed many of the free exiles by stating the self-evident truth that many of the principles of Marxism were in harmony with the evangelical spirit of dispossession and communion. He and his successors worked out a *modus vivendi* with the authorities that, in a sense, continued the prior Romanian tradition of close political collaboration (in the 1930s, for example, the patriarch was the prime minister of the state and another bishop headed its State Department of Religion). The practice of the faith flourished, and was deeply rooted in the personal lives of millions of ordinary Romanians. Church activity was officially hampered, but one-third of the salaries of the clergy was paid by the state. In 1955, when the Church of Romania celebrated its seventieth anniversary of independence, the government made much fuss about it as a symbol of national pride. At the same time, however, thirteen bishops and hundreds of priests languished in Romanian gaols.

From time to time the flourishing condition of the church drew disapproving remarks from the central Soviet leaders, resulting in periods of church demolition and visibly heavier oppression. The state secret police, the Securitate, were especially brutal in communist Romania, and there have been many examples of the suppression of individual dissidents, monks, and priests, which have amounted to many bloodless (as well as bloody) martyrdoms in the course of the last two generations. In 1958 there was a sustained crackdown against the church, as the authorities took fright at the programme of renewal over which Patriarch Justinian was presiding. Five hundred priests and leading monks were arrested and subjected to the infamous communist show-trials. Two mass trials were held, inflicting sentences of between eight and twenty-five years in gaols and labour camps. The aspirants of the women's monastery at Agapia were taken from their college, and sent en masse to a labour camp. Legislation subsequently demanded that no aspirant to the monastic life should be under 60 years of age. Approximately 1,200 monks and nuns were expelled from their religious houses and many monasteries were forcibly closed.

From 1948 onwards the authorities had generally made it immensely difficult to recruit new monastics, recognizing the importance of the monastic life in Romanian church affairs, but after the fall of the communist regime there was a rapid increase. Monasticism in Romania has generally been closely bonded to the diocesan life, under the care of the local bishops. The monastery of Agapia contains several thousand nuns following a range of lifestyles, from the cenobitic to the completely eremitical, in an extremely beautiful wooded valley. In other houses of men, such as at the historic centre of Sihastria, or the beautiful Transylvanian community at Rohia near Satu Mare, the hesychastic life is followed with admirable fervour. Romanian monastic architecture is a wonderful hybrid of Gothic–Orthodox, and the painted monasteries of the north of the country[101] supply some of the world's greatest examples of Christian cultural achievement.

The spiritual and mystical life of the Romanian monasteries was inspired by the hesychastic movement, and St Paisy Velichovsky widely disseminated copies of the Philokalia (a large collection of Orthodox ascetical and mystical writings from the Fathers) from his base at Neamts. One of the great modern Romanian theologians, Father Dimitru Staniloae, began the issuing of a modern Romanian Philokalia (a new edition of the patristic writings from critical editions), and the new version ran to many volumes more than the original, presided over by SS Macarius of Corinth and Nicodemos the Hagiorite in the eighteenth century, with new commentaries and critical notes that were a testimony to how well the intellectual life of the Romanian Church was flourishing under such difficult circumstances. In Romania today there are several nationally regarded monastic elders (*startsi*), many of whom endured years of persecution for the faith.[102]

After the fall of communism the incumbent patriarch, Theoctist, offered his resignation to the holy synod (acknowledging student protests over the past conformity of the church to communist policy) and retired to monastic life. The loss of his skills and acumen was soon felt, and his return was requested by the church at large. He subsequently presided with a skill and energy remarkable for his advanced years over the important transition of the church to post-communist freedom. Romanian Orthodoxy has traditionally had a lively intellectual life. Its theologians are today rebuilding their devastated libraries and schools, and can be expected to offer a substantial, and vital, contribution to the character of world Orthodoxy in the years ahead. The national census taken after the fall of communism showed 20 million people declaring themselves to be Orthodox Christians, worshipping in about 8,300 active parishes, which makes Romanian Orthodoxy the second largest of all the Eastern churches, and arguably the one with the most open and outward-looking mentality, and with vigorous and educated bishops.

Romania is one of the liveliest members of the family of Orthodox churches with a desire to engage with the rest of Europe, of which it feels itself to be an integral part: the only example of Orthodoxy among a Latin people. The current social-ethical problems in Romania (the street children, chiefly a result of the appalling communist orphanages), which are the legacy of the communist autocracy, face the Romanian Church as a pressing future agenda which it is beginning to address, and will focus on more directly when it has re-established the base infrastructure of its churches, monasteries, and schools. The rebuilding of the ecclesiastical life and structures is proceeding with extraordinary rapidity and vigour, which is a testament to the love and respect in which the church is generally held by the ordinary people. The country is rich in natural resources, as well as in the resources of the native intelligence of its people and clergy. The impoverishment of such a fertile land after fifty years of misrule is testimony in itself to the lunacy of the post-war political administration that squandered such vast gifts in the tyrannical oppression of its own people. The church has much good will in the country at large, and is regarded as a hopeful force for the rebuilding of Romanian pride and national self-direction.

The Church of Georgia

The ancient Christians of Georgia were known as the Iberians. They became a distinct people after migrating in the fourth to the third centuries BC from the regions of the Euphrates and the Tigris, to their present homeland in the mountains between Russian and Armenia in the southern Caucasus. The church was founded in the fourth century by St Nina, the 'equal to the apostles'. There had also been missions in the time of Constantine the Great, and local traditions assign a foundational role to the apostle Andrew. At first it was jurisdictionally dependent on the patriarchate of Antioch. The Georgian homeland was a place of transitions and struggles of empires, beginning with the conflicts between the Byzantines and Persians, in whose midst the Georgians found themselves, and as a result the history of the Georgian Church has been full of martyrdoms and suffering, not least in the annals of the last century. From the seventh century onwards the predominant influence on the Georgian Church came from Constantinople, but it also established its effective autonomy at that same time, with a katholikos[103] of its own as senior hierarch. Georgia's nominal subordination to Antioch continued until the eighth century, when it became effectively autocephalous. It was ravaged by Timur in the fourteenth and early fifteenth centuries, and, shortly after him, by the expansion of the Turks, who took control after the sixteenth century. It was incorporated into the Russian Orthodox Church in 1811, after Tsar Alexander I had annexed the entire country to Russia. At this time the resident katholikos was forcibly retired by the Moscow synod, and they appointed in his place a Russian to act as exarch. The use of Georgian language in both church and state was forbidden, and for a century all the exarchs were Russian nationals. Understandably this did not encourage warm relations between the Georgians and their perceived oppressors. On the eve of the revolution, Tsar Nicholas II issued a decree of religious toleration, and the Georgian hierarchs were unwise enough to trust it. They sent in a formal appeal to the throne for autonomous status for their church. The result was the exile of the pro-independence hierarch who drafted the protocol, a setback which resulted in great disaffection among the people, and many stirrings of Georgian nationalists. The Russian exarch of the Georgian Church was himself one of their assassination victims at this time.

Immediately after the Russian Revolution in 1917, the Georgian Church again asserted its autocephalous status and elected Bishop Kirion as its first restored katholikos. In 1917 there were 2,455 Orthodox parishes operating in the country, with fifteen diocesan bishops in the synod. In 1919 Constantinople acknowledged the autocephaly, but Moscow refused to do so. In 1921 Georgia fell under Bolshevik Soviet control.

After initial resistance, severely repressed by the harsh imprisonment of the clerical leaders, the hierarchy settled into a conformist relationship with the communist powers, that was rewarded in 1944 when Patriarch Sergius of Moscow officially recognized the Church of Georgia's autocephalous status. It endured a long suffocation under the Soviets. By 1970 there were only eighty state-recognized churches in operation, but this period also saw the start of a revival of church life. The church had always kept the affection of the Georgian people, who knew it had been one of great preservers of Georgian identity. In 1991 Georgia declared its political independence. The katholikos Ilya II was a charismatic leader at this time, and presided over a call to return to faith. The revival gained symbolic publicity in 1992 when the Georgian president, Shevardnadze (a former atheist and member of the Russian Soviet Politburo), accepted baptism in the Orthodox cathedral of T'bilisi. But Georgia's progress to democracy was a difficult one, and the country began to suffer great instability because of the close-following civil war of 1993, its own separatist movements (there are over a million Muslims in the eastern parts of Georgia), and great economic difficulties. Today the church consists of 600 parishes, and about 3,011,600 faithful, forming the vast majority of the Christians of the country. There has been a sizeable ethnic Armenian Orthodox presence in Georgia from ancient times. They number about 340,000 faithful.

The Church of Poland

The Polish Orthodox Church traces its origins back to two chief periods of formation; the first in the tenth century, and the second revival after the union of Lithuania and Poland in the fourteenth century. When Poland was dismembered politically in 1722, its Orthodox population was absorbed by the Russian Church. When the country was reconstituted as a sovereign independent state, after the cessation of the First World War in 1918, her new borders contained about 4 million Orthodox faithful, mainly Ukrainians and Belorussians in the eastern part of the country. They had hitherto belonged to the jurisdiction of the patriarch of Moscow. At that time, Patriarch Tikhon was willing to grant autonomous status to the new church, but the new government was pressing the Polish hierarchy to establish its complete independence from Russian control by declaring autocephaly. In 1923 the senior Polish hierarch, Archbishop George Yoroshevsky, was still arguing for a greater degree of autonomy when he was actually assassinated by a crazed Russian monk who felt such a move was scandalous. The degree of scandal this, in turn, caused, occasioned the Polish government to appeal directly to the patriarch of Constantinople for the award of autocephalous status, and this was given by Constantinople in a *Tomos* of 1924. The Moscow patriarchate did not recognize this until the country came under its own political control once more in 1945, and, in 1948, Patriarch Alexei wrote to the Phanar announcing that the Russian Orthodox Church had itself conferred autocephaly on the Polish Orthodox. Attempts by the Catholics in the pre-war years to over-zealously persuade the Orthodox to come back into union (they were regarded by the Polish Catholics as former Uniates who had been pressured to enter the Orthodox Church in the nineteenth century) involved many cases of lawsuits to claim back churches and buildings, and forcible closures of institutions. This heavy-handedness extensively soured relations between the Orthodox

71

and the Catholics for many generations afterwards.[104] Prior to 1918, the Orthodox had ten bishops in their synod, five dioceses, fifteen monasteries, and about 2,000 parishes with 4 million faithful. By 1960 the Orthodox totalled only 4,500 faithful. Today, there are 400 parishes with 1,021,000 faithful. The senior hierarch of the Polish Orthodox is now known as the Metropolitan of Warsaw and All Poland. The church retains very close links with the Moscow patriarchate.

The Church of Albania

Originally part of the patriarchate of Constantinople, the Albanian Orthodox Church became autocephalous in 1937. It is a religiously mixed country. After the fifteenth century there were extensive Muslim conversions from among the Orthodox population. Today, of the total 3.6 million Albanians in the homeland, official statistics suggest that approximately 60 per cent are atheist or radically secularized. Just less than 20 per cent of the country is Orthodox, with the other half of the religiously active citizens represented by Islam and Roman Catholicism. The Orthodox of this land took their origin ecclesiastically from the famed missionary centre of Ohrid. But in 1767, pressured to it by the Ottoman political masters, the patriarchate of Constantinople absorbed the church and thereafter directly appointed its metropolitan bishops, all of whom until 1922 were Phanariot Greeks. The local church pressed for more independence, first in 1908 when the Young Turk movement disrupted Ottoman control, and again after the Balkan wars of 1912–13. In 1922 a synod of the local church demanded the grant of autocephaly, and the Greek hierarchs left the country. By 1926 the Phanar had agreed to afford autocephaly under certain terms, but the head of state, the Muslim Amadh Zoghu, refused to countenance them. He would later assume the title of King Zog of Albania, and (though a Muslim) patronized the Orthodox, confirming their right to officiate as bishops, just like the sultans had before him.

In 1929 the local Albanian synod proclaimed autocephaly independently, and was excommunicated for its pains by the Phanar, a state of affairs which brought about the immediate state-ordered exile of the exarch of Constantinople, Metropolitan Hierotheos, then resident in the country. The patriarch of Serbia recognized the autocephaly eventually, and fostered a reconciliation with the Phanar. Constantinople accepted the state of autocephaly in 1937. In the years after the Second World War, Albania fell under the heavy hand of severe communist oppression. There was extensive persecution in the years after 1945, with several leading Orthodox hierarchs murdered by the communists, and in 1967 the government declared the complete and final closure of all Christian places of worship (a premature statement as it turned out). The state policy during the 1950s was to bring the church under the jurisdictional care of the Moscow patriarchate, and several Albanian hierarchs who resisted that policy were forcibly deposed. The Orthodox currently represent about half a million faithful, worshipping in 909 parishes. The senior hierarch is His Beatitude the Metropolitan of Tirana and Durazzo, Archbishop of All Albania. There is also an Albanian diaspora which continues under the jurisdictional protection of the patriarchate of Constantinople. The communist rule, as was usual elsewhere, succeeded in bringing an already poor country down onto its knees, and the Orthodox Church in Albania, like the rest of its people, is only now beginning to emerge from the chaos of its recent nightmare.

The Church of the Czech lands and Slovakia

Orthodoxy was present in Moravia, the medieval forerunner of Czechoslovakia, from the time of the mission of SS Cyril and Methodios in the ninth and tenth centuries, but the majority religion of the region had always been Roman Catholic. The stirrings of the Reformation secessions were severely controlled by the Habsburgs in the early seventeenth century when they gained power over Bohemia and Moravia. Czechoslovakia was constituted as an independent nation in the years following the First World War, part of the break-up of the Austro-Hungarian empire. The Orthodox churches of recent times were founded in Prague in the mid nineteenth century, and since then have come under, at various times, the patronage of the patriarchates of Serbia, Constantinople, and Moscow.

In 1918 the vast majority of the population was Roman Catholic. During the First World War Orthodoxy had been suppressed in the country, and it was also to endure some element of persecution again during the Second World War. When the Czechoslovakian Orthodox Church was reconstituted in the aftermath of the First World War, approximately 40,000 declared themselves and a bishop (Gorazd Pavlik) was appointed for them by the Serbian patriarch. Bishop Pavlik succeeded in rallying together most of the Orthodox faithful under the jurisdictional care of the Serbian patriarch, but in 1942 he and several of his clergy were assassinated by the Nazi invaders.[105] By 1946 the political mantle of the Soviets had fallen over the country, and the patriarch of Moscow acted independently to assume jurisdictional charge of the Czechoslovakian Orthodox. This was one of the reasons the Phanar at first looked askance, for many years, on the canonical status of the churches of Czechoslovakia and Poland, although now relations are fully restored. The concept of a separate Czechoslovakian Orthodox Church had been shrunk significantly by the Soviet annexation of much of its former territory in Podcarpatska Rus, but was soon after swollen in 1950 by the 'supposedly' free return to Orthodoxy of the Byzantine-rite Catholics of the diocese of Preshov in Slovakia. These reunited congregations demonstrated their true opinion in 1968 when large numbers elected to return to the Roman Catholic Eastern rite communion. In 1951 the patriarchate of Moscow declared the Orthodox Church of the country to be thenceforward autocephalous under the guidance of the metropolitan of Prague. The country separated politically once more into its chief constituent parts of the Czech lands and Slovakia after the collapse of communism in the last decade of the twentieth century. The Orthodox remained united across the national divide. There is a smaller Orthodox presence in Slovakia, with ten parishes and 23,000 faithful, while the Czech Republic has 100 parishes and 51,000 faithful who use the Slavonic rite. The total number of Orthodox in the region amounts to 74,000 faithful.

The three autonomous Orthodox churches

1   The Orthodox Church of Finland

The Church of Finland petitioned to come under the Omophorion of the patriarch of Constantinople in 1923, as part of its reaction to the communist oppression of the Russian Church, and the achievement of its own political independence in 1919. Before that, Finland's small Orthodox community had historically looked to the patriarch of Moscow. The Moscow patriarchate did not accept the legitimacy of this exchange of jurisdictions until 1957. Most of the Christian Finnish population since the Reformation have been Lutherans, but the birth of Orthodoxy in Finland long pre-dated the Reformation, originating from the missionary work of the Russian monks of the famed monastery of Valamo on Lake Ladoga, who evangelized the pagan tribes of this region in the thirteenth century. The church is a relatively small one. There are forty parishes, with about 70,000 faithful, but it is a vigorous community which has for centuries known itself in the context of a much larger Lutheran majority, which itself has given way to an increasingly extended atheistic secularism. The Finnish Orthodox Church has experience, beyond many others, of the issues of witnessing to, and dialoguing with, a profoundly secularized environment which will prove invaluable for other Orthodox communities in a new age of 're-evangelization' and ecumenical dialogue.

2 The Orthodox Church of Japan

Orthodoxy in Japan was initiated by the Russian priest (after 1906 archbishop, and since 1970 canonized as 'saint') Nicholas Kassatkin (1836–1912). He was sent in 1861 by the patriarchate of Moscow to serve the pastoral needs of the Russian consular offices in Hakodate, Japan. Once there he decided that he should work as a missionary priest among the local Japanese too, and mastered the language and culture, beginning translations of the sacred books into Japanese. In 1868 he performed his first baptism of a Japanese convert, and a mission was established in 1871. In 1872 he was able to witness the ordination of two indigenous Japanese priests. Since his foundation the church has grown, through periods of stagnation and setback, to the point where it now has forty parishes in three dioceses, and about 38,000 faithful (28,000 were listed in 1904). The political effects of the Russo-Japanese War of 1904, then the Russian Revolution, and then the Second World War, disrupted relations between the patriarchate and Japan. The Japanese government, in 1939, also put a heavy nationalistic hand on the constitutions of all societies, and pressed the church to draw up a new constitution for itself that diminished reliance on foreign intervention. Accordingly the archbishop at that period, Metropolitan Sergei (Tikhomirov), resigned his charge (along with many other non-Japanese church leaders) and handed over the property of the church to Japanese ownership.

The Professor of Russian Language at the Japanese military academy, Arsenius Heikichi Iwasawa, was appointed as head of the new episcopal committee to find a new chief bishop, but remained administering the church until 1941, to the accumulating protests of a significant group of clergy who, representing the 'All Japan Church Council', had elected Archpriest James Shintaro Tohei as the legitimate episcopal candidate. Having approached the Russian synodal hierarchs (ROCOR), Iwasawa's group secured the episcopal consecration of Archpriest John Kiichi Ono. He and his wife (daughter of the first Japanese priest ever ordained) took monastic vows on the same day, and he received episcopal ordination, as Bishop Nicholas, shortly after. When he returned to Tokyo cathedral for the first Pascha service, however, he found the doors of the church locked against him. Persuasion from the government led to a reconciliation between the two parties, and Bishop Nicholas was acknowledged as presiding bishop. Archpriest James was put forward for episcopal consecration too, but died before this could be effected. At this time the government formally approved the new constitutions. After the Second World War, Bishop Nicholas retired (some said he was pressured to it by enduring opposition), and a movement was quickly inaugurated to separate the Church of Japan from the supervision of the ROCOR synod, and open dialogue with the Metropolia Church (the Russian Church in America, eventually to become the OCA). A group within the church clung to the jurisdictional link with ROCOR and for a short time Bishop Nicholas joined them as their head, setting up a tendentious schism. In 1954, however, he reconciled with the Church of Japan, which was then under the wing of the Metropolia Church in America. It was the Metropolia which helped it towards its present ecclesiastical status, when in 1970 the patriarchate of Moscow officially granted full autonomous status to the Church of Japan, under its own renewed spiritual patronage.

3   The Orthodox Church of China

Christianity in China dates back to antiquity. It is said that the apostle Thomas preached the Gospel there in the first century. But concrete evidence of the once massive extent of the missionary work of the Syrian Church can now only be found rarely, for example in the surviving stele of Xian, set up by Nestorian missionaries to mark their work in China, in 781. The records that would have clarified how extensive this Eastern Christian mission once was were extensively burned in the later period (sometimes by later missionaries), a profound loss to the history of Christianity in China.

The modern history of the Orthodox in China begins once more with the Russians. In 1685 the Chinese emperor resettled in the capital a group of some thirty or so Russian cossacks who had entered his service after his capture of a few Siberian border towns. Among them was the priest Maxim Leontiev, their chaplain, who subsequently built the first Orthodox church in Beijing for himself and his companions. In 1715 a Russian archimandrite, Hilarion, began a mission in Beijing, and it appears in official records in 1727 as part of a Sino-Russian treaty. Its purpose was largely to provide pastoral services to Russian diplomatic staff resident in the Chinese capital. An estimate of the mid nineteenth century suggested there were still only about 200 Orthodox faithful resident in Beijing, most of whom were ethnic Russian descendants. The latter part of the nineteenth century witnessed a revival, following on the cultural work of the priest Hyacinth Bichurin and the monk Archimandrite Palladios, who became masters of the Chinese language.

The Boxer rebellion of 1898–1900, where Christian converts in general were a target of violence, saw 222 Orthodox Christians martyred for their faith. The library of the Beijing Orthodox mission was also burned to the ground. Nevertheless, by the year 1902 there were an estimated thirty-two Orthodox parishes in China with a body of about between 5,000 and 6,000 faithful. By 1949 this had risen to about 106 Orthodox parishes in China. There was also a seminary, and several Chinese priests working in the parishes. The 1917 revolution in Russia increased the missionary activity in so far as many fleeing the turmoil in Russia, came east via Siberia. By 1939 there were estimated to be 200,000 Orthodox in China, with five bishops, and one Orthodox university operating at Harbin. Most of the clergy and people were ethnic Russians. The advent of repressive communist masters to China altered this situation of slow growth. At first the communist government ordered the repatriation of all 'foreign' missionaries working in China. Many of the Russian ethnic Orthodox clergy were sent back at that time to the USSR to meet a difficult fate, though others escaped to America. Later the Cultural

Revolution savagely crushed all forms of the surviving Chinese Orthodox Church. In 1957 the Chinese Orthodox Church was given autonomous status by the Moscow patriarchate. This occurred despite its tiny size, and its still struggling condition, because of the political necessity of having verifiable independence from all 'foreign powers'.

Today Orthodoxy is not among the official forms of Christianity acknowledged by the Chinese communist state, but a small body of the Orthodox continues nonetheless. There are Orthodox parishes in Beijing and north-eastern China that still meet despite official disapproval, as well as parishes operating in Shanghai, Guangdong province, Hong Kong, and Taiwan. The Russian Orthodox church of SS Peter and Paul resumed services in Hong Kong, and the ecumenical patriarchate has also sent a bishop there recently. The Orthodox mission church in Taiwan is also operating freely. The Chinese Orthodox have had an immensely difficult time under a heavy yoke that still has not lifted from them.

The various Orthodox diaspora communities

The diaspora consists of the Orthodox faithful of all the above patriarchal, autocephalous, or autonomous Orthodox churches (known practically speaking as 'the jurisdictions'[106]) who have moved elsewhere in the world and are, in their new countries,[107] looked after by bishops appointed by the home synods of their originating churches. All Greeks living in the diaspora (a large number indeed) now fall under the jurisdictional care of the patriarchate of Constantinople, which has exarchates and missions in most Western countries, given that the modern Greeks (like their ancient forebears) travelled far and wide. The Russian Orthodox also had a large diaspora population (especially after the political disruptions of the early twentieth century), but its diaspora situation was fragmented, because of its political troubles, into four major divisions which will be discussed shortly. The other larger churches that had a considerable number of faithful living abroad either set up pastoral missions for them or knew that they could be pastorally cared for by the existing Greek and Russian church provisions. In recent times, for example, there has been much mobility among younger Romanians (following the political relaxation of the country and its entrance into the European Union), and, naturally, an extension of the pastoral provision for Romanian Orthodox in Europe and America has followed. It has been, typically, organized by the patriarchal synod of Romania, with specific reference to the pastoral needs of the Romanians in the diaspora, with an archbishop in western and central Europe respectively, and also in America. All of them are members of patriarchal synod. The political problems of Romania in the twentieth century caused the diaspora churches across America to experience some of the fragmentation known among the Russians: with parts of the diaspora wishing to remain in communion with the home synod and other parts wishing to break the link on the grounds that the communist secular powers had infiltrated the mother churches to an unacceptable extent. What was true about the Russians and Romanians was true also of the other churches whose hierarchies came under the Soviet oppression, but who had extensive communities in America and elsewhere.

Diaspora church in this sense means an outlying 'mission' of the original church. Problems arise as to how long a church mission can be established in a land without becoming indigenized. It is invidious, to the Orthodox, to establish churches where the church has historically already been established under the protection of an ancient patriarchate (the West falling under the aegis of the Roman patriarchate). The over-laying of a separate ecclesial structure (indigenous dioceses and synods, for example), is regarded by the Orthodox as proselytism, not true missionary activity, and is taken as a sign of a profoundly defective ecclesiology when it is forced upon the Orthodox in their own countries by so-called Western Christian 'missionaries'. This situation holds, even after the long-established secession of the Roman patriarchate from the pentarchy. Diaspora churches, therefore, which are in the traditional territories of the Roman patriarchate are in a different situation from those in the 'New World' (Asia, the Americas) a situation which was envisaged canonically by the Fathers of Chalcedon in 451, who laid responsibility for authentically 'new' missions with the patriarchate of Constantinople.[108] Indigenous Orthodox hierarchies will not, then, be declared in the traditional regions of the Western Church but can and ought to be declared in the 'new lands' that are part of neither Western nor Eastern Christianity. One example is the large and energetic Syrian diaspora in America, part of the patriarchate of Antioch. Over the course of time this has grown more and more acclimatized in the American cultural scene. It has attracted many converts, even among its clergy, who have no ancestral connection with Syria. The expanding grant of 'autonomous' status (without a formal declaration of autonomy being made) often marks this level of acclimatization of such a community which was once truly a mission. As a partially autonomous church, however, it retains its organizational links with its founding community, even though its day-to-day governance may be wholly in the hands of the local hierarchs.

Apart from these continuing 'mission' churches of the national Orthodox bodies, for example the Serbian or Romanian Orthodox churches with their parishes in England, or America, which all look back to the authority and jurisdiction of the patriarch and his synod (but through the administration of a small resident hierarchy set up for the pastoral oversight of that particular diaspora in western Europe) the concept of Orthodox diaspora churches comes most into view in the cases of the Greek and the Russian Orthodox, who are the most numerous.

The Greek churches of the diaspora are the simplest to account for. As mentioned earlier, all of them are under the immediate jurisdiction of the patriarchate of Constantinople. The largest of them are the archdiocese of North and South America, the Greek Orthodox in Australia, and the archdiocese of Thyatira and Great Britain. They each have a large measure of autonomous government, but are, canonically speaking, simply extensions of the Constantinopolitan Church in foreign parts.

The other largest single group comprising the 'diaspora' is the Russian Orthodox outside of Russia. This diverse and extended community of Orthodox faithful has been to a large degree 'problematized', ecclesiastically speaking, mainly because of the communist revolution of the early decades of the twentieth century, and the immense hold that these hostile masters placed over the Russian Church within its borders over the course of an entire lifetime. Resulting from this time of persecution, and the considerable refugee problem resulting from it, the Russian Orthodox community abroad fragmented into four divisions that continue to cause considerable disturbance among the affairs of the Russian Orthodox world-wide.

Of the four major groups the first is composed of those dioceses outside Russia that have remained loyal to the allegiance of the Moscow patriarch. There are a small number of such parishes, in America, western Europe, Britain (the archdiocese of Sourozh[109]), and elsewhere. They were never attached to the Karlovtzy synod and in places (such as America and Britain) the disunion between these two groups was always a public sign of the wider troubles of the Russian Church under communism.

The second is the group of churches organized after the Karlovtzy synod (1921). Tikhon, the last patriarch of Russia before the communist yoke was imposed with a vengeance, disseminated an encyclical in 1920 that laid down emergency plans if communication between the Russians abroad and the patriarchate at home should become difficult or impossible. He was acting out of the foresight that a long darkness was about to descend. Just how long that would last perhaps escaped even his saintly perception. In 1921 the bishops of the Russian Orthodox Church outside the borders of Russia, who were free to act, met at the invitation of the Church of Serbia, to discuss how to organize themselves in those difficult times. It was decided that the final authority over this 'Russian Church Outside Russia' (ROCOR) would be vested in the holy synod of the free bishops, who should meet every year at Karlovtz (Sremsky Karlovtzy)[110] to discuss the condition of the churches under their control and their relation with the church of the motherland, which they now knew to be more and more under the thumb of autocratic political controllers, who were inimically hostile to the church and the Christian religion. Archbishop Antony Khrapovitsky, the former metropolitan of Kiev who had been exiled by the Bolsheviks, was elected as the synodical president. They had the allegiance and good will of many of the Russian exiles abroad, but by no means all of them, and not all were willing to recognize their authority when they constituted themselves, more and more, as an 'alternative' to the Russian hierarchy in Russia. In 1921 a statement they issued declaring themselves for the restoration of the monarchy, and pledging the support of the church for the return of the Romanovs (as a matter not only of political right, but ecclesiastical polity), made their identification as 'reactionaries' easy for Bolshevik propaganda at home, and caused much unease among the wider Russian Church, which did not universally have rosy memories of life under the tsars.

Tikhon, who retained a high standing in the eyes of all the Russian bishops overseas, was meanwhile arrested and imprisoned (1922–3) by the communist authorities. Most have presumed that they exerted extreme psychological pressure on him in this time of incarceration. In the following year, he issued (or was ordered to issue) a statement expressing dissatisfaction with the way the Karlovtzy synod had arranged matters, even though it had gained the assent of most of the hierarchs outside Russia. Instead he appointed one of the leading Russian hierarchs, Metropolitan Evlogy (Georgievski) of Paris, to work out a new plan for the governance of the ROCOR. This too was adopted by the synod outside Russia, but received no official endorsement from Tikhon. Tikhon established Evlogy as his personal representative for western Europe, and Bishop Platon (Rojdestvensky) for North America. At first the ROCOR synod was very anxious to keep Evlogy and Platon closely bound to its decisions, but the tension was soon to prove too much. After Tikhon's death in 1925 the succession to the newly re-established patriarchate[111] was somewhat irregular. While alive, Tikhon had nominated three potential successors, only one of whom survived by 1925, namely Sergius, a prelate whose career had already manifested a certain willingness to 'bend' to the new political masters.

The hierarchs of the ROCOR synod had little confidence in him, and would not recognize the legitimacy of his election or that of his immediate successors (under a synod that was no longer free). They have also claimed, following the logic of this rejection, that the decrees of the patriarchs under Soviet control lacked canonical force, being merely the political tools of communist oppression. In 1927 the ROCOR synod issued a condemnation of Evlogy and Platon. In the following year it flatly refused any ecclesiastical obedience to Patriarch Sergius following on his demand that all exiled Russian bishops should cease from political activities of any kind, and was in turn condemned by the patriarch and the Russian synod as a result. Evlogy was reconfirmed in his role as representative of the Russian Church in western Europe by Sergius, but in 1930 he was relieved of his duties in a blatantly political move. From the death of Tikhon onwards the ROCOR synod has been immensely suspicious of the Russian hierarchs, regarding them as tools of the state. In their turn they have been denounced and excommunicated, and pilloried as reactionary monarchists. In the decades following the fall of communism in Russia, however, there were encouraging signs of reconciliation between the hierarchs of the synod and the Moscow patriarchate. Patriarch Alexis made every effort to restore union, and the results of that 'dialogue of love' advanced to the point that, in the autumn of 2006, the hierarchs declared their decision for the restoration of full canonical union with the patriarchate, though retaining the autonomous administration of their parishes and clergy. The reunion finally took place in 2007, and now the ROCOR synod will receive the chrism from the hands of the patriarch of Moscow, and its bishops will be given seats as part of the Moscow holy synod. This welcome reconciliation marked the end of a long chapter of sufferings resulting from the severe persecution of the Russian Church throughout the twentieth century.

The third group of the Russian Orthodox diaspora was led by the aforementioned Metropolitan Evlogy of Paris. At first he had been a significant part of the hierarchy of the synod, but after 1926 he ceased to attend its meetings. Separating from them, he had intended to keep lines of communication open with Patriarch Sergius in Moscow, but in 1927 he was denounced by the ROCOR synod for vacillation, and in 1930 he was personally disowned by Sergius for having had the audacity to pray in public for 'persecuted Christians in Russia', when there was, as everyone knew, 'no such thing'. By 1931, therefore, Evlogy realized that his hope of keeping formal lines of connection open under such bizarre circumstances was not realistic, and he placed himself and his parishes under the jurisdictional care of the patriarch of Constantinople, despite the loud protests of both Moscow and the ROCOR synod.

Evlogy was never happy with this arrangement, however, and at the end of his life was personally reconciled with the Moscow patriarchate, but the parishes of his jurisdiction had no desire to follow his example, seeing the communist powers in Russia gaining more and more of a stranglehold over their church and homeland. The ecclesiastical arrangement of Constantinopolitan supervision of the Russian parishes abroad was suspended in 1965 (one presumes after protests by the Moscow hierarchs), but even at that stage the Russian parishes harboured deep suspicions of the intentions of the Moscow patriarchate, and refused to return to its allegiance, continuing their independent existence. In 1971 the patriarchate of Constantinople once more assumed a supervisory role. It was the French group of Russian Orthodox who had a massively important role in raising the consciousness of the Western churches in regard to

Orthodoxy after the Second World War. The White Russians in Paris were among the first to bring to the attention of most Europeans (especially French Catholics and British Anglicans) the beauties of the Orthodox liturgy, and the strengths of Orthodox theology. Many theologians were among the group of exiles,[112] and their works gained a large and sympathetic audience in Europe.

One of them, Sergius Bulgakov, was instrumental in founding the Society of SS Alban and Sergius which did so much to open up friendly relations between the Anglican Church and the Russian Orthodox in exile. Bulgakov was a brilliant teacher and writer, a protégé of Evlogy of Paris, who appointed him as a professor in the Theological Institute of St Sergius which he had founded in 1925. Bulgakov's trial and condemnation for heretical teaching[113] by the Karlovtzy Synod hierarchs was a cause célèbre at this period, and further complicated relations among the Russians in exile.

The fourth group of the Russian diaspora was formerly known as the Metropolia Church (The Russian Orthodox Greek Catholic Church in America) and has had a lively and dramatic story of growth, to the point that it is now known as the Orthodox Church in America (OCA). It is undoubtedly the largest body of the four we have been considering that originally grew out of the Russian patriarchate 'abroad', and the one with the most interesting history in recent years.[114] Its size and importance today are such that we ought to consider it apart from the ethnic diaspora origins it once had, and list it under its own classification as a church that has claimed autonomous status, even though the whole Orthodox world has not yet recognized that autonomous position.

The Orthodox Church in America

The Russian Orthodox in America, even before the Russian Revolution, were constituted into a formal diocese of their own as an integral part of the synod of the Moscow patriarchate. The pre-revolutionary metropolitan in America, Archbishop Platon, had his residence in New York. In 1924 he too severed relations with the Moscow patriarchate, but in the year after his death, that is, in 1935, his successor Metropolitan Theophilus joined with the Karlovtzy synod, and so things remained until a synod of the American Russian Orthodox, held in Cleveland in 1946, caused a major rupture among them. Five of the nine constituent bishops of the American Russian synod affirmed their loyalty to the ROCOR synod but were only followed by a minority of the parishes. The other four bishops voted to rejoin the Moscow patriarchate, and so they separated. When the pro-Moscow bishops made their offer, however, it was on condition that the patriarchate should acknowledge their extensive autonomy *de facto* (they meant their synodical form of self-government 'free from communist interference').

The patriarchate refused to grant this, and so the group continued in an autonomous fashion generally known as the Russian Metropolia, the Greek Catholic Russian Orthodox Church in America. To this body belonged a cadre of eminent theologians who were very important in the self-articulation of this group as having a consciousness of its own destiny beyond being simply a colonial extension of the Russian 'mission' in the United States. Among them were Fathers Florovsky, Schmemann, and Meyendorff, known as much for their theological writings as their work in establishing the Russian Orthodox seminary of St Vladimir's, in New York.[115] It was this ecclesial group which, in 1970, was granted autonomy by the official decree of the Moscow patriarchate. At that time the patriarchate went even further, and granted autocephalous status too. Few of the other Orthodox churches have acknowledged the legitimacy of this grant of autocephaly by the Moscow patriarchate. This was without prejudice to the regard in which the OCA was held, generally speaking, in terms of its doctrinal purity and Orthodox legitimacy. But 'autonomous' status was one thing that could be granted to the Metropolia by the Moscow patriarchate. To go beyond that with either a grant or a declaration of autocephaly was tantamount to the OCA laying claim to be the representative and indigenous 'Orthodox Church of America' of which, according to the ancient canons of the Orthodox Church, there can only be one such body in a nation, never more. This claim for autocephaly was thus regarded by many of the other Orthodox in America (certainly by the large number of Greeks) as transgressing on the rights and privileges of the American Orthodox who wished to retain allegiance to their ancestral traditions, and not be an autocephalous church.

More than one other body, it is true, joined in the 'synthesis' which made the OCA more than simply the Metropolia Church which it had been prior to 1970,[116] but the extent of the 'coming together' entirely left out the vast Greek archdiocese which remained under the jurisdiction of Constantinople, and that alone meant that the passage to autocephalous status (at least as recognized by the wider Orthodox world) will hardly be a *de facto* condition without the Phanar's future agreement. In 1970 there was very little interest among the Greek Orthodox in America to separate from Constantinople, and join with the OCA project, and there is no indication this situation has altered since.

The considerable size of the OCA, however, with over a million faithful, and its vigour in pushing for the establishment of an indigenous American church, have raised the pressing and controversial matter of how long an Orthodox church can pretend that it is a diaspora, or a mission. At what stage does a church cease to be a collection of immigrants and move towards an indigenous establishment? This is, of course, exactly what constituted the Russian Orthodox themselves in the sixteenth century; and many would argue that it is exactly what ought to be happening in America today. While some lament the very idea of severing historical and cultural ties, many others of the Orthodox, in one of the largest, and arguably the most powerful, countries on earth are finding it a natural thing to progress towards the establishment of an American Orthodoxy.

While it is normal that many groups would prefer not to be wholly Americanized, but retain cultural and religious ties with the ancestral homeland from which their churches were first established as overseas missions, the problem becomes exacerbated, generation by generation, as the younger Orthodox belonging to those ethnic groups cease to regard themselves in any residual sense as Russians, Serbians, Albanians, and so on, and think and speak of themselves only as Americans. The continuing use of the ancestral languages, Greek or Slavonic or Romanian, in the liturgy in America, thus stands as a comfort and an important symbol to some, while to others it has become a real stumbling block, which seems to contradict the historical principles of Orthodoxy, which encourage the establishment of worship in the natural language of the people. Many younger Orthodox see their church experience as hopelessly immured in 'past-looking' nostalgia, which has little interest for them, and makes their catechizing of their thoroughly Americanized children increasingly difficult within a living ecclesial environment.

What makes the situation even more confused (and confusing) however, is that America in the third millennium continues to act, as it did in the nineteenth and early twentieth centuries, as a massive magnet for immigrants from eastern Europe, the traditional Orthodox countries who first established missions there for the first wave of American Orthodox immigrants. Many OCA churches have had to revert to more and more use of Slavonic in the liturgy, after having spent many decades evolving towards an English-language liturgy, simply to accommodate the pastoral needs of newly arrived immigrants in their churches. The new arrivals, for the most part, have not the slightest interest, yet, in the establishment of an indigenous American Orthodox Church.

In addition to all of this, the growing number of Orthodox groups (every national church of the Orthodox world has some representation in America), all with their own separate episcopal jurisdictions in the United States, continues to contradict fundamental canonical principles of the establishment of the church in a 'new territory',[117] not least among which is that there must be only one Orthodox bishop in any city, to whom all the Orthodox faithful should give allegiance. This principle of 'one bishop, one church, one Eucharist,' is day by day being muddied by the overlapping confusion of 'jurisdictionalism' in America. Attempts to resolve this contradiction, by the establishment of a Standing Conference of Canonical Orthodox Bishops in America (SCOBA) which would represent all the Orthodox hierarchs in international communion meeting together to find a common mind on all issues important to American Orthodoxy, have so far produced little more than a small movement towards the 'appropriate' situation, towards which the OCA (perhaps prematurely, some of its hostile critics sometimes say) pointed the way with the notion of an indigenous American Orthodox church.

Notes

1 The term now more commonly designates the Roman Catholic 'Eastern rite' churches.

2 A mystery typified in the icon of the Anastasis, or 'Harrowing of Hell'.

3 In the sense that the world was made for beatific union with its God.

4 Acts 2.2–4.

5 Matt. 28.19.

6 Christians have historically read the Old Testament through the lens of the New, up until the rise of the historical-critical method in the schools of the West.

7 See the account of the healing of the blind man in John 9. Many modern scholars read the regular references in this story to community tension with the Pharisees

(John 9.22) as revealing the concern of the evangelist in his own day with the problem of expulsion of Christians from the synagogues.

8 Barrett 2001.

9 See Ignatius of Antioch: *To the Magnesians* 6.1; *To the Smyrnaeans* 8.1–2; *To the Ephesians* 20.2.

10 For a more detailed presentation see McGuckin 1989.

11 Cf. 1 Pet. 2.1–3; 2 John 1.7–11; Matt. 24.24; Rev. 2.2.

12 And, of course, some that were in use then have since been allowed to fall into abeyance.

13 Originally the name of a division of provincial Roman territory. Christianity followed

a pattern of assigning a single bishop to each of these areas. Today the word has come to mean primarily the 'ecclesiastical' division of a single bishop's territory.

14 The term cathedral comes from the Greek *kathedra*, or 'seat' signifying the church where the bishop's throne of doctrine was situated. In antiquity the famous orators sat on 'thrones of doctrine' and the bishop's signified his role as apostolic successor and source of Orthodox teaching for the diocese.

15 The exchange was known as the Quartodecimans Controversy. Further: see McGuckin 2004a.

16 1 Tim. 3.1–7.

17 The battle of the Milvian Bridge, 28 Oct. 312. On his way to this critical fight for control of the Roman empire, the church writers Lactantius and Eusebios tell us that he either saw a vision in the sky or had a revelatory dream, instructing him to adopt the chi-rho (a cipher for the name of Christ) as his army's battle standard.

18 Now continued in the ritual of the consecration of a Christian king or queen.

19 Further, see McGuckin 2003.

20 The ancient church was eventually to recognize the super-city status of five great sees: Rome, Constantinople, Alexandria, Antioch, and Jerusalem (the last as a nominal symbol). Their bishops were afforded the title 'patriarch' or 'pope'. The highest level of international consensus of the faith was lodged in the communion of the five popes. When the Pope of Rome separated from the communion of the other four Eastern popes, Orthodoxy regarded the ancient unity of the Eastern and Western churches as having been broken: a disunity which still continues. The four popes are still an integral part of the Orthodox system of governance. The Western Church, of course, also still looks to its pope, the only one the Latin world had in antiquity or in the present. In more recent times the number of Eastern 'patriarchs' has been added to, recognizing the importance of the growth of new patriarchal sees as countries have risen in status since ancient times.

21 1 Cor. 2.16.

22 Now collected in the volumes known as the Paterika. The collection gathered in the eighteenth century, known as the Philokalia, is one of the Paterika sources best known in the West.

23 For its creed and decrees (and those of the other ecumenical councils) see Percival 1900, or Tanner 1990; for more on their history and theology see Tanner 2001 and Davis 1987.

24 The word derived from a bishop's seat, or throne of teaching (*kathedra*), that designates a diocese.

25 For more detail see McGuckin 1994b.

26 Since ancient times there have been many attempts at reconciliation. At the end of the last, and during the present, century, there have been renewed efforts, based upon a newly advanced claim presented by scholars from both churches that the Coptic Christology (founded upon the writings of St Cyril of Alexandria and those of Severus of Antioch) can actually be reconciled with the meaning of the statement of faith issued by the Chalcedonian Fathers. The results of this theological dialogue need to be much more disseminated through the Orthodox world before they can be objectively considered, and assessed, by the faithful at large.

27 His treatise on the *Mystagogy of the Spirit* is an important text articulating the Orthodox sense that the *Filioque* doctrine (the teaching that the Spirit proceeds from the Father and the Son as from two distinct sources) is a radical subversion of the patristic doctrine of Trinity.

28 Dvornik 1948.

29 Cited in Runciman 1955: 139.

30 Innumerable relics of the saints, and icons, and other treasures were taken back to Latin churches in the West in the manner of 'spoils of war', a fact which sent shock waves of scandal all over the Eastern Christian world.

31 Cited in Ware 1987: 71.

32 Words he would come to regret when he fell into the hands of Mehmet the Conqueror, who treated his family unspeakably.

33 See Obolensky 1971.

34 Constantine adopted the new name on his tonsuring as a monk.

35 Barrett 2001.

36 Namely the anti-Chalcedonian churches in Syria and Egypt. as discussed in de la Taille 1926: 281.

37 In older English books they used to be called collectively the 'Oriental Orthodox' churches.

38 'The one concrete embodiment of God the Word in flesh.' See Newman 1874; Romanides 1964–5.

39 The term *Mia physis* means the one concrete reality of the Christ, God-Man, whereas 'Monophysite' is a term applied to them from without as a logical extrapolation of their refusal to assent to the conciliar formula of 'two natures in one person'. The deeper and more accurate understanding of St Cyril, and the conciliar agenda is a critical need for Eastern Christians today. Cf. McGuckin 1994a.

40 Which reflects the fact that they tend to base their Christological position on St Cyril of Alexandria's early theology.

41 Once called Jacobite (from a famous early bishop, Jacob Baradeus), but as an 'outsider' descriptor.

42 Only one legitimate ruling bishop in each city according to the ancient principles of church order. Other bishops arose in the course of history on the claim that the incumbent bishop was not teaching Orthodox faith. But Orthodox ecclesiology is still based on this principle: one faith one bishop. If there are two or more ruling bishops in a given city, only one can be authentic, only one can be Orthodox.

43 Especially canon 34 of the apostolic canons; canon 6 of Nicaea I (325); canon 2 of Constantinople I (381); canon 28 of Chalcedon (451); canon 36 of the synod in Trullo.

44 Rom. 12.5; Gal. 3.28.

45 Tribalism, or nationalism, in the sense that it erects human prejudicial categories over and against the ancient demand of catholicity, and the mystery whereby Christ dissolves human barriers by unanimity of mind and heart in the allegiance to his common lordship. There were some sceptical voices heard at the time, in the Orthodox communion as well as outside it, that suggested the patriarchate was being severe to nationalistic phyletism among the Slavs, and had been rather blind to it among the Hellenes.

46 That is, an autocephalous church, as distinct from an exarchate or a mission designed to serve the needs of Eastern Christians who happen to live in western Europe.

47 Rome, of course, which was the oldest see, is no longer held to be in communion.

48 Excepting the ancient Church of Nubia (modern Sudan) which had, from antiquity, ties with Byzantium but which was submerged under Islam, and lost to the Christian world in the fifteenth century; and (of course) the ancient and most venerable Church of Ethiopia, which is now one of the anti-Chalcedonian Eastern churches.

49 The patriarch of an autocephalous church will have a supervisory power (not divorced from the national synod, but in its context) of serving as a court of appeal out of the dioceses, and the decisions of local bishops. The same locus of appeal continues often from the churches that were once 'founded' by those patriarchates originally. The patriarchate of Constantinople was given, by the Council of Chalcedon in 451, a right to serve as the final court of appeal for the whole Eastern Orthodox world.

50 It may be easiest to adopt the distinction of an 'inviolable jurisdictional power', applying to a ruling bishop in his own diocese, and a 'supervisory power', limited by the canons and interpreted by the synods, applying to metropolitans and patriarchs.

51 The patriarch of Alexandria, actually is designated as the 'Pope of Africa', but what is meant here is that there is no papal equivalent of a jurisdictionally monarchical super-episcopacy in Orthodoxy.

52 Autocephaly signifies the right of a local church to be completely self-governing, and elect its own hierarchs without the

intervention of any other ecclesiastical supervision other than its own local synod. Autonomous status can represent a degree of self-regulation lower than autocephaly, where the supervisory oversight of an older patriarchate can still be combined with more or less complete local self governance in day-to-day affairs. The word 'autocephaly' means 'head of its own affairs': with its own ruling synod. Such synods will be led by a metropolitan archbishop or a patriarch.

53 Given a certain precedence of honour according to the date of the establishment of their ecclesiastical independence. But some of them such as Russia, Romania, and Greece, are much more significant than the others in terms of their magnitude.

54 The church is so tiny (one monastery), that some regard it as autonomous rather than autocephalous. It is technically the latter since its archbishop has no supervisory senior other than his own synod.

55 Bulgarian, Georgian, or Serbian Orthodox living in foreign parts, for example would often not require a separate church, since the Russian liturgy was celebrated in the same church Slavonic they knew at home, and they often joined with the existing Russian diaspora churches. They might only have their 'own' church building in a particularly large city where a sizeable local expatriate population justified it.

56 Now known, politically, as Istanbul in Turkey. Formerly it was the centre of the eastern Roman empire and the headquarters of the emperor. The Great Imperial Church (once the church of the patriarchate too) was Hagia Sophia. After the conquest of the city by Islamic forces in 1453, the emperor was killed, and his dynastic rule was ended, and the patriarchate took over (under the sultans) political and religious supervision of all the Christians of the eastern Islamic dominion. After many vicissitudes and sufferings, the patriarchate came in 1603 to be established in its present location in the modest church of St George at the Phanar in Istanbul.

57 'Following in all things the decisions of the holy Fathers, and acknowledging the canon, which has been just read, of the One Hundred and Fifty Bishops beloved-of-God (who assembled in the imperial city of Constantinople, which is New Rome, in the time of the Emperor Theodosius of happy memory), we also do enact and decree the same things concerning the privileges of the most holy Church of Constantinople, which is New Rome. For the Fathers rightly granted privileges to the throne of old Rome, because it was the royal city. And the One Hundred and Fifty most religious Bishops, actuated by the same consideration, gave equal privileges to the most holy throne of New Rome, justly judging that the city which is honoured with the Sovereignty and the Senate, and enjoys equal privileges with the old imperial Rome, should in ecclesiastical matters also be magnified as she is, and rank next after her; so that, in the Pontic, the Asian, and the Thracian dioceses, the metropolitans only and such bishops also of the dioceses aforesaid as are among the barbarians, should be ordained by the aforesaid most holy throne of the most holy Church of Constantinople; every metropolitan of the aforesaid dioceses, together with the bishops of his province, ordaining his own provincial bishops, as has been declared by the divine canons; but that, as has been above said, the metropolitans of the aforesaid Dioceses should be ordained by the archbishop of Constantinople, after the proper elections have been held according to custom and have been reported to him.' Canon 28, Council of Chalcedon (451).

58 Making exceptions for ancient custom (where once glorious Christian capitals have been overthrown by non-Christian power, for example) it is expected that the senior hierarch of a church should be seated in a leading city, not a backwater.

59 It argued (although it too had risen in importance in Christian affairs because of its own geo political position) that an apostolic foundation imparted a superiority of juridical charism. This was the germinal

60 foundation of the claim for Petrine primacy that would develop in late antiquity into the theology (what the Orthodox would call the *theologoumenon*) of the Papacy.

60 Inappropriate nationalism.

61 Kidd 1927: 305.

62 The statistics of the *World Christian Encyclopedia* (Barrett 2001) clearly show that the nineteenth to twentieth centuries have been the era of the greatest number of martyrdoms in Christian history.

63 John 17.22–3.

64 The first among equals. Outlining his rank in terms of the position of other Orthodox bishops.

65 Then numbering 1.5 million souls, many of whom were murdered.

66 Rhodes, Leros, Kos, and Karpathos.

67 As the recent catalogue of Byzantine and post-Byzantine religious art from the Holy Mountain can demonstrate: Karakatsanis 1997.

68 An idea can be gained from the illustrated book by P. Sherrard (1985): *Athos: The Holy Mountain.*

69 See McGuckin 2004b, 2005a.

70 Further, see McGuckin 1994b.

71 Those who followed the faith of the king, that is the emperor of the Byzantines, and in other words accepted the Council of Chalcedon (known as dyophysites because they professed the two natures, divine and human, of the Incarnate Lord).

72 A corruption of the Greek word for Egyptian. Known also to their enemies as Monophysites because they would not accept the formulation of 'two natures [in Christ] after the Incarnate Union'.

73 In the fifth century Christian ascendancy the archbishops had taken over parts of the Serapeum in Alexandria as their residence. The obelisk now in Central Park, New York, was once found gracing the steps to their palace.

74 The story of the foundation of the church, by indigenous initiators, who were then supported by the Alexandrian patriarch, is told briefly in Ware 1987: 196–8.

75 Between 1600 and 1720 six patriarchs of Antioch made professions of allegiance to the pope.

76 It is a commonly used word (though one that is regarded as pejorative by the communities themselves) to describe those churches, formerly Orthodox, who acceded to the jurisdiction of Rome. Thereby they technically became Roman Catholics of the Eastern or Oriental rite.

77 The Orthodox patriarch used to reside at Damascus, the Latin at Rome, the anti-Chalcedonian at Mardin, and in addition there were the four Uniate communities of the Greek Melkites, the Armenians, the Maronites, and the Syrians. The residences are now more mobile.

78 The ancient Antioch is now Antakiya, a small, provincial and massively Islamic town.

79 The Roman imperial province of the *Oriens.*

80 Founded by Origen of Alexandria and Bishops Theoctistus of Caesarea and Alexander of Jerusalem. It had many luminaries holding its headship after that point including the great church historian Bishop Eusebios of Caesarea.

81 In the West it is more commonly called by its medieval name: the church of the Holy Sepulchre.

82 The later Crusades were in part stimulated by the act of the mad Caliph Hakim, who destroyed the tomb of Jesus in the eleventh century. The Al Aksa mosque built on the platform in Jerusalem where the Temple once stood (actually on the site of the southern portico of Herod's Temple complex) incorporates the Crusader church of the Templars.

83 For a good modern narrative see the sobering account in Dalrymple 1998.

84 Patriarch John of Antioch had also heavily censured their collective behaviour at the synod, and was himself regarded as canonically irregular in his behaviour by refusing to join in the conciliar sessions.

85 Once they were Christians, as were the surrounding lands, part of the Byzantine empire, but for centuries past they have been Muslim.

86 The 'Mountain of Moses' is sacred to all three religions: Judaism, Christianity, and Islam.

86

87 See Baddeley and Brunner 1996.

88 Old Rome (fallen, that is in its separation from the Orthodox fold); and New Rome (Byzantium), fallen in subjugation to the Ottomans. The Russian monk and political theorist Philotheos of Pskov wrote, in 1510, a letter to Tsar Basil III which included the following lines: 'I will add a few words on the present Orthodox empire of our ruler. He is on this earth the single Tsar of the Christians, the leader of the Apostolic Church which stands no longer in Rome or Constantinople, but in the blessed city of Moscow. She alone now shines in the whole world brighter than the sun. . . . All Christian Empires are fallen and in there place stands only the empire of our ruler, in accordance with the prophetical books. Two Romes have fallen, but the third stands, and a fourth there shall not be' (cited in Baynes and Moss 1961: 385).

89 In 1472 Ivan III (Ivan the Great) married Princess Sophia, niece of the last Paleologan emperor of Constantinople. From this time the grand dukes adopted the title of 'Junior Caesar' (tsar is a corruption of Caesar) and used the heraldic device of the Paleologans, the double-headed eagle (the dominions of Rome in East and West). More and more they came to see themselves as the continuing might and legitimacy of the Roman emperors, with rights over church and state based on those of the Christian emperors.

90 Those (like Princes Boris and Gleb) who have elected a path of suffering rather than the assertion of their rights, in honour of the suffering Lord of Humility.

91 Bouteneff 2004: p. vi.

92 Mark 10.45.

93 See Meyendorff 1981; Obolensky 1971.

94 The Holy Wisdom: in emulation of Hagia Sophia in Constantinople, though architecturally it was more in the form of the Byzantine church of Holy Apostles.

95 What has been called the 'Northern Thebaid' after the first exemplar of monasticism in the arid heat of the Egyptian desert.

96 Many of the old guard remained in power after the fall of Russian Soviet communism and the Ukrainian declaration of independence, relabelling themselves superficially.

97 Moldavia today is normally used as a regional designation for the parts of the ancient Moldovian principality still remaining in the territory of Romania, and the new republic now detached from the Soviet Union is designated as Moldova.

98 The word connotes 'tribalism' and opposed the notion of ethnic groups claiming to be separate churches on the basis of ethnicity. Its strong point is that the Church of Christ cannot be subdivided along 'ethnic' lines. The communion of the Gospel has (or ought to have) transcended this way of humanly thinking about society, as something merely tribal, divisive, and self-protective. But the patriarch's denunciation, at the time, overlooked the two significant perspectives: (a) that many of the Slavic churches under the jurisdiction of the Phanar as it conducted itself under the yoke of the Ottomans, seemed to be suffering from Greek phyletism, and (b) that the ancient canonical principle of independent secular administration, meaning independent ecclesial administration (which had given birth to the ancient patriarchates themselves), had not evaporated in the modern age, leaving only the old privileges unassailable, but on the contrary was rightfully being applied to new political realities in a world where the Byzantine emperor was long dead.

99 St Sava managed to maintain the warmest relations with both the senior patriarchs.

100 Henry 1930; Joanta 1992.

101 Chief among them are Neamts, the central church of Moldavia, rebuilt by Stephen the Great in 1497 (the printing press of Paisy Velichovsky was based here: Humor, founded in 1535); Putna monastery, built by Stephen the Great in 1466, who is himself buried here; Voronets (1486), built to replace the wooden cell where Daniel the Hesychast (Stephen's confessor) had spent his last

years, and to house his tomb – it received its magnificent frescoes in 1547 under Prince Petru Rares – the monastery and the numerous Hesychast cells in the surrounding hills were destroyed by the Austrian armies in 1786; Sucevitsa (1583–6); and Moldovitsa monastery (1546), rebuilt under Prince Petru Rares.

102 See Stebbing 2003.

103 A title originally used by the primate of the Armenian Church to signify the leader of an autonomous church – one which was largely in charge of its own affairs, but which recognized the right of an older patriarchate to appoint its senior hierarch.

104 Bolshakov (1940) puts it in these terms: 'They were repelled for ever by the methods used to turn them into Roman Catholics' (cited in Attwater 1962: 126 n. 8).

105 On the charge of protecting the assassins of the infamous Gestapo chief Heydrich.

106 There are, of course, no 'denominations' in Orthodoxy, which regards such a thing as a heresy, since the Church is one, and cannot be other than one.

107 Generally speaking that means the non-Orthodox lands of the West, but even in Orthodox countries the various national churches tend to have a pastoral oversight of their own faithful, at least in terms of offering a church where the liturgy can be celebrated in their language (although this is never set up as a independent church in another Orthodox church's territory). So, for example, in Athens there is a Russian-language church staffed by Russian priests, a fraternal arrangement between the hierarchs of both countries.

108 It has never been as simple as this in 'real life' however, as the establishment of Orthodox mission churches has always followed the natural process of the establishment of trade with new countries, that immediately required the setting up of churches to care for the pastoral need of the traders from the different national churches. This particularly had reference to the Russians, who had an expanding empire of great proportions while the rest of the Orthodox world was politically in bondage.

109 Formerly led by the widely respected metropolitan, Antony Bloom. Throughout his life he retained full relations with the Moscow patriarchate. After his death parts of the Sourozh diocese preferred to place themselves under the jurisdiction of the Russian archdiocese of western Europe under the Omophorion of the patriarch of Constantinople.

110 Sremsky Karlovtzy in Yugoslavia. Its first meeting was held at the invitation of the patriarch of Serbia. After the Second World War, and the fall of Yugoslavia to communist control, it moved its meeting headquarters to Munich, and after 1949 to buildings on the Upper East Side of New York City.

111 The Muscovite patriarchate had been abolished by Peter the Great several generations before, who replaced it with synodical government, and it had only just been reconstituted when Tikhon was elected as the first incumbent of the restoration. After Tikhon's death, Stalin delayed the reassignation of patriarchal status for many years until he had observed how Sergius would behave.

112 Bulgakov, Florovsky, Lossky, Zernov, Evdokimov among them.

113 Especially his Sophia speculations, which have never been received by Orthodoxy at large. His condemnation, however, was more than an act designed to ensure purity of doctrine, and was politically motivated to weaken Evlogy's prestige. One of the results was to identify (rightly or wrongly) ROCOR as the group that tolerated no new thought, and wished to recreate Russia in the Romanov mould out in the West, while the Evlogy group was producing fascinating writings and engaging in the complicated ecclesiastical world they now discovered in the West. That tension is still in evidence today, a peculiarly enduring pathology of the communist legacy in relation to the validity of Orthodoxy's

relationship to its non-Orthodox intellectual environment.

114 See Bogolepov 2001.

115 This, growing from small seeds in the classrooms of Union Theological Seminary, New York, moved to a fine campus in Crestwood, near New York, and today is one of the leading Orthodox seminaries of the world, with one of the most important of all English-language Orthodox presses.

116 The OCA currently includes within its organizational unity parishes of Romanian, Albanian, and Bulgarian tradition.

117 How long one can go on regarding America as a 'new world' is also a matter of some speculation.

Chapter 2

The Orthodox Sense of Tradition

THE HOLY TRADITION

One of the most commonly used phrases in the theological vocabulary of the Orthodox is 'The Holy Tradition'. In former times this notion had some resonance with Western Catholics,[1] but perhaps a little less in the present era of extensive theological and cultural changes affecting Roman Catholicism. For Protestants, the term usually brought to mind many of the reasons they had originally challenged Latin Catholicism in the Reformation era, charging it at several instances with corrupting the biblical tradition of Christianity in favour of its own 'customs and traditions'. For most of the non-Orthodox, therefore, the concept of the Holy Tradition probably suggests, at best, a somewhat stultified churchly mentality that looks always to the past and is not able to address the present era, and, at worst, a readiness to hang on to the 'customs of men'[2] more passionately than to the word of the Lord.

The Orthodox do not understand the concept of tradition in that way. For the Eastern Christian world tradition is the gateway to the theology of revelation. It may be the case that some of the less educated Orthodox equate the tradition with every-thing that happens in church as they currently experience it (for better or worse, good practice or bad) and so may be unable to discern the difference between the incidental customs of their national churches and the universal tradition of the apostolic faith, which is a matter transcending any difference of custom and forming the essence of what Orthodoxy is universally. But this does not change the fact that Orthodox faith teaches that the Holy Tradition is something far different from 'the customs of men' about which Jesus spoke so disparagingly. Orthodoxy understands the Holy Tradition to be the essence of the life-saving Gospel of Christ brought to the world through the church by the power of the Holy Spirit of God. The tradition is, theologically speaking, how the Spirit is experienced within the Church of Christ as the charism of Truth.[3]

Tradition in this sense is not something that is past-looking only (obsessed with traditions and precedents). It bases its claims to authenticity on the fact that it speaks the words of Christ in the here and now, faithful to his own Spirit; but as much as it looks to the past and stands in unbroken continuity with it, thus 'passing on' the Gospel of life (which is the root meaning of the word 'tradition'), it also looks to the

90

future. The tradition is the Spirit's energy of proclaiming the Gospel and energizing the church's worship and knowledge of God in the present generation, and for future generations to come. The Orthodox, therefore, understand the Holy Tradition to be venerable and hallowed from times past, but to be essentially charismatic, and alive, and full of the power and freshness of the Spirit of God, concerned with bringing new generations to Christ until the end of time: one of the basic functions of his earthly church.

Orthodox tradition is understood be to built up from many parts, but all together making a single harmonious whole. No part of the tradition is in conflict with any other part, or could be, but the harmony of all the legitimately different parts cohering together is a sign and proof of the health and authenticity of the tradition. St Irenaeus, in his treatise *Against the Heresies*, described this approach to tradition as a sense of 'knowing before one looks'. For him it was comparable to how a person took in all the pieces of a mosaic and recognized instinctively how together they harmoniously made up a perfect portrait of a king. Devoid of the overall sense of what that portrait was meant to be, and faced with only the random blocks of material (such as the mosaic tesserae), any kind of picture would be conceivably possible but it would not be the authentic portrait. For Irenaeus, only the apostolic churches had the 'charisma of truth'.[4] This was manifested above all in the manner in which they interpreted the Scriptures, soberly, and with catholic consensus.

It was in this context that he developed his famous image of the 'interpretative key' (*hypothesis*) which the church has and others outside do not possess. It was to grow into the fuller patristic concept of the *Mens Ecclesiae*, the 'Mind of the Church', what St Athanasios was to call the church's 'instinctive knowing' (*dianoia*) and its sense of the overall 'intentionality' (*skopos*) of Scripture and tradition, namely the comprehensive overview given to the Spirit-illumined faithful, which was radically partialized and distorted by heretical dissidents. For Irenaeus, the heretics were those who did not possess the 'key' to the Scriptures. They reassembled the pieces of the mosaic of the King and made it up again from the original parts, but now representing a dog, claiming that theirs was an authentic image because their mosaic squares were original.[5]

Irenaeus added further to the fundamental vocabulary of the theology of tradition when he developed the argument that the key to biblical interpretation was the 'canon of truth',[6] which in the Latin version of his works gave to the West, decisively so in the hands of Tertullian,[7] the principle of the *Regula Fidei*, or *Regula Veritatis*.[8] This 'Rule', Irenaeus says, is the strongest refutation of Gnostic variability, for it is maintained in all the churches and goes back to the apostles. Apostolic succession, then, is not primarily a matter of succession of individual bishops one after another, but the succession of apostolic teaching from the time of apostles to the present. His view is simple and robust: 'The apostolic tradition in the church, and the preaching of the truth have come down to us.'[9]

For Irenaeus the touchstone of a test-case of apostolic tradition lies in comparing Christian doctrine with the proto-credal Regula Fidei. He gives as the basic framework of this apostolic *kerygma*: belief in God as Father and Creator of heaven and earth; Jesus Christ his Son who came in the flesh to save humankind; the Virginal Conception, the Passion, death, and Resurrection of Jesus, the Holy Spirit who revealed this dispensation by means of the prophets.[10]

Orthodoxy does not just hold to the tradition, in this sense. It *is* the tradition. It does not simply find the tradition in its fundamental sources (such as the Scriptures, the councils, the canons, the Fathers, and the liturgy); it exemplifies and reveals the tradition in its ongoing charismatic life. It is synonymous with the tradition, because the tradition itself is the communion of grace. Orthodoxy's life, as a church, is no more or less than a life lived in the grace of the Spirit of God, and the illumination of the Spirit is essential to that Truth, conferring on the illumined servant of God the capacity for spiritual discernment, the knowledge of the difference between the ways of Christ, and the ways of the world. Orthodoxy has 'the mind of Christ', and the possession of that *phronema* is what inspires the constant passion of the faithful to cling to the sacred gift of Christ's communication of the Gospel to the church.

The tradition is at once a mystical grace (for the presence of the Spirit across time and space within the earthly church cannot be limited to visible and material phenomena, or organized and controlled as if it were bureaucratically 'biddable', for the Spirit blows where it chooses'[11]) and also a concrete, quantifiable, reality. This is because the essentially free and charismatic openness of the Spirit does not mean that the Christian tradition is formless or uncontainable. The restless Spirit of God, creative and constantly energizing all things, was the very one who brought order and form to the chaos of the dark waters, in the Genesis Creation account,[12] and that ordered form was, we are told, a matter of bringing light: *lux fiat*. So it is with the tradition. It is free and energized like light, but it also runs like the blood of the veins in the body of the church to bring life and oxygen to the Christian experience.

Yet it is also something that exists in a strict form, a shape of the Spirit's own making, echoing the concrete shape the Holy Word himself took in the Blessed Virgin. Tradition is like the shadow of the Lord's Incarnation; but it is the 'overshadowing' that itself gives light, a mark of the presence of God himself, active among his people.[13] The tradition always hovers between its charismatic and intangible quality and its concrete exemplification in distinct and easily found loci within the church's systems of governance and authoritative reference. The issue of sacred tradition is of such fundamental importance that it is hardly surprising that it has been the subject of much comment by modern Orthodox theologians.

Among those, the British priest Archimandrite Lazarus Moore was highly focused on the inner quality of holiness which is distinctive of the tradition, and he also speaks of the 'dynamic of salvation' which tradition connotes, using the vocabulary of Irenaeus in the process:

> By Holy Tradition the Orthodox Church means the divine revelation given by God to his people, through the mouths of his holy prophets and apostles. This divine revelation is the body of truth which God Himself has revealed to men, so that they may rightly and savingly believe in Him, love serve and glorify Him, and do his holy will.[14]

Father John Meyendorff strongly distinguished between the traditions which partially manifest the church's inner principle of the life of salvation, and the Holy Tradition properly understood, which is the acting out of this life. Meyendorff goes further than Moore in connecting tradition explicitly with the Christological principle of the salvation of historical creatures (the church as the Body of Christ, the manifestation of the eucharistic principle of the world's redemption). Speaking of the historical forms which the Byzantine ecclesiastical polity assumed, he says:

> Theirs were human historical achievements, accepted and 'received' by the church as manifestations of her unchangeable divino-human Being, but this being itself was present only in the eschatological reality of the Eucharist, and manifested in the experience of the saints.[15]

Metropolitan Philaret of Moscow had taught the same distinction when he differentiated the visible form of traditions from the inner principle of holiness which lay behind Holy Tradition, which accordingly:

> does not consist uniquely in visible and verbal transmission of teachings, rules, institutions and rites; it is at the same time an invisible and actual communication of grace and sanctification.[16]

Archpriest Georges Florovsky, who was influenced by Philaret in this regard, spoke of tradition as the process of the church's advancement into the Life of Christ. For him it is Christ in his risen presence as Lord of the church that is at the root of all that is important about the Holy Tradition, illuminating all that is alive and salvific about ecclesial traditions:

> Faith alone makes formulas convincing; faith alone makes formulas live. It seems paradoxical, yet it is the experience of all observers of spiritual things: no-one profits by the Gospels unless he be first in love with Christ. For Christ is not a text but a Living Person, and He abides in His body, the church.[17]

The Greek theologian Bishop Papadopoulos also points to this when he speaks of the sacred tradition as essentially that dynamic and salvific mystery of the divine 'enclosure' in Christ. This is, for him, the root reason that the indwelling of the Holy Spirit can be recognized as the heart of the church's life, and the very 'constitution'[18] of the tradition:

> Only in the general conscience of the church can the essence of the faith be dynamically reinterpreted for the situation in which we are called to live. This is the true life of the church, our life in the Holy Spirit. In this way we affirm the traditional belief that the church of Christ, in the totality of His members, reflects the holy life of the Triune God, which seeks in Christ to embrace the whole created order. The faith of our creed... sees in the witness of the Spirit, the very presence of God in our midst, which presence alone constitutes the true Tradition. Holy Tradition is a divine process; it is not ours but God's, reaching out from the *soma* to the fullness of the *pleroma*. Holy Tradition is not something static, to be safeguarded by dogmatic formulas; it is the dynamic movement of God in history, in which man shares as part of the perfect humanity of Christ.[19]

Vladimir Lossky was interested in the entrance into tradition as a mystical initiation, governed by the Orthodox person's immersion in the life of the sacraments:

> In fact, the revealed truth is not a dead letter but a living word: it can be attained only in the church, through initiation by the mysteries or sacraments into the 'mystery hidden for ages and generations and now made manifest to his saints'.[20]

The mysterious process of sacraments in the spiritual life of the church is an analogy to this wider and deeper notion of the tradition as cipher, or sacrament, of the very presence of the Spirit. For Lossky, the believer's entrance into this sacramental initiation (and here Lossky richly glosses St Basil's original meaning) is comparable to the comprehension of the true gnosis, and reveals to the illumined Christian the fundamental enthronement of the divine Spirit at the heart of the process of the saving tradition. Holy Tradition, therefore, is the *methexis*, or participation, of the church in the life of the Spirit of God:

> The unwritten traditions or mysteries of the church mentioned by S. Basil constitute, then, the boundary with Tradition properly so-called, and they give glimpses of some of its features. In effect there is participation in the revealed mystery through the fact of sacramental initiation. It is a new knowledge, a 'gnosis of God' that one receives as grace; and this grace is conferred in a 'tradition' which is, for St Basil, the confession of the Trinity at the time of baptism: a sacred formula which leads us into light.[21] Here the horizontal line of the 'traditions' received from the mouth of the Lord and transmitted by the apostles and their successors crosses with the vertical, with Tradition, the communication of the Holy Spirit, which opens to members of the Church an infinite perspective of mystery in each word of the revealed truth. Thus starting from traditions such as S. Basil presents to us it is necessary to go further and admit Tradition, which is distinguished from them.[22]

A closely parallel idea is at the heart of Florovsky's doctrine on the 'essential tradition'. Florovsky begins by drawing attention to the fundamental characteristic of true tradition as sharing in the dynamic and vital nature of God himself. It is the witness of the Spirit, the Spirit's continual advancement of the dynamic of salvation. In the end it is nothing other than the voice and presence of the divine Spirit within the world, and particularly within the Church of Christ:

> Tradition is not limited to church archaeology. Tradition is no outward testimony which can be accepted by an outsider. The church alone is the living witness of tradition; and only from inside, from within the church, can Tradition be felt and accepted as a certainty. Tradition is the witness of the Spirit; the Spirit's unceasing revelation and preaching of good tidings. For the living members of the church it is no outward historical authority, but the eternal, continual voice of God, not only the voice of the past, but the voice of eternity. Faith seeks its foundations not merely in the example and bequest of the past, but in the grace of the Holy Ghost, witnessing always, now and ever, world without end. As Khomyakov[23] admirably puts it: 'Neither individuals, nor a multitude of individuals within the church preserve tradition or write the Scriptures, but the Spirit of God which lives in the whole body of the church.'[24]

The identification of the essential mystery of tradition with the indwelling presence of the saving Spirit, does not, of course, contradict the Christological principle of the coherence of the church as the Body of Christ, for he is none other than the Spirit of the Risen Christ who informs the inner dynamic and vitality of his church. Florovsky, then, can equally well express the same sentiment in Christological form:

> To accept and understand Tradition we must live within the church, we must be conscious of the grace-giving presence of the Lord in it; we must feel the breath of the Holy Ghost in it. We may truly say that when we accept Tradition, we accept, through faith, our Lord, who abides in the midst of the faithful; for the church is his Body, which cannot be separated from him.[25]

The point of connection between the Christian believers, both individually and corporately, and the indwelling divine presence (what Lossky evoked with the image of points of vertical and horizontal intersection) is described by the majority of these thinkers in terms of the 'spiritual communion' that characterizes Holy Tradition as its inner life. It is a concept that has been extensively developed in Metropolitan John Zizioulas' recent study of the church that prioritizes the concept of *koinonia*.[26] Before him, however, Zernov had spoken eloquently of the tradition as coming to life in the mystical ecclesial communion:

> The Holy Tradition is identical with that knowledge of the truth which is granted to the redeemed portion of mankind. The Incarnate Lord has transformed and purified the human race. Christians have the mind of Christ. Tradition is the awareness of the unbroken bond of faith and love enjoyed by those who fully participate in the life of the One, Holy, Catholic, and Apostolic Church.[27]

Zernov went on to point up the essential cohesive principle within this model as provided by the living tradition of holiness that the Spirit inspires within the church to make it co-inhere, with a constant identity in Christ, across the long and varied ages of its historical journey:

> The Holy Spirit keeps watch and reveals the same truth to every age and race. There is therefore no better guarantee for Christians that they are following the right path than their preservation of loving fellowship with the saints, the holy men and women of the past generations who have lived in communion with the Holy Spirit.[28]

Zernov was influenced in his views by a modern master of the theology of the discernment of the Spirit, Father Sergei Bulgakov, who had earlier argued:

> Tradition is not a sort of archaeology, which by its shadows connects the present with the past, not a law, it is the fact that the life of the Church remains always identical with itself. Tradition receives a 'normative' value precisely because of this identity. And as the same spirit dwells in each man living the life of the Church, he is not limited to touching the surface of Tradition, but, in so far as he is filled with the spirit of the church, he enters into it. But the measure of that Spirit is also the measure of sanctity. This is why sanctity is an interior norm used to determine what constitutes church tradition. The light of sanctity thus illumines Tradition.[29]

It was a strong point of Father Lazarus Moore's brief essay that it brought out this synonymity of tradition and the inner life of holiness within the church (the holiness of her members as they enter into the mystery of the holiness of her God) as the master theme of almost every paragraph. For him the tradition of holiness, and the *askesis* which it constantly demands of the earthly members of the church, is the dynamic forward thrust of true tradition, a movement and vitality inimical to all inertia and conservative narrowness:

> To live in the stream of holy tradition in the Kingdom of God requires perpetual repentance, revival, and renewal by the Holy Spirit. The true traditionalist is not a person who lives in the past, but one who is open and alert to the voice and activity of the Spirit today. By living in the Spirit he is right up to date and alive to what God is doing now.[30]

And again:

> [Tradition] is not a sum of past experience, but a living experience of God's action today. It is not a dead dependence on the past but a living and total dependence on the Holy Spirit.[31]

Lossky, too, had argued how the relationship with the Holy Spirit was demanding of *askesis*, and restlessly progressive in the manner in which it demanded judgement (*krisis*) from the true believer, and that engagement with the concerns of the Kingdom of God that follows from this discernment. Lossky takes his point of origination from the historical lessons learned from the development of the 'canonical' principle:

> The fact that the canon of the writings of the New Testament was formed relatively late, with some hesitations, shows us that the Tradition is in no way automatic: it is the condition of the Church having an infallible consciousness, but it is not a mechanism which will infallibly make known the Truth outside and above the consciousness of individuals, outside all deliberation and all judgement. In fact, if Tradition is a faculty of judging in the Light of the Holy Spirit, it obliges those who wish to know the Truth in the Tradition to make incessant efforts: one does not remain in the Tradition by a certain historical inertia, by keeping as a 'tradition received from the fathers' all that which by force of habit flatters a certain devout sensibility. On the contrary, it is by substituting these sort of 'traditions' for the Tradition of the Holy Spirit living in the Church that one runs the most risk of finding oneself finally outside the Body of Christ. It must not be thought that the most conservative attitude alone is salutary, nor that the heretics are always 'innovators'.[32]

The true tradition, therefore, as it is close to the presence of its divine Lord, and life-giver, always bears this character of living and vitalizing energy. This, in a real sense, gives the present age of the church no inferior place to previous ages, even the times of the apostles and the Fathers. It cannot be otherwise if the church is fully identical with itself in every age, and is, essentially, the eschatological sign of salvation rather than a merely historical institution.

Florovsky develops on some of the problematics of the fact that tradition demands the past and present of the church be *homotimos*, equal in stature, while at the same time the church of the latter ages is committed to preserving the apostolic teachings as authoritative. He expresses it as follows:

> Not everything within the church dates from Apostolic times. This does not mean that something has been revealed which was 'unknown' to the Apostles; nor does it mean that what is of a later date is less important and convincing. Everything was given and revealed fully from the beginning. On the day of Pentecost Revelation was completed, and will admit of no further completion till the Day of Judgement and its last fulfilment. Revelation has not been widened, and even knowledge has not increased. The church knows Christ now no more than it knew Him at the time of the Apostles. *But it testifies to greater things.* In its definitions it always unchangeably describes the same thing, but in the unchanged image ever new features become visible. But it knows the truth not less and not otherwise than it knew it in the time of old. The identity of experience is loyalty to tradition. Loyalty to tradition did not prevent the fathers of the Church from 'creating new names' (as St Gregory Nazianzen says) when it was necessary for the protection of the unchangeable faith.[33]

Such vitality as it is experienced in the church must not merely be related to the individual holiness of its members, but also to the necessary outreach of that holiness (just as the holiness of God inevitably reaches out into the salvation of the world in the trinitarian revelation). In other words, the Spirit-filled vitality of this tradition is seen most significantly in the manner in which the church fulfils its kerygmatic task. Lazarus Moore puts it succinctly:

> Tradition is authority to teach and make disciples, to save and sanctify, and to bear witness to the truth. The church bears witness to the truth not by harking back to the past, but by sharing the fruits of its own living experience.[34]

The same concern is strong in Bulgakov, who adamantly refused to subordinate the mission of the contemporary church to any previous generation. In the church's confidence to speak words of salvation from the depths of its experience of God, he sees the dynamic and vital nature of tradition being enacted. Bulgakov speaks about this in the context of how theologians in the present period must conceive their task in relation to ecclesial tradition. He says:

> A personal religious consciousness, personal theological thought, seeks to enlarge, to deepen, to affirm, to justify its faith and to identify it with the super-individual perception of the church. This faith tends to be united with its primary source, the integral experience of the Church, attested by ecclesiastical Tradition. This is why theological thought, which, in its quality of individual creative work and of individual perception in the Church, has necessarily an individual character, cannot and should not remain egotistically individual (for this is the source of heresy, of division) but should tend to become the theology of Tradition and to find in the latter its justification. It is not that these thoughts should simply repeat in other words what already exists in tradition, as it seems to formal and narrow minds, the 'Scribes and Pharisees' of our day. On the contrary, that thought should ever be new, living, and creative, for the life of the church never stops and Tradition is not a dead letter, but a living spirit. Tradition is living and creative: it is the new in the old, and the old in the new.[35]

Florovsky also calls attention to this primary sign of the vitality of the church's kerygmatic witness as something that testifies to the abiding presence of the animating Spirit. If this is the case, the present *kerygma* must in no sense be subordinated to the past *kerygma*, yet has a seamless unity with it, though expressed in widely different circumstances:

> That is why loyalty to tradition means not only concord with the past, but, in a certain sense, freedom from the past, as from some outward formal criterion. Tradition is not only a protective, conservative principle; it is, primarily, the principle of growth and regeneration. Tradition is not a principle striving to restore the past, using the past as a criterion for the present. Such a conception of Tradition is rejected by history itself, and by the consciousness of the church. Tradition is authority to teach, *potestas magisterii*, authority to bear witness to the truth. The church bears witness to the truth not by reminiscence or from the words of others, but from its own living, unceasing experience, from its catholic fullness.[36]

The contemporary witness of the church is a sign of the life of the Spirit of the Risen Christ which it can claim to experience. The saving *kerygma*, therefore, cannot be located in any given age, or given priority in the past alone, as it is an eschatological mystery that is 're-enacted' always in the present *kairos* of God's grace. As Florovsky puts it:

> The scriptures need interpretation. Not the phrasing, but the message is the core. And the church is the divinely appointed and permanent witness to the very truth and the full meaning of this message simply because the church belongs itself to the revelation, as the Body of the Incarnate Lord....
>
> But this witness is not just a reference to the past, not merely a reminiscence, but rather a continuous rediscovery of the message once delivered to the saints and ever since kept by faith. Moreover, this message is ever re-enacted in the life of the church.... Salvation is not only announced or proclaimed in the church, but precisely enacted. The Sacred History is still continued.... The ultimate end of revelation, its *telos*, has not yet come.[37]

He continues, prophetically,

> The sacred history of redemption is still going on. It is now the history of the church that is the Body of Christ. The Spirit-Comforter is already abiding in the church. No complete system of Christian faith is yet possible, for the church is still on her pilgrimage. And the Bible is kept by the church as a book of history to remind believers of the dynamic nature of the divine revelation, 'at sundry times, and in diverse manners'.[38]

It is, essentially, this spiritual *sobornost* (or communion) of the encounter of believers with the divine Spirit within the history of the church, and witnessed in its active *kerygma* from age to age, that is the guarantee of the church's essential catholicity. Because of its communion in the Lord, it has communion with itself across the ages, and through the different forms of its historical existence. Florovsky elaborates on this from the perspective of the theology of Christic *theosis*:

The church is completeness itself; it is the continuation of the theanthropic union. The church is transfigured and regenerated mankind. The meaning of this regeneration and transfiguration is that in the church mankind becomes one unity 'in one body'.[39]

Florovsky also expresses an argument similar to Bulgakov's, arguing the same ideas about catholicity, from the perspective of how the individual theologian or believer is called on to fulfil the apostle's injunction and 'conform to the mind of Christ'.[40] At the end, the conformity to God, effected in the life of the saint by the Spirit of Holiness, is coterminous with the true tradition:

Catholicity is no denial of personality, and catholic consciousness is neither generic nor racial . . . catholicity is a concrete oneness in thought and feeling. Catholicity is the style, or the order, or the setting, of personal consciousness which rises to the 'level of catholicity' . . . We must not say: 'Everyone in the church attains the level of catholicity', but 'Everyone can, and must, and is called to attain it'. Not always and by everyone is it attained. In the church we call those who have attained it Doctors and Fathers, because from them we hear not only their personal profession, but also the testimony of the church; they speak to us from its catholic completeness, from the completeness of a life full of grace.[41]

That communion which is the soul of tradition is, therefore, spiritual enclosure within the mystery of God. This *sobornost*, what the Byzantine Fathers called the redemptive mystery of *theosis*, is what constitutes both the church's ability to recognize itself from age to age, and its capacity to continue to offer its apostolic and saving *kerygma* to contemporary society, as from a living spring within itself, not as if taking words from a dead repository.

In the end, therefore, this double form of the concept of tradition, both as a concrete, canonical matter, and as a fundamental mystery of salvation (the kerygmatic mysteries and forms blessed by God, as well as the Living God himself present in those mysteries, not least the mystery of his church) finds a reconciliation and a harmony. Lossky expresses it well as a 'dynamic of interdependence'. The 'tradition' (namely the presence of the animating Spirit of Christ within his church, which energizes and vivifies it from age to age and conforms humanity to the common mind and life of Christ), and the ecclesial 'traditions' which sing of this, have an inner relation and a tensile dynamic which presents a constant challenge to the church of the present time. Lossky warns, and it is an important message to note, how arch-conservatism is not to be mistaken for fidelity to the tradition, but in fact can be a force that is hostile to it:

There exists an interdependence between the Tradition of the catholic church (the faculty of knowing the truth in the Holy Spirit) and the 'teaching of the fathers' (the rule of faith kept by the church). One cannot belong to the Tradition while contradicting the dogmas, just as one cannot make use of the dogmatic formulas received in order to oppose a formal 'orthodoxy' to every new expression of the Truth that the life of the church may produce. The first attitude is that of revolutionary innovators, of false prophets who sin against the expressed truth, against the Incarnate Word, in the name of the Spirit to which they lay claim. The second is that of the conservative formalists, Pharisees of the church who, in the name of the habitual expressions of the truth, run the risk of sinning against the Spirit of Truth.[42]

The dynamic and mysterious character of the sacred tradition, as it is understood in the Eastern Church, is thus clearly something that exposes well-known statements like that of St Vincent of Lerins (tradition is 'that which is believed everywhere, at all times, and by all'[43]) as somewhat wooden and lacking in their capacity to capture the essence of what is going on.[44] As a result tradition, as it came to be understood in the later West, was reduced to being a matter of the 'sources of authority' for Christian faith. Roman Catholic thinkers spoke widely of two sources of the faith: Bible and tradition.[45] This was a doctrine that even affected some Orthodox theologians in the eighteenth to nineteenth centuries, though in reality it is not so much true to Orthodoxy as redolent of Latin scholasticism.

It was inevitable that as Latin reflections on the sources of authoritative teaching were expanded out of the canon of Scripture and the varied liturgical formulae and patristic writings, they should eventually become subject to the overarching umbrella of papal authority. Even the 'right interpretation of the Scripture' was subjected to the theory of papal authority in the end; and in many ways the Protestant rejection of the significance of tradition was related to this resistance of false dichotomies that had been erected by the late medieval Western Church. Orthodoxy's sense of Holy Tradition may offer a way forward for ecumenical dialogue among the separated Western churches. Meanwhile it proclaims its inner system of truth with confidence, even though it knows it is a notion that has hardly had a hearing outside its own communion, and may be difficult for others to listen to with unclouded attention.

Sources of Authority in Orthodoxy

If one were to leave this broader discussion of the nature of sacred tradition underlying Orthodoxy's apprehension of its 'enclosure' in Christ, and its grasp of its self-identity as bearer of the Gospel *kerygma* to the world, and come down, as it were, to the more concrete examples of 'where' this tradition is manifested and exemplified, then it would be relatively easy to synopsize. The fundamental bulwarks of the Orthodox faith are: the lives of the Spirit-filled elect, the Holy Scriptures, the ancient traditions manifested in the sacred liturgy and the church's ritual practices, the creeds and professions (*ektheseis*) of the ecumenical councils, the great patristic writings defending the faith against heretical positions, the church's ever-deepening collection of prayers that have had universal adoption and enduring spiritual efficacy and, by extension, the wider body of the spiritual and ascetical writings of the saints of times past and present, the important writings of hierarchs at various critical moments in the more recent past which have identified the correct response that ought to be undertaken against new conditions and movements prevailing after the patristic period. This last category is often known as the *Symbolical Books* of Orthodoxy. The 'maintenance' of the sacred tradition is the responsibility of the whole church. Its holistic conscience of the faith (sometimes referred to in Latin as *sensus fidelium*) makes it alert to the preservation of apostolic order from heterodox dissidence of all types. Within that charism of the *sensus fidelium*, however, the office of bishop as teacher and defender of the true faith is particularly elevated within Orthodoxy. This, and the eucharistic presidency of the churches, are the primary offices of the episcopate, wherein the bishops serve as stewards and ministers of church unity and fidelity.

Figure 3   The Divine Liturgy. Patriarch Pavle of Serbia (centre) together with Bishop Artemije of Kosovo (right) and Bishop Atanasije of Hercegovina, praying before the holy altar at Gracanica Monastery.
Photograph: www.kosovo.net

Within the list of these great bulwarks of tradition, there are hierarchies of importance, of course.[46] The Scriptures stand as far greater in moment, and richness, than any writing of the saints. But there is not a profound difference in order, and not a dissonance of quality, for it is the same Spirit who inspires his saints in each generation, and inspires in them the same mind of the self-same Lord. Protestantism has generally elevated the Scripture as something far and above all other things in the church. Assigned as a composition of the Spirit of God (often understood in a sense of inspiration detached from the ecclesial community rather than within it) it is made to stand out alone, towering over any other thing that could be ascribed to church traditions. The one is seen as the infallible Word of God, the other as the words of fallible human beings. While Orthodoxy ascribes infallibility to the Scriptures as the Word of God, it does not divorce them from the tradition at all like this. Nor does Orthodoxy separate out Scripture from tradition in the manner of the Roman Catholic doctrine of the twin sources of revelation: tradition alongside Scripture. Scripture, for the Orthodox, is one of the purest manifestations of tradition. It is constitutively within sacred tradition, not apart from it.

The Scriptures stand at the head of other bulwarks of the Holy Tradition because they were the first written and didactic expression of the tradition after the generation of Jesus and the apostles. But the church existed before it actually had a recognized New Testament, and the evangelical writings themselves were the first outflowings of the Holy Tradition presided over by the Spirit of God. Similarly, the writings of the saints and Fathers which have been gathered together across time, were written under the inspiration of the same Spirit, offering clarifications of the same truth in different forms for different eras. Scripture is qualitatively the highest expression of the Holy Tradition, but Orthodoxy does not 'close' the ever-flowing river of inspiration from the Spirit in ways that other traditions seem to us to do. For such reasons the various bulwarks of the sacred tradition are approached in a holistic and organically united fashion. Scripture is read for what it is, part of the celebration of the mystery of Resurrection within Christian worship. Equally, the conciliar formulations of doctrine are read for what they essentially were, exegetical commentaries on the Holy Scriptures that underlie them all. It is impossible to read any patristic text at all without recognizing that they are all, without exception, talking incessantly of either Scripture or Christian worship.[47]

All the elements of the Holy Tradition are coherently bonded together in Orthodoxy, and they function to provide the church's sense of its inner identity as Christ's people. The fragmentation of the different parts of tradition has always been regarded by the Orthodox as a sign of heterodox 'loss' of the sense of the true spirit of Christianity. None of the individual bulwarks of the tradition can be set up in isolation. For example, no single sentence or argument of an individual Father of the Church carries with it an infallible authority, just because it came from a Father of the Church. Even more so, no individual bishop is afforded such infallible authority at any time in the church. Just as Homer could nod, so could some of the saints. Even the best works of the greatest among them contain matters, and isolated propositions, which the Orthodox gloss over at times out of reverence for their 'overall' contribution to the majestic exposition of the faith.

It is the consensus of voice that matters: reading the Fathers within the Scripture; the Scripture within the horizon of the church; the liturgy within the context of prayer: all together forming a 'seamless robe'. The seamless harmony of the whole tradition shores up all the different parts, self-correcting and self-regulating in its wholeness. It ever converges to what it essentially is: not a systematician's 'reduction' of Christian faith in millions of propositions, but rather the record of a whole people's long pilgrimage towards God across the desert horizons of a long history, as well as a compass for keeping the right course for the future.

ORTHODOXY'S READING OF THE SCRIPTURES

The Holy Scripture is the primary archetype of the tradition manifested concretely. In discussing its manner of impacting the Orthodox Church we could do no better than to point at every line of the church's worship service and show how almost each instance is a quotation or paraphrase of the sacred text. If ever all the bibles in the world were lost, sacred Scripture could be rewritten by reference to the service books of the Orthodox Church. The monks would single-handedly be able to recite the entire Psalter by heart. The ordinary faithful would reconstitute the Gospels verse by verse; and what was left lacking from the other apostolic and prophetic literature would be readily discoverable in the liturgies and offices of prayer. In what follows in this present section, however, instead of taking a liturgical trajectory through this important issue, I shall approach the question through the lens of hermeneutics: how the Orthodox think it is appropriate to 'read' the Bible in the light of the controversies that are presently circulating in academic circles about biblical authority and interpretative methodologies. I offer the remarks in four chief subheadings: what is the Orthodox ecclesial reading, and how the church understands three critical 'principles' in the correct reading of Scripture: the principles of consonance, of authority, and of utility.

An ecclesial reading

The present era has witnessed a welter of warring interpretations of Scripture. New 'critical methodologies' have come and gone over the last 200 years, largely under the horizon of interest of the Orthodox schools. Most of what has interested the Western Christian world in recent generations about scriptural interpretation has arisen in a Protestant context of thought which has (curiously) presumed a large 'separation' between the Bible and the early church. Many aspects of Protestant readings of Scripture have been more recently carried on, often unconsciously, into secular academic readings of Scripture that have approached them largely as historical texts to be deconstructed by specialists (often using a hermeneutic of suspicion with which to approach them), and as texts that have to be wrenched away from any notion of inherent holiness or inspiration. The Protestant elevation of the principle *sola Scriptura* (Scripture alone) has, over the centuries since the Reformation, been taken to such lengths that unforeseen practical results came from it, not least the way that professors of scriptural exegesis have tended to replace the ancient saints as oracular voices whose latest discoveries almost supersede anything that has gone before. The secularized pundits who came after them, specializing in predominantly 'non-religious' readings of the Christian Scriptures in university schools, could arrive at a position (often manifested in the writings of the so-called 'Jesus Seminar' in the USA) where the Lord was presented as little more than a 'Galilean peasant', entirely explicable by reference to first-century politics and religion.

Orthodoxy has no reason to distance itself from any reasonable and useful hermeneutical methodology that is a reverent way of reading the sacred texts. Nevertheless, those methods that intrinsically grow out of ideological positions that are inherently alien to Orthodoxy are part and parcel of a globally heterodox view of the Scriptures that Orthodoxy will oppose instinctively. Methods that treat the Scriptures as a simple body of historical literature, Orthodoxy resists. The Scriptures, within the church, are always to be seen as inherently sacred and especially revelatory, and always (and utterly) Christocentric. The Orthodox do not cling to the texts 'fundamentalistically', however, perfectly understanding the need to interpret this complex library of sacred literature in broad symbolic ways sometimes, and in precisely historical ways at other times, and in moral ways on yet other occasions. Some of the texts have a direct and pressing application; others have a more indirect significance today; while yet others need care in the attention given to their application so that disastrous results do not follow from a foolish literalism in reference to them.

Many preachers of sacred Scripture, for example, might advocate the text on Paul's authority: 'Children, obey your parents'[48] and claim that it had an enduring value. Few, other than fundamentalists who were enslaved to a 'biblicist principle', would apply the same apostle's injunction in the adjacent verse for slaves to 'obey their masters' as something pleasing to the Lord.[49] The right reading of the Scripture, from age to age, in differing conditions, is part and parcel of the ongoing mystery of revelation, as far as the Orthodox are concerned. The book is not a rigid, closed, repository that dominates the church but part of the ever-flowing mystery of grace that enlightens the body of disciples. For this reason Orthodoxy advocates a faithful and attentive reading of the Holy Scriptures, as something profoundly sacred and authoritative. But it does not affirm that the literal text of any isolated verse is to be an unyielding law for the church, nor that every verse is equally significant. No other parts of the scriptural canon, for example, approach the sacredness of the four Gospels, and Orthodoxy always reads the Old Testament through the resolving lens of the New. The Gospels and apostolic writings are a theological 'key' to the whole rationale and meaning of the totality of sacred Scripture as far as Orthodoxy is concerned. The Word of God, ultimately, is not mere words; but a harmonious consonance of how earthly words reveal the Word Incarnate, Jesus. All Scripture, in so far as it is Scripture, serves this Christocentricity faithfully, and unswervingly.

One key element of a genuinely Orthodox biblical hermeneutic is that the academic 'critical' presupposition that each previous age has obscured the truth that now at last is to be laid bare by 'objective' historical research, or newly sharpened philosophical acumen, is both arrogant and uninformed, misunderstanding the nature of history and textuality, as well as deliberately cutting itself off from any communion or solidarity with the originating community of discourse. No historical context, or text, exists in some disembodied space that can be objectively scrutinized by an infallible academic voice. Neither do text, context, and interpretations merge into one another, in a form of intertextuality where it is no longer proper to speak of meanings. Nor is it an acceptable axiom to believe (as many modernists came to affirm) that Protagoras was right, and that 'Man is the measure of all things'. The recognition and perception of meaning are undoubtedly driven by human epistemological systems that have only recently come to be more fully understood through the critical efforts of postmodernist philosophers; but the philosophical step forward from this, namely that humans have created meaning rather than recognizing it (one so central to the relativism that postmodernism wished to inculcate) is a secular 'act of faith' (not fact) that stands in contradiction to much that is held valuable in human culture at large, and most of what the church would recognize as the patterns of revelation within the created order.

Far from text being detached in a disembodied space, text (at least ancient text such as the Scripture) is the collective 'song of the community'. The interpreter who understands this is one who is sensitive to the community of meanings that constitute the 'community's meaning'. In Orthodox terms this means that the text of the Bible 'belongs to' the church, as much as the church belongs to the Bible; and the ecclesial reading of the Ekklesia's song, therefore, is very much a matter of conformity to the appropriate modalities of interpretation. Much contemporary academic criticism finds this highly objectionable. The ancients, especially the Christian Fathers, never failed to argue that true interpretation demands a *symphonia* of understanding between the discourses brought into association: that 'like can only be known by like'. We might express it today by the dictum that the insightful critic has to have deep empathy for the subject. A music critic, for example, certainly does not need to be a performer. If he or she is not an empathetic musician, however, their criticism is hardly worth reading.

Nevertheless, a key result of much modern 'hermeneutic of suspicion' in the Western academies has been has been the systematic rejection of other perspectives that conflict with the axiomatic ideologies of the new hermeneutic that is being applied, and an unwillingness to subordinate the critical commentator to canons of judgement other than his or her own pre-selected 'principles'. From the first, this visibly resulted in an exile of patristic analysis. The vast collection of patristic sermons on Scripture was banished from all serious academic discussion of biblical hermeneutics as hopelessly irrelevant. At a stroke the community which strenuously elevated the canon of the Bible, and faithfully preserved it in kerygmatic preached discourse, was eliminated from our considerations of how to interpret it. Today, very few biblical commentaries seriously consider how a pericope has been interpreted in the past. The rich and nuanced body of patristic material has been caricatured as all of a piece 'allegorical' or 'typological' analysis, and set aside. Such crudity of categorization can only be the fruit of repressive ideology. The same is suggested by the observation that only towards the end of the twentieth century were serious scholarly analyses of patristic biblical hermeneutics making their appearance.[50]

Orthodoxy can always look afresh at the sacred texts applying parts of the herme-neutic of suspicion (how much the role of apostolic women in the earliest age of the church has been enhanced by feminist readings of texts, for example), but the funda-mental 'ideology of dissonance' behind that hermeneutic (and many others) will always be resisted, since the consciousness of communion with the church of the originating age of the biblical texts is one that underpins the whole Orthodox ethos of consonance in biblical reading; and behind that, underpins its awareness of being the self-same church as that in the apostolic period (though of course in a different environment). It is not so much a hermeneutic of suspicion that is active here in Orthodoxy, but a hermeneutic of familial trust. This is what contemporary criticism would call 'grand narrative imposition' of a high order, but what Orthodoxy would recognize as its primary drive and instinct of self-recognition across the ages. In Orthodox reflection this would be recognized as a fundamental aspect of the sacred tradition that underpins the reception of the apostolic Gospel proclamation, the creation of the biblical canon[51] in response to that, and the ongoing developmental life of the church across the centuries: its worship, its intellectual life, as well as its socio-historical forms.

If we can call this primary principle of Orthodox hermeneutics the principle of the 'ecclesial reading',[52] we will see how basically it matters that an Orthodox interpreter shares a 'consonant' motivation for interpreting the sacred text, consonant that is with the kerygmatic motive of the earlier saints, preachers, and biblical commentators whose works have been 'received' by the church at large. This commits Orthodox interpreters, of course, to a large body of biblical interpretation which may not be particularly 'accurate',[53] but which remains good in so far as it proved its utility in building up the faith of the community, and entering into the heart of the community. If previous meanings have fallen out of the heart (and memory) of the community, so be it. It would be ridiculous in the name of authenticity to patristic tradition, for example, to resurrect some of the patristic biblical homilies that were warmly welcomed in earlier centuries, but which to modern congregations would simply sound fanciful, and prove a barrier to the comprehension of the core biblical message of salvation. Some element of falling out of memory, and falling out of favour, in the life of the church is an important aspect of the self-renewal of the tradition of the saints, and ought not to be interrupted by the work of 'archaizers'. Orthodox clergy who simply read out patristic sermons in the course of the liturgy, for example, as a response to the demand to preach the Gospel, surely have a deep need to examine their praxis. It is not a habit the great Fathers themselves would have allowed to become established, as they themselves originated powerful new interpretations of the message in contemporary Greek rhetoric of their own.

The principle of consonance

Consonance with the ecclesial tradition, as the primary requirement for the Orthodox Christian biblical interpreter, is exactly what the great Athanasios meant when he wrote this axiomatic passage about biblical interpretation in his treatise *On the Incarnation of the Word*. It stands to this day as a charter for the Orthodox conception of attaining to the biblical meaning by an underpinning of 'that virtue[54] which is of Christ', and by 'consonance with the saints'. For this reason it is worth quoting despite its length:

> What are the requirements for the searching of the Scriptures, and for true knowledge of them? An honourable life is needed, and a pure soul, and that virtue which is of Christ. For the intellect must apply this to guide its path and then it shall be able to attain to what it desires, and to comprehend it, in so far as it is possible for a human nature to learn of things concerning the Word of God. But, without a pure mind and the modelling of one's life after the saints, a person could not possibly comprehend the words of the saints. If we wanted to see the light of the sun, for example, we would certainly wipe our eyes to brighten them, and would purify ourselves in some appropriate way related to what we desire. So, for example, the eye by becoming light would then be able to see the light of the sun. Or take the case of a person who wanted to see a certain city or country. Such a person would surely journey to the place in order to be able to see it. It is exactly the same for someone who desires to comprehend the mind of those who speak of God. Such a person must begin by washing and cleansing their own soul, and by addressing their manner of living. They should approach the saints by imitating their own works. By such consonance with the saints in the conduct of a shared life, a person may understand also what has been revealed to them by God.[55]

St Basil the Great also says much the same thing in his *Treatise on the Holy Spirit*[56] when he describes how the interpreter of the oracles of the divine Spirit needs to be rendered clear by the working of the same Holy Spirit (just as glass when clear can mediate the sun). This kind of interpretation requires 'consonance'. In other words, the communion with the Holy Spirit who inspires the text is a fundamental precondition for the authentic 'opening up' of the sacred book. Without that, there may be many levels of historical and morphological comment possible on the biblical text; but no *exegesis* properly understood.

This leads us to the conclusion that, for Orthodoxy, biblical exegesis belongs properly to the community of the church, which is defined by the possession of the charism of the Spirit. Individual biblical interpreters supplement their own possession of the charism of the Spirit's illumination, with the gift of illumination that over the centuries has been granted to preceding generations of the church. For this reason alone, no Orthodox interpreter can presume to disregard, or ridicule, the interpretative efforts of previous generations, least of all those of the saints who have been preserved in the tradition as particularly worthwhile. Consonance in this case is certainly not the same as monotonous repetition of past utterance, which would amount to strict conformity, and would signal the end to intelligent development of biblical analysis; on the contrary, what is meant is that new applications of biblical interpretative methods proceed reflectively 'within the communion', just as variations on a theme are self-evidently linked to the master theme which they in turn set out to elaborate, illuminate, or extend. This principle of course allows Orthodox interpreters to make use of a large range of biblical readings, methods, and styles that have not been produced by those within the church's communion, and perhaps not written with much regard for what one might call the 'inspired' character of the sacred text, but it commits the Orthodox interpreter to view and process all of that extrinsic material in the light of the church's inner principles of receptivity. In all things the method is an interpretative tool, merely a tool. The guiding metaphysic (the process towards authentic reception of the exegesis of the Bible) has to be the reception of the sacrament of revelation in the present moment: what the Fathers called the 'Mystery of Christ'.

The principle of consonance (which we could also call the principle of communion) is extensively set out, and most elegantly so, in the first of the *Five Theological Orations* by St Gregory the Theologian,[57] who elsewhere throughout his work describes the biblical commentator as a priest who is allowed entry into a temple, but the deeper the progression into the sacred areas (beyond the veil no human can go in this earthly life) the more pressing is the need for purity of heart and acumen of mind. Both things, moral and intellectual power, are seen by Gregory to be significant charisms that cannot be neglected, and if they are not present in the manifested works of the interpreter, the priestly act of biblical exegesis will be debased into sacrilege.[58] These patristic writers who speak of consonance with the mind and spirit of the biblical author are largely echoing Origen who, in turn, is developing his principles of biblical interpretation from the starting point of 'seeking the mind of Christ', since for him, that mindset is a matrix which the *energeia* of inspiration lays down in the mind of the apostolic author. His starting point for this is, of course, the apostolic dictum in 1 Corinthians 2.16, which is itself the climacteric of one of the first ever considered essays on the Christian theology of inspiration, from the hand of the apostle himself.[59]

This is not to imagine that sophisticated biblical theologians such as Origen, Athanasios, and Cyril of Alexandria, or the Cappadocian Fathers, ever envisaged a direct or literal transference of information from God to the human author (something the icon painters have somewhat naively depicted); rather that they imagined inspiration as being a divine *energeia* that vitalized the charism of 'comprehension' of the things of God in a human heart. Such comprehension was seen to be always partial (inevitably so, since no human mind could fully comprehend the purposes of God) but substantively accurate, and differing in quality from saint to saint. Accordingly, the Fathers understood the differences in the biblical accounts of Jesus, for example, as fundamentally related to the quality of the inspiration of each of the various evangelists. John and Paul were always recognized, in almost all patristic literature, as being clearly more in possession of the 'mind of Christ' than most of the others.

Many of the Fathers expressed this sense of degrees of inspiration among the biblical writers[60] in a regularly repeated image, that some of the apostles were called to the

107

mountain with Christ to see things that the others could not witness directly, but had to hear of only through later report (as in the episode of the Transfiguration in Mark 9). The patristic idea of consonance, however, was fundamentally one that resisted the atomization of biblical texts into disparate trends, or parts. It is this fundamental vision that accounts for the church's refusal to allow Marcion and the Gnostics to divide the Testaments, or the suppression of the Diatessaron[61] of Tatian in favour of restoring the four synoptic voices in the Syriac Peshitta. It is also at the heart of building and defending the biblical canon: that whatever is recognized as canonical literature is endorsed as sharing in that communion of spirit which is authentically the Jesus tradition. Not all parts of the scriptural tradition share the same level of inspired greatness, this implies, but they all share the same communion of authority. It follows that the contemporary principle of affording the highest level of authority to chronologically earlier materials (such as the so-called Jesus Seminar endlessly arguing over what is or is not an 'authentic utterance' of the historical Jesus) is deeply inimical to Orthodox principles of biblical interpretation. There is no hidden canon within a canon, a pure core of historically verifiable materials (as distinct from what later disciples added to the ur-tradition) to be established by the sagacious historian; but rather a collegiality of *kerygma* beginning with the preaching of Jesus and from there extending back over the whole comprehension (or reception) of the Old Testament itself, and extending forward over the whole unrolling of Orthodox Christian civilization (the culture of the church).

The principle of authority

There is another area in which there will always be radical difference between Orthodox biblical interpretation and so-called 'independent academic criticism', namely the issue of the authority seen to reside in the text. The difference arises in so far as Orthodoxy is fundamentally defined by its allegiance to evangelical and apostolic authority, and modern scholarship (by and large) is not. The principle of authority is robustly resisted in modern critical hermeneutic precisely because the contemporary interpreter is given the highest status of authority. If it is necessary to share that authority among others (as in cases of controversial points of judgement) then a cabinet of academics can be convoked (strangely echoing the historical movement of Christianity from apostolic to synodical principles of judgement-making). One can see this process operating consistently among biblical critics, from the unshaken confidence of the nineteenth-century liberals to the more tentative dogmatism of the Jesus Seminar, which votes on what is to be considered (or not considered) authentic.

Common to both is the sense that the putative academic judgement is the last and highest court. No reference ought to be made to any other type of authority to elucidate 'authentic meaning'. Bishops are irrelevant, the faithful beside the point. If there is such an appeal to 'outside factors' it is often regarded as a professional foul. This fundamental attitude has survived even its most rigorous twentieth-century attack (mainly by ignoring it), in the form of the protest from Liberation Theology that such academic self-enclosure cut off the voice of the poor and dispossessed who did not share in this type of discourse, and could see in it only the age-old marks of the oppressive disregard of the rich for the poor. Even so, for most of the lifetime of higher

108

criticism the concept of 'apostolic' witness has been merely of a piece with 'patristic' or other forms of medieval or modern piety, at best irrelevant to the elucidation of the quest for authenticity (considered as chronological priority[62]), and at worst evocative of systemic forces of historical oppression.[63] Orthodoxy does not admit such perspectives, though it is open to isolated insights for the good that can emerge even from such deeply flawed methodologies.

For Orthodoxy, the apostolic authority is certainly not an oppression, but a liberative lens through which the church, and its biblical interpreters in the present age, can share in a commonality of experience of the Christ Mystery. Dominical and apostolic utterances become, as it were, the set key signatures within which the present music of the re-expression of the evangelical *kerygma* can be performed: that music which is the essential self-expression of the church from age to age.[64] It is an 'oppression' only in the sense that fugal form necessarily guides the composer in the creation of a fugue, or in the way a sonnet is specifically required to rhyme in a fourteen-line structure.

As we have noted, St Irenaeus was highly influential in developing the concept of the church's possession of the charism of truth[65] which could not be presumed to be at work elsewhere.[66] For him, this essential *charisma* was manifested above all in the manner in which the leaders of the great churches interpreted the Scriptures with sober catholic consensus. It was in this context that he developed his famous image of the interpretative 'key' to the Scriptures (*hypothesis*) which the church has, but which others do not possess. For Irenaeus, the chief thing that was wrong about Gnostic exegesis was its lack of a harmonious sense of direction.

The principle of utility

Beyond the principle of consonance, many other Fathers pointed regularly to a most important aspect of undisputedly Orthodox biblical interpretation, which is its edificatory character. The biblical commentary is not, essentially, a historical essay or semantic analysis, but an expression of the charism of preaching within the church. We might call this the principle of utility: how the proclamation of the faith is rendered 'appropriate' from age to age; how in one era the discourse is suitably Semitic and symbolically imagistic, while in another the framework of Greek rhetoric and hymnody works most effectively, and in another age does not work so well, and may require simpler forms of re-expression. Origen (who certainly saw the act of biblical commentary as an extension of the prophetic charism of preaching the word) expressed this principle in his own time by describing the commentator as a 'spiritual herbalist' whose duty was to know the values of all the contents of the herbarium, and be able to make a potent mix for the benefit, not the bane, of the recipients:

> The saint is a sort of spiritual herbalist who culls from the sacred scriptures every jot and every common letter, discovers the value of what is written, and its use, and finds then that there is nothing in the scripture that is superfluous.[67]

This, in short, is a caution to Orthodox biblical commentators of the future, that commentary cannot be separated from the task of kerygmatic proclamation; and, since the latter includes dogmatics at its heart, a caution that Orthodoxy must be very careful indeed not to allow the same divorce between systematic theology, biblical interpretation, and pastoral theology that has so painfully and so decisively marked much of Protestant and Roman Catholic theological development in the aftermath of the New Hermeneutic in the present age. The Orthodox sense of the liturgical rooted-ness of all theology serves as a counterweight to processes that tend to erect systematic division between fields and subfields. It may be that the life of the academy was unable to cope in any other way with the burgeoning complexities, and increasing literature, of its subfields; but the progressive atomization of domains of expertise has been a defect of twentieth-century curricular philosophy.

Patristic and Conciliar Authorities

While the body of conciliar doctrines (most particularly the decrees and decisions of the seven ecumenical councils) and other major patristic literature are not regarded as being of the same order of importance as the Holy Scripture, in the mind of Orthodoxy this does not set them apart from the Scriptures as radically as other Western churches seem to have thought. Some forms of Protestantism, for example, would not ascribe much authority at all to this venerable literature, and many modern evangelicals have never read or been influenced by it at all.[68] Even Anglicanism and Roman Catholicism, while they hold the Fathers in high esteem, do not afford them more significance than as part of a range of muffled historical voices in the ongoing elaboration of theological discourse.

Orthodoxy sees the ecumenical conciliar theology and the greatest of the patristic theology as sharing in the charisms of the Holy Spirit's truth, and therefore as possessed of a high and venerable authority for the universal church. As we have noticed earlier, the individual writings of each patristic theologian are not afforded the status of an infallible guide to the truth, but the decisions of the ecumenical councils are, in the sense that it is unthinkable that the Spirit of Truth should ever abandon his high priests assembled in solemn liturgical adjudication of matters of fundamental concern to the definition of truth for his universal church. The patristic writings are seen as 'sharing in' the charism of the Spirit's own truth, in so far as they are in 'consonance' with the tradition, and emanate from men and women whose lives are mirrors of the Spirit's indwelling grace: the same grace, and the same Spirit who revealed his mysteries to the prophets and apostles before them. Truth can barely shine through a lens that is filmed over with grime. A human being who has become transparent to the love of God, and conformed to the gentleness of the humble Saviour, can hardly fail to be a beacon of the Spirit's truth. In many eras of the church the prophetic and theological witness of the great saints has stood out against all opposition to hold fast to the truth, winning through even when they seemed to be in a minority. One thinks especially of the ancient leaders such as Athanasios, Gregory the Theologian, Basil of Caesarea, Maximos the Confessor, John of Damascus, Theodore Studite, Gregory Palamas, and Mark of Ephesus, teachers who spoke for truth even in the face of powerful 'established' pressures. There have been men and women in every century of the Orthodox Church to correspond with them in prophetic foresight and courage.

Athanasios' career in the fourth century, struggling against an Arian establishment, seemed to present him as a man swimming against the tide of common opinion.

110

He was the bearer of the tradition, the others were not. Those innumerable other bishops such as Eusebios of Nicomedia (a contemporary Arian thinker more highly placed than Athanasios) or Eunomius of Cyzicus (a radical Arian bishop who claimed the miracles manifested in his circle demonstrated his authenticity of doctrine) were all certain that their teaching was in correspondence with Scripture and logic, and they pursued their agendas forcibly. Athanasios knew that his doctrine of the deity of the Lord Jesus was in harmony with Scripture, as well as in consonance with the liturgy, the writings of the saints of previous generations, the lives and witness of the best of his current generation, the tenor of the international consensus of the Western bishops. That wider sense of consonance made the difference: it demonstrated the essential quality of the 'patristic mentality', a prophetic voice which leads the community forward and with the evident grace of the Lord's own Spirit.

These then are the chief sources of the Orthodox understanding of what other traditions have called the 'deposit of revelation': the Scriptures, the conciliar decrees, the patristic writings, and the sacred liturgy, with the rich body of 'non-textual' symbolic witness that the divine liturgy constitutes for the church. Here in the liturgical and prayer life of Orthodoxy is the book for the unlettered, the library of theology that is sung in the praise of God from the assembly of the faithful. To be a regular participant in Orthodox worship is to be exposed over successive years to a vast body of the deepest theology imaginable. This is communicated in ways that transcend the merely cerebral, and have proved their effectiveness over centuries before literacy was common in the world. Orthodox Christians have long known how to sing their faith, even if they could not write or read it. To illustrate an authentic part of the Orthodox tradition it is enough to point to its manifestation in the liturgy of the church. To consult the liturgical books is a wonderful experience. There are so many of them, each with its own distinctive spirit: the Euchologion, the Lenten Triodion, the Pentecostarion, the Festal Menaion, the Octoechos, the twelve-volume Menaion, the Synaxarion, to name only a few. They are a veritable treasury of prayers, hymns, canons and antiphons, exorcism rituals, sacramental celebrations, and blessings. The 'mind' and attitude of these books is profoundly illustrative of the sacred tradition, although (in the same way with the Scriptures or patristic material) they are to be approached holistically, and using the evidence 'in consonance with' the other windows of the Holy Tradition.

THE SYMBOLICAL BOOKS

The so-called 'symbolical books' of the Orthodox Church would probably appear on most Orthodox lists of authoritative sources, towards the end of that list, after the fundamental springs of faith we have been discussing above. These do not have the same status as the great patristic and conciliar statements but are nonetheless held by the Orthodox to be substantive and significant theological statements, as from important later synods of the church (or its leading hierarchs) when faced with theological problems that needed immediate resolution. They were predominantly put together in the late sixteenth and the seventeenth centuries, when the effects of the Protestant Reformation were first being dimly felt to impinge on life in the Eastern churches. But there are some from before that period, and after it. All of them are characterized as having been stimulated either by Roman Catholicism, or the Protestant churches, addressing Orthodoxy with different suppositions, which the Orthodox felt must be clarified and restated from an Orthodox perspective. One of the central texts in the list was the result of the explicit impact of the Reformation. One of the seventeenth-century patriarchs of Constantinople, Cyril Lukaris, had issued a statement of faith which many at the time believed had moved towards being an implicit endorsement of Calvinism. It caused considerable alarm among the Orthodox. In the aftermath of Cyril's fall,[69] Patriarch Dositheos of Jerusalem moved to make the position of the Orthodox Church clear on some fundamental aspects of Protestantism. The acts of his synod of Jerusalem in 1672 have been widely accepted by the Orthodox ever since as having a high didactic authority.

The symbolical statements from this period of conflict, a period when generally speaking the intellectual and political resources of world Orthodoxy were at a low ebb, have increasingly visible limitations nowadays (which is why they are, perhaps, no longer clung to as closely as in previous generations). The Protestant ethos had travelled into the Eastern Christian world by the seventeenth century, and several Protestant theologians were trying to secure agreement from Orthodox hierarchs on points of the faith, so as to strengthen their own apologetic with Roman Catholicism in the West. Most, if not all, the Eastern hierarchs had only the slightest sketch of what Protestant religion actually was. The delegations that came before them were ceremonious, highly courteous, and putting on the best 'ecumenical' face on all aspects of their dialogue. When the Reformation was offered to them as a legitimate protest against the sovereign rule of the Papacy the Orthodox hierarchs listened with sympathetic ears at first. But, generally speaking, it was only later in the seventeenth century that the Eastern bishops began to gain a clearer sense of what was really involved in the Protestant movements. At first hearing, they had placed certain Reformation ideas piecemeal into the overall structure of Orthodox thought, and even when they gained a truer understanding of the extent of the divergence between the Protestant and Orthodox ecclesial mentalities, they still (understandably) continued to describe and approach Protestantism from the horizons of the Orthodox world-view.

In addition to this, Orthodoxy itself at that period of its history had been heavily influenced by the systematic theological treatises of Western Catholicism, which it had adapted and reused even in its own seminaries. Ukraine was a particular example, where Peter Moghila, the great hierarch of Kiev, used Polish Jesuit works of theology (with a few emendations) as the training course for his clergy. This gave to the whole manner of Orthodox reflection and style of theologization in this period a very baroque cast, which in many ways was foreign to the natural way Orthodox theology had grown up before that point, as a broad and holistic system rooted in the soil of the Scriptures and the ancient patristic tradition. It had been many centuries, as far as the Orthodox were concerned, since any crisis of a serious dogmatic nature had ever shaken the church. Not so in the West, where religious divisions and hostility had reached an extraordinary pitch. The marked and bitter context of church disunity and mutual apologetics in the West, which had initiated the first encounters of the Reformed theologians with the Orthodox, called for sharp answers to particular problems, which were not always in the natural focal range of what the Orthodox regarded as 'real issues'. All in all, while the symbolical books present the church with an authentic and accurate response of the Orthodox world to central tenets of the faith (as an answer to Catholic or Protestant principles, for example, in relation to the church, authority, grace, and the sacraments) the Orthodox today who accept their guidance are not bound to believe that their form of expression was the most felicitous possible.

Many Orthodox theologians have looked back and called this period of 'Westernization' (it would be better to call it the admission of heavily scholasticized method) in Orthodoxy as the 'Great Captivity'. Several Orthodox theologians are of the position now that this very title of the 'symbolical books' is misleading and ought to be discontinued. Zankov, citing the pre-revolutionary Russian theologian Glubokovsky, puts it this way:

> As Glubokovsky says,[70] 'The Orthodox church has no symbolic books; its only creed is that of Nicaea. Considering the so-called Orthodox "symbolic" books as symbolic in the western sense of this term,[71] leads to mistakes and misunderstandings.' As the result of this many important points of Orthodox Christianity take on a very different sense and meaning. The Catechisms of different local churches, for example, have no credal authority, not even the best known and widest spread, the catechism of Platon, Metropolitan of Moscow, and especially the greater and lesser catechisms of the famous Metropolitan of Moscow, Philaret. But they are important, because they present the modern official view of the objects of the faith.[72]

Zankov's noticeable anxiety to put the symbolical books at arm's length is best explained, now that we are at the beginning of the twenty-first century, in the sense that it was not so much that there was material here that the Orthodox would now wish to renounce, or consider was 'wrong' in any sense, but rather that the terms of the symbolical books, and the local church catechisms which in turn put these partially decontextualized apologetic utterances into even more decontextualized and gnomic form so that they could be learned parrot fashion in the schools, led to a certain bankruptcy of Orthodox thought in the academies.

It was this occlusion of the true roots and springs of Orthodox theology (which lay in the greater oceans of the Scriptures, the liturgical hymns, the rituals of the mysteries, the patristic writings, and the lives and witness of the ascetic saints), that lay behind Zankov's unease, as well as that of many other theologians of the time as well. Father George Florovsky, also referring to this period of the theological 'captivity' of Orthodoxy, called for a renaissance in the theological formation of church teachers, in which he imagined a widespread return to the broader and deeper traditions of theological reflection, rooted in the Bible, the Fathers, and the liturgy. Today in the Orthodox world the limited understanding of 'theology' as apologetics, if it once had currency, has indeed withered away in most places, and there has been a widely experienced desire to re-source theological utterance in the Scriptures and Fathers.

Nevertheless the symbolical books are still important elements of the historical defence, and an expression of the Orthodox understanding of central matters. They derive their status from the character of the local councils of the church. Formally speaking, Orthodoxy attributes an indefectible character of the truth only to the decisions of ecumenical councils. These cannot be revised, annulled, or even partially set aside. They belong to the core of the confession of the Orthodox Christian faith. But the last of these was held in 787. Since then the synodical life of the Eastern Church[73] has continued with the decisions and decrees of local councils. These are different to national synods in so far as, for a local council, hierarchs of other national churches travel to be part of the deliberations and give their statement a more solemn authority. While not being infallible of themselves, these important local councils are character-istic of all episcopal synods in that the bishops present speak charismatically, out of their hearts, on the nature of the ancient faith of the whole body of faithful. As a result, their decisions will usually be recognized by the Orthodox at large (and across historical periods) as having far more than a merely local effect. In the case of many synods of the Orthodox Church that have been held since the last ecumenical council, this has indeed been the case. Their teaching has been held up as having a large relevance.

The same thing applies to the decrees even of single bishops who have in times past written encyclicals in response to pressing matters.[74] Local and individual utterances of bishops can assume such an elevated significance too if they are accepted ecumenically, that is by a large proportion of the faithful over a significant time, as important statements of faith. While the ecumenical councils cannot be taken piecemeal, however, the decrees of the local councils may well be. In other words their authority is recognized, but not the 'whole package' needs to be adopted. As Metropolitan Kallistos puts it: 'The church has often been selective in its treatment of the Acts of Local Councils: in the case of the seventeenth century councils, for example, their statements of faith have in part been received by the whole Orthodox church, but in part set aside or corrected.'[75]

The symbolical books, are represented by the following:

1   The Confession of Faith of Gennadios Patriarch of Constantinople (1455–6)
2   The Responses of Patriarch Jeremias II of Constantinople, to the Lutheran Theologians (1537–81)
3   The Confession of Faith of Metrophanes Kritopoulos (1625)
4   The Orthodox Confession of Peter Moghila (as revised and endorsed by the Synod of Jassy[76] in 1642)
5   The Confession of Dositheos, Patriarch of Jerusalem, as ratified by the Synod of Jerusalem (1672)

In addition to this core, the Orthodox have generally also recognized the following statements as also carrying great authority to 'speak for' all Orthodox:

1   The Encyclical Letter of St Photios, Patriarch of Constantinople (867)
2   The First Letter of Michael Caerularios, Patriarch of Constantinople, to Patriarch Peter of Antioch (1054)
3   The Acts of the Councils of Constantinople (1341 and 1351) relating to the Hesychastic Controversy
4   The Encyclical Letter of St Mark of Ephesus (1440–1)
5   The Responses of the Orthodox Patriarchs to the Non-Jurors (1718 and 1723)
6   The Response of the Orthodox Patriarchs to the Letter of Pope Pius IX (1848)
7   The Response of the Synod of Constantinople to the Letter of Pope Leo XIII (1895)
8   The Encyclical Letters of the Patriarch of Constantinople (1920 and 1925) on Christian Unity and the Modern Ecumenical Movement

The Russian Church has also, since the early nineteenth century, given great weight to the Catechism of Philaret.[77]

THE PEDALION (HOLY CANONS)

To the above we might even add now (since it was assembled in the eighteenth century, and became more commonly available in an English translation of the early part of the twentieth century) the evidence for the Holy Tradition that is given by the canons (or rules of discipline) of the various councils and synods of church history. The canons have a more direct authority than the symbolical books, of course, but stand in need of a more 'refracted' exegesis, as sometimes changing historical conditions have left some of the rules stranded on the shore. The canons were collected together in a volume known as the Rudder (Pedalion) by SS Nicodemus the Hagiorite and Makarios of Corinth. They are a welter of legislation (sometimes confusing, and sometimes 'inapplicable'[78]) accumulated over centuries of past synods. Orthodoxy has never thrown away any of its synodical legislation, and rarely updated it or made it streamlined and strictly consistent, in the way that Roman Catholic popes and legal commissions have regularly overhauled Latin canon law. Some of the disciplinary texts have the highest universal value for the church today (such as the canons of St Basil that govern the church's approach to marriage law, or the canons of Nicaea governing church polity), but others approach the quality of dead letters from a bygone era (such as injunctions for clergy not to eat with non-Orthodox, or not to be present when music is performed). Their application is, most properly, the function of the local bishop who is called upon by the grace of his office to exercise 'discernment' as to when and where to insist on the strict application of the canon law (*akribeia*[79]) or on its judicious relaxation according to different circumstances (*oikonomia*). The exercise of this function of merciful judgement is one of the most gracious attributes of the episcopacy today, and signals that they too, even as a present generation of hierarchs, share in the same charism of governance that once inspired the ancient Fathers. Their application of discretion is a clear manner in which they 'stand for' the gentle Christ in the midst of his needy people today.

Sadly, the wide availability of this thick tome of canons and rules (one that requires so much learning and discretion to enter into it properly) has tended to make it in recent years something of a club for more fundamentalistic mentalities to hold over and against other Orthodox whom they dislike. The blatant use of the book of canons as a threat for others demonstrates immediately, however, that many are misusing the holy texts. It is invariably the case (in my opinion) that self-appointed lawyers should be energetically encouraged not to open the *Pedalion*. Its use should be governed by the hierarchy. An exception would be if interested enquirers would open the book to see how it applied to improving their own lives, rather than correcting those of others. This is an old question of logs and splinters.[80] A chief 'problematic' here that needs to be addressed is the falsification that necessarily occurs in such a project as the *Pedalion* where ancient canons are 'systematically' cross-referenced by topic, and accumulated as sources towards a global answer, with little regard for the historical, occasional, or apologetic context of the original rules being proposed by the conciliar Fathers. The infrequent and very unsatisfying attempts by St Nicodemus to provide background context at certain points on issues which he himself felt were controversial only demonstrates the need to undertake this task thoroughly, systematically, and from a basis of the proper academic training.

TRADITION AND REVELATION

The survey of these fundamental aspects of what the Orthodox understand as Holy Tradition, even if it has been rapid, may leave readers with a sense of the complexity of basic matters that comprise the living reality of Orthodox faith. The Western systematic tradition would probably have entitled such a chapter as this the 'doctrine of revelation'; but while Orthodoxy recognizes a definitive 'change' from the apostolic period that saw the closing of the New Testament canon, onwards into the later eras of the church, it does not wish to create an over-elaborate barrier between those periods such that the inspiration of the Spirit of God in the apostolic period substantially ceased with the end of the apostolic age. Western theologies of revelation usually either do that, or struggle in some way to account for an ongoing 'development' of church doctrine from ancient times into the present. Orthodoxy does not subscribe, either to the notion of the end of the age of revelation, or to the theory of the development of doctrine. The Spirit breathes in his church to this day, and his revelation continues; in different modes, and at different levels, but ever the same in so far as it is the direct energy of the Holy Spirit at work creating the vitality of the church. The Orthodox certainly do not see that revelation as an extraneous body of things that go on accumulating, or changing, or developing; rather as an experience of God that is entered into in new ways in each generation, but always found to be the same 'familial experience' of the self-same Lord, in each era of the church. Christ, always new; ever the same.

To that extent the very notion of revelation-tradition remains mysterious and to a degree unapproachable, uncontainable in the Orthodox experience: like picking up a raindrop from a window pane. It is untouchable, and at the same time entirely apprehensible. Those looking in on Orthodoxy from outside sometimes experience a sense of frustration that Orthodox faith is not as neatly packaged as the credal expressions of Western Christianity. But this is partly because of the 'mysterious' nature of the tradition itself, that rightly reflects the charismatic nature of its mysterious Lord. Instead of logical neatness there is to be found a deep organic coherence and a lived-out sense of the mystery of grace. Orthodox theology and doctrine are first and foremost expressions of Christian praxis: they are tested as much in the living of them as they are in their logical sense. The mysterious tradition, for all that, remains clear, sensible, approachable, discretely recognized and citeable. It pervades all aspects of Orthodox life and is known to the children as well as to the learned. Its complex range shows quite clearly that Orthodox theology is at one and the same moment *apophatic* (turning away from speech as defective, and preferring the silence of worship) and yet dogmatically proclamative (*kataphatic*). It is, in other words, simultaneously formal and charismatic. It is unshakeable, and yet bends down (as God himself does) to catch up even the smallest intellect, the most doubting heart in its embrace. The greatest of all the intellects of Christian history have contributed to it substantially; but no intellect, however great, could ever exhaust its richness, for in the end it is an invitation to enter into communion with none other than the divine Sophia, and to be conformed in his image and likeness as members of his holy Church.

Notes

1   Up to the Vatican II declaration on revelation, Catholicism had taught the twin springs of Christian faith were Bible and tradition.
2   Mark 7.7.
3   Very fine explanations of Orthodox tradition can be found in Florovsky 1972 and Meyendorff 1978. A fuller discussion of issues in this chapter can also be found in McGuckin 1989 and 1998.
4   *Against the Heresies*, 4.26.2.
5   Ibid. 1.8.1.
6   Ibid. 3.2.1. The *Kanon tes Aletheias*. He speaks of the church having the 'body of truth': *Against the Heresies*, 2.27.1.
7   Tertullian pressed the legal context much more than Irenaeus. For him tradition was transmitted within the churches that were linked by 'familial' apostolic relationship. Tradition is thus the legal patrimony of the apostolic churches: a patrimony that is the legacy of the legal founder of a corporation. It belongs only to the legitimate heirs. False pretenders to the legacy, such as the heretics, must be excluded by a legal *praescriptio*: that is, their claims are voided by default. *On the Prescription of Heretics*, 19–21.
8   The Rule of Truth, or of Faith.
9   *Against the Heresies*, 3.3.3; cf. ibid. 4.26.2 and 4.33.8.
10 Ibid. 1.10.1; Tertullian reproduces this in *On the Prescription of Heretics*, 19–22.
11 John 3.8.
12 Gen. 1.1–4.
13 Luke 1.35; Matt. 17.5.
14 Moore 1984: 3–4.
15 Meyendorff 1989: 377.
16 Metropolitan Philaret, cited in Florovsky 1937: 178.
17 Florovsky 1972: 14.
18 Which I take to mean something akin to the Irenaean sense of *hypothesis*: the interpretative key.
19 Papadopoulos 1964: 101.
20 Lossky 1975: 147, citing Col. 1.26.
21 Basil, *On the Holy Spirit*, 10.
22 Lossky 1975: 147–8 (citing St Basil's treatise *On the Holy Spirit*).
23 Khomyakov, 'Essay on the Church', in Birkbeck 1895: 198.
24 Florovsky 1971: 46.
25 Florovsky 1971: 47.
26 Zizioulas 1985.
27 Zernov 1961: 97.
28 Zernov 1961: 97.
29 Bulgakov 1935: 26.
30 Moore 1984: 10.
31 Moore 1984: 11.
32 Lossky 1975: 155–6.
33 Florovsky 1971: 49–50.
34 Moore 1984: 16.
35 Bulgakov 1935: 71.
36 Florovsky 1971: 47.
37 Florovsky 1971: 26.
38 Florovsky 1971: 36.
39 Florovsky 1971: 39, citing Eph. 2.16.
40 Cf. Phil. 2.5.
41 Florovsky 1971: 44.
42 Lossky 1975: 165.
43 *Commonitorium*, 2.3.
44 Though what he meant was more of an appeal to the idea of spiritual 'consensus' in Christianity than a literal claim that everyone everywhere believed the same.
45 Some scholastics also added in a third 'Book of Nature'. The extension of the 'sources' of revelation was primarily intended to serve as an apologetic against the Protestant theory and principle of revelation by 'Scripture alone'.
46 For a good recent discussion of authority-sources in Orthodoxy see Bouteneff 2006.
47 The manner of the Fathers has been appropriated in west European academic traditions, largely as a formulator of controversial dogmas, and this has heavily falsified their original intent; while Orthodoxy is glad that a patristic revival has taken place in recent centuries, it often hardly recognizes the Fathers in the way they are presented as some kind of antique systematicians.
48 Col. 3.20.
49 Col. 3.22.
50 Such as Simonetti 1994; Stylianopoulos 1997; Trakatellis 1996; Panagopoulos 1994; Hauser and Watson 2003.

51 For Orthodoxy, the Christian canon is only apparently historically 'subsequent' to the canon of Hebrew Scripture. In fact, from its inception (and this was why the concept of the reception of the canon took some time for the nascent church) the whole corpus of Scripture was received collectively. The New Testament, in other words, is not an 'add-on' to the Hebrew canon, but the whole canon (a textual shorthand for the biblical consciousness of covenant election) is adopted in the church through the very process of the reception of the Gospel, which both constitutes the church and is demonstrated in the appropriation of Israel's sacred history as its own. By virtue of this history being read exclusively through the climacteric covenant event of Jesus, the meaning of that history will be significantly different from that of the synagogue, in any age.

52 The prevenient notions of divine inspiration and apostolic authority are not, strictly speaking, hermeneutical, though of course they too impact upon Orthodox understandings of appropriate interpretative process.

53 Some of it, frankly, is historically inept, and based more upon elaborate rhetorical plays upon the texts than on serious contextual analysis. There are some exegetical Fathers whose works have stood the test of time, of course. With the Scriptures themselves, and certainly with the large body of patristic exegetical material, the exercise of discretion, and 'quality control', is an important part of our contemporary entrance into the Spirit's ongoing charism of revelation. Those who neglect this task of discernment do not show themselves to be 'more faithful' to the Spirit of Wisdom, simply to be less educated. The Fathers themselves would be first in the line to edit and adapt their works for today, if they were on earth.

54 *Arete* here is not simply moral probity, but connotes the energy of direction, and instinct for knowing when one has arrived, elements of the divine power of the Logos communicated to the church,

which Athanasios is deliberately adding in to his account.

55 *On the Incarnation,* 57.1–3.

56 *On the Holy Spirit,* 9.23.

57 Oration 27.

58 See McGuckin 1996: 145–52.

59 See 1 Cor. 2.3–16.

60 His central insights into the process of biblical criticism were collected by the Cappadocians Gregory and Basil and assembled in the *Philocalia of Origen,* English translation G. Lewis (Edinburgh, 1911).

61 A conflated version of the different Gospels.

62 And often notoriously built on the flimsiest of evidence bases, that makes other serious academics outside the biblical field look askance at the methodologies being applied here to historical literature.

63 The rise of patriarchy, or the suppression of the Gnostics, for example, or the resistance of the Reformers' theology, or countless other incidences.

64 Including its spiritual and liturgical life, but also its intellectual and social culture.

65 *Charisma veritatis. Against the Heresies,* 4.26.2.

66 This does not mean to suggest it is always absent elsewhere, but that it cannot be presumed to be consistently operating elsewhere.

67 *The Philocalia of Origen,* 10.2.

68 Something that could not be said of the classic Reformers.

69 He was strangled on the orders of the sultan, and the prestige of the patriarchate of Constantinople was much damaged at the time.

70 Glubokovsky 1913.

71 That is, as systematic expositions of the fundamentals of faith.

72 Zankov 1929: 35–6.

73 So too has that of the Western Church, needless to say. But Orthodoxy will not recognize its synods as having been anything other than local councils since 787, even though for the Catholic West, Vatican II was listed as the twenty-first 'ecumenical council'.

74 The same thing might be said as well about the witness of priests or lay theologians who

in times past were afforded 'patristic' status, and could well be again, since the age of the 'Fathers' and 'Mothers' of the church continues as long as Christ raises up saints and teachers in his charismatically endowed community. But bishops are called to teach by virtue of their ordained office, and it is their role, above all, to represent the truth collectively, in synodical and prophetic harmony, for the church's guidance.

75 Ware 1987: 211.

76 Iasi in Romania.

77 It is freely available on the internet at the Christian Classics Ethereal Library (CCEL) site.

78 In the sense that no hierarch would insist on their universal literal application in today's circumstances.

79 Literally: exactness.

80 Matt. 7.3–5.

Chapter 3

The Doctrine of the Orthodox Church I: The Glory of the Lord

THE CHRISTIAN GOD

The word 'God' was very often on the lips of men and women in our last, tormented, century, and in recent times too. But usually it has been as a problem, or as a desire (like that of the crazed Nietzsche) to bid a less than fond farewell, or even as a simple and unreflecting blasphemy. For several centuries past Western civilization has seemed to grow weary of God, and has, accordingly, been taken by surprise when other religious communities in its midst (such as Islam in Europe) regard its secular *ennui* as a decadence rather than a sophistication, and show no desire to ape it. Rarely has such a quest for a post-God culture gone anywhere, except to set up the human heart or mind on a throne, and pretend that humanity come of age is as a new god. And yet, all this hubris and shouting in the desert which we made of the twentieth century, wherein the new high priesthood of science still tries to mask the close relation of its technological progress with the cult of death that went with it, hand in hand.[1]

Even so, secularism itself is now showing signs of that death it so earnestly wished upon God. So, who or what is this persistent God? It is a vast and difficult question for modern culture. It is the same manner of difficult path that humanity has had since the dawn of spiritual intelligence when the wonder of the stars or the natural world, or the sense of the nearness of a powerful providence beyond themselves, first led humans to raise 'the question' of God. That kind of questing for the divine has always been a thorny path, whose vagaries can be the subject of scrutiny through the history of religions or of ancient philosophy. The Orthodox Church has always known that God has left more than his fingerprint in the heart and soul of the human being. Rather, the very fabric of human consciousness is 'tuned' to the receptiveness of the presence of God. The Divine Logos, as part of the very making of the human creature, left an abiding affinity with the Godhead in the ontological constitution of humanity. It is the sense of the loss of this, a cultural alienation from it, which is the source of humanity's root sense of sin and alienation – what the Scripture connotes with the story of the Fall. Unlike the Western Church, however, Orthodoxy has never so heavily stressed the destructive aspects of the Fall as to insist on the utter depravity of the human soul or race (*massa damnata*). Even in the fallen condition, Orthodoxy insists, the flames of the divine yearning flickered in the human species. The Fall did not, and could not, remove the fundamental condition that the human creature was a graced and miraculous being, substantively created in the divine image and likeness, and given the hope of an ontological destiny of communion with God. Perhaps it is partly because of the traditional emphasis that Catholic and especially Protestant theology has given to the notion of a wholly corrupting fall from grace, that the Western cultural image of the search for God today has become so problematic. So much so that to speak of the 'quest for God' usually denotes primarily the sense of spiritual desolation that has turned much of Western civilization's religious consciousness into mere bewilderment.

Orthodoxy is not in thrall to such a 'quest' for this God, who in fact usually turns out to be 'many gods and many lords'.[2] Orthodoxy does not call out to such a God of speculation and abstraction, but knows the name of this God, because it has been gifted and consecrated with it, and so cries out: 'Abba, Father.'[3] This is the case because there is not only a spiritual knowledge of the Divine Father, but a relationship of intimacy: 'For all who are led by the Spirit of God are sons of God. For you did not receive the spirit of slavery to fall back into fear, but you have received the spirit of sonship. When we cry, "Abba! Father!" it is the Spirit himself bearing witness with our spirit that we are children of God.'[4] It is not the case, therefore, that the path to the perfect obedience of God is an easy one for the Orthodox, for it is a difficult road for all human beings, and at times confusion may reign even when the heart is true. But, within the Orthodox Church, God is not a question to be agonized over, but a joy to be celebrated; a Father to be blessed (and importuned); a Lord to serve and in whose service to find liberation and true delight. Because of their knowledge of this Father, Orthodox Christians are not alien in this cosmos. Whatever terrors it still may have (and religious faith is not any form of opiate for the difficulties of earthly existence[5]) they are terrors that are accepted, sufferings that are redeemed, within a cosmos that is at once clearly not a home,[6] and yet a sufficient oasis for our onward pilgrimage to the same Father.

The manner of finding this perfect knowledge of God, and spiritual intimacy with him, was given to the church by Christ the Lord. It is the gift of the knowledge of the Father which marked the reconciliation between the Father and creation, and which was signed in the covenant of the church's very coming-into-being. The knowledge of the Father in the inner life of the church is entirely Christ's gift; his own spiritual accomplishment in the fabric of time and space. It was incarnated among us as his church in the historical propaideusis of the Old Covenant,[7] and brought to a new perfection in the covenant of his own Incarnation. This was the root of the birth of his church on earth; itself the fruit of the glorification of the Son by the Father, and the outshedding of the Spirit over the world. This was also the time of the revelation of the Trinity, the perfect manifestation of God-in-Himself, to the consciousness of Christ's purified elect. Since that time, the age of the manifested Trinity, the church has been in being, sustained in being, by the praise of the Father which is its very essence: the source of its delight and its spiritual power, given through the Son, and brought to harmony within the church by the consecration of the Holy Spirit.

121

The Orthodox Church knows that God is its Father, because it knows its Father. It is able so to know because it senses the surge and pulse of the life of the Trinity within its variegated spiritual existence. Christ's Church is the functioning of the grace of the Holy Trinity, and therefore the source of praise on earth of the divine mystery of the Trinity. This perfection of spiritual knowledge rises out of the sacred communion the church has in and with the Trinity. It follows, then, that when Christian communities decline from their essential being as church, the loss of trinitarian impulse, and the loss of the doxology of the Trinity, become more and more marked in them. This is an infallible symptom of loss of ecclesial being, and is always something that Orthodox hierarchs wish to place high up on the agenda of any contemporary ecumenical discussion. In its own liturgical life, its mystical sense, its culture of the divine awareness, the Orthodox Church is quintessentially the community that celebrates the joy of the Holy Trinity, as the nearness of the transcendent Father, the Lordship of the humble Saviour, and the concreteness of the ineffable Spirit. Such a God of contradictions and closeness; of enigmas, and clarity. Such is the mystery of his being made present in the spiritual life of Orthodoxy.

For an Orthodox to admit that God is a problem, or a distant absence, or an enigma, is not, therefore, a testimony to 'existential honesty', but rather the admission of a profound spiritual problem. An Orthodox person telling an elder that he or she feels the absence of God and has little surviving faith (presuming such a confession was motivated by some form of regret or desire to experience faith again) would be graciously heard and sympathetically comforted, but they would be advised to find a path home by fasting and repentance and encouraged to return to their prayer life. This is because God does not meet us primarily in our heads, but rather in the clarity of a humble and merciful heart, since he himself is pure humility and mercy. This is not to denigrate the spiritual importance of the intellectual life in any way (or the searching honesty that is part and parcel of true intellectual perception). It is merely to state that Orthodoxy places great emphasis on the unshakeable primacy of the faithful heart in that complex synthesis which is the human being. Many 'problems' in faith, in ethics, in one's understanding of religion and philosophy, can affect the Christian on his or her way forward, especially in this age of vastly increased 'alternative sources' of spiritual teaching, but the Orthodox Church holds fast to its belief that all problems, difficulties, and dark confusions can be illuminated and healed only by the return to prayer, along with ascetical repentance and the unceasing petition for our Father to restore us to that radiance he has given freely, and preserved in the purity of his church.

Does this mean that the Orthodox are always filled with the immediate sense of the presence of God? Or that they never experience times of apparent abandonment or spiritual confusion? Hardly that. Just a glimpse at the book of Psalms will show that even the depths of faith have moments of confusion and loss. But what sustains the church, collectively (as it did Israel in the words of the Psalmist), is the unerring faith in, and fidelity to, the mercy of God, even when such a merciful countenance is not always immediately visible. *Pistis*, the word for 'faith' mentioned so many times in the New Testament, is ultimately a word that connotes 'trust'. When the Lord commanded his disciples 'to believe' in the Father, and to believe in himself, it was not a demand that they should assent to propositions, or dogmas, but rather that they should put their hands, their lives, their total confidence in the Lord and his ability to speak for and on behalf of God the Father. After that moment of total dedication, there can only be one aftermath – discipleship. We follow the one we love, and in whose hands we have placed our lives and our hopes. This is the path of the Orthodox Church. It has followed this trail from the beginning, despite all temptations to deviate.[8] It will continue to make its pilgrimage along the same path until the end of time, regardless of whether the world thinks it wise or foolish, socially important or regressive. The voice of praise will never be silent from the earth, and that is the way in which the track of the Orthodox throughout history can be traced.

But the praise that rises up to the throne is not a mere 'praise of God' or a generic reverence for the divine principle, as far as the Orthodox are concerned. Orthodoxy would not, by instinct, rush to stand alongside those who think that all 'spiritual attitude' is a good thing in society, and they would certainly not endorse those who believe that all religions offer praise to the same divine force along different and legitimate tracks. The pagan philosophers Celsus and Symmachus both raised such an apparently reasonable position in the times of the early church and were sceptically challenged by both Origen and Blessed Augustine, two of the most inclusive and sharpest thinkers of the patristic era (and both of them much greater minds than Symmachus or Celsus). This is not to say that Orthodoxy does not respect men and women of varied religious belief, and does not respect their creeds and codes. In charity it is called to meet them in a communion of love, and in so doing prove its own universality. That charity, as far as the Orthodox are concerned, does not extend so far that one is obliged to affirm the old (and untrue) cliché that: 'All religions are the same' or 'We all worship the same God.' There is an ancient and deep-seated sense in Orthodox thought that the patterns of the Logos, the seeds of the true knowledge of God, are deep in the heart of every creature. The Orthodox generally believe that many aspects of other religions can serve to moisten and cultivate those seeds of our Lord and Master, the Logos, and can lead the devotees of other religions onwards in truth. Equally, however, many aspects of those religions can serve to obfuscate and delay this advance to wisdom.[9] The early church had great pastoral experience dealing with polytheistic religions and philosophically speculative monotheisms in late antiquity. It is certainly not the case, as some would have it, that Christianity has, for the first time, become aware of the issue of multicultural religion in the twentieth century. From antiquity the church placed 'religions' in the category of varying degrees of 'approximation' to the gift of covenant. The concept of 'religion', almost as something originating as a complex of ideas and rituals meant to evoke a divine consciousness, is alien to the Orthodox understanding of how God gifts his presence to the human heart. Religions, in this sense, are shades of approximation to truth, that often can slide off (since all approximations are not the truth but guesses) into some forms that are more wrong than they are right.

The ancient church knew, for example, that the monotheism of the philosophers was incomparably better as an 'approximation' to God than the animal sacrifices of the polytheistic cults (which it saw as little better than demon-worship). As the Lord said, some who were not yet his disciples were, nonetheless, 'not far from the Kingdom of God'.[10] The church, nevertheless regarded even the best and greatest of the philosophers as stumbling approximaters. Lactantius, the fourth-century Latin Father who was one of the early church's greatest advocates of how 'pure religion' could bring pagans into the orbit of the Gospel, was impressed by some of Plato's theology but ultimately dismissed him as someone 'who had only dreamed of God, but clearly had never known him'.[11] For such reasons the Orthodox, customarily, will not join in with multi-faith religious services. The chief reason for this unwillingness is that the God invoked by all, in such circumstances, cannot possibly be named as the God who is the 'Father of Our Lord Jesus Christ'. This being the case, the Orthodox would be implicitly abandoning the economy of the Trinity by which they were saved. Men and women of other religious systems, in such a multi-faith service, might well make such an invocation to the one God in good faith. The Orthodox do not believe they could. The Orthodox Church knows, and recognizes, and serves only one God. It knows and follows only the Father, in the grace and mercy of the Lord Jesus, by the power of the Holy Spirit. What this means, in short, is that the utterance of the simple word 'Abba', Father, has placed our hand in that of the Loving Father, through the sole mediation of the Lord Jesus, who first showed the church the meaning of the Father's love, and brought about the Father's presence to us, by the outpouring of the Spirit on the church. The very uttering of the word Abba is the sign and cipher of the 'consecration into truth'[12] which marks the Orthodox believer, but (as Jesus himself said[13]) also confers, along with the possession of truth, the duty of sharing that inestimable gift with others.

Orthodoxy knows one Father: one Lord Jesus, one Holy Spirit. All three are God. The Son and Spirit are God of God, Light of Light, Mercy of the Mercy, Presence of the Presence. Not gods of God, though each is divine with the single deity. Not three distinct parts of a divine complex Triad. But each the manifestation in a distinct economy to the world, of their unique and mystical bond, before the world was ever made, as a single being in a communion of hypostases, or subsistences, who possess one and the selfsame ontological life, which is the power of the Father's love. And yet what can this mean to those who have not experienced it already? 'To those outside' all comes in parabolic riddles which are not capable of being pierced except by those to 'whom the secret of the kingdom has been gifted'.[14]

The ascent to the knowledge of this God is not an easy one, even though it has been graced to the Church of Christ, certainly not won by its own cleverness or purity of heart. Even so, it is a knowledge that can be possessed by mere children (and lost by sages who turn aside to idols of their own making), but, if kept faithfully, it will preserve the church, the elect of Christ, their whole life long in innocence of heart and youthfulness of soul.[15] The divine ascent is initiated always by God. For this reason it is always a grace; entirely a gift of love. It is in the character of love that we find the one whose glory and transcendence would otherwise so vastly elude us. Irenaeus put this wisely in the second century: 'We cannot know God through his greatness, for the Father cannot be measured. Even so, by his love (for it is this which through the agency of the Logos leads us to God) we constantly learn, by obeying him, that this great God exists, and that he himself (by his own will and act) disposed, ordained, and yet governs all things.'[16] The medieval English priest who wrote the *Cloud of Unknowing* was repeating this (through the mediation of Dionysios the Areopagite), when he penned some of the most memorable words in English theology: 'By love he may be gotten and holden, but by thought, never.'

The Orthodox Church is steeped in the theological truth that God is, by nature, incomprehensible. All theological utterance is fragile and tentative at best, the stammerings of our praise. The Fathers never tire of repeating this truth. St John of

Damascus says: 'That there is a God, is a clear fact; but what he is by nature and essence is altogether beyond our comprehension.'[17] And St Dionysios the Areopagite adds: 'God is not some kind of being. Certainly not. But in a way that is simple, yet indefinable, he gathers into himself, and anticipates every existence.'[18] If one ever thinks one might solve that *aporia*, he has another one ready for his reader: 'The Pre-existent One is not a facet of being; rather being is a facet of him. He does not possess being; it is being that possesses him.'[19] In other words, our thought can hardly grasp that which is its very condition of possibility, infinitely exceeding it. This is why Orthodoxy looks with a raised eyebrow on the numerous attempts throughout the history of Christian apologetics to 'prove' the existence of God by demonstrable scientific or rational syllogisms. As the Russian theologian Evdokimov said:

> The insufficiency of the proofs for the existence of God can be explained by the basic fact that God alone is the criterion of his own truth. God alone is the argument for his own being. God can never be subject to logical demonstrations, or enclosed in chains of causality. . . . This means that faith is never invented: it is always a gift.[20]

Orthodoxy does not reject the attempt to demonstrate the rationality of belief, therefore, but it finds ridiculous the thought that even thought itself could encompass the eternal majesty of the maker of the mind.

In order to understand this ascent to the knowledge of the True God, the Father of Our Lord Jesus, it is necessary to be moved in the path of the economy by which the gift of the knowledge of God was given to the world. In its most precise form this path is a triadic economy of grace. It begins with the universal Spirit of the Father, manifested and hovering over the chaos of the world order in the act of governance of all created being, which is the order which the Divine Logos brings to material being. The book of Genesis suggests this poetically in its opening stanza: 'In the beginning God created the heavens and the earth. The earth was without form and void, and darkness was upon the face of the deep; and the Spirit of God was moving over the face of the waters. And God said, Let there be light; and there was light.'[21] Orthodoxy understands the spoken word of God to be the Logos. So it appears from the opening words of the Scripture that the power of God's creative will, in the root of all material being, is manifested from the Father's will through the action of the Word in the power of the formative Spirit. This was (in the sense of a broad analogy), like a universal 'incarnation' (or more properly 'enspiration') of the presence of God among his creatures. It was initiated by the Will of the Father, set into action by the Word of the Logos, who enlightens all things with his Father's light, and empowered and diffused among creation by the energy of the Divine Spirit. Such is how the pattern of the knowledge of God always works. Always in this order and with this energy of direction.

As God the Father moves out to creation through the Son and in the Spirit, so it is meant, and destined as the communion of our grace, that the highest levels of the creation (spiritual intelligences above all, though the pattern is noticed in other parts of the sensible creation) themselves move towards God the Father. The movement to the Father directly is impossible: such is his transcendence and glory that no creature can make that pathway without mediation. One moves to the Father through the promptings and guidance of the Spirit. The movement is perfected by the Spirit's incardination of each spiritual intelligence in the image of the Logos, whose pattern forms our substrate of being, and our perfection of enlightenment. So the Spirit brings us to the Logos, and the Logos initiates us into the meaning of God, the love of a child for its Father. It is a simple movement. It is the energy of direction that accounts for all created being. Yet it is the most complex and mystical element of all life: far greater in its intensity and complexity than the vast array of cosmological space that so enthrals us, or even the impenetrability of the microcosmic world that has so engaged us of late. This triadic movement to unity (the return to the One, in the power of communion, not unicity) is the great revelation given to the church: the revelation of Trinity that is the unique possession of the people of God.

For this reason the correct path to understand the great mystery of the Trinity is by reflecting on the process of the three hypostases of the gift of God among us: the Spirit, the Son, the Father; most notably how they work to vivify and enlighten the soul. God himself is not in the grasp of our comprehension;[22] but God as our Father, our Healer, our Animator, is more close to hand and can be observed from his economic mercy at work among the church. Although this threefold splitting up is an artificial way to reflect on the ever single-triadic economy of grace, it may lead us more easily into the character and tonality of the grace of the Trinity itself. Accordingly, we will devote some discussion on the character of God as Father, Son, and Spirit, before returning to the fundamental and complex Christian revelation of God as Triune Majesty. The God of the Orthodox is the Trinity. But his life is not an abstraction; and so we cannot invoke the name of God as Triunity, or imagine that Triunity is the highest name of all. We can only approach the mystery of the Divine Trinity, that threefold oneness, by the progressive invocation of each of the divine names in their proper order: that triadic energy that powers the doxology of the church at prayer: showing us the glory of the Father by the face of the Blessed Son, in the grace and vitality of the sanctifying Spirit. In other words: 'To the Father, through the Son, in the Holy Spirit'. And in this way our chapter will proceed.

THE HOLY SPIRIT

The Orthodox Church confesses the Spirit as 'The Lord and Giver of Life'. Both titles connote his divine glory, and the initiation of life he presides over in the creation which is characteristic of God. He is the Illuminator, not from a reflected glory, in the manner an angel or saint can illuminate the soul of another, but as from the heart of God's own being. The Spirit instantiates life: all spiritual vitality is his gift. The chief blessing of life[23] which he gives to the created orders of intelligences (angels and humanity) is the knowledge of the Living God, through the mediation of the Divine Logos. To this extent he is also called the Spirit of the Father, and the Spirit of the Son. The dogmatic statement of the first ecumenical Council of Constantinople (381) states the basic Orthodox affirmations very succinctly (in fact very baldly): 'And [we believe] in the Holy Spirit, the Lord and Giver of Life, who proceeds from the Father. Together with the Father and Son he is worshipped and glorified. He has spoken through the prophets.' Some twentieth-century scholars have suggested that this basic level of statement represents a certain hesitancy over the nature and role of the Spirit of God in the pre-fourth-century church. This follows largely from the logic of late nineteenth-century theories of the 'development of dogma' as they were emerging from the conflict between liberal Protestant theologians and Catholic dogmaticians. Orthodoxy has never approached its pneumatology in this reductionist, linear way. Even in terms of historical scholarship the theory is peculiarly blind to the manner in which the entire fourth-century patristic theology is woven from the fabric of the magnificent New Testament theology of the Holy Spirit, seen in all the Gospels and most of the Epistles, but especially majestic in the Gospel of John and the Pauline Letters. One result of the impoverished 'linearity' of developmental thinking, as it has held sway in recent critical European historical theology, is that pneumatology has waxed and waned in a remarkably unstable way in the latter-day history of Western theology, with long periods when writers hardly touched upon the subject. Several Western theologians have commented sadly on the manner in which the Holy Spirit, and indeed the doctrine of the Trinity itself, has become a 'neglected' aspect of Christian confession.

Orthodoxy understands the theology of the Spirit of God in a different way, and with a different tonality. The Spirit of God is the heart and soul of the church's love for its Lord, and accordingly the vitality that keeps the church young and spiritually alive. It is a profound gift to the church. Certainly the articulation of a nuanced theology of the Spirit took several centuries for the church to explicate fully (as did its Christology) but each and every aspect of the great pneumatological synthesis of the fourth-century patristic age is simply an exegesis of the great profundities already revealed in the biblical account. Moreover, the doxological hymns to the Spirit already prevalent in popular worship of the second and third centuries (one thinks for example of the vesperal hymn Phos Hilaron[24]) show that this theology was not something waiting for the fourth century to manifest, but was already a major part of the very context of the Church's inner ponderings.

And yet the 'depiction' of the Holy Spirit is not something that can be approached in a simplistic linear manner. If it perennially escapes the attempts of the mind and tongue to encompass it, neither can it be graphically summated, despite banal attempts by many artists to encapsulate the power of God in the symbol of a dove.[25] In other words it cannot be approached or seen directly: as if, like looking at crystal, one needs to look at it slightly askance so as not to look through it. The Spirit is akin to the creative medium of nurture in which all spiritual perception can take place. The Spirit, that is, is comparable (in the material order) to the medium of air which we breathe and through which we see all other things, most of the time hardly conscious that we are seeing through any medium at all. Change that environment, however, and attempt to see through the medium of the sea (for example as if swimming underwater), and one appreciates the way in which the medium through which one understands spiritual realities can also be the very capacity for apprehending those things; just as air mediates our vision while simultaneously providing our ambient life as oxygen.

Vladimir Lossky, pointing up the strong connection between the work of the Holy Spirit, in Orthodox theology, and the eschatological dimension of Christian life, argued that in the present age the Spirit has no appropriate 'image', since that 'icon' is a work in progress. Though the life of holiness in the lived experience of the saints is certainly an 'icon in the making' within this present era, Lossky is here arguing that the full unveiling (*apokalypsis*) of what this means can only to be revealed in the glory of the Eschaton:

> The Holy Spirit, as person, remains unmanifested, hidden, concealing himself in his very appearing.... The Holy Spirit is the sovereign unction upon Christ, and upon

127

all the Christians called to reign with him in the Age to come. It is then that this divine person, now unknown, not having his image in another member of the Trinity, will manifest himself in deified persons: for the multitude of the saints will be his image.[26]

As we cannot see the medium by which we see, directly, or nakedly, so it is, in a sense, with the Spirit of God. The work and energy of the Spirit is so intimately the substrate of our creaturely capacity to apprehend the divine that it is difficult to focus on the Spirit as a divine *hypostasis* in his own right. Christians feel and mark the Spirit of God's presence in the effect and impact he has on their lives, in the way he forms and alters their spiritual consciousness; but they cannot have a direct vision of the Spirit, or a concrete incarnation of this Lord, who is so utterly transparent, universally present, resistant to all material embodiment, being the principle of the supreme spirit that animates materiality and renders it transcendentally transformative; the energy and drive that leads materiality onwards beyond itself, never resting within itself, as Jesus himself taught.[27] As the supreme Spirit of God, he knits[28] material forms together, to greater complexity capable of the ascent to divine illumination. He is thus the source of that common energy that moves onwards the ranks of angels and the chorus of the earthly elect in their ascent to God. This aspect of his effect on creation is why he is most commonly called the 'Sanctifier'. What is operative here is a sense of the perfecting of holiness in sentient creatures that emanates from the Spirit's essential being as the utter Perfection of Holiness, God himself. The presence of the being, in this case, is the gift of communion.

For the Spirit, that presence to the created order[29] is the gift of sanctification, beginning with purification[30] and enlightenment, and ending with the ineffable mysteries of the divine communion among the saints,[31] each in their own degree of glory, that cannot be apprehended by those of a lower degree. This sharing of his own energy in his elect saints is known to the Fathers as *methexis*: participation (or communion) in the divine. It is union with the Spirit of God which deifies the elect creation, makes it into church, and realizes all redeemed intellective existence into the image and likeness of Christ (thereby admitting it to the realization of the Transcendent Father, whose image Christ himself is). The Spirit of God, therefore, not only sanctifies the elect in Christ, it 'deifies' the true believer. The Orthodox hymn to the Holy Spirit in the office of Vespers of Pentecost expresses it in these terms: 'Spirit of wisdom, Spirit of understanding...God, and making us god.' This deification is the gift of the Spirit's own presence, and through that presence, a share in its own energy and capacities. To express this great mystical truth of the deification of the believer (*theosis*) we could either speak about it as the indwelling of the Holy Spirit in the soul of the believer, or as the manner in which the Spirit forms Christ in the church, and conforms the believer to the Lord. Both things are synonyms, yet again manifesting the intimate bond between the work of the Spirit and that of the Lord, in the economy of the Holy Trinity.

The doctrine of the Spirit of God was always one of the most important *arcana* of the church from its earliest days. These were the 'secret doctrines' that it was not permissible to share with the uninitiated. The first time most neophytes were even told of the existence of the Spirit of God was at their pre-baptismal Lenten catechesis, when it was the custom for the local bishop to explain to them (only a matter of days away from their baptismal initiation) that they were going to be immersed into the threefold name, and thus what the mystery of the Spirit of God meant. Several of these catechetical lectures have survived, among them interesting works from the hands of St Cyril of Jerusalem and St Gregory the Theologian.[32]

The first source of theology of the Spirit, of course, comes from the Lord himself, especially in the great initiation he gave the apostles, as recounted in the final sections of the Gospel of John. From this point[33] one is able to look backwards to the profound riches of the Old Testament theology of God's *ruah* (or living breath) which animates and inspires Israel in all its history. The New Testament presents the Spirit of the Lord as the one who has inspired all the prophets and the saints from times past.[34] This is based upon the teaching of Jesus himself.[35] This doctrine is repeated in the credal acclamation from Constantinople I (381) in the simple words 'Who has spoken through the Prophets'. The intimate and irrefragable union of the Lord and the Spirit (which Paul evokes in his famous phrase in 2 Corinthians 3.17) is seen at every turn in the Christian-inspired reading of the Scriptures when the Old Testament prophets evoke the Christ-mystery in types and symbols. It is the Spirit who speaks in the soul of the Psalmist-prophet, for example, but the words uttered are those of the suffering Lord: 'My God, My God, why have you forsaken me?'[36] A corollary of this important doctrine is that the Spirit of God is the soul of the Scriptures.

Many people have attempted to interpret, exegete, or explain, the 'real meaning' of the Christian Scriptures in times past and present. For Orthodoxy only those who are Spirit-filled (*pneumatophoroi*) can do so authentically. All the others are merely singing songs, the meaning of which escapes them. Theologians, as distinct from scholars, therefore, (that is those who have this charism from the Spirit who is Lord of the Scriptures), are not seen as qualified for this task solely from their intellectual acuity, but mainly from the manner in which their lives in general manifest the charisms of the Spirit-filled. For the Orthodox, one of the chief preparations for this task of theologizing is the 'purification' the Spirit gives through repentance, which leads to clarification of the spiritual intelligence.[37] But its most concrete manifestation is the principle of 'consonance'. Those whom the Spirit has inspired are given the *phronema Christou*[38] and are conformed to the character and mindset of Christ. When the saints teach, therefore, they are in harmony with one another, since together they compose a harmonious picture (and living mystery) of the same Lord. This is why Orthodoxy knows a rich communion of patristic theology, one that itself interprets the holy Scriptures, and which forms a richly coherent tradition that is being continued into the present moment in harmonious unanimity. For Orthodoxy, all the authentic teachers of Christ, from the apostles to the present moment, mystically stand in this same harmony of the one *phronema*. It does not mean that there can only be repetition of the former words of the biblical or patristic writers (though these remain luminous and form the substrate of our doxology in formal gatherings), but it does mean that all theological utterance is known for its veracity when it is clearly seen to stand in the faithful line of the same inspiration of the saints and apostles of old. This *energeia* of truth emanates directly from the indwelling Spirit.

The task of looking into the Scriptures therefore remains to the church as a primary way of experiencing the grace of the Spirit; but it is not automatic. The Spirit blows where it wills.[39] It seizes, it is not grasped. It comes readily to those who are receptive in humility,[40] and resists the proud and self-sufficient.[41] Jesus marks the strongest of distinctions between those who merely 'search' the holy texts[42] and those who have the mysteries 'opened' for them.[43] The Old Testament Scriptures describe the divine *ruah*, or breath of the Lord, as the powerful force that charges the inner life of the prophets and leaders of ancient Israel,[44] as well as (perhaps a less noticed detail but nonetheless revealing) inspiring all the quest for beauty and gracefulness, that was seen in acts of great valour or skill in craftsmanship.[45] The Spirit who breathes over the church through all generations is shown in the biblical type of the rejection of Saul and the election of David, as God's anointed.[46] Not through any dynasty or caste does the knowledge of God come to the church, but in each generation afresh the Spirit of the Lord speaks to the souls and minds of the young and the old, leads them to the Gospels, shows them patterns and loci of holiness, and brings them forward as the new singers of Christ's song. In this way: 'You send forth your Spirit and they are created, and you renew the face of the earth.'[47]

In the New Testament the Spirit of God is the great agent of the Incarnation of the Saviour, forming the Lord's body in the womb of the Virgin,[48] and thus revealing her as the great mystical sign of the disciple 'conformed' to the life of her Son and Saviour: she who is the greatest of the *pneumatophoroi*, or Spirit-bearers. The Spirit also is presented as the constant inspiration of Jesus' powerful prophetic acts, his healings and miracles.[49] This is underlined in the Gospels so that there is absolutely no suggestion (as was so prevalent in other forms of late antique literature at the time of the Gospels) that Jesus' works were done out of some form of 'innate magical power'. The later Fathers, especially St Cyril of Alexandria, were very forceful in correcting some of the Syrian writers of their time, on the point that Jesus did not 'receive the Spirit' like a mere prophet of Israel, but was himself the source of the gift of the Holy Spirit to the world. Nevertheless, in his own *kenosis* (the humility of his incarnate condition), his power of working miracles was part of the Spirit's energization of his own created flesh. He who was the giver of the Spirit, was also the receiver of the Spirit's blessing, and not simply for himself (as if he had need of sanctification) but more precisely in his capacity as Second Adam, acting for the benefit of the whole of humanity, as whose High Priest he served when he called down the consecration of the Holy Spirit upon his flesh.[50]

As St Gregory the Theologian, St Athanasios, and St Cyril never tired of pointing out, it is necessary to understand the evangelical references to the humility of the Incarnate Lord in their 'economic' sense. In other words, every reference to Jesus' receiving the Spirit refers to his earthly humility as God's servant, and ought not to be read (as the Arians tended to do) as referring to his status as an inferior being to God. The Orthodox Fathers are very insistent that the Lord Jesus is at once the Giver of the Spirit to the world (as the Word of the Father) and receiver of the Spirit (as Word made flesh in his historical ministry). His majesty being most manifested in his humility is yet another sign of the irrefragable union and harmony of the Son and the Spirit in the economy of the revelation of the Father.

To show this distinction between Jesus as the mediator of the Spirit to the world, and the condition of creatures as receivers of the Spirit, the evangelist John makes it clear that the Lord is 'the one who baptizes in the Holy Spirit'[51] and who 'gives the Spirit without measure' which thereby brings life.[52] The Spirit, though he moves over the face of the earth, is nevertheless not a gift indiscriminately given. His beneficence is universal, but his sacred gift of indwelling is only for the elect. Such a descent of the Spirit is invoked only over the disciples through Jesus' own glorification[53] and because the Lord himself calls down in a solemn priestly *epiclesis* the gift of the Spirit from the

Father's side, upon the hearts of the disciples.[54] Without that gift, it is impossible even to be a disciple.[55] But although the Father has to be asked for the Spirit, he gives that gift willingly to his church.[56] Without the consecration that the Spirit brings (that assimilation to the presence of Christ alive in his church) it is impossible, so the Lord tells us, to enter the Kingdom; for the gift is tantamount to 'being born', that is, coming alive. Those who have not come alive, as yet remain dead; and the Kingdom is comprised only of those who are alive in God.[57] This is the birth of 'water and the Holy Spirit'[58] that is spoken about, and also that 'worship in spirit and truth'[59] which the Lord says distinguishes true religion from false.

The great climacteric of the Lord's high-priestly prayer in the Gospel of John is the revelation that the Spirit of God will guide the church into the fullness of truth in the course of its earthly journey after the Lord's Ascension. Jesus himself sends the Spirit as a second Counsellor and Advocate (Paraclete)[60] and the Holy Spirit 'teaches all things' to the church, and presides over the holy tradition of Jesus' Gospel.[61] The Father sends the Spirit in the name of Jesus, and the Spirit in turn affirms and vindicates the Lord by taking from the store of what was Jesus' and animating it over and again in the life of the disciples.[62] It is such a proof of the living charism of truth, or that life of the Spirit animating the church through all history, that is summed up in the great sign of forgiveness that is given to the apostles in Jesus' act of breathing upon them the Holy Spirit, and the transference of this power of reconciliation through them to others.[63] For as Paul teaches, if the Spirit of Jesus dwells within a person, life flourishes; not simply moral life, not even only a transcendent bodily life that reverses our nature's ruinous path to death (since the elect shall share in the Resurrection that the Spirit manifested so powerfully in the body of the Lord himself[64]), but a life that moves 'from glory to glory'[65] in the endless beauty of the entrance into God which is the destiny of the saints.

The apostle Paul's doctrine of the Spirit is almost as profound as that recorded by the evangelist John, though it has something of a more 'personalist' stress. The apostle is reflecting more closely on the activity of the Spirit of God in the heart of the believer, and the transformative processes that occur once that initial consecration (of the gift of the Spirit) has led the disciple through the door of an ever-deepening initiation into the Christ life. So, for example, the apostle teaches that the Spirit's presence in the genuine disciple is marked by a character of gentleness, peacefulness, hopefulness, and joy.[66] What is distinctive about all these charisms, it is worth noticing, is that they cannot be faked or 'acquired' by life-study (neither in the church, or in the culture of the world outside, which is so desperate to appear to have conquered joy). Joy is one of the most 'give-away' marks of Christ's saints, and the invariable sign of the presence of the graceful Spirit; just as malicious agitation is a sign of the opposite spirit, as many of the desert Fathers have taught.

The apostle to the Gentiles is overcome by the great work of salvation he has witnessed: how the Spirit has consecrated the Gentiles to the service of God in Christ,[67] making a new covenant of salvation: a 'law of the Spirit' which has set the church forward into freedom.[68] The motif of freedom is never far away from Paul's mind when he reflects on the power the Spirit has given to the disciple. Wherever the Spirit is, there is freedom.[69] He takes careful note of how the Spirit alone is able to raise up the soul of a believer to demonstrate the ultimate knowledge of God by calling out: 'Abba, Father'.[70] In an important text,[71] the apostle teaches that in the Spirit, becoming co-heirs with Christ, the knowledge of the Father (and the very ability to call

131

out to him as Abba) is perfected. Once again the mystery of the Triunity of the saving Lord is shown to be part of the economy of the Divine Spirit. Approaching the Spirit otherwise than through the mystery of the economy of salvation in Christ, or other than through Christ to the glory of the Father's love, is not part of the church's confession, and constitutes an anti-theology rather than the reception of the life-giving Gospel. For it is Christ alone who has brought his church peace and given it access to the Father.[72] This is what the gift of the Spirit is. This is the whole stress and import of the Pauline pneumatology. The apostle's teaching, accordingly, has a deeply doxological cast. It is in the act of prayer that the believer manifests (or fails to do so) the prophetic inspiration that proves his or her consecration. In the believer the Spirit of God himself prays, interceding for the saints in the living mystery of God's salvific presence.[73] It is the consciousness of the Spirit, possessed in the heart of the ecclesial mystery, which is the 'guarantee' of salvation.[74]

In the Spirit the church is able to recognize Jesus as Lord, and confess him as such.[75] It is this gracious Spirit who forms and moulds, in the believer, the 'mind of Christ', without which all the knowledge of God that the soul possesses remains unformed, embryonic.[76] The believer consecrated by the Spirit becomes the temple of God's own presence.[77] The indwelling Spirit, most characteristically, makes the believer 'one spirit in Christ'.[78] This is that love of God which informs the hearts of all the believers, and is poured out as the gift of the Spirit's blessing on the church,[79] making in itself and of itself the bond of the church's union.[80] The Spirit of God is the unity of the church.[81] This is exactly why schismatic division and heretical scission of Christ's church inevitably results in the loss of the grace of the Spirit. The church of Christ is not a bourgeois corporation or a formalistic society: rather, it is the communion of the life of God; and if communion is ruptured the Spirit 'is grieved'[82] and departs. The presence of the Spirit makes and marks the church's life; rendering it hot instead of cold, and alive in the glow of Christ's own fervour.[83] It is the presence of the Spirit in the church which energizes its mission and rouses its charisms of outreach,[84] for the Spirit is not manifested in timidity but in freedom and power,[85] and will constantly inspire the saints to bear witness to the courage of their Lord[86] in the trials that will inevitably mark the church's passage through earthly history.

The Fathers of the Church in their turn have a deep and very beautiful pneumatology. It is an elaboration of these profound teachings that they found in the Scriptures, and also (which is why Orthodoxy venerates their writings and their persons) an experiential encounter with the Holy Spirit which they lived out in their own lives as disciples. They spoke from the Spirit both as reflective theologians, and from what they had learned in the secret place of their own spiritual lives. Some of the earliest Fathers are so concerned to elaborate the Spirit's presidency over Scripture (at a time when the authority of the Scripture was itself being contested by Gnostic apocrypha and pseudepigrapha) that they often describe the Spirit in broadest terms (much less acute than the Scriptures themselves). So, for example, the second-century writer Athenagoras the Apologist describes the Holy Spirit as:

The one who inspires those who utter prophecies. He is an effluence from God, who flows out from him and returns to him, like a ray of the sun. How can [outsiders] possibly call us atheists, therefore, when we confess God the Father, God the Son, and the Holy Spirit, teaching their unity in power and their distinction in order.[87]

The much greater thinker St Irenaeus, similarly writing in the second century, is also much exercised against the Gnostics[88] in explaining to the church how the Spirit of God first established the apostles in the mature understanding of the Christian Gospel, by his consecration of their minds and hearts at Pentecost, and thereafter has presided over the stable manner in which the Gospel is authentically preached and preserved in the church, in contrast with the vagaries of heretical doctrines that constantly produce sects that bring dissension into the church.[89] Irenaeus teaches that this gift of Truth preserved in the church is the sacred tradition (*paradosis*). It is shown in the manifest fact that the church still contains the life-giving and regenerating Gospel of Christ within it, through and across history. For Irenaeus, this charism is directly presided over by the Spirit of God. As Life-Giver, the *paradosis* is his own vitality which he ensures Christ's church never loses:

> The *kerygma* of the church continues on an even course. It has been demonstrated that it follows the testimony of prophets, apostles, and all the disciples, a witness which includes the beginning, the middle and the end,[90] in short the whole divine economy and that operation which is directed at the salvation of human kind. This is the very thing which provides the foundation of our faith. We have received this faith from the church, and carefully preserve it. By the Spirit of God it continually renews its youth. Like a precious treasure in a fine container, it causes the containing vessel to renew its youth as well ... The Holy Spirit has been distributed through the church as the means of communion with Christ, the means of confirming our faith, as the pledge of incorruption, as the ladder of ascent towards God.... Those who do not join themselves to the church do not participate in the Spirit. Where the church is, there is the Spirit of God. Where the Spirit of God is, there is the church and every grace.[91]

Irenaeus established, in most of the patristic teaching that followed him, the distinction that the Divine Word was the power of the Trinity that, following the will of the Father, established the reality of being in the world, while the Spirit of God established the refinement of being's ordering.[92] In the elaborated tension between the establishment of 'what is', therefore, and its proleptic extension to perfection, there emerges in the writings of this ancient theologian an immensely refined sense of collaboration between the Word and the Spirit in the unanimity of the Trinity's actions within the world, but also a clear sense of distinctness of operations:

> There is, therefore, One God, the Father, who is uncreated, invisible, the maker of all things: above whom there is no other, and after whom there is no other God. Since God is rational, he made all things that were made, by his Word, and adorned all things by the Spirit. As the prophet says: 'By the Word of the Lord the heavens were established, and all their power by his Spirit.'[93] The Word, therefore, establishes, that is gives body and grants the reality of being, and the Spirit gives order and form to the diversity of the powers. So it is right and fitting that the Word is called the Son, and the Spirit is called the Wisdom of God.[94]

Irenaeus tended to see the descent of the Divine Logos into human history almost as an encouragement of the Divine Spirit to descend into the material creation (to rest therein for the first time – although it had visited the cosmos before in acts of power and inspiration). Irenaeus employs this graceful image of the Logos, as it were, coaxing down into the world the timid dove of the presence of holiness.[95] His idea is that the perfection of divine grace in the life of the Redeemer served almost as the 'persuasion' for the Spirit to inhabit the saints, and constitute the spiritual life of Christ's Church as a new beginning in the covenant between God and humanity. After Irenaeus, many other Fathers sustained and clarified this intimate link between Christology and pneumatology, chiefly by laying various stresses on the distinct roles of the Word and the Spirit in the historical economy of salvation (and their inseparable unicity in the inner life of the Triune Godhead). The Logos established the archetype of the icon of God the Father in humankind. The Spirit consecrated, sanctified, and perfected the image in the church. By this synergy both the Spirit and the Lord brought the elect saints into the knowledge and grace of the Unapproachable Father.

Irenaeus, however, is one of the first to clarify and elaborate the 'order' of the trinitarian economy (*taxis*): 'Through the Spirit we rise up to the Son. Through the Son we rise up to the Father.'[96] Or again, describing the path to salvation initiated by the Father: 'So the Father decides and commands; the Son carries out the Father's plan; the Spirit supports and facilitates the process.'[97] Here the ancient bishop was influenced by the pattern of the doxologies of the church liturgies over which he presided, and which have retained their essential character to this day in the Orthodox Church: in all things 'To the Father, through the Son, in the Holy Spirit'. Irenaeus describes this triunity of the outreach of God's own being as follows:

> The Father supports creation and his Word. The Word, supported by the Father, bestows the Spirit on all, as the Father wishes... and so there is revealed the one God the Father who is 'above all, through all, in all'.[98] Above all is the Father, and he is the head of Christ. Through all is the Word, and he is the head of the church. In all is the Spirit, and he is that 'living water'[99] which the Lord bestows on all who rightly believe, and who know and love him.[100]

This progressive drive of the work of the Holy Spirit is seen in all his energy of transforming, purifying, sanctifying, facilitating, leading onwards into the fullness of Christ, who himself perfects us in the grace of the Father. In turn, the Lord manifests to his saints that this perfection of the grace of the Great Father is none other than the indwelling of the Spirit and Logos in the souls of believers which deifies them and renders them 'near to' the inaccessible Father himself. All of this drive and élan is a difficult rhythm to express in words. It is none other than the whole complexity of the Christ-life, and it cannot be expected that it could be summed up simply; no more than the nature and character of the Holy Spirit could ever be described easily. Irenaeus' words are full of depth and suggestiveness, but were, to a certain extent, neglected by the third-century theologians who came after him. It is in the fourth-century Fathers that once again we find a concern to set down the traditional teaching of the church in simplicity and clarity. Sharp controversies that were operating at that time over the divine status of the Son and the Spirit account for this.

In his *Catechetical Lectures*, Bishop Cyril of Jerusalem in the mid fourth century advised his catechumens to be circumspect in their understanding of the Spirit, and to follow the lead of the Scriptures above all.[101] He himself, he says, will not go beyond what the Holy Spirit desired and decided to say about his own person (that is he wishes to say nothing more than is contained in Scripture). Here Cyril raises an interesting characteristic of the Spirit, his gentle modesty,[102] for he will not speak of himself, only of the Lord.[103] Cyril then sums up the church's doctrine to his neophytes as follows:

> There is one Holy Spirit, the Comforter...and no second spirit equal in honour to him; just as there is only one God and Father, and one Only-Begotten Word and Son of God, who has no brother. Now the Holy Spirit is a power most mighty, a being divine and unsearchable. He is living and intelligent, the sanctifying principle of all things that have been made by God through Christ. He illumines the souls of the just. He was in the prophets, and he was also in the apostles of the New Testament.[104]

He says later in the same lecture:

> The Father gives to the Son; and the Son communicates to the Holy Spirit.[105] The Father through the Son, with the Holy Spirit, confers all his gifts. The gifts of the Father are none other than those of the Son and those of the Holy Spirit. For there is one salvation, one power, one faith; one God, the Father; one Lord, his Only Begotten Son; one Holy Spirit, the Paraclete. It is enough for us to know these things. Do not be curious about the Spirit's nature or hypostasis. If it had been explained in Scripture I should have spoken of it: let me not venture on what has not been revealed. It is enough for salvation to know that there is a Father, a Son, and a Holy Spirit.[106]

It is clear from other passages, however, that Cyril's own experience of the joy of the Spirit was more advanced than he was admitting in this initial lecture to the unbaptized. At times, describing the activity of the Spirit in the heart, he is unusually lyrical:

> The Spirit works...always tending to what is good and salvific. His coming is gentle. The awareness of his presence is fragrant. His burden is most light. Beams of light and knowledge shine out before his coming. He comes with the kindness of a true guardian. He comes to save, and to heal, to teach and to admonish, to strengthen, to exhort, and to enlighten the mind: first of the one who receives him, and then through him others too. Imagine a person who has been sitting in darkness, then suddenly sees sunlight, and his eyes are illumined and he can at last see things clearly. Well, so it is with a person who receives the gift of the Spirit. Such a person is enlightened in the soul and sees things which are beyond human sight, things he had not even known about. Such a person finds that though his body is on the earth, even so his soul mirrors the heavens.[107]

For Cyril, the Holy Spirit penetrates the 'innermost recesses of the soul' not just like water that flows around an object, but like fire whose heat and radiance penetrate the essence, such as in iron, when it transforms the whole thing into fire.[108] He notes, for the benefit of his catechumens, that just as the Eucharist is not simply 'ordinary bread' so too the baptismal chrism is not simple oil, but an anointing which, while it is being applied to the five bodily senses, marks the process of 'the soul's sanctification by the holy and life-giving Spirit'.[109]

The pneumatology of St Athanasios, a contemporary of Cyril, was largely determined by the controversial nature of his whole life. Fighting a constant war with Arians who denied the divine status of the Logos of God, he only turned to explicating his pneumatology later in his life. As the Arians denied a distinct divine subsistence (*hypostasis*) to the Logos, it followed, even more, they refused to sanction the confession of the divinity of the Holy Spirit. As this became clear to him, St Athanasios turned his attention more explicitly to the doctrine of the Holy Spirit, and his late *Letters to Serapion* have become important texts for the Orthodox ever since. Athanasios made a close exegesis of the scriptural teachings and brought them to a refined focus: How can it be possible not to accept the deity of the Holy Spirit when he is clearly understood in all the church's tradition to be the power of God that sanctifies and gives life? He who gives life from his own grace is not to be classed among the creatures:

> The Blessed John has taught us, writing: 'And so it is that we know we abide in God, and he in us, since he has given us of his Spirit.'[110] So, if it is by participation in the Spirit that we are made sharers in the divine nature,[111] what madness would it be to conclude that the Spirit has a created nature, and not the nature of God himself? For those in whom the Spirit dwells, are from that very fact made divine. If he makes creatures divine, it cannot be doubted that his nature is that of God.[112]

Such is St Athanasios' consistent doctrine, and he draws his inspiration not only from the close reading of the Scriptures, but from the prayers and liturgical practices of his church, for he too was a bishop. This drawing out of theology from doxology was a method that St Basil the Great would follow soon afterwards in his own influential treatise *On the Holy Spirit*,[113] showing, in a more detailed way, how the liturgies and prayers and unwritten customs of the church of Christ had unanimously confessed, and implicitly understood, the Holy Spirit to be divine from the very beginning; and how it was merely the heresy of the Arians (those who denied the deity of Christ) that had led to confusion in some quarters about correct pneumatology in the fourth century. If St Athanasios had begun to make necessary clarifications about the unanimity of the Son and Spirit of God in the singleness of the Father's divine nature, while all the while they were possessed of subsistent distinctness[114] in their *hypostases* and in the economic operations of the Trinity's single salvific power, then it was nonetheless left to the Fathers of the later fourth century to explicate this trinitarian theology more openly.

For the Cappadocian Fathers[115] who were the younger heirs of Athanasios and the second-generation defenders of the Council of Nicaea, the distinction of the divine nature in the Trinity was a matter only of the 'personal relations' among the *hypostases*. Other than that, the nature was absolutely one, undivided, coequal, and in absolute harmony of action and will. The Cappadocians, in other words, insist that because the Holy Spirit is an active force of sanctification, and is spoken of as 'third' or as 'being sent', this does not mean he is 'inferior' within the Godhead. They were concerned to correct a very widespread belief in late Roman antiquity that 'work' invariably connoted servile status.[116] When Christ and the Spirit were shown to be actively 'at work' in the economy of salvation, several Arians had seized on that to imply they had a servile (that is non-divine) status. It is high among their many achievements that the Cappadocian Fathers show that Christ and the Spirit are the face of a God who is not ashamed to stoop down in pity to a fallen world. For them the economy of salvation is not derogatory to the majesty of God, but one of the most supreme manifestations of his glory.

Among these great Orthodox writers was the scintillating rhetorician St Gregory the Theologian who, with an eye for the simplest of all statements to serve the widest number of people, brusquely demanded that the Orthodox should admit that the Son and Holy Spirit were God of God and both *homoousios* with the Father:

> If the Spirit is a creature how can we say we believe in him? How can we be made perfect in him? For it is quite a different matter to believe in a thing as to believe about it. The one belongs to deity, the other to any common or garden thing. But if the Spirit is God he is certainly not a creature; not a created being; not a fellow-servant of us. None of these lowly things. There! Now I have thrown the word among you.[117] Get your slings out if you wish. Start weaving your syllogisms...[118] but the Gospel says 'The Holy Spirit who proceeds from the Father'.[119] Because he proceeds from that source, he is no creature. Because he is not begotten, he is no Son. Because he is between the Unbegotten and the Begotten, he is God. And thus, escaping the laboriousness of your syllogisms, he has manifested himself as God in a way stronger than your distinctions. So, you might ask, 'Then what is this procession?' Well, you tell me first what is the Unbegottenness of the Father, and then I will make clear to you the process of the Son's generation and the Spirit's procession. But then we shall both be struck down with madness for having dared to pry into the mystery of God. Who are we to even attempt such things when we cannot even see what lies at our feet, or count the sand of the sea, or the drops of rain, or the days of eternity?[120] Much less can we enter into the depths of God and supply an account of that nature which is so indescribable and so transcends all human speech.... But is the Spirit God? Most certainly so. Well, then in that case is he Consubstantial? Undoubtedly, if he is God.[121]

In his turn, St Gregory of Nyssa, works from the principle of the identity of operations in the Trinity, to the demonstration of the singularity and coequality of the undivided divine nature:

> We believe and confess that in every deed and thought, either of this world or beyond this world, either in time or eternity, the Holy Spirit is to be understood as joined with the Father and Son. Nor is he lacking in any form of will, or energy, or anything else that can be implied in a devout conception of the Supreme Goodness. And so, we believe that, except for the distinction of order [*taxis*] and person [*hypostasis*], no variation in any point can be understood. We maintain that while the Spirit's place is counted third in mere sequence after the Father and Son, third in the order of the transmission, in all other respects we acknowledge his inseparable union with them: that is, one in nature, in honour, in godhead, in glory and majesty, in almighty power, and in all devout belief.[122]

The culmination of their teachings was the credal affirmation of the deity of the Holy Spirit at the ecumenical council of Constantinople I in 381, at which the two St Gregories were present. The Creed shouts it out: 'And [we believe] in the Holy Spirit, the Lord and Giver of Life, who proceeds from the Father. Together with the Father and Son he is worshipped and glorified. He has spoken through the prophets.' Putting together a series of extensions on the more simple pneumatological statement of the Nicene Creed, the conciliar Fathers here adopted the language of St Athanasios and St Basil, in preference to the more robust terms of the two Gregories. 'Lord and

Life-Giver' is a shorthand to accept the argument of St Athanasios, well known to them all from his *Letters to Serapion*, that the Scriptures affirm, through the ascription of divine functions and titles, the divine status of the Spirit. The affirmation of 'homodoxy' (conglorified and co-worshipped) falls back on Basil's well-known argument: that if the Spirit is worshipped with divine honours in the universal *cultus* of the church, it is because the church has always recognized him to be God. In other words to conglorify the Spirit alongside the Father and Son is to affirm, in as many words, his coequality of divine being.

Although the Emperor Theodosius had entertained hopes of reconciling the Macedonians (who refused to admit the deity of the Spirit) at the Council of Constantinople, they were not to be realized. In the years after the council, the theological works of the two Gregories came to the fore, and were reflected more and more in the works of later Fathers such as St Maximos the Confessor, and St John of Damascus. The great Latin theologians, after this time, also began to produce substantial works on the Trinity and the role of the Holy Spirit, not least the Blessed Augustine, Pope Leo, and Pope Gregory I. The Eastern Church, however, did not give them much notice. Already the problem of languages was asserting itself. After the fourth century it became increasingly rare for any bishop from the eastern or western empire to be able to communicate bilingually. Also, the rise of the Latin concept of the 'Double Procession' of the Spirit[123] gave the Eastern Orthodox grave disquiet, and served to reinforce their more or less complete reliance on the Scriptures and the Greek Fathers for this most central and important doctrine of God. By the time of St John of Damascus in the eighth century the church's doctrine of the Holy Spirit was being assembled as a compendium of all the earlier patristic statements, laying its heaviest stress on the coequality of the Spirit's divine glory. John's summary, made its way into the West too, for his book *On the Orthodox Faith* was used as one of the primary sources of St Thomas Aquinas in his own *Summa*. It shows, at one and the same moment, a brilliant synoptic quality, evoking the Spirit's universal sustenance of the creation, but also a certain scholastic denseness:

> Likewise we believe also in one Holy Spirit, the Lord and Giver of Life, who proceeds from the Father and rests in the Son. He is the object of equal adoration and glorification with the Father and Son, since he is co-essential and co-eternal: the Spirit of God, direct, authoritative, the fountain of wisdom, and life, and holiness: God existing and addressed along with Father and Son: uncreated, full, creative, all-ruling, all-effecting, all-powerful, of infinite power, Lord of all creation and not under any lord: deifying, not deified: filling, not filled: shared in, not sharing in: sanctifying, not sanctified: the intercessor, receiving the supplications of all: in all things like to the Father and Son: proceeding from the Father and communicated through the Son, and participated in by all creation, himself creating, and investing with essence and sanctifying, and maintaining the universe: having subsistence, existing in its own proper and peculiar subsistence, inseparable and indivisible from Father and Son, and possessing all the qualities that the Father and Son possess, save that of not being begotten or born.[124]

The writings of the church theologians have often been pushed this way, towards scholastic precision, because of the exigencies of the times in which they lived, and the need to counter the arguments of heretics. In the ascetical writings of the monastics, however, and certainly in the liturgical texts, the spirit of controversy is itself pushed to the background, and in these sources there is a much greater lyrical celebration of the beauty of the Spirit of God. John of Damascus himself was a fine poet, and knew the place of systematic theology, but also when rhapsodic song could serve better. The Byzantine mystic St Symeon the New Theologian turned aside from scholastic precision to say more simply that he did not know the Spirit of God in terms of definitions, but rather from the intimacy of direct and immediate experience:

> Come, for your name fills our hearts with longing, and is ever on our lips,
> Yet who you are and what your nature is, we cannot say or know.
> Come, Alone, to one who is alone.
> Come, for you yourself are the desire that inspires me.
> Come my breath and my life,
> Come, consolation of my humble soul,
> Come, my joy, my glory, my endless delight.[125]

The ascetics of the Orthodox Church have long described the Christ-life in simpler terms than the doctrinal theologians, as the 'acquisition of the Holy Spirit'.[126] Theodore, the disciple and successor of Pachomius the Egyptian monastic founder, expressed that simply in the words with which he used to advocate the monastic life: 'Come, for what can be greater than to possess the Spirit of God?'[127]

For the Orthodox today, one of the most vivid examples of the recommendation of the 'life in the Spirit' is that given by St Seraphim of Sarov (1759–1833), the great Russian *starets* and mystic. In a dialogue with one of his lay disciples, Nicholas Motovilov, Seraphim began to glow with unearthly radiance.[128] It communicated itself to the astonished disciple too, who was told: 'When the Spirit of God comes down to man, and overshadows him with the fullness of his presence, then the man's soul overflows with unspeakable joy, for the Holy Spirit fills with joy whatever he touches.' Earlier, as they were walking through the snow-filled forest together, St Seraphim also told him:

> Prayer, fasting, vigils, and all other Christian practices, however good they may be in themselves, certainly do not constitute the aim of our Christian life: they are but the indispensable means of attaining that aim. For the true aim of the Christian life is the acquisition of the Holy Spirit of God. As for fasts, vigils, prayers, and almsgiving, and other good works done in the name of Christ, they are only the means of acquiring the Holy Spirit of God. Note well, that it is only good works done in the name of Christ that bring us the fruits of the Spirit.[129]

Vladimir Lossky once described these words as a definition that 'sums up the whole spiritual tradition of the Orthodox Church'.[130]

The graceful joy of the Spirit permeates the holiest places of the church's existence (creating that holiness by its own presence) namely the activity of prayer that rises from the church like a daily offering of incense, and above all in the great events of the mysteries, the sacramental consecrations that invariably call upon the grace of the Spirit to effect their sanctifying power.[131] Not one prayer service, either in church or in the Orthodox person's private home, begins without the invocation of the Holy Spirit.

The prayer, known by heart by all the Orthodox, which serves as this *proem*, acts as the very invocation which makes prayer possible, for without the Spirit praying within us,[132] prayer never rises into the eloquence of the children of God, but remains a small, squeaking thing:

> O Heavenly King, the Paraclete, the Spirit of Truth, who are present everywhere, filling all things, Treasury of the Good and Giver of Life, come and dwell in us, cleanse us of every stain, and save our souls, O Good One.

The Divine Spirit who descended on the church at Pentecost[133] is shown as reversing the chaos of the tongues of Babel. In that energetic descent the church was at one and the same moment brought into unity of a single purpose, and yet the charisms of each of the apostles were raised to a higher force. Metropolitan Kallistos Ware, commenting on this double aspect of the Spirit's 'hypostatization' of the Christian (the bringing of the soul into the light of true identity as child of God) has this to say:

> The Spirit brings unity and mutual comprehension, enabling us to speak 'with one voice'. He transforms individuals into persons ... [T]he gift of the Spirit is a gift of diversity: the tongues of fire are 'cloven', or divided, and they are distributed to each one directly. Not only does the Holy Spirit make us all one, but he makes us each different. At Pentecost the multiplicity of tongues was not abolished, but it ceased to be a cause of separation; each spoke as before in his own tongue, but by the power of the Spirit each could understand the others. For me to be a Spirit-bearer is to realize all the distinctive characteristics in my personality; it is to become truly free, truly myself in my uniqueness. Life in the Spirit possesses an inexhaustible variety; it is wrong-doing, not sanctity, that is boring.[134]

The Romanian theologian Archpriest Dumitru Staniloae also touched upon the same mystery of 'personalization' in the light of God, saying:

> Revelation is also the work of the Holy Spirit as one who continuously makes us spiritual, strengthening us more and more in that loving freedom which is liberated from the automatism of nature'.[135]

The Spirit is the perfection of personalism: and in that outflow of his perfection on the world, which is the grace of his transfiguring presence, he elevates all things to the supreme perfection of the Ultimate Persons, the glory of the One Godhead in the mystery of the Trinity. This is why his most distinctive act in the noetic creation is the deification of God's elect.

In the eleventh century, exiled to a small village opposite Constantinople for daring to say to the church authorities of his day that it was possible to live in the Spirit as powerfully in the present era as the apostles did in the past, one of the Orthodox Church's greatest mystics, St Symeon the New Theologian, composed a book of *Hymns of Divine Eros*. They are among the most rhapsodic of all Christian mystical celebrations of the love of God.[136] At the beginning of his book he stands an *epiclesis*, a quasi-liturgical prayer for the descent of the Spirit, not only to inspire his writing, but chiefly to seize his heart and soul. We noticed a brief section from it above. Its character demonstrates well the élan that the soul feels when the Spirit of God works most acutely within it: what St Macarius described as 'sober drunkenness'. It can serve here to close a chapter of theology that will actually never close, for the Spirit's glory will blaze endlessly in all the radiance of God that serves to delight the saints and angels, through countless ages, and which is the ineffable heart of God's own inner beauty. Over this mystery, words of description falter, and doxology is the appropriate modality, celebrating communion and union, divine and human. The *epiclesis*, the summoning of the great eschatological cry, 'Come!' (one remembers the earliest of prayers: 'Maranatha! Come Lord Jesus!'[137]), is appropriate to honour the Spirit who is the Lord of the beginning time,[138] and Lord of the Eschaton when the radiance of God will be perfected among the saints gathered around the Risen Christ:

> Come true light,
> Come eternal life,
> Come hidden mystery,
> Come nameless treasure,
> Come ineffable deed,
> Come inconceivable One,
> Come endless bliss,
> Come unsetting Sun...
> Come untarnishing crown,
> Come royal purple of our great King and God,
> Come crystal belt studded with gems,
> Come unapproachable sandal,
> Come royal purple and right hand of the King,
> Come you, whom my poor soul has longed for, and longs for still,
> Ah! what thanks I give that you have become one spirit with me.[139]

THE LORD JESUS

The confession of the Lord by the Orthodox Church is inspired only by the Spirit. What the Spirit gives rise to the church to say about its Saviour[140] is its only concern. Its confession of Jesus, largely rising in doxology, but also present in the controversial refutation of those who have falsified his name and message within history (and how many of them have there been, just as there are many of them continuing to distort and fight against it today), is part of its most sacred preservation of the Truth into which the Spirit of God has led it, established it, and secured it. This is the sacred *paradosis* which the Lord has delivered to the Orthodox Church by the medium of the Spirit. This, it is Orthodoxy's duty to proclaim once again in a bewildered age. All other confessions, exegeses, interpretations, novels, or fantasies about the Lord, it knows have not come to the world from the Spirit; though it suspects where they have come from. For such reasons the Orthodox Church fences around its confession of the Lord, known in the Western churches (somewhat narrowly) as 'Christological doctrine', with solemnity and reverence.

One of the most prevailing trends in contemporary English-language 'Christological' writing, and the great cult of fantasy about the so-called 'historical Jesus' which once lay at the heart of liberal Protestant thought and now has come to a debased form in popular secular consciousness, is the premise that Jesus was just an

141

ordinary, relatively ignorant, Jewish peasant, a child of his time. A symbol of a god-seeker, doubtless, but no different to any other good rabbi of the day, and elevated into a 'deity' only because of the credulous 'gentilism' of the Hellenists of the primitive church. Moving on from that grand axiom, the Christology of this 'new' movement[141] dispenses altogether with the Holy Spirit, as being yet another superfluous reference to the abstract force of the divine, and ends by showing its full features as a blend of Gnosticism and Arianism: reducing the evangelical tradition to an alleged 'core' of what Jesus is supposed to have actually said,[142] establishing the vagaries of self-styled intellectuals (many of them of dubious academic reputation) in place of the reverence for the apostles and prophets that has guided the church from the beginning, and year by year presiding over a Jesus cult of their own devising that has become increasingly devoid of any sense of prayer, reverence of the mysteries, respect for the tradition of the church, or of any apparent interest in the power of the Resurrection living on in the world as anything other than a feeble myth of idle minds, or a misplaced cipher for social action.

Nevertheless, the so-called 'quest' for Jesus did not entirely take hold of the academic world. There were still numerous examples of serious scholarly work that continued to be marked by spiritually faithful exegesis, witnessed in numerous evangelical and Catholic schools; although many departments of Bible and theology in the West at the beginning of the millennium demonstrated clearly, notably, and unarguably, in the quality of the works they produced about the Lord Jesus, that a radical shift had taken place. The so-called 'Death of God' school of the middle of the century was replaced at the end of it by a self-styled 'post-Christian religion'. Soon popular culture adopted this wave, with an added twist of resentment and hostility to the church added in (if it was not already there), and elevated it into careless myths of 'Christian origins' of the type that regularly featured Mary Magdalene, conspiracy theories, and lost books that once told the 'whole story'. So it was that Arianism and Gnosticism finally celebrated their long-delayed marriage at the dawn of the third millennium.

The Orthodox Church has eyes with which to see, and ears with which to hear the Gospel. It knows the icon of its Lord, not merely by distant repute (a rumour from a far land) but from daily familiarity. It has entered into the heart and soul of its Lord through the Spirit's grace which has conformed it to Christ across generations of saints. It does not need to be told that these new Christs are counterfeit.[143] It is not at the beck and call of a cadre of elite intellectuals (though it has many of its own serious scholars, and is hostile to any obscurantist interpretations of faith) who are blown here and there with every gust of academic fashion. Its understanding of the Lord Jesus is stably rooted on the rock of the Gospel, and the living prophetic spirit of prayer. The Orthodox Church is itself in the power of the Holy Spirit, the prophetic judge and arbiter of the authenticity of the gift of God to the world; this is why its task of proclaiming the truth about Jesus (and mainly by living in the Truth of Jesus) is perhaps one of its most pressing missions to the world of today. Its Christ is not an antiquity; not someone needing to be dug up from the dust of oblivion and falsification; not merely a prophetic servant of God; not merely some religious sage; but rather an ever-present power and guiding force, who remains Lord and Master of his community, correcting it and leading it onwards in and into his own Spirit.[144]

The Church of Christ, therefore, knows its Lord in the light of the Spirit. Out of its careful attentiveness to his teachings, it wrote out its first confessions of the Master.

Illumined by the Spirit, these records of the earliest believers, the Gospels and Epistles, have been established as the fundamental Scriptures of the New Covenant, and have served the church ever since as the keys to the unlocking of the Old Covenantal texts. These were the oracles that charted the long pilgrimage of history, through the icon of God's mercy depicted in the election of Israel, to the fullness of the revelation of the Father in the person of the Lord Jesus. The church did not follow after the Scriptures, however; the Scriptures flowed out, by God's grace, from the heart of the church's living tradition of faith in the Lord: a faith which was far more than mere belief in the correctness of his doctrine, but was a physical and spiritual assimilation to the consecration of body, soul, and spirit that Jesus presided over in his transfiguration of raw humanity; first into elect nation, and then into chosen Universal Church, his own mystical body extended in space and time: his spiritual incarnation in the noetic world by the work of the Divine Spirit.

The predominant 'tone' of the evangelical picture of the Lord is one of obedient trust, culminating in the absolute trust of the Son who follows the path of ministry and service even to the point of the Cross. The predominant tone of the apostolic letters, alongside the Gospels, is one of triumphant victory. Both the confession of the Lord as Suffering Servant, and as Victor are equally canticles of glory, and together make up the rich harmony of the whole New Testament corpus in terms of its 'song of Christ'; for this is a rich weave, rather than a simplistic or monolithic picture. Much modern interpretation of the Gospel Christology has seized on this or that detail, pointing to alleged contradictions or later 'inauthentic' elements. Orthodoxy, however, has taken to heart the whole apostolic tradition. It can understand its coherence in the 'Great Tradition' for it is itself in that same tradition. Even in the second century Irenaeus complained of those who took only one element of a rich mosaic and made up from the dislocated tesserae a distorted picture of something else.[145]

For this reason Orthodoxy understands that the picture of the suffering and humiliated Lord which the Gospels offer is no less glorious than the Saviour who appears resplendent on Thabor or the Mount of Ascension. For Orthodoxy, the Christ of Mark is the same as the Lord of St John's Gospel. It follows the evangelist John's understanding that the *katabasis* (the descent, or 'coming down') of the Word is not simply a *kenosis*, but an epiphany of condescension. And the *anabasis*, or exaltation of the Lord, is not merely a prophet's reward of blessing (like Elijah in the chariot) but a return to the 'bosom of the Father' which the Logos had left only 'economically' to complete the incarnate ministry. The Exalted Lord is the Servant of God: the Humble Servant is the Lord of Glory. To mark this holistic understanding of the Scriptures, the Orthodox Church continues the most ancient pattern of the Christian use of the Scripture, that is, it reads the evangelical accounts primarily in liturgical contexts: the doxological setting for which the accounts were first composed. Many Orthodox, of course, read the Scriptures privately, but in public the Orthodox Church always 'proclaims' the scriptural accounts of the Lord in the Liturgy, as doxologies, out of which, and from which, it interprets all the other scriptural readings, since all things in the Church take their meaning from the revelation of the Father in the face of the Lord Jesus.[146]

The confession of the church's faith in the Master was assembled, of course, from the rich collection of distinct confessions, songs, and creeds that comprise the whole array of evangelical and apostolic writings. But this confession grew first in the soil of the hearts and minds of disciples who were set on fire with love of the Lord. This was an experience they all knew when the Lord spoke to them,[147] and it remains one of the signs of the Spirit's opening up the heart of the contemporary disciple to the service of the Lord. It is this ever-present *pistis*, or act of submission to the Lord in complete confidence, that originally defines the scriptural word for 'faith', not the allegiance to doctrinal statements which modern thought has largely tended to read into the word. The church follows Jesus. All its statements about the Lord, therefore, are either celebratory of his mighty works (doxological) or designed to explain to itself (or others) how to walk the path of discipleship. The biblical material about Jesus shows this double character of being either *kerygmatic* (missionary and proclamative), or *paraenetic* (didactic). And so it is with the confession of the Master in the ages afterwards.

The formal Christology of the Orthodox Church (as distinct from its own songs of glory that it uses in prayer) is a long story of elaborating a defence of the evangelical icon of the Lord against a series of alternative pictures proposed, which have been rejected by Orthodoxy as heretical. The controversy surrounding each of these numerous debates in antiquity, as they succeeded one another, has left behind a vast body of literature. Much of it is very complex, and this chapter will only be an attempted summary of a part of it in its most essential elements. Yet even at its most rhetorically 'precise', the patristic language about the Lord Jesus retains the spirit of the Gospels and Epistles. And this in two strong senses: first it is a literature that confesses the power of the Lord. That is, it is soteriological in concern. It does not speculate about Christ for the sake of intellectual curiosity. It only makes statements about the Lord to clarify aspects of how his saving power has been experienced. To that extent it is a Christological language of action, and even when speaking what seems to be 'very high' theory, the patristic theology is always one of praxis. From the beginning to the present we know Christ immediately in his *energeia*, and that *energeia* is communicated so as to be universally accessible even in the contemporary world by the presence of his Spirit. Doctrinally speaking, this is why the Orthodox Church holds strongly to the confession that the Head of the church is the Lord. Christ has not abdicated his regnant power over the community. He remains among it. He does not need an earthly vicar. He is himself Lord of the church on earth and in heaven: ever present and immediate to his faithful. The church has always insisted that, to know Christ, one begins from the salvific effect he has on his world and his church. The 'what' he has done, reveals the 'who' the Master is.

The second way in which the patristic confession of Christ retains the evangelical spirit is the manner in which it constantly reverts to doxology. The confession of the great deeds of the Lord for the liberation and purification of his people, and their ultimate *theosis* is essentially about praise of the energy of the Trinity's life-giving revelation among humans and their social history. This language of praxis, for all its complexity, therefore, retained the essential character of doxology. This is how it could so easily enter into the fabric of the Orthodox liturgy at an early stage and why the eucharistic *anaphora* are profound Christological discourses, using the most elevated theological language with effortless ease. This doxological character of patristic Christology has been generally obscured in most available English-language textbooks, which have tended to excerpt Christology into small dialectical propositions. This wholesale scholasticization of method (operative for the best part of two centuries) is shown up as radically falsifying to those rare souls who read the Fathers from the primary sources. The great difference between their presentation as philosophical controversialists and their reality as spiritual pastors is immediately obvious.[148] For the Orthodox, the writings of the Fathers about the Lord have the character of inspired and grace-filled writings. They are seen to be the 'testimonies' of the saints, to the Lord of all saints.

For the Orthodox Church, Christ is first and foremost the Saviour. The Nicene–Constantinopolitan Creed expresses the fundamentals of necessary belief:

> [We believe] in One Lord, Jesus Christ, the only-begotten Son of God, begotten from the Father before all ages, Light of Light, True God of True God, Begotten not made, of one essence[149] with the Father, through whom all things were made; who for us and for our salvation came down from heaven and was incarnate of the Holy Spirit and the Virgin Mary, and became man. He was crucified for us under Pontius Pilate, suffered and was buried. On the third day he rose again, in accordance with the scriptures, and ascended into heaven. He sits at the right hand of the Father, and he will come again in glory to judge the living and the dead: of his Kingdom there shall be no end.

The whole of this liturgical song[150] celebrates the saving act of God in Christ. Each stanza is a direct biblical exegesis, a clarification and collation of the New Testament confession, for an age that demanded greater precision after the teaching of Arius had tried to pass off Jesus as a great angel of the Father. It is a synopsis of the New Testament *kerygma* about the Lord and his economy of salvation and, as such, the basic dogmatic structure of Orthodoxy's teaching about Jesus. As almost all the great Fathers insisted, Nicaea 'is' the standard of Orthodoxy; not just another dogmatic synopsis of useful belief, but the authentic boundary stone that safeguards the biblical and doxological confession of all subsequent Christianity.

Orthodoxy confesses 'One Lord Jesus Christ'. The obvious implication of this is that there are not two. What this means simply is that Jesus, and the Lord, and the Christ, are one and the same person. He who was the humble Son of Man, who suffered and died, is the self-same subject who was 'with God in the beginning' as Word and Wisdom of the Father. It is this simple axiom that marks the heart of Orthodox Christology. It has always been a matter of great tension in Christian history as almost all sectarian heresy has wished to reverse it, and underscore a profound distinction between 'the Lord' and 'Jesus', finding it a difficult matter to ascribe the honour of divine adoration to such a humble earthly figure. The 'separatists' of the past have been teaching from the beginning: the Docetists, the Gnostics, the Photinians, the Arians, the Nestorians, the Monophysites, the Monothelites; the list goes on and is still active to this day. The church worships and adores one Lord, in both his humanity and his divinity. The 'historical' Jesus born in Nazareth, and executed on a cross in ancient Palestine, is the one to whom the cosmos bows its knees.[151] The Word of God made flesh is 'God of God, Light of Light, True God of True God'. This, of course, is a scandal to many who are outside the church; for its 'particularity'[152] is too extreme, but for the Orthodox it is the heart of the 'Good News' of salvation. For in literal, and marvellous, precision, God himself has stooped down to save us. As Irenaeus said: 'God became man, and it was the Lord himself who saved us.'[153] This emphatic confession that the Son is God of God, coequal to the Father in terms of the divine being, is the whole thrust of the first third of the Christological clauses of the Nicene Creed,[154] culminating as they do in the attribution to the Son of the *homoousion*, consubstantiality with the Father. This doctrine was the very hallmark of authenticity of Orthodox belief in antiquity, and it remains so to this day. As consubstantial with God the Father, the Son is born timelessly, eternally, from God,[155] and is united to the Father in the totality of the single and self-same divine essence, as well as in the irrefragably united will and love that constitutes the union of the Son and the Spirit in the being of the Father.

It is obvious, of course, that there is some Christological distinction to be made between statements which are appropriate to the earthly incarnate economy of the Lord, and those which apply to his state as divine pre-incarnate Wisdom (the Divine Logos, or *Sophia*), or to his current glory as Enthroned Saviour (bearing the glorified flesh still) sitting at the right hand of the Father. But this distinction is not one of person or identity; only of the economic manner of the revelation to the church. All the attributes of the Divine Word apply to the Son, in all times and states, except that a proper acknowledgement ought to be made of the self-emptying undertaken by the Word, 'in the days of his flesh'.[156] For Orthodoxy, the Word remained immortal even when, in his humanity, he accepted death on the Cross 'in the body'. The immortality of the Word was conferred even on the body, for the body itself rose again on the third day and lives in the unconquerable power of God.

The Archimandrite Eutyches in the fifth century misunderstood this to mean that the humanity was so flooded with the divinity that it was almost magically transformed. He called it a 'heavenly body' and suchlike. The church (especially in the writings of Pope St Leo I) censured this view (however piously meant) as being a denial of the real and true humanity which the Word accepted: a veritable *kenosis* for all the limitations and suffering that choice involved.[157] But, as a result of this tendency to insist on the 'separateness and discreteness of natures', certain later Latin theologians progressed over the centuries towards a view that over-strictly differentiated both spheres: to a certain extent hermetically isolating the humanity of the Lord from the divinity, or only mechanically relating them. It was St Cyril of Alexandria, above all others, who insisted that the Orthodox belief in the Christological Union meant exactly that: a union (*henosis*) having taken place in Christ of two previously disparate realities: divinity and humanity. For St Cyril the fact that Christ confers deification on the human race through his Incarnation is a reality that first happens in the Lord's assumption of a human body. He speaks of the deification of Christ's own flesh through the power of the indwelling Godhead. Many of his own contemporaries (and many critics of Orthodox Christology following their steps to this day) have complained that this 'transfiguration of the humanity' must have meant the annihilation of authentic manhood. St Cyril argued consistently that not only was this a false conclusion, but that his opponents' premise (that the divinity and humanity remained untouched by one another in Christ, perfectly and mutually intact after the Incarnation) was a meaningless and dead theology that took no account of the basic motive for the entire Incarnation: namely, to render a dying race immortal.

St Cyril pressed the conclusion (and his thought remains central to all Orthodox theology) that while the divine and human natures preserve their integrity in complete fullness: their interaction is the whole power behind the dynamic force of the Incarnation's soteriological effect.[158] In Christ the humanity is transfigured by the indwelling Godhead. His human hand (one that will suffer pain in the Crucifixion) is

146

the same vehicle of light and healing when he stretches it out to Lazarus, the disciples on Thabor, or the blind man to whom he gives sight. His spittle, simple human saliva, is not 'merely' human saliva, for it is part of the humanity of the God-Man, and gives sight to the blind and speech to the dumb.[159] The impossible has taken place in the Incarnation of the Logos: creaturely materiality is now revealed as perfectly united to Godhead. This mystery in Christ is, in and of itself, the archetypal icon of what will happen to the race which will soon be given the grace of the Incarnation: the restoration of what was 'once far away' to become 'near'[160] to the divine communion. St Cyril often speaks of the *henosis* (or dynamic union) of the natures in Christ, in terms that emphasize its total perfection. The natures are one in the way the perfume of a lily is one with its shape; or in the way the Holy Eucharist is both earthly material (bread) and yet the life-giving power of God; or in the way in which a human being's soul is 'one' with his flesh. Time and again, however, he insists that a monolithic understanding of 'being one with' in the sense of 'being changed into' is certainly not what he means. He wishes to connote what the earlier Fathers had celebrated as the glory of the Incarnation, namely its transfigurative effect on the humanity which is thereby raised to new potentialities.[161]

The attributes of the deity, therefore, are by no means 'proper to' the Lord's humanity (for otherwise it would have been a sham human life, a mere masquerade as man) but are nevertheless 'shared' to a certain extent with the Lord's body. This 'sharing' was called the 'hypostatic union' in the ancient church, and was meant to convey the manner in which, while retaining their own proper characteristics intact, the divine and human natures of the same Lord were indissolubly bonded in a vital communion by the self-same Person who lived through and in both natures: eternally in the divine nature, and after the Incarnation within history also through the glorified human nature.

The matter had caused the greatest of controversy during the fifth century, and for this reason the credal definition of the Council of Chalcedon,[162] so carefully explaining the integrity of natures and their 'indivisible' correlation in the single Person of the Word, sounds like a very careful exercise in rope-walking. The Fathers of the second Council of Constantinople (553) summed up the matter once more in the tersest of terms:

> If anyone says that the Word of God who worked miracles was someone other than the Christ who suffered,[163] or that the Divine Word was joined with the Christ who had been born of woman, or that he was in him as one person within another,[164] and does not rather say that he who was made flesh and became man is the one, self-same, Jesus Christ our Lord, the Word of God; and that both the miracles and the sufferings which he voluntarily endured in his humanity are his: let such a one be anathema.[165]

The Fathers consistently synopsized this concept of the single subjectivity of the Son of God in a principle of Christocentric biblical interpretation: all the lofty statements concerning the Son throughout all Scripture (his mediation of the whole creation, for example,[166] or his unity with God[167]) are to be understood to refer to his divine condition as Word of the Father; while all the humble references (such as his tears, or his ignorance of the Last Day[168]) refer to his condition as Word Incarnate, that is enfleshed and subject (of his own choice and *kenosis*) to the limits appropriate to the humanity he had assumed in the flow of history. St Gregory the Theologian expressed this as follows:

> Consider the many scriptural titles of the Son. Walk through them. Peruse those that are lofty in a godlike spirit, and those that are corporeal in a corresponding fashion. Or rather, treat all of them in a godlike fashion so that you yourself may become a god.[169] For you should ascend from lowly things for his sake who came down from on high for our sake. In all, and above all, keep to this and you shall never err, either in regard to the loftier or the lowlier titles; 'Jesus Christ is the same yesterday and today'[170] in the incarnation, and in the Spirit, forever and ever. Amen.[171]

This is why, as one and the same Son of God and Lord, the Saviour is able to simultaneously express immortal power (his resurrection from the dead), and suffering mortality (his real death upon the Cross). He lives an authentic and appropriately limited human life, teaches, suffers, and dies. All of which demonstrates his full and authentic humanity. He is no divinity visiting the earth, as in the old myths, who only adopts human appearance for temporary ends, but is rather the true incarnation of the divinity. And so, having truly died, in his bodily life, he nevertheless breaks the power of death in his glorious resurrection. Having become human within history, without ever relinquishing his divine and eternal status, the Incarnate Word does not leave the humanity unchanged; but transfigures it in light. His own flesh is life-giving, and light-emitting (and could be seen as such by those who had the eyes to see). Its touch restores life and health. Its words give life in the Spirit.

For the Fathers, the entire motive and purpose of the Incarnation of the Word in history was that the human race might be redeemed from its subjection to sin and death. The Fathers express this in biblical terms: that the Word assumed flesh in order to heal flesh that had been subjected to death. Christ is the embodiment of the impossible: that human creaturehood should be so united with the Creator. In his own person the flesh and the Godhead are so irrefragably united, and permeated, without the one losing its identity in the face of the other, yet with both perfectly acting and operating within the other that the actions of the divinity in Jesus were always mediated through his assumed body, and the actions of the humanity were endowed with the grace of divine power.[172] Such an Incarnate Lord walks on the sea with his bodily feet, and raises the dead with a word of command. Such a Divine Lord weeps for grief at the tomb of Lazarus, and needs to sit by the Samarian well in the heat of the day, for weariness. The second Council of Constantinople, again with an eye for the terse synopsis, affirmed this principle of the Christological union in the memorably dramatic phrase of Cyril of Alexandria's: 'One of the Trinity suffered in the flesh.'[173]

It is, therefore, the faith of the Orthodox Church that the divinity of the Logos (eternally 'God from God, and Light from Light') is just as present in the Logos-made-flesh in the person of Jesus the Christ. Jesus is thus the 'Word made man', to demonstrate the power and presence of God to humanity in the making of a new and decisive covenant. The entire presence and power of the divinity is in Jesus (the Logos 'hominified' as Athanasios liked to describe him[174]), in a direct and unlimited manner. It is precisely because of this that the Orthodox insist that one of the most succinct confessions of ecumenical faith in Jesus is the admission that the Blessed Virgin is rightly called 'the Mother of God' (Theotokos).[175]

As God the Word, even as a man in Nazareth, he ruled the cosmos with his will.[176] This does not preclude the equally obvious fact that his assumption of human life in the time of his earthly incarnation was an assumption of genuine limitation (true humanity, that involved suffering and loss). But it was not an absolute limitation. The Word did not 'change into' a man, in the time of the Incarnation of Christ, with the Logos being suddenly reduced to all the limitations of an ordinary man. The Orthodox Church teaches that the Incarnation was not a mythopoeic 'changing into' but an adoption by the Eternal Word of the forms and media of an individual human life. There were thus two natures in Christ (a divine *stasis* or condition, and a human one, both intimately harmonious[177]) but only one single person presiding over both: and this person the Eternal Logos of God.[178]

The Council of Chalcedon (451) expressed this classically (though, as we have noted, in a complex and defensive manner, given the controversial situation of the fifth century) in its ecumenical credal confession:

> And so, we follow the holy Fathers in all things and we confess one and the same, our Lord Jesus Christ. We all teach in harmony that the same one is perfect in Godhead, the same perfect in manhood, truly God and truly man, the same of a reasonable soul and body; that the same one is consubstantial with the Father as to Godhead, and consubstantial with us as to humanity, 'like us in all things except sin'; that he was begotten before ages of the Father in Godhead, and the same one in the last days born for us, and for our salvation, of Mary the Virgin Mother of God, as regards his humanity; but that he is one and the same Christ, Son, Lord, unique; acknowledged in two natures without confusion, without change, without division, without separation; the difference of the natures being by no means taken away because of the union, but rather the distinctive character of each nature being preserved, and concurring in one person and hypostasis, not divided or separated into two persons, but one and the same Son and Only-Begotten God, Word, Lord Jesus Christ; as the prophets of old and the Lord Jesus Christ himself taught us about him, and the creed of the Fathers has handed down to us.[179]

All this is perhaps more simply communicated in the biblical icon of the wounds in the hands of the Risen Saviour as he appeared to the disciples in the upper room.[180] The Victor and the Crucified are one. The Lord who is radiant in the Spirit is still endowed with the holy flesh. His body is glorified, not abandoned. His earthly life is universally transcended, not abrogated. He is the human face of God and the divine face of man, for in this union and unconfused synthesis of the divine and human in his own personal life, he is the archetypal icon of our race's own transfiguration, and all our earthly struggles and achievements will be lifted up in him into a new dimension. Our lives and discipleship may be the child's building blocks of the Kingdom of God, but God, in his mercy, accepts and validates them as part of the architecture of his own glory.

Because of the immense scope of the work of redemption that Christ accomplished through his incarnate ministry, it follows as something basic to Orthodox Christology that the Son is not in the ranks of the creatures,[181] either in his pre-incarnate state or in his earthly economy, when he bore the flesh that he himself had made. As St Athanasios expressed it:

> The Son would not have been worshipped or spoken of in the way the scriptures speak of him,[182] if he had belonged merely to the ranks of creatures. But he is not a creature. He is the child of the God who is worshipped, a child proper to God's own substance, and a Son by nature, not adoption. This is why we worship him and believe him to be God, and why he is the Lord of hosts, and has authority, and is All-sovereign, just as the Father is. He himself says, 'All things that the Father has are mine.'[183] Indeed it is proper to the Son to possess all that the Father has, and to be the very manifestation of God the Father.[184] It is also the Son's unique role that 'through him all things were made'[185] and that in him the universal salvation was accomplished and established.[186]

But it is very important to understand that his is not a separate deity, as if alongside the Father's. It is the single Godhead of the Father which is given to the Son-Logos in the 'mystical begetting' that constitutes the life of the Trinity. St Basil described it in this way:

> There is one source, and one being derived from that source; one archetype, and one image. Thus the principle of unity is preserved. The Son exists as begotten from the Father, and in himself naturally representing the Father. As the Father's image, he shows a perfect likeness; as an offspring, he safeguards the consubstantiality.[187]

And as St Gregory the Theologian put it:

> He is called Son because he is identical with the Father in essence, and also because he is from the Father.... For this reason the Son is a concise demonstration, an easy exposition, of the Father's nature.[188]

The sharing of the same being is why the Son and Father do not constitute two gods, but are one power and being of God manifested in distinct *hypostases*.[189]

> The Father is the principle of unity, for from him the other two derive their being, and in him they are drawn together: not so as to be fused together, but so as to cohere. There is no separation in the Trinity, in terms of time, or will, or power. These factors make human beings a plurality, each individual at odds with others and even with themselves. But unity properly belongs to those who have a single nature and whose essential being is the same.[190]

Basil the Great notes that the single divine essence (conceived as Light) which is common to Father and Son (and the Spirit), makes it a unity without distinction in being (being God), yet with distinction in characteristic manners of being (being God *as* Father, being God *as* Son):

> The Godhead is common. Fatherhood and Sonship are, as it were, individual properties; as a result of the interweaving of the two, the common and the particular, the

apprehension of the truth comes, arises in us. And so, when we hear of 'ingenerate light', we think of the Father; while 'generate light' conveys to us the notion of the Son. In respect that both are light there exists no contrariety in them.... yet there is one underlying substance, and these special properties do not alter that substance, and do not produce disunity.[191]

Since the Son is the archetypal icon of the Father, the world (which could never see the essentially invisible Father because of its metaphysical limitations), is able to 'see' him through the Son-Logos, whose role in the Trinity is to manifest the Utterly Transcendent to both the noetic and the material cosmos. The Son is the authentic mediation of the Infinite; infinite in himself, yet mediating a comprehensible revelation of the sublime to finite creaturehood, which has derived its own power of being 'through him'[192] and subsists in being because of him. Cyril of Jerusalem expresses it simply to his fourth-century catechumens as follows:

He who has seen the Son, has seen the Father, for the Son is in all things like him who begot him. He is begotten Life of Life, and Light of Light, Power of Power, God of God; and the characteristics of the Godhead are unchangeable in the Son. Whoever is found worthy to behold the Son's Godhead, attains the fullness of the Father.[193]

Already in the second century St Irenaeus had put it even more memorably: 'The Father is the invisible of the Son, the Son the visible of the Father.'[194]

But the Son comes to work on creation, not simply to reveal the Godhead of the Father which had also been manifested within history by manifold paths,[195] not least the shape and structure of the human mind, and heart, and conscience. The incarnation of the Son-Logos was for the repair and healing of a damaged world. This is one of the reasons why the mystery of salvation was accomplished in obedience under suffering. The pain of the world in its alienation from the love of God was met and 'spent' in the person of the Crucified and Victorious One.

The Fathers understand that this was quintessentially the role of the Son-Logos, who had first designed the created order (putting into all things the 'seeds' of 'Logos-purposes' in their root being). All things were designed to accumulate to the glory of God; and this was sufficient to their fulfilment. When it ceased to be so (notably among the angels and humans who desired self-glorification at all costs) the harmony of the world was tilted. For all the Fathers, and the Orthodox tradition of Christology which follows them (just as they followed the New Testament), the Logos stooped down to his own broken world in order to heal it. Since the source of human pain had been felt most intimately in the flesh, and in the suffering of death, the Incarnation of the Word of God was seen as the 'stooping down' of a surgeon to a sick patient. The very act of assuming flesh, living as a man within time, was understood as a personal remaking of humanity's being: now as a new Christ-being which was forged in the person of Jesus himself, God made man, and passed on to the church as Christ's new creation. This was the origin of the disciple's destiny, which meant to live henceforward in the potentialities of the Incarnation's grace, and thereby in a 'New Humanity', namely assimilation to Christ, the Victor over death.[196]

St Gregory of Nyssa finely expresses this image of the Logos Doctor in a sermon to catechumens:

> Those who submit to surgery or cautery are often angry with their doctors as they smart under the agony of the operation. But if restoration to health follows, and the pain passes, then they are grateful to those who brought about the cure. In the same way, when after tedious processes the evil which had been mixed with human nature and had grown up with it is finally expelled, and when the restoration to original perfection has taken place for those who are now lying in wickedness, at last there will arise a unison of thanksgiving from all creatures. This will come even from those who have suffered chastisement in the process of purification as well as from those who perhaps needed no purification at all. Such are the benefits conferred by the great mystery of the divine incarnation. By mingling with humanity, sharing all the distinctive features of nature (birth, nurture, growth), and going right through to the experience of death, Christ brought about all those aforementioned results, freeing humanity from wickedness and even healing the inventor of wickedness himself.[197] For the purification of the disease, however painful, is the healing of infirmity.[198]

The motive of healing resonates also in Athanasios, who speaks of the Incarnation as the embodiment of God's pity:

> Our guilt was the cause of the descent of the Word, and our transgression called forth his loving-kindness, and this was why he came to us, and why the Lord was manifest among humans. Our trouble was the reason for his embodiment. Because of our salvation, he went so far in his love for humankind as to be born and be manifest in a human body.[199]

Even earlier St Irenaeus had talked about the motive of the Incarnation as the Logos artist wishing to remake the beauty of the 'lost icon of God' that was formerly the human soul. The icon had to be redrawn if humanity was to be restored to a divine potentiality (the possibility of communion with God), and the fresh icon-writing is perfectly accomplished in the Lord-Servant, the God-made-man, who having perfected the icon in himself and his own life goes on to re-establish it by grace in the human race that comes after him:

> In the very beginning the Word existed with God, and 'through him all things were made'. Also, he was always present with the human race, but in these last days,[200] according to the time appointed by the Father, he has been united with what was his own handiwork and 'he was made man',[201] capable of suffering. . . . He was incarnate and made man; and then he recapitulated in himself the long line of the human race, winning for us a comprehensive salvation, which meant we recovered in Christ Jesus what we had lost in Adam, namely, the state of being 'in the image and likeness of God'.[202]

For Irenaeus this restoration of the lost glory of the race meant above all the return of humanity to the knowledge of God, and the consequent breaking of the power of corruption that had resulted from our alienation from the divine. For almost all the Fathers the loss of the divine knowledge intrinsically brings with it a loss of the power of life[203] (*ptharsia*, or corruption of existence) since the vision of God is the 'proper' ontological source of all human and angelic being. For Orthodox theology, therefore, the great victory of Christ is manifested above all in the restoration of life given to the redeemed race. This 'life' (no mere symbol but a powerful reality) is culminated in the gift of resurrection, and in the transfigured life of the communion of the saints, but it is manifested even here and now in the church, in the form of many charisms – the conquering of the fear of death, the willingness of the saints to prefer heavenly things to earthly, cheerful self-sacrifice for the sake of others, the offering of the warm joy and simplicity of Christ to those one meets in an overarching philanthropy that constantly seeks out the poor to 'hear' them and lift them up to the common table from which they have been pushed away, in the love of poverty and humility for the sake of Christ and in the charisms of celibacy and chastity: things which St Athanasios describes as 'unnatural' in the common world order, but as signs of 'new life' in Christ.[204] These are, each one singly, great signs of the power of life in a human being. Taken collectively, within the body of Christ's disciples, they are the witness of the enduring power of the Resurrection in the world.

St Irenaeus describes the Incarnation in terms of a conquering Greek hero stripping the corpse of the defeated enemy (death):

> God the Word restored Man in himself, for it was his ancient handiwork, and did so in order that he might bring to death sin, strip death of its power, and give back life to Man.[205]

In his own account of the motive of the Incarnation, St Athanasios echoes Irenaeus:

> If the works of the Godhead had not taken place by means of the body, mankind would not have been made divine. If the properties of the flesh had not been ascribed to the Word, humans would not have been thoroughly freed from them. But as it is, the Word became man and took as his own the properties of the flesh. Thus, because of the Word which has come in the body, these attributes (death and corruption) no longer adhere to the body, but have been destroyed by the Word. Henceforth humans no longer remain sinful and dead according to their own attributes, but they rise in accordance with the Word's power, and persist immortal and incorruptible. Whence also as the flesh is said to have been begotten from Mary, the Mother of God, he himself is said to have been begotten, he who bestows birth on all others so that they come into being. This is in order that he may transfer our birth to himself, that we may no longer return as earth to earth, but, as being joined with the Word from heaven, may be carried up with him into heaven.[206]

Here is one of the first synopses of what that 'economy of salvation' by means of the Incarnate Logos, actually signified for the redeemed race. One notices in Athanasios' first paragraph, above, the phrase taken from 2 Peter 1.4 referring to 'becoming partakers of divinity'. For the Fathers, beginning with Irenaeus and Athanasios, and cascading into a major soteriological theme in all of their later successors (especially the Cappadocians, St Cyril of Alexandria, and the Byzantine Fathers), the Word's redemption of humanity through the assumed body can be exactly epitomized as the 'deification of the race'. For those brought up under the terms of Western Christian redemption theory (with its heavy stresses on atonement and sacrificial substitution) this theme of deification-*theosis* can often sound startling. It is a synonym in Orthodox theology for much of what Western Christianity will choose to express in terms of its theology of grace. Deification in patristic and Orthodox thought always means the manner in which humankind, through Christ's redemptive grace, is caught up into a divinely initiated communion with God himself in his prevenient love and beauty. Nevertheless Orthodoxy uses the stark term *theosis* in order to connote just what a radical transfiguration of the old human nature has been brought about. Adam's nature has died away in Christ.[207] What remains after its dross has been purged is a radiant new nature, a deified humanity: a 'Christ-ed' humanity, which now no longer has death as its natural end, but the very communion of God as its destiny and goal. St Irenaeus was one of the first to sum up this entire Incarnation theology as *theosis*, and he even sums up the whole nexus of *theosis* theory in a memorably graphic line:

> Our Lord Jesus Christ, the Word of God, out of his boundless love, became what we are that he might make us what he himself is.[208]

St Athanasios wished to elaborate the same thing a little more fully for his own audience:

> He assumed a created human body, that, having renewed it as its creator, he might deify it in himself, and thus bring us all into the kingdom of heaven through our likeness to him.... We should not have been freed from sin and the curse, had not the flesh which the Word assumed been by nature human (for we would have nothing in common with what was alien to us). So too humanity would not have been deified, if the Word who became flesh had not been by nature derived from the Father and his true and proper Word. For it was for this reason that the conjunction was of this kind, that he might join him who by nature was human, to him who naturally belonged to the Godhead, that his salvation and deification might be sure.... There would have been no profit to us humans if either the Word had not been truly and by nature the Son of God, or the flesh which he assumed had not been real flesh.[209]

But he remembered the succinctness of Irenaeus, and was himself the author of a phrase that has since become famous in all Eastern Christian theology:

> God was made man that man might become god.[210]

The Incarnation is thus fundamentally a life-giving paradox and mystery. The Incarnation of God is rendered the deification of the new race of mankind: Christ's elect. In Christ, the church is caught up into the very life of the Trinity, and shares in its power of life.

So far, then, this chapter has discussed the first two-thirds of the Nicene Christological clauses, set out as the basic agenda of Orthodox faith: namely, that the One Lord and Divine Son is consubstantial (*homoousios*) with the Father, and that he 'came down' for the salvation of the human race. But the Creed also contains a cryptically short reference to eschatology which completes its Christological section:

> [And we believe that He] Sits at the right hand of the Father, and he will come again in glory to judge the living and the dead: of his Kingdom there shall be no end.

It was the first two sections of the Creed that caused most controversy in the fourth and fifth centuries and to them, primarily, that much patristic attention was directed, elucidating and expanding in many beautiful writings, the philanthropy of God, in Christ. But it would be too 'formalist' a picture of Orthodox Christology to leave without an explicit mention of the eschatological context the Creed points us to, for the complete understanding of the Lord. That Jesus will come again as Judge of the World no one now believes except his elect faithful. The fact that they do believe this is the sure sign of the eschatological flame of the Spirit that burns in their hearts, and leads them to cry out still: 'Maranatha! Lord Jesus come!'[211] This continuing trust that the Lord is active for justice over the world (he will come as Judge to vindicate righteousness on earth), and also actively present for the continuance of his mercy on earth (for he will not leave us orphans[212]) is the power of belief that activates the spiritual life of all the faithful, their moral life, and their passion for mercy and justice.

It is in this certain knowledge of the Lord's presence in his glory, as well as in the humility of the believer's heart and soul, that all dedication to prayer and ascetical devotion is made possible. The Orthodox do not pray in desperation to an empty throne, or to a vacant vastness: they lift up heart and soul to the Lord who is ever near to them; who constantly speaks through the Spirit to bring the wandering mind back to its home. One remembers the Blessed Augustine's immortal words: 'You have made us for yourself, O Lord, and our heart can find no rest until it rests in you.'[213] The church's Christology, therefore, is just as powerfully contained in the praises of the saints as it is in the ecumenical documents of the faith. To reproduce all of that rhapsody would be a task exceeding any book. But it is important to note that Orthodox spirituality returns to the central theme of its love for Jesus like a moth to a flame; and through and from that love of Jesus, to the love for the other.

It is almost a cliché to say that Orthodox spiritual writing is profoundly Christocentric in character. It has a tonality in all of it, whatever century it comes from, of profound trust in the mercy of the Lord. How rarely in the writings of the great Orthodox saints do we find strident denunciations, and threats to sinners that they will face the terrible judgements of the Lord. Very alien is that form of so-called Christian rhetoric that takes a delight in harshness, threat, and acerbic judgement in the name of Christ. Predominantly we find a sense of great compassion; one that has been learned from the Lord himself. The face of Jesus, as known to Orthodoxy, is one of deep compassion. It is not an easy visage, like the smiling faces one sometimes sees on saccharine and rather emotional depictions of the Christ. The face of the Saviour on the ancient icons which Orthodoxy knows is one that is traditionally severe, even unsmiling. It is the Lord whose gaze pierces the soul; who sits in judgement on the world; the Lord Pantocrator (master of all).

This image is given pride of place in all Orthodox churches, either inside the roof dome or on the main iconostasis. Before it all Orthodox stand regularly in prayer. But if the Lord here has a severe countenance, the book of Gospels that he always holds open in his hands is more often than not laid open at the page which speaks the words: 'Come to me all you who labour and are heavy burdened and I will give you rest. I am meek and humble of heart and you shall find rest for your souls.'[214] If not this, then the other usual text is: 'I am the Light of the World; whoever follows me will not walk in darkness.'[215] This is the message that the Lord of severe mien offers to those who stand before his judgement. The book of Gospels is held in the Judge's left hand (the

155

Figure 4 *Deisis* icon of Christ Pantocrator from the church of Hagia Sophia (The Holy Wisdom) built by emperor Justinian in the sixth century in the heart of Constantinople. Until the completion of St Peter's in the Renaissance era, this was the largest of all Christian churches. It was the centre and capital of Eastern Orthodoxy for 900 years until the fall of the city to the Ottomans in 1453.
Photograph: Eileen McGuckin

symbolic side of the reprobate) and gives out our judgement as a grace. The right hand (symbol of the elect who stand at the right of the Saviour) is held out in blessing. By their complex synthesis of all these symbols, the Orthodox icons of the Pantocrator speak out a clear theology that the Lord's very judgement will be an act of his mercy: an economy of our healing.

The iconic Christology, therefore, despite the apparent severity of the Lord's appearance and throne of judgement, is one of immense hopefulness, and childlike trust. In the icons of the Deisis, the throne of the Last Judgement, the Christ is depicted seated in great glory, holding his hand up in blessing and once more opening the Gospel at heart-warming words. At his side there are depicted the Blessed Virgin and John the Baptist, both bending in with willow-like grace to 'intercede' (such is the meaning of the Greek term *deisis*) for the souls who appear before the Righteous Judge. The Orthodox faithful tend, by instinct, to have a deep trustfulness of the Lord and an almost careless expectation of his gracefulness. It is not without foundation: the Orthodox read every page of the Gospels as a continual hymn to the compassion and mercy of Christ, whose anger was never raised, unless against the hard of heart who oppressed the poor, or the hypocrites who confused the ways of God to the simple. Even in the Lord's agony of death he cried out in clarity to the throne of God on behalf of his enemies: 'Father forgive them, for they do not know what they do.'[216]

The presence of the Lord is known and proven by the grace of mercy and compassion. Such is the perfume that emanates, always, from his presence; and always seeks the reconciliation and healing of all those whom he draws close to himself. For these reasons the Lord Jesus is the consolation, the confidence, the reconciliation, and the hope of his church. More than this, he is its joy, its blessed delight, its radiance, and its proud boast through the ages. 'No man has ever spoken like this';[217] No one has ever lived as luminously as this. No Lord has ever cared so mercifully for his disciples (even those he has led with great compassion down the road of suffering which he himself walked). Wherever the presence of the Lord is; then there is light and joy, and peace, and hope, and love. Wherever men or women have closed the door to him, there the weeds of all that is opposite start to grow. But even then his restless energy for seeking out the lost constantly has him turning up in the oddest places:

> Behold, I stand at the door and knock; if any one hears my voice and opens the door, I will come in to him and eat with him, and he with me. He who conquers, I will grant him to sit with me on my throne, as I myself conquered and sat down with my Father on his throne. Whoever has an ear, let him hear what the Spirit says to the churches.[218]

It is this most profound sense of 'incorporation' into the embracing mercifulness of its righteous Lord that animates the hearts and minds of Orthodox disciples with the twin signs of authentic belief in Christ, namely, their own passion to bring his compassionate mercy, and the spirit of his righteous vindication of the poor and suffering, into the busy marketplace of this world. Without this aspect of the 'dynamic following' of the Lord's own pattern of life, discipleship remains unformed, undirected, uninspired.

We shall leave the final words on the Lord Jesus to the great Syrian saint, Mar Isaac of Nineveh. They could, perhaps, be matched and paralleled in their rhapsody and eloquence by countless other instances of the writings of the innumerable saints who make up the library of Orthodox theology, and who sang so powerfully of the love for the Saviour, in times reaching down from the apostles to the martyrs and confessors of our own age. In a newly discovered work[219] the Syrian hermit points us towards the 'Christ of humility', and indicates how, for those who wish to understand the deeper mysteries of the presence and person of the Living Lord, it is the Lord himself who will teach them in prayer:

> O Christ who are 'covered with light as though with garment',[220]
> Who for my sake stood naked in front of Pilate,
> Clothe me with that power which you caused to overshadow the saints,
> And with which they triumphed in this conflicted world.
> Divine Lord, be gracious to me, and lead me above this world to be with you.
> O Christ, the many-eyed Cherubim are unable to look upon you
> Because of the glory of your countenance,
> Yet because of your great love you accepted scornful spit upon your face.
> And so Lord, remove my shameful timidity,
> And grant me a faithful countenance
> When I come before you at the time of prayer.[221]

THE IMMORTAL FATHER

The Lord and Holy Word of God, as Irenaeus informed us, is the 'visible of the Father's invisible'.[222] Who and what the Father is, therefore, is mediated to the church entirely through the revelation of the Divine Logos to the creation, especially as that revelation is manifested so luminously in the radiance of the Incarnation. For Orthodoxy, and in this it differs considerably from later Western Christian traditions, the face of God manifested in the creation is above all the face of the Logos of the Father.[223] The epiphanies of God in the Old Testament, for example, are also taken, by and large, in the Orthodox tradition to be the manifestations of the Divine Word. The Word is the approachability of the Unapproachable and Utterly Transcendent God. He is the Revealer, and (with the Spirit) the Revealing of the Unseen Father. This is why the Christian revelation of God is always as Trinity. All Christian apprehension of God, therefore, is initiated by God himself. Our God is never an object of our own discovery; always a gift of his own graciousness. All knowledge of God, whether it be spoken of as mediated to human consciousness 'directly' (meaning in the deepest spiritual intimations of the heart and soul) or through the rational meditation on creation as a witness to the majesty of the Creator-God, comes to the same thing, a mediation of the presence and grace of the Father to the world, and especially to the elect church, through the Son and Word, by the grace of the Spirit.

That the Father can only be approached through the Son is the quintessential heart of Christian religion. The Father's unapproachability, however, is not that of his self-distancing, for our God is one who shares the gift of being with a vast and incomprehensibly rich array of creaturehood, and wishes all the noetic orders to come to divine awareness,[224] and all the non-noetic material orders of creation to be filled with the blessings of life, or at least non-conscious existence, in the vastly generous outreach of cosmic reality. The Father is, before ever the creation was, the source of the outreach of the being of the Holy Trinity: the *arche*[225] of the Son and the Spirit, who share his own single being, and thereby demonstrate the quintessential character of the *God Who Is* as a communion, and who ever reaches out as source of life. The Father who is unapproachable to his creation (yet who ever wishes to draw near), has so structured the existence of all things that he can be made known to noetic vision therein. God's inner life, as an outreach that lies outside all created knowledge and is known only to the Trinity itself, is therefore imaged through the Son to the created order. This he patterns into being as that mode of existence which comes to life by the outreach of God beyond himself: God's beneficence to creation. Communion with God is life. For the noetic creation, communion with God is meant to be life eternal: the deification of humankind, and the angelic order's permeation by the bliss of the divine vision.

The unapproachability of the Father, as far as humans are concerned, is a question of the divine nature that cannot be fully apprehended by limited creaturehood. St Gregory Palamas expressed this gulf between the creature and the Uncreated One in the clearest terms: 'Nothing whatsoever of all that is created has, or ever will have, the very slightest communion with the supreme nature, or nearness to it.'[226] The gulf, however, is not 'an impossible' one, for it has been bridged by the condescension of the Word. He is the true icon of the Father, who has made himself known to the creation, especially the noetic domains, among whom he has placed his own image and likeness (and thus that of the Father) in the very depths of their beings. Even in the heart of non-noetic creation the order and beauty of the Logos remains as a trace: a fingerprint of the potter enduring in the clay; recognizable to those who follow the traces from the vantage point of a rational and inspired searching of the 'scripture' of the material orders.[227]

Orthodox theology customarily describes this gulf and this bridge in terms of the distinction between the essence (*ousia*) of God (utterly unknowable to all outside the persons of the Trinity) and the energies (*energeia*) of God. The latter describe the impact the divine nature and trinitarian persons have upon the cosmos, both in its making and in its regeneration. The nature is unapproachable, the energies reach out to all corners of the cosmos and penetrate all being.[228] In the saints the energies are radiant to the point of transfiguring the creaturely being into the new life of the deified elect. God's nature is transcendent, in other words, and his energies are immanent. But as these energies are uncreated, they are, nevertheless the true and direct presence of God at work in his creation. God is thus known accurately in both his immanent and transcendent dimensions. It follows, then, that the Father, as the most supremely distant being by virtue of his incomprehensible transcendence, is also the most intimately near reality. He is the paradox of the ground of our being, remaining uncontained yet containing us.[229] It is also the case that only Jesus can make known this God, as Father. Not simply the revelation of deity as a 'fatherly being' (which many religious systems might presume to deduce) but precisely as 'The Father': 'All things have been delivered to me by my Father; and no one knows the Son except the Father; just as no one knows the Father except the Son and any one to whom the Son chooses to reveal him.'[230] Without this voice of the Logos telling us that the Supreme God is our Father, theology would have remained locked in the sterility of ancient Greek thought about the 'Uncaused Cause', or would have remained infantile, using only anthropomorphisms to speak of God.

The semantic terms of this revelation of the Word, regarding this known and yet unknown God, this stranger who is more familiar to us than ourselves, is at once the most sublime and the most homely, the most exalted and most humble: 'Our Father'. In these two words lie the complete mystery of the Lord's revelation to his church of the nature of God. It is a theological revelation which is an instruction in prayer, not metaphysics. 'Hallowed be your name' is the only fitting response if the message has been received and understood. 'Our Father': two words which are at once completely understandable by the most simple of minds,[231] and yet remain transcendent in their depth and ramification. 'May your Kingdom come; your will be done on earth as it is in heaven.' Who can begin to imagine this, other than the Lord? When this eschatological mystery is complete, the revelation will correspond to 'common sense'. Until then it remains an insight reserved fully for the beloved of God only (who alone are able to enter into that relation of complete trust of the Father wherein life changes its aspect eschatologically), but 'for all others on the outside it is given in riddles'.[232]

The Lord tells the church that, like the love of a true Father, God's care overflows in restlessly energetic actions for the benefit of his children: 'If you then, who are evil, know how to give good gifts to your children, how much more will your Father who is in heaven give good things to those who ask him!'[233] The equation is simple. God stands over the world like a father over a family. The very instinct in humans to care, derives from the archetype of God's watchful care of his beloved: something the apostle repeats when he says: 'For this reason I bow my knees before the Father, from whom every family in heaven and on earth is named.'[234] Perhaps there are those, even in the church, who might regard this as a simplistic statement; in the light, doubtless, of the vast amount of lack of love that appears to be in evidence in so much of the world's dealings. But it was given to the church as a profound revelation of the character of the Father, by the Lord himself, in the agony of his suffering in the Garden when he said, 'Abba, Father, all things are possible to you; remove this cup from me; yet not my will, but yours be done.'[235] It was not given to the church by the Lord in a careless way or a random moment of optimism, but as a pattern of truth from the heart of the economy of his suffering. In joy, or in sorrow, the Lord taught that all things come to the beloved of the Father, as from the hands of one who gives the gifts of love, for: 'Are not two sparrows sold for a penny? Yet not one of them falls to the ground without your Father's will.'[236] This teaching is meant to give us courage: 'For even the hairs of your head are all numbered. Do not be afraid, therefore; you are of more value than many sparrows.'[237] And it does: even though it was spoken with great challenge from the Lord to the disciples, as he invited them to walk with him to Jerusalem, where they (rightly) suspected he would come to his death, and set them on the road to theirs.

What a difference was manifested between his and their embrace of the gift of the Father in the time of his Passion. For them chaos reigned, in that last week; for him the gift of the Father steadily unrolled. The Lord nevertheless modelled for them the disciple's illumined understanding of the nature of the Father's dealings with his beloved ones, challenging them to adopt his own perspectives of faith: that nothing comes by fate or chance, all comes from the invitation of the love of the Father, and it is manifested to them in love, and through love, for their perfection as children of God. If the disciples rise into this faith, accept it from the Lord's hands, so it becomes a luminous metaphysical reality for them. God is not merely revealed as their Father, they themselves are now revealed as the children of God in whom only the love of God is manifested, and fate is overcome and cast aside, in favour of a God-graced destiny. What it is for those who are not the beloved children is not said, and is obscure to theology; though God is all-merciful and infinitely generous.

Our God is the Father of Mercies,[238] the loving Father of the beloved; outside that relationship there is no knowledge of the true God – intimations of a self-made God, perhaps, which *de facto* prove to be false. Those who have glimpsed the light of this most simple of revelations of the inner structure of God's dealings with his cosmos understand in the same moment that they are lifted out of childish passivity to become 'as gods' for others in their turn: 'Be children of your Father who is in heaven', the Lord told his church, 'For he makes his sun rise on the evil and on the good, and sends rain upon the just and the unjust alike.'[239] This is why the Lord's command (otherwise so impossible) can be fulfilled: to 'be as perfect as the Father is',[240] by loving as the Father does. The summation of all ethics is this vital knowledge of how loving the Father is: 'Be merciful, even as your Father is merciful.'[241] Only the Father's love can make men and women rise to the stature of the beloved children of light,[242] for this is more than a mere philanthropy, it is a mystically graced lifestyle (seen abundantly *in concreto* in Jesus) that begins to embrace all men and women in a power of love that exceeds the ordinary human capacity for affection, and takes on the character of the selfless 'willing of the good of others' that marks God's character vis-à-vis his creation.

Only in this stature, as God's children of light, acting from the light of the Spirit and in the communion of the Son, can men and women understand the nature of God, as it is at its heart: 'in spirit and in truth'.[243] For those who have become the children of God, in Christ and his transfiguring Spirit, all is changed. The world is utterly changed in that moment: essentially and metaphysically altered. The face of God is shown to be other than it could possibly have been understood to have been from the evidence of the world. Fate dies on the vine in that instant and destiny flowers out in a binding together of creature and Creator, a fashioning of a new covenant that grows from the placing of the child's hand in that of the Father, following the example of the Son *par excellence*, who trusted his Father in all things, and made of the dark and bitter Cross a source of light for the cosmos, challenging his disciples not to lose faith: 'Let not your hearts be troubled; trust in God, trust also in me.'[244] This light falls upon a troubled and darkened world where humans continue to hold others in enduring bondage, and it reveals to the children of God the will, and the ways, to subvert the manifold forms of dark fate for the enlightenment and liberation of the suffering. So it is that the 'children of the day' fulfil the Lord's own urgent prayer: 'May your kingdom come! May your will be done on earth as it is in heaven.'

The New Testament revelation of the Father is, therefore, at once a most simple and an immensely complex one; one that is bound up in the Lord's own pilgrimage to his Cross, and in the disciples' unfolding understanding of what the Lord himself meant by 'trust' (*pistis*) in God. It remains the case to this day, in the ongoing spiritual life of the church, that the Lord's faithful make their own progress into the active understanding of God's Fatherhood as they walk alongside their Lord, and learn total abandonment to the will of the Father for their good (the Father who knows what we need before we ask him[245]). The understanding of God as Father is a given revelation. It is also an ongoing mystery of the Spirit which is only accessible to those who walk with the Lord, and thus share in his own Sonship. For it is through his Sonship that we have all become co-heirs; and in no other way.[246]

The Church Fathers pondered this mystery of God the Father most deeply and left their characteristic mark on all subsequent Orthodox theology. For most of them the two primary truths theology ought to confess about the Father are, first, the fact that it is he himself who directly wills and blesses the creation of all things as a good and light-filled act of beneficence, through the medium of his Son and Logos; and, secondly, the manner in which the human mind falters in the face of describing God truly. The first thesis was designed to stand against all manner of Gnostics who believed that they could only defend the divine transcendence by denying a directly divine volition of creation. The second was comparable to the building of a fence of 'reverent diffidence' around those affirmations that the feeble human mind could assert about the One who ultimately transcends.

The Greek Fathers, in particular, are very cautious about the possibility of the human mind posing as an 'expert' on God. 'Although the deity is without form, and nameless, we use theological descriptions', Clement of Alexandria says,[247] 'mainly so that our mind will have something to rest on, so as to stop it wandering at random.' This is the so-called 'apophatic' tradition of Orthodox thought, deriving its name from the Greek term 'to turn away from speech'. It is most clearly exemplified in the theologian Dionysios the Areopagite,[248] but it was a tradition within the church's theologians long before him. In the apophatic approach, the titles of God ('Lord' connoting his power,

'Light' connoting his mercy, 'Fire' connoting his restless energy, and so on) always describe the actions of God in the cosmos, rather than the nature of God in himself, which remains beyond the scope of human enquiry, except in so far as some of the revelations of the Logos have 'imaged' it to the church in specific revelations. God, as the originator of all being, who is outside the limitation of being which describes and defines all created existence, abides by definition as incomprehensible in being, and mysterious in effect. His essence is wholly unknowable (except to the Son and Spirit) and his energies in the world are ineffable and life-giving to the creation, whereby it knows the power and presence of its God, intimately and joyfully. Later in the medieval period, the Greek hesychast writers would refine this argument by insisting that, as the 'energies' of God were uncreated (that is, divine), when they were experienced within the world this was equatable with a genuine and authentic experience of God available within the created orders of existence, even though the perfect apprehension of God's essence remained unknowable. Thus, God was perfectly unknowable (in himself) and yet known intimately and authentically in his economy of revelation to his creation.

Although the Scriptures, in perhaps a simpler medium of discourse, are full of the sense of God's nearness as a 'Shepherd of Israel' leading his people through their history, the later writings of the Church Fathers who speak about apophatic theology were equally impressed by the need to emphasize the Father's ultimate transcendence. This character of combining the simpler affirmations of the Scriptures about a God who acts brusquely and directly within history, with more sophisticated reflections on the nature of the Absolute Transcendent One who is Lord over history and not contained by it, has been distinctive of Christian discourse from the earliest times, and is a rhythm of Orthodox theology to this day which is invoked easily and smoothly in both private prayer and formal worship. Most of the exegetical writings of the great Fathers of the Orthodox Church are concerned with this double level of discourse about God: what is appropriate for simpler believers, or appropriate to the heart's outpourings in times of prayer and thankfulness; and what is appropriate to the mind when wrestling with the deeper mysteries of creation, and with the incomprehensible mystery of our God. The Father is, at one and the same moment, the loving parent who has given us 'our daily bread', and also the Almighty Pantocrator, the Cosmic Lord who has left us creatures of flesh and blood standing awed, as it were, in a vast universe, blinking with our minds over the vast complexity of it all.

Clement of Alexandria refers to our mental bankruptcy facing such a God when he says:

> Since the First Cause of everything is exceedingly difficult to discover, the original and supreme cause is very hard to describe, the cause which is the reason of the coming into being and of the continued existence of all things. For how can that be spoken of which is not genus, differentiation, species, individual, number, accident or subject of accident?[249]

Because of the 'difficulty' of knowing God, theology (as the Orthodox understand it) has a strict duty imposed upon it to be profoundly humble and tentative. It has often failed abysmally in this regard, and in so doing has departed from its vocation to ascend as theology, usually degenerating into religious speculation, which is something very different indeed. St Gregory the Theologian spends much time in his *First Theological Oration* insisting that the words of theology, rising to speak about God, become so sacred that they are powerfully sacramental: and accordingly can only be handled by those who have been 'consecrated'. Such a consecration, for Gregory, is provided by the 'purification' of mind and life (through Christian ascesis), that must necessarily precede all speech about God. It is a sacred matter. If it is carelessly engaged in, or launched as speculation by those who have not allowed their hearts to be quietened by the finger of God, then it can be a sacrilege:

> Discussion of theology is not a matter for anyone, only for those who have been tested and have solid foundations in learning and, more important, have undergone, or are in process of, purification of body and soul. It is as dangerous a thing for someone to lay hold of pure things who is not pure himself, as it is for weak eyes to look at the sun's radiance.[250]

When one uses the many scriptural descriptors of God, and deduces something of the Lord's power from them, such as his unity,[251] his all-powerfulness,[252] his omnipresence,[253] his wisdom,[254] his invisibility,[255] and so forth, it is important, therefore, to realize that first and foremost these theological terms describe the economy of the Father's salvation among us: not his essence.[256] They are 'relative' attributes (however 'all-embracing' they set out to be as 'infinite-sounding' words) of the Father who escapes all finite human thought and speech; and can only be rightly apprehended in the love of the Son, fostered by the grace of the Holy Spirit. The highest level of theology is to follow the divine commandment itself: 'Be still, and know that I am God.'[257] How sad it is when theology forgets its need to be quiet, and humble, and becomes ashamed of its 'stammering character' (what St Gregory of Nazianzus called 'fisherman's rhetoric'), and then begins to bluster. How much sadder still, and wearily tiresome, when it becomes a matter of denunciations and hateful speech, or a shoddy slopping together of citations and verses of evidence.

One of the greatest of patristic theologians, St Gregory of Nazianzus, expressed how theology always needed to remember it was 'praxis' never 'theoria' when it came to discourse about God. It did not express how things were in the divine essence, but only how God's energy and grace effected his creatures:

> God is light: the highest, the unapproachable, the ineffable. It cannot be conceived in the mind, or spoken with the lips. It is the light which gives life to every reasoning creature. God is, to the noetic world, what the sun is to the material world. He presents himself to our spiritual intellects to the degree that we have been purified. He is loved to the degree that he is presented to our spiritual intellects, and understood to the degree that we love him. He contemplates and comprehends himself and pours himself out upon what is external to him.[258]

Orthodox theology tries to preserve its fidelity to 'fisherman's rhetoric' by never breaking the link between theology and doxology. If a statement about God cannot (without the slightest of difficulty) be 'translated back' into prayer and acclamation, it is surely suspect. If it is not a glorification, it is surely false. If it does not proceed from the overflowings of the heart, it is unquestionably otiose. If it is not an affirmation of mercy, it is not Christian. The most reliable springs of Orthodox theology, accordingly, have always been the sources of doxology: the prophetic and apostolic writings, the

Divine Liturgy and hymns of the church, the writings of its saints. In the following excerpt from St John of Damascus, it is clear that, while the theologian attempts to sum up all the 'positive affirmations' one can make about God in the clearest and shortest way, what results is not a scholastic list of the 'attributes of God' as much as a song of praise. The titles become, as it were, a litany of wondering prayer. In the hands of this masterful theologian we find dense thought about God turning almost into a liturgical song:

> We believe, then, in One God, one beginning, having no beginning, uncreated, unbegotten, imperishable and immortal, everlasting, infinite, uncircumscribed, bound-less, of infinite power, simple, uncompounded, incorporeal, without flux, passionless, unchangeable, unalterable, unseen, the fountain of goodness and justice, the light of the mind, inaccessible; a power known by no measure, measurable only by his own will alone for all things that he wills he can accomplish, creator of all created things, seen or unseen, the maintainer and preserver of all, and for all the provider, being master and lord and king over all, with an endless and immortal kingdom. He has no contrary, filling all, encompassed by nothing, but rather himself the encompasser and maintainer and original possessor of the universe, occupying all essences intact and extending beyond all things, and being separate from all essence as being super-essential and above all things and absolute God, absolute goodness, and absolute fullness: determin-ing all sovereignties and ranks, being placed above all sovereignty and rank, above essence and life and word and thought: being himself very light and goodness and life and essence, inasmuch as he does not derive his being from another, that is to say, of any of those things that exist: but being himself the fountain of being to all that is, of life to the living, of reason to those that have reason; the cause of all good to all things: perceiving all things even before they have become: one essence, one divinity, one power, one will, one energy, one beginning, one authority, one dominion, one sover-eignty, made known in three perfect subsistences [*hypostases*] and adored with one single adoration; believed in and worshipped by all rational creation.[259]

While it would be possible to find innumerable Orthodox prayers to the Lord Jesus with which to illustrate the Orthodox Church's understanding of its Christology, it is a much more difficult thing to find almost any prayer that succinctly illustrates Orthodoxy's sense of the Father. This is because almost every prayer is addressed to the Trinity as a whole; coming at the Father through the Son and the Spirit. The great exception, of course, is the Lord's own prayer: the 'Our Father', which in a few syllogisms teaches us the essential mysteries we have already spoken of: that the Father is to be glorified because he is our loving Father; that the heart which understands this launches out thereby into ecstatic praise of the holiness, earnestly calls for the will of the Father to be manifested on the face of the earth, and in the meantime trustingly calls upon God to provide and protect. The Father is the focus, however, of perhaps the greatest and most solemn prayer in Orthodoxy after this, namely the Anaphora or great eucharistic prayer. All this prayer (and, without exception, any prayer invoking the Father in Orthodoxy) is set in a trinitarian context, if not explicitly so, then by the final doxology, but those doxologies of prayers which end 'And this we ask through your beloved Son, with whom you are blessed together with your all holy, good, and life-giving Spirit' demonstrate those invocations which have specifically 'begun' with the address to the Father. The Anaphora, and one of the intercessions from the priest's

'Prayers of the Lamplighting' taken from Orthodox Vespers, will illustrate the typical Orthodox celebration of the mercies of the Father-Creator.

The first is the invocation of God as Father that begins the eucharistic Anaphora:

> It is fitting and right to hymn you, to bless you, to praise you, to give you thanks, and worship you in every place of your dominion; for you are God, ineffable, incomprehensible, invisible, inconceivable, ever-existing, eternally the same, You and your only-begotten Son, and your Holy Spirit. You brought us out from non-existence into being, and when we had fallen, you raised us up again, and left nothing undone until you had brought us up to heaven, and granted us the Kingdom that is to come. For all these things we give thanks to you, and to your only-begotten Son, and to your Holy Spirit; for all the benefits that we have received, both known and unknown, manifest and hidden. We thank you also for this liturgy which you have been pleased to accept from our hands, even though there stand around you thousands of archangels and tens of thousands of angels, the Cherubim and the Seraphim, six-winged and many-eyed, soaring aloft upon their wings, singing the triumphant hymn, shouting, proclaiming and saying: Holy, Holy, Holy, Lord of Hosts. Heaven and earth are full of your glory. Hosannah in the highest. Blessed is he who comes in the name of the Lord. Hosannah in the highest.[260]

The theme of the prayer is clearly the trinitarian access to God through the Son and Spirit, but celebrates the Father as the Unapproachable One who approached his world to give it life and healing, and whose continued approach sends the heart and soul of the creature who recognizes him into the ecstasy of praise: that song of the angels[261] which is left speechless (before the Ineffable God) except for the incantation 'Holy!' The prayer connects the majesty and ineffability of God most directly with his intimate and loving providence. Such is Orthodoxy's essential understanding of God as 'Father'.

All seven of the Lamplighting Prayers address God as Trinity except the fifth. This one, addressed to the Father specifically, is, nevertheless, thoroughly trinitarian in character. At this point of the Vespers' service the priest prays silently while the congregation sing Psalm 103 to celebrate the beauties of the Creator seen in the creation:

> Lord, Lord, who hold all things in the hollow of your hand, and who are long-suffering to us all, yet grieved by our wickedness; remember your compassion and your mercy. Look down on us in your goodness and grant that through the remainder of this day, by your grace, we may avoid the varied and subtle snares of the evil one. Guard our life from all dangers through the grace of your all-holy Spirit; through the mercy and philanthropy of your only-begotten Son; with whom you are blessed, together with your all-holy, good, and life-giving Spirit; now and forever, and to the ages of ages. Amen.[262]

One notices, yet again, the recurring sense of how God's Fatherhood is seen to cover the world through the grace of the creation, and the mercy of his active providence.[263] This prayer goes further in taking up the concluding themes of the Lord's Prayer itself: namely that God's Fatherhood is also seen to be active in his dispensation of forgiveness, and in his protection of his beloved from the machinations of the evil one.

Perhaps we may sum up with the very simple observation that for Orthodoxy the understanding of God as Father is a matter for praise and blessing: a celebration of

God's providence that, in the act of celebrating it, confirms the disciple's understanding of it, and reveals it as ever-extending through the economy of the Son and the Spirit. In the act of appropriating it, it also stimulates the disciple's vocation to bring that light of justice and mercy to the dark places of the world.

Attributed to the very early writer St Ioannikios is one of the shortest and simplest of all theologies. Like the best of Orthodox confession, having said little, and having said enough, it returns to the silence of wonder:

> The Father is my hope.
> The Son is my refuge.
> The Holy Spirit is my protection.
> O Holy Trinity: Glory to you !

THE HOLY TRINITY

The prayers and liturgy of the Orthodox Church sum up its doctrine of God – its theology therefore – almost at every instance, by either calling upon God as the Holy Trinity, or by asking the Lord Jesus' intercession for the grace of the Spirit to lead the church to the mercy and graciousness of the Father. In either case, the entire conception of God is witnessed in the day-to-day life of the church to be essentially trinitarian. There is no other way to conceive of God, for the Orthodox, and certainly no other way to invoke him. Accordingly there is no tendency in Orthodoxy, as in some aspects of Western Christianity for example, to have a 'Jesus-centred' cult, or 'Spirit-centred worship' which seem, in many ways, disconnected from a trinitarian foundation. The doctrine of the Trinity, which for so much of Western Christianity seems an odd, intellectualist conundrum, almost a meaningless part of religious life that is barely mentioned in the churches, is, for the Orthodox, a basic and regular rhythm of private prayer and liturgical life. It goes without saying that, in each and every church service, one will hear the trinitarian doxologies repeated many hundreds of times. The Orthodox grow up with the embedded sense of the dynamism of 'God as Trinity' in their lives; and it is no disconnected theological theory that they understand by that term, but rather the nearness and graciousness of God active in their life: by the grace of the Spirit, in the glory of Jesus, to the mercy of the Father's embrace.

Orthodox instinctively wish to speak of the Trinity whenever the notion of 'theology' proper is raised, often to the perplexity of their listeners who might not share the same ethos. The Russian theologian Fedorov raised many eyebrows in the World Council of Churches during an ecumenical discussion some time ago, when he replied to a question about the Orthodox Church's 'social policy' and gave the answer back that it was the Divine Trinity! What he meant by that was immediately obvious to the Orthodox, though perhaps not to many others. God in his very essence (he who is as communion of eternal persons) and in his economy of salvation (he who is to us as Maker, Saviour, and Life-Giver) gives the constant witness to the world of the fundamental nature of the spiritual life as the communion of love. Being, in its most elevated and fulfilled form, is the communion of love. All in human society that is not radiant as an icon of loving communion is contrary to the purposes of God's Kingdom and must be steadfastly opposed by his church.

166

Human social and cultural life (as a spiritual force) demonstrates this quality of seeking depth through complexity, and greater richness through interconnectedness. All wisdom and insight is nurtured in communion. What the Trinity reveals to us, as a flashing sidelight of its infinite mystery, is something beyond this: that the spiritual perfection of humanity will be in the communion of the saints gathered around the love of God. Love, therefore is the abecedary of life: its most basic cell and its most complex goal. God, in his most personal, is community. In his eternal thrice-hypostatic communion 'He Is Who He Is'. Accordingly, Christ's saints finally become themselves when they leave aside the false ego in favour of the true self that finds itself in love for others. The Lord told us this truth[264] most simply in terms of loving service to the poor: since to love one's neighbour is 'worth more than all burnt offering and sacrifice'.[265] Love is the *epektasis*[266] or 'extension' of creaturely being, when it finds this *mimesis* of God's life in communion, that renders us capable of experiencing the eternity of the Next Age, even though we are finite creatures. The *epektasis* into God's communion (our *theosis*) is the eternal experience granted to the finite, our true encounter with the love of our God. Its corollary on earth, the striving to live in communion, and live out the ideals of loving communion, which is the Kingdom of God, is what makes us become more than human. It is our *epektasis* from being self-referential beings, focused on gain, and our transfiguration into the communion of saints, focused on mercy. This is our communion with God as Trinity: and the love of the church, on earth and in heaven, reflects this mystery as we grow ever deeper in it. Without commitment to this life of loving the other (specially Christ's poor in our midst) our relationship with the true God is profoundly frustrated.

It is only by approaching the mystery of the Trinity in this way, as the mystery of our salvation, and God's life-giving outreach to humanity, that it can be saved from becoming, for us, a mere conundrum, of the type that is often parodied in books of catechism, where all the facts of the Trinity are rehearsed as if they were mathematical formulae: three persons in one God, each person wholly divine, making not three gods or three parts of one God, but all who are one God, possessed of the self-same nature in three coequal hypostases and expressing a single power, and glory, and will. This, the solemn patristic doctrine of the Trinity, is a mystery full of significance and symbolism. Without the prior understanding, however, that the Trinity is first and foremost our focus of praise in the liturgy, and our call to have compassion on the other, then it is doomed to scholastic sterility: a fate which has affected many parts of Christian culture globally, where trinitarian faith is often little more than a formalist relic of Christian belief.

The apostles and Fathers of the first three centuries were content with little formal elaboration of the trinitarian mystery. It was enough to state the majestic power of the Father, revealed to perfection in the Son, and manifested among his faithful by the power of the Holy Spirit. The trinitarian doctrine of the Gospel of John, for example, is at one and the same moment the most advanced trinitarian theology in the history of the church, and yet undeveloped in the sense of what would come later from the Greek Fathers. This articulation was conducted at an immensely high pitch of philosophy, and in an atmosphere of intense controversy. Patristic trinitarian theology was forged as part and parcel of the great fight of the Nicenes against the Arians. Those who consistently argued for a monist view of the Godhead, denying the hypostatic deity of the Son, and that of the Spirit, obviously had little time for any concept of the Tri-unity of the deity. Those, however, who had 'searched the Scriptures' and seen the regular affirmations of divine status for the Son and the Spirit of God, were anxious to know how this confession of the divine glory shining out in the different persons could be reconciled with their fundamental faith in monotheism.

This was a question that was at once difficult in the extreme (understanding how God was 'our God' and related to us in the economy of salvation in history) and perfectly impossible (trying to perceive how the Son and the Spirit related to the Ineffable Father in the transcendent life of the deity). It was a question of the utmost importance, however: a question of our life and our life's focus, and thus a question that was no mere idleness, or obscurity, but one of the most pressing issues of theology. Trinitarian theology, more than any other aspect of the Christian faith, thus still bears the chisel marks of those who wrote as if they were carving this doctrine out of stone by the highest efforts of the mind and soul. It can easily be mistaken for 'high scholasticization' or neglected because of its demanding nature. Those who reflect on it, like the Virgin Mary 'pondering these things in her heart', may find that it is profound, mysterious, and life-giving: a well of salvation that offers the believer living water that is unique to the Christian faith.

The Orthodox confession of the Trinity is easy to state (difficult to exegete). St John of Damascus put it most succinctly as follows:

> There is one essence, one divinity, one power, one will, one energy, one beginning, one authority, one dominion, one sovereignty, made known in three perfect subsistences [hypostases] and adored with one single adoration; believed in and worshipped by all rational creation; united without confusion and divided without separation a thing which surely transcends thought.[267]

The Fathers are clear that the divine persons, or *hypostases*, are not merely names, or aspects of God, but veritable persons whose titles signify something profound and 'distinctly real' (perhaps the best modern equivalent of the ancient word). Gregory the Theologian expressed it like this:

> We do not speak of the Son as Unbegotten, for there is only one Father; nor do we speak of the Spirit as a Son, for there is only one Only-Begotten, so that the persons have their singularity in a divine manner; the one in respect of sonship the other in respect of procession, not sonship.... The Father, the Son, and the Holy Spirit have this in common: that they are uncreated, and they are divine. The Son and the Holy Spirit have this in common: that they are derived from the Father. Proper to the Father is his ingeneracy; proper to the Son, his generation; and proper to the Holy Spirit, is his being sent.... Be content to know this about God: that the Monad is adored in the Triad, the Triad in the Monad.[268]

Orthodoxy holds strongly to the belief that the 'names' of the *hypostases* of God are part of the deposit of divine revelation. For this reason it refuses to follow the advice of some modern theologians of Western traditions who advocate an abandonment of the traditional terms in favour of a feminist rearticulation of God as Mother, Daughter, or other titles invented so as to avoid gender reference. The Orthodox tradition does not ascribe gender to the divinity in any sense. The Word alone assumed a gendered body, but the Word as divine *hypostasis* is not subject to the earthly concept of gender.

But equally, it regards the titles as more than merely formalist and socially constructed. The titles Father, Son, and Spirit, since they are the revealed names of the *hypostases* of the divine, are, as such, worthy of adoration. The name carries the power of God within it, as the Scriptures of the Old Covenant rightly sensed, and its invocation endows prayer with the power of holiness. The Orthodox of both sexes will never cease to use the threefold and correct name of God in all their prayer and invocation.

For the Orthodox the Trinity is not a static or problematic concept, in the way it can be to those who wish to comprehend its logic first, before experiencing its effect in prayer. This is not to say that any Orthodox would be able to give a good account of trinitarian theology if asked, but they would be able, in some sense or other, to explain how the Trinity was the substrate and process of all the spiritual life of the church. The Fathers envisaged the life of God revealed as a power that flowed out over the world, to give life and light. The doctrine of Trinity especially expresses this outflow of mercy: from the Father, through the Son, in the Holy Spirit. In such a way only is the truth of God's presence given to the world. Only in like manner – in the Spirit, through the Son, to the Holy Father – can humans give glory and so become the children of God. The immersion in the Trinity is like the lung of prayer, breathing in and out in a rhythm of life: God gifting his presence to us in the economy of revelation, and that gift in turn drawing us back to the Father, in the Spirit's sacred consecration of the believer in the Christ-mystery.

For such reasons, although the theological synopses of the Fathers, such as John of Damascus, serve to defend and prescribe the limits of trinitarian orthodoxy, the church's substantial experience of the Trinity is found, almost in contradistinction, in the vast richness of the creation, and in the boundless generosity of the spirit of prayer. The theological complexities serve to wall around. The Trinity itself flows over the cosmos in indescribable greatness and generosity; and illumines the church as the light of the world. Trinitarian orthopraxis is thus critical for the Orthodox. We may not comprehend the greatness of the God who has revealed his own life, and demonstrated his great love by offering to share it with humanity, but we can certainly celebrate it. By doxology the Orthodox grow slowly in the power of the Name, and in the comprehension of its saving power. This, theology in action, is enough. Within the Orthodox Church, therefore, the tree of trinitarian doctrine is both massive and alive with green leaf. It shall always be so. It is one of the supreme marks of the living church. Where faith in the Trinity is static, dead, or formalist, doxology of the True Name of God cannot occur, and the gifts of power and grace begin to wither.

For such reasons all the Orthodox are very anxious, in ecumenical discussions, that the doctrine of the Trinity be respected profoundly. It is one of the 'sticking points' in the dialogue of East and West that from the ninth century onwards, the Western churches (the Protestant communions still following Rome in the main) adapted the Nicene Creed to express a novel trinitarian confession known as the *Filioque*. The word is a Latin term that means 'And from the Son'. It refers to the clause that was inserted into the original Niceno-Constantinopolitan Creed immediately after the words 'And we believe in the Holy Spirit ... who proceeds from the Father'. The Western version of the Creed, now read in all Catholic and many Protestant churches each Sunday, thus reads: 'And we believe in the Holy Spirit ... who proceeds from the Father and from the Son'. This is why the *Filioque* doctrine is also known as the 'Double Procession'. From early times, especially in the patriarchate of St Photios (810–95), the *Filioque* doctrine, as it began to gain ascendancy in the West, greatly troubled the Orthodox. Some of the reasons for this were related to the manner in which the great statement of Orthodox faith, the Creed itself, was being treated in a cavalier fashion (so it seemed) by being altered to suit the mood of the times.

Eventually many Orthodox writers would connect the rise of papal power to this instance of authorizing the changes to the Creed, and see in the admission[269] of the *Filioque* a deleterious example of how papal monarchy had 'overthrown' ancient Christian synodical governance,[270] and resulted in doctrinal innovation. This line of argument is why, to this day, many Orthodox connect the *Filioque* theology with the rise of papal power and see the two things as great divergences from Orthodoxy, the one almost accounting for the other. In short: if one's view of God's being is incorrect, it follows, like night follows day, that one's ecclesiology will go astray. Orthodox currently engaged in the *Filioque* debate argue, therefore, that it cannot be treated *in abstractu*, merely as an arcane point of historical theology, but has to be broadly contextualized in the whole weave of how one understands revelation to be communicated to the church, how tradition functions, and how hierarchs are meant to preserve it.

The Orthodox theology of the single procession of the Spirit is articulated clearly by St Gregory the Theologian, who followed the dogmatic statement of John 15.26: 'That Spirit of Truth who proceeds from the Father'. It was also defended strongly in the ninth century by St Photios the Great. St Gregory argued that 'procession' is the *proprium* of the Spirit, just as Sonship is uniquely characteristic of the Son's *hypostasis*. The Son issues from the Father by manner of generation, just as the Spirit issues from the Father by manner of procession. Both Son and Spirit come from the self-same Father, and have the nature of that Father as their own nature. There is thus one single nature of Godhead in the Divine Trinity (none other than the divine nature of the Father) with three *hypostases* expressing it characteristically: the Father expressing his own nature as the unique Uncaused Cause of Godhead (*Monos Aitios*); the Son expressing the Father's nature (now his own) as Filiated *Hypostasis*, and the Spirit expressing it as Processed *Hypostasis*. The single procession of both Son and Spirit from the Father alone thus preserved the Christian sense of one supreme Godhead. What is more, the terms and concepts Filiation and Procession are sacred elements of revelation, given in Scripture, and not to be replaced or re-expressed as descriptors of the life of God as Trinity.

For the Orthodox, the association of the Son with the causation of the divine *hypostasis* of the Spirit (a factor, one must say, that was not always, or necessarily, intended by the Latin profession of the *Filioque*[271]) was a disruption to the very coherence of the doctrine of the Trinity, and was regarded as a very serious matter by the Orthodox East. This was a perspective not generally shared in the West. At one time in the high Middle Ages Latin controversialists charged the Greeks with themselves having altered the Nicene Creed so as to remove the *Filioque*, and it was a charge that resurfaced in the time of the mutual excommunications of Patriarch Michael Caerularios and Cardinal Humbert in 1054. The Latin theologians generally were aware that many of the earlier Fathers had linked the Spirit to the Son most intimately, and from the vantage point of a profession of *Filioque*, which by then had become normative in the West, they began to exegete the patristic trinitarian sense along these lines. Athanasios and others, for example, had called the third divine *hypostasis*: the

'Spirit of the Son'.[272] In this the Fathers were generally referring to the mission of the Spirit within the saving economy, whereas the credal statement about the Spirit's procession (and the biblical text on which this hung) was referring to the emanation of the *hypostases* within the eternal life of the Godhead.

Even so, the concept of the Spirit proceeding from the Father 'through the Son' was known in the East.[273] It was included in the statement of faith sent by Tarasius, patriarch of Constantinople, to the other Eastern patriarchs in 784 and endorsed by St John of Damascus in his own great *summa* of theology.[274] This statement was implicitly acknowledged by the second Council of Nicaea (787), which examined it. But once again, the overarching context here ought to be understood as the soterio-logical mission of the Spirit in the church and the world, not the issue of the emanation of the *hypostases* in the eternal Godhead. It was the ninth century that really saw the issue sharpening up as the Western and Eastern churches grew more alienated. In 867 the Patriarch Photios came across the *Filioque* in the context of a dispute with Latin missionaries in Bulgaria who were advancing claims of jurisdiction against the rights of Constantinople. Photios examined the doctrine carefully, realizing that something significant had happened to the old harmony of the theological tradition of the churches, and at a council in Constantinople in 879–80, with delegates present from Pope John VIII, the notion of the *Filioque* was condemned. Photios composed a Synodical Letter on the subject[275] as well as a specific treatise entitled *The Mystagogy*, attacking Latin views.[276]

The notion of the double procession of the Spirit, however, was an element of Latin speculation from an early time. It first appeared in Tertullian, an important architect of Latin systematic thinking on the Trinity.[277] Hilary of Poitiers also argued that the Spirit is an expression of trinitarian unity, or bonding, because: 'He receives from both the Father and the Son'.[278] Other Latin Fathers suggested similar things.[279] In all the cases where there can be seen 'intimations' of a doctrine of double procession in the early Latins the immediate context was of the soteriological mission of the Spirit in the world, what the Orthodox would call the 'economy' of salvation. In Latin thinkers after Augustine, however, this began to change and the *Filioque* started, more and more, to be referred to the eternal relations of the Divine Trinity. In the context of 'economic' or soteriological discourse about God, the Orthodox too believe that it is perfectly correct to speak of the Son sending the Spirit,[280] just as it is to speak of the Spirit 'driving the Son into the wilderness',[281] but that context has to be distinguished from statements that concern the eternal intra-hypostatic life of God: *theologia* proper, not *economia*. The elision of reflection about the inner life of God (which for the Orthodox remains an illegitimate subject of speculation) and ideas about God's trinitarian work of salvation became more and more marked in the late antique Latin world. This trend was strengthened incomparably by Augustine's monumental work, his highly influen-tial book *On the Trinity*.

In this Augustine taught the whole West, ever afterwards, that the Father was the principal source of the Spirit, but that 'by the Father's gift' the Son also serves as a source of the Spirit's procession such that there is a 'common procession' of both.[282] It was only a matter of time before these influential theologians of the Latin Church impacted on the public liturgy and declarations of faith. The term *Filioque* is first publicly encountered in the Latin Church in the acts of the third Council of Toledo (589), and was defended against criticism by Paulinus of Aquileia at the Council of

Friuli (796). It came to a higher level of ecumenical 'problematic' when Pope Martin publicly alarmed the leaders of the Eastern churches by referring to the doctrine of double procession in a synodical letter to Constantinople in 694.

In the Western provinces the *Filioque* clause was introduced into the liturgically chanted Creed at the court of Charlemagne, and from there, in 807, Latin monks introduced it into their liturgical practice at their monastery on the Mount of Olives. The patriarch of Jerusalem, alerted by Orthodox monks from St Sabas, immediately protested this practice to Pope Leo III, maintaining that it was an unauthorized change to an ancient conciliar statement, and that it professed dubious doctrine. Carolingian theologians under the pope's instruction considered the question and reported that it was rather the Greeks who were in theological error, and that changes were only forbidden to conciliar statements in terms of orthodox meaning, not matters of exact words. Accordingly the pope issued a decision defending the orthodoxy of the *Filioque* doctrine, while diplomatically dropping any charge of error against the Greeks. But at this time he also refused to allow the addition of the clause into the Roman liturgy and advised the Frankish and Spanish churches gradually to discontinue their innovatory practice for the sake of peace.

The Frankish court continued unabashed, however, and by the early eleventh century the *Filioque* finally made its way into Roman liturgical custom too. There have been several historical attempts to resolve the controversy. Greek theologians at the Council of Lyons II (1274) and Ferrara-Florence (1438–9) agreed on the potential orthodoxy of the *Filioque* if it were not being used to affirm the double causality of the Spirit, though they refused to countenance the legitimacy of its addition to the Creed. Even so, in both cases these councils were strongly disavowed, almost immediately afterwards, by the Orthodox clergy and people. Since that time the *Filioque* has become seen widely in the Orthodox world as a 'test case' of doctrinal correctness, while in the West it has dwindled in significance to a rarely travelled bywater of theology, seen as at best arcane, at worst irrelevant, and part of the overall neglect of trinitarian thought and spiritual culture in many parts of Western Christendom.

Why it matters still to the Orthodox can be digested to some central refutations of certain propositions. First is the notion that the sacred tradition is susceptible to upgrading and updating, largely on the basis of a theological theorist (however great such a thinker may be, as in the case of Augustine), and without reference to a General Council. Second is an objection to the notion that papal authority is such that it can extend to serve as an international arbiter of the tradition of faith. Third (and most importantly) is the belief that to abandon the patristic and conciliar confession of the Father's single causality of the Godhead weakens the bond of trinitarian unity as being lodged in the sole being of God as Father, and fractures to coherence of unity in diversity, which the Trinity constitutes by being *as* a communion. In the Orthodox estimate, the *Filioque* controversy was equivalent to an 'opening proposition' in a long future series that progressively falsified and distorted the theological tradition about God that grew from it. To this day it stands as one of the significant spiritual and intellectual dividing points between East and West. It also explains why the Orthodox Church has a dim view of the otherwise great saint, Augustine of Hippo, his impact on theological thought in the various areas of original sin, atonement, and trinitarian theology being widely regarded as disastrously misguided by the Orthodox.

The whole richness of the Orthodox trinitarian theology is expressed in this prayer, from the Vespers of Pentecost Sunday, attributed to the Emperor Leo, and with which we shall end our present, and all too incomplete, consideration of the most ineffable mystery of faith:

> Come all you peoples and let us worship the Godhead in three *hypostases*:
> The Son in the Father with the Holy Spirit.
> For the Father timelessly begot the Son,
> who is coeternal, sharing the same throne as he;
> And the Holy Spirit was in the Father, glorified with the Son.
> There is one power, one essence, one deity,
> Which we all worship in these words:
>
> Holy God, who created all things through the Son,
> with the co-operation of the Holy Spirit;
> Holy Mighty, through whom we have known the Father, and through
>   whom the Holy Spirit came into this world;
> Holy Immortal, the Comforting Spirit, who proceeds from the Father,
>   and abides in the Son;
> O Holy Trinity, glory to you.

Notes

1   Oppenheimer's naive dismay when he saw the results of the bomb; or the strange exultation that Down's Syndrome had all but been eradicated in parts of Europe (only as a result of pre-natal screening and abortion); or the gross annual income of armament manufacturers exceeding that of national net worth in many cases. The Prince of the World (John 12.31; Eph. 2.2) wears many masks, but they all have the same hue, and can be spotted by the combination of their surface allure, yet their innate hostility to human joy and the spirit of life.

2   1 Cor. 8.3.

3   Mark 14.36; Gal. 4.6.

4   Rom. 8.14–16.

5   What could have possessed Marx to come out with this nonsense? Had he never spoken to any men or women of faith?

6   Heb. 13.14.

7   Gal. 3.23–6.

8   'So Jesus asked the twelve, "Do you also wish to leave me?" Simon Peter answered him, "Lord, to whom would we go? You have the words of eternal life. We have come to believe and know that you are the Holy One of God." ' John 6.67–9.

9   The second-century philosopher Justin Martyr expressed this in *Second Apology*, 2.13, saying: 'All those writers [viz. the pre-Christian poets and philosophers] were able through the seed of the Logos implanted in them, to see reality darkly. But it is one thing to have the seed of a thing, and to imitate it up to one's capacity; and a far different matter to have the thing itself, shared and imitated in virtue of its own grace.' His robust conclusion was: 'Whatever has been spoken rightly [about God] in human discourse belongs to us Christians: for we worship and love, next to God, the Logos who is from the unbegotten and ineffable God.'

10   Mark 12.34.

11   *Divine Institutes*, 5.15.

12   John 16.13, 17.17.

13   John 17.17–19.

14   Mark 4.11–12.

15   'Blessed is the man who walks not in the counsel of the wicked, nor stands in the way of sinners, nor sits in the seat of scoffers; but his delight is in the law of the Lord, and on his law he meditates day and night. He is like a tree planted by streams

of water, that yields its fruit in its season, and its leaf does not wither.' Ps. 1.1–3.

16 *Against the Heresies*, 4.20.1.

17 *On the Orthodox Faith*, 1.4.

18 *The Divine Names*, 5.4.

19 Ibid. 5.8. St Maximos the Confessor in the *Ambigua* (*PG* 91.1180) echoes the same idea: 'All existence derives from God, but he himself is not existence. He is beyond existence itself, whether expressed or conceived simply or in any particular mode.'

20 Evdokimov 1980: 46.

21 Gen. 1.1–2.

22 Irenaeus, *Against the Heresies*, 3.24.1. 'It is by his love and infinite kindness that God has come within the grasp of human knowledge. This knowledge, however, is not in respect of his greatness or his true being; for no one can measure or grasp this. Rather we know him in this way: that we recognize the one true God is the same as he who made all things and fashioned them and breathed into his creatures the breath of life, and who nourishes us through his creation, who establishes all things by his Logos and binds them together by his Wisdom.'

23 As the scriptural writers indicated, especially the Gospel of St John, when they differentiated the word *zoe* (the life-giving knowledge of God) from the word *bios* which connoted the blessing of the ordinary vital principle in the world.

24 Which culminates in the very clear phrase: 'We sing to God: Father, Son and Holy Spirit.'

25 The leaping flame (of Pentecost) used so much in contemporary religious art is no happier a device, since here all iconic motifs falsify the more profound truth that the apostle suggested: 'The Lord is the Spirit' (2 Cor. 3.17), and 'Christ is the image of the Unseen God' (Col. 1.15), in other words the Incarnation of the Divine Logos is the true iconographic realization of the manifestation of the Spiritual Godhead, and our preferences for graphic representations of the Spirit fall infinitely short of his own graphic and didactic representation of the divinity to humanity,

in the Incarnation of the Logos within history. Christ is the final revelation of God, and that revelation is trinitarian. The elucidation of the nature and character of the Holy Spirit, therefore, is part and parcel of our exegesis of the Lord Jesus and his meaning and presence to the church.

26 Cited in Ware 1979: 138.

27 John 6.63.

28 Ps. 139.13.

29 What the Spirit is to the Father and Son in the eternal life of God exceeds the capacity of our imagination, since who can explain what it is for God to rejoice in his own glory and the communion of the beauty of the hypostases? All spiritual joy and delight in the love of the Creator is only a small reflection of this essential beauty in the life of God.

30 Wisd. 12.1–2: 'For your immortal spirit is in all things, and so, little by little, you correct those who go astray.'

31 2 Cor. 3.18: 'And we all, with unveiled face, beholding the glory of the Lord, are being changed into his likeness from glory to glory for this comes from the Lord who is the Spirit.'

32 Cyril's *Catechetical Lectures* are available in several English versions, and the homilies of Gregory *On the Lights* and *Holy Theophany* are the sermons he gave to his baptismal candidates in Constantinople in 381.

33 For the Christian, inspired reading of Scriptures means that the book is for us eschatological not historical (or merely chronological), and so we begin the meaning of the Old Testament from the starting point of the New, at least as far as the revelation of the (trinitarian) Person of God is concerned.

34 Matt. 22.43, 10.20; Mark 13.11; Luke 1.41, 1.67, 2.25–7.

35 Mark 12.36.

36 LXX, Ps. 21.2.

37 The most important ancient elaboration of this fundamental principle is given in Gregory the Theologian's *First Theological Oration* (Orat. 27). He does not oppose intellectual qualification against spiritual inspiration (indeed he demands that the

preparation of the intellect should strenuously precede any attempt to speak theology) but he insists that only the Spirit's prior purification allows the mind to see the divine truths that are withheld from the 'uninitiated'.

38 1 Cor. 2.16.
39 John 3.8; Isa. 40.13.
40 Isa. 57.15, 66.2; Ps. 34.18, 51.17.
41 Job. 22.29; Prov. 15.25; Sirach 3.28; Luke 1.51.
42 John 5.39.
43 Luke 24.32, 45.
44 Num. 11.17, 25, 29; Deut. 34.9; Judg. 6.34, 14.6; 1 Sam. 10.10; 2 Chron. 15.1; 4 Ezra 14.22.
45 Exod. 31.3–5, 35.31; Ps. 104.30; Isa. 11.2.
46 1 Sam. 16.1.
47 Ps. 104.30.
48 Matt. 1.18–20; Luke 1.35.
49 Matt. 3.11, 3.16, 4.1, 8.16, 12.18 (citing Isaiah), 12.28–32; Mark 1.12; Luke 4.1.
50 Elaborated throughout his treatise, *On Adoration in Spirit and Truth;* also see his *Commentary on the Gospel of John,* Book 12.1.
51 John 1.33.
52 John 3.34–6.
53 John 7.39.
54 John 14.15–18.
55 Rom. 8.9, 8.4–8.
56 Luke 11.13.
57 Matt. 8.22.
58 John 3.5–8.
59 John 4.23–4, 6.63.
60 John 15.26.
61 John 14.26; 1 Cor. 2.10; Rev. 2.7.
62 John 16.13–15; 1 Tim. 3.16.
63 John 20.22–3.
64 Rom. 8.11.
65 2 Cor. 3.18.
66 Rom. 14.7, 15.13; Gal. 5.22–5.
67 Rom. 15.16.
68 Rom. 8.2; 2 Cor. 3.6.
69 2 Cor. 3.17.
70 Gal. 4.6.
71 Rom. 8.14–17.
72 Eph. 2.17–19.
73 Rom. 8.27.
74 2 Cor. 1.22, 5.4.
75 1 Cor. 12.3.

76 1 Cor. 2.14–16.
77 1 Cor. 3.16, 6.19; Eph. 2.22.
78 1 Cor. 6.17.
79 Rom. 5.5.
80 Eph. 4.3.
81 1 Cor. 12.13.
82 Isa. 63.10; Eph. 4.30.
83 Rom. 12.11.
84 Rom. 15.19; 1 Cor. 12.4–11.
85 2 Tim. 1.7.
86 John 15.20, 26–7, 16.7–14; 1 Peter. 4.14.
87 *Plea for the Christians,* 10.
88 The heretic Valentinus taught that the Spirit was a mere angel of the Father.
89 *Against the Heresies,* 3.1.1.
90 The Old Testament, the New Testament, the Eschaton.
91 *Against the Heresies,* 3.24.1.
92 Accordingly, Irenaeus teaches that the fashioning of a body in the Virgin was predominantly an act of the Logos. The patristic tradition tended to follow this, though stressing more clearly in the later centuries (especially in the work of St Gregory of Nyssa, and Blessed Augustine), the inapplicability of human reasoning 'differentiating' the holistic action of the Trinity.
93 Ps. 33.6.
94 *Demonstration of the Apostolic Preaching,* 5.
95 'And the Spirit descended from God onto the Son of God who was made the Son of Man, and with him it grew accustomed to dwell among the human race, and "to abide" on men, and to dwell within God's creatures, working the will of the Father in them, and renewing them from their old state into the newness of Christ.' *Against the Heresies,* 3.17.1.
96 Ibid. 5.36.2 and 4.20.4–6: '(4) The Spirit prepares man for the Son of God. The Son leads man to the Father. The Father gives man immortality...(6) Thus was God revealed, for in all these ways is God displayed. The Spirit works, the Son completes the ministry, the Father approves.'
97 Ibid. 4.38.3.
98 Eph. 4.6.
99 John 7.38–9.
100 *Against the Heresies,* 5.18.1.

101 *Catechetical Lectures*, 16.2.

102 As with Christ, the ultimate manifestation of glory, in the humility of our merciful God.

103 John 14.26.

104 *Catechetical Lectures*, 16.3.

105 Matt. 2.27; John 16.13, 14.

106 *Catechetical Lectures*, 16.24.

107 Ibid. 16.15.

108 Ibid. 17.14.

109 Ibid. 21.2.

110 1 John 4.13.

111 2 Pet. 1.4.

112 *First Letter to Serapion*, 24.

113 Also in Letters 125 and 159. Basil's Letter 189, on the Trinity, is now usually attributed to St Gregory of Nyssa.

114 The distinction of Nature and Person in the Divine Trinity, which followed as a logical corollary from increased insistence among the Orthodox Fathers on the Son and Spirit's subsistent deity. In other words, the more the fourth-century theologians left the realm of the older 'theology of discretion' which contented itself simply with the biblical phrases, and strenuously defended the church's belief in the deity of the three hypostases against the Arians, the more they found it was incumbent on them to explain the interrelation of the Persons within the Divine Triad.

115 Chiefly: St Basil the Great, St Gregory the Theologian, St Gregory of Nyssa, St Amphilokios of Ikonium. Other theologians in their kin group included St Macrina and St Peter of Sebaste.

116 It was a philosophical notion that originated with Aristotle and was very common in intellectual circles of the time.

117 The title 'God'.

118 He is ironically addressing the Arian logicians who misapplied quasi-mathematical syllogisms to insist that if the Son and Spirit were divine, one would thus have to believe in three gods.

119 John 15.26.

120 Sirach 1.1.

121 Oration 31.6–10 *passim* (the Fifth Theological Oration).

122 *On the Holy Spirit: Against the Followers of Macedonius*, 14; See also *On the Holy Trinity* (formerly attributed to Basil the Great), Letter 189.

123 After the nineteenth century the Latin Church increasingly began to stress this aspect of Augustine's speculative trinitarian thought, that the Spirit proceeded from the Father 'and from the Son'. The so-called *Filioque* controversy (from the addition of the Latin word *Filioque* into the Nicene–Constantinopolitan Creed) was widely seen, in the Eastern Church, to contradict the Scriptures, the Creed, and the formative theology of the Cappadocian Fathers, by disrupting the single 'flow' of the outpouring of the Father's own being in the hypostases of the Son and Spirit. It was one of the causes of the eventual schism that has not been healed to this day. See the following section on the Divine Trinity for further discussion.

124 *On the Orthodox Faith*, 1.8.

125 Preface to the *Hymns of Divine Eros: Mystical Prayer of Our Father St Symeon*.

126 See Kontzevich 1988.

127 *First Greek Life of Pachomius*, 135.

128 See the account given in English translation in Motovilov 1953.

129 Ibid.

130 Lossky 1957: 196.

131 Chief among them, and representative, may be the great eucharistic epiclesis, which signals the consecration of the holy elements: 'Again we offer you this spiritual and bloodless worship and we ask you, and pray you, and implore you, send down your Holy Spirit upon us and upon these gifts here set forth, + and make this bread the precious body of your Christ, + and what is in this chalice the precious blood of your Christ, + changing them by your Holy Spirit.' Liturgy of St John Chrysostom.

132 Rom. 8.16, 26–7; Eph. 3.20.

133 Acts 2.1 ff.

134 Ware 1979: 126.

135 Staniloae 1998: 29.

136 McGuckin 2005a.

137 Rev. 22.20.

138   Gen 1.1–2.

139   Preface to the *Hymns of Divine Eros*:
      Mystical Prayer of Our Father St Symeon.

140   Matt. 10.20; John 14.26, 16.13. It hears
      the sevenfold prophetic cry of John:
      'Whoever has an ear let them hear
      what the Spirit says to the Churches.'
      Rev 2.7 and *passim.*

141   But only revival of the second-century
      heresy of Photinianism, which shocked
      the sensibilities of the early church by
      claiming Jesus was 'merely a man' (Psilan-
      thropism), via the now threadbare 'Jesus
      of history' writings of the Victorian age.

142   The professors who formed the American
      'Jesus Seminar' met in conferences and
      voted on what *logion* of the Lord ought to
      be regarded as 'authentic' or not; as if they
      were a new college of apostles assembled at
      an ecumenical council, deciding to rewrite
      the Scripture.

143   Matt. 24.5; 1 Tim. 6.20–1; 2 Pet. 2.1–2; 1
      John 4.1; Rev. 2.2.

144   The Fathers understand Christ's gift of
      the Holy Spirit to the church to be one
      of the great motives of the Incarnation.
      As he possesses the Spirit's presence by
      his nature as Word, as well as by his total
      openness to the Spirit's blessing in his
      bodily ministry, so he gives it as a bles-
      sing to the New Humanity he fashions
      in himself. Athanasios of Alexandria,
      Against the Arians, 1.46, 1.48; Cyril of
      Alexandria, *Homily on the Gospel of
      Luke,* 10, and Epistle 17.

145   'Their manner of acting is just as if one,
      when a beautiful image of a king has
      been constructed by some skilful artist
      out of precious jewels, should then take
      this likeness of the man all to pieces,
      should rearrange the gems, and so fit
      them together as to make them into
      the form of a dog or of a fox, and even
      that but poorly executed.' *Against the
      Heresies,* 1.8.1.

146   'I heard some people say: "If I do not find
      it in the Scriptures [archives], I do not
      believe it in the Gospel." And when I said
      to them: "It is written," they answered me:
      "That is precisely the question." But for
      me the Scriptures are Jesus Christ. The

inviolable Scriptures are his cross and
death, and his resurrection, and the faith
which comes through him; by these
things I want, through your prayers, to
be justified.' Ignatius of Antioch, *To the
Philadelphians,* 8.2.

147   Luke 24.32, 4.22, 20.39; John 7.46.

148   A recent attempt to offer a broad-cloth
      presentation of the patristic teaching
      on the Nicene Creed (Trinity, Christo-
      logy, pneumatology, anthropology, and
      eschatology), is to appear in five volumes
      beginning in 2009, from IVP Press,
      entitled *Ancient Christian Doctrines.* The
      second volume in the series, devoted to
      Christology, is edited by myself. The
      third, dedicated to Christological soterio-
      logy, is edited by M. Edwards.

149   *Homoousios,* or consubstantial.

150   It began as a baptismal creed recounting
      the 'mighty deeds' of the Lord's New
      Covenant.

151   Phil. 2.10–11.

152   The once-for-allness of the incarnation
      of God in Christ.

153   *Against the Heresies,* 3.21.1.

154   'We believe in One Lord, Jesus Christ,
      the only-begotten Son of God, begotten
      from the Father before all ages, Light of
      Light, True God of True God, begotten
      not made, consubstantial with the
      Father, through whom all things were
      made.' Creed of Nicaea.

155   Athanasios of Alexandria, *Against the
      Arians,* 1.24–5, 3.63, 66; Gregory the
      Theologian, Orations 29.2 and 39.12;
      Gregory of Nyssa, *Against Eunomius,*
      1.26, 1.42.

156   Heb. 5.7.

157   In the seventh century the third ecume-
      nical council of Constantinople taught
      that Christ possessed two wills (insepar-
      ably bonded to one another), divine and
      human, simply in order to insist once
      more on the full and complete humanity
      of the Logos Incarnate. The dogmatic
      symbol of the council describes it as
      follows: 'We preserve in every way the
      Unconfused and Undivided Lord. We
      briefly set out our confession: we believe
      the Lord Jesus Christ, our true God, to

be one of the holy Trinity even after his assumption of flesh, we declare that his two natures shine forth in his one hypostasis, in which he displayed both miracles and sufferings through the whole course of his incarnate life, not in mere phantasm but truly, the difference of nature being recognized in the same one hypostasis by the fact that each nature wills and works what is proper to it, in communion with the other. On this principle we glorify two natural wills and operations (in the Lord) combining with each other for the salvation of the human race.'

158 Cyril of Alexandria, *Against Nestorius*, 1.1; id., Letter 17; id., *Letters to Succensus*.

159 John 9.6; Mark 7.33.

160 Eph. 2.13.

161 See, for example, Gregory of Nyssa, *Against Eunomius*, 5.5.

162 Held at the so-named suburb of Constantinople in 451. The *Dogmatic Definition* (*Tomos*) of the council is cited in full below.

163 The council was censuring the Nestorian view that a distinction ought to be made between the historical (suffering) Jesus and the Divine Lord and Word, and argued, to the contrary, that the Incarnation is a mystery of the union of the two natures in one selfsame divine person.

164 Some of the Syrian theologians had spoken of 'Two Sons': the Son of God, and the Son of Man. They had initially intended to convey, by this, the two natures (humanity and divinity). The council is determined to remove any suggestion that there could be two 'persons' in the single Christ.

165 'Anathema' meant to be subject to ecclesiastical censure. The main censure in the ancient church was that lay folk were deprived of communion, and clergy were deposed from ecclesiastical office if they did not maintain the common (i.e. 'catholic') faith. *Acts of the Council of Constantinople*, 553; *Anathematisms against the Three Chapters*, §3.

166 John 1.1–3; Col. 1.15–19.

167 John 1.1, 10.30, 17.21–2.

168 John 11.35; Mark 13.32.

169 John 10.34–5.

170 Heb. 13.8.

171 Oration 30.21. See also the words of St Cyril of Alexandria that were given synodical confirmation at the ecumenical council of Ephesus in 431: 'We do not divide the terms used in the Gospels of the Saviour as God or man between two *hypostases*, or persons, for the One and Only Christ is not twofold, though he is thought of as out of two, and as uniting different entities into the indivisible unity, as man is thought of as of body and soul, and yet not as twofold, but one out of both. . . . For if it is necessary to believe that, being God by nature, he became flesh, that is, man ensouled with a rational soul, then why should some be embarrassed by some of his sayings that are appropriate to his humanity? . . . All the terms used in the Gospels are to be referred to one Person, the one incarnate *hypostasis* of the Word. There is one Lord Jesus Christ, according to the Scripture.' Epistle 17 (*Third Letter to Nestorius*).

172 The patristic doctrine of the Hypostatic Union.

173 'If anyone does not confess that our Lord Jesus Christ who was crucified in the flesh is True God and Lord of Glory and One of the Holy Trinity, let him be anathema.' Second Council of Constantinople (553), anathema 10.

174 *Against the Arians*, 3.30; *On the Incarnation of the Word, passim*. The title of the latter treatise in the original Greek is: 'On the En-man-ment of the Divine Word'.

175 'If anyone does not confess Emmanuel to be very God, and does not acknowledge the Holy Virgin consequently to be the Mother of God [Theotokos], for she brought forth after the flesh the Word of God become flesh, let him be Anathema. If anyone does not confess that the Word which is of God the Father has been hypostatically united to flesh, and is One Christ with his own flesh, the same one being both God and man alike, let

him be Anathema.' Cyril of Alexandria, *Epistle* 17. (Synodically affirmed at the Council of Ephesus, 431). See also id., *Against Nestorius*, 1.1, and Gregory the Theologian, *Epistle* 101.5, *To Cledonius*.

176 Eusebios of Caesarea, *Oration on Constantine*, 11.15–16, 12.4–5; Cyril of Jerusalem, *Catechetical Oration* 11.24; Cyril of Alexandria, *Epistle* 17.

177 Athanasios of Alexandria, *Against the Arians*, 3.31; id., *Letter to Serapion*, 4.14. Dionysios the Areopagite, *Divine Names*, 26; Constantinople II (553), Anathemas 4 and 8.

178 Gregory of Nazianzus, *Carmina Arcana*, *On First Principles*; id., *Epistle* 101.5–6; Eusebios of Caesarea, *Oration on Constantine*, 14.9–12; Cyril of Alexandria, *Homilies on the Gospel of Luke*, 10; id., *Epistle* 4; id., *Epistle* 17 (*Third Letter to Nestorius*); id., *Against Nestorius*, 1.1.

179 Council of Chalcedon, *Dogmatic Symbol*.

180 John 20.20.

181 Athanasios of Alexandria, *On the Synods*, 23.

182 Referring to Heb. 1.6; Isa. 45.14; John 13.13, 20.28.

183 John 16.15.

184 John 14.9.

185 John 1.3; Col. 1.16.

186 Athanasios of Alexandria, *Against the Arians*, 2.24.

187 Basil of Caesarea, *Homily* 24.3; see also Gregory of Nazianzus, *Oration* 29.2; Gregory of Nyssa, *Against Eunomius*, 1.36. 1

188 Gregory of Nazianzus, *Oration* 30.20.

189 *Hypostasis* is the patristic word for 'individuated reality'. It is usually translated by the English word 'person' but in contemporary language a 'person' connotes a separate psychic entity, a sense of distinction not implied by the Greek in a trinitarian context, which spoke of a single and selfsame Divine Being, individuated in three 'modes of discrete existing' (*tropoi hyparxeos*, as St Basil called them).

190 Gregory of Nazianzus, *Oration* 42.15. The Son and Spirit have no other being (or nature, or essence) than that of the Father, and so are essentially one with the Father, while still being personally (hypostatically) distinct. This is Gregory's classic account of why Christians who confess the threefold divine hypostases of Father, Son, and Spirit, are nevertheless confessing only one Godhead.

191 Basil the Great, *Against Eunomius*, 11.28.

192 John 1.3; Col. 1.16.

193 Cyril of Jerusalem, *Catechetical Oration* 11.18.

194 *Against the Heresies*, 4.6.5; see also ibid. 4.4.2.

195 The economy of salvation found in the Old Testament, for example.

196 See, for example, Cyril of Alexandria, *Letter to Succensus*, 9.

197 Namely, Adam.

198 Gregory of Nyssa, *Catechetical Oration* 26.

199 Athanasios of Alexandria, *On the Incarnation*, 4; see also Cyril of Alexandria, *Letter to Succensus*, 9.

200 Heb. 1.2.

201 John 1.14.

202 Irenaeus, *Against the Heresies*, 3.18.1.

203 See Athanasios of Alexandria, *On the Incarnation*, 4–5.

204 Ibid. 27; 29; 47–48; 51.

205 Irenaeus, *Against the Heresies*, 3.18.7.

206 Athanasios of Alexandria, *Against the Arians*, 3.33. See also *On the Incarnation*, 9, 20, 44.3–4.

207 The Fathers spoke about the Virgin birth as one of the signs that Christ became New Adam: as Adam rose by the hand of God from 'untilled soil', so they described Christ coming from the Virgin's womb (the new and 'untilled earth' of the New Creation of humanity). Irenaeus, *Against the Heresies*, 3.21.10; Athanasios of Alexandria, *Against the Arians*, 2.7.8.

208 Irenaeus, *Against the Heresies*, bk. 5, preface.

209 Athanasios of Alexandria, *Against the Arians*, 2.70; see also ibid. 1.42 – 'He deified what he put on; and, more than that, he bestowed this gift upon the human race' – and 3.38.

210 Athanasios of Alexandria, *On the Incarnation*, 54.3.

211 Rev. 22.20.
212 John 14.18, 27.
213 Augustine, *Confessions*, 1.1.
214 Matt. 11.28–9.
215 John 8.12.
216 Luke 23.34.
217 John 7.46.
218 Rev. 3.20–2.
219 St Isaac lived and wrote in the seventh century. The newly discovered work has been tentatively called *The Second Part*. Not all of Isaac's works are currently available in English.
220 Ps. 104.2.
221 Isaac of Nineveh, *The Second Part*, (II) 5.22–3, cited (with adaptations) from Alfeyev 2000.
222 Irenaeus, *Against the Heresies*, 4.6.5, 4.4.2.
223 Clement of Alexandria summed it up in *Miscellanies*, 4.25 (156.1): 'God is undemonstrable and therefore is not an object of knowledge. But the Son is Wisdom and Knowledge and Truth, and thus he admits of demonstration and explanation.' See also ibid. 8.2.5.
224 1 Tim. 2.4.
225 Beginning, principle, or origin.
226 Gregory Palamas, *The 150 Chapters*, ch. 78. *PG* 150.1176.
227 For St John of Damascus (*On the Orthodox Faith*, 1.1) God left sufficient information about himself in nature, apart from anything the Scripture records, that no human being could claim ignorance of God.
228 Gregory Palamas, *The 150 Chapters*, ch. 78. *PG* 150.1176.
229 'One God and Father of us all, who is above all and through all and in all.' Eph. 4.6.
230 Matt. 11.27.
231 Matt. 11.25.
232 Mark 4.11.
233 Matt. 7.11; Luke 11.11–13.
234 Eph. 3.14–15.
235 Mark 14.36.
236 Matt. 10.29.
237 Matt. 10.30–1.
238 2 Cor. 1.3.
239 Matt. 5.45.

240 Matt. 5.48. 'You, therefore, must be perfect, as your heavenly Father is perfect.'
241 Luke 6.36.
242 1 Thess. 5.5.
243 John 4.24.
244 John 14.1.
245 Matt. 6.8.
246 Rom. 8.17.
247 *Miscellanies*, 5.12 (82.4).
248 See for example the short but dense treatise *The Mystical Theology*.
249 *Miscellanies*, 5.12. (82.4). In his second theological oration (Oration 28) St Gregory the Theologian discusses how all 'definitions' are inapplicable to God since definitions derive their meaning from inherent limitations and God is essentially infinite.
250 Gregory the Theologian. Oration 27.3.
251 James 2.19; Rom. 3.30.
252 Gen. 17.1; Ps. 91.1; Rev. 4.8.
253 Wisd. 19.22
254 Job. 12.13; Ps. 104.24; Rom. 11.33.
255 Rom. 1.20; Col. 1.15; 1 Tim. 1.17; Heb. 11.27.
256 See John of Damascus, *On the Orthodox Faith*, 1.4, 1.9, 1.14.
257 Ps. 46.10.
258 Gregory the Theologian, Oration 40.5.
259 John of Damascus, *On the Orthodox Faith*, 1.8.
260 Liturgy of St John Chrysostom.
261 Isa. 6.1–3.
262 Prayer 5 of the Lychnapsia prayers of Vespers.
263 For a fuller discussion of the Orthodox understanding of God's providence see John of Damascus, *On the Orthodox Faith*, 2.29 and 3.1.
264 Matt. 5.43–6, 22.39; Luke 6.27; John 10.17, 13.34–5, 14.21–3, 15.9–12, 17; Eph. 3.19, 5.2; 1 John 4.7–8, 4.16.
265 Mark 12.33
266 The term used in the Fathers to denote the endless 'reaching out' of creaturehood to God.
267 *On the Orthodox Faith*, 1.8.
268 Oration 25.17.
269 Though it is significant that the first time the credal addendum came to

papal notice it was not at all favourably received.

270 The Orthodox and patristic concept of the General Council as the supreme earthly instrument of ecclesial governance.

271 Further, see Vischer 1981.

272 Athanasios, *To Serapion*, 1.24, 3.1; Gregory of Nyssa, *Against Eunomius*, 1.378; Basil of Caesarea, Epistle 38; John of Damascus, *On the Orthodox Faith*, 1.12

273 See Berthold 1985.

274 *On the Orthodox Faith*, 1.8.

275 The text is in *PG* 102.793–821.

276 See Farrell 1987; Haugh 1975.

277 *Against Praxeas*, 4.1.

278 *Historical Fragments*, 2.31.

279 For example Marius Victorinus, *Against the Arians*, 1.13, and Ambrose, *On the Holy Spirit*, 1.11.120.

280 John 15.26, 16.7.

281 Mark 1.12.

282 *On the Trinity*, 15.26.47.

Chapter 4

The Doctrine of the Orthodox Church II: The Economy of Salvation

HUMANITY AND ITS SUFFERINGS

The weeping of the poor has never ceased on the face of the earth, especially in our previous vaunted century of progress when so many life-enhancing discoveries led the human race, (once again), to regard itself as having god-like status. Humanity is a god with clay feet, however. The century that has seen such wonderful progress in terms of political stability and equity, the protection of international common rights, the eradication of so many scourges of disease, and the increasing dissolution of the longevity of tyrants has also proved to be one of the most bloody and war-torn eras of human history. The petty brutality of tribal conflict, to which our species is prone, has been elevated to new levels of damage by smiling demons in Armani suits, selling weapons in one of the most lucrative global markets of the age. Crippled children hobble, one-legged, far away from the elegant conferences and luxury hotels used by landmine manufacturers, and kept strictly out of sight. But God sees, and is not mocked.[1]

The world is poised, as never before since the dawn of the nuclear age, on an edge of development where unstable regimes lust to acquire global destructive capacity, aping models and patterns of super-government (offered throughout the second half of the twentieth century by ageing empires) that have bequeathed them a legacy of armed and arrogant stand-off as the default discourse operative between nations. Fissures of the extremes of 'having' and 'not-having', as well as chasms of understanding between the twin ignorances of consumerist secularism and chauvinistic religiosity, threaten the peace of the world more deeply than ever before, when a plethora of hi-tech images of surfeit and decadence constantly fuels the dreams of the poorest villagers still living lives of medieval deprivation. There has hardly been a year that has passed in the twentieth century, or in the opening decades of the twenty-first, when the sound of weeping has not been heard; and always, it seems, from the innocent in the front line of war. How wistful that cry still seems: 'Happy the people with such blessings...no ruined wall, no sound of weeping in the streets.'[2] Ancient ogres, long thought to have died in legendary obscurity, have walked the hills once more in living memory, the mythic beasts of genocide, jihad, enslavement, imperialist invasion, and mass starvation. The poorest and most obscure weep unheard by the powerful and by the well-fed of the world, the ravaged populations of Africa especially, where fatal diseases rage through generations like an unchecked fire.

But God is attentive to the voice of the poor raised in desperation,[3] and wonders why the fire of compassion in the hearts of the faithful has not stirred his church more urgently to reach out to the woe of the world.[4]

The scourges of war, famine, and disease, to be sure, are not blemishes that can be simply cast away with a careless benignity by human power, but they are certainly more within the grasp of a 'humanity come of age' than ever before in history: and to this extent the outreach of God's children to the suffering and destitute has become, in this day and this era,[5] a chief mark and a new standard of Orthodoxy. Yet again, this is nothing new, simply the old criterion of mercy by which the Spirit judges the quality of the faith of the church: 'Come into the joy of my Father, for when I was hungry you gave me food.'[6] From the beginning, in the Lord's conception of the new Kingdom of God on earth, the love of God has been expressed in and through the love of the poor and the care of the neighbour. It has always been the charter and focus of the life of the Christian, that *orthopraxis* and *orthodoxia* (the balance of right behaviour following from right understanding) have been inseparable. Their alienation has led to all the innumerable falsifications of the Christian message throughout history. This is not a new message, or insight, although it is one that has been proclaimed with new urgency by many theologians in the Western churches in recent times,[7] and has comprised a powerfully prophetic call for the *church* to hear the call to liberation which God has addressed to his people: to be set free above all from servitude to a selfishness that prefers ease and security to the stemming of the tears of those who weep. It is a compassion that, of course, calls on the surrender of the privilege of ease that has often caused, or colluded with, those sufferings in the first instance. And in that resistance to the surrender of privilege and ease, there comes a stalling of the desire for change, a fearfulness of what hearing the Gospel might demand, and a consequent preference for self-protective apathy. How well the apostle described this protective indolence that leads to the choice of wickedness, as both a spiritual sickness and a cause of the suffocation of the true self that cried out for the liberation of the Saviour.[8] The close bonding of *orthopraxis* and *orthodoxia* is not something that Orthodoxy has to discover as a novelty, as it has always known it: though Orthodoxy knows that the two are not synonymous, and that one cannot replace the other; but the intertwining correlation of *orthodoxia* and *orthopraxis* must be insisted on once more, and much more volubly, by contemporary Orthodoxy in the face of the cry of the poor.

Centuries of obscurity during which the Orthodox nations have lost lands and institutions and power to overwhelming forces of oppression have now come to an end for many. May it last for generations to come. The old somnolence and isolationism in the Eastern churches that was a natural result of such political overshadowing must also now come to an end. Equally an Orthodoxy that is re-emerging on the world political stage must be careful to avoid the dead ends of attempts to return to pseudo-Byzantine posing, such as is represented by neo-nationalisms of all stripes. It is the call to a corporate philosophy of mercy that will most fully represent the renovation and renascence of Christ's Church on earth in this present age (as in all previous ages).

It is this movement towards mercy and the mission of compassion, more than the (laudable) refurbishment of icons and baroque church fabrics that ought to be the inspired prophetic vision of our present generation of bishops and church leaders. Christ's faithful will respond to the call, such is our faith, since the Spirit never ceases to energize the church and renew it in the mercy and love of Christ day by day. But the prophetic summons to such a global programme of mercy must be heard so that the people can be taught its implications in a newly energised *paideia*; not least because it is by such a re-prioritizing of its goals and foci that the hierarchy of the church will also renew itself in the grace of the Spirit. Then, once more (as in earlier ages of civilization) they may grow to the stature of being worthy to be heard as significant voices of global leadership in a world where false prophets have set up their shrines all too easily in the groves of mass communications.

The war has never been so acute as it is in the present time, between the prophets of the Lord and the priests of Baal; and one of our tragedies is that so few Christian leaders show signs of having been made aware of the pressing nature of the problem, and that even fewer are capable of proclaiming the message globally, taking advantage of those mass communications to enhance the work of the evangelical *kerygma*. Orthodoxy remains the biggest secret in world Christianity. Few of its international leaders have the necessary preparation to assume a major role in speaking to the world in truth. Orthodoxy will never set up any single leader who will be comparable to the pope, for example, believing as it does in the great importance of local communities and the principle of subsidiarity.[9] But there is much need for the elaboration of a clearer and louder voice of communication from the Orthodox hierarchs on the world stage. What is more, a common call to the faithful to join together with the other Orthodox churches of the world, a pan-Orthodox initiative, would serve to energize great outpourings of mercy. The faithful of the Orthodox churches in the poorest of the countries of eastern Europe are among the most generous of all peoples. The will is not lacking. What is lacking is a common call, and model of action, from the highest spiritual leaders, designed to energize a prophetic coming together of the world Orthodox to serve the poorest of the poor. It is this, more than endless debates on the rightness or wrongness of the Gregorian calendar, or the appropriateness of praying with the heterodox, that God is interested in; and the agendas of our synodical meetings and national laity congresses need urgently to be changed so as to reflect the evangelical priorities rather than ecclesiastical introspection.

Patriarch Bartholomaios of Constantinople is an example, today, of a highly educated and inspiring world leader who might set a new international standard of understanding in this, although the strictures of the political limitations that are set upon his religious role remain a great hindrance to him. The hierarchical leaders of the eastern European churches will also play an increasingly important role in the future. But only if they realize that a modern world audience will no longer listen to a bishop simply because he is a bishop. The great Orthodox leaders of the future must first prove to the world by the quality of their lives, the refinement of their minds, and the energized moral passion of their Christian commitment that they are worthy of being listened to. One must also add that it is necessary to have in place a common system of communication where the Orthodox can gladly speak as one on global issues of pressing importance. For too much of history (especially after the collapse of the structures of Eastern Christianity in the face of the advance of Islam) the Orthodox leaders have been content to be quiet (and sometimes they had to be so for their very lives' sake) and work in isolation from one another, using the ancient system of intercommunication of the bishops merely as a kind of ceremonial play-acting where formal visits were made to one another clouded with arcane rituals and banquets, but hardly affecting the real lives of millions of people, who paid no attention to it.

Those days are, rightly, over. Orthodoxy's chief spiritual leaders, in this new world order, are well poised to show the fulfilment of the model of servant leadership in simplicity and poverty, representing, as they do, the refining purification of the alliance of the monastic and the episcopal lifestyle. The active observance of the monastic lifestyle will, more and more, come to characterize the hierarchical character in the modern world; especially in the way that this lifestyle advocates simplicity of manners, modesty of lifestyle and philosophy, and a freedom that allows the highest leaders access, at one and the same time, to the courts of the powerful and the tin shacks of the poorest. To be a hierarchical leader in the church of this day and age is to serve a crucified Lord in a crucified world, and to run the risk, no less, of crucifixion from hostile powers. The laying aside of old pretensions to Byzantine aristocratic status and imperial trappings becomes easier in this perspective; since it was not a cross of gold our Lord received as his reward, but one of wood. It is this daring and engaged form of life which is the true apostolic ministry for the present troubled world order, prophetic in its essence and powerful like a fire in its effects, which St Paul describes when he names such leaders as 'prophets of whom the world was not worthy'.[10]

This is by no means simply a vocation of the hierarchs. The call to see the poor at the door is a test of faith, a standard of Orthodoxy, which presses itself upon all the faithful. I have focused on the hierarchs mainly to make it clear how important is the role of apostolic leadership in this regard. The love that motivates the faithful is not lacking. Sometime, perhaps, the understanding is lacking, and the ability to look beyond one's own back yard and one's excessive concern over immediate needs. And this is why the clear call to the asceticism of love (which always presses on believers to leave behind comfortable self-regard and become ready to respond to Christ's call to serve the poor) is so very important; and most urgent of all, undoubtedly, in areas of the world where church members are ranked among the wealthy and the comfortable. It is this call to serve the poor that will serve to bring together a new sense of world Orthodoxy and inspire the hierarchs of the church with a re-energized vision of the church in a new world order. The mission of the Gospel in the third millennium will call us to re-examine many of our old presuppositions about communicating the truth in a global society which, sometimes, seems to have forgotten the basic syntax of the language of God.

It may seem strange to begin a consideration of the Orthodox understandings of the human being and society (anthropology in the religious sense of that term) with this call to hear and respond to the voice of the poor, one that is heard with sharp cries in our age; but it is not so strange when one takes the wider view and looks at the condition of the world today, where economics has moved up the scale of philosophy and become the one international code which governments automatically respond to. Religion, ethics, and culture (even philosophy, but usually in the frightful guise of ideology), which were the older international codes that once governed the affairs of nations, have all given way to the primacy of the religion of Mammon. For Orthodoxy,

185

this obsessive cult of prosperity and ease, at the cost of the impoverishment of the invisible poor, is not merely a neutral ethical or religious matter, however, but one that strikes at the very heart of what the destiny of the human being is: for it overturns the right order of worship.[11] The prevalence of the cult of economic expansion, and the consumerism this induces in a personal lifestyle, is inimical to the Gospel injunction to prefer nothing in the entire universe to the love of God, and to allow no force to disrupt the love of the neighbour. This is why I have suggested the importance of the element of apathy and the 'closing of the eyes' which characterizes this false cult. It would otherwise be impossible for the Church of Christ to engage itself in idolatry. Mammonism, therefore, masks its true face, and leads the good, whom it has thus bewildered, to the altar of the false god as it were blindfolded.

It is, accordingly, a high prophetic task of the hierarchy to name the hostile powers that have enslaved the minds of the people, and offer evangelical models of how to change (*metanoiein*). This will be a complex task, limited only by our apostolic imaginations, of course. But it will all be held together by the common basis of an Orthodox understanding of who the human being is, and how selfhood functions: materially, psychically, intellectually, and noetically. Orthodoxy sees the single human being as a complex made up of all these elements. To be unaware of the force and sphere of action of any one of them is to make fundamental errors about the destiny of the whole. It is in their correct alignment, and ultimate harmonization, that Orthodoxy believes the song of God's glory issues forth as a perfection of cosmic life. This glory, once perfected, will be the Kingdom of God on earth. Its approximation is the goal of the church's polity in this as in every other age. In short, religious anthropology is of immense importance in understanding how to respond to the challenge of God's will in the present world.

Here, Orthodoxy's attitudes have not only been formed by the Scriptures and patristic writings, but also by centuries of ascetical experience. The monastic writings, especially those from the fourth to the ninth centuries, contain much that is of profound interest for all those who wish to know the archaeology and architecture of the inner self. Christian ascetical philosophy is a major movement which advanced Hellenistic philosophy from its classical bases, in the light of the Gospel teachings, with deep reflections on the ethical character of the inner person, its recurring problem of freedom, and the irrepressible aspiration for transcendental destiny that characterizes the complex that is the human person. This complex is destined for joy in the communion with God, and this aspiration can never be wholly silenced while the human being is alive on earth, although repeated rebellion against God can stifle it to apathetic depths. If frustrated, the longing for the divine causes endless sorrow, because the human being senses deeply inside, from the earliest years, that this cosmos is not its ultimate home. St Augustine described this paradox in one of the most famous, and most beautiful, of all patristic aphorisms: 'You have made us for yourself, O Lord, and our hearts can find no rest, until they rest in you.'[12] That primal 'instinct' requires that, if the aspiration for God and the communion of the saints is stifled, it needs to be replaced with some form of counterfeit, such as the quest for sex, or money, or power, none of which remotely measures up to the capacity for ontological harmony which the vision of God confers on the believer. This is a cause of great suffering in humanity.

Orthodoxy understands humanity in a highly personalist sense. It is not so much the abstraction of 'Mankind' that reveals the inner workings of the race, but the encounter with a man or woman. I am not writing this as if it were some universal law of anthropology, but rather to demonstrate the nature of the Orthodox approach to anthropology, which always starts from the concrete, the personalist, and asks how the spiritual history of the individual reveals his or her 'nature'. In this approach Orthodoxy (although it has heavily borrowed from Aristotle's categories over the years) actually reverses the methodological principles of Hellenism. Greek philosophy generally sought to understand the individual by reference to the collective. The issue of human nature was all-important. The concept of the individual (*to idion*) was not generally seen as a proper category at all – rather something eccentric and peripheral. Accordingly, it was felt that whatever was peculiarly individual was not something that essentially belonged to human nature at all, and so could not illuminate it. Thus, one proceeded from the abstract generality about human nature, to the definition of how a person fitted within that nature.

Along with its disregard for the eccentricity of the particular (*to idion*), Hellenism also scorned the concept of the person. It was Christian philosophy and theology that actually provided a substantive identity to the concept of person, supplying the very words[13] to the vocabulary of the intellectual tradition, and moving the idea of personhood from the periphery to the centre of philosophical enquiry and interest. It was, of course, the Christological debate that saw the conception dawning of personhood as a vehicle of substantive truth. Aristotle could never have dreamed of such a development, nor could the Hellenistic tradition of polytheism in its wildest tales. It was the Gospel tradition of the Incarnate Lord which alone had the sobriety and the nerve to suggest that personhood was not only a centrally important 'revelatory', but also a transcendent substantive.

Orthodox Christianity, therefore, reversed Hellenism in this crucial regard: by refusing to believe in the strict limitation of the *ousia*, or nature, of separate things, and by teaching, instead, the complex character of humanity as a nature rooted in two distinct characteristics (matter and spirit) which gives it a *meontic* status[14] with the capacity for transcendence. It was St Athanasios of Alexandria who most developed his thought on the peculiarly meontic character of the human being, developing on the roots of this philosophy in his intellectual sources, Irenaeus and Origen, and in turn having a great influence on the anthropology of the Cappadocian Fathers. Hellenistic thought had tended to depict a bleak polarity in ontology. Things were either in being (*to on*), or not in being (*to ouk on*). Athanasios was formed by the Scriptures, however, and was particularly anxious to correct the local Egyptian views of his time, which suggested the soul of the individual was naturally immortal. For him, there was no such natural immortality, even of the spirit of the human being. All was a conditional gift. If immortality was achieved by the individual, it was solely as an external gift to the human nature, which was self-evidently corruptible. Plato's theory of the immortality of the soul has often been so enthusiastically received by Christians of different ages, that they have sometimes forgotten that the church has never taught or sanctioned such a pagan idea. The human being, as Athanasios knew, was conditionally immortal, but naturally corruptible. To connote such a novel concept, he added to the vocabulary of the Hellenist ontologists a third, middling category, calling it *meontic*. The adjectival suffix 'ontic' derives from the Greek word for being. The prefix 'me-' is the Greek conditional negative: having the effect (which English is not so succinctly capable of doing) of connoting a state or condition which is fundamentally tentative.

Something that is meontic, therefore, is poised between polarities. The human nature is thus depicted as a reactive force, an energy, rather than a fixed substantive category. Athanasios regards human life as existence (becoming), not being: something that we sense is called towards 'making a response' in order to define and claim its hold on reality.

Aristotle had introduced to his idea of natures (*ousiai*) the notion of teleotic development within set forms,[15] but had not gone as far as the Christian Fathers in seeing the very nature of human beings as itself an energy (*energeia*) that had been sent out by God for the purpose of lifting the very nature of mankind into a transcendence of itself in communion with the deity. In patristic thought humanity, therefore, hung upon the will of God for its proper existence in a way completely unlike any other nature that had been formed within the material creation.[16] Reflecting also on the startling concept of the creation of man from nothing (*ex nihilo*, or *ek ouk on*),[17] Athanasios considered the human nature as made up out of the very stuff or fabric[18] of nothingness, and with an innate ontological tendency to revert to nothingness. This tendency he called *ptharsia*, corruption or corruptibility, understanding it primarily ontologically rather than morally; although he always saw the moral dissolution of men and women as a direct result of their lapse of ontological energy.[19] To this extent, early Christian ethics is always a subfield of anthropology, and rooted in the sphere of ontology, something which makes it very intriguing, although difficult to communicate in modern terminology, where the syntax of argument has changed so much in contemporary discourse.

When the human being followed the natural tendency to dissolution, it was occupied with wholly material concerns. The end of the material life, however, was the corruption of both body and mind which was fixed within the material entity as an inescapable law of death. When the human being responded, on the other hand, to the deeper instinct which was planted within it by the direct gift of God, it found a different form of life that began rooted in material humanity, but rose out of it in a grace-filled existence that brought it into direct communion with God and the angelic beings. When the human lived such a life (Athanasios called it a life lived in 'accordance with the image of God') the material boundaries of the human nature (*ousia*) that were otherwise inflexible (death being a prime example of our limit) proved to be permeable to a new *energeia* of being. A new ontological rule was experienced, of which the gift of the Holy Spirit, and the anticipation of resurrection that flowed from this, were the primary (eschatological) signs in the present world order.

This dawning experience of the new life of Christ, graced with the intimation of immortality, was itself the first experience of the Resurrection which will be more fully graced to Christ-filled human beings in the next age, when their very material form will be radically transfigured. In the interim, the space of time between this present age and the next age, the human race serves as a testing ground of *ascesis* (athletic labours) where men and women prove and demonstrate the 'kind of nature' they possess by the quality of the different lives they manifest. This time of testing and manifesting shows humanity not to be a fixed condition, but more of a 'sliding scale', as it were. This is what Athanasios meant by our meontic state. We are, as the Fathers understand, what we become. And the more we become habituated in the good, the more established in that state we find ourselves to be. If we become aimless and directionless (become nothing, as it were) then we oscillate all the time, and are immensely unstable and impotent in being. If we tend towards a material lifestyle and its concomitant mentality, we inevitably embrace the dust of nothingness from which we were put together in this most fragile of all ontological conditions. If we embrace our destiny to be the communicant of the divine vision, on the other hand, we become no less than 'deified'[20] creatures. Even in this present lifetime such a person begins to transcend the limitations of material humanity. Athanasios particularly appeals[21] to the examples of the martyrs' courage, or the Christian virgin's chastity, or the desire of the believer to part with money and power, as examples of extraordinary grace that show the nature of such believers has already transcended the natural material limitations of an earthly nature, one that is made up from a response to basic instincts for self-preservation and pleasure.

In the patristic tradition of Irenaeus, Athanasios, and their followers, and thus in the mainline understanding of the Orthodox Church to this day, there is a deep optimism in this understanding of human life as an athletic context. In the Latin Western tradition, on the other hand, dominated as it was by St Augustine and his local church's pessimistic theories about the 'mass of perdition' which was the human race after the Fall, there is not the same sense of expectation and hopefulness. Orthodoxy, needless to say, never wholly endorsed Augustine's views of the Fall, or the *massa damnata* of a deeply damaged humanity that resulted from the Fall, and always retained a tradition more faithfully in line with the wider sentiment of the Greek Fathers. In this consistent view, humanity contained within itself, even after the Fall from grace (as recounted in the story of Adam and Eve[22]), the innate gift of the Image of the Divine which was the particular charism that marked out the *proprium* of human being (as distinct from angels or all other material entities).

This gift of the image is rooted in the psychic consciousness of the embodied soul that is the human creature.[23] Athanasios describes it as a shining mirror of the divinity that is within.[24] The person who wishes to see God need only turn the spiritual gaze interiorly, and there in the clarity of the God-seeking mind and soul will the image of God be radiant, and instructive. Of course, Athanasios implies that the 'mirror' is such as he would have known in his own time and place, fourth-century Alexandria. The mirror, therefore, is understood to be made of highly polished silver. And here lies the force of his analogy, in his treatise *Against the Nations*, about the effects of the Fall. After humanity turned its face away from the quest for the divine, and the grace-filled life of love that flowed from this, it embraced corruption, both morally and ontologically. At this instance the mirror began to tarnish and corrode. Soon it was impossible to see any reflection at all in the depths of the inner life. The loss of orientation that resulted from this became so deeply ingrained in the race that the whole covenant of prophetic instruction, and the system of the Law, was instituted by God to provide remedies for the innate orientation that humanity had lost.[25] Even this was not sufficient, and so the creative Logos himself came into history as Incarnate Lord, to reconfigure the inner structure of humanity's being, and redraw the fundamentals of psychic and moral teaching. The loss of the mirror, however, was not a wholesale collapse of the human ability to see God. The mirror was useless because it was no longer functioning, not because it was taken away.[26] St Athanasios, and many of the other Greek Fathers in their ascetical doctrine, calls for a 'cleaning of the surface'[27] so that it can function once again as a bright and reflective surface.

More on this, however, in a later discussion of Orthodoxy's ideas of redemption, for here it is enough to note that the significance of the divine image in humanity was taken to a pitch in the masterful work of patristic theologians such as St Cyril of Alexandria, who demonstrated the perfectly close weave between anthropology and the gift of deification.[28] For the moment I wish to draw attention to the principle that runs throughout Athanasios, and indeed through all the great Fathers of the Church, that the mirror remains in the interior consciousness even when tarnished. It can be cleansed, and will again function as a clear revelant of the divine presence. Anthropology is thus a sacred thing; part of the fabric of revelation. Creation itself is the first revelation of the divine light to the human creature. The light of the divine presence is thus lodged in the very fabric of the ontology of the cosmos. This is in no way akin to Gnostic panentheism (the doctrine that an all-pervading deity inhabits, or co-inheres within, the cosmic structure), but in the sense that God's divine energy, the reflected image of his action of loving outreach (and thus an accurate image of his own presence), is within the very fabric of material and rational being, as its ontological foundation and (for the ensouled creation) its destined goal (*telos*). From the moment the human being was aware, therefore, the sense of the divine nearness was part of the essence of human experience and awareness.[29]

For such reasons, therefore, Orthodox thought resists a dominant aspect of Western religious philosophy that has tended to elevate so-called supernatural revelation over and against 'natural religion'. For Orthodoxy the two things are so intimately woven together in the very substrate of the creation, and most particularly in the constitution of the human creature, that there can never be anything, in relation to either the human or angelic orders, that is simply 'natural'. All being, for both ontological orders, is an effluence of the divine grace, an expression of both species' complete ontological reliance on God, and finds its true harmony and purpose when it manifests itself as a quest for appropriate communion through the glorification of so great a Father. A later discussion of the Orthodox liturgical ethos will explore some of these insights. Suffice it for the moment to note that while many external critics find fault with Orthodoxy's liturgical centrality (those who are hostile call it a form of ecclesiastical introversion), the Orthodox themselves understand that, in the unfolding experience of the communal sacred liturgy, the very fabric of the universe is passing by in epiphanic revelation. The ranks of angels gather with the church on earth. What happens, far from being 'ecclesiasticism run riot' is, for those taking part with a refined sensibility, no less than the height of existential engagement.

The great patristic prayers comprising the Anaphora of the sacred liturgy also show this cosmic dimension of faith in almost every instance. In this sense the liturgy is the re-enactment of the sacred drama of creation and revelation, culminating, as it does for our radical Christian philosophy, at the Cross and the tomb of the Lord. It is this moment of world history (the *kairos* of grace which the sacred liturgy is), to which the act of creation runs as its original *telos*.[30] The church, finding its gathering-force in the holy liturgy therefore, learns to gather its understanding of life and society from that focal point onwards, rather than the reverse, which argues, falsely, that liturgical 'style' ought to be a reflection of the sociological condition of the Christians in their present generation. Liturgy, for the Orthodox, is not primarily a pedagogical experience, or a community act of conforming to new requirements of the historical mission; rather, it is the immersion in the great narrative of creation and salvation; a participation in the formative energy that made and saved the world, and which, in its ever-renewed epiphany, reorientates the individual and the community to the authentic springs of their being.

This anthropology suffused with the light of God's energy is at the heart of all Orthodox thought. The Orthodox Church has always believed that the individual is the energy of the image of God, and this is also the root of all its ethical understanding. Above all else it suggests how mysterious is the human creature: a being that is mysterious even to the deepest self who individuates (or hypostasizes) it. In fact, in the individual, especially in the root consciousness of the divine that is the highest aspiration of men and women, lies the supreme force of individuation, as well as the path towards ontological fulfilment, which Christianity understood to be the *telos* of the human nature that Aristotle had talked about as being the ultimate definition of the concept of nature. This supreme instance of individuation is sacred, unlike anything else in the cosmos, and forms in the human race the reason why the perfection of humanity is its transcendence,[31] and why the consummation of individuated identity is also the common ground of communion.[32] Non-Christian, or defectively Christian, anthropologies are unable to sustain harmony in this essential paradox of humanity. They either run to a philosophy of individuation in which the person wars against the environment and strives to excel among other innumerable 'persons' who are its rivals; or they look to forms of Gnostic transcendentalism that seek to leave behind material conceptions in the quest for the divine, or else they bury themselves totally in an existentialist shortening of the human horizons into an all-consuming materiality. At the end of the day, Orthodoxy insists on the perennial freshness and beauty of the human being, even in the fallen condition, not for the sake of human pride or self-confidence but in order to ensure that the essential truth of the human person is never forgotten: their luminous *energeia* as a song of God's mercy and philanthropy and, because of that, a mysterious entity who is innately beautiful, glorious, and alluring.

Because of their biblical rootedness, and their insistence on the starting point of the personal, the ancient Fathers followed closely after the scriptural way of describing 'man' in terms of 'Adam'. The name and the state are one and the same. Modern theological sensibilities to gender bias in language have today demanded more sensitivity than used to be shown to the concept of using 'man' to signify 'men and women'. To avoid this kind of gender obscuring, many writers will now prefer to use 'humanity' in place of 'man', and 'humankind' in place of 'mankind'. Throughout all the patristic writing, however, the first of those synonyms is used, not accidentally, but with deliberate emphasis. The Fathers read the story of the Fall and restoration of the race as the drama of a single individual. They are, of course, constantly thinking of the Genesis story when they argue that man was made not in the abstract, but in the particular and in the personal. God, that is, entered into relationship with a man, a particular Adam. With this man, and because of him, the relationship was also damaged. To effect its repair was the task of the second man, the New Adam.[33] This is highly symbolical theology of course, but it is taken by the Fathers with great seriousness that in some sense or other there are two human beings that count: Adam and Jesus. No matter that history tells us that there have been countless generations; there are still only 'two' that constitute the history of the world's salvation.

It is suggestive, for in our own history of salvation, we too are either Adam or Christ. If we are faithful we experience the progressive leaving behind of Adamic being and the

191

constant 'putting on'[34] of the New Adam's gracefulness. In Orthodox anthropology, therefore, we find this constant allusion to the oscillation in human experience between the collective (or the familial), and the personalist (or the individual). Sometimes, especially when reflecting on accountability for moral lapses, the oscillation is significant for its middle ground (what we might today think of as the 'social guilt' for sin and defect in the world, or corporate sinfulness), but sometimes for its separate poles. At one pole we experience how sin creates defect in the world that brings heavy suffering on the individual who is not personally responsible for the suffering at all. War is a primary example. At the other pole, we see how individual wickedness inevitably damages the integrity and grace of the one who commits it, and can bring immediately caused sufferings in its train (addiction or sexual infidelity are common instances of faults leaving a broad wake of misery after them). This is not to suggest that all suffering is the direct result of sin, even less to suggest that anyone who suffers is paying price for their own sin, though such views can be found in some of the ancient authors and are sometimes voiced by moralists today who, in my opinion, lack the prophetic gift, as well as being deficient in pastoral charity. Such a view, generally, represents the dim-wittedness of the consolers of Job, and was rebuked by the divine voice itself: 'Who is this that darkens counsel by words so devoid of knowledge?'[35]

The Orthodox Church understands the complex range of sufferings that beset mankind and form a backdrop to human existence in the material world, as it were, as an acute form of spiritual problem or better, a mystery of the spirit. For if it were not an attitude constantly springing from the spiritual intelligence of human beings that such sufferings 'ought not' to happen, there would be no 'problem of evil' at all. It is the confluence of the church's faith in the supreme kindness and providence of God, allied with the intensely personalized sense of the individual's hypostatic being, that raises the problematic of suffering as an acutely theological question. While animals, and angels for that matter, can be said to suffer, there is not a problem of suffering that besets them alongside the physical or psychic pain of the experience.

Many of the range of human sufferings are seen by Orthodoxy as the result of wickedness, and the alienation from a loving lifestyle that was our ideal; but not all evils that beset humanity can be seen to derive from this collapse, except in so far as generally speaking, the Fall is understood as the 'alienation' from a primeval immortal and joyful existence, and an exile into the material domain.[36] Some of them arise from the very fact of our transitional ontology: the fragility of the material order in which we exist as a feather on the wind, blown on the one side by massive forces such as tsunamis and earthquakes, and on the other hand by tiny forces such as bacteria, viruses, and defective gene connections. To such suffering, diffused through the world, Orthodoxy has no definitive 'answer' other than to advocate compassion that mirrors the ultimate philanthropy of God, and fervent prayer that calls out to God to ameliorate sorrow, in the belief that the alleviation of suffering is always in harmony with the generous and merciful character of the God who wishes to give his children bread, never a stone.[37]

Just as God has reached into the heart of death and pain that is part of the human experience of being alive, and has offered its redemptive transfiguration in love through the Cross of the Lord, so too the church, following in the steps of its Lord, is called to meet human suffering with personal courage and communal philanthropy, and alleviate the pains of the suffering in whatever way it can: physically, morally, or emotionally. This is why the church's involvement in the social institutions of mercy (hospitals and schools) or suffering (prisons and places of enslavement) is a primary element of its mission. Relieving the suffering caused by natural disasters and chronic disease constitutes a major element of the church's necessary response: a major way of manifesting among society its belief in the glory of the human being as the radiant image of God. Some of the greatest sermons of the most eloquent of the Fathers, especially St Basil the Great, Gregory the Theologian, John Chrysostom, and Pope Gregory I,[38] have been devoted to this aspect of theology as the praxis of philanthropy.

It is clear enough, however, that the removal of pain from this world order is not wholly in our human power. Part of the very essence of the limitation (*horos*) that defines and prescribes our natures as material beings is bound up with the fact of suffering. The exquisite sensitivity of the cornea, part of our basic capacity to see at all, is exactly what causes so much distress to those with eye disease. And the incredible refinement of our consciousness is, for that reason, a curse for those whose awareness has become excessively depressed or unbalanced. To be human is to suffer, and ultimately to die. To be human in the form of the New Adam is to learn not to be afraid of that startling realization that life-wisdom brings, for the Christian faith constantly teaches us to hope for the transfiguration of that suffering alongside all our earthly experience, including the joys that so often outweigh the amount of suffering most of us witness in the course of our life; and that (along with the effort of the community of believers to alleviate suffering in love and consolation) can indeed be the greatest comfort to the sorrowing and agonized. But, even so, suffering remains a problem of the theological order; an ultimate question which was asked even by the Lord himself: 'My God, My God, why have you forsaken me?'[39] For it is not only the understandable disorder and collapse of the fabric of the self that makes us cry out in bewilderment, but also, and particularly so, the allocation of the degree of suffering that falls to any particular individual in the course of a life's journey that is problematic.

There seems to be no reason for some suffering, especially that of children, the old, the innocent generally. Nothing in it seems to be able to be refined easily. For those who have known a suffering that has proved elevating, or reformatory, there are innumerable others who have been crushed or spiritually annihilated by their suffering. Also, in many instances the power of evil is attracted to the site of human suffering and adds to it, clouding and darkening the experience of suffering even more with the fog of wickedness. The interwoven histories of the famines of Africa and civil war are a case in point. Those who have any experience of life know that the tired cliché that pain ennobles is simply not true. Even so, many voices in the church, in times past, have felt driven to account for every single element of suffering in the world as either a 'righteous chastisement' of God for hidden sins, or the 'opportunity for spiritual strengthening' sent by God to those who might otherwise grow cold in faith. These attitudes (inspired by a desire to keep faith with the God of mercy and justice) have often been disastrously and callously inflicted on the suffering by self-righteous 'comforters' who thereby risk the serious alienation of the wounded they speak to, not least because of the very contradictions of the image of the God of mercy which they have represented. The Old Testament, it is true, has numerous texts that offer this vision of suffering as chastisement for sins,[40] but our Lord himself spoke with much more discretion and reserve about the mysteries of God's allocation of suffering to pilgrims on this earth when he told his disciples not to be so sure that those who suffered misfortune were 'evidently' under the anger of God.[41] His repeated instruction was for the believer to repent, to pray for the deliverance from evil, the passing away of the chalice, if it could be possible.[42]

This is why the Orthodox Church's deepest response to the problem of suffering (and its own history has been one of great sorrow as it has made its way through this world, so it does not speak of this as from a culpable naivety) is to ask God for that 'deliverance from evil' each and every day. This is with an honest sense that there is indeed within human suffering the clear and often palpable manifestation of a power of evil that is part of the world order since the Kingdom of God has not yet fully arrived. The 'scandal of suffering' is exactly this intimation (within the church certainly, but also in the wider world too) that physical suffering that oppresses and diminishes the unique and sacred mystery of the human being is a kind of sacrilege, as well as an affront to the 'proper' order of being. But, if God has permitted this to afflict humans, it is not the same as saying God has willed it, or sent it. All the church's prayers for physical healing involve the exorcism of malign spiritual forces which, if they have not stirred up the problem to begin with, often flock to the side of the sick person to make life more wretched. The discernment of this element of malignity in the problem of suffering was, of course, one of the chief marks of the Lord's own ministry of healing through exorcism, which he left as an example to his disciples in all later generations.

No prayer service in the church takes place without the constant petitioning of God to 'help, save, and have mercy on' his afflicted people. If an Orthodox person becomes ill, either in body or spirit, they will usually, immediately, ask for the prayers of the priest and the church. The first reaction to illness, along with seeking medical help as appropriate, is to turn to God in repentance,[43] and to use the illness to lift up to God the 'incense-offering' of our own fragility, and from the dark place of our weakness to call on the mercy of God with special fervour. Those who have no present suffering attribute it as a blessing from God, and double their prayers for those who are currently undergoing difficulty and grief, that God may alleviate their pains swiftly. This network of prayer and compassion is part of the very fabric of the communion of the saints (an inner mystery of the church's presence on earth) and flows out beyond the visible boundaries of the church to be a blessing invoked day and night on the entire world. Just as the forces that are hostile to the Kingdom of God gather to make an impact on the world, so too the love of the communion of the saints gathers and swells in the world, making an impact for the good, establishing once more, in this fallen world, that the ultimate law of being is the doxology of God from the joyful hearts of the saints. Orthodoxy is entirely and deeply serious about its attitude to the hostile powers, as well as its awareness of the beneficent force of God and his angels and saints. These are not archaic elements of mythology for Orthodoxy, but part of the fabric of the universe seen in the light of the mysterious destiny of the 'third creation'.[44]

Allied to this awareness of the spiritual essence of suffering is the deep-seated belief in the Orthodox Church that its prayers are effective.[45] In other words the prayer of the church alleviates and banishes pain and sorrow, through the mercy of God. One of the unfortunate aspects of the modern era is the manner in which the hi-tech hospitals of the West have become so spiritually desolate, and even hostile to prayer as little more than eccentric magic in the mindsets of many doctors. The attitude that suffering ought to be accepted stoically, or with resignation to the inevitable breakdown of a neuro-chemical system is instinctively resisted by Orthodoxy; so too is the agnostic apathy that sullenly regards pain as a betrayal by God, or as an excuse to curse the Father as being no father at all. Sorrow and pain that are 'sent' by God, such as endure regardless of the fervent prayer of the church, both personal and collective,[46] is ultimately seen by Orthodoxy as a mysterious invitation to enter into the sufferings of the Lord himself, so as to share in his glory.[47] Even in this spiritual embrace of suffering, however, the emphasis in Orthodoxy is always on the hope of the Victory which Christ has already won.

It is the incomprehensible allocation of pain in such different degrees to different people in life which is the mysterious thing that is so often perplexing, and has troubled even the great saints from time immemorial. The jubilant optimism of the Psalmist who says that he has 'never seen the just man forsaken, or his children begging for bread'[48] is a very 'long perspective' of faith that few people would readily share, or perhaps voice, today when the wicked are indeed seen to prosper, and the innocent and the poor endure more than their share of the griefs of the world. But when the Lord himself addressed this problem of trustfulness in God, in the face of sorrow and pain,[49] he spoke invariably about the need for the courageous facing of suffering in the overall light of a profound and irrefragable certainty that God's eye was not elsewhere, but rather more closely and compassionately on the suffering disciple than others.[50] To accept suffering, as if from the hand of a loving God, is an intensely mature spiritual capacity. It is the willing assumption of the 'chalice of God's anger' as the Scripture phrases it; the chalice the Lord himself tasted of in his Passion.[51] It was his own advice and example to us to pray fervently that it would not fall to us as individuals to taste that cup on earth;[52] that is why the central petition of the Lord's Prayer is that we should be delivered from evil.

Orthodox anthropology (and the problem of suffering is one acute manifestation of this principle) thus sees the human being as a work in progress, not a fixed reality. The true reality of our being is in course of being unfolded here. Everything that affects us is the material for the ultimate purpose of our life: our unfolding into beings that will live by eternal doxology, and no longer on the basis of chemical processing. We are, from the moment of our birth, in the process of dying, but that dying is a process of new forms of living taking over from the old. Out of our youth grows maturity. The one does not come in spite of the other, but through and because of it. So, with the Christian life, the constant perspective of life as a movement towards transfiguration does not denigrate the validity and beauty and immediacy of this present life, but neither does it allow us to limit our perspective on what humanity is to the affairs of the present. Orthodoxy understands that life emerges fully only when human beings have clarified their understanding sufficiently to see God and accept God's beneficent rule in every aspect of that life. Such a vision, and the obedience to act upon it, once seen, demand a high level of asceticism from the disciple. Dimness of sight, and reluctance to follow the call of God, are often thought of as more comfortable and secure lifestyles, and to overcome this tendency to inertia the disciple requires the great grace of God, and a regular habit of discipline which church life provides (the reading of the psalms and the ecclesiastical prayers, fasting, attendance as a community at the Holy Liturgy and sacraments, and active interaction with other Christians who are on the same path of growth). Only by the faithful dint of regular practice, and incessant yet hope-filled repentance and reorientation after our mistakes, can the Orthodox break the bonds of self-interest and find an ever-growing eagerness to follow the path of the Lord, who walked along such uncomfortable tracks.

The ancient Orthodox writings, found in the Byzantine ascetics and philosophers, describe this 'process' which is the human being as a lifelong struggle to allow the 'higher' parts of human perception to predominate over the more material instincts. The ascetics described a human as comprised of *nous, logos, psyche*, and *soma*. We might translate that complex synthesis as the correlation of spiritual awareness, intelligent awakening, soul-perceptiveness, and bodily grounding. Each of those primary functions, as the Byzantine anthropologists understood them, were profoundly related to one another in a hierarchical correlation that immediately affected its nearest 'neighbour' (the body conditioned soul-states, soul-states directly affected intellectual perception, which in turn closely informed spiritual states). One could not go directly from body state to spiritual awareness (so drug-induced ecstasy, for example, was a spiritual delusion, not an advancement) but none of these states was 'separate', and all interrelated through a regularly working hierarchy of being. The presiding genius of the system was 'meant to be' the human spiritual instinct: obedience to God and love for the divine presence that would condition all human interactivity as a society of love. However, with the Fall, the wise presidency of the spirit over the mind and heart of human beings was frequently overthrown in favour of the wilder governance of theories, immediate gains, comforts, desires, and obsessions. When a human being is 'ruled' by the lower orders, then chaos and the self-interest that elevates itself over others (even at their cost) are the order of the day.

The Fathers went on to say that this inevitably produced a life of sorrow, for persons who had so overthrown divine order in their own life both made others full of grief and caused untold suffering for themselves too. When, on the other hand, the primacy of spiritual and intellectual sense was established, then the body was taught sufficient discipline to join in the church's living movement towards a harmonious self-alignment with the values of the Kingdom. The Fathers knew that the body or the mind might regularly rebel against the governance of the *nous* (the spiritual instinct) because their own immediate satisfactions seemed preferable (a preference established, therefore, by the 'sense of order' of a materialist consciousness), and the value of personal asceticism, regularly practised as part of a Christian lifestyle (prayer, fasting, and the quest for simplicity in favour of excess) was thus always necessary to ensure balance in the ethical and spiritual life of a disciple. We were like ships, the Fathers said, blown across the seas of great desires, and ideas, and the task of making sure the ship moved in harmony with the heavenly path was a one that required constant 'watchfulness' (*nipsis*). The Christian life that has little understanding of the complex synthesis which constitutes the human being, or which has little place for ascetic 'attentiveness', is one that is out of harmony with fundamental Orthodox attitudes.

Orthodoxy, in this respect, shows itself to be a close and compassionate student of human psychology, but resists many aspects of contemporary psychological characterizations that tend to leave out of the picture the human being's instinctive spiritual compass. When it is properly understood, in the light of this overall anthropological matrix, Orthodox asceticism is a joy-making process, aimed at the clarification and liberation of the human psyche, and its elevation to deeper perspectives and values. It is invariably marked by a turning to greater simplicity in individual and communal life, and a growing desire for compassion. If an individual Orthodox life, or that of an Orthodox community (such as a parish) does not manifest such basic growth signs and tendencies there is surely something 'undeveloped' about it, for this movement to the simplicity and joy and selflessness of the Lord himself is an inescapable charism of Christian truth.

This sense of humanity as an endless pilgrim's progress deeply marks Orthodox prayer services, from the baptismal rite, which speaks of the fall from grace and the rendering of the human life into a labour of 'return' to God, even to the funeral service, which speaks of the human passage as a life-long 'burial procession' that shuffles past but which takes as its song the cheerful motif 'Alleluia, Alleluia, Alleluia'. The journey is often difficult and laden with sorrow, but the hope of the church takes its song in the major key and thereby makes of the journey an Alleluia.

The Fathers of the Church write about the transcendent soul with great poetic élan. Gregory the Theologian, for example says:

> The soul is a breath of God, and while being heavenly it endures being mixed with what is from the dust. It is a light enclosed in a cave, though still it is divine and inextinguishable.... The Word spoke and having taken part of the newly-created earth with his immortal hands he formed my image, and gave to it his own life; for he sent into it the spirit, a ray of the invisible deity.[53]

Despite the apparently dichotomous language that is often used (body–soul), the Eastern Christian writers more commonly use the notion of a complex synthesis of spiritual, intellectual, psychic, and corporeal elements that together make up the human reality, and which together will work towards the transcendence of human life into the next age, which is salvation, and which is the deification of the race promised in Jesus' gift of the Holy Spirit. Orthodoxy does not teach that the soul is divine, nor that it is intrinsically immortal in the way Plato imagined, but 'conditionally immortal' in dependence on God's promise of the gift of life. The ancient controversy as to when the soul was made was never solved decisively by the Orthodox tradition. It preferred to leave the matter without comment, except to mark a strong refutation of Origen's speculation that the soul was pre-existent and fell to earth as part of its pedagogical punishment, destined once more to rise to heaven and shuffle off the body in the process. Orthodoxy has a perennial suspicion of dichotomists who so quickly divide the one from the other, when the whole Christian tradition of the incarnation of God in the flesh so dramatically distances itself from such residual Platonism.

We are not angels. We are not simply animals alongside the other animal orders who are not driven by the noetic instinct (the divine image and likeness placed in the core of their being). Gregory the Theologian calls mankind the 'third creation', a mixture of the other two orders of creation, the spiritual (angels) and the material (the cosmos and animal life), and he sees this conjunction of opposites as a source of much conflict and sorrow in a human life. But he also envisages it as the ontological ground of our ascent: for the mixture of our being is part and parcel of God's invitation to this tensile ontology (our human race) on its fragile planet, to ascend to the vision of glory through the love of the Lord. To this extent, belief in God is part and parcel of a

197

transcendent belief in oneself. The Russian theologian Pomazansky puts it in an interesting observation:

> The more lively is one's faith in God, the more firm and undoubting is [a person's] faith in the immortality of soul... One who completely loses or stifles faith in God usually ceases to believe in the immortality of the soul, or the future life at all, and this is surely understandable. A man receives the power of faith from the very source of life, and if he cuts off his tie with this source he loses this stream of living power.[54]

Our God is the One Who Is. When the disciple is in ontological harmony with this God, the disciple also comes into life. What that life means begins at our conception, and flowers out of a simple biological striving towards life, and food, into a wonderful blossoming of psychic and intellectual complexity. In its ascetical and anthropological doctrine, the Orthodox Church also wishes to insist that this blossoming is not ended here, in the beauty of a pacific and merciful human culture, and the constant and vigilant suppression of humanity's tribal bloodiness, but is actually taken further into the blossoming of the human being into the true and final identity of eternal glory. On that day, the body is not forgotten, or superseded, but truly transcended in a new glory, comparable to that shown in Christ's own transfigured body. Such metamorphosis begins here and now. Its supreme manifestation is the selfless compassion that was so readily seen in Jesus.

SALVATION AND THE CALL TO ASCENT

Orthodoxy sees the human being, therefore, as a dynamic of ascent: a creature whose destiny is open-ended and always in process of being fulfilled. God's word of creation for men and women is still being spoken in an active present tense: 'Let us make Man in our own image and after our own likeness.'[55] St Gregory of Nyssa spoke of this ascent as *epektasis*, a complex term that evokes the endless 'stretching out' of the terms of human nature as the creature always 'reaches out' to the God who exceeds all created limits. He saw this *epektasis* as one of the delights of heaven. This concept of the ascent of men and women to their divine destiny, something that is called the 'doctrine of salvation' in Western systematics, is more usually conveyed by the Orthodox concept of the deification of the human race in Christ. The word is deliberately strong. It was meant to raise eyebrows, and seemingly still does when those from outside Orthodoxy, especially evangelicals, first encounter a classically articulated patristic doctrine that seems to them so daring and so apparently divergent from the usual paths of atonement theology that have so dominated post-medieval Western Christian discourse.

Deification in Orthodox theology does not mean that humans 'become God' in a pagan sense of *apotheosis* that the pre-Christian Romans spoke of; what it does mean is that the grace of God 'conforms'[56] the saints to his presence so that they can see and enjoy the divine radiance which is impossible for the unclean to witness except as a torment. The divine presence itself so changes the nature of the creature in this radical cleansing that this metamorphosis has to be spoken of as a transfiguration by grace. *Theosis*, therefore, is what the Orthodox East means by the perfection of the power of grace so irradiating the being of the redeemed saints that they too become light-filled, perfected by the mercy of God, in order to be conformed to the divine presence. The difference in nature between creature and creator is never annihilated or forgotten,[57] but the 'chasm' between God and his beloved is diminished, and this because it is God himself who makes the step towards the creature. In its concept of *apotheosis* pre-Christian Roman paganism taught that humankind could step towards God. Orthodoxy teaches, instead, that the unapproachable Creator actually steps towards us: and that is the difference. The divine presence does not simply delight, it utterly changes, the saints.[58] *Theosis* is the high road of how Orthodoxy approaches salvation theology.

It is not that Cross-centred atonement theology is lacking in the Eastern Church: far from it. The Orthodox know the significance of the Lord's work of atonement as the bestowing of the profound gift of reconciliation with the Father mediated through the Son's gift of the Spirit to his church.[59] But the Crucifixion is never seen (as seems to be the case in some recent Western thought) as the 'abandonment' of the Son by the Father. Those who reiterate the Lord's words from the Cross: 'My God, My God, why have you forsaken me?'[60] to support such a strange view, have never read to the end of that same prayer from the Psalms that he was reciting as he died, or seen the power of the triumph of faith that is represented in the last verses. Atonement was the apostle Paul's great theological theme in all his writings. But the theology of atonement as it developed after Anselm of Canterbury, in the Western churches, and especially as this has been taken up in the high medieval Latin Church, and fought against in the writings of the Reformers, has, to a certain extent, brought much of Western reflection on this theme into a problematic condition.

From the Orthodox perspective, the dissonance began with Anselm's introduction into the biblical idioms of atonement (that deeply sacramental and joyous theology of celebration and purification) the muddy Norman sense of feudal obligations and punitive satisfaction theory. The strange mix that resulted can be seen in many variants in the later pieties of the West, from the bloody crucifixes held up for emulation and empathy in Mediterranean Catholicism to the severe ethos of Reformation thought on justification and redemption. These are great themes indeed, and cannot be justly summed up here, but it is no exaggeration or mere cliché to say that Orthodoxy's first response to the concept or symbol of the Lord's Cross is to associate it with victory. Almost every patristic hymn and writing celebrates the Cross as the Lord's 'trophy'; and approaches his sufferings through the lens of his glory. It does not exegete the Resurrection through the lens of the Cross, but the Cross through the gateway of the glory: the glory that was his from eternity as Only Begotten, and the glory that he won bodily, as the church's hero and liberator, in his incarnate ministry as Beloved Servant. The theme of victory does not underestimate the impact of the Lord's suffering (we do not wish to hurry over the Cross in order to arrive painlessly at the joy of the Resurrection) but equally the church does not become lost in the sufferings, or overcast by the gloom of a religion of suffering and satisfaction of an angry God. The Lord's wounds are his glory in the struggle not with his Father, but with the forces of evil. The Passion of Christ (and so it calls out to all his believers) is undertaken for us to be our encouragement: for the Lord was glorified; his suffering and rejection was the warrior's blow that reduced him to his knees, but he stood up again and won the fight.

He won it decisively, on behalf of his people: and resurrectional joy shared in the church is, not least, a light that floods into every aspect of believers' lives, that they will never, ever, have to walk in the darkness in which he walked, that darkness of complete lovelessness and triumphant evil, for he has broken the victory of loveless evil, and brought love even into the depths of hell. Even if the Lord sends a share of his sufferings to each of his friends during the course of their lives (large or small it may be according to the challenge he has set for each one), no disciple ever walks again in hopeless darkness,[61] for his presence is always as the giver of light, the warrior who won triumph; and the Cross is his sign of victory that casts away hate-filled gloom, and sends the forces of evil flying in panic. The poor are never forgotten by the Lord of Humility, and even their ongoing sufferings, their apparent continued occlusion by the forces of evil and oppression, serve only to diffuse the light of Christ's blessing over a darkened world. All Orthodox know this be true as a basic element of their faith, and of their practice of prayer. The Cross is their victory, and their hope, and often has been their consolation in the long dark night of suffering. The marking of the self with the sign of the Cross is one of the most distinctive things any observer will see if they ever look at the Orthodox at prayer.

This sense of confidence in God is the essence of what the New Testament describes as faith (*pistis*). Confidence, however, needs to be distinguished from naive optimism, that often can become self-centred, and forget the cry of others in distress. A strong belief in God's victory characterizes Orthodox faith, but it is born out of a sense of suffering and dependence, not meant to replace those things. Orthodox believers are not meant to close their eyes to doubt, or to sing 'Hosannah', when their hearts are weeping. There is need for a mature sense of how providence works, to distinguish it strongly and passionately from such aberrations (as have appeared in modern Christianity) as the 'Gospel of Prosperity' and other comparable heresies.

The Orthodox believe that God is attentively careful in his overarching providence of the world. He is not tired, incapable, distracted, or neglectful. Neither is the divine providence meant to ensure our species enjoys every delight and pleasure and happiness as it makes its way through history. God's providential care does not equate with him being the genie in a bottle to resolve all our problems and hardships. We are sentient, corporeal, creatures in a dangerous material cosmos. Living things eat one another on this earth; the predators around us that are larger than us (sharks) or smaller than us (bacteria) are not endowed with the innate intelligence to recognize the spiritual priority of humans, and hence attack us as yet another part of the food chain. We also act with deeply irrational behaviour patterns that can cause immense suffering in addition to what is destined to come our way 'naturally'. In addition to hunger and disease, for example, we have often added war and brutality, because we preferred violence to peaceful negotiation of a civilized exchange of goods, and because we have often, as a species, closed our hearts to the other in preference to having the pain of opening oneself out to the other and attending to the weak as the chief goal of a system of culture. In addition to all these 'complications', there is an evil abroad in the world (human and daimonic) that accumulates as an increasingly perverse force throughout history, attempting to make a counter-culture to the Kingdom of God. Its manifestations are variegated and diffuse in the world, and are always endowed with a spirit of malice and hostility to humanity's finest aspirations. Though it is a damaging and dangerous force, and can often destroy many of the attempts to achieve the good, and can even test the elect by scandalizing them with the appearance of a world masquerading as a hostile joke,[62] it is ultimately chained to futility by the command of God. Nevertheless, evil has not lost all its teeth: a fact that calls out to the elect to be as aware of cosmic evil as they are aware of material evil. One needs to know how to cross a road safely; equally one needs to be taught how to recognize unerringly the smiling face of wickedness.

In spite of all the hardships that life in a fragile body brings (this 'poor bone-house' the Old English poets used to call it), and all the sufferings that are further fomented by the presence of evil in the world's affairs, the Orthodox believe that there is a deep-seated instinct, or power, that puts the world to rights, like the centrifuge that keeps a top spinning vertically, and will right it again after imbalances. This, we believe, is the great 'governance' of the wonder of creation that God has instituted, making creation the profoundly good and holy thing that it is,[63] and the awe-inspiring wonder that lies in the macro-structures and micro-structures of all sentient and non-sentient reality. Orthodoxy believes implicitly that God, having made this wondrous world, 'contracted' or covenanted with it in the sense of retaining his sheltering hand over the wholeness of the created order. This applies to all things, not simply humanity in the world. All is blessed by the hand of God, and all things are the 'songs' of God's glory: even things that humans find odd, and perhaps disgusting. Ugly insects are as much part of the song of glory as graceful trees. Sin alone is not part of the song of glory. Alone in the creation it cannot sing at all.

But, although one can discern the touch of the maker in the symphony of what has been made, it is by no means true that the face of God lies, waiting to be easily discerned, behind the fabric of the material creation. The cosmic creation is a mani-festation of God's power, certainly, but never of God's essence. Nature theologies, of various kinds, but especially of the pantheistic form, are following a radically divergent track from Orthodoxy. Although Eastern Christianity affirms the beauty of the world as a 'sign' of the mystery of God's activity among us, nevertheless it insists that the world cannot reveal to us the unapproachable nature of God himself. It is in the trinitarian mystery alone, that is, only from and through the starting point of the Incarnation of the divine in the cosmos, that we find the difficult and partial revelation of God's purposes in a world that otherwise seems merely 'natural' to a non-believer. To the Orthodox, the material world is not 'natural' at all, for all is a miracle of providence. The existence of the human being's spiritual intelligence is the most miraculous part of the earthly creation. Ignorance of it is the most awful example of frustrated development conceivable. All is sustained on the breath of the power of God, like a feather floating on the air. All is so regular (we wake every morning and begin again) that we presume it has a 'natural' stability of its own regardless of faith in God, but the truth is that although the feather may not comprehend how it is sustained in perfect rest, it is nevertheless a dynamic energy of God that supports all being. The Orthodox vesperal prayer expresses it as: 'All things are held in the spotless hollow of your hands.'[64]

St John of Damascus defines providence as 'the care that God takes over all things', and he describes it as something 'both fair and most excellent in itself.'[65] For St John, the provident power that rules the world's affairs is simply 'God's good will' towards his own creation. He makes a distinction, in affairs that relate to humans, between those that are 'within our power' to determine in life and those that are not. The former, he says, lie outside the providence of God (though always are contained within his prescience and destiny) because they have been commended into our hands as agents of free will. This honour (and challenge) marks our rise into awareness and the rank of co-creative agents alongside God: like the angels we are called to act as priests and spiritual connoisseurs of the cosmos. But with regard to those things that properly lie within the providence of God, all the material regulation of the cosmos, and all human affairs that are greater than human choice, certain rules apply. The overarching call to the church is to believe that God's providence is always 'fair and excellent', and demonstrative of fatherly love. So how, then, do human beings approach 'difficult' providence? That is, when something horrible happens?

St John makes an important distinction between God's providence of 'good will', that is his default condition of beneficence towards creation, and his providence of 'permission', when he allows the forces of evil to have a certain latitude (acknowledging even here the extent of the dominion of free will afforded to the creatures) despite the fact that such perverse will is aimed at fostering and extending the domain of evil within the cosmos. So at times there is a direct and beneficent providence from God expressed in fatherly gift, and at times God defers to the free will of agents that have deeply set their faces against the Kingdom of truth and righteousness, just as he often defers his providence over the righteous, in favour of those who elect self-determination in place of reliance on the provisions of divine good will.[66] It is basic to the Orthodox faith, however, that even when God allows latitude to a free will that seeks to aggregate things to itself, he will subject all things to the overarching power of the Kingdom of God. So, however much 'the nations rage and kings conspire'[67] the Lord will ultimately 'laugh them to scorn' in the defence of his righteous on earth, and their final vindication. Though this, it appears from Scripture (and from life's experience), may not be the case here on earth for every life and family, and never without an apocalyptic struggle, in all periods, and in every life, against the forces of evil that are never dormant.[68]

Even for the elect who submit themselves to God's providence as entirely as they are able to conform themselves to it, and as best they can discern it (the aim of an advanced spiritual life) the path of life will not necessarily be smooth and painless. God's active providence especially blesses those who commend and conform themselves to it. For them the angels of God have a specially active ministry[69] and there is a growing sense how all the twists and turns of life are becoming more transparent to the action of God (even, and especially, the difficult parts). But even for those who live fully under the default of the 'fatherly providence' of God, as St John calls it, he reminds us that a father's care for a family involves a fatherly love that at once blesses and chastises. It is to be seen as a blessing even when God corrects and turns our life in certain directions, making us 'learn wisdom' by a variety of means. St John lists the numerous examples from the New Testament of different, and difficult, providences, that amount to life-challenges that have a didactic quality. Some disciples are brought low in order to set them off on a better path. It is always a profound matter to discern the message from the varieties of challenges one is faced with (whether God is correcting us simply, or whether we are being subjected to the assaults of evil and malice). There is always a lesson to be learned in suffering (though not always at the time), but when a human being is in great distress there is need for a deep sense of trust in the divine mercy, and a profound spiritual wisdom that can explain the mysterious ways of providence as an invitation to move into the Kingdom. To reduce all this spiritual complexity and mystery to the blanket advice that 'God must be punishing you' is offensive to Christian faith as well as scandalously foolish advice to those who are spiritually vulnerable. Regrettably, many think that they are being zealous when they insist on being naive in this way; and they greatly obscure the mysteries of God.

Orthodoxy sees the best way to conform to faith in a providential and merciful God as not to engage in long metaphysical speculations, but to immerse oneself entirely in the works of mercy as part of one's own commitment to belief in the infallible mercy of God. Each act of mercy from the believer is an affirmation that God's mercy and God's Kingdom will have dominion, and that ultimately 'God will not be mocked'.[70] The Orthodox seek to conform themselves to the work of God within the world by joining the ongoing struggle to affirm the joy of the Kingdom in the face of the remaining evil in the cosmos. This is why the works of mercy are an essential part of the church's witness of prayer. Without the concrete, material acts of mercy, the spiritual ascent of prayer is made defective. The elect cannot simply worship God in the mind or the spirit: they must worship the Incarnate God in the flesh too: and worship him by making their physical resources available to his service as much as their intellectual and spiritual faculties.

It is easy to mislead oneself that one is at rights with the Lord, while at the same time being blind to the needs of others. The Letter of the apostle James sounds a loud warning against that *prelest* or spiritual delusion.[71] His stirring words are still a challenge to believers: 'If a body is devoid of a spirit, then it is dead; and faith that is devoid of works is dead.'[72] The body is often a proof of the spirit's love for God, though, just as truly, the body cannot move to righteous deeds until the heart and spirit have been moved to them by God's inspiration and mercy. In short, both things are inextricably intertwined, and a living faith is one that grows in wisdom and insight into the affairs of God, as well as in mercy and compassion to the needs of others. The body and the spirit are often described as at variance with one another: at times they may be in the life of a Christian, when the desire for bodily ease sometimes stifles the aspirations of the spirit to which God is speaking a message of transcendence. But often, so the Orthodox believe, the body and the spirit assist one another greatly. At times the spirit inspires the believer to do great deeds, the body delighting to do the work; at other times the spirit may be sluggish, but the body's own generosity of heart may give away some cherished money, or engage in a labour of love for someone in need, and immediately the heart and spirit can be rejuvenated. The influence works both ways. What is necessary is to be in a 'stream of life' in a living spiritual community where one's family, and friends, and colleagues continually assist one to refine the sense of the righteous life, and to have the courage to affirm that one wants to adopt it. When God sees the heart is willing, he will extend its courage and its capability to grow in the understanding that faith and ethics are one and the same mysterious life for the elect believer.

To have access to such a community is a chief function of the church, and each parish must seriously assess itself, on a regular basis, to see that it is sustaining this basic function of mutually challenging each other to live more justly and more courageously, just as faithfully as it is observing the celebration of the sacred liturgy and the proclamation of the Holy Scriptures. It is in this way that the Christian life, lived fully in a generous and developing spirit, becomes a liberation for the individual believer, and equally a liberation for all around them. Without this grounding in love and grace, the path of ethical liberation can often be undertaken by the generous in heart, but it soon becomes a pathway dominated by anger and resentment, as believers encounter the full extent of the resistance of the world to the light of God's love, and its deliberate intent to baffle the liberation of the suffering. This spiritual anger frequently consumes the elect and diminishes them: for the work of love has to be accomplished in love (sometimes hard love being necessary, but always offered in a spirit of love). The Lord is the example to look to, as always. He was under no illusion how the Temple priesthood were corrupt and needed to be shown reform by table-turning and a knotted rope;[73] yet he breathed out his last words as compassion on the stupidity of their malice.[74]

Orthodox ethics focuses strongly on the individual's freedom to rise into the spiritual perception that the righteous life opens out, progressively, according to the degree of wisdom possessed at various periods in life. It also understands how much of ethical 'resistance' (knowing the good but being sometimes inert in the capacity to adopt a better path) is a matter of difficult diagnosis and prescription; requiring the joining together of training (*ascesis*) as well as repentance and willingness. For such reasons Orthodoxy advocates that those who wish to live a deepening life in Christ need to avail themselves of the wisdom of those who are more deeply rooted in the spiritual life and can serve as their guides (*startsi*). They especially need to review their lives regularly, with kind guidance and advice, in the sacrament of confession, where the priest may assist them to advance their commitments and choices in ways appropriate to their different callings. Orthodoxy has the deepest respect for prayer as the honour due to God alone, and its understanding of ethics is based on the fact that mercy to the poor and assistance to the oppressed is one of the greatest forms of prayer. It allies the believer with the Father of mercy; and allows each disciple a little way to 'stand beside' the God of righteousness, in the company of Christ and his saints: a good company to be in.

It is a perennial struggle of church communities to keep this vision of faith lived through an ethical life firmly before the eyes of all worshippers, over and against the ever-present danger of 'sleepiness' that can affect the church in its local parishes. Orthodoxy believes, very strongly indeed, that a regular practice of prayer, fasting, and almsgiving is absolutely necessary for Christians of all ages, to avoid this sleeping sickness. God is ever calling his elect into a new life: a life of transfigured grace that will begin here and transcend even the greatest limits we can imagine. The Christ-life is always a condition of love and communion, and there is much to be done to work energetically on this earth to make love and communion more widespread than they are, and to defend them vigorously when they come under attack. One of the chief marks of such a life is that it is radiant (the great saints often were radiant in a literal sense) and compassionate. Another way to express it is that such a person is one who lives 'fully awake'. If we cannot live fully awake, all the time, at least we need to ask God to wake us up regularly to see the state of our world, and to recognize the calling he has given to each chosen soul to become an ally of the Kingdom.

THE SONG OF CREATION

From what has gone before it may have become evident that the Orthodox do not understand the world as a simple arena in which the salvation of human beings is worked out, with little reference to it in theology other than as a passive backdrop for the human race. Human beings are a 'crown' of creation, certainly, but they are not the spoiled child of the cosmos, or the whole *raison d'être* for its being. To adopt such a grossly self-referential view would scorn the angels, just as much as it flies in the face of the teeming abundance and immense beauty of all life around us. Self-referentialism in our species has been largely responsible for the way in which so often humans have been obtuse before the wonder of the world, and have not only refused to learn from it, but have set out on paths of destructiveness of towering proportions. Even in this present generation, our world is wounded by the rush towards an economy of greed and surfeit. For the first time in history the human race holds in its little hands the capacity of damaging the fresh springs of the entire world's water and oxygen. In the face of such realizations it has seen the rich nations' pretend ignorance, so as to avoid the call to change, and unless things do change dramatically that 'pretended ignorance' will eventually give way to a more explicit state of the world understood as heavily armed camps, divided between those enjoying a lifestyle of surfeit and the poor who are struggling for subsistence. Signs of that polarization and the slide to the violence it will initiate are already before the eyes of those who care to observe today.

For Orthodoxy the world itself is a holy and blessed thing. Adam's 'dominion' over the beasts and plants was meant to be a stewardship of love, not a tyranny of oppression. Trends of theology that have suggested otherwise, especially those which argue that mankind, as 'head' of creation, has all of the world order laid at its feet and at its disposal, have drastically misunderstood the concept of 'headship' in the New Testament, which connotes the manner in which Christ laid down his life for the love of his church.[75] Such trends in the post-Reformation West, in some instances, led to a deep-seated sense in secular industrialized consciousness that the world was a mere thing, devoid of 'spiritual value' in and of itself, a base material commodity that could be used without regard for any sense of what human 'footprint' was left behind. These views have given Christianity a bad reputation with many contemporary ecological thinkers, some of whom have actually turned to the (re-)invention of earth goddess cults to attempt a rehabilitation of ecologically reverential attitudes. Orthodoxy regards this form of neo-paganism, obviously, as a heretical deviation; but so too it regards the distorted view that the world is merely a material resource for exploitation.

This has been a very unbalanced view of the past which grew, in the hands of nineteenth-century (largely Protestant) industrialists, to be tantamount to the heresy of the depredation of the earth. This heresy has now been continued into the present age in the form of global capital exploitation. No other thing matters than unrestricted economic growth. The earth will pay the costs of excess. Even when there are other planet-friendly ways of harnessing power, the profit margin is more important than responsibility to the earth, or compassion to the poor, who always are the ones who pay the real cost (a very high one) for 'cheap fuel'. As long as the defilement of the earth is left out of sight of those who are most benefiting from the 'product' that is extracted all shall be well. And indeed all was well, until the pollution of the springs and wells began to effect even the 'home' village. The extent of the corruption of the world has now broken, dimly but assuredly, into world-wide consciousness. It has dawned on even the greatest of the exploiters. Yet still to this day vested interest groups are able to persuade powerful governments to block enlightened efforts to agree on a very modest reduction of world-wide carbon gas emissions. Almost incredibly, a political race is now beginning, at the dawn of the third millennium, to open up the Alaskan and polar wildernesses for more aggressive oil extraction, which would mean that the wholly outmoded reliance on fossil fuels would continue unabated for another century. This is not merely political and economic wrong-headedness; it has all the marks of a serious moral deficit, and as such comes (or should come) into the remit of the church's interest and comment.

From Orthodoxy's perspective this sad state of affairs is the result of a long marriage to a heresy which first begins by corrupting sound doctrine, and ends by introducing moral paralysis. The Eastern Christian tradition has always tended to regard the world as first and foremost an icon of God's mercy and love. As such, it is a primary sign of the divine glory. It is, indeed, a song of God's glory. The dawn of each new day begins with all the species of earth singing out their lives to the glory of God. Trees and rivers, though not conscious, also sing out a song of glory which God hears,[76] and in return blesses the earth. When the rivers are filled with filth of our making, the song of creation is unquestionably diminished: a blasphemy is put in its place, and only the spiritually blind and deaf are unaware of it. Because of this theological instinct for the holiness of the earth, Orthodox religion has within it many examples of how the believer has to be formed in a consciousness of cosmic beauty and grace.

The sacramental life of the church is one way in which this is inculcated. One can think immediately of its rituals of blessing water, as well as oil, and wine, and wheat, and fields, and cattle, and bees, and springs and rivers and forests. There is a deep love, witnessed in the saints of the church, for the glory of this world, and a deep satisfaction in its beauty. For most of its existence Orthodoxy has lived in pre-industrial societies where nurturing earth traditions were instinctive. The cycle of natural events, such as harvests and planting, mirrored closely the cycle of the festivals of the church. A sense was built into the hearts of believers that they were transient enjoyers of the earth: not its possessors. The psalm was taken with utmost seriousness: 'The earth is the Lord's and its fullness.'[77] Since the blight of communist totalitarianism, however, Eastern Orthodox lands have known their share of the rape of the earth. The countries around the Danube have made that ancient lifeline one of the most polluted rivers in the world. Against the backdrop of the exquisitely beautiful mountains of Transylvania, the deadly by-products of mining run down freely into the water table. The rusting and neglected waste piles of the former Soviet states contain deadly pollutants (and nuclear detritus) of such proportions that it has only avoided causing world-wide panic by being obscured from common view, and not openly discussed. Against the context of this vast madness of the previous policies of world resource abuse, some ascetical common sense needs to be reasserted. As always, God's intent for the world, a design where human beings could enjoy its beauties and fertility alongside other species of life, is a better and happier way of existence than those we have badly built for ourselves, spurred on by rapacious greed.

Two of the most central instances of that approach for the Eastern Christian tradition can be found in the Cappadocian Fathers. The first is the *Hexaemeron* of St Basil, which takes delight in discoursing about the world to an audience of fourth-century workers, as a marvellous example of exquisite craftsmanship from God the Supreme Artist and lover of beauty. The second is the hymn to the wonder of the world given in St Gregory of Nazianzus' *Theological Discourses*, where he argues that it is not merely the divine mysteries that exceed the capacity for human fathoming, but even the mysteries of divine beauty hidden in what we take as the 'natural order', but which is more truly seen as a gate to revelation of the infinite beauty of God set in the exquisite beauty of the wonder of life. His poem is a sustained comment on the great Hymn of the Creation in the book of Job.[78] In both these Fathers' cosmologies, the world is not presented as a 'natural order' at all (or considered as something defective in comparison to the 'spiritual' realities Christians can aspire to). More properly understood it is a sacramentally charged mystery of presence. The defects and pervasive extent of the Fall from divine harmony which sin has introduced into the world can certainly be heard in the continual 'groaning'[79] of the earth until it finds its fulfilment. Nevertheless, the song of the birds, the glorious flowering of different species of plants and flowers, the majestic power of rivers and mountains (not least the beauty of the craft and care of humans when they respect the environment and 'work with its grain' rather than plunder and ravage its resources) all conspire to sing together of the original intent of God who wished such incredible beneficence upon his people, even when they had to 'earn their bread in the sweat of their brow'. The labour itself could become a source of order and vigour in human life, and the innate testimony to immense prodigality and overflow everywhere one looked in the surrounding environment (the teeming seas, the pure rivers, the wooded hills) was a powerful indication that the world in all its wonder was not merely there for the satisfying of immediate human needs, but had a purpose of its own. The vast varieties of life and their orders and natures are not, and never have been, solely justifiable in terms of their utility to the human species. God has clearly delighted in diversity and play, and has invited his rational creation (the angelic and human orders of being) to share in that wonderment, by adding to the sum total of beauty and purpose.

Accordingly when humanity understands the iconic witness of the deep holiness of the so-called 'natural world' (a world which when seen by those who have eyes to see reveals how much beyond the simply 'natural' it is), it is not merely the world which assumes a new and liturgically radiant vesture; it is men and women themselves who suddenly become irradiated with the glory of the divine creator, and enter into a new level of relationship with the living God, precisely as they enter into a new relationship with the world, donning new priestly vestments as they deal with it. Partly this means a new training (the *paideia* of our seminary of life) which alerts the priestly mentality to the need for reverence and dignity in the very handling of the 'sacred vessels' of the world order. Orthodox tradition is deeply aware of this sacredness and the power it has for training the heart and soul to begin to see the presence of God in the fabric of the holy creation. One example is the reverence and delight it attaches to iconic 'things' in daily life: what I have in mind are the frequent blessings of food and drink that mark all regular meals with the presence of the Lord, and the regular sanctifications that attend all aspects of life and craft.

In the Orthodox Church material gifts are elevated as sources of spiritual blessing. One example is the blessing of oil for healing, vials of which are often kept in the houses of the Orthodox for use in times of illness or despondency, to anoint oneself and loved ones. The same is true of holy water (*agiasmos*), frequently used by the Orthodox, who drink it or sprinkle it in houses. In such instances they do not only seek healing and grace from the Lord through blessed and holy objects, but also act as consecrators themselves. They receive blessing and bestow blessing. Such is one form of realization of their priestly status. The sign pre-eminent of the transpenetration of the divine grace in the world order, however, is the deliberate choice by the Lord himself to signify his enduring and glorious resurrection presence in the cosmos and the church through the primary medium of bread and wine in the Holy Eucharist. Here, in Orthodox understanding, is not merely a symbol of the presence, but its whole reality and glory in the antitypes of bread and wine which have been transfigured by the blessing of the Spirit to become the gift of the Lord of Glory: the Holy Mysteries *par excellence.* How typical of the humility and cheerfulness of the Lord to assume these things beyond all others as the gift of presence and the focal point of priestly transfiguration: that the most humble gift of the food of the poor, the richness of the gift of earth in alliance with the labour of hands grimed in dirt (for neither bread nor wine falls off a tree in and of itself) should be invested with a sacred transfiguration that the proud and inattentive could never see, let alone understand.

Another focal point of the Orthodox understanding of this sacred quality of a transfigured and transfiguring world is the evangelical account of the metamorphosis of Jesus on the mountain: when his earthly clothes became white with a heavenly radiance and his true flesh and blood emitted light in the sight of his astonished disciples. Here, in the luminous epiphany of Jesus, is the perfect icon of a new world and a new humanity gifted 'to those who have ascended with him'. Christ's saints see the world, literally, in a different light. Nothing is the same any longer to those whose hearts have been priested with this understanding. The result is, along with all understandings and gifts of mystery, a profound realization of the need for purification. Just as Isaiah called out for it in the face of the divine epiphany and was cleansed with a red-hot coal by the Seraphim,[80] so too the disciple caught up into the luminosity of the Transfiguration is brought to a deep sense of how the 'new world' requires repentance. The voice of the Father passed over the mountain and, silencing Peter's enthusiasms, gave a simple message: 'Listen to him'[81] – and this not generically, or nominally, but precisely to 'listen' to what he had just told them, and what they had chosen to ignore because of its demands of *metanoia,* namely: 'If anyone wishes to follow me let him renounce self and follow me.'[82] The true priestly disciple, in the face of the beauty of the sacred world, is called upon to exercise constant vigilance in the use of the gift of creation. Rapinage, waste, hoarding, excess, violence, exclusion, monopolies, theft, expropriations, and all manner of unequal and privileged 'processing' of the world order, as if it were a purely 'natural', dumb thing, there to be ravished at our whim: all of this is the mark of the Beast.

The true disciple stands in wonder at the white knuckles and clenched fist of the unbeliever who so desperately feels the need to grasp and seize what was meant as the common weal. Our laughable tendency to hoard what we cannot possibly need or use, and our darker tendency to wish to express ourselves by possessions and consumerism at the cost of the necessities of the poor elsewhere, are all tokens of our failure to believe, our failure to adopt the path of the holy fool, as the Lord invites his disciples to accompany him on the fateful road to Jericho and beyond. Such ingrained resistance to the call of the disciple, however, cannot easily be overcome. This is why rapinage and consumerist greed (presiding over appalling and fatal inequities that most of us pretend are 'not our fault' or simply part of 'how the world has to work') have become the established order of world economies today, and why the greatest nations on earth devote so paltry a percentage of gross product to the relief of the poor. It requires *metanoia,* and to bring forward a favourable condition for *metanoia,* in so far as this lies in our power (as distinct from the proactive mercies of God), requires asceticism.

The priestly understanding of the sacredness of the world, therefore, is in part dependent on the willing adoption of simplicity and ascetic 'abstention'. This can come in many forms. It is not the asceticism of the monk of which I am speaking now, it is the refraining from excess that most acutely characterizes the 'new secularism' of the consumer throw-away culture that is burning up the patrimony of the world order; one that is literally burning the rain forests, and all other carboniferous fuels, and living like the 'rich fool'[83] by using up the resources of generations and centuries as yet unborn. The cost of our prodigality has not only impoverished the world of the present, shutting our door in the face of the poorest nations who look on amazed at how our table groans, and how little of it seems to be available to them when they ask for a crust, but it has impoverished the world for generations to come. No other generation of humanity has been able to do this before ours. No other generation bears the guilt of it in the same way. The signs of our sickness are clearly apparent now: except of course to those who choose not to see. Our oceans are polluted, species are extinguished at an accelerating rate, the gases we have pumped into the highest atmosphere rebuff the very sun, our source of cosmic life under God. We worry about etiquette, but fail to see the vast sacrilege we have committed in marring the earth. Repentance becomes ever more difficult, as the addiction to excess becomes more engrained in younger and younger 'consumers'.

The Fathers, especially St Gregory of Nyssa and St Maximos the Confessor, speak of humanity as God's intended 'priests' who would bring the whole song of creation to its perfection of purpose by offering up the incense of praise in the face of the beauty of the world. Much Western Christianity has been overwhelmed, in the face of the world's iconic witness, by the drama of the separateness, even the alienation, from God which it can signify. The deep consciousness of sin present in the minds of some theologians has often overflowed to a world-denying attitude that has regarded the earthly creation as a mass of perdition. In part this has arisen from a mistaking of the biblical idiom of the 'world' which stands in resistance and opposition to God. This *kosmos* as it is found in the texts of the Scripture is not the creation which we see, the fundamental structures of the existence of all things, all of which are intrinsically beautiful and wondrous in their complexity and God-given order; rather, the *kosmos* as Scripture means it negatively is comprised of those hostile forces of spiritual powers that are at work in the world producing attitudes that are adept at reducing the creation from its iconic status and priestly capacity to a dull secularism: the image of a humanity separate from God. The rebellious *kosmos* is not the beautiful creation, but rather the fallen angels, and a humanity that (like them) tries to make itself an independent god over earthly things, and in so doing mimics the primal rebellion of Adam. To refuse this idolatrous service, as a priest of the beauty of the creation, is a pressing call on all Christians today, and one of the instincts that daily Orthodox life, with all its rituals that love and cherish earthly things that are radiant with God's energy, might assist to inculcate more widely.

Orthodoxy has a great deal of work to do in future generations, renewing its call for ascetic simplicity of lifestyle among believers, and correlating that with a call to reverence the earth and to denounce its abuse as sacrilegious and sinful. It will be a long educational task, but it is one that has already been begun, in full harmony with deep Orthodox traditions. Patriarch Bartholomew of Constantinople has already made very positive efforts, sponsoring publications and raising international ecological awareness to the extent that he has been called 'the Green Patriarch'. The Moscow patriarchate has also initiated new educational efforts (not currently translated into English[84]) and the works of several Orthodox theologians[85] have focused powerfully on this theme. Future generations will look back and judge this present age on how it assumed and fulfilled its duty to make the earth capable of feeding nations, and retaining its beauty and sustainable and God-given richness. Previous ages which began the cosmic damage could at least plead ignorance (for ignorant they truly were); but the time for that excuse has now passed. The eyes of God are upon us to account for what we have done with the world: and the church of God has a duty not only to give an account, but also to teach others how they can make right again the dissonant traditions that have led us all so badly astray.

THE BLESSED THEOTOKOS: JOY OF ALL CREATION

A deep devotion to the Virgin Mary is one of the distinguishing characteristics of the Orthodox Church. It is taken, by the Orthodox at large, to be one of the evident signs of health in the state of the catholicity of a church; and accordingly, for the Orthodox, the antagonism to the Blessed Virgin, or a more generalized indifference to the figure of the Mother of God, that is sometimes found in parts of the Western Christian world, raises disturbing questions. In the Orthodox understanding, the church's devotion to Mary is something kerygmatic: deeply biblical, and resonating with how one understands (and responds to) the offer of salvation in Jesus. The veneration of the Mother of God is, to that extent, for the Orthodox not merely a peripheral matter, a form of piety that one can take or leave depending on one's psyche, gender, or religious preferences. It is understood, rather, to be a foundational sign of 'belonging' to the Ekklesia, in the same sense that a believer's attitude to icons, or the sacramental mysteries, or the veneration of the saints, reveals the completeness and maturity of one's Orthodox faith. External critics of the role the Virgin plays in the faith life of the Eastern Orthodox Church often bring up anachronistic apologetics that have been at play between Roman Catholicism and Protestantism for centuries past. Orthodoxy shares the same deep veneration of the Mother of God that is found in Western Catholicism, but it does not know the devotional approach through the so-called 'troubadour' tradition (prevalent in the Western medieval period) that led, perhaps, to emotional excesses that are alien to the Orthodox veneration of the Mother of God.

Avoiding apologetics, time is better spent directly studying the Orthodox understanding of the Blessed Virgin as a guide to an authentic understanding of the Gospel, in so far as she herself is understood to be the perfect image of a disciple; herself perfected and redeemed by her divine Son, and rendered luminous among, and above, all saints and angels by the perfect harmonization of her life with that of the Lord.[86] The Blessed Virgin Mary figures as a dogmatic element supporting several aspects of the Christian faith, therefore, but she herself is a figure who belongs to what some Orthodox theologians have called the 'inner tradition' of Christianity. This signifies a mystery of intimacy; things that are known to the elect and the illuminated, but not necessarily understood by those further out in the 'wings' of Christian mystical experience. The Russian theologian Vladimir Lossky put it in the following words:

> The mystery of [Christ's] Mother was revealed only to those who were within the church.... It is not so much an object of faith as a foundation of our hope, a fruit of faith, ripened in Tradition.[87]

The New Testament shows, evidently enough, that Mary was one of the leading figures of the Good News. If she does not feature strongly in the writings of the apostle Paul, the deficiency is more than made up by the manner in which the evangelists Luke, Matthew, and John paint her icon in profoundly deep theological colours. In the New Testament texts of the Annunciation, the Nativity, the wedding feast of Cana, the Crucifixion, and the account of Pentecost, we find major streams of evangelical tradition that set out the counterpoint of music which the Holy Virgin plays in response to the invitation of her son.[88] The pattern of her own discipleship is recounted there as a model and archetype of the 'true disciple'. It is amazing to consider that some thinkers have regarded her as a peripheral figure, compared, for example, to Peter or the other apostles, when so much focus is given to her within the New Testament texts themselves, that she clearly emerges as *prima omnium* among the disciples.

She is the one alone who is admitted to an effective ancillary role in the revelation of the glory of her son, in the time of his ministry, when all other apostles are excluded from it. On two supreme occasions this can be seen in the Scripture: the first when she gives her assent to the angel at the Annunciation, for the great mystery of the economy of salvation to 'be done' in her according to God's will;[89] the second when she asks and thereby initiates her Son's manifestation of his glory in the world at the wedding feast of Cana.[90] Both signs are associated with the mystery of the Lord's Passion. In the first, Mary announces herself as the servant of the Lord in conformity with her role as Mother of the Suffering Servant of God who will achieve the economy of salvation. In the second, the overflowing wine of the wedding, the symbol of the new Kingdom which the Lord's ministry has initiated on earth, is also the first of the seven great signs which initiate the economy of the Passion from the very beginning of his preaching and miracles.[91] After the revelation of the glory at Cana, there is a relentless movement in the Gospel of John to the supreme manifestation of the glory of the Lord in the mysteries of his death and resurrection.

In both instances, therefore, at the Annunciation of the Good News, and at the moment when the secret revelation of the glory is shown among the apostles gathered at the wedding, cardinal points in the evangelical story, the Mother of Jesus is brought in by the various evangelists to serve as the herald and prophetess of her Son's hidden meanings. Luke the evangelist depicts her for this reason as one who pre-eminently 'pondered the word'[92] in the depth of her heart. She is the first exegete and mediator of the meaning of the hidden signs of the Lord to others: to Joseph her husband, to the disciples at Cana, to Elizabeth, and to us, who listen to the Gospel, when we see and hear her acting in prophetic ecstasy and magnifying the Lord's wonders in his works of salvation. Her prophetic utterance of the simple word *chaire* (rejoice) makes the younger prophet, John, leap for joy in his mother's womb, startled into life by the return of the power of the Living Spirit to Israel, as witnessed in her repetition of the angelic evangelization.[93]

It is for reasons such as this that the Blessed Virgin and St John the Forerunner are constantly associated in the iconic tradition of the Orthodox Church. Both are seen as the pre-eminent intercessors and mediators with Christ, the judge of all things, at the Last Judgement of souls. The great icons of the Virgin and John the Forerunner pleading at either side of the judgement throne of Christ is known as the Great Deisis (or Intercession). Her upraising of prophetic hands when she teaches Elizabeth

211

(and us) the meaning of radical prayer in her Magnificat (the New Hannah instructing the mother of the New Elijah) shows, in her, that virginal force (so far removed from the naivety we moderns mistakenly associate with virginity) that celebrates the downfall of the mighty and proud, and the merciful relief of the poor who have called out in grief on the name of God.[94]

There can be little doubt that the Blessed Virgin was one who actively shaped the transmission of the Gospel traditions after the death of her son. Modern biblical exegesis has been strangely reluctant to admit anything of this, despite Luke's repeated insistence that it was Mary who treasured the significances of the story of her Son's birth, Mary who initiated his education in the understanding of the Torah and the Prophets, and Mary who was one of the towering figures in the first organization of the church of Jerusalem in the time of James the brother of the Lord. The silence about her role in contemporary Western biblical criticism is positively deafening.

In the Orthodox understanding of the Scripture, however, it is not simply historical accuracy or semantic exactitude that matters most: it is prophetic insight. The Scriptures are only partly records lying within history; in their deeper significance they are eschatological mysteries in and of themselves; charged with the revelations of the Holy Spirit, which are opaque to those outside, all wrapped in riddle and enigma[95] but luminous to those who are illumined by the Spirit of God, and perspicacious in the spirit of prophecy which so abundantly inhabited the Blessed Virgin. In this light the symbol of the Virgin gathered with the apostles for the Ascension of the Lord and afterwards in prayer in preparation for the descent of the Pentecostal Spirit[96] is profoundly symbolic of her role as the Mother of Sion. In the Orthodox icons of the Ascension, the apostolic church is gathered around the Virgin in centre position on earth, while the Lord ascends above them all. Her hands are once more upraised in the figure of prayer. In the earliest iconography of Christianity the female Orant is the symbol of the church at prayer. The sign derives from the apostolic role of Mary in the days after the Resurrection in Jerusalem.

In the later conciliar tradition of the church the Holy Virgin's role was defined over the course of several councils, and thus appears in the Creed or Acts of the councils of Nicaea (325), Ephesus (431), and Constantinople II (553). In the Nicene Creed the Gospel teaching of the virginal conception and birth of Jesus is affirmed in a special way. The subject of the Christological clauses is the 'One Lord Jesus Christ, the Son of God ... begotten of the Father before all ages' who is then confessed to have 'come down from the heavens and was incarnate of the Holy Spirit and the Virgin Mary, and was made man'. Here the extraordinary synergy of the Virgin and the divine Spirit is stressed in that extraordinary phrase (often weakened in the Latin and English renderings of the Creed at this point): 'incarnate of the Holy Spirit and the Virgin Mary'. The other aspect which the Creed insists on most powerfully is the identity of subject between the Eternal Son of God who was 'with the Father before all ages', and the Son of God, the Lord, who 'came down ... was incarnate of the Holy Spirit and the Virgin Mary ... and was crucified for us'. This is a centrally important confession: namely, that the Orthodox understanding of the Lord Jesus begins and ends with the statement that the child born of Mary is one and the same as the eternal Son of God. The eternal Word of God became flesh of Mary in the person of Jesus; Jesus is himself the Word now appearing within history and space. This also means that Mary's status as Mother of God is a definitive part of the Christian Creed.

In the early fifth century the Syrian archbishop of Constantinople, Nestorius, was anxious to 'reform' the traditional language of the church in relation to the Christ. He forbade his people to use terms that seemed to confuse or mix together the three concepts he thought ought to be held separate: the Everlasting Word, the Christ of God, and the man Jesus. His short tenure as reformist bishop came to a disastrous end over this issue. St Cyril of Alexandria pointed out to him in 428 that if one introduced a differentiation of persons between the Eternal Word and the historical Jesus, one had not only introduced something alien to the faith of Nicaea, but had voided the church's hope in the divinely supra-human value of the life, death, and resurrection of the Lord. If the resurrected Christ was really distinct from the divine Son of God, then his crucifixion and resurrection would have only nominal significance as the witness and reward of yet another righteous servant of God. Nestorius countered violently with the charge that Cyril's preferred Christological polarities, the sets of opposites and juxtapositions that he loved to use in normal speech (such as the 'tears of God', or the 'sufferings of God', or the 'death of the Immortal') were either heretical (confusing the categories of divinity and humanity) or foolishly inept, and not suitable for a theologian of any sophistication. The dispute between Cyril and Nestorius over this matter grew to a crisis that was resolved at the Council of Ephesus in 431.[97]

Here the assembled Fathers declared that Cyril's dogmatic letters were authentic expressions of the Nicene faith. St Cyril's central antinomy was given conciliar status when the Virgin was defined as 'truly Theotokos'. The word means God-birther, and is more usually rendered as 'Mother of God'. In fact after Ephesus the 'new' term,[98] because of its newly important Christological significance, replaced the older designation Meter Theou (Mother of God), leaving the latter intact only on the icons of the Virgin Mary, where it still remains as the traditional superscription. To address Mary as the 'Mother of God' was exactly one of those apparently 'shocking' polarities that so delighted Cyril of Alexandria. His point was that what was once impossible, even contradictory, before the Incarnation, was rendered not only possible, but grace-filled and vivifying, after it. So, for example, the chasm between Godhead and humanity on the one side (what we might call the chasm between Creator and creaturehood) once so absolute in all monotheist religions before the advent of Christ, is now rendered no longer an absolute chasm: since he who is the Eternal Word, God of God, from the Father's own being, is now equally truly and authentically, a man of the house of David, and born of a human mother. Cyril also pointed out that the Incarnation equally voided other 'impossible contradictions', not least the 'death of the Immortal One': for he who was immortal by nature, died by free choice on the Cross. In the same way the power of the mystery of the Incarnation meant that what was impossible had now become a reality: that God who was motherless by nature (since divine being has no origin other than itself, and the Divine Word had no parent other than the Father) had now become the child of a mother in the economy of the Incarnation.

Nestorius, and many other theologians since his time, wanted to 'clarify the logic' of this manner of speaking and add something to the effect of 'Yes, but motherless as God, and mothered as a man', but Cyril would not budge an inch, and the council agreed with him. Jesus and the Eternal Word were not two persons, or two different subjects, only one person. The Divine Word, in adopting humanity by choosing to be born as a man, did not adopt a new person alongside his divine being; rather, the same person adopted a new set of circumstances (embodied life within history) alongside his natural manner

213

of living, which was as the Eternal Word in transcendent power. This new set of circumstances opened out new and divinely paradoxical possibilities within embodied time and space, not least among them the possibility of the redemption of the whole human race, which had been the entire point and purpose of the Incarnation, as Cyril never tired of pointing out. To sum up this complex set of arguments about the single subjectivity of the Divine Word made flesh, Cyril hit upon a clear and scintillating strategy. If one did not accept that Mary was the Theotokos in the full sense, one could not be Orthodox in the understanding of the Incarnation.

During his pre-conciliar arguments with Cyril, Nestorius is said to have complained (in relation to the Theotokos title) that 'Strictly speaking Mary is not the Mother of God, rather the Mother of Christ, or the Mother of Jesus.' When Cyril heard this he countered with the sardonic reply: 'But if Mary is not "strictly speaking" the Mother of God, then the one who is born from her is not, "strictly speaking" God.' During the debates at Ephesus, in the summer of 431 just before the formal conciliar sessions opened, Nestorius lost his temper with some bishops who were berating him about the excessive complexity of his language and, in exasperation at their use of Theotokos as a marker of faith, was reported to have burst out: 'I cannot call an infant of two or three days old my God!' But for Cyril this is exactly what faith in the divine person of Jesus, the Incarnate Word, demands of the Christian. The scandal ('to the Greek a foolishness and to the Jew a stumbling block'[99]) is not that of a deficient semantic on the part of theologians: the scandal is entirely that elected by God who so 'emptied himself out'[100] that he who was immortal and omnipotent chose to live and die within the limits of a mortal and suffering human life, in time and space.

For these reasons Cyril projected the title Theotokos for the Virgin as the summary and chief bulwark of Orthodox Christology. Mary's status as the Mother of God proclaims prophetically to the church that her Son is no less than the Divine Word, and that he who is eternal in the Father's own being has now come among humanity as a true child of the Jewish Virgin of Nazareth. Again that which is to be seen is more than can be seen by mere eyes. It is the eyes of faith alone that can see the Jewish maiden as truly Theotokos; just as it is the illumined heart alone that can see her Son as the Living Word of God. When the church confesses her (a word that rightly means to join in prayerful praise to celebrate the wonders of God) it confesses, therefore, the essence of the mystery of redemption in Christ. The praise and confession of Mary is, to that extent, entirely a celebration of the fundamental *kerygma* of our salvation: that God himself came in our midst as Emmanuel, to rescue us.

The council of Constantinople II stressed the doctrine of Nicaea more firmly in 553, to afford her the title Aeiparthenos, meaning 'Ever Virgin'. It is axiomatic to Orthodox belief that the Blessed Virgin was not merely virginal before the conception of Christ, but remained so for all her earthly and heavenly witness afterwards (for as it is with the greatest of the saints and angels, Orthodoxy understands her to be active and powerful in the guidance and help of the earthly church even to the present). For this reason Orthodoxy understands the New Testament references to the brothers and sisters of Jesus[101] to signify his immediate family in the wider kin-group, but not the biological children of Mary, as if conceived after him (and this is something which is certainly in accordance with the biblical idiom, and not in contradiction of it).

Again, in the iconic tradition, in almost all the images of Mary that one finds throughout history, she is depicted wearing three stars on her *maphorion* (or the garment that covers her head and shoulders). These stars are the artistic evocation of her threefold virginity: before, during, and after the birth of Christ. Roman Catholicism also knows the doctrine of the threefold virginity. In Orthodoxy there is a slight difference: in order to offset any suspicion that a virginity *in partu* might render the birth of Jesus excessively 'magical' or docetic (a concept that haunted parts of early Asia Minor Christianity, namely that Jesus was a spirit merely appearing to be flesh), the theologian-iconographers habitually painted the child's body over the third star, obscuring it and leaving only two stars to be witnessed by the observer. In this, their instinct for Orthodoxy was unerring.

With the Blessed Virgin there are many mysteries, and not all of them for prurient scrutiny. The icon of the Dormition (known in the West as the Assumption) shows Mary lying on her bier, grieved over by the apostles and carried off in spirit by her glorious Son. In some icons of the scene there is a figure, the doubter. He tries to find out if this renowned woman was truly a virgin as her devotees have claimed. As he creeps up to the bier an avenging angel descends and lops off his impious hands. It is a useful, though somewhat gruesome, symbol that virginity as it ultimately 'signifies' in Christian theological tradition, is far more than a biological witness. The church's assertion of Mary's perpetual virginity is a strong statement that the annunciation, the birth, and the very person of Jesus her Son are transcendent. He is the virgin Son of the virgin Mother, and his life and person are not reducible to that of a Jewish Mediterranean sage, wholly explicable from and within his own historical culture. The virginity of Mary and the miracles of the Lord must always be dismissed quickly by such Christological 'demythologizers' as pure 'folk legend'; despite the evident historical reality that the New Testament texts themselves show signs of anxiety over how the tradition of the virginity of the Lord's birth was already offering easy fodder to the enemies of the early Christian movement, in terms of the obvious apologetic that he was born 'outside the law', illegitimate and unworthy to assume religious leadership.

The Matthaean genealogy, the Lukan annunciation, birth, and circumcision narratives, which are paralleled with those of John the Forerunner, all give evidence that the evangelists who record the virgin birth tradition are 'more than anxious' that it should be communicated publicly in a way that will offset its 'almost unbelievable' character. This is not something that one finds in the reading of the apocryphal Gospels of the second century, where anything that is weird and wonderful can be legitimately attributed to the Christ child and the holy family. In these later apocrypha Joseph is such a bad carpenter that his divine child stretches table legs where the old man has been unable to level them off with his adze. In his free moments the child casually makes clay birds which then fly off into the air; and so on. The evangelical virgin birth tradition is quite unlike this. Critics and rationalist exegetes have long tried to explain it away in terms of *origo explicat omnia*: find the source and all will be reducibly comprehensible. To this extent *Religionsgeschichte* critics of the nineteenth century drew parallels between the virginal birth and the mystery religions, where the divine hero was virgin-born. In any sober reading, there are absolutely no convincing parallels at all, and critics' attempts to force them are pathetically obvious. The literary allusion to the 'virgin who gives birth', as the evangelist Matthew heavily points up, is the Isaian text,[102] which 'originally' (in its first historical context) signified new hope to much-oppressed Israel, by the fact that the royal court of Hezekiah had produced an heir to the throne from one of the younger royal concubines. This is a severe criticism of the reigning king whom the prophet saw as a rather useless messianic (or royal) symbol for the nation. When the evangelist Matthew uses it, and it is exactly the same when he throws a highlight on his other Old Testament 'proof texts' in the same chapter of his birth narrative, it is abundantly clear to any open-minded reader that he is 'searching through the Scriptures' to find out-of-the-way texts that will truly illustrate the narrative he has received about the birth of Jesus, rather than the other way around.

It is, therefore, not that the scriptural prophecies have so weighed down on the birth narrative of Jesus that they have more or less conditioned its complete form and detail. On the contrary, the evangelist has been pressed to tell the story he has received about the premonitions and extraordinary birth of Jesus with reference to the 'expected' biblical data, and has had to go very far afield to find scriptural materials that illustrated it. This is why, if one isolates the Old Testament prophecies related to the birth of Jesus in both Matthew and Luke, one sees the evangelists walking through the byways of scriptural narrative rather than the normal 'highways', as it were, of the messianic proof texts that would have so readily sprung to the mind of an ancient Jewish theologian who was composing an account of the expected Messiah. Add to this the evident fact that Mark the evangelist has elected simply to delete the entire birth story from his Gospel account[103] rather than having to deal with the burden of apologetic that would be required to keep it afloat in his Gentile environment, and one is faced with the historical implication that the evangelists received the tradition of the virgin birth from the very sources of the *kerygma*,[104] and, knowing that they would have an uphill battle against all manner of later apologetic,[105] they did their best with it. In short, to dismiss the annunciation and birth narratives (and the tradition of the virginity of the Blessed Virgin along with them) out of hand, as hopelessly non-historical and mythic parts of a Jesus story that is long overdue for refurbishment in a 'rational' and 'non-miraculous' fashion, is simply to act in an perverse counter-historical way with the scriptural record: a record that is deeply sober and responsible in its customs of telling the story of Jesus.

It is an enduring character of the church's tradition, running on into the later centuries to retain this sobriety of history in its basic faith-proclamation, and it is for this reason that the host of apocryphal gospels (of Judas, Mary Magdalene, and numerous others) were rejected, instinctively rejected, from the canon of Christian Scripture because they played fast and loose with received traditions from sober sources. This is only a brief argument using scriptural indications to speak about historical tradition soberly received and reverently passed on. It will hardly convince a generation of so-called historical scholars who have mutilated the scriptural record they set out to comment on, using the premise that 'nothing unusual can happen in the world, that is not entirely explicable by reference to things that are usual'; and thus 'explaining' the Virgin birth for their readership as a 'magical' explaining away of an illegitimate birth. But the Akathist hymn gave a good response to this in ancient times:

> Wise orators stand mute as fish before you Theotokos; for they are unable to explain how you could remain a virgin and yet give birth. But we who marvel at the mystery of faith can cry out to you: All hail, you who are the chosen vessel of God.

The Virgin Mary stands not only as a Christological bulwark, epitomizing the ultimate 'scandal of our faith' that if she is called the Theotokos, her Son must be confessed as divine (God of God, Light of Light, true God of true God, as the Creed has it). But in many ways she is a 'Bronze Gate' in a contemporary world abounding in reductionist and faithless exegesis. She who treasured all these stories and tales of wonder about her Son in her heart, as the evangelist tells us, is still one who refuses to allow the sacred *kerygma* of the Gospel to be watered down and made palatable to the tastes and conceptions of those who are far from being deeply rooted in the strange and paradoxical ways of a God who, with the world's salvation in the balance, chose a simple and innocent heart which was ready to say to him: 'Let it be done in me, as I am your servant.'[106] The choice of an unmarried first-century Jewish woman from a rural backwater was a contradiction of the 'wisdom of this world', and still is. It is perhaps, why theological reflection on the Theotokos (so prevalent and powerful in the early church) has fallen into relative silence today. Nevertheless, those disciples who know that God does not see as humans see, but looks into the quality of the heart and faith of human beings, know that the divine election follows ways that often seem surprising, incredible, or plain bizarre to the rational gaze.

We do not have to be as radical as Tertullian (who once said 'I believe it precisely because it is absurd!') to sense that the virginity of Mary is the symbol of faith that shows her Son to be the True Servant of the Most High. As it is with Jesus himself, the entrance into the understanding of his glory and radiance only comes with the acceptance of his Passion as Suffering Servant. So it is with Mary too; the paradox of her virginity is only partly the biological miracle of the gift of an unexpected Messiah child to the world; more than that, it is the essence of a faith and obedience which is entirely and purely virginal in the sight of the demands of her God. Only such a totally and generously given heart could have made such a response in such a time and climate when unmarried pregnancy might well have meant expulsion, shame, and even mob assassination. That she gave her heart so willingly was the proof positive that she was a virgin in the sense that God finds important and significant. When the disciple of Christ himself, or herself, also finds that virginity of heart, such that the Spirit of the Most High is able to overshadow and shape the soul into the ways of the Kingdom, then, and then only, will that disciple gain an inkling into that mystery of virginity which is faith, and the *renovatio*, the refashioning of life that always accompanies genuine faith. Only then will the disciple gain a deeper understanding of the mystery of the virginity of Mary.

This is not something publicly accessible from the *kerygma* of the church. It is something inside, mysterious, and deep. It is absolutely related to the gift of the heart in totality, the essence of discipleship as Christ himself taught it.[107] For this reason the Blessed Virgin Mary, in her spiritual virginity, is the perfect icon of the perfection of discipleship. When a voice in the crowd cried out to Jesus: 'Blessed is the womb that bore you and the breasts on which you sucked', he did not contradict them when he replied, 'Rather you should say – Blessed are those who hear the word of God and keep it.'[108] It was precisely in defence of his mother's honour that he made that retort: glorious in her virginity, but even more glorious in that virginity of her faith whereby she had moved the heart of God himself to intervene for the salvation of Israel and the whole world. In the process, her own heart and soul became consecrated as the temple of the Lord. In this, the scene of the activity of the transfiguring Spirit of God, she is the great symbol of the transfiguration that is called for in all the disciples of God, who are equally destined to be consecrated by the Spirit. For such reasons she is always addressed in Orthodox thought and prayer as someone who transcends the achievements of even the greatest of the other saints and apostles. She is the greatest *pneumatophoros* (Spirit-bearer) of the Creation. This is why she is associated so fundamentally, in the Orthodox perception of the divine economy, with the Spirit's work in the Incarnation, and also in the eschatological judgement (when she intercedes for the church at the end-time) when the elect, Spirit-filled, are gathered together in the Lord's glory. She is called 'More honourable than the Cherubim, and more glorious than the Seraphim' and the devotion that is given to her is described as *hyperdoulia*,[109] connoting a degree of reverence that exceeds that which is honorifically offered to angels and saints in the church's devotions.

The titles of the Blessed Virgin given to her in the faith life of the Orthodox Church reflect this whole mystery of ongoing transfiguration. We have noticed the two 'conciliar' and dogmatic titles (Ever Virgin, and Theotokos) but the common name for the Holy Virgin in Orthodox countries is the 'All Holy' (Panagia). In the liturgical services of the church she is often called upon in prayer. Each time, as if in a formal act of acknowledgement and honour, she is given a full roll of her titles, and never referred to informally simple as 'Mary'. She is, always, 'Our All Holy, Immaculate, Most Blessed, and Glorious Lady, the Mother of God and Ever Virgin Mary'.

The celebration of the Mother of God as immaculate (*achrantos*), is a clear and universal recognition of her exceptional and iconic sanctity. Orthodoxy did not follow the path of Roman Catholicism in moving towards a confession of her Immaculate Conception. This was a late (nineteenth-century) decision and was not welcomed by the Orthodox hierarchs of the time, who saw it as an example of 'over-elaboration' of the faith tradition. In the Western Christian context the Immaculate Conception is closely related to aspects of St Augustine's theory of original sin and inherited guilt and moral stain passed on down through the human race by means of generative concupiscence. Orthodoxy has never accepted that Augustinian theory as a good guide to the understanding of the Fall of the human race from God, and, accordingly, not a particularly good model of our understanding of the processes of redemption. For such reasons the Orthodox acclaim the Blessed Virgin as Achrantos, the Immaculate One, without teaching the doctrine of the Immaculate Conception of the Virgin Mary.

Orthodoxy did, however, bring to Western Catholicism after the eighth century a deep devotion to her feast of glorification, a festival which was established and popular in the East by the fifth century. Glorification, in Orthodox literature, primarily means 'canonization'. In reference to the Blessed Virgin, it signifies an ancient tradition of the church (which by the fourth century was beginning to be developed in extended literary narratives) that after her death the apostles buried her,[110] and when the tomb was opened shortly afterwards, to allow a latecomer to the funeral to view her corpse, it was found to be empty. The Feast of the Virgin's 'Falling Asleep' (Koimesis) as it is called in Orthodoxy, is one of the greater of the secondary-cycle liturgical festivals of the church (those not connected primarily to the cycle of the Lord's ministry and Passion). It occurs on 15 August. In Roman Catholicism, the same feast is called the Assumption of Mary. It is always observed as a great national holiday in Orthodox countries.

Theologically it is another symbol of the hope a true disciple can sustain for a heavenly glorification, after death, with the Lord. The theology of this feast is clearly set out in the icons of the Koimesis. The Mother of the Lord, asleep in death, peaceful on her bier, is wept over by the gathered apostles, while unseen by them Christ, in the radiant glory of his resurrection, comes down to lift up her soul (dressed in swaddling clothes like a little baby) and take it into heavenly glory. In a charming reversal of the normal icons of the Mother and Child, it is now Christ himself who 'shows'[111] his mother to the church as an object of veneration and wonder. The icon celebrates the Theotokos in the communion of saints, and is widely understood in the Orthodox Church to be a consolation that at our deaths (often called the moment of our last solitude) none of us will be left alone. The tenderness of the Blessed Virgin and the mercy of her Son will watch over the disciple's last journey.

St John of Damascus explicitly links the Koimesis to the remarkable discipleship of the Virgin. He sees it as a 'debt of honour' paid by Christ so that he would not be outdone by his mother's gracious hospitality:

> For it was necessary that she who had entertained God the Word as a guest in the chamber of her womb, should finally be brought home to the dwelling of her Son. Just as the Lord said that he had to be in the place that belongs to his Father, so the Mother had to take up her abode in the palace of her Son, in the house of the Lord, in the courts of our God.[112]

In the early eighth century St Germanos of Constantinople explained the Koimesis in terms of the inability of death to keep captive a soul of such great beauty and holiness, and its powerlessness to interrupt her intercession on behalf of the church:

> As it has been written: 'You are indeed beautiful'[113] and your virginal body is entirely saintly, entirely chaste, entirely the dwelling place of God. Accordingly it shall be entirely free from the dissolution to dust. Rendered changeless in regard to all that is human, it is now exalted into immortal life; that very same body, now living and glorified, and sharing without loss in the perfection of life. For it was not possible that the vessel which had carried God, that living temple of the sacred deity of the Only Begotten, should be held a prisoner of death's tomb. So it is, O Theotokos, that we believe you still go about among us.[114]

The Koimesis of the Virgin thus presents her in one of her roles as an intercessor for the soul of the believer after death. She who is with the Risen Lord body and soul in heaven (whereas the other great saints and apostles are present with the Lord in spirit only until the Final Resurrection) is presented to the church as the most powerful of all intercessors for those on earth. Like the Lord, she is believed to be always ready to listen to those in distress.

Throughout Christian history the Blessed Virgin has been one of the most powerful symbols of protection for the distressed and the oppressed, for women in general, and all people of faith. Throughout long patriarchal ages, when women were even regarded as unworthy to be educated, it has been the image of the Theotokos that has elevated the figure of a young girl, and the quiet serenity of a woman of courage, in the face of loss and adversity, to the pre-eminent position among all the disciples of Christ.

Some of the earliest Christian Fathers celebrated the Virgin's role as 'reverser of Eve'. The later Latin Fathers delighted in playing on the semantics that the 'Ave Maria' reversed (literally so) 'Eva', the Latin name of Adam's wife. By the middle of the second century the scriptural symbol of the woman of faith who crushed the serpent (the

Theotokos as one who undoes the damage done by Eve's rebellion) was becoming a standard theological theme.[115] From the early second century her name is found scrawled as an invocation in cemeteries and pilgrim shrines, among the recognizable Christian graffiti of antiquity, and a second-century papyrus preserves the earliest known liturgical prayer to her.[116] It is in the Greek of the poor classes, though it is commonly known among scholars as the *Sub Tuum Praesidium*. It has survived (in a slightly developed form) as one of the most common prayers to the Blessed Virgin in contemporary Orthodoxy:

> Open to us the gates of your compassion O Blessed Theotokos. In that we have placed our hope in you, may we never be confounded. Through you may we be delivered from all adversity, for you are the salvation[117] of the race of Christians.

And her titles expanded as time went on. In the third-century writer Hippolytus of Rome she is the True Ark of the Covenant made of incorruptible wood.[118] In other writers she is *par excellence* the 'Burning Bush'[119] wherein the Lord appeared to Moses at Sinai. Ancient Christians always understood the epiphanies of God in the Old Testament to be revelations of the Divine Logos. And so it followed, that the Logos who inhabited the form of fire in an ordinary acanthus bush which he did not consume, thereby gave a 'type' (a mystical symbol) of his incarnation from the womb of the Virgin. She bore the fire of the Godhead but was not consumed by it. As this revelation of God's name through the sign of the burning bush inaugurated the covenant, so it was with Mary, who typologically stands as the door to the inauguration of the New Covenant, when God does not come merely in epiphany to humankind, but comes bodily and personally present through the Virgin. By the fourth century, in poets such as Ephrem the Syrian (especially his splendid Eighteenth Hymn on the Blessed Virgin) or the sixth-century poet Romanos the Melodist, her titles are expanded in popular liturgical songs.

One of the longest of these, perhaps the most famous of all, is the Akathist hymn. The word means 'not sitting down' and refers to the fact that it was one of the processional hymns to the Virgin that were regularly sung in the church of Constantinople. This is one of the greatest of all the Eastern Christian hymns to the Mother of God, and is still regularly recited by many of the faithful today, as well as being liturgically sung in a special service during the Fridays of Great Lent. The rich variety of the many forms of the icons of the Virgin spring either out of the Scriptures themselves, or the apocryphal work known as the Proto-Evangelium of James (which gives many popular legends about her childhood), or from this great hymn of the Akathist. The initial stanza of the Akathist can be taken, briefly, as an example of its finely crafted style. The poem at large consists in a series of salutations all beginning with *Chaire* (All Hail!), introducing a whole list of honorific titles, with the recurring refrain of 'Hail, unwedded bride'. It is almost as if the angel of the Annunciation is stammering out praises, unsure of what to say. The reason for this is given in the opening stanza:

> An angel of the highest rank was sent from heaven above
> To say to the Mother of God: All Hail![120]
> And seeing you, the Lord, taking bodily form,
> He stood in awe, crying aloud to her, with his bodiless voice,
> And saying such things as these:

> All hail to you through whom joy shone forth.
> All hail, you through whom the curse was blotted out.
> All hail you who are the restoration of fallen Adam.
> All hail, you the redemption of the tears of Eve.
> All hail, you who are a height hard to climb for human thought.
> All hail, depth impenetrable even to the eyes of angels.

The Annunciation is presented in a new slant. This manner of telling the biblical story over again paraphrastically and from a novel angle is an ancient Semitic technique (originating from the church of Antioch and the Syrian Christian poets) known as *Midrash*. Here in the Akathist, the Divine Logos has commissioned his archangel, Gabriel, to give the Virgin a simple message: 'Hail, highly favoured one'. But he does not seem to have let the angel in on the secret of what was to happen. Accordingly, as Gabriel starts to deliver his instructed message, he sees his own Divine Lord, the Logos himself, who has beaten him to earth, as it were, assuming flesh in the Virgin's womb right in front of the archangel's 'bodiless' eyes. This puts him into such a state of shock (the whole mystery of the Incarnation that is beyond the imagination of angels since it is the unfathomable compassion of God himself worked out in flesh) that he forgets his original message and begins to stammer out a massively long series of 'praises'. These liturgical hymns were very popular indeed in Byzantine times, and today remain a central feature of Orthodox liturgical services, where they are sung as verses ands responsorials, sometimes by a double choir.

The Blessed Virgin's status as 'higher than the angels' is celebrated in what is perhaps the most popular of all Orthodox prayers to the Theotokos:

> More honourable than the Cherubim, and more glorious beyond compare than the Seraphim, inviolate you gave birth to God the Word. Truly the Theotokos we magnify you.[121]

Other hymns call her the 'garden enclosed', or 'the sealed well' applying to the mystery of her virginity the biblical types of the Song of Songs.[122] Once again virginal motherhood is not simply presented as a biological paradox, but rather as a mysterious symbol of mystical faith. It is not without meaning that Jesus' reaction to her suggestion at Cana is to associate her alongside him in the revealing of the time of the 'hour of revelation'. Such is the meaning of his question to her when she asked him to multiply the wine: 'Woman what is this to you and to me? – for my hour is not yet come':[123] that is, why do we concern ourselves with peripheral matters when the advent of the Kingdom is about to be announced? From the Gospel itself, the Virgin is shown to be intimately associated with her Son's redemptive work: she is someone who is expected by her Son to know the mysteries of the Kingdom in a way that the disciples cannot yet attain. And in the immediately following passages of the Gospel of John, their groping path to understanding is contrasted implicitly with her serene comprehension. As St Gaudentius of Bresca put it:

> The most blessed one ... understood the mystical sense of his question ... otherwise she would never have said to the attendants: 'Do whatever he tells you.' This was because, after her divine child-bearing, she remained full of the Holy Spirit, and so knew the meaning of Christ's answer, and also foresaw the entire course of his making

the water into wine. What could be hidden from the Mother of Wisdom, from one who was able to contain God himself, one who was the very temple of such great power?[124]

This last reference of Gaudentius' is to the Greek title of the Virgin as Platytera, another paradoxical concept the Greek Fathers loved to employ. Platytera means 'Wider than the Heavens'. Icons of the Virgin Platytera are often found in the apses of Orthodox churches over the altar area. In them the figure of the Virgin is often deliberately spatially distorted. The theological point the icon and the title are making is that God, the One 'whom the heavens could not contain' and who could certainly not be held within the small space of a temple sanctuary,[125] was now (in the Incarnation) contained snugly in the womb of the Virgin Mother of God. The Theotokos is thus clearly 'wider than the heavens'. St Cyril of Alexandria gave voice to this in a famous sermon on the Mother of God, in which he says:

Hail to you who contained in your womb, one who cannot be contained; you through whom the Holy Trinity became glorified and adored throughout the world. You are one through whom heaven rejoices; through whom angels and archangels are made glad. Through you the demons are put to flight, and all creation that was once held fast in the delusion of idolatry, has come to the knowledge of the truth.[126]

In a famous fifth-century homily delivered at Constantinople (the centre of fine weaving in the eastern Roman world) St Proclos called her

The awe-inspiring loom of the Incarnation on which the weaver, the Holy Spirit, ineffably wove the garment of the hypostatic union. The overshadowing power from on high was the interconnective thread of the weave; the ancient fleece of Adam was the wool; the undefiled flesh from the Virgin was the threaded woof; and the shuttle – no less than the immeasurable gracefulness of her who bore him. Over all stood the Logos, that consummate artist.[127]

Perhaps the most revealing, and most celebrated, of all the many Orthodox acclamations of the Blessed Virgin, however, are those by which she is most commonly known by the faithful in prayer: 'She who is Ever Ready to Help', and 'Theotokos the Joy of All Creation'.

THE DANCE OF THE BLESSED: THE ANGELS AND THE SAINTS

In one of the greatest poet-theologians of the early church, there is a renowned and rhapsodic hymn describing the nature and work of the angelic orders. In it Gregory the Theologian synopsizes the Orthodox understanding of these creatures of light:

Shall we pass through the first veil, and step beyond the realm of senses? Shall we look into the Holy Place, the noetic and celestial creation? We will not see it in an incorporeal way, though it is incorporeal itself, since it is said to be, and indeed is, both fire and spirit[128] ... For an angel is called spirit and fire. It is spirit, since it is a creature of the noetic sphere. It is fire, since it is itself a purifying nature. I know that these same names belong also to God as First Nature. But even so, at least as regards the angels' relative status compared to our own humanity, we should reckon the angelic nature to be incorporeal (or at any rate as nearly so as possible). How quickly we get dizzy over this subject, and are unable to advance to any point, except to state categorically that we know there are Angels and Archangels, Thrones, Dominions, Principalities, Powers, Splendours, Ascents, Intelligences or Intelligent Powers;[129] all of them pure and coherent natures that cannot be moved by evil, or scarcely moved. Eternally they circle in chorus around the First Cause, and are illuminated from its purest light, each one in a degree appropriate to its nature and rank. They become so conformed to that primal beauty, so shaped by it, that they themselves become secondary lights, and begin to enlighten others by the abundance and largesse of the First Light. As ministers of God's will, they are strong with an innate, as well as an imparted, strength. They can cross all space because of their agile nature, while their pastoral zeal makes them eager to be readily present to all humans in all places. Different individuals among them prefer different parts of the world, and are appointed over different regions of the Cosmos, as only God knows who has appointed and ordained all these things. In their ministry the angels weave all things together according to the goodwill of God. They sing their hymn to the majesty of the Godhead, ceaselessly contemplating his Eternal Glory.[130]

The Orthodox Church looks to the angels to give it a clearer picture of its own identity as church of the next age, for it is only there that it will be rendered luminous and transfigured in the complete fulfilment of the praise of God. But also for this reason it is difficult to form an image of the angels, since they are wholly eschatological beings, radically different from humanity and its limited form of existence and perceptive consciousness. We, that is the human species, are called into an eschatological hope from out of the central gift of our life which is material existence in the space-time continuum of the present universe. As a result, there is something profoundly ambivalent and tentative about human life. It is fragile and precarious. We know this to be true in material terms, of course (or at least we do when we cease deluding ourselves). Our life has a set term, and most of us approach the gift of death after long years of decline of powers that rob us of the fundamentals of our physical energy and sensibility. We are not so clear, perhaps, that we are also ontologically fragile because we are a composite creation. We are not constituted from one thing. St Gregory the Theologian[131] put it in terms of the precariousness of being of the 'third creation'. Angels were the first, and were made from one single substance: a spiritual power which affords them a nature we can only imagine. Their origination, according to the Fathers was unimaginably long before the making of the material heaven and earth which is referred to in the book of Genesis.[132] They are of the Aeon, not of the material time-bound cosmos.[133] They are close to the spiritual being of God and accordingly have an ontological simplicity.[134] The second creation came next, that making of the cosmos, the sun and moon and stars and so on. All of this was made up out of material stuff, the *hyle* of matter that God put together in the orders and ranks of innumerable different beings. The limits of their own orders were set; limits to their development and outreach were imposed that are predetermined.[135] Yet each being worked within that limit and was coherent within it. In short all the second creation is a material construct that finds its fulfilment, meaning, and truth within the material order. Like the angelic first creation, the second creation of animals and things is coherent and uni-substantial.

223

And then came humanity, the third creation. It was a decision by God, says St Gregory, which is very puzzling indeed. For the human being is an animal endowed with an immensely refined spiritual consciousness. The fixed order of the human nature is meant also to give way at certain points to allow for a spiritual transcendence and transfiguration that has been allowed to no other life form on earth. In this transfiguration, humanity leaves behind the animal orders, with which it shares so much else, and enters the company of the angels. Angels and the material cosmos, however, are both orders that rise in their being from their respective single coherent fabrics (*hyle*). Humanity, on the other hand, has a double ontological structure: a material substrate, with a intellectual consciousness woven within it that is gifted with the further capacity of the engagement with God, and to which (in the case of the elect of the covenant) has been given the awesome promise of communion with the divine. The ancient Fathers called this unique element of spiritual transcendence in humanity its 'ensoulment' as a noetic consciousness.[136] Although other animals might be said to have 'souls' (*psychai*), or that element of consciousness that directed their higher intellectual and emotional lives, they insisted that only humans had souls endowed with the capacity for divine perception. This 'admixture' in so intimate an alliance of fundamentally different ontological structures (spirit and flesh as they were called in the biblical terminology) made humanity alone a 'mixed nature'; a *tertium quid* in terms of the levels of specific creations. St Gregory finds this juxtaposition of almost incompatible natures a great paradox. Human beings, therefore, are to some degree an even greater mystery than angels, who, although they are immense and radiantly powerful, are simple and coherent, whereas humankind is not. Humans are thus a mystery to themselves, and certainly a mystery (in large degree) to the angels, who in their own turn have to learn to understand the strange pattern of material existences partially through the medium of the human being who serves as the priest of the material order, bringing it to a spiritualization in the peculiar way humanity conse-crates matter to the service of God.[137] Gregory also sees this 'mixing' as a source of great suffering for the human race, which can never, as a result, be truly at home in this material cosmos which otherwise so perfectly provides a home for all other species of life, and all other inanimate things that are bound together in harmony by inflexible laws of physics.

Given that the angels are eschatological spirits of praise, we find naturally that when the same vocation to be transfigured in praise is, even approximately, approached in the life of the church on earth, the faithful sense the presence of angels very closely. It is a form of spiritual exultation which is profoundly deep, and sober, and peaceful. It can be sensed at moments of great grace in the divine liturgy, at which they also serve, according to the apostle's teaching,[138] and on other occasions when the grace of God has been perfectly fulfilled by a disciple's obedience; for all such occasions are the result of the assistance of the angels of God. Evagrius the Theologian said that the feeling of inner warmth during prayer was also a sign of the presence of an angel taking note of our prayer and joining in with us. Angels are first and foremost the company of beings who were first-born in the cosmos. They are God's elder children,[139] and express their root of existence out of the energy of prayer. Their ontological force is the vision of God that gives them life and joy. The beauty of the Unapproachable is seen by them more clearly and radiantly than humans are ever able to glimpse while in the body, and because of that their state of being is incomparably more mobile (some theologians

224

speak of them as possessing almost unlimited motility[140]) and more beneficent. They are creatures of light and a goodness which is now so deep in them[141] that it has approached the *stasis* of being an innate character. Their chosen forms of epiphany in the material cosmos tend to be as a beautiful young human or as radiance. They are described as 'young men' in the New Testament accounts.[142] Here, their faces are 'like lightning' and their robes are described as 'dazzling white'. This character of *astrapé*, a brilliance so great that the eye cannot look upon it, is the biblical way of signalling that they share in the nature of God's light, and are 'not of this world'.

In historical epiphanies, therefore, they adapt to human conceptions of how they ought to appear. No human being has yet seen their form directly,[143] since within time and space we who are embodied do not have the capacity for such a vision of the 'Bodiless Powers'.[144] The word 'angel' itself derives from the Greek of the Septuagintal Old Testament, and the many New Testament references to the work of angels in the establishment of the church. In the Greek Scripture it means 'a messenger' of God. In the Syriac-speaking church they were known as 'the Watchers' who looked over God's creation and his church with special care.

Orthodoxy teaches that the angels are immortal beings.[145] Once again this aspect of the angels' character was used by the Lord as a symbol of the transfiguration to immortality which will be the lot of the saints in the eschatological mystery.[146] According to Jesus' remarks about there being 'no marrying in the Kingdom', the church has traditionally understood the angels to be sexless, undifferentiated beings, who do not multiply except by direct creation from God. For this reason the icons depict them as 'genderless' eunuchs, with the masculine force of powerful bodies and the feminine grace of hairstyle and features. It was a duty allocated to the imperial bodyguard of eunuchs in the Great Cathedral at Constantinople, to sing the 'song of the angels' (the Cherubikon hymn) during the liturgy, and their eerie *castrati* song was said to evoke the sense of awe among the faithful that, at this solemn moment of the eucharistic celebration, unseen angels were descending among the church. The text of the Cherubikon is as follows:

> We who in a mystery,
> Are icons of the Cherubim,
> And sing the thrice-holy hymn,[147]
> To the life-creating Trinity,
> Now lay aside all earthly care,
> To receive the King of All
> Who comes invisibly,
> Borne up[148] by angelic hosts.
> Alleluia, Alleluia, Alleluia.

The Lord himself attached much significance to the presence of angels in prayer. Some of the great phrases of the Our Father illustrate the significance of the advent of the Kingdom of God by means of the example of angels. 'May your Kingdom come. May your will be done on earth as it is in heaven'[149] is an Aramaic duplication of a phrase in which the second instance ('May your will be done') illustrates more of the implications of the first ('May your Kingdom come'). In this case, the Lord is teaching that the angels give humanity an example of the perfection of the Kingdom, for they serve the will of God their Father perfectly, exactly, with heartfelt joy.[150] The Lord's injunction to his disciples to 'Love the Lord with your whole heart and your whole soul'[151] is something the blessed angels of God do instinctively, almost naturally. As a result, the Kingdom has truly 'come' among them. They stand within the Kingdom of God, and day by day (as it were, for they are outside of the limits of time) their self-consummation to fulfil the will of the Father forms part of the fabric of the Kingdom itself, which spills out even over the material cosmos, in the form of the beneficent mercy that accompanies the grace of God given to mankind.

It is an ancient belief of the church, based partly upon the Lord's prayer in Gethsemane where he taught his disciples to expect heavenly assistance[152] and on other of his sayings[153] (as well as upon the Psalms[154] and apostolic literature[155]), that the faithful on earth are given an angel to watch over their spiritual lives. This angelic care also extends, in many instances, to physical protection of the lives of the elect, though it is mainly given to the church for the purpose of having a mentor for the transfigurative process that is the guiding purpose of the lives of the faithful within history. Several of the early Fathers and ascetic teachers also said that we can weary the angelic guide, especially if we knowingly neglect our spiritual vocation. Such angelic guides are often portrayed in sentimental literature and painting as if they were a comforting blessing. In the patristic writings they serve more as pedagogues in the ancient style, where a pedagogue was certainly not 'a figure of fun or comfort', but someone who pushed the learning process hard.

It is also taught, and from the ancient tradition of the church, that some of the fallen angels are particularly malicious towards those who are seen to be making spiritual progress. Originally spirits of light, some of the angels have fallen so as to become spirits of darkness.[156] Modern society has not only ignored the significance of angels, but has extensively demythologized the concept of demons,[157] and accordingly has rendered itself relatively inarticulate in charting the mysteries of spiritual development in individual lives. Even the cleverest of people sometimes appear to be remarkably spiritually illiterate. In relation to the church's doctrine of angels, the central thing involved, from our point of view, is the need for assistance in navigating mysteries that take our understanding of our own being to its very limits. In this regard, the presence of beneficent beings who will assist those who are ready to learn, as well as malign forces who are always ready to cause harm to the innocent, is something that is far removed from the 'homeyness' associated with angels in the popular consciousness.

The Scriptures describe encounters with angels, such as those known by the prophets or patriarchs, as encounters with eschatological warriors which drain the life-force away, so awesome and uncanny they are.[158] But the angels, like the Lord himself with the gift of the grace of the Holy Spirit, do not force the holy presence upon the inattentive, or those who imagine (because they have so little conception of the complexities of it) that they need no mentor and no assistance in the task of rising into the deeper levels of prayer, or psychic vision. When such people feel no presence of angels it is, perhaps, not surprising, though undoubtedly sad. The Orthodox believe that the power of the sacramental mysteries, especially the great initiating mysteries of the baptismal washing, chrismation, anointing, and the Holy Eucharist, are 'seals' on the body and spirit of a human being to protect the elect from any oppression by the fallen angels: to mark the member of the church out as God's protected one. As the power of prayer, perhaps, diminishes in the broader fabric of an increasingly secularized society (which finds the concept of demonic oppression foolish), and as the extent of the mysteries is reduced, the Orthodox are not surprised that the influence and malignity of the hostile powers is also more commonly found to be at work. Self-hatred and despair are among the most common forms of such oppression, and so too the forms of self-destructive behaviour that incarnate these malign inspirations. Chief on the list of such 'signs' are addictions that destroy human happiness and lives in a wide swathe of damage, but there is also work that delights in war, violence, and impoverishment. Evagrios the monk noted that 'agitation' is the clear revelatory signal that such power is at work. We might add that a progressive alienation from simplicity (and a loss of 'creativity' that springs from direct contact with material of some form that is to be transfigured[159]) has also led to a burgeoning of the loss of human value in many parts of Western society. The Orthodox theologian David Bentley-Hart, for example, recently described the all-consuming globalist economic consumerist thrust (where many multinational corporations now have greater assets than whole countries, and behave as new imperial masters) as opening up a new agenda of world history where the dominance of the 'hostile powers' over humanity's interests is once again made visible.[160] He was not, I think, speaking merely metaphorically.

The Orthodox Church retains a deep devotion to the angelic guardian spirits. It understands them not only to be concerned with the mentoring of believers, but also with the governance of the material order, within their powers.[161] Orthodoxy understands that in some sense, not wholly understood, and not mechanically assured, the angels, and indeed the great saints, continue to serve a ministry of compassionate guidance for the church on earth. It is, however, always a governance of mercy, even if sometimes it may be 'corrective' in ways that the person praying had not anticipated. To this degree it is legitimate, the Orthodox believe, to call upon the glorified saints and angels for assistance in life, always understanding their mercy to be a gift from the one God and Father of us all part of that 'communion of the saints' to which humanity is in the process of being transfigured. In the night prayer of the Orthodox Church one of the last invocations said addresses the guardian angelic spirit in words that ask for help, and also signal that the angel is a mentor and fellow-traveller on the road to the vision of God.[162] And in each divine liturgy the assembled church asks God to send to each one: 'An angel of peace, a faithful guide, a guardian of our souls and bodies'.[163] The last mystery attending a believer who has fallen asleep is the great funeral service of the Orthodox Church. In this too the angels are spoken of as those who come out to greet the soul of the departed and guide it in its new and strange paths.

Orthodoxy has classified the angels from Scripture,[164] as well as from the highly influential work by St Dionysios Areopagite, the *Heavenly Hierarchy*, into nine choirs in turn divided into three hierarchies. The hierarchies are the orders in which the entire angelic species 'ascend' to closer unity with the Godhead. Their ascent is compared by Dionysios to a helical process of deepening purification, enlightenment, and 'drawing closer' to God, not only as the source of their being, but as the 'understood' source of their being, as their initiation deepens and so clarifies their own spiritual essences.[165] To this extent, all the heavenly life of the angelic order (and so it will be for the earthly saints as many of the Fathers have suggested) is one endless *prokope* or advancement. Heaven is not a static place, but one where the endless joy of discovery, constantly unfolding, gives to the created order the closest experience of the infinite it can have: namely, that of endless extension. It is comparable to the use of the term 'bounded infinity' in contemporary science. The first angelic hierarchy

227

contains those closest to God, the Thrones, Cherubim, and Seraphim, in ascending order. The Seraphim are so close to the throne of God that they are depicted in the icons as beings of pure fire. The Cherubim are described as the seat of the Presence on which the majesty of God reclines. The first of the three orders is understood to be entirely occupied with the presence and service of the Most High. The middle hierarchy, in ascending order, are the Authorities, Dominions, and Powers. The lower hierarchy is comprised of those angels who are most concerned with the direction of the affairs of earth, and the mentoring of the human elect. They are, in ascending order, the Angels, Archangels, and Principalities. In some parts of the New Testament[166] the Principalities were regarded as hostile angelic powers who had been brought into submission by the Lord's Resurrection. By the time of Dionysios, however, the title has been entirely reserved for the higher order of the elect angels, who are different from the 'hostile powers' (fallen angels) which the early apostolic literature was talking about.

Dionysios categorized the Christian angelic doctrine most fully, bringing together all the various 'titles' entirely from Scripture, and it is his system which the Orthodox Church observes today. The lineaments of his teaching can also be found in the more scattered remarks about the angelic orders found in St Ignatius of Antioch from the early second century, as well as significant writings from the fourth, not least the Apostolic Constitutions, and St Gregory the Theologian, and later in Pope Gregory I, St John Chrysostom, and John of Damascus, among the most notable.

Church tradition lists the names of seven individual angels are known through Scripture or the non-canonical literature. Michael signifies 'Who is like to God?'.[167] Gabriel is Hebrew for 'The Man of God'.[168] Raphael (The Help of God),[169] Uriel (The Fire of God),[170] and Salathiel (Prayer to God)[171] are also joined by two other angels from the hagiographic literature: Jegudiel (The Praise of God), and Barachiel (The Blessing of God).

Orthodoxy, therefore, takes the existence and intervention of the angels of God with utter seriousness. It does not understand them to be mere symbols of something else, or mythological anachronisms. It accepts the substantial testimony of the Scriptures about their involvement with God's plan for the salvation of the earth. As it does with the existence of evil in the world, it sees the communion of goodness around it (admittedly dimly at times as it tries to see with the eyes of the spirit instead of the eyes of the flesh or the mind) as a living web of influence. The members of the church sense the presence of living saints among them, and on the same principle can sense the presence of angels gathered to 'watch over' men and women who are themselves rising into the presence of the holy. The Russian theologian Bulgakov expressed this eloquently when he said: 'The spiritual world, and the existence of good and evil spirits are evident to all those who live the spiritual life. And the belief in the holy angels is a great joy and consolation for the Christian.'[172]

Orthodoxy in all its generations knows, and deeply respects, the sanctity that is so evidently seen in the human lives and activity of several living elders, of both sexes.[173] They are not usually known at all to the outside world, their hidden lives and careers passing by largely unnoticed; but their names are certainly known within the homes of the faithful, who often travel on pilgrimage for many miles to meet with them, and ask their advice. Even when Orthodox believers cannot be in direct contact with these elders they are often aware of their spiritual force and influence at several removes. It is the same with the heavenly saints and angels too. There are many stories current among the Orthodox of men and women of prayer who have encountered the angels. It is not regarded as a phenomenally 'strange' thing that this should be so, just as the continuing interest of the heavenly saints is not regarded as something unusual in a great and benign spirit. It would, on the contrary, be a major self-contradiction for a great spirit not to have any philanthropic interest, given that the Lord to whom all the church, in heaven and on earth, looks to as its Master and exemplar, is himself the Megas Philanthropos, the Lord and Lover of Humankind.

This is the reason Orthodoxy has a great devotion to the saints. In its calendar of festivals, there is no single day that is not filled with commemorations of great men and women of the Christian past who are celebrated as having 'excelled' in their love of Christ. The New Testament writings designate all the believers as the 'saints of God'.[174] In this it continued the Old Testament custom of referring in this way to the holiness of the Elect People. While Orthodoxy recognizes that this holiness is collectively given to the faithful in their consecration through the mysteries of baptism, chrismation, and Eucharist, as well as in their ongoing initiation in the Christian life, it also knows that some of the saints are exceptional witnesses to the sanctifying grace of the Holy Spirit. In their lifetimes this can be manifested through extraordinary works of mercy they achieve for other people in prayer. Their prayers are powerful beyond the ordinary. Some of them are great miracle workers, and are known as *thaumaturgoi*.[175] Others have the gift of clairvoyance, and the ability to read souls and direct consciences. Some of them have been entirely unknown during their lifetimes and posthumously appeared by strange deeds and philanthropic miracles. Recent examples of great saints in this category are St Charbel Mahklouf the wonder-worker of Lebanon, a *myroble-tes*[176] who has cured many souls after his holy life as a Maronite hermit; or St Ephraim the New Martyr of Greece. Most of the others were famed in their own lifetimes as Christian heroes. Many of the leading saints of the Orthodox calendar are the martyrs and confessors[177] from the early ages of the church. But the list of them extends even into the present. They are usually not officially declared to be saints until their veneration has become a widespread matter in the churches: that is, a lot of Christians agree over a long space of time that here in this particular life was a true example of God's glory. For this reason the official service declaring them to be saints of God is known as their 'Glorification'. In antiquity their glorification often was a matter of immediate acclamation. Certainly this was the case after martyrdom, for it is the ancient belief of the church that a martyr, in his or her suffering, receives immediate spiritual admittance into Paradise.

The church does not teach with complete clarity of detail about the state of the soul after death. It has partial suggestions, and intimations. In this reserve it is being faithful to the apostle's confession[178] that the glorification of the faithful soul is a gift of God that is a profound and secret mystery that cannot be described mechanically. It affirms as part of its faith that the soul of the departed believer 'lives in God' who is a God of the living not of the dead;[179] nevertheless it often refers to the state of the faithful Christian after death as a 'time of repose'.

The early Christians invented the word 'cemetery' to describe the graveyards of the believers. The word means 'sleeping grounds'. The early church also referred to the saints who died before the Second Coming as 'asleep in the Lord'; terms which are still in use among the Orthodox. The funeral service of the church speaks of the faithful dead as being 'given rest' by Christ 'in the place where the just repose', 'in a place of brightness, a place of refreshment and repose, from which all sorrow sickness and sighing have fled away'. This connotes a place and state of awareness,[180] certainly, but the emphasis is clearly on resting. In some of the ancient non-canonical writings, as well as in several liturgical texts and customs, it is suggested that the afterlife is divided into several zones. Paradise itself is to be distinguished from the general resting place of the righteous dead.[181] The righteous dead will be admitted into the heart of Paradise only after their final purification after the Last Day and after the resurrection of the body has occurred. In the meantime they rest peacefully, with a lesser degree of the vision of Paradise, (where the angels and great saints abide), than the one they will later receive when fully glorified.[182] This is in some sense like an anticipation of glory, one that is a delightful repose, and not burdensome because the passage of time and spatial distance is abrogated after death. There is not as much energy expressed in their being there, compared to the angels and the great saints, because the ontological state of the righteous dead is incomplete before the final resurrection when they will be transfigured into their final and newly 'coherent' stage of being. Until the End, there-fore, the church on earth prays for the righteous dead, and for the repose of their souls. On the other hand, those it has recognized as great saints, already active in Paradise, it does not pray for in the same sense:[183] it asks assistance from them. The great saints, although equally not yet fully 'coherent' in their final glorified body, still have a more active ministry in the glorified life, and are closer to the enjoyment of the full freedom of Paradise, because the energy of the Spirit of God that was in them has brought them closer to the condition of the finally glorified body already. 'Star differs from star in glory', as the apostle said.[184]

The saint, therefore, is sensed by the earthly church as particularly great because their experience of Paradise still involves this active philanthropy for their separated brothers and sisters on earth. Their ministry is probably limited to the guidance and protection of the elect, while that of the angels is more diverse and free-ranging. The power of love which motivates the paradisal saints is a testament to the greatness of their discipleship, and the charism of the Spirit they enjoyed on earth. As the Lord himself described it,[185] there is a great gulf between Paradise and the other 'places' of the afterlife, which the elect cannot cross (even if they wanted to). It also seems that there is a large gulf which makes it a matter of some labour for the angels and saints to continue working between Paradise and the earthly sphere.[186] That the angels and saints continue to do so is the chief testimony to their philanthropy and large energy of spiritual power. The Orthodox Church venerates many thousands of saints, but knows some of their number to be particularly active still.[187] All the Orthodox are given a saint's name at baptism, and this 'name day' is celebrated in preference to their actual birthday in most Orthodox countries to this day. Their patron saint is appealed to in regular prayer, and is believed to take a special interest in the welfare of the Christian that makes intercession to him or her. Whereas angelic intervention has been heard of in many unsolicited cases, it is thought that the intervention of a saint usually follows only after a specific invocation of the saint in times of need: either by the person who seeks help, or by friends and loved ones who have prayed to the saint on behalf of the person. There are several services of intercession (*paraclesis*) used in the church specifically dedicated to asking the intercession of the Blessed Virgin and the saints.

The Orthodox regard it as natural that the great saints should continue to exercise loving benevolence in this way. It also gives theological testimony to several important aspects of the Orthodox understanding of the church as the communion of saints. First of all it shows in a very practical way that Christ arranges our salvation not in a narrowly individual manner, but in a way that is deeply interconnected with the family of souls around us with whom we live and interact. None of us gets to Paradise alone. Our pilgrimage there is a long trail of dependencies, and philanthropies. St Symeon the New Theologian called it a 'golden chain' in which we were always initiated into the love of Christ through other members of the communion.[188] We know that this merciful interaction (the growth of holiness in society), both its negative side (all the damage we do to other people by our lack of faith and our sinfulness) and its therapeutic side (the way we manage to atone, and find forgiveness and reconciliation) are all an integral part of the Great Communion (*koinonia, sobornost*) which consti-tutes the spiritual interconnectedness of all Christ's elect: the angels in heaven, the faithful on earth, and the chosen ones in Paradise. Many parts of Western Christianity have lost the sense of the close involvement of the saints in the ongoing daily lives of Christians. Some even think that devotion to the closeness of the saints in this way is a distraction from a direct engagement with the presence of the Lord in a Christian consciousness.

It is a great mistake to think that the soul finds Christ nakedly and alone. The Lord always comes to us in the family, and through the medium of the love of other members of the communion. He came to his world through the Holy Virgin. He comes to us in faith, even to this day, through the ministry of those who have loved us and nurtured us, and formed our minds and characters in a thousand ways. He comes to us in the Scriptures, directly, yes, but also through the countless hundreds of thousands who have transcribed, collected the texts, and preached them to society over centuries. There is no direct and solipsistically solitary path to the Christ. If we find Christ we find the heart of love and communion. Those who wish to find the Lord alone, and possess him alone, have not found the true Lord. In some places in the world superstition may indeed have perverted the cult of the saints, so that it has degenerated into a disturbingly non-Christian phenomenon. Orthodoxy does not generally manifest that social condition. If it does appear, the clergy correct it energe-tically. The Orthodox veneration of the saints is widely understood by all levels of the faithful, educated or not. And the celebration of the saints is deeply integrated with the sense of the church as a communion of word and sacrament. This has been a pattern of Eastern Christian life since the earliest centuries, when the tombs of the martyrs grew into being the local parish churches.

Orthodoxy, in its heart, does not understand a personalist attitude that issues in the form of a latent (or not so latent!) hostility to the saints, and finds it to be defective in its comprehension of the communion of salvation. It is difficult to express the significance of family to those whose experience of earthly families has been insignifi-cant, or worse, damaging. But the action of the saints, still philanthropic and still assisting the lives of Christians on earth, is a fact of authentic Christian family life, and for the Orthodox is part of their very faith-confession that Christ has saved not a host of solitary righteous people, but rather an elect communion of beings: humanity and angels, who are brought together in him and through him[189] in a bond of love that constitutes the New Being of the Kingdom. Love, and the communion that grows from

231

it in a strenuous commitment to justice and mercy, is thus the fabric of the light that upholds the being of the next age. The saints and angels are already living, or learning to live, in that luminous element. We on earth are in a more primitive state of *paideia*, and both our justice and our mercy is erratic. It is, therefore, very useful to study the lives and deeds of the saints in order to see how flesh-and-blood people like ourselves responded in their own particular historical conditions to the demands of the Gospel imperative.

To this extent, while the lives and teachings of the ancient saints are often starkly instructive, the witness of saints nearer our own time is even more useful, perhaps, in showing us patterns of behaviour. The achievements of the ascetic desert Fathers and Mothers, for example, makes for jaw-dropping reading. To mimic their kind of disciplining of the body would probably make most modern people ill within a very short time. But they serve to give the church a perennial warning about the dangers of conforming to the soporific luxuries of society. In this consumerist age, rather than sinking into the pit of anachronism, their testimony takes on a new relevance, and power. More recent saints, especially the numerous Orthodox martyrs of the communist yoke, give us examples of a standard of courage and freedom that is deeply inspiring.[190] Be that as it may, Orthodoxy understands the saints to be more than simple examples from history. They live on near us, even when parted from us in their degree of glory. Like the Lord they served, they are merciful and gracious, and not only do they offer us a model to look to, they can, and often do, answer prayer, and delight in bringing to us the grace the Lord himself has given them for our benefit.

The saints too are regarded by the Orthodox Church as supreme theologians. This is not to say that all the saints are authoritative theologians, or that everything they had to say should be taken as serious axioms. Some of them may have excelled more than others in the quality of the life of the mind, and in the character of preaching and teaching. Nevertheless, the church regards the saints as having lived out the full implications of the Orthodox faith, as clearly manifested in the quality of their apprehension of the Divine Spirit. It is, therefore, impossible to conceive of a saint who is deficient in theology. The doctrine represented by the saints is the same as that known by all the Orthodox in communion with one another. Indeed the church has always regarded the greatest of the saints as being particularly imbued with the inspiration of the Spirit. Their theological writings, therefore, are given 'patristic' status. They are not simply the works of famous old theologians from the past, but are writings that breathe the presence of the Holy Spirit, with a quality of inspiration similar to, though not in the same degree as, the Holy Scriptures. The saints present Orthodox doctrine in graphic form, as a life-enhancing philosophy that deifies and illuminates all that it touches (intellectually, morally, and physically). The writings of the Fathers of the Church, and the great ascetic teachers, therefore, have always been given special status in the Orthodox Church, and continue to be read carefully: not as windows onto the past (as historians often approach them), but rather as guides to the spiritual pilgrimage written by great travellers who have made the journey successfully before us.

The same is true about the icons and relics of the saints. These are seen to be charged with a grace that flows over from association with these Spirit-filled beings, and so they serve as focal points of encounter with the saints in prayer. Orthodoxy does not recognize the old Latin conception of the supererogatory merits of saints: as if they had accumulated a store of benefits and merits while on earth, which they are now able to spend on posthumous acts of philanthropy. Orthodoxy sees the power of saints as a habitual effluence, through them, of the energy of the Holy Spirit of God which so absorbed them in life that it has now wholly irradiated them by grace after death.[191] The relics of the saints are carefully preserved in the Orthodox churches. The faithful will make long pilgrimages to greet them, and when they come to their shrines will kiss the relics attentively, as if they were kissing a much-respected loved one or teacher. The relics and icons have a power of blessing in them that can sanctify and pacify troubled souls and restore peace, or can bless houses or other things and places that are filled with malign energy and bring the clarification and calm of love back to them. Clergy are often to be found conducting such services of blessing in the churches and homes of the faithful, using the icons and relics in this way.

Sometimes the bodies of the saints are found incorrupt many years after their repose. This is always taken as a sign of the special favour of the Lord, showing that their Christian lives were indeed 'incorruptible'. Physical incorruptibility of the relics, however, is not an invariable sign of great sanctity. Recently deceased saints will often be laid out in the churches on their feast days in their open coffins, with the face covered with a liturgical cloth, and the hands available to be kissed by the pilgrims. The incorrupt bodies of many saints can also be seen in the Kiev Caves monastery (Pechersky Lavra) in Ukraine, some of them centuries old. Every Orthodox church, however, has relics of the saints; so do many of the houses of the Orthodox faithful. They are always in each church's Holy Table[192] and the *antimension*[193] on which the Eucharist is celebrated. Those that are kept in private homes are found on the icon shelf, the so-called 'Beautiful Corner', which is that place in the home where prayers are customarily said and the family icons are hung.

On some occasions the relics of the saints emit perfume, or a holy myrrh which can cure the sick who use it with faith and repentance. This phenomenon is widely attested among the Orthodox throughout all the past centuries, and still occurs today. The invisible spiritual presence of a saint is often signalled to the Orthodox faithful by a perfume that fills a house or chapel. Such things are called *thaumata*, or wonders. The Western word 'miracle' is too grandiose for them.[194] The Orthodox regard them as more natural than the word miracle would suggest, which has been taken so much in past centuries to suggest a 'supernatural reversal' of the world order. Orthodoxy, however, understands that these signs of the inbreaking of the next age into this age are small, because our comprehension and capacity are small; but they are nevertheless real signs that the 'normal' world order is that which is established by Christ in the eschatological mystery of the Resurrection. The church, therefore, understands the regular visitations of the saints and angels in the sense that they also serve to manifest this mystery of the Anastasis as a loving grace. Far from being 'miracles' of a supernatural order, therefore, Orthodoxy regards such *thaumata* as being the most normal things possible,[195] signs that normality is actually returning to our alienated consciousness. Most Orthodox, if asked to speak of such things, would have stories to share of times when their spiritual sensibility has glimpsed through the veil, and become aware of the Lord and his saints drawing near to them. And the stories they would tell would all have the same character, would all accumulate to the same generic theological point: that we are not alone on our pilgrimage but are assisted by a loving and intimate 'cloud of witnesses'.[196]

OUTSIDE THE GATES: DEMONOLOGY AND THE ENIGMA OF EVIL

The prophetic visionary St John on Patmos puts in very dramatic fashion the distinction between those who are within the Kingdom, and those without:

> Blessed are those who wash their robes, that they may have the right to the tree of life and that they may enter the city by the gates. Outside the gates are the dogs and sorcerers and fornicators and murderers and idolaters, and every one who loves and practises falsehood.[197]

His vision is of the heavenly Jerusalem, but it is just as true on this earth that evil has no kinship with the good. The power of God's grace and holiness shuns and repels evil. Evil cannot enter the presence of the Living God, and cannot harm, in any ultimate sense, and only in immediate senses which are closely controlled by God, the saints of God who are marked with his grace through the sacraments. But it is also true that on this earth the forces of goodness and evil mix more fluidly than in the Kingdom of the saints, where God has established an absolute barrier between them.[198] The face of evil is urbane and habitually masks itself in the present aeon of world history. It can even seek to mimic the good, and tries to fool even the elect, if such a thing were possible. Evil always betrays itself, however, for the simulation of the good is difficult for it, and its innate characteristics of agitation, spitefulness, lies, and hostility to what constitutes the peaceful good of others cannot help showing themselves at critical junctures. It is, nevertheless, an important part of the unmasking of evil that the elect have to recognize its presence, discern its intention and scope, and name it for the warning of the common good. All too often even good people are led astray, thinking that there is no such force as real evil in the world, or that wickedness is merely a word for mistaken or unfortunate behaviour. There is that, of course; but it is a foolish myopia not to be able to admit the palpable presence of evil in our world, and an even more lamentable failing not to be able to point the finger at it in the cause of unmasking its pervasive effects. The good are especially prone to this mistake, as they live, generally, in atmospheres of gracefulness and cannot imagine some of the character of real wickedness that is always on the prowl.[199]

Orthodoxy takes seriously the doctrine of the elemental spirits spoken of so extensively in the Gospels,[200] and elaborated in the later Epistles[201] where their role in the propagation of 'false teaching' that confuses and leads astray large portions of humanity is stressed.[202] The discernment of evil in the midst of society, and its public exorcism, was part of the fundamental ministry of Jesus in his time in Galilee, and the victory over evil that was effected by his Cross remains a consolation to the Orthodox. But this struggle with the force of evil is not yet completed. Each Christian, throughout life, is faced with a myriad of 'offers' to align with the persuasive rhetoric of evil. Its lying promises, like false advertisements for the cult of greed in which it so often thrives and hides itself, are hardly, if ever, sustained in reality, but it seems to matter little. Men and women often willingly subject themselves to the domination of illusion as their primary guide in life: and the shackles of illusion, once willingly adopted, are hard to shake off. The cult of consumerist happiness, so prevalent in affluent Western societies today, is one instance of a primal lie that masks its illusionary nature by failing to spell out commonly what oceans of oppression and suffering lie beneath the alleged happiness of the top level of consumers of the world's resources. Most of the printed resources of Western society (by volume of print and dissemination at least) serve to propagate this false culture, the manifold masks of evil, and its visual form in Tinseltown philosophy tries desperately to mask its intellectual bankruptcy with superficial devices. One leading New York television producer said to me not so long ago: 'Sex and violence, and personal gratification, are what sell. Nothing else. I am interested in nothing else.' It was in the course of a dark afternoon spent among the bright lights of a major American media company. I have rarely felt so ill at ease in any place on God's earth.

St John of Damascus articulates how, for Orthodoxy, evil is the negative face of the doctrine of the communion of the angels and saints. Because the reverse of this is 'breakdown of communion' the forces of evil cannot wholly unite even among themselves to prove a strong and credible opposition to the love which is the Kingdom of God. Their coherence is driven by malice and greed. But even so, this negative force still attracts large numbers of men and women, of each generation, into it by means of illusion and deceit. The results are desperation, but one that usually only reveals itself when the trouble has already been caused. Drug addiction is a primal example of the programmatic policy of evil. The drugs are 'cool' and used by 'interesting' people. They lead to the realization of high feelings of spiritual elevation, ecstasy, and enhanced intellectual states that are a godlike condition, to which men and women were surely destined. What is never said is that, in the end, the hard drug addict loses love, society, freedom, self-respect, and eventually their very teeth; something which is decidedly not 'cool' in any way at all.

The Damascene explains that evil is presided over by Lucifer, one of the greatest of God's angels of light, who was appointed one of the great guardians of the cosmic balance, but turned away in an unalterable will to defy God by fomenting rebellion in the world:

> He who from among these angelic powers was set over the earthly realm, and into whose hands God committed the guardianship of the earth, was not made wicked in nature but was good, and made for good ends, and received from his Creator absolutely no trace of evil in himself. But he did not sustain the brightness and the honour which the Creator had bestowed on him, and by free choice was changed from what was in harmony to what was at variance with his nature, and became set against God who created him, and determined to rise in rebellion against Him. Lucifer was the first to depart from good and become evil. ... but along with him an innumerable host of angels subject to him were torn away and followed him, sharing in his fall. They who once had the same nature as the angels became wicked, turning away at their own free choice from good to evil. Yet they have no power or strength against any one, except what God in his dispensation has conceded to them.[203]

The path to transcendence, for a Christian, is made up of innumerable steps, demanding *ascesis* and discipline, the adoption of a simple and loving attitude before the world, strong fidelity to prayer, faithfulness to the Gospel teachings and commandments, and regular involvement in the church's sacramental and liturgical life, so that by all these means one's life may slowly be turned and directed in the footsteps of Christ and his saints. It is exactly the same when it comes to a life led astray by evil. It cannot happen all at once or in a flash. The soul is seduced by evil little by little. Its poison all in one moment is too much for humanity to stomach; so it distils itself into men and women by small degrees over a long period. It takes many forms in its seduction: the allure of many possessions; the will to power over others; the desire for indolence over the energy needed to be creative. Whatever stultifies, hardens, embitters, or frustrates the ascent of human beings is the primal programme of evil. Many humans around us are in the various stages of being either willing or unwitting collaborators in this programmatic philosophy to diminish the realization of human life as a sacrament of grace.

Behind them all, however, lie darker forces of malign spirits.[204] Once they were bright angels; after aeons of alienation from light and love they have diminished greatly; but when men and women turn from the paths of light and perversely orientate their lives to worship them, they gain new strength (as in the times of Roman paganism when the great Fathers recognized them behind the mask of the old sacrificial cults). They are very much alive today and active in the mockery of Christianity; and in its portrayal as a dead or dying religion (another lie in the era when the church has never grown so much or been so extended on the face of the earth). Orthodoxy, in its daily prayers and in its formal prayer services, still recognizes the presence of evil malign influences and is not ashamed to pray against them. In this context the invocation of the power of the Cross is an invariable part of the prayers. It is manifested in that most common of daily Orthodox prayers: 'Jesus Christ conquers, and scatters every evil.' It can be found everywhere in the church and among Orthodox: the square cross in which each quadrant has the phrase inscribed in abbreviation IC XC NIKA: Jesus Christ Victorious.

This systemic programme of evil, and its corruption of humans into it, is always given away, so the Fathers tell us throughout the ascetical literature, by the character of agitation it has and brings with it to create a micro-ambience. That which is heavenly, is peaceful, loving, joyful, and works for the good of all that it meets. What is the opposite can never know joy, since this is a charism reserved only for that which is filled with the presence of life and grace. Evil is agitated and agitates all around it; it is joyless, suffocatingly self-referential and pompous; it does not know how to laugh except when laughter is a cruel mockery of others; it cannot properly build (for it is devoid of the notion of communion) and has a force only in deconstructing and diminishing. It is easily recognizable when one knows what to look for.

In Orthodox Church life, if a believer is feeling oppressed in particularly heavy and despondent ways they often resort to the prayers of exorcism. Liturgically the greatest of the prayers of exorcism are contained in St Basil's Great Exorcism (used in services for healing) and in the prayers of the Exorcism of Catechumens used today in the ritual immediately preceding baptism. There is also a lesser and much more common form of exorcism of evil used many times in Orthodox life, in the form of the blessing rituals that are so much a part of Orthodoxy. Families often call in a priest for the blessing of the house and family. This is not in some ridiculous 'horror film' fashion, for the elemental forces hold little power over God's beloved, and the services of blessing and exorcism are quite normal parts of church life, taking place (outside special times of distress) at every yearly cycle of Theophany (6 January). These blessings are used in

236

cases of sickness of family members, cases of despondency, family disunity, cases of failures of crops or plans that have gone astray unpredictably. The Orthodox also make regular use of blessed water (to drink as well as to sprinkle their homes with), and they offer incense in their homes before the icons to invoke the power of Christ and his saints to guard themselves and their loved ones. The sprinkling of the blessed water and the holy incense are seen as purifications of the home and the environment. The Orthodox also constantly pray for others so that the grace of God and the protection of the angels and saints will guard them in all aspects of their lives. Modern Orthodox are often aware that many in the West (even Christians among them) regard this aspect of their faith as residual superstition. They, in their turn, are intrigued that a sense of the discernment of the various types of evil is so undeveloped around them, and that there is so little sense remaining in the West of how prayer and the intercession of the saints and angels so dramatically interacts with human life for our good.

Sergei Bulgakov referred to this obliquely in his own consideration of the demonic aspect of life:

> Side by side with the angels of light there are fallen angels or demons, evil spirits, who strive to influence us, acting upon our sinful inclinations. Evil spirits become visible to those who have attained a certain degree of spiritual experience. The Gospels and the whole of the New Testament give us unshakeable testimony on this point. Orthodoxy understands this testimony in a manner wholly realistic; it does not accept an allegorical exegesis, and even less refuses to explain these texts by the simple influence of religious syncretism. The spiritual world, and the existence of good and evil spirits, are evident to all those who live the spiritual life.[205]

There are innumerable examples in the accounts of the saints and the spiritual elect of all generations of Orthodoxy, where his words are borne out as true. A critical matter in all of this is the role of the *starets* or *starissa*, who can give guidance to the perplexed or troubled Orthodox Christian. The prophetic discernment required for the unmasking of evil is an important charism required in the Christian communities; for it is only by the finger of God, ultimately, that evil can be cast out effectively,[206] and it always longs to remain active by passing unrecognized, or as 'unbelievable'.

In the church all forms of human fallibility are forgiven; no sin is outside the range and capacity of God's mercy and healing grace. It is, consequently, the church's duty to welcome sinners, not to judge and condemn them (for who in the church is not in that company?), and to encourage their trust in God's encompassing forgiveness. The weakness of sin in this sense, however, is one thing: evil is another thing that has taken root and become chronically opposed to God's will. Evil, in this sense, the church abhors. In the ancient discipline of the canons there were certain sins that called down 'exclusion' from the community automatically: among these were the crafts of the sorcerers, the makers of potions (usually referring to abortionists), even the matter of belonging to the army in the earliest days of the church. Today we would find it peculiar to refuse baptism to a soldier solely on that basis; but there ought to be a more lively sense in the church that their 'equivalents' are still around: those who thrive on the sexual slavery of others, those who manufacture munitions and land mines that devastate the lives of the innocent poor; those who foment global schemes of exploitative devastation of whole eco-environments, those who glory in racism and dedicate themselves to antagonistic divisions within society: these are the servants of something more than just sinful weakness.

These are the modern collaborators with evil, and for them the church has only words of resistance – not welcome, not soothing. This level of sin has gone beyond individual culpability to become a deep-seated corporate wickedness that rebels against God's deepest ordinances. It ranks among those things that Scripture identified as 'sins to the death' because they were so chronic and deep-rooted. Scripture tends to reserve this damning indictment for one evil above all others: the fomenting and fostering of false belief that blinds and muddles people. Perhaps never since the age of Gnosticism in the early generations of the church has there been an age such as this one where fundamental doctrines of Christianity have been so controverted and muddied. In the midst of all of it, especially in the face of contemporary pseudo-philosophers who have dared to claim that Truth itself is a redundant concept, the Orthodox are unmoved; instead they point the finger, and name the smiling demon.

The Church: Bride of the Lamb

Although we live in a world where the very concept and term 'church' has become bureaucratized and formalized, so that most people would immediately think of either a building or an administrative society when they hear the word; the Orthodox have retained the older and infinitely more dynamic understanding of church which is found in the Scriptures. These describe the church as a mystery of the 'life in Christ'; a society of believers, certainly, but more fundamentally, the extended power of Christ's saving work as manifested and concretized in the world, and in the next age.[207] The church, rooted as it is in this age, yet moving already out of it to its transcendent destiny with the glorified Christ, is at heart an eschatological mystery that cannot entirely be at home in the present world order, and cannot fully be glimpsed within it. The Scriptures prefer to come at this mystery of renovation (what we might call the full depth of the experience of Christ's salvation and the Spirit's communion of grace) through a whole variety of metaphors and similes. Taken together a rich and deeply suggestive understanding of the church emerges from them. Accordingly the Church of Christ can be understood as organic and extended body,[208] a vineyard where the vinedresser keeps the stock nurtured and productive,[209] a flock of sheep under the care of a good shepherd,[210] a household,[211] the energy of spousal love[212] and even a project under construction with foundations and cornerstones.[213]

The Scriptures provide the fundamental material for Orthodox ecclesiology (the doctrine of the church) but that dogmatic and central phrase of the Nicene Creed is also very important, where the church is defined as a central mystery of the Christian faith (whose acceptance is necessary for salvation in so far as the church is the experience of 'belonging' to Christ). The Creed affirms that it is necessary to believe in: 'one, holy, catholic and apostolic church'. The Orthodox Church describes itself, from its inner consciousness, as being that one, holy, catholic, and apostolic church of Christ on earth. It knows, and teaches, that it is the self-same communion of saints founded by the Lord in the course of several mysteries in his earthly economy,[214] and empowered for its historical and saving mission in the world[215] at Pentecost. It has this self-awareness of its powerful spiritual and physical identity not least because of its awareness, embodied in time and space, of the transcendent Lord's resurrectional presence within its midst. This the *phronema Christou*,[216] that 'mind of Christ' which it has as its own spiritual consciousness by the gift of the Spirit, and into which it is constantly transfigured, both collectively, and in the personal lives of holiness of each of its members. This Lord remains the sole Head and Supreme High Priest of the Church of Christ,[217] and directs its continuing pilgrimage through time and space.

Many Western Christians (perhaps used to the perception of the churches as denominations and communions scattered in organization and to a certain degree disunited in doctrine and polity[218]) have found this to be a presumptuous idea, and an outrageous claim. But it is meant, simply enough, to say that Orthodoxy 'knows itself', through the paths of its own sacred history on earth. It is the church of the apostles and Fathers, continuing on its journey; aware of its own times and conditions, and ready to respond to them, but always out of the continuously preserved heritage of its communion with the ancient saints. This communion is something that is a spiritual bond, as well as a doctrinal harmony. The saints of the past, and the church of the present, have this harmony of love, and belief, and teaching, precisely because they have, as their innermost inspiration and communion, the self-same love of the Lord as inspired in them by the same grace of the Holy Spirit.

The church knows itself because it knows its Lord who called it into being as the church, and knows him as living in the present moment by the gift of the Spirit which is the soul of the church. For the same reason, it knows the truth of the Gospel tradition, and defends it passionately, preferring the truth to 'negotiated harmony' and understandings of ecclesial unity which are bureaucratic or chiefly political in character. In an age when some Western scholars would even laugh aloud at the very notion of someone being able to 'know' the Gospel tradition (either claiming it was ungraspable, non-existent, or irreducibly multiform) the Orthodox Church affirms its knows exactly what that tradition is, since the Lord who taught his Gospel remains the Teacher and Master of the community which continues to hear, ponder, live out, and proclaim that Gospel as a life-saving message, not a recondite archaeology.

Orthodoxy refuses to concur with a conception of the church that has become increasingly common in the West since the Reformation – and that is the tendency to strictly demarcate the heavenly and the earthly church into separate entities. In such a view, if we may generalize and caricature a little, the 'invisible' church is thought of as the glorious, and glorified, communion of saints – all that Christ intended his church to be, while the 'visible' earthly church staggers on through history, mired in compromise, scandals and corruption; constantly requiring some beneficent reformer, or other new committee of action, to rescue it from its present generational decadence, so as to reform it once again, and polish up the battered paintwork so that, at least, it might not scandalize the world too much. In its earthly state it is seen as liable to present a very sinful face to the world. The invisible church, in this approach, is understood to be the kernel of the elect within the church; but it is often overwhelmed by the husk and bureaucratic chaff which threaten to stifle it. The invisible church is imagined to be what the Scripture referred to in glowing terms, whereas the visible church is simply an earthly society capable of being led astray by powerful factions and blown off course by the prevailing winds of the age. This is a widespread preconception, particularly Protestant in form,[219] and is often found operative as a default understanding in many Western writings about the church. Nevertheless, it is one that is inimical to the Orthodox understanding of the church, and does not correspond to its own lived experience.

Orthodoxy refuses to admit a dichotomy of this magnitude between the heavenly and earthly conceptions of the Church of Christ, or between its invisible and its visible characters. The visible church can be distinguished from the heavenly church, in the sense that one is still in the struggle to be perfectly conformed to the will of God on earth, while the other has found its transcendent glory with the Lord, but the two cannot be separated, since they are organically linked together as one and the same family, or communion, living in one and the same energy of God's salvific grace, albeit in different 'stages' and 'orders' of discipleship.[220]

It applies, against this dichotomous understanding, the typological understanding of the Incarnate Lord's unity with his own body. The church, as the apostle clearly taught, is the mystical Body of Christ.[221] Similarly, the visible and invisible characters of the church are bound together in an indissoluble union ('a consilience into unity' as St Cyril of Alexandria put it) that cannot be set apart. Such ecclesiologies of division have about them the same dichotomous character as the Christological heresy of Nestorianism. Orthodoxy thus sees the church as the living icon of Christ. This iconic character of manifesting Christ (among itself and to its own communion, and also to the world in the form of its evangelical mission) is seen at its highest pitch in the mystery of the Holy Eucharist, which is the apex of the *koinonia* of the church. The one bishop, with the local churches gathered round him in the celebration of the holy mystery of communion, has always been seen as a great icon of the unity of the church. This is the context of the very first time the word 'Eucharist' ever appeared in reference to the mystery of the Lord's body and blood, as when Ignatius of Antioch said to the Philadelphian faithful:

> Take great care to preserve one Eucharist. For there is one flesh of Our Lord Jesus Christ, and one cup to unite us by his blood, one sanctuary, just as there is one bishop together with the presbytery and deacons, my fellow-servants. In this way all your acts will be done in accordance with God's will.[222]

The very function and purpose of the gift of the mystery of communion in the Lord's body and blood is to bring unity among his flock, and it is no small part of the church's work on earth to be the locus of the Eucharist, in so far as this is the unity of Christ, from which all other unity devolves.

After receiving communion, Orthodox greet one another with the customary words: 'Christ is in our midst'. The words are demonstrative that this communion moves from being iconic to substantive, since the Eucharist is not merely an icon of the Lord's presence, but the actual gift of the presence. Similarly, the church as the icon of Christ to the world, expresses a good sense of the way in which it is called upon to present a true and beautiful image of its Lord to a wider society which seeks (perhaps unknowingly) this healing beauty. On occasion the members of the church may significantly fail in this task of iconizing their Lord successfully, but the Lord ensures that the church never loses its iconic veracity and power as a whole. The individual moral failings of members of the church in any generation (and equally its moral successes as a society of believers) represent the church's iconic witness, and can be powerful or weak in any particular time or place, just as an icon can be radiantly beautiful, or rather badly done, while still remaining an icon.[223] So too the individual member of the church can be a poor icon of the Lord, while never losing the fundamental iconic character (as long as repentance still keeps that believer in the harmony of the church). But the mystery of the whole church as icon of Christ is indefectible, in a way analogous to the Holy Eucharist. Its iconic role is also related to its ontological status: its 'being' as the Body of Christ, knitted together in oneness with the living Lord by the power of the Spirit which makes new life. So it is with the church as the icon of Christ. It involves a moral character of the disciples' collective obedience and fidelity to the Lord, but also an ontological character (in which the indefectibility of its holiness lies) in so far as it is the mystical body of the Risen Lord in the world, and bears all the beauty of his own glory, unfailingly delightful to the eyes of the Father, in the perennial springs of the Spirit's grace.

Orthodox thought has also used the typology of the Holy Trinity in its ecclesiology. The church is, then, to be understood as the icon of the Holy Trinity also. This is a far more difficult image to visualize, just as the icon of the Trinity in the history of iconography has proved to be a supreme challenge to the theological vision of the iconographers. Most will know St Andrei Rublev's magnificent evocation of the iconic theme of the 'hospitality of Abraham'.[224] Here the icon tries to depict the supremely peaceful energy of union in love, as it issues in the salvific action of God, out of philanthropy for the world. So it is with the church as the icon of the Trinity. Simply put, the concept of individuation (the three *hypostases* of Father, Son, and Spirit) demonstrates a mystery of such profound union that there can only be one God. The power of love dispels disunion. The supreme individuation (hypostatization) of the three Persons is manifested not in separateness but in the ontological communion of singularity. Similarly, in the local church is manifested the totality of the being of the church, but this individuation is not set against, but rather consummated in, the union with the universal church. Its hypostatic identity, as local church, is not as a 'part' of the wider whole (just as the three *hypostases* are not cumulative 'parts' of the single Godhead). Such a trinitarian mystery of the church was revealed in Jesus' own description of the inner energy of ecclesial unity as a mystery that flowed from the very love and unity which he and his Father shared, which is no less than the power of the divine life of the Trinity:

> I do not pray for these only, but also for those who believe in me through their word, that they may all be one; even as you, Father, are in me, and I am in you, that they also may be in us, so that the world may believe that you have sent me.[225]

This divine union, which among the persons of the Holy Trinity is the coequal power of the divine essence, is, in the case of the church, not so much an 'essence' of sacred union, but a participation in it, as of creatures sharing in the divine life through grace. The Greek word for essence is *ousia*; that for participation, *metousia*. It is near enough a synonym for 'communion in grace', or the deification of the believer that the Christ-life conveys. It is the church's possession of such a *metousia* in the Holy Trinity itself that is the heart of its irrefragable union on earth. It is also the root of its ministry and witness as an icon of the Trinity among all mankind.

On the same trinitarian principle (of the perfect coequality of all the divine *hypostases* in communion) the church's power of government and self-discipline is not

Figure 5 *Hospitality of Abraham* by St Andrei Rublev.
Tretyakov Gallery, Moscow. Photograph: Bridgeman Art Library

'subordinated to' another, but seeks to be the servant of the other, and so, in mutual *kenosis*, the local churches find commonality of heart and action in the concerted standards of their collective *phronema*, especially as these are manifested in the canons they all willingly observe and maintain. This is an evocation of how the supreme glory of the Father is manifested not in superior power but in the absolute coequality of all the Persons.[226] Yet the equality of the Son and Spirit is manifested in their loving service of the Father's will, and their mutual forms of humble *kenosis* in the extension of God's salvation to the world. This icon of power is highly paradoxical, contrary to the world's expectation and experience, for within the world power seeks to be superior and to subordinate, and individuation seeks to be separate and to disconnect. In the church, however, identity is found in the harmony of communion. Great stress is laid, within Orthodoxy, on the concept of freedom within communion, and it is one of the reasons that models of church authority based upon monarchical centrality have always been rejected, as not in conformity with the being of the church as an iconic witness of freedom.

Power learns from Christ to be transfigured as service, and individuation blossoms out as the true flower of loving communion, when it can then have the authority to be truly free. This is why church structures are required to demonstrate a pattern of authority which rejects dominance, and seeks rather to be based upon mutual service and humble pastoral love.[227] The Orthodox revere the leaders of the church, the

242

threefold priesthood[228] as well as the monastics, and those who are clearly Spirit-filled teachers within the communities. The authority of all these leaders is seen in most elevated terms. The bishop, following the words of St Ignatius of Antioch,[229] is revered as the voice of Christ in the local church. But their authority is not that of the army superior,[230] but rather (and this is not merely a 'wishful' generalization but a genuine experience across the Orthodox world) a loved and respected father of a family. There is a profound reverence for, and valuation of, personal freedom in the ways an Orthodox Christian decides to follow the Gospel path. At the same time, each of the Orthodox know themselves to be bound by a large number of customs, rules, processes, and laws, extending from the fundamental 'canons' of the scriptural injunctions, down to synodical regulations governing forms of prayer, fasting, and minutiae of church behaviour.

The existence of these canons and clearly set out protocols[231] belies the assumption of many outside observers that the great freedom that is found in Orthodoxy is one that is born out of indiscipline or chaos of governmental structure. Nothing could be further from the truth, and the bishops govern their churches and their relations with sister churches within the communion of world Orthodoxy, within the guidance of clear and precise canonical charters. These extensive rules regarding behaviour, that have accumulated over many centuries,[232] are not so much a 'burden' on the lives of the Orthodox; it is rather that most believers find themselves freely valuing these 'guides' to the spiritual life, as the charter handed down to them that will protect the common spirit of Orthodoxy from the many forces in each generation that seek to secularize and mislead the children of God, and deflect them from the narrow path. Far from being a burden, the canons function as challenges to excellence. The rules of fasting are one small example. Multitudes of people in all conditions and walks of life align themselves with the fasting rules, in varying degrees according to their ability and fervour. The monastics observe them with strict care. In the 'togetherness' (the *sobornost* as the Slavic languages express it) the canons become a description of the actuality of the church's praxis.

Like all rules and laws their 'enforcement' on the church's members is done in accordance with the 'mind of the Lord' and the pastoral benefit of the believing community. It is a matter of the supreme discretion of the ruling bishop, or the synod, who adjudicate problems in accordance with this *phronema*. Orthodoxy is thus a communion of the saints where the tradition and teaching of the ancient saints is treated with extreme seriousness. They are not thrown away or discarded as irrelevant, but studied with close and affectionate attention as powerful guides to the same experience of Christ that drives on the present generation of the church. This is why Orthodoxy calls itself the church of the Bible, the Fathers, and the seven councils. This harmonious experience of the ancient saints remains alive and Spirit-filled, a living and important guide along the paths of the Spirit in the present age.

How to account for 'corruption' within the church therefore? It is important to clarify what exactly are the marks of corruption that we mean. If it is a question of moral scandals caused by church members, such things are signs that the standards of Christian living have decayed, or have been forgotten, or smothered, in the lives of individuals. Berdyaev reminds us how necessary it is to always consider the 'dignity of Christianity' alongside the 'indignity of Christians'. Spiritual vacuity, especially in the case of those whom one might have expected to be spiritual leaders and standard-bearers for a generation, can also have a widely felt depressive effect on the quality of life and zeal in a local church. While scandal and corrupt behaviour call out to the rest of the church members (especially the church hierarchs, priests, monastics, and prophetic visionaries) to discipline and correct it (to denounce the faults to the degree the occasion demands, but always with the motive of charitable rebuilding, and humble pastoral love for the lapsed member) they do not give grounds for seeing the church itself as corrupt. The lapse from the highest moral standards always occasions scandal in the minds of the wider world, precisely because the church's moral teaching is itself of the highest moral calibre. It is not the teaching which has changed, in the case of Orthodoxy, merely the individual who has proved unfaithful to the tradition, and may have hidden behind the façade of the church as a cover for un-Christian behaviour. However, if it is more a case of corrupt practice or doctrine that one means, Orthodoxy offers for scrutiny its principles of operation for all to see. It follows the ancient apostolic faith of the Scripture, the patristic saints who have interpreted it, and the disciplinary guidelines that have been laid down in the holy 'canons' of the councils and synods that in each case were guided by motives of the constant encouragement of the Christians to excel. These foundational principles remain Orthodoxy's primary guides. This has not changed, been diluted, or ever forgotten. We have confidence in its indefectibility. This is why Orthodox claims to be none other than the apostolic church: unreformed because uncorrupted (*numquam reformata, numquam deformata*[233]).

The Orthodox believe that even when Christians fall from the path of grace, they will (unless the turning away is deeply rooted and perversely followed) be caught back up into the love and reforming power of the Spirit of Christ which unfailingly courses powerfully, and ever without defect, through his church. The church, in this sense is the immaculate[234] Bride of the Lamb.[235] It never falters, or ceases to be the arena of radiant grace, prophetic charism, and burning love, even when some members within it personally decline from the inner consciousness of what they know to be their destiny and vocation: deification by grace within the communion of the holy family of grace. As they decline from the Gospel, of course, they also decline from their radiant existence as active and living members of Christ's body. It was the Lord himself who warned his disciples, from the very beginning, of the danger of this state of corruption, and pointed to the inevitable law that those who decline from life, incline to death:

> Abide in me as I abide in you. As the branch cannot bear fruit by itself, unless it abides in the vine, neither can you, unless you abide in me. I am the vine, you are the branches. He who abides in me, and I in him, he it is that bears much fruit, for apart from me you can do nothing. If a man does not abide in me, he is cast forth as a branch and withers; and the branches are gathered, thrown into the fire and burned. If you abide in me, and my words abide in you, ask whatever you will, and it shall be done for you. By this my Father is glorified, that you bear much fruit, and so prove to be my disciples. As the Father has loved me, so have I loved you; abide in my love. If you keep my commandments, you will abide in my love, just as I have kept my Father's commandments and abide in his love. These things I have spoken to you, that my joy may be in you, and that your joy may be full.[236]

To the degree that they sense the church's unfailing Christ-energy in the world, the Orthodox faithful expect themselves to be reformed by the church, rather than look to see how they can constantly reform it. It is not an experience which leads them to immediately think of the church as *ecclesia semper reformanda*;[237] rather, they experience its inner life as evidence that it is *ecclesia semper reformans*.[238]

This is not to make a naive statement that there is nothing ever 'wrong' with the church at any time in history. Clearly, from generation to generation, throughout its long earthly pilgrimage, the church has sometimes shone more brightly with the love and mercy of Christ than at other times. Sometimes church leaders (and ordinary Christians) have made lamentable compromises with the powers of the world of their time. It was so in the times of the early martyrs (which were also times of the early apostates) and it is so now. Sometimes one finds in the local parishes examples of radiant kindness, apostolic zeal, and loving compassion which are reminiscent of Christ's own presence in our midst. Sometimes, one has to say, one finds narrowness, bigotry, self-righteousness, and racism. The answer to such defects is to call the believers back to the Gospel they hear preached to them week by week; call them back, in effect, to the purity of the church. To this extent, the ongoing educational effort of the church leadership (the ministry of teaching the Christian standards, and proclaiming the Gospel, and interpreting its demands for each generation) is a critical one in every age. People are only brought to Christ in one way: by conversion. Even those who place great stress on their being 'cradle Orthodox' must confess that they came to Orthodoxy from the unredeemed state of the non-baptized, and were admitted freely, having once been no-people, and as an act of grace, into the Orthodox Church. There is, therefore (or at least should be), no caste mentality in Orthodoxy.[239] It is a question of our own honour, as Orthodox in this present generation, to make sure that we emulate the greatest of the generations of the saints with the quality of our own response to the Gospel demands.

Some traditions of Western Christianity customarily denigrate the church as a defectible and highly fallible side-issue to the centrally important question of a personal Gospel commitment. One might, for example, hear critiques of the ancient church for its 'failures' to see, let alone respond to, fundamental issues of human rights in times past and present. People point out that the burning of heretics and the church's immensely woolly response to the institutionalized form of mass slavery that ancient Mediterranean life worked from were defects of a large failure of spiritual vision. We can be glad, today, that the exposure of the wickedness of slavery, and the refusal to oppress others for religious motives have entered widely into the church's, and wider human, consciousness. It is clear, however, from all we read of ancient Christian writing, that the church has never advocated those things from its foundational charter; rather, its leaders from time to time have succumbed to such compromises with the 'spirit of the age' from a disastrous misreading of its charter. It is equally clear that its most elevated members (its saints and visionaries) always knew they were profoundly wrong things, inimical to the clear message and spirit of its merciful and loving Founder. It is not that the sources the church was drinking from were corrupted. It is more a case that Christians did not listen to them. There have been times when high authorities have advocated indefensible things. In such times the higher authorities of the Gospel and the inner conscience have never failed in the Orthodox Church. As a result Orthodoxy has not witnessed in its past (for example) the contradictions of warrior bishops going to the Crusades. If the clergy spill blood, they are canonically debarred from celebrating the mysteries. It is a sign that something has happened at the very sources, and needs rectifying. The church is so rooted in its ancient procedures that sometimes it needs a nudge to catch up with new circumstances. Some critics find that its attitudes to women need renovation, and that is something that Orthodox women themselves will have to adjudicate with more and more consideration as time goes on. It is equally the case, however, that from time immemorial the church (even in patriarchal times) has constantly defended the rights and dignities of women in social circumstances which militated against this. Christ's Church professes a standard of profound equality, even if, at times, it has not lived up to it in practice. Christian attitudes to other religions which in times past came under its dominion (and one thinks especially of the Chosen People of the Jews) may not always have been the models of charity and hospitality that we might wish to establish today, but the ecclesial canons (unlike many of the secular laws) have generally tried to protect and preserve the 'stranger in your midst' in accordance with biblical injunctions.[240] In this light, therefore, and conscious that such a response is not a charter for stagnation in the face of changing social conditions (for the prophetic energy of the Spirit of God constantly blows refreshing winds into all forms of self-satisfaction), Orthodoxy affirms that the church itself is neither corrupt, defiled, or wandering, but even though its members may be dim or radiant from age to age, there is within the church an unfailing spring of regeneration that makes it always function as the arena of conversion, reconciliation, grace, and progressive development in morals and spiritual perception.

The faults of the leaders of the Christian community have always been more disastrous than those of its more lowly members. But it may also be necessary to be aware that a reforming zeal that is ready to use its own historical hindsight to point an accusatory finger at the myopia of the ancient church (or the medieval church, or the nineteenth-century church, or that of our parents, or wherever we wish to point the finger) is itself going to have to answer some very uncomfortable charges from the generations of saints that come after us. Some of those questions come to mind very pressingly in these early years of the twenty-first century when there is widespread tension between the West and Islam, not to mention war in several places, and relate to exactly those same examples that were offered earlier: slavery and other religious-social oppressions. Why, one wonders, has the contemporary secular West reinvented forms of slavery unheard of for centuries and opened up widescale trafficking of human beings for sexual exploitation? Why did the emancipation of African Americans who were already allegedly free only take place after the most profound social struggles in the latter part of the twentieth century? Why has the voice of the West, so nobly active in the pursuit of human rights in common dialogue among its own nations, been more supine before the appalling travesties of rights in countries where slight intervention could have resulted in massive liberational changes? One thinks of the genocide of Rwanda, the radical oppression of Christians in Sudan, and the genocide of Darfur that followed: things that took place in full view of almost acquiescent Christian civilizations elsewhere.

What the response of the church was to these injustices is an important thing to note, for it is an unfailing mark of the quality of its Christian life in its own generation. Reformist zeal is a powerful charism of the Holy Spirit. In Orthodoxy it must begin in having the humility to realize that we have a treasure of the limpid water of the faith, even though it is carried in poor pots. The apostle's words are taken to heart:

> For it is the God who said, 'Let light shine out of darkness,' who has shone in our hearts to give the light of the knowledge of the glory of God in the face of Christ. But we have this treasure in earthen vessels, to show that the transcendent power belongs to God and not to us. We are afflicted in every way, but not crushed; perplexed, but not driven to despair; persecuted, but not forsaken; struck down, but not destroyed; always carrying in the body the death of Jesus, so that the life of Jesus may also be manifested in our bodies.[241]

The Orthodox Church is able, therefore, at one and the same moment, to acknowledge its own deficiencies, as a society of believers, to confess its own individual shortcomings from the embodiment of the pure Gospel in the lives of all its members in each generation, and yet, at the same time, to confess that the church itself never becomes corrupt, or loses the gift it has from its faithful Lord, of the unfailing springs of the Spirit's own purity and grace. This confession of the church's indefectibility, however, must always be safely (and vigorously) preserved from the bourgeois mentality that seeks to guard itself from all criticism with automatic responses to the effect that the 'church is beyond all criticism'. Far from it. In times past clerical introversion has often led to a culture of secrecy in some parts of the church. In modern times this culture is increasingly difficult to sustain. In next to no cases has it proved to be beneficial (as may once have been claimed), and the church generally will be far better (as is true of all families) with a more diffused spirit of openness and discussion. The organizational charter for most national churches now allows for full participation of clergy and laity at the synodical meetings called for its local government, and this is a welcome development which returns more faithfully to ancient Christian practices.

The ability to be conscious of the demands and radicalism of the Gospel is an awesome matter for a disciple, one that relates directly to the quality of the prophetic renunciation of the old self, with its constantly pressing desire for ease and self-congratulation. A disciple that takes up the Gospel in the light of the Spirit will take up a cross. There is no alternative to that. It is the old self which regards it as a cross. The new self, in Christ, regards the new life as an immense joy, and wonders why the old self-imprisonments seemed, at the time, so attractive, and so absolute. But this question of 'perception' is not automatic. It cannot be mechanically guaranteed, or stimulated (let alone effected) by committee decree, or episcopal letter. It is something that has to be embraced in the ultimate realm of freedom: the heart's freedom to say yes to the invitation of Christ, to be transfigured in a new manner of life. And that is why the constant prayer of the Christian will be that of the publican in the Lord's parable.[242] This is the life the church offers to those who hear the voice of the Lord. It provides it in the form of keeping the Scriptures ever fresh and ever before the minds of the faithful, and by its constantly sustained ethos of prayer, and ethical encouragement (and most radiantly in its celebration of the sacred mysteries in which the loving grace of the Spirit is poured out abundantly). But it cannot automatically supply the divine grace. It requires the ultimate gift of the freedom of the believer, to accept and assume the crucifixion of the old self in obedience to the call of its crucified and glorious Lord. For this reason the church can often seem impotent, even geriatric and out of touch with the real pulse of society. The prophet Hermas, a leader in the ancient Roman church, described the Ekklesia, in his visions,[243] as bearing at once the features of an old woman and a young virgin. And so it is with the mystery of the Ekklesia to this day. Those who denounce it, often from the outside, as a withered old woman perhaps have failed to see (and thus to have personally experienced) the powerful currents of its vital energy and graciousness. Its inner powers are often hidden from those who scrutinize it with hostility or superficiality. To some it might even seem corrupt and self-serving. Many people today have little time for the external 'ecclesiastical culture', and it must be said that in many respects an 'ecclesiastical mentality' that seems divorced from the lives and problems of ordinary people is a complaint raised by many Orthodox too against their clerical leaders; sometimes in a justified sense, sometimes not.

But, in reality, the church as the Orthodox understand it is the unfailing spring of the regenerative power of the Spirit. It is God's unfailing offer of *metanoia*, and salvation; but it is not an ideology of force. It will not step on that sacred ground of ontological freedom. It can teach the pure Gospel, and can recognize its counterfeit. But it cannot ensure that everyone, at all times, sustains that standard, for such a mystery is too deep, and accordingly it takes the church far away from the concept of being simply a club for the moral and the pious. It would be truer to reality to see it as a sanatorium for those who wish to rise from their sick-beds and live a full life. One thing that powerfully emerges from this sense of the immaculate nature of the church as the Bride of the Lamb is that the Orthodox do not ever fall victim of the presupposition that the church is ultimately, or even 'more purely', represented by its clerical members. Far from it. The deeply rooted notion that the church is an unfailing spring of holiness and grace is not a charter for abuse by any section of the church claiming the right of being beyond criticism or correction by virtue of 'representing' this spirit of indefectibility. Such a claim is one that is robustly resisted among the Orthodox. No one among us has that infallibility; no lay person, or priest, or bishop, or patriarch. None among us has that power of superiority. Together we sense that indefectibility of Christ's regenerative power. For anyone to claim it personally is a heretical arrogation of a mystical charism that pertains to the Lord's body as a whole.

This does not, in turn, argue that such indefectibility can never be concretely manifested. It most surely can: in the authoritative teaching office of the bishops for example, and in the witness of holiness among countless ordinary people. But those manifestations are exactly that: manifestations of a charism that flows out of the mystery of the church. A bishop is not automatically teaching from the fountain of the church's spring whenever he says anything, even when intending it to be heard widely by the faithful. Nor is a Christian's holiness a mechanistic thing. True charism flashes out in extraordinary ways. By such means the Lord renews the life of his church, and from age to age it is able to resist the encroaching weight of bureaucracy and formalism that can threaten its deepest spiritual instinct of graceful freedom. It is at once a wonderful thing and yet a historical burden, to have such a profoundly ancient heritage to sustain. Outside observers, noting this aspect of the Orthodox Church, have often found it difficult to assess, or understand. It is more clear to the Orthodox themselves: how at one and the same moment they know themselves to be bound to numerous standards, and canons, and authorities and yet at the same time completely free. The Orthodox monk Father Lev Gillét[244] once put it in eloquent terms, as follows:

Equally far removed from authoritarianism and individualism, the Orthodox Church is a church both of tradition and freedom. She is above all a church of love...a strange church so poor and so weak...a church of contrasts, at the same time so traditional and so free, so archaic and so alive, so ritualistic and so personally mystical, a church where the pearl of great price is so preciously preserved, sometimes under a layer of dust, a church which has so often been unable to act, but which can sing out the joy of Easter like no other...[245]

This is a spirit that has given to the Orthodox a general freedom from subservience (even to the highest leaders of the churches) while at the same time having a profound sense of respect for the leaders and teachers of the faith. It is also true, though it may seem paradoxical to those who have not experienced it, that the Orthodox believer's unshakeable faith that their sacred tradition is authentic and true sets their faith free in ways that allow it to be more courageous in dialoguing with the philosophies and obsessions of any given generation, proclaiming to all generations, as its core vocation, the joyful news of the Gospel of Christ.

The visible-invisible church dichotomy that is much favoured in many forms of Western Protestantism can sometimes be applied in ecumenical contexts to suggest that the church remains 'one' mystically, or invisibly, or spiritually, as it were, while in actual historical reality it has been divided among itself so much that denomination-alism has become the basic fact of ecclesial life. The sum total of the denominations (or at least the sum total of the 'mainline' denominations) is thus felt to be the only surviving vestige of any real sense of what one might mean in this day and age by talking about the 'One Holy Catholic and Apostolic Church of Christ'. It is on the basis of such a model, presumptively operating at least, that ecumenical organizations such as the World Council of Churches or the national councils of churches in the West, have sometimes hoped to come together for a concerted Christian action. Orthodoxy, though belonging to these organizations, never has, and never will, concur with such ecclesial theories that sometimes underpin them. This is one of the chief reasons why the Orthodox presence in the ecumenical movement was not a tranquil one in the twentieth century. It also explains why the desirability of continued involvement in the WCC and similar organizations has recently been passionately questioned in several different parts of world Orthodoxy. Some of the Orthodox, of course, are equally passionate about the great usefulness of being involved in the ecumenical dialogue, seeing it as a required labour of love and a duty of mutual respect among Christians. Others have denounced it as a movement that too often covers over harsh truths of disagreement on fundamental principles, with the rhetoric of conciliation.

Because it does not admit the dichotomy of the visible and the invisible church, Orthodoxy is bound, on the basis of its own conception of identity, to claim that it is, in itself, the one single holy catholic and apostolic church of Christ on earth. It claims, therefore, at one and the same moment, a concrete historical identity and a spiritual glory that grows out of this embodiment, not separate from it or parallel to it. Orthodoxy understands its innate holiness not simply to be a matter of the collective virtue of its members but, more substantively, the gift of the Holy Spirit which has drawn the church into communion with the divine, in a profoundly intimate way, a marriage with the Lamb, who has rendered the Bride spotless and chaste. The personal holiness of the body of believers is an important thing: though if any individual

Orthodox was asked; 'And how do you, yourself, represent the holiness of Christ's Church in the present moment?' they would habitually respond with the only truth they could: '*Kyrie eleison me hamartolon*' (Lord have mercy on me, a sinner). No living Orthodox would ever dare to claim holiness as a charism they could clearly represent to others. This does not mean to say that such a charism could not be clearly seen to shine out of them: but they would never claim more than being a sinful disciple still on pilgrimage. Nevertheless, each one also knows that they are the radiant elect of the Philanthropos, the Loving Lord who has redeemed and saved them, and gathered them into the heart of the church. Individual holiness is the same mystery as the collective holiness that has been given as a charism to the Body of Christ on earth: it is the grace of the radiant and transfiguring presence of the Lord himself. The individual, as well as the whole assembly of Christians (especially the local church family gathered around the eucharistic celebration week by week) undertakes its call to be so transfigured that the beauty of the church shines out more and more fully on the eyes of the wider world.

In this context the many lapses from the radiant Gospel that are found in the life of the church are certainly a stumbling block, and a hindrance to the evangelical mission of the church in society. Even so, however, the lapses of the individual Christians who fall away from the Gospel standard cannot mar the church's radiant soul and true depths. It is always a deep disappointment to hear public revelations of the crimes of people who have been significant 'Christian' leaders. The *dénouement* of such people, however, simply manifests that they have *not* been significant Christian leaders, only masquerading as such in a formalist way. Talk is always cheap. Living the Christ-life is not counterfeitable for long. The exposition and ejection of such figures from the heart of the church is a natural and organic process, though only if the local church community is a healthy one. If it is not, it needs to rely on other parts of the church to correct and reorientate it. Orthodoxy has a robust sense (clearly expressed in its ancient canons of procedure) that if officers of the Christian community do not live up to a higher standard of life, to the extent that they cause public scandal, then they are to be deposed from the office they hold. Ordinary members of the faithful, if they persevere in lives that are significantly, and publicly, at variance with the ethical standards of the church, will invariably be debarred from reception of the Eucharist, until such time as repentance re-establishes them as fully communicant members. There is a mutual duty of correction ever present in the Church of Christ.

Many people have, on hearing this unyielding claim of Orthodoxy over the generations to be the one historical Church of Christ, especially in the last century when rapprochement between the Orthodox churches and Western Christianity has become more common, wondered what could be the point of dialoguing with a church that can make the statement that it is identical with the One and the Holy Church of Christ. Is not the claim intrinsically insulting to other churches with their own ancient traditions? Well, the Orthodox statement is not meant to be insulting. It is uttered with humility, not from *hubris*, and spoken in the profundity of awareness that its charisms are given to it as graces, not from its merits, and that it can claim the truth as simple disciples not as arrogant purists. The truth is that Orthodoxy is better at knowing itself than it is at knowing what the other religious communions are. It waits for them to clarify more fully what they themselves see to be the essential charism of the church, and how they each represent that within history and in their own traditions.[246]

In today's pluralistic ecumenical environment Orthodoxy is always ready, and eager (or at least ought to be if it is filled with the love of God who desires the expanding of the communion of love), to hear from other Christian communions[247] what their understanding is of how they relate to the foundations of the evangelical tradition. In this mutual 'scrutiny' Orthodoxy applies exactly the same standards to the communions it discovers that are apart from itself as it does *to* itself, standards based upon the cornerstone of Gospel fidelity, and the harmony with apostolic and patristic teaching, such as is represented in the ecumenical tradition.[248] Orthodoxy is thus very clear what is heresy, and knows the heretic not to be part of the Church of Christ. It is more than puzzled, however, when it finds in many parts of the other Christian communions it encounters elements which seem to it exactly like the heresies of former ages; though in the present they are often sustained by Christians of great sincerity who (we might say) do not always have a very clear awareness of what they are maintaining.[249] As a result, because contemporary ecumenical dialogue involves the consideration of many varied traditions of Western Christianity with elements that are simultaneously sometimes fully in accordance with the tradition of Orthodoxy, and sometimes deeply at variance with it,[250] Orthodox theologians have faltered greatly in being able satisfactorily to describe and characterize the nature of non-Orthodox churches.

The useful element in this is that Orthodoxy has thus been more articulate (as a result of its encounters with the pluralism of the believing, as well as the unbelieving, West) as to how it understands itself to be the church. What deviates from its expression of the fundamentals of faith it declares to be heresy; but it also knows that there are many Christians, of other communions, who sincerely hold teachings that it may classify as such, because that is what their own path to Christian faith has handed down to them as a foundational tradition. Orthodoxy does not necessarily declare these Christians to be heretics, in so far as they have not originated doctrines in contradiction of the ancient tradition; although it seeks around for a category in which to balance an 'economy of charity' and an unyielding defence of the apostolic tradition from which it lives. It often falls between stools, regarding the other Christian churches as something akin to 'schismatic'. This is not a fully accurate or clarifying position to adopt, however, in so far as schism is a precise technical word for a division within Christianity that is largely organizational or disciplinary in character, and one that could be resolved relatively easy by reconciliation. But where central doctrinal differences or important ethical matters are concerned, divergence in the confession of the faith is not schism, but heresy. And heresy brings with it proof positive that the charism of union with the church has been lost. For such reasons, some of the more 'zealous' of the Orthodox (and sadly their zeal is not often matched by understanding of, or sympathy with, the religious communions they somehow feel able to criticize so freely) have declared all non-Orthodox Christians to be heretical and deprived of the action and grace of the Holy Spirit. In such a viewpoint, they are, logically speaking, false churches. This, however, is far from being the attitude of the Orthodox as a whole.

Part of the ambivalence here is not that the Orthodox do *not* affirm themselves to be the single Church of Christ according to the ancient canons and criteria of the apostolic tradition, which it embodies: for they do; rather, when the Orthodox look out on their Christian brothers and sisters in the West, they see men and women who are evidently moved by the graciousness of the same Spirit of the Lord whom it knows and serves itself. It would, thus, be running counter to basic common sense (and spiritual perceptiveness) to follow the road of the zealots who deny the title and character of Christians to 'separated brethren' of other communions. Orthodox theology, nonetheless, affirms that the fundamental ethos of the church is a mystery of oneness which cannot admit any degree of disunity in fundamental matters. It makes that statement, not meaning that the church ideally 'ought not' to admit divergence from its fundamental union, but precisely that the church 'cannot' admit divergence from union; that the charism of union is so fundamental to the ontological structure of the church that when such union has been broken, the bond of belonging to the Ekklesia has also been fractured.

Orthodoxy is, therefore, deeply hostile to theories of the division of the churches which have appeared within the modern ecumenical movement, such as the well-known 'branches of the one Church of Christ' theory, which has proposed that all the different denominations are branches of varying thickness and antiquity of the single 'tree' of Christ's Church. This model of 'ecclesial economy' is entirely rejected by Orthodoxy both as not representing the truth of its own experience, and also as being completely defective regarding the comprehension of the historical tradition of the Gospel of truth. Orthodoxy is equally hostile to reductionist models of the church which see it as a bureaucratic corporation, a purely human 'representation' of a society of believers who have gathered together for various reasons. Its own understanding of the mystery of the Ekklesia is a profoundly mystical one that clashes with the predominant Protestant conceptions of a defectible earthly society of believers, and clashes to some extent, also, with Roman Catholic understandings of the union of the Ekklesia as provided by organizational principles, especially as revolving around communion with a single historical 'see', or supra-episcopal focal point, such as is represented by the Papacy.

Orthodoxy is certain that it represents the fullness of the apostolic tradition, and that (while peripherals of its collective mentality, mode, and behaviour are always open to the need for correction and reform[251]) the substantive heart of the church and its life (its doctrine, its ethos, and its spirit of holiness, for example) are not in need of reform, but on the contrary are absolutely authentic and serve to reform the members of the Body of Christ, day by day, through the endless outpouring of the Holy Spirit, given abundantly in the living communion of the church. When Orthodoxy claims that it is simply identical with the single church of Christ, it provokes a scandal of mutual appreciation in relation to the problematic condition of the unity of the church in the modern world. That pathology of church disunion, however, is not something that falls clearly within the consciousness of the Orthodox Church. It is, itself, essentially a communion of unity, nurturing the charism of unity which the Lord has given to it, and doing so with great care. Just as sin itself is largely incomprehensible in the eyes of God (the illogic of the choice of non-being in the face of the possibility of the gift of life), so too is it the case that disunion is something that does not, and cannot, fall clearly within the consciousness of the church, for it is existentially altogether held in being as a communion of oneness.

The Orthodox Church is, for this reason, to a deep extent unable to focus clearly on the pathology of disunity that is so abundantly witnessed in the state of Christian communions throughout the world. It is also hindered because its vocabulary of disunion has not been extensively developed. The major problems it faced in its earliest centuries with those who taught a series of false gospels, and wanted to sow the field with the weeds of disunity, gave it a bipolar syntax of heresy and schism.[252] Today, with large national communities of Christians in the West who have followed complex paths towards the denominational stances they now represent, this twofold terminology is simply not refined, or extensive, enough to give a clear and satisfactory picture.

For such reasons, some Orthodox have taken a very hard-line stance and concluded that since the Orthodox are the presence of Christ's Church on earth, it logically follows that all non-Orthodox are 'non-church'. This deduction, of course, does not follow as simply as some like to argue it does. It is a form of logic about which the Orthodox understanding of itself as the living communion in Christ does not fully stretch to. It would be much more accurate to say that while Orthodoxy is able to, and does, affirm that it is identical with the One Holy Catholic and Apostolic Church, it is not sure what is the state of other Christian religious communions which are not in spiritual harmony with it, for a multitude of reasons and causes. It is, one has to say, always of the opinion if that a large body of Christians fall away from the canons of truth which Orthodoxy recognizes in itself, they are to that degree liable to have deviated from the apostolic tradition. The extent of that degree, that deviation, is something that can only be clarified by extensive studying of the denominations, which is something Orthodoxy in general has not fully completed, to date. It cannot be done by studying denominational seminary textbooks; it has to be done by looking at the theological tradition in the overall light of the denomination's spiritual and sacramental life and vitality, which is a more intimate and more difficult matter by far. Orthodoxy, however, does not look back nostalgically to an ancient and primeval time when the church was one in communion across the Mediterranean world, and from Syria to Ethiopia, a time of the 'Great and Undivided Church', which might one day be restored. It argues, on the contrary, that the Great and Undivided Church is still one in doctrine and practice across the world to this very day, and that the Orthodox Church is it; unchanged in doctrine and habit from the times of the early Fathers who nurtured and kept that union with careful fidelity. Those doctrines and habits are also preserved, in many forms and manners, among the separated bodies of the various Christian communions. The common faith of Nicaea, for example, is still an aspiration and a standard that brings together most Western Christian bodies. To this extent (and to the extent that such apostolic quality of doctrine can be proven in practice) Orthodoxy does still recognize the charism of Christian truth shining in the wider Christian world.

Perhaps too many large generalizations and clichés have too often been applied to the way the Orthodox have looked on other Christian bodies. This is because they tend to look immediately to the places where the traditions of the denominations contradict, or depart from, the apostolic tradition. It is possible, on a principle of the economy of charity, to recognize that there are many degrees of difference, some of them even applying in terms of legitimate style of worship or national character,[253] and to that extent many of the denominations are 'closer' to the heart of Orthodoxy than others. It is one thing to be able with clarity, and honesty, to say that many aspects of a denomination's profession of faith and order do not seem to the Orthodox to be part of the apostolic tradition; it is another thing to feel compelled to deny such a denomination any share in the Spirit of the Lord of grace. For such reasons there is a sharp tension felt in many parts of world Orthodoxy today, about the attitude that ought to be taken towards Western forms of Christianity in general, and the ecumenical movement in particular.

Orthodoxy feels empowered, because it is the communion of truth, to assert the canons of authentic judgement of what constitutes the one Church of Christ: especially in terms of ethics and doctrine, and spiritual fidelity. It is thus able, with a fair degree of accuracy, and a clarity that does not call for profound or expert adjudications (it arises rather out of the ecumenical consensus of the people of God, protected by the hierarchs who serve as its doctrinal guardians) to affirm the truth, and demarcate significant deviations from the truth. If a deviation from the evangelical standard of doctrine or ethics is substantial enough it has, throughout history (and continues so to do despite the unfashionable status of the term), readily categorized a position as *hairesis*. This word, originally meaning a simple disagreement in Hellenistic philosophy, has, from the outset been used in the apostolic writings to signify a fissure in substantive matters of Christian identity, such that those who have originated this kind of teaching have changed the fundamental ethos of the Gospel tradition. Accordingly, to uphold, or tolerate, such a position would radically overshadow the clarity of the authentic tradition, and could not be allowed within a communion of truth that was given the commission to preserve all that the Lord had taught his disciples, in order to pass it on as a life-saving grace across many generations. It is for such reasons that the Church of Christ has always reacted to heresy, first and foremost, by naming it as such. Orthodoxy did not invent heresy: it invented the naming of heresy, because of its powerful instinct of preserving the tradition of the Gospel.

In accordance with the apostolic writings, therefore, Orthodoxy regards the arising of heresy (always a substantive matter of doctrinal or ethical deviation) as a sure sign that the propagators of the movement are heralds of another spirit than the Spirit of God who gives the church the charism of adhering to the truth, with great force and passion. Heresy is, in and of itself, the sign that its protagonists have left the communion of the church. Orthodoxy's position on this is just as it was when St John wrote the following:

> Those rivals of Christ came out of our own number, but they had never really belonged; for if they had belonged they would have stayed with us. But they departed so that all could see that they are not of us.[254]

It was this biblical spirit of a sharp and prophetic concern to stop the earliest Christian movement from degenerating into a host of aimless sects and speculations,[255] that continued in the writings of the early Fathers such as Irenaeus, Tertullian, and Cyprian, who were among the first to lay down a foundation for the public discernment of what constituted the borders of the church's historic identity. Irenaeus, deeply aware in his own community (over which he presided as bishop) of how the Gnostic teachers were inventing new gospels devoid of apostolic authority, set out in his treatise *Against the Heresies* a clear and comprehensive doctrine on the nature of identifying apostolic tradition.

First of all, the true tradition would be recognized as 'One' (that is it tended to coherency and stability across the generations). This inner unity was recognized as a clear sign of grace and spiritual life, given that the 'doctrines of men' were unstable and changeable across the generations.[256] Secondly, it would be guarded by the faithfulness of the apostolic witnesses: the Christian leaders who first and foremost saw it as their duty to listen carefully[257] to the saving message, then pass it on, uncorrupted, to their own generation, from where it would pass on to the next generations. Irenaeus argued that this was a duty being massively neglected by the speculative theologians of his day, and was, for that reason, more faithfully to be seen in the teaching charism of the bishops, who were thus demonstrated to be the heirs of the apostles. This 'apostolic succession' was also demonstrated in other concrete ways: especially in the fact that the bishops sustained the fundamental doctrine in an authentic succession (Christians knew who their teachers were, and knew that each shared communion with the others in a line that joined them as legitimate heirs of the apostolic preaching). This is what Orthodoxy means by calling the bishops the 'successors of the apostles'. It is partly that their succession of consecration can be demonstrated,[258] but mainly indicates their full and entire harmony with apostolic doctrine (not least as this has been subsequently laid down in the Holy Scriptures, of which the bishops are the churches' authorized interpreters and preachers).[259] It was a 'sameness' of doctrine and behaviour that was proven when one compared it with the doctrine taught in the adjoining churches which were also apostolic (it was thus universal, *katholikos*, or 'catholic') in the sense of being sustained by the communion of love and fellowship that each local church had with its neighbours so as to make up the universal Church of Christ.

The fullness of the Ekklesia is thus manifested in each local church; which is itself, in every way, the fullness of the Body of Christ, and from its own life witnesses all the charisms of the Lord and the Spirit, and possesses all the completeness of the Mystery of Christ's church on earth. Collectively, in their single communion, all the local churches add up to the same fullness. They do not add up, as different parts and fragments, to a greater whole; they add up from completion to make one completion, as one ocean added to another makes a single ocean. This is how the Orthodox understand the mystery of the church's unity (as one, holy, catholic, and apostolic) to be manifested across four charisms which are really one and the same mystery. The holiness is dependent on the unity (the church's unity with itself in communities spread across time and space; as well as its transcendent unity with its Lord); the apostolicity is dependent on its catholicity. It would be the same if other combinations were made among these four great 'marks' of the church.[260] The unbreakable harmony of each of them coalesces into the living experience the church has that it manifests the original apostolic tradition in the present age. Because each local church knows that this is the case, it is able to recognize all the other Orthodox churches as its sisters and its very self. Orthodoxy does not derive its identity from the collective, or the centre, as if it were a bureaucratic society. It spreads its local unity outwards in evangelical outreach, and finds its unity mystically reflected in the same experience of the Spirit in its sister churches in other cities and lands.

As St Cyril of Alexandria put it, the Spirit of God is itself the unity of the church.[261] While the church has the Spirit as its soul and the principle of its life, so it is a communion which (from the core of its being) cannot tolerate disunion, cannot comprehend it, or live with it. So it is that the church is found to be local as well as universal. But the local is not a branch of the universal, it is the universal in particular. Catholicity therefore, is a mystical communion of all, proven by many definite signs (common doctrine and allegiance to the ancient canons of the church being the most practical and important elements) but ultimately grounded in its mystical immediacy in the resurrectional presence of its Lord, who lives in it and through it in the society of

255

all generations, by the energy of the Holy Spirit, until the End Times, and who is thus the unending source of the church's vitality and renewal.

Orthodoxy's understanding of the unity of the church especially looks to St Cyprian of Carthage (c.200–58) for its classical patristic exposition. In this it differs in tonality from the West, which has tended to make St Augustine its chief ecclesiological voice. Its current public statements on ecclesiology are, not surprisingly, predominantly based upon Cyprian, whether consciously or not. One of the very first of all the twentieth-century Orthodox statements[262] concerning the nascent ecumenical movement began with this statement of the nature of the church that more or less synopsized Cyprian's teaching:

> It is a truism that the holy catholic and apostolic is founded upon the Apostles and preserved by the divine and inspired fathers in the Ecumenical Councils, and that her head is Christ the Great Shepherd who bought her with his own blood; and that according to the heaven-tending Apostle she is the pillar and ground of the truth,[263] as well as the body of Christ. This holy church is indeed one in identity of faith and similarity of manners and customs, in unison with the decisions of the Seven Ecumenical Councils, and she must be one and not many that differ from each other in dogmas and fundamental institutions of ecclesiastical government.[264]

Cyprian himself was elected to the episcopal throne of Carthage in a time of immense tension in the church. He had been relatively recently initiated into the faith. He was an adult pagan, highly educated as a rhetorician and administrator. His attitudes as a neophyte Christian bishop consistently show a conservative and hesitant instinct. His primary concern was to protect and cherish the community which he saw to be under great threat from outside and from internal traumas. He was not inclined to take the wider or broader view, for his critical time, at least.[265] He had only been bishop for two years when, in 250, an edict of the Emperor Decius ordered all citizens to sacrifice to the gods of Rome or face a severe penalty. The period of persecution that followed led to numerous lapses from the faith among the people. Cyprian went into hiding and escaped arrest. After the persecution abated, the lapsed asked for reconciliation to full sacramental life, which Cyprian was unwilling to allow. Unfortunately for his situation, Cyprian also had a council of presbyters, many of whom regarded his popular election with disfavour, thinking him insufficiently grounded in his new faith. They undermined his episcopal decisions by encouraging the lapsed to accept the prophetic assurances of the Carthaginian 'confessors'[266] that their sins had been forgiven.

But not only was his own see in conflict in this critical time, but the see of Rome was simultaneously split in two by the Novatianist schism. Pope Cornelius was fighting the rigorism of the theologian Novatianus, who actively propagated a view that any sinfulness inherent in Christians de facto alienated them from the Church of God which was solely and exclusively a communion of the holy. Cornelius himself taught, in a very moderate way, the doctrine that seemed scandalous to many at the time, that a system of reconciliation ought to be established in the churches to benefit the many who had proved weak in the face of adversity and threats. This controversy would run for many centuries, causing a schism in many parts of the church. Its effects were immediately noticeable in Carthage when some of Cyprian's dissident presbyters moved to elect an anti-bishop, Fortunatus, and set him up as a rival. Cyprian's immediate reaction to this was that the sacraments and authority of a schismatic bishop were utterly void and fruitless. His ordinations were null, his right to belong to the church was forfeit. The threat of a new persecution in 251, under Gallus, made Cyprian suddenly change his position on the issue of restoration, and he called for a general reconciliation among the church of all the lapsed, and of all the dissidents, fearing that they would otherwise have to face the persecutor unprepared. His change of view was motivated by deep pastoral care, but was interpreted by some as another sign of inconsistency. During this time Cyprian exchanged letters with Pope Cornelius and was surprised to find that his views on the validity of schismatic sacraments were contested by the pope. This alarmed Cyprian and made him adhere to them all the more. For Cyprian the office of the bishop was one of the load-bearing pillars supporting the unified coherence of the Christian community. He was terrified that any 'wobble' in the pillar could be disastrous to the church (not least in times of persecution and stress). So, he says:

> The Apostle Paul describes this sacrament of unity when he says: 'There is one body, one Spirit, one hope of our calling, one Lord, one faith, one baptism, one God.'[267] It is our duty to hold and defend this unity, especially us who preside in the church as bishops. In this way we can prove that the episcopate is also one in itself, and undivided. Let no one deceive the brethren by falsehoods, and let no one corrupt the truth of our faith by unfaithful transgressions.... The church is one, and by her fruitful increase she is extended far and wide to form a plurality. It is just like the sun which has many rays but one light; or a tree that has many branches but one trunk and whose foundations are the deep-seated root; or as when many streams flow down from a single spring... But try and cut off a ray from the sun's disc, and see how the light refuses the concept of division. Break a branch from the tree, and see how the broken member cannot bud. Cut off the stream from the spring and see how it immediately dries up. So it is with the church, flooded as it is with the light of the Lord and which extends her rays over the whole world.... The Bride of Christ cannot be made into an adulteress. She is always undefiled and chaste. So, whoever stands apart from the church and is joined to an adulteress, is cut off from the promises given to the church. Whoever leaves the church of Christ, cannot arrive at Christ's rewards. Such a person is an outcast, an alien, an enemy. No one can have God for his father, who does not have the church as his mother. Did anyone escape [the deluge] who was outside Noah's ark? Escape is no more likely for someone who is outside the doors of the church.[268]

In a later epistle he demonstrates the episcopal charism of unity just as robustly:

> The church never departs from Christ. And the church is made up of the people united to their bishop,[269] the flock clinging to its shepherd. This is why you ought to know that the bishop is in the church, and the church is in the bishop, and that if anyone is not with the bishop, such a person is not in the church.[270]

In harmony with Cyprian, Orthodoxy sees the episcopal office as inherent in the nature of the church, not as a bureaucratic or historically conditioned form of government that can be dispensed with. His words, however, originally intended as they were to characterize and resolve the problem of anti-bishops within Carthage and

Rome, have been used by many of the Orthodox to analyse (to say 'resolve' would be stretching a point) the condition of ecclesial disunion in the west.

On the basis of this some of the more zealous Orthodox have presumed that no one who is not a visible member of the Orthodox Church can be called a Christian in any sense at all. Nor can such a person experience, in any way, the saving power of grace in any of the sacraments, prayer services, or broader Christian life. Such a view is, unfortunately, a wooden and immensely narrow application of a patristic giant who needs interpretation as does any other single source of the Orthodox tradition. The actual practice of Orthodoxy shows a view that does not wholly adhere to this apparent strictness which Cyprian offers. He, of course, does this to sustain his point that the one guilty of committing heresy and schism has utterly been cut off from the church.[271] But, simply put, the great multitudes of non-Orthodox Christians cannot crudely be regarded as 'having committed' either heresy or schism. At most they can be said to have inherited such elements in their faith traditions. And if their communions have historically sustained basic elements of Christian practice and doctrine which the Orthodox would regard to be both heretical and schismatic, then that is clearly the cause of an enduring, sorrowful, separation. But it is not necessary, even then, and even in the light of the direct words of Cyprian himself, to claim that all non-Orthodox have no claim to be Christian. This not only runs counter to charity[272] but actually runs counter to common sense, and to basic spiritual apprehension of the power of the Holy Spirit which is manifested in so many, so beautiful, and so varied ways among the non-Orthodox Christian communions and confessions.

Such a view that the non-Orthodox are 'wholly and utterly outside the Church of Christ' is, therefore, a harshly rigorist and decontextualized misreading of what even Cyprian meant to say. Those who most strictly adhere to Cyprian seem to have forgotten the canonical epistle of St Basil the Great, which has ecumenical authority in the Orthodox Church. In writing to his relative the newly elected bishop, Amphilokios of Iconium, Basil set out the best way to approach the numerous problems of ecclesial division that were already affecting the Christian churches of the fourth century. He begins from the basic understandings of the distinctions of heresy, schism, and illicit assembly, and also accepts that a deliberate breach from the church's union implies the loss of ecclesial identity. But then he clearly moves on to a more actively 'economic' sense of how to bring about union within a disunited environment. What is important to Basil is the degree of communion in practice and doctrine that a different body of believers still retains. If this is still recognizable in terms of biblical, liturgical, and conciliar standards, then the great churchman is willing to advocate that the young bishop should exercise 'discretion'. It is this same discretion which many Orthodox offer to other Christian communions in the so-called 'ecumenical dialogue'. Basil's letter is worth quoting at length on this point because it is both foundational and offers a more generous economy than reliance on St Cyprian alone:

> With regard to your query about the Cathari group[273] it has already been said (as you rightly reminded me) that we ought to follow the custom of each particular region because those who, at the time, gave rulings about such matters were divided in their decisions about the status of their baptism.[274] In my judgement, however, the baptism of the Pepuzenes[275] has no validity at all. And I am amazed that this fact

escaped Dionysios the Great,[276] skilled though he was in canonical matters. Earlier generations had decided to accept a baptism which in no way swerved from the path of faith. So it was that they applied the names heresies, schisms, and illicit assemblies, to the various groups.

Heresies referred to those who had completely broken away and were alienated in respect of the very faith. Schism applied to those who had separated from the rest for some reasons of church policy or questions that were capable of adjustment. Irregular assemblies was the term used for congregations gathered by rebellious presbyters, or bishops, or unformed laymen.... It was decided, then, in ancient times, to reject the baptism of heretics, while accepting that of schismatics in so far as the latter still had some link with the church.... Those attached to irregular assemblies were to be reunited with the church after amendment by adequate repentance and reformation. Accordingly, in many cases, when men who held office had detached themselves and joined the rebels, they were received back on showing repentance, even in the same rank. But the Pepuzenes are clearly heretical, for they give to Montanus and Priscilla, the title Paraclete... and how could one justify accepting as valid a baptism of those who have baptized into Father, Son, and Montanus, or Priscilla?... The Novatianists, on the other hand, are clearly schismatic, but earlier authorities, including Cyprian and our own predecessor Firmilianus[277] decided to give a blanket rejection to Cathari, Encratites,[278] and Hydroparastatae,[279] on the grounds that the origination of their separation arose from schism and that those who had apostatized from the church no longer had upon them the grace of the Holy Spirit, since the gift ceased to be imparted when the continuity was broken. The original separatists, therefore, had received ordination from the fathers, and possessed the spiritual gift through the laying on of their hands. But those who break away become laymen, lacking authority either to baptize or to ordain, because they cannot confer on others the gift of the Holy Spirit from which they have themselves defected.

So it was that those who had been baptized by them were instructed to come to the church to be purified again, as if they had been baptized by laity.[280] Nevertheless, since some of the brethren of Asia[281] have definitely taken the line that their baptisms are to be accepted (so as to make it possible for them to deal with the majority) then indeed let them be accepted. We should take note, however, of the intolerable behaviour of the Encratites, because, as if to make themselves incapable of being received back by the church, they have decided to anticipate baptism by a peculiar baptismal rite of their own, an action that involves the abrogation of their own customary practice. My opinion (since no clear pronouncement has been made about them) is that their baptism should be rejected. If someone has received baptism at their hands and then comes to the church, such a person should be baptized.[282]

Even so, if this threatens to become an impediment to the general order of the church, we shall have to fall back on custom and follow the practice of the fathers, who here provided precedents for our guidance. This is because I am anxious in case, by trying to discourage them from baptizing, we ourselves become an obstacle to those who are being saved, by the severity of our ruling. Even so, the fact that they accept our baptism must not be allowed to disquiet us. We are under no obligation to reciprocate the favour. Our obligation, rather, is to observe the canons strictly. In any event, it must be decreed that those who come to us from their baptism should be anointed (at the hands of the faithful obviously) and on this condition alone allowed to approach the mysteries.[283] Even so, I am well aware that I myself have already received the brothers Zois and Saturninos into the episcopal chair,[284] and they belonged to that community. I am therefore, prevented from excluding from the church those who were attached to their company, since by my acceptance of the bishops I have already, as it were, promulgated a canon of communion with them.[285]

This important text, explains the (still differing) practice of the Orthodox churches when they receive members of other Christian communions who come seeking admission to communion. Some receive all non-Orthodox by baptism. Other Orthodox churches receive certain Christians by chrismation alone, but members of other communions by full baptism. Investigation is always made into the liturgical practice of the various communions (did it involve trinitarian baptism with threefold immersion or not?) and investigation is also made into the doctrinal 'closeness' of the communion to the apostolic faith, as synopsized by the Scriptures, the Nicene Creed, the ecumenical councils, and patristic writings (were such communions 'sacramental' in character for example?). Depending on this adjudication Christians from other communions can be admitted to Orthodoxy by full baptism, or by chrismation alone.[286] Dissident Orthodox can be readmitted to communion with the larger church (depending on the nature and severity of their lapse or schism) either by chrismation, or by act of penance, or simple profession of allegiance. It falls to the apostolic discretion of the local bishop in such cases, or, in issues of greater significance (more communities being involved, for example), to the decision of a regional synod of bishops. In each case the bishops are guided by the ancient canons, although, as can be seen, often the canons themselves leave large room for pastoral discrimination, which is always meant to have at its heart the care for charitable communion, and an active desire to see Christ's Church united in love (though never at the cost of sliding over truths).

The Great Church of Constantinople has long been pressing for a greater commonality of accepting a broader ecclesial 'economy' than a strict adherence to the letter of St Cyprian would suggest. In its own protocol, for example, and it is a practice widely concurred with among the Orthodox, it accepts the validity of Roman Catholic and Anglican trinitarian baptism, and will only administer chrismation to mark the reception of such converts to Orthodoxy. Baptismal initiation, however, is regarded by all the Orthodox as such a serious matter that 'economies of charity' are wholly inapplicable here. The acceptance of the baptism, then, is a clear sign that the gift of the Spirit is seen to be still operative in those churches: just as the gift of chrismation is the clear sign that Orthodoxy welcomes them into the completion of the gift of unity as it admits them to the heart of the one church. Nevertheless, it is true that those parts of the Orthodox world which insist on baptizing, as if for the first time, converts coming from any source (Western Christendom, Judaism, Islam, or paganism, it would appear to make no difference) are a source of much puzzlement to observers. Their behaviour in this matter is explicable on the basis of the strictness in the way St Cyprian's principles are applied in practice, as distinct from the manner in which St Basil's concept of economy can be set to work in the cause of reunion. Those requiring baptism are anxious to err on the side of greater severity and strictness, a principle which can be traced also in St Basil's canonical letter, even though the greatness of his spirit causes him time and again to err on the side of an economy of charity, for which he has many patristic precedents.[287]

Many Orthodox theologians, representing both sides of the baptism question, would argue that if it ever became a matter of whole Christian communities discussing a reunion based on the wholesale confession of the apostolic faith, as sustained by the Orthodox throughout the centuries, then a different set of canons would be applied than would apply to the (normal) issue of an individual or small group seeking to leave their former bodies in favour of admission to Orthodox communion. It seems to me that the practice of the Great Church of Constantinople is the one that captures an essential understanding in Orthodoxy, namely that Christ's truth is not always preserved best by the strictures of logic, but rather is captured in the expansiveness of love.[288]

Notes

1 Gal. 6.7.

2 Ps. 143.14–15.

3 Ps. 68.5, 146.9.

4 Isa. 1.17.

5 What the Scripture would call this *kairos*, this moment of grace offered to the generation as its destiny of the finding of grace.

6 Matt. 25.35.

7 Notably, Boff, Cone, Freire, Gutierrez.

8 Rom. 7.18–24.

9 Namely: that ought not to be commanded, or taken over by the central or by the superior power, which can be done with perfect competence by the local and normal factors in a society.

10 Heb. 11.32–8.

11 Another meaning of the word orthodoxy, especially in its Slavic form, *pravoslavie*, is 'right glorification'.

12 *Confessions*, 1.1.

13 *Persona* in the Latin tradition (which beforehand had semantically connoted an actor's mask) and *hypostasis* in the Greek tradition. The latter is literally a 'substantive' (derived from the terms 'to stand underneath' something). It is the key Christian Greek word for individuation.

14 Tentative being.

15 The nature of a tree, in other words, was seen from the study of its whole life-cycle from acorn to mature specimen; and this path of growth was its *telos*, or life-goal. The *telos* gave the idea of energetic development to the Aristotelian idea of Nature.

16 Athanasios, *On the Incarnation*, 3.3. 'For God is good, or rather is essentially the source of goodness. He that is good could hardly be miserly, and so he begrudges existence to none. He has made all things out of nothing by his own Word, Jesus Christ our Lord. And among his earthly creation he has especially taken pity on the human race. Having perceived its inability to continue in a single stability, because of the condition of its origination [from nothing], God gave mankind a further gift. He did not simply create man, as he did all the irrational creatures on earth, but he made us "According to his own image", and gave us a communion even in the power of his own Word. In this way, since we have in ourselves a kind of reflection of the Word, and are thereby made rational, we are given the capacity to stand stable in an abiding blessedness, living the true life which belongs to the saints in paradise.'

17 A point which St Gregory of Nyssa also insists on in the *On the Making of Man*. Patristic anthropology thus entirely stands on the observation that the human being is afloat in the universe of being without self-subsistent resources, and only by a miracle of divine grace. There is therefore no simply 'natural' life for such a being: only the existence as a graced creature which depends on the relationship with God that has been established in the core of the type of being that has been gifted (different for material entities, angels, and humans).

18 *Hyle*, or matter. It was nigh on impossible for the ancients (as for us today!) to conceive of the making of anything, least of all humanity, from nothing whatsoever. Athanasios, therefore, imagines God making the human being from a substrate stuff which is 'nothingness', and which has characteristics appropriate to nothingness, especially a tendency to ontological dissolution.

19 Athanasios, *On the Incarnation*, 5.1–2: 'Not only did God create us out of nothing, but through the grace of the Word, he also gave us the free grace of a life in communion with himself. Even so, humanity rejected eternal realities and was led by the counsel of the devil to turn to corruptible realities. So it was that we became the cause of our own corruption in death. This followed, as I have said, because humanity's being was naturally corruptible, even though it was destined by the grace the follows from communion in the Word, to have escaped this natural condition if it had persevered in the good. Since the Word was dwelling with the human race, even its natural corruption could not come near it. But note how Wisdom also says: "God made mankind for incorruption, and as an image of his own eternity, but through the envy of the devil, death came into the world." '

20 The Fathers often use this dynamic language to connote the transfigurative power of redemptive grace that elevated us ontologically to be capable of the divine communion. Cf. 2 Pet. 1.4. It wholly contradicted the Hellenistic theory of *apotheosis* (humans achieving divine status), and connoted the prevenient gift of graceful redemption from God.

21 *On the Incarnation*, 27–9.

22 The Orthodox tradition about the Fall differs from that of the West in several respects. Adam is seen in the Fathers as a more simple creature. His fall is the lapse of an undeveloped innocent. As Irenaeus says: 'He was a child, whose understanding was not yet complete, needing still to develop before he came to fulfilment'

(*Demonstration of the Apostolic Preaching*, 12). After the Fall, the whole human race is spiritually damaged, as Paul teaches (Rom. 6–7), and especially left prey to the prevalence of desire and its force to make mankind deviate from the quest for God. This force of desire sets up the power of *pathemata* (disordered drives, or passions) that progressively damaged the spiritual harmony and power of the human being. This is the primary 'original sin' and its effects throughout the human race have been so deleterious that they ultimately called down the necessary rescue of God in the form of the Incarnation. But there is no 'original guilt' as Augustine taught. There is no attributed sin that is not individually merited. Nor is the human being after the Fall utterly depraved and incapable of communion with God. Augustine's view (*On the Perfection of Human Righteousness*, 4.9) that fallen man is under the 'harsh necessity' of committing sin is wholly rejected; although the resistance to sin, before the advent of Christ, was profoundly weakened, and Orthodoxy would agree with Augustine's sense of the prevenience of God's grace, though with a much more robust sense of the necessary synergy of a human response to grace for the virtuous life to make sense. Nor does Orthodoxy accept that the fallen human nature lost its freedom. Orthodox believe that humanity inherited Adam's punishment of corruptibility, and thus mortality, but not some form of generic guilt. It thus prefers to describe the problem as 'ancestral sin' (*to proporatikon hamartema*) to distance itself clearly from the Augustinianism that took such different 'forked paths' in the later history of Roman Catholicism and Protestantism, and their respective theories of redemption based upon this notion. Further see Pomazansky 1997: 154–66; Ware 1987: 227–30; Romanides 1957.

23 The Fathers had long debates on the precise anthropological location of the 'image', most preferring the *nous*, the

262

spiritual intellect, or the spiritual con-sciousness. Some later Fathers, especially St Gregory Palamas, also argued that, after the Incarnation of the Divine Logos in the flesh, the image could also be said to abide in the whole human being, body, soul, and *nous*, because of the immensely close union (*henosis*) that the Divine Lord had made between the deity and the flesh. Further, see Ware 1987: 225.

24 *Against the Nations*, 34.

25 *On the Incarnation*, 11–12.

26 To clarify this, the Fathers, following Ori-gen, distinguished between the possession of the 'Image' of God in the human being, and the enjoyment of the 'Like-ness' (see Gen. 1.26, where both concepts are mentioned). The Image was innate, the Likeness was that correspondence with the call to sanctity that the indivi-dual was required to make (one's life in the Holy Spirit according to grace). A rebellious life could result in the loss of the Likeness, though not of the Image. See John of Damascus, *Exposition of the Orthodox Faith*, 11.12.

27 By which they invariably mean that the believer ought to correspond with the prevenient grace of God in an active (if unequal) synergy with the divine grace of redemption and mercy that has been given in Christ. Almost all the ascetical Fathers argue that the gift of God's grace is given in measure, appropriate the degree of seriousness with which the believer responds to the initial grace, and with which he or she continues on the Christian path of responsiveness. God calls his people to himself, but expects them to respond, and does not generally force the presence on the unwilling or the unresponsive (except in cases of extraordinary mercy and conversion).

28 See Burghardt 1957.

29 Such a thing can even be instantiated from palaeohistoric studies: the sense of awe that characterizes archaic graphic depictions of the external world, the con-cept of human culture deriving from the irrepressible character of *homo narrator*, and the primitive custom of inhumation with burial goods.

30 The ontological goal, or purpose, as manifested in the existential energy and direction of a life-force.

31 The perfection of a human life is its ful-filment in the glorified state of the Resurrection.

32 The redeemed soul is rendered so perfectly 'In the Image' that communion is thereby established with all noetic creation—the communion of the saints. Through the ontological root that all share in the Being of the Divine Logos, all redeemed creation becomes the true family of God, by authen-tic 'genetic link', we might almost say.

33 Rom. 5.14–21; 1 Cor. 15.22, 45. The sec-ond Adam's reversal of the arrogance of the first is also behind the great hymn of Phil. 2.5–11.

34 Rom. 13.14; Gal. 3.27.

35 Job 38.2.

36 Origen explicitly envisaged the original creation of humanity as a spiritual bles-sedness in the angelic condition, and understood earthly material existence as itself part of the punishment and correc-tion given by God to us as lapsed spiritual intelligences (*noes*) whose physical embo-diment in time and space was not the least of our griefs as we sought to return to the sphere of Paradise. His views were gener-ally rejected by the church after the later third century, however, and the theory of pre-existence decisively rejected by the Fathers of the fifth ecumenical council, Constantinople II in 553. His metaphysic was not an idle one, nevertheless, but an attempt to account for suffering (especially innocent suffering) on earth. The more generally sustained view in the Fathers was that all suffering devolves from the fallen state of mankind, but not necessarily that it all derives from individual guilt.

37 Matt. 7.7–12.

38 Further see Phan 1984; Shewring 1948.

39 Ps. 22.1

40 Deut. 6.14–15; Ps. 78.31; Ezek. 5.15–17, and *passim*.

41 Luke 13.1–5.

42 Mark 14.38, 35–6.

43 As in the context of Isa. 1.15–17. It is customary for the individual Orthodox to acknowledge his or her own failings, when ill, and to repent of all moral evil in the course of seeking physical healing. But it is wholly inappropriate to attribute the physical suffering of any other person to their possible moral failings. Orthodoxy always uses the customary form of prayer in the first person; 'O Lord have mercy on me a sinner.' But when prayer is made collectively, no one may ever presume that anyone else in church is a sinner, except themselves only!

44 What St Gregory the Theologian called Humanity. Angelical and material realities were the first and second respectively.

45 Matt. 18.19–20, 21.22, 26.37–9; Mark 11.24–5; Phil. 4.6–7; 2 Chron. 6.29–30; Ps. 65.2–3; Ben Sira 21.5.

46 Orthodoxy has numerous prayer services focused on healing, chief among which are the Eucharist itself, as well as Confession, and the Mystery of the Seven Unctions, three of the greatest sacraments of the church.

47 Rom. 5.3–5, 8.18–26; 2 Cor. 1.5; Phil. 3.7–15; 1 Pet. 4.12–13.

48 Ps. 37.25.

49 Matt. 6.25–6, 7.7–11, 8.26–7, 14.29–32, 16.21–3.

50 Luke 12.6–7.

51 Matt. 20.22, 26.39.

52 Matt. 26.39–41, 6.13.

53 Oration 7, On the Soul.

54 Pomazansky 1997: 133.

55 Gen. 1.26.

56 2 Pet. 1.4

57 A false inference that has sometimes made evangelical theologians misguidedly attack the doctrine of *theosis* as heretical. A good explanation is found in Ware 1987: 236–42.

58 For more, see Russell 2004; Gross 1938, 2002; McGuckin 2006c.

59 See, for example, Pomazansky 1997: 196–208 for a wider discussion on Orthodox theology of redemption.

60 Ps. 22.1.

61 Ps. 23.4.

62 Some of the greatest challenges to faith in a loving God have been raised by the sickness or death of innocent children. Yet for all those who have concluded such an experience was a scandal of faith that could not be sustained there are others who have found in similar immense suffering a mystery of mercy and reconciliation in the midst of suffering. What had threatened to destroy entire families has mysteriously led some to faith, and some to the casting off of faith.

63 The recurring phrase 'And God saw that it was good' of Genesis 1.

64 Fifth Lychnapsia prayer of Vespers.

65 *On the Orthodox Faith*, 2.29.

66 See also ibid. 3.1.

67 Ps. 2.1–4.

68 1 Pet. 5.8.

69 Ps. 91.9–16.

70 Gal. 6.7.

71 James 1.22–7, 2.12–26.

72 James 2.26.

73 John 2.15.

74 Luke 23.34.

75 Mark 12.10; Eph. 1.22, 4.15; Col. 1.18, 2.19.

76 Ps. 147.15–18, 107.33–8; Isa. 43.19–20; *The Prayer of Azaraiah* 56 expresses it: 'Bless the Lord, seas and rivers, sing praise to him and highly exalt him for ever.'

77 Ps. 24.1.

78 Job 38.33–39.30.

79 Rom. 8.22.

80 Isa. 6.1–7.

81 Mark 9.7.

82 Mark 8.34.

83 Luke 12.16–20.

84 Shlenov and Petrushina 1999.

85 See Chryssavgis 1999, 2004, and also Guroian 1987.

86 One of the major recurring criticisms of the Protestant Reformation to the devotion that the church pays to the Blessed Virgin is that attention to the Theotokos allegedly diminishes full commitment to the basic evangelical principle of the single mediatorship of Jesus. This has never been the experience of Orthodoxy, which understands the intercessory power of the Theotokos to derive exactly, and entirely,

from the singular power of her Son the Mediator. Orthodoxy's delight in calling upon her assistance, however, marks a clear difference in conception over the deeper understanding of the mediatorship of Christ, for in Orthodoxy the fruits of Christ's victory are sensed to be given to the church in a profound communion of spiritual love, especially as manifested in the saints.

87 V. Lossky, 'Panagia', p. 35, in Mascall 1949.

88 A learned priest once described to me the relation of Mary to her Son as comparable to the second violin's creative matching and reflection of the melodic line of the first, in Bach's double violin concerto adagio.

89 Luke 1.38.

90 John 2.3–7, 11.

91 A fundamental literary and intellectual structure of the Gospel of John, whereby the unfolding of the Seven Signs leads the reader into the mystery of the progressive manifestation of the Glory.

92 Luke 2.19, 51.

93 In Orthodox tradition the 'Annunciation' is called the Evangelismos of the Virgin, with its intrinsic word-play on the meanings of 'receiving good news', and 'being evangelized' (initiated) thereby.

94 Luke 1.46–55.

95 Mark 4.11–12.

96 Acts 1.5–14, 2.1–4.

97 For a more detailed treatment see McGuckin 1994b.

98 It had appeared before in the writings of Origen and Gregory of Nazianzus, among others.

99 1 Cor. 1.23.

100 Phil. 2.7.

101 Mark 3.31.

102 Isa. 7.14; Matt. 1.22–3.

103 Certainly not that he represents the 'original tradition' which did not have it, whereas the other two synoptics added it individually.

104 When the deeds and wonders of Jesus were being collected in the aftermath of the Resurrection, most probably in Jerusalem, and under the supervision of Mary herself and the family of Jesus who had good reason to know these familial traditions.

105 The Talmud still retains a (somewhat garbled) tradition within it that Jesus was the illegitimate son of a Roman centurion. The cynical dismissal of Jesus, recorded from his own lifetime, that he was a 'friend of prostitutes' (Matt. 7.19) may also reflect some of this hostile apologetic.

106 Cf. Luke 1.38.

107 Matt. 22.37–40.

108 Luke 11.27–8.

109 The terms *latreia* (adoration), *hyperdouleia* (high reverence), and *douleia* (reverence), were worked out in detail by the seventh ecumenical council at Nicaea in 787, to make it clear that adoration was due to God alone; although the Virgin, the angels and the saints could be offered reverence as great heroes within the Kingdom of God. It was insisted on at the council that the reverence appropriate to the Virgin exceeded that due to all other creatures, and thus her superiority to all saints became part of the ecumenical dogmatic tradition.

110 History has suggested two rival sites, those of Jerusalem near the garden of Gethsemane, which most Orthodox regard as the rightful place of pilgrimage, and that of Ephesus, near the tomb of the apostle John.

111 The normal icon of the Mother of God presents her 'showing' Christ to the observer. In these icons she is called the Hodegitria: 'She who shows the Way'.

112 John of Damascus, *Homily on the Koimesis of the Theotokos*, 2.14 (*PG* 96.740–1).

113 S. of S. 2.13.

114 *On the Koimesis of the Theotokos*, 1.

115 Justin Martyr, *Dialogue with Trypho*, 100; Irenaeus, *Against the Heresies*, 5.19.1; Tertullian, *On the Flesh of Christ*, 17.

116 Excepting the *Chaire Theotoke* (similar to the Latin 'Hail Mary'), which is composed of the biblical verses taken from the story of the Virgin's meeting with Elizabeth.

117 The word may strike a non-Orthodox ear as very abrupt; but Orthodoxy never attributes the grace of salvation to the Blessed Virgin as if it were distinct, or autonomous, or separate from the single and sole salvation found through and in her Son. It is always perfectly well understood among the Orthodox faithful that the Theotokos leads disciples to salvation as a grace of the Saviour of all, her own Son who first perfected her own salvation, and then elevated her as an advocate for later disciples. If the Blessed Virgin is an aid to our salvation it is precisely because Christ himself gifted to her this eschatological role.

118 Exod. 15.10.

119 Exod. 3.2–3.

120 The word also means: 'Rejoice' or 'Be happy!', the beautiful greeting of the ancient Greeks. It is based on the words the angel spoke to the Virgin in Luke 1.28: 'Hail to you most highly favoured'. It is a pun in the original Greek (*Chaire kekaritomene*: 'Rejoice most graced one').

121 Liturgy of St John Chrysostom.

122 S. of S. 4.12.

123 John 4.12.

124 Sermon 9.2, *On Reading the Holy Gospels*.

125 1 Kgs 8.27.

126 Homily 4, *On the Blessed Theotokos*.

127 *Encomium on the All Holy Mary, Mother of God*.

128 Heb. 1.7.

129 The nine ranks, or choirs, of angels. The systematic arrangement of Dionysios the Areopagite would become the classically accepted one in Orthodoxy.

130 Oration 28.31.

131 Gregory calls human beings 'another kind of angel' (Oration 45.8). Also see John of Damascus, *On the Orthodox Faith*, 2.3.

132 See also Job 38.7: 'When the stars were made, all my angels shouted in praise.'

133 Cf. Basil the Great, *Homilies on the Hexaemeron*, 1.5. Dionysios says that because of this aeonic origination, they stand 'Mid-way between those things that are, and those things that are coming-to-be.' *Divine Names*, 10.3.

134 St Gregory of Nazianzus describes them as: 'Simple in some measure and more fixed in good than humanity, owing to their nearness to the highest Good.' Oration 31.15.

135 The Fathers understand each thing to have its determined *ousia* or nature. This is a flexible and dynamically 'growing' reality that can contain several distinct stages and developments (infancy, youth, maturity, old age, or acorn, seedling, plant, and tree), but has a boundary beyond which it cannot pass. In this respect Orthodoxy does not wait in anticipation for chimpanzees to 'develop' consciousness in human style, as if this were a natural and to be expected part of their species' evolution. Humanity itself, when trying to deny this set limit to its being, has a tendency to self-deification, something in which its *hubris* inevitably calls disaster down on its head.

136 For the Fathers the *nous* was that element of the human consciousness (*logos*) in which it was aware of the Divine Logos; accordingly the *nous* was the place where the divine image was most profoundly known and experienced, the bridge between human consciousness and the awareness of God. Gregory calls the ensouled *nous* of the human being 'a worshipper of blended nature, who is an initiate of the material creation, but a neophyte in regard to the noetic world'. Oration 45.8.

137 Staniloae 1998: 146–9 discusses the manner in which angels and humans know the patterns of the cosmos, humanity mediating spiritual insight through material forms, angels perceiving spiritual essences directly. Each form of knowledge assists the other species in some way. Just as the angels once mediated the knowledge of the Godhead to humanity (in the old dispensation presided over by the pre-incarnate Logos) so too humanity (now through the mystery of the Incarnation of the Logos) has mediated more of the purposes of God's loving creation to the

angelic order which did not know this before, and which had never seen the 'embodied' face of the Logos before. The opening stanzas of the Akathist hymn finely express the 'amazement' the angelic order felt before the revelatory act of Incarnation.

138 The meaning of Paul's enigmatic instruction for women praying to be veiled out of respect for the angels (1 Cor. 11.10) who attend the church's prayer and carry it to the throne of God (Rev. 8.3–4) so that it can be a part of their eschatological liturgy also.

139 A common biblical name for them is the 'Sons of God'. They iconize God's immaterial power, while human beings (by virtue of the Incarnation of the Logos among us) iconize the embodiment of God's love. Both icons are necessary. The Fathers disputed which one was superior, but neither one is self-sufficient or cut off from the other: they have a mutual communion of destiny. The Incarnate Lord in his glorious body serves to reveal more of the deity to the angelic order (see Eph. 3.10; Gregory Palamas, *Triads in Defence of the Holy Hesychasts*, 2.3.29–30), while the 'glorified body' in which he transfigures the saints in the next aeon will extend their materiality into spiritual dimensions which are presently impossible to imagine, but which will be more closely attuned with the angels (Mark 12.25).

140 They are circumscribed, according to John of Damascus, *On the Orthodox Faith*, 2.3, and so cannot claim the omnipresence of God; but their refined spiritual nature makes much of what is impossible for us, because of our cosmic limitations, quite possible for them.

141 The Scriptures and the Fathers speak of a great test of the angels in pre-ancient times which caused some of them to rebel. In turning from the vision of God, and the song of his glory as the meaning of their lives, they lost their own glory and stability of being, and fell to the depths of demonic mutation.

The angels of God who remained faithful have progressed in the love of the Lord so powerfully over aeons of presence in the Kingdom that now their goodness is stabilized, in ways comparable to the stabilizing effect of grace within the great saints.

142 See, for example, Matt. 28.4; Mark 16.5.

143 As with the epiphany of Raphael (Tobit 12.19), the adaptation to human expectation is an economic one.

144 The angels are usually called the *Asomatoi*, or Bodiless Ones, in Orthodox reference.

145 Not innately immortal, but deathless as from the gift of God to their natures, as distinct from elect humanity which receives the gift of conditional immortality, over our nature.

146 Luke 20.36.

147 'Holy, Holy, Holy.' See Isa. 6.1.

148 The imperial bodyguard would acclaim the Byzantine emperor by lifting him up on a shield as they carried him among the military camp. It is an image of royal acclamation and coronation.

149 Matt. 6.10.

150 Tertullian comments thus: 'May your Kingdom come, Lord, with all speed. This the prayer of Christians, the confusion of the pagans, the exultation of the angels.' *On Prayer*, 5.

151 Luke 10.27.

152 Matt. 26.53.

153 See, for example, Matt. 18.10; Luke 15.10.

154 Ps. 90.11.

155 Heb. 1.14.

156 2 Pet. 2.4. describes the fallen angels exiled to Hades. It is not presumed that they are inactive there, but that their power is limited by the bonds God has set upon it.

157 Or marginalized the idea with exotic horror films. One of the most chilling phrases to come out of our own century's close association with the demonic, however, was the description of Eichmann, at his trial, as the face 'of the banality of evil'. Malice of cosmic proportions is often like the more domesticated version one finds in

ordinary life, chillingly twisted and mutilated; unable to conceive a living work of its own, but adept in sowing dissension and discontent in the works of others. Its presence is always given away, according to Evagrios, by the agitated unease it causes in the minds of the discerning who are in its presence, and the restless anger it permanently foments in those it has seduced.

158 The angelic epiphany is usually accompanied (as in the prophet Daniel 10–12) with the offer of help, as the earthly prophet 'fails' before the awesome and unearthly encounter, and has to be stabilized before he can hear what the messenger says. The ancient Israelite liturgical symbol of the Seraphim used to be the cobra: its awesome fascination and terror being used to evoke this eerie encounter with unearthly and life-threatening power.

159 Not necessarily 'the soil' any longer, but in some sense a human being must 'till the soil' to produce his or her own material creation. Such is the priestly ministry given to a material life, which, if renounced, or stolen, leads to a profound 'rootlessness' among human society. The spiritual power of vocation and work cannot be neglected without deep harm following to the springs of self- and communal love.

160 Bentley-Hart 2003.

161 Gregory the Theologian, Oration 28. It is a concept that derives from reflection on Rev. 7.1, 14.18, and 16.5, as well as Dan. 10–12.

162 'O holy angel, accompanying my poor soul and afflicted life, do not abandon me though I am a sinner, and do not depart from me because of my recklessness. Do not allow the evil spirit to overcome me by the oppression of this mortal body. Rather, take me by ... my outstretched hands and lead me in the way of salvation. ... Intercede with the Lord on my behalf that he might strengthen me in the fear of God and make me a worthy servant of his goodness.' Office of Small Compline.

163 Liturgy of St John Chrysostom, Great Ektenia.

164 Especially the apostle, as in Rom. 8.38–9; Col. 1.16; Eph. 3.10.

165 A lively discussion of the angelic orders can be found in Staniloae 1998: 119–55.

166 Eph. 6.12; Col. 2.15.

167 Dan. 10.13, 12.1. Jude v. 9; Rev. 12.7–8.

168 Dan. 8.16, 9.21; Luke 1.19, 26.

169 Tobit.3.17, 12.12–15.

170 3 Esdras 4.1, 5.20.

171 3 Esdras 5.16.

172 Bulgakov 1935, 1988: 127.

173 The men are known as *startsi* (Russian), or *gerontes* (Greek) and the women are known as *starissa*, or *gerontissai*.

174 Matt 27.52; Acts 9.13, 32, 41, and *passim*; Rom 1.7, 8.27, and *passim*.

175 The Greek term for wonder-worker (Slavonic: *chudotvorets*). St Nicholas is particularly known as 'The Wonder-Worker' in Orthodox countries.

176 The relics of great saints sometimes emit sweet-smelling myrrh which is then used in healing services in the churches near the saint's tomb.

177 A confessor is a hero of the faith who either survived martyrdom or lived after the age of martyrs, and who is regarded as having been a martyr equivalent by the quality of the Christian witness of their day-to-day lives.

178 1 Cor. 2.9.

179 Matt. 22.32.

180 The church understands that the righteous dead behold the Lord's glory (cf. John 14.2–3) even before the Final Judgement when the Great Transfiguration will take place and they will be translated into their glorified spiritual bodies; that is, their new natures that transcend earthly materiality, and are comparable in glory to the angels.

181 Sometimes called 'Hades' in the old church hymns, though understood to be separated into different zones so that the righteous in Hades are far apart from the wicked, who are held in Hades until the Last Judgement. As one part is filled with light and blessedness, so the other is seen as a gloomy and

desolate place full of the malice of its inhabitants. St Basil the Great explicitly ruminates that there are also different zones in the experience of Hell: where the lamentation and punishment differ according to the wickedness of the different kinds of inhabitants. In this way God's mercy also reaches into the depths of Hell (*The Brief Rules*, 267), though the luminous grace of the Holy Spirit does not shine there (*On the Holy Spirit*, 40).

182 Even in the final glory of Paradise there are 'many mansions' (John 14.2) corresponding to the different achievements of the elect. Clement of Alexandria. *Miscellanies*, 6.14.108 and 114.

183 It commemorates them honorifically, as for example the great commemorations of the Blessed Virgin, the prophets and martyrs, that are made immediately after the consecration of the holy gifts in the Eucharist. Here, the saints are certainly 'prayed for' but not in the normal way that asks God to give their spirits forgiveness and peace. The saints have already transcended that need. Like the elect angels who have passed through their test, they too have eschatologically anticipated the Judgement, and this is why they are free to continue to operate on earth after their earthly histories have been completed.

184 1 Cor. 15.41.

185 Luke 16.26.

186 Luke 16.29. Abraham refuses the appeal of Dives for a convenient miracle and paradisial visitation, when so much already exists within the normative historical order for the right ordering of our spiritual and material needs.

187 Many Orthodox know members of their own families who have departed to the repose of Christ who continue to exercise a philanthropic oversight of grace among their ancestral kin, and they pray to them as their 'local' saints accordingly. This does not always follow after the expected pattern of those who were closest family members on earth, but is related, as always, to the quality of the charism of the Spirit those

Christians enjoyed on earth, something that was not always obvious to the other family members when they were alive.

188 *Centuries*, 111.2–4. 'The Holy Trinity permeates all humanity from first to last, from head to foot, and binds all together....The saints of each generation are joined together with those who have preceded them, and like them they also are filled with light, so as to become like a golden chain, where each saint is a separate link, united to the next one by faith, deeds, and love. In this way, in the unity of God, they form a single chain which is immensely strong.'

189 Col. 1.13–22.

190 See Plekon 2002; Bouteneff 2004.

191 St Basil the Great expresses the principle of how the saint is one who becomes a clear lens for the light of the Holy Spirit in this important passage: 'Shining on those that have been wholly purified, the Holy Spirit makes them spiritual through communion with himself. Consider a sunbeam falling on something that is already bright and transparent, how it immediately becomes even more brilliant, and starts to emit a fresh brightness from out of itself. So it is with souls which have the Spirit dwelling in them and illuminating them. They themselves become spiritual, and send out their grace to others.' *On the Holy Spirit*, 23.

192 The Orthodox term for the Western Church 'altar'.

193 The sacred cloth depicting the Passion of the Lord on which the chalice and *diskos* (paten) stand during the liturgy.

194 The term *thaumata* follows the New Testament word for the 'wonders' of Christ. These were acts of healing or liberation from oppression whose primary philanthropic effect was illustrative of a greater message. The healing of the sickness led to the 'awe' that fell on the witnesses (see Matt. 17.6, 27.54; Mark 4.41; Luke 5.26) as they understood the presence of the holy to be near. The *thaumata* caused by the saint's presence are sometimes small and insignificant in nature (though they too can

consist of great cures), but even then they have the effect of reminding those who have the eyes to see it that the gift of God is very close to them.

195 The Orthodox faith regards the so-called 'natural' life of humankind as a miraculous state of being to begin with: constantly upheld by the grace and energy of being afforded it by a loving God. There is, therefore, no such thing as a 'natural' event that is not already suffused with the divine presence. Only sin, that most unnatural of all phenomena, can be said to be outside this communion of the divine power.

196 Heb. 12.1.

197 Rev. 22:14–15.

198 Luke 16.26.

199 1 Pet. 5.8.

200 Matt. 8.16, 31, 12.28; Mark 5.2–19; Matt. 24.29.

201 Gal. 4.9; Col. 2.8, 15, 20; Rom. 8.38; Eph. 6.12; 1 Pet. 3.22.

202 1 Tim. 4.1; 1 John 4.1.

203 *On the Orthodox Faith*, 2.4.

204 For more on this see Pomazansky 1997: 149–61.

205 Bulgakov 1988: 127.

206 Luke 11.20.

207 It is precisely because the church is the body of the saved that the old aphorism took its force: *Extra ecclesiam nulla salus* (Outside the church—no salvation), though the Latin ought more accurately to be rendered: 'Outside the church - no safety'.

208 Eph. 1.22–3, 4.16.

209 John 15.1–8.

210 John 10.1–6.

211 Eph. 2.19; 1 Tim. 3.15; Heb. 3.6.

212 Eph. 5.32.

213 1 Cor. 3.11; Eph. 2.20–2.

214 The foundation of the church is often seen to have occurred visibly and dramatically at Pentecost; but there are other mysteries which initiated it, and which reveal different characteristics of Christ's Church, such as the raising up of prophets and priests in the Old Covenant, the selection and commissioning of the apostles, and the mystery of the death and resurrection of the Lord pre-eminently, as well as his own Great Commission to the disciples (Matt. 28.18–20). The birth of the church, therefore, is figured in a nexus of mysteries which cannot easily be separated from one another, just as the nature of the church itself cannot easily be reduced to the monochromatic level of the bureaucratic or the 'visible'. Pentecost is the dramatic manifestation of the consecrated Church of Christ to the world, and the birth of its universal mission. It is a mystery of consecration which allows the church to be the 'New Creation' of its Lord, and from which moment of grace (continuing to this day) it is empowered both to celebrate the Eschaton of the Eucharist, and to preach the saving word to the world in the power of the Spirit.

215 Its primary *raison d'être* being threefold: first, to be the locus of the glorification of God on the face of the earth; second, to form the family of God as communion of saints, helping one another on the pilgrimage to salvation and being assisted in turn; and third, to bring the lost sheep into the fold by evangelizing in the power of the Spirit until the Last Day when the Lord returns to gather his own.

216 1 Cor. 2.16; Phil. 2.5.

217 Any other claim that hierarch or prince could ever be the 'Head' of Christ's Church, being rejected by Orthodoxy as alien to the evangelical tradition, and as suggesting that Christ has abdicated his everlasting royal power, a position contradicted specifically by the credal phrase: 'Whose Kingdom shall have no end', and by numerous biblical teachings such as Matt. 16.8, 28.20; Eph. 1.22–3. Orthodoxy also rejects the suggestion that any single bishop can represent Christ in a 'vicariate' sense (endowed with the Lord's plenipotentiary powers over his church) as if there was some sort of absentee landlordism involved. Christ has not abdicated his authority, in the Orthodox

conception, and that authority is shared among many different offices and vocations among the body of the faithful, according to the various gifts and responsibilities of each Christian, and for the overall service of a ministry of love. There is, accordingly, a major problem, for the Orthodox, with the concept of the papal office as currently understood as a juridical supremacy in the Western Catholic Church.

218 Something Orthodoxy regards as a pathology of ecclesiology, and not its normal condition.

219 Though it has its roots in the ecclesiology of St Augustine, in so far as that was produced under conditions of immense tension, forced as he was to make an answer to the Donatist schismatics who were using the ecclesiology of St Cyprian as a rod to hit him with. See *On Baptism*, 5.38.

220 In the seventeenth century, in answer to formal approaches by Calvinist theologians who had submitted their teaching on the 'one invisible church' to the Eastern hierarchs, the *Dogmatic Epistle of the Eastern Patriarchs* made the following statement of ecclesiology: 'We believe, as we have been instructed to believe, in what is called (and what in actual fact is) the holy, catholic, apostolic church, which embraces all those, whoever and wherever they might be, who believe in Christ, who being now on their earthly pilgrimage have not yet come to dwell in the heavenly homeland. But we do not in the least confuse the church in pilgrimage, with the church that has reached the homeland just because (as certain of the heretics think) one and the other both exist, that they both comprise (as it were) two flocks of the single Chief Shepherd who is God, and are sanctified by the one Holy Spirit. Such a confusion of them is out of place and impossible, inasmuch as one is battling, and is still on the way, while the other is already celebrating its victory, and has reached the Fatherland, and has received the reward, something which will also follow

for the whole ecumenical church.' Cited in Pomazansky 1997: 230–1.

221 Rom. 12.4–5; 1 Cor. 12.12–27; Eph. 1.23, 2.16, 4.4, 12, 16, 5.23, 30; Col. 1.18, 24, 3.15.

222 Ignatius of Antioch, *To the Philadelphians*, 4; see also id., *To the Smyrnaeans*, 8: 'Shun divisions as the beginning of all evils. All of you follow the bishop, as Jesus Christ followed the Father, and follow the presbytery as you would the apostles. Respect the deacons as the ordinance of God. Let no one do anything that pertains to the church apart from the bishop. Let that be considered a valid Eucharist which is under the bishop, or one whom he has delegated. Wherever the bishop shall appear, let the people be there; just as wherever Jesus Christ may be, there is the catholic church. It is not permitted to baptise or hold a love-feast independently of the bishop, but whatever he approves, that is also well-pleasing to God. In this way all your acts will be sure and valid.' And see id., *To the Ephesians*, 5–6, and *To the Magnesians*, 6–7. There is a fine discussion of this principle of eucharistic ecclesial unity in Meyendorff 1978: 84, and Zizioulas 1973, 1985.

223 One might justifiably say that many of the icons in our churches are far from being inspired works of art, though they still function as channels of grace. How wonderful it is to find a graceful icon which is also of an inspired artistic standard: here form and function join together in a powerful harmony.

224 Abraham and Sarah at the Oak of Mamre, who serve the three angels 'who are as one Lord'. Patristic exegesis from ancient times accepted this as a biblical icon of the Trinity. Gen. 18.1–15. The icon is finely discussed in Chryssavgis 1999: 134.

225 John 17.20–1.

226 Dragas 2004: 20 expresses it eloquently as follows: 'Being in God the church reflects on earth God's unity in trinity. What is natural to God is given to the church by grace. The grace of the Trinity

is the starting point for understanding the nature of the church, and especially her unity in multiplicity, as the trinity shares one life and one being.'

227 This is not to say that all exercise of power within Christ's Church attains this standard; but that when it lapses from this into self-aggrandisement or (worse) a desire to lord it over others who are regarded as 'inferiors' to the ecclesiastical 'superior', the Orthodox recognize the lapse abundantly clearly. Their most loved hierarchs, and probably the most obeyed, are undoubtedly those who manifest the loving humility of Christ in their ministry and (thanks to God) they are the many.

228 More precisely, a single priesthood, particularly manifested in the degrees of bishop, presbyter, and deacon.

229 'When you are obedient to your bishop, as to Jesus Christ himself, it is clear to me that you are not living as ordinary mortals, but living according to Christ.' *To The Trallians*, 2.

230 Regrettably that model of authority could be found in several places where the pattern of relation between hierarchs and priests seemed to take its cue from the civil service or the army: wholly inappropriate and secularized paradigms, and corruptions of how authority is to be exercised within Christ's Church.

231 An English version exists of the historical canons of the councils and synods, originally compiled by St Nicodemus the Hagiorite, called the Pedalion (Rudder), and one can see there, even from the abridgement, just exactly how many, and how explicitly detailed, the canons are. It falls to the ministry of the local bishop, and the priests, to see how these are applied in given circumstances. They cover matters ranging from immediate family life (such as marriage, divorce, childcare) to more recondite matters of church discipline.

232 Unlike Roman Catholic canon law, the Orthodox canons (devolving from the decisions of the apostles, and the great synods of the ancient church) have not been regularly systematized or 'updated'. Their application depends upon the pastoral discretion of the ruling bishop as part of the ongoing prophetic charism of his sacred office.

233 The motto of the Latin Carthusian order: 'Never reformed, because never deformed.'

234 Eph. 5.25–7.

235 Rev. 19.7, 21.9–10.

236 John 15.4–11.

237 The church must always be reformed.

238 The church is constantly reforming.

239 Although 'nationalism' in its various forms troubles the Orthodox churches a great deal, and often degenerates into a form of tribalism that is a sad denigration of the church's true identity as catholic and thus universal. The issue of 'phyletism' (in the worst sense of ethnic separatism, not confusing it with the rights of national churches to legitimate self-expression of their own cultures, and their own ecclesial governance systems) has divided and certainly weakened pan-Orthodox consciousness.

240 Exod. 22.21, 23.9.

241 2 Cor. 4.6–10.

242 Luke 18.13.

243 Written in the late first century, and entitled *The Shepherd of Hermas*.

244 1892–1980.

245 Sermon on the anniversary memorial for Monsignor Irenée Winnaert, March 1938. In V. Bourne (ed.), *La Quete de Verité et I. Winnaert* (Geneva, 1970), cited in Coniaris 1982: 11.

246 Father Stylianopoulos put it well when he wrote: 'The Orthodox Church is the true church of God on earth and maintains the fullness of Christ's truth in continuity with the church of the apostles. This awesome claim does not necessarily mean that Orthodox Christians have achieved perfection: for we have many personal shortcomings. Nor does it necessarily mean that the other Christian churches do not serve God's purposes positively: for it is not up to us to judge others, but to live and proclaim

the fullness of the truth. But it does mean that if a person carefully examines the history of Christianity, he or she will soon discover that the Orthodox Church alone is in complete sacramental, doctrinal, and canonical continuity with the ancient undivided church as it authoritatively expressed itself through the great Ecumenical Councils' (Stylianopoulos 1976).

247 For it clearly recognizes other churches as 'Christian' in their ethos, and holds their historic Christian achievements in high regard and honour.

248 The seventeenth-century *Epistle of the Eastern Patriarchs* put great stress on the 'confession' of faith which constituted the body of believers, as follows: 'We believe that the members of the catholic church are all the faithful, but only the faithful. This means only those who undoubtingly confess the pure faith in the Saviour Christ (that faith which we have received from Christ himself, from the Apostles, and from the holy Ecumenical Councils) even though certain among them may have submitted to various sins…'. Cited in Pomazansky 1997: 238–9.

249 There are many parts of the Christological confessions of contemporary Western Christianity, as seen in popular books, or scholarly writings, for example, which are clearly redolent of the heresies of Gnosticism, Arianism, or Photinianism, to name only the more common. Most Orthodox would react to these elements very strongly, and immediately, while most contemporary Western Christians would have difficulty knowing what any one of these 'isms' actually meant.

250 For example, Orthodoxy regards Roman Catholicism as sharing with it, substantially, the catholic ecclesial ethos in relation to the saints, and the sacraments; but as departing from its understanding of core traditions about the nature of the church and juridical power, as well as significant traditions about the Trinity. Similarly it regards Anglicanism as

having a profound relation with the apostolic tradition in core matters of the faith, yet as simultaneously demonstrating significant deviation from its awareness of the holy tradition in terms of many of Anglicanism's contemporary positions in relation to Christology, revelation, ethics, the veneration of the saints, the understanding of sacraments, and so on. In its wider relations with the heavily diffracted forms of Protestantism, Orthodoxy recognizes the powerful Christian charisms present there of joyfulness, prayer, and evangelistic zeal that motivate it, but is bewildered by the extent of so many deviations within Protestantism from the historic and sacred tradition such that can result in hostility to the cult of the saints, and the drastic reduction of sacramental practice, not least the rejection of ordained priesthood and episcopacy. In Orthodoxy's attitude to all three forms of Western Christianity it remains more puzzled than certain about the resolution of how the West embodies its vocation to be church. It thus falls back on its own primary duty, which is to articulate and demonstrate with clarity, and honesty, how and why it has maintained its own spiritual identity, as the present embodiment of apostolic tradition.

251 It is not so dim as to have forgotten the difference between 'traditions of men' (Mark 7.3–15) and the 'tradition of the saints' which its knows to be its apostolic heritage.

252 To which the Orthodox also later added the category of 'illicit assembly' to signify a church community led in prayer or worship by someone resistant to a local bishop's authority, that was disunited from the whole, but in a lesser degree than schism. Canon 33 of the Council of Laodicea forbade members of the church to join in prayer services with schismatic groups. Some Orthodox today, especially those who are hostile to the ecumenical movement *in toto*, argue that this is still applicable as a veto on ecumenical prayer services.

253 The Greek East and Latin West in ancient times were quite different in many external forms of worship and intellectual culture, for example, without being divided in faith or practice.

254 1 John 2.19.

255 Gnosticism has always thus been seen as the archetypal and primal heresy.

256 Cf. 1 Cor. 2.13–14; Col. 2.8.

257 The apostolic charism derives from having 'heard' the Gospel from the Lord.

258 The early churches began to draw up lists of their authentic bishops, in a provable line of succession, in order to meet the growing threat from speculative Gnostic innovators who claimed that they had received true apostolic tradition (from other and more dubious sources, not least their own imaginations).

259 Orthodoxy differs from the Roman Catholic conception of apostolic succession in so far as it understands it less in the formalist manner of lines of succession radiating out via a pedigree of consecration (though not denigrating the importance of this model of continuance). Orthodoxy understands apostolicity more in the issue of historical fidelity to apostolic doctrine and practice. Thus, a church is apostolic in so far as it primarily demonstrates its own apostolic fidelity and purity in its ongoing life, and as that is proven by communion with the other apostolic churches. Clearly, therefore, all the local churches of the Orthodox world are 'apostolic sees' (whether or not they were actually directly founded by a missionary apostle). Orthodoxy does not accept the argument that apostolicity can be guaranteed in a formalist fashion by organizational allegiance to a central 'apostolic see', such as Rome, from which apostolicity derives as from a central fountain. Such an argument presupposes that when a church is not in communion with that source, it has lost apostolicity. So, the Roman Catholic ecclesiology tends to deny apostolic fullness on the basis of how churches relate to the peculiar theologoumenon of the Petrine primacy (which it has itself elevated as a central axiom of the faith).

260 The catholicity is dependent on the holiness, in so far as the holiness derives from unity with Christ, as given in and by the Spirit, and closeness to that Lord is the proof of its fidelity to his teaching, and thus its apostolicity.

261 'Christ is the bond of unity, since he is God and man in one and the same person. In speaking of this unity of the Spirit I shall follow the beaten track of the church's doctrine and repeat that we all receive one and the same Spirit, the Holy Spirit, and thereby are mingled with one another, and with God. Though we are many, and Christ makes the Spirit of the Father (which is his own Spirit too) to dwell in each one of us individually, nevertheless the Spirit is One and is Individual. By his own being, therefore, he joins into unity those spirits which by the terms of their own nature as individual persons are cut off from unity with one another. Through his activity they are manifested as a kind of single entity in himself. For just as the power of the holy flesh [the Eucharist] incorporates its participants with one another; just so, in my view, the one indivisible Spirit, who dwells in all of them, brings them into a spiritual unity.' *Commentary on John*, 17.21.

262 Encyclical of the patriarch of Constantinople, Joachim III, 1902.

263 1 Tim. 3.15.

264 Ibid. Patelos 1978: 30.

265 How different the episcopal instinct of St Gregory the Theologian, who when he became the Orthodox bishop of the deeply Arianized see of Constantinople in 381 advocated the 'economic' reception of Arian baptism, and the continuance in office of all Arian clergy who would submit an Orthodox profession of faith.

266 Those who had been tortured for the faith and survived. In early Christianity it was popularly believed that they had the privileges of martyrs among

the community, and could successfully intercede with God for the forgiveness of sins.

267   Eph. 4.4–6.

268   *On the Unity of the Catholic Church*, 4–6.

269   Cyprian's term *sacerdos* here signifies the episcopal office.

270   Epistle 66.7.

271   A position which Orthodoxy still maintains.

272   Some Orthodox believe that an 'economy of charity' ought to be observed in treating non-Orthodox Christians as if they 'really were' Christians, while holding that they are not. This further complicates matters of important truth-telling, draping a web of false rhetoric over issues that ought to be spoken out in honesty and lovingkindness.

273   Novatianist rigorists who excommunicated the larger church assemblies because they advocated post-baptismal penance and reconciliation.

274   Equivocation about the status of the different baptisms can be seen in the earlier Fathers and some of the conciliar canons. Nicaea's canon 19 prescribes rebaptism for the followers of Paul of Samosata, who used trinitarian baptismal formulas but whose doctrine of the person of Christ was that he was an elevated 'man' caught up into the grace of God. St Athanasios regarded the baptism of the Arians (who did not believe in the co-equal deity of the Son, or that of the Holy Spirit) as wholly defective because of their lack of trinitarian belief, and needing to be given *de novo* as for the first time. But the seventh canon of the Council of Constantinople accepted the validity of Arian baptism, while rejecting the baptism of the Arian Eunomians (who only used one immersion) and that of Montanists and Sabellians, although the latter groups used the evangelical formula, but had a Unitarian doctrine of God. St Cyprian and Pope Stephen in the third century both regarded all heretical baptisms as invalid; but Stephen believed that the 'majesty of the divine name' worked sacramentally over and above defective intentions, and he advocated that if a baptism had been conveyed outside the church, though using the trinitarian formula and three-fold immersion, only 'the laying on of hands' should be given to such converts, to perfect the grace of baptism. This view became standardized in the ancient Latin Church in the seventh canon of the Council of Arles in 314, and was propagated widely by St Augustine. This position of the ancient Latins is accepted by the Orthodox, of course, as part of the One Undivided Church of the Fathers.

275   Montanists.

276   Famed canonist and archbishop of Alexandria (d. *c.*263). Dionysios supported Pope Stephen, against St Cyprian, that the baptism administered by heretics and schismatics could, in some circumstances be valid.

277   Bishop of Cappadocian Caesarea, 230–68. He supported Cyprian on the issue of schismatic baptism, in opposition to Stephen and Dionysios.

278   A sect which denounced marriage as sinful and forbade it to the baptized.

279   Also known as Aquarians, because they would not use wine in the eucharistic celebration, employing water instead.

280   In other words to come for chrismation, not for a second immersion.

281   The bishops of Asia Minor, modern-day Turkey.

282   That is with immersion and chrismation as if they had never received the sacrament at all.

283   Holy Communion.

284   That is, received these two bishops of an Encratite community, along with their flocks, into communion with the catholic church and allowed them to continue as (Basil's own) bishops.

285   Canon 1, Basil of Caesarea, Epistle 188 to Amphilokios.

286   Sometimes, in Slavic practice, converts from Roman Catholicism are initiated by confession and communion (a practice initiated by Peter Moghila in seventeenth-century Kiev).

287 St Gregory the Theologian admitted Arian clergy into his communion in 381 if they would only give verbal assent to the Nicene faith, and he accepted as valid the Arian clergy's administration of baptism over several generations in the church of Constantinople, even though these clergy had not even hitherto professed the Trinity. Like other Fathers, he knew that the Church of Christ has an immense healing power that can overflow for the benefit of many ostensibly outside it.

288 John 13.34–5.

Chapter 5

The Holy Mysteries and Liturgies

GREATER AND LESSER MYSTERIES

Orthodoxy does not use the word 'sacrament' with the same frequency as the Western churches. Its preferred word is *mysterion*. The word means 'thing to be silent about', and was used by the apostles and Fathers with deliberate analogous reference to the pre-Christian mysteries, or mystery religions, where the element of the *arcana* (refusing to divulge the contents of the initiation) became a very important identifying mark of the adherent. Orthodoxy uses the word, in a comparable sense, still. In earliest Christianity the believer was forbidden to divulge the content of the mysteries to the uninitiated non-believer, even if such a one was under instruction to be baptized. They were regarded as too sacred for utterance to the unbaptized. Even well into the fourth century the catechumens only received the final elements of the faith from the baptizing bishop, who would give to them the Creed a few days before their baptismal liturgy, and require them to memorize it. It was only in these final days of initiation that the doctrine of the sanctifying effect of the Holy Spirit was conveyed to them, and the manner in which their baptismal immersion[1] conveyed his mystical grace and cleansing. To this day in the eucharistic liturgy the deacon will cry out publicly before the beginning of the Anaphora[2] for all the catechumens to leave the building so as not to witness the mystery of the eucharistic consecration. The concept of *mysterion* thus also connotes a 'passing by'[3] that produces awe[4] in the hearts and minds of those who witness it, and understand it, that results in the quietness of deep reverence for the holy. The mystical[5] reaction of the silence that 'ponders in the heart'[6] is exactly that which is initiated by the mystery itself. It is a small sign of the inner consecration that has also taken place, as God in his mysteries has 'passed by'. Like Moses before the burning bush at the Sinai theophany, those present at the mystery have to learn the syntax (the *politeia*) of the divine 'passing by', and so are told, and slowly learn it through their subsequent Christian lives, that it is necessary to take off one's shoes in humility and reverence,[7] for here one stands upon holy ground.[8]

The mysteries are experiences of Christian initiation that are not easily explicable, and are deeply resonant with the grace of the Lord who has empowered them by his Holy Spirit, so as to use them as primary ways of manifesting his life-giving presence and energy within the earthly church until the Eschaton. As Sergei Bulgakov once described it, the sacraments are the continuing signs that Pentecost is still occurring within the heart of Christ's Church, and their youthful, unfailing freshness, is a sure sign of the authenticity and truth of the church.[9] All the Christian mysteries are eschatological in essence. They stand, as does the earthly church itself, poised between the two ages, this age of conflicted loyalty to God, the expectation of the Kingdom, and the next aeon where the Kingdom of God will be revealed as all in all. Although the mysteries are 'hidden' in character, and profound, the term does not predominantly mean a conundrum, or something that eludes comprehension. Such is merely the contemporary, secularized significance of the word 'mystery'. Mysteries, in the church's understanding, are the particularly empowered means the Lord has left his church to grow into the supreme mystery, his own eschatological presence in the world, a deifying grace that is conferred on the elect church by the Holy Spirit. All the mysteries are forms of theosis, and encapsulate, in different ways, the same experience of deification of the believer, which is assimilation to Christ. Each one, to that extent, is a synopsis of the Kingdom, and the path to it. Each one is a metamorphosis, transfiguring the faithful into eschatological newness of vision, and being.

Orthodoxy has preferred the vocabulary of *mysterion* as being more apostolic in character and scripturally original than the secular word *sacramentum* that the early Latin Fathers pressed into service to describe the Christian initiation in terms drawn from the soldier's oath of loyalty. Tertullian, himself the son of a centurion, who had witnessed all the pagan army rituals, was partly responsible for this development. This Latin theology of sacrament and grace also belongs to Orthodoxy, for the church of the first thousand years shares the same spiritual heritage. It is clearly manifested in the profoundly rich theology of worship that exudes from the ancient Latin ritual. Orthodoxy, however, although its teachers were sometimes bilingual until the end of the fourth century, generally became less and less aware of the intellectual and liturgical currents of the West from the sixth century onwards. By the time the Eastern and Western parts of the church rediscovered one another, it was with a profound cultural shock in the medieval period, when political friction and the religious wars known as the Crusades, not to mention the great extension of powers the Papacy had assumed by that period, had deeply soured relations with a mutual hostility that would soon lead to the Great Schism. As a result, the Latin liturgical tradition did not have a great influence on the foundational period of the East's development.

Linguistically and culturally Orthodoxy was deeply rooted in the Greek Scriptures, and knew the term *mysterion* from the Septuagintal Bible as specially related to the revelation of the hidden things of God[10] or the deep secrets of a person's heart.[11] In the evangelical tradition the word was given a new baptism, to connote the revelation of the inner principles of the Kingdom that were only available to the elect disciples of Christ. It was a special and particular form of initiation into that very mystery of the Kingdom, as well as the manner of entering the initiation. So the Lord tells his disciples that in their reflection on his parables they have already been given the 'Mysteries of the Kingdom'.[12] The apostle Paul uses the word[13] to designate the secret plan God has for the salvation of his people, one that began with the election of Israel and will conclude with the reconciliation of Israel before the end time, and whose scope is of such vastness it can escape the less percipient, who may have forgotten that the Jews: 'as the chosen people are still loved by God . . . who never takes back his gifts or revokes his choice'.[14]

For the apostle, Jesus is, in and of himself, the 'revelation of a mystery kept secret for long ages'.[15] This usage, the 'Mystery of Christ' which is revealed as the salvation and consolidation of his people in the New Age, becomes the standard post-Pauline use in the Scriptures.[16] The mystery of the living faith of the Christian is, therefore, 'Christ in you, the hope of glory'.[17] To this extent, all the mysteries of the Orthodox Church are one and the same: just as Christ is one and the same, and sends the same Holy Spirit into the heart of the faithful individually and collectively to constitute them as his own Mystical Body.

Nevertheless the *epinoiai*,[18] or aspects, of the Lord are manifold and diverse. These are the ways that Christ adapts himself to the needs of his people in time and space, who are at various stages of spiritual growth, and different levels of mystical perception. So it is that the mysteries are varied in form. They have the same character of the holiness of Christ, and because they emanate directly from the energy of the Holy Spirit, they are indefectible in essence and absolutely pure in quality (even though they may pass by 'unperceived' in some instances by those whose hearts and eyes are not prepared to see them[19]). Even when the believer approaches them formalistically, however, they have an unfailing power and grace, since it is not the faith of the believer that energizes the mysteries, but rather the mysteries, celebrated in the glory of the whole church's doxology, which bring the disciple into the presence of the Lord of Glory. It is because of this diverse character of the paths to our common and singular salvation that there are several different forms of mystery within the church.

Orthodoxy has generally not been willing to enumerate them and classify them strictly, in the manner of the medieval Western Church,[20] but in recent centuries, especially in theological writing after the seventeenth century when Latin scholastic influence was prevalent in the Eastern churches, it has tended to agree with the scholastic formulation that there are seven great mysteries in the life of the church: this largely to stand against the post-Reformation reduction of the understanding of the mysteries to merely the 'two sacraments' of baptism and Eucharist, something that has been found in some forms of Protestantism. Nevertheless, when it is reflecting within its own tradition and not looking outwards to the issue of external apologetics, Orthodoxy has preferred a wider view that sees the great mysteries not as things that are strictly bounded and formally delineated in the church's life, but rather as the central experiences of worship and doxology found in the salvation history of the Orthodox, in which the grace of the Holy Spirit shines out in particularly glorious ways. These moments of the central mysteries turn around the charter stages of initiation and Christian growth into God (the path of the deification by grace of the believer), and also fan out (as it were) into doxological moments of encounter which can be lesser in character. These lesser mysteries share the lineaments of the great mysteries. So it is, for example that Orthodoxy fully recognizes the central mysteries of the church as the three great initiation experiences: baptism, chrismation, Eucharist (the mystical supper), and the two mysteries of healing (the seven anointings) and *metanoia* which relate to them in a primary way.[21] Then there are also the two great mysteries of vocational consecration (the more specific sacraments of initiation as this develops into the particularities of a disciple's allegiance to the Lord), namely holy orders (the 'laying on of hands'), and matrimony.

The primary mysteries of initiation are still strictly observed in their liturgical form. Baptism and chrismation are meant to be celebrated together. The Eucharist itself is the initiation mystery *par excellence*, though only given to those already illuminated as the completion of their initiation. So it is always meant (for the first time at least) to be celebrated immediately after baptism. Thus, in Orthodoxy, if infants are baptized then they must also immediately receive the Eucharist, and continue receiving it from that day onwards, as the unrolling of their initiation and their new life in Christ.[22]

This triadic unity of the three separate mysteries, and the unity that flows out from them to the other mysteries too, is seen to reflect something of the character of the Church of Christ itself, which in the mysterious quality of its own unity in diversity knows something of the life of God as three distinct *hypostases* in one self-same being. Similarly the mysteries are distinct in scope, but singular in function, being energized by the same Spirit of grace and leading to the same illumination in Christ (the *theosis* of the believer). Also, they are seen to iconically represent the mystery of the Incarnation (again a similar way to that in which the church as the Body of Christ does this), that is in so far as the mysteries have a double nature and a single reality. As the Incarnation is understood to be the Logos' own supreme spiritualization of matter, in which the flesh of the Lord is taken up into the power of the Godhead to become 'God's very own flesh' (as St. Cyril of Alexandria put it), so the mysteries begin in physical materialities[23] and lead directly into the presence of the divine. The Eucharist is itself a supreme mystery of the spiritualization of matter (not merely a symbol of it, but rather its concrete realization). Baptism and chrismation do not merely symbolize the death of the old nature and the new birth of the Christ-initiate; they actually effect it, and seal that character in ways that are permanently visible to the bodiless powers and the elect saints.[24] The mysteries of marriage and ordination (and monastic profession) are similarly powers of the transfiguration of structures of living and working, into patterns of 'living out' the Kingdom.

This double character of a visible material act and a spiritually charged energy suffusing it is compared often in Orthodox thought to the paradigm of the Incarnate Lord. His finger, or his face, according to the mystery of the Incarnation, is not a material thing inhabited by, or used by the Lord of time and space, it is more truly the finger of God, the very face of God, the form of the energy of God within the world. So it is when the blind men felt this finger on their eyes,[25] they were able to see again. This was the ultimate paradox of the 'finger of the living God', not metaphorically, but really so, and thereby full of life-giving power. The material form of the mystery is, of course, closely related to the specific *epinoia* of Christ which it celebrates. The explication of that relation is one of the chief ways one can exegete the inner workings of the mysteries for those who have not experienced them directly. The Eucharist, for example, is a 'burning of the heart'[26] which directly relates to the loving covenant meal's bread and wine, heady and potent, consumed reclining on the bosom of the Lord, yet eaten within the shadow of the High Priest's dungeon, under the gloom of the betrayal of a chosen apostle.[27] The mystery of confession uses the materiality of words of repentance to unravel words and deeds of denial, and to find the unwavering forgiveness of the same Master who led Peter to restate his profession, 'deeply moved', on the shores of the lake.[28] This exegesis will be attempted below. It is a task that is greatly assisted by the liturgical texts that so solemnly enwrap the celebration of the mysteries within the Orthodox Church. All of the great mysteries have ancient and revealing rites and ceremonies that are full of mystical symbols, and poetry of great beauty that has been added to them across so many generations. Invariably, after the celebration of one or several of the great mysteries in the churches, the Orthodox will be found together continuing the celebration, sometimes eating and drinking (and usually talking animatedly) together near the church. The elation is tangible and communicable.

Even the 'repeatable' mysteries, such as the Holy Eucharist, are prepared for carefully in advance, with stipulated prayer and fasting rituals. No adult Orthodox would ever think of going to the altar unprepared or as a matter of course. These moments of great grace are an 'event': in fact they are a *kairos*, one of the moments in which the Kingdom of God is felt to have manifested itself in concrete from within the fabric of history. As such they are eschatological mysteries, that for a moment (but decisively so and irreversible in their tendency[29]) have brought the aeon of the next age into the fabric of the present era, and wholly changed it with a terrible beauty. At these moments the Orthodox know the truth in complete fullness: that 'To you has been given the secret of the Kingdom',[30] and also that 'The Kingdom of God is within you.'[31]

All the mysteries convey the self-same character of consecration, so that believers may assume the full extent of their destiny as spiritual beings who share the life of Christ in the world; yet each one of them configures that 'process' of deification in a different way. Baptism is such an archetypal form, an unrepeatable 'sealing', that can never be reiterated.[32] The others, in a manner that stretches across the whole space of a Christian life,[33] lead the Orthodox forward into the deepening experience of the life of God. Such a life of discipleship is charted by the 'markers' of one's regular participation in the repeatable mysteries, especially those of the Holy Eucharist, *metanoia*, and the anointing of the sick. Many Orthodox theologians have also spoken of the entrance into the monastic state (the profession of a complete renunciation for the love of God, and the reception of the angelic habit) as a lesser mystery. To this extent, like the mystery of *metanoia*, the monastic profession is understood as a form of the renewal of the once-for-all baptismal profession, and as a renewed sharing in its renovatory power. The same concept has been seen to apply to the mystery of the funeral rite for the believer. It too shares elements from the other mysteries, especially related to the consecration of the iconic body of the believer, and the celebration of the forgiveness of sins. The ritual of the 'Great Blessing of Waters', on the feast of Epiphany, is also seen as an especially solemn mystery in church. In addition to this, however, there are a number of other experiences in which the Orthodox would recognize the character of a mystery, without necessarily articulating them as the greater mysteries. This would apply, for example, to the use of blessed oil and water in the homes of the faithful, the offering of incense to Christ,[34] the reception of the blessed *antidoron*,[35] the asking for blessings from a bishop or a priest, the experience of the blessing of God at a place of pilgrimage or the shrine of a saint. All of these lesser mysteries share the same character (and are thus mystically recognized as significant and sanctifying) of the enlightening grace of the Spirit of God.

Orthodoxy has, then, a rich and deep 'sacramental theology' which is more akin to Western Catholicism than it is to the Protestant Church's experience, where sacramentalism has been diminished in the post-Reformation age – not only organization-ally,[36] but also in terms of their interior understanding: sacraments and prayer services are seen predominantly in symbolic fashion, the Eucharist understood mainly as a 'commemoration' of the Lord's Supper, and baptism as a symbolic initiation into the community of disciples. On the other hand, post-medieval Western Catholicism has increasingly turned its theological attention to the sacramental mysteries, classifying them as seven in number, and sometimes using a heavily scholasticized method to explain their relevance and functionality. Orthodoxy has not given the same scope to the scholastic approach; and accordingly, the profound way the Orthodox Christian experience is 'guarded about' by mysteries is harder to convey to those who have not had extensive experience of this form of Christian living (or who tend to see it through the lens of their own comprehension of their own ecclesial sacraments), because it is more hidden from plain sight. Mysteries can only be 'mystically' apprehended.

The mystery of baptism

This great mystery is commonly seen by all who call themselves Christian as a foundational initiation. *Baptisma* was a ritual that was found in Judaism in the New Testament period, designed to serve as the initiation rite for pagan females[37] who wished to convert to Judaism. Its root symbolism was related to the Judaic rituals of purification. It was a 'sprinkling' for purification, and admittance into the number of the elect people of God. This 'typological' understanding carried on into the church as well.[38] Baptism, which essentially means 'the washing', was partly rooted in the experience of the Lord himself, when he entered the waters of Jordan and gave the great theophanic sign of the Trinity, in the sight of John, the prophet and forerunner. The Orthodox Church teaches that here the old dispensation was consummated, and the material order consecrated in its root element (water). The ultimate mystery of the Trinity (the voice of the Father, the descent of the Spirit on the head of the Master) at work in the manifestation of a new world order[39] was shown to a yet uncomprehending world,[40] although the prophet recognized what had transpired and ushered his own disciples forward to become the apostolic followers of their new Lord. 'Behold the lamb of God',[41] John was able to say after his initiation at the baptism (for Orthodoxy sees the baptism as the initiation of the prophet not the initiation of Jesus), and so they too passed into the mystery of the encounter with Christ.[42] This, then, is how Christian baptism is rooted in time, though it also opens a door that reaches beyond time into the Kingdom. The historical baptism of the Lord is its 'archetypal' form.

Baptism is also rooted in an act and command that lie outside time, poised between history and the eschatological present of that moment when the Risen Lord gave the command to his disciples to become a new future, by evangelizing the whole world through teaching the observance of his commandments and by baptizing new disciples in the threefold and singular name of the Trinity.[43] From this mystery of evangelization that corresponds with the sacred initiation of the teachings of Christ and the consecration into the threefold name, there immediately follows the corollary of Christian identity: that mystical experience that alone makes the authentic reality of the church, namely the presence itself: 'For then see: I am with you always, even to the consummation of the world.' The Lord taught Nicodemus that baptism, as a spiritual rebirth, was necessary for entrance into the Kingdom of God.[44] And elsewhere the Scripture makes it clear that baptism is a fundamental requirement for Christian initiation.[45] It is the low lintel of repentance through which door all must enter stooping down, or else they cannot enter at all. The believer, by this mystery, is given a new life that transcends and transfigures the physical, that is, the 'species identity' they have received from their parents. In many debased estimates of baptism it might be presumed that this is merely a little ceremony of welcome for a new baby, comparable to an ancient pagan naming service. Nothing could be further from the Orthodox understanding of the mystery. The adult or child is actually understood to be reborn,[46] passing from the shared human nature that is our common physical inheritance into a new nature. Theologically, this is the passage from the Old Humanity, Adamic nature, to the New Creaturehood which is given in Christ, through the consecration of the Holy Spirit. For this reason the church's ritual frequently describes baptism, typologically, as the passage through the Red Sea from the slavery of the Egyptian exile into the freedom of the children of God. This image of the people of God making their way through waters which were life to them, yet death-dealing to the enemies of God,[47] is basic to the ritual of the Orthodox baptism ceremony. Orthodox theology is very serious about its presupposition that there must then be two types of human nature present on earth and within our species. One is the Adamic nature which still groans to be liberated, and which still lives under the lesser light of a more material conception of the meaning and destiny of life. The other is the Christ nature into which his elect in the church have been initiated, and into which each believer strives to grow to the 'fullness of the stature of Christ'.[48] It is for this reason that the Orthodox Church takes seriously the task of evangelization in the world. It does not see all religions as equal, or as equally valid paths to God. It strives, on the contrary, to witness to and proclaim that path to God which God himself instituted on earth for his faithful to come to him. It hopes for the entrance of all humanity through the 'narrow door'[49] that leads to life. This single-minded fidelity to its own charter of salvation, the Holy Gospel, as a gift for the entire world, does not preclude it from being able to respect other religions for the many aspects of truth and civilizing power they may contain. But Orthodoxy's canon of judgement on this remains the Gospel alone.

As the apostle Peter also taught his hearers, in the full charismatic gift of the pentecostal Spirit,[50] repentance and baptism precede the full remission of sins and the gift of the Spirit of God. The spreading practice of infant baptism took away from many celebrations of the baptismal mystery the clear element of repentance and remission of sins that came so clearly before the eyes of the ancient Christian congregations when adult pagans (for soon the candidates[51] for the church were largely gentile and dubiously formed in their moral upbringing) stood before the font and made their renunciation of their past lives of sin, along with their formal dedication to Christ. Adults coming for admission into Orthodoxy are still required to study with the parish priest and learn to be familiar with the faith, and especially open their hearts and minds to the priest,[52] in great privacy and discretion, so that their moral values and habits can be brought into harmony with the standards and practices of the church. All of this is an essential 'preparation' of the spirit before entering into the mystery. In the ancient church this time of preparation was particularly associated with the Great Lent leading up to Pascha, and this is still the most fitting time for adults to be initiated.

The large first parts of the rites (still observed even for infants today) consisted of a turning to the west, symbolic of the domain of the Prince of this World, and a renunciation of Satan. The candidates spat,[53] facing the west, and were exorcized from demonic possession, understood as having manifested itself (at the very least)

283

in their previous worship of false gods, and their lack of a true sense of moral order. The exorcisms, once completed, led on to the solemn consecration of the baptismal waters, in which they were led and immersed as a vital type of their death to the old order and their rebirth to the new life in Christ. The bishop conducted all these ceremonies in antiquity, after he himself (with the assistance of his priests and deacons) had conducted a long and rigorous programme of education and moral 'scrutiny' of the new candidates, one that sometimes would last for several years as the pagans were acclimatized into the new lifestyle, and new moral demands, of Christian *politeia*. Nowadays the celebration of the mystery is generally delegated to priests in parishes. Its dependence on the episcopal charism is nevertheless demonstrated by the fact that the chrism (necessary for the completion of the sacrament) must be consecrated by the celebration of bishops alone, although it is conferred at the hands of a priest. Baptismal immersion can be administered by a layperson in a case of urgent necessity,[54] but it cannot be performed on another by those who are not themselves baptized. This possibility of lay baptism is, in fact, in virtue of the common priesthood of all believers which is conferred on them through their own baptismal chrismation. Without that priestly gift, the grace cannot be offered, and this is why the non-baptized cannot confer the sacrament, and also why the non-ordained cannot confer any of the other sacraments, which are reserved to those who have been given the gift of a radiant, particular, and elevated priestly charism, through their admission to the mystery of holy orders in the apostolic succession.[55]

Infants, of course, are not expected to prepare. Their sponsors are 'standing in' for them in all things. It is the sponsors who are expected to prepare, and both they and the officiating priest should fast and ready themselves by prayer for several days before the mystery takes place. The parents of the child who is presented for baptism are expected to do this out of their own zeal for the faith, and the desire to enter into a greater communion of love with their own child, by means of sharing the presence of Christ with it. It stands to reason that they are expected to bring up their child as someone rooted in the customs and practices of the faith from their earliest days. It is a burden that parents impose on their children, not a mark of love, if they offer a child for baptism and are then careless about its religious formation. The sponsors of a child in baptism are required to be Orthodox themselves, and are undertaking a serious obligation to 'keep an eye' on the spiritual and moral development of their 'children' as well as on their educational and social development. In Orthodox countries this entrance into the role of godparent (*nounos, koumbaros*[56]) creates a kinship between the families, and especially between the *nounos* and the newly baptized. It is seen as a lifelong relation of great force. It is a 'spiritual relationship', of affinity (*syngeneia*) for example, that precludes all possibility of a subsequent marriage between the two persons.[57] The sponsor is like a father or a mother: a guardian to that soul, not its partner on the road.

In ancient times Christian parents would enrol their children as catechumens, who would attend all the church services, marked with Christ's Cross, and dedicated to him, but not yet taking that personal step of conforming all their life to Christ's service. The catechumens stayed in the outer part of the church building and did not receive the eucharistic mysteries. They had such a profound sense of the holiness of life required of the baptized that they often delayed baptism until their last years; looking to its sanctifying effect to atone for all their past sins. This custom of a lifetime of catechumenate was denounced by the great Fathers so successfully[58] that infant baptism became the standard path to initiation in Christian countries afterwards. With this success, perhaps, came a relaxation of the awe that once attended baptism as the once-for-all commitment and remission given of sins. Today Orthodox Christians have the great benefit, which was not always available for their Christian brothers and sisters in all parts of the ancient church, of ready access to the sacrament of confession, through which they can charismatically experience the grace of repentance and the consecration which Christ himself gives them as part of the 'Spotless Bride' of the Lamb.[59]

In the liturgical rite of Orthodox baptism, after the exorcisms have concluded, and the renunciations and professions of faith have been witnessed by the wider church, the candidate is led to the font where solemn prayers of blessing over the water are said, and oil is mixed in with it. The font is large enough to hold enough water completely to cover the person to be baptized. In some of the ancient churches of the East the font was a cross-shaped pool set into the floor, into which the baptizer and candidate would descend. Such a one can still be seen in Nazareth, and in many other parts of the Eastern Christian world. Just before the baptism, in ancient times, the candidates would be vigorously and liberally anointed with blessed olive oil, by male or female deacons respectively. This, the so-called 'oil of the catechumens', now more generally referred to in Orthodoxy as the 'oil of gladness'[60] was a symbol of the new strength the candidate would bring to the prosecution of the Christian life. Most of the ancients associated bathing with an anointing of this form. In later times the day-to-day symbolism of such an anointing (it is not the anointing of chrismation) fell away more and more. In the contemporary ritual there is only a very small amount of oil used, whose purpose is to convey a blessing of healing, and a reminder that the newly baptized is an 'athlete' of God, who needs to prepare and 'warm up' just as the ancient athletes once did by anointing themselves for action. The candidate first hears the prayers of blessing over the oil, and is then anointed on the forehead, the breast, the upper back, the hands and feet. Then the celebrant leads the candidate into the water and says the formula of baptism: 'The servant of God (Name)[61] is baptized in the name of the Father, Amen; and of the Son, Amen; and of the Holy Spirit, Amen.' Each time the name of one of the Divine Trinity is mentioned, the candidate is laid under the waters and brought up high again. If it is a baby the child is immersed feet first, until its head is also washed, and then lifted up.[62] If it is an adult, he or she is usually laid backwards under the surface and lifted up. In antiquity the candidates would enter the water naked. Women faithful would be escorted and assisted by deaconesses, men by male deacons. In present-day practice male or female sponsors will help adults who are being baptized, but some form of 'shift' is usually worn out of modesty. Babies alone continue boldly, in the ancient manner, like a new Adam or Eve. Three times the name of God is invoked over the candidates, three times they are immersed and raised up. The newly baptized comes out from the waters to put on a radiant white robe,[63] and Psalm 31 is sung by the choir.

The mystery of chrismation

After the immersion, the newly baptized stands in the middle of the church in white robes, with bare feet, as the service moves on to a focus on the royal and priestly dignity[64] that has been conferred on the New Creature. Sacred chrism is used to anoint the gateways of the human senses with the mark of the Cross: the forehead, the eyes, the nostrils, the lips, the ears, the breast, the hands back and front, and the feet. Chrism (*myron*) is regarded as a most sacred element in the Orthodox Church. It is made only on solemn occasions by the most senior of all the bishops of each region,[65] who invoke the blessing and power of the Holy Spirit upon this fragrant mixture of oil and balsamic myrrh. It endures in the church in similar ways to its typological usage in the Old Testament: as a sign of the conferral of particularly powerful charisms and spiritual gifts.[66] The consecration of the chrism is reserved for bishops, as the successors of the apostles. Just as the apostles once passed on the gift of the Holy Spirit by the 'laying on of hands'[67] so their successors today reserve the apostolic privilege of consecrating the chrism, through which (by the laying on of hands of the present-day bishop or priest) the same gift is conferred. In the ancient church the gift of baptism and chrismation was an act reserved for the bishop alone. Later centuries saw the administration of this sacrament also passing to the presbyters, in ways similar to the manner in which the presbyters (as Christianity greatly expanded) also assumed the presidency of the eucharistic celebration in parish churches. The strict reservation of the making of the chrism,[68] which is then given by the presiding bishop to all his presbyters, is an enduring sign of the ancient baptismal practice. The sacred chrism is kept in special vessels in each parish, within the holy altar, for use primarily within the initiation mysteries.[69]

At each anointing of the baptized person the priest says: 'The seal of the gift of the Holy Spirit.' The gift of the Spirit of God, given in this sacred moment, is not understood, therefore, to be a passing charism, or an occasional assistance (as is the case with many graces from the Lord for the varied opportunities or temptations of our lives as disciples). This consecration is a fundamental reorientation; an abiding consecration that is 'sealed' into our flesh and soul, and our spirit's very structure, by the sacred chrism. It cannot be lost. It cannot be damaged in its core except by the deliberate renunciation of the faith which is apostasy, whose seriousness is so great it should not be confused with careless lapses from the practice of the faith that can occur in the course of a lifetime and can be dealt with by the mystery of confession. In this case it is often thought that the reconciliation of such an apostate believer needs to be prepared through another chrismation. Baptism itself can never be repeated.[70] The anointing with the sacred chrism is the gift of grace that initiates the kingly, prophetic, and priestly charism of the individual Christian's knowledge of God. It is this knowledge of the now indwelling presence which the apostle speaks about: 'I write this to you about those who would deceive you; yet the anointing which you received from him abides in you, and you have no need that any one should teach you, since his anointing teaches you about everything, and is true, and is no lie, just as it has taught you to abide in him.'[71]

The royal and priestly charism shared by all the faithful after chrismation demands its exercise in all members of Christ's Church, not merely those who have been called through the mystery of ordination to a more explicit priestly office. This priestly work which is at the heart of the church's vitality in the world is, in essence, the transfiguration of the material cosmos by the introduction into time and space of spiritual consciousness. This metamorphosis is also the priestly activity of angels; but it falls to human beings particularly, the median species whose constitution is the mixture of materiality and spirit, to perform the priestly office of the consecration of matter within the material universe. Such a metamorphosis is accomplished through the power of love, and the conscious consecration of all human vitality and communion to the glory of God. When all will be subject to the glory of God, and when the will of God is 'done on earth as it is in heaven'[72] then the Kingdom will have been consummated on earth. Until then, the church labours to be faithful and each of the baptized, within his or her communion, and through the individual character of each one's vocational path, moves on the pilgrimage road to the Kingdom by their own priestly ministries, consecrating matter as they move from the forms and limits of the old Adamic life into the new attitudes, potentialities, and practices of God's children.

Love and justice are the primary signs of this priestly work. When they are introduced into the social and political equation, all is transformed. After baptism, the Christian cannot, therefore, 'see' anything that remains secular or irrelevant to the life of discipleship. All has been utterly changed. The vision of the world that formerly had been in place is now wholly subjected to the will of God. After the initiation given to the eyes of the soul by the chrismation, the illumined Christian is no longer able to pretend ignorance that all humanity calls out for mercy and compassion. They understand that from that moment a life of merciful compassion, as detailed in the evangelical teachings of Jesus, is the expected master-plan of the rest of a disciple's career. Much effort, and energy, and interest is expended by most of us in the prosecution of our ordinary careers. The care for the development of the priestly vocation that is committed to all the faithful in chrismation is something that is far more important, and requires an even higher level of energy and commitment. It is the vocation of vocations. This is the knowledge of God communicated to believers to make them prophets and priests after the chrismation. This knowledge could be described as a 'new instinct' for the will of God among us. It is a spiritual capacity for insight into the Scriptures, and into the very syntax of prayer, that must now be carefully nurtured (or developed in an infant by Christian parents who have already experienced it). If this freshness of vision, this miraculous capacity to transfigure the world around us, is obscured or dimmed by our later meanderings away from fidelity to God, it can only be rediscovered with labour, through repentance, and fasting, and prayer.

The newly illumined believer is led around the font three times by the priest[73] while the choir sings the *troparion* hymn, 'As many as have been baptized into Christ, have put on Christ, Alleluia.'[74] The words of the apostle[75] are spoken by the priest to the newly chrismated believer: 'You have been washed, you have been sanctified, you have been illuminated'.[76] The newly baptized has been justified in the name of the Lord and by the Spirit of God.[77] Buried in the waters of a death to the old Adam, they have risen out of the water-grave into the new life of the Risen Master, and now inhale and exhale not merely by material means but by the *pneuma*,[78] or breath, of the Divine Spirit which was the inspiration of the Lord himself. This union of baptism and chrismation fulfils the command of the Lord to be 'baptized with water and the Holy Spirit'.[79] This intimacy of the synergy of breathing in the very *pneuma* of God is an awesome thing. The new Christian is set upon the road to the Kingdom, and must demonstrate in the fabric of his or her life, whether that baptismal synergy has become even closer as life progresses through the fires and trials of the faithful disciple,[80] or whether love is destined 'to grow cold',[81] and the awesome gift neglected.

287

The newly baptized will finally be led to listen to the scriptural readings, and towards the end of the ceremony will have part of their hair cut off, in the shape of a cross. This is the 'tonsuring', an act that will happen again if they are initiated into the minor orders. The tonsure is a symbol of the dedication, the fulfilment of the vow of allegiance the new Christian has made to God in the sight of their fellow Christians. The baptismal mysteries will finally be brought to their mystical completion by the reception of the Holy Eucharist. In this act the person is fully initiated into the mystical communion of the church. In a mystical type, and thus in a spiritual reality that has been deeply imprinted onto the very form of their souls, the new disciples have passed through the experience of the Passion and death, and risen with Christ out of the grave, so as to stand with him in the eschatological life of the transfigured saint. All of the rest of the Christian life is a working out of this seed, this kernel experience. These initiatory mysteries are the condensed pattern and gift of God's gift of deification by communion (*metousia Theou*). To this gift of new life is now added the invitation 'to live': to actually unfold the gift of the Lord's presence in the uniquely different ways that all of Christ's elect are called to manifest in their own world era, and by their own specific talents and powers of love. The bond with the Beloved is forged, and from this moment on all other love, all achievement, all other communion and aspiration are mediated, refracted, and perfected through this fundamental mystery of grace.[82] It is as the prophet Joshua said: 'But as for me, and my house, we will serve the Lord.'[83]

The mystical supper: communion in the Holy Eucharist

If baptism and chrismation are the mystical synopses of the whole pattern of the Lord's economy of salvation, by means of which his church is brought in to the shared experience of his saving death and resurrection, and in to the pentecostal gift of his most Holy Spirit, then the Eucharist is the mystical drama of that salvation given to us, as a renewable feast, in a great spirit of joy. The celebration of the Eucharist in the churches is the repeated entrance into the one great act of Christ's self-sacrifice in his Passion. It is not the death and resurrection of the Lord happening time after time (for this mystery was once and for all and cannot ever be repeated[84]); rather, it is the recurring admission of time-bound creatures into the once-for-allness of the supreme eschatological mystery of the Lord's redemption. The church experiences the Eucharist, therefore, as truly the sacrifice of the Lord's body and blood, his sacred and redeeming Passion. But it is a joyful experience; for this death and sacrifice are at one and the same moment the glorious Resurrection, and the effusion of the light and energy of the Resurrection on the worshipping church in the gift of the Spirit. Orthodoxy does not understand the Eucharist as sacrifice in quite the same way as the later Latin tradition, which developed a more lugubrious theology in which Christ was seen to be making atonement in some way to an angry God. These biblical images of the divine satisfaction had been, in the sentiment of the East, overly emphasized by some of Franco-Latin theology after Anselm, and led to a certain amount of distortion. In Orthodoxy, the sense of sacrifice is much as it was for the conception of the 'sacrifice of praise' in the Old Testament,[85] where the sacrificial cult was a much more joyous affair than most moderns can conceive it as being.[86]

The Orthodox Church believes that the Eucharist, while certainly being a sacrifice in the sense of the entrance of the church into the great sacrifice of praise that Christ offered to the Father from his obedience on the Cross,[87] is also a sacrifice to Christ, as well as to the Father and the Holy Spirit.[88] There is none of that sense of transactional sacrificial bargaining[89] left, only the joyful sense of rendering obedience and allegiance in love and in praise.[90] It has long been understood, and accepted, in the church, that the offering of this great 'sacrifice of praise' is for the physical support of the believers (the blessing of their homes and lives) not simply for spiritual benefit; and so those who are in need will often ask the priest to pray particularly for them. We can see this practice at work from ancient Christian times. This statement of the broader sacrificial theology of the Eucharist was one of the first things to be raised as a matter of 'difference' between the Latin and the Greek churches as they grew apart after the Great Schism. It can be seen, for example, in this excerpt from the Council of Constantinople in 1156:

> The life-giving sacrifice has never been offered only to the Father of the Only Begotten who is the Source of all things, neither when it was first offered by Christ the Saviour, nor at any subsequent time even to the present day. It has always been offered also to the Word, who became incarnate; and the Holy Spirit is not left out of so divine an honour. The oblation of the mysteries which is consecrated on each occasion by the power of the Trinity, has been made (and is still made) to the Godhead over all, in the Trinity of *Hypostases*, which is known to us as united and as one in the same nature, and as co-eternal.[91]

In the course of the liturgy, therefore, all the elements of the Lord's saving ministry are summed up, recapitulated, as it were, and re-experienced by his faithful throughout history. The eucharistic liturgy begins with prayers, moves on to the record of the earthly ministry through the reading of the Scriptures and the Gospel, recalls the high-priestly prayer of the Lord, and his Mystical Supper,[92] witnesses the descent of the Spirit, and shares the eucharistic gifts to the sound of hymns of the Resurrection. All the prayerful oblation of the church runs to the Father, but only with and through the Spirit, and with and in the Word who became flesh for this very purpose, to bring all the world back to the knowledge of the One God. This is why the ancient prayers are so fundamentally trinitarian in their structure and conception (something that is especially seen in the constantly reiterated trinitarian doxologies).

All the liturgy moves in a solemn unfurling that resists being split up into discrete divisions. All is a seamless union of parts.[93] The Passion is thus made one with the Resurrection and Ascension. At the Epiclesis the Supper of the Lord is mystically perceived as one with the descent of the Holy Spirit also; for in the Lord's economy of salvation there is neither disruption of chronological time nor separation of spatial dimension. This economy has the character of the Eschaton, but is fragmented by the lesser comprehension of creatures who are still temporally and spatially bound. The Person of the Saviour is the church's gate to the glory of the Father, but only through the spiritual deification conferred on his eucharistic community through the Holy Spirit. In fact, it is in the course of the liturgy that the church is most clearly revealed to be (and constituted as) the communion of praise that lives out of the doxology of its God, and finds within this glad thanksgiving (*eucharistia*) the power of its communion of love with one another,[94] and the source of its energy of compassion towards the world. Thus, every moment of the liturgy tends towards a holistic in-gathering of the church into the seamless unity of Christ's own person (his divine and human condition theandrically united), as well as the deepening unity of the Trinitarian oneness of hypostases, of which the church (as we have already noted) is also the living icon on earth.

All the prayer services of the Orthodox Church have an element within them that marks off time, tries to sanctify sections of time, as it were, to make the day conform more fully to the service of the Lord. Thus there are morning prayers, midday prayers, evening prayers, midnight offices, and so on. The mysteries, however, are not, in any sense, attempts at sanctifying the hours of the day. They stand outside, and over the normal course of, the unfolding of the hours. They are eschatological events, partly within time but predominantly beyond time. The Eucharist is a clear example of this. The ritual takes place within time, apparently. The church gathers, usually on a Sunday morning in the parishes (more frequently in the monasteries and cathedrals) and so the rite begins. But each of the Orthodox experiences it unfolding outside of time. It is supremely eschatological. As each parish celebrates the eucharistic liturgy, it is within the same mystical celebration of the same liturgy that took place in the upper room in Jerusalem when Jesus first presided; the same liturgy that took place in Emmaus when the bread was broken before the startled apostles; the same moment in trans-cendent time that saw the patristic liturgies taking place; the same moment that saw the angels joining in with the eucharistic descent of their Lord and trailing clouds of glory; the same moment that binds us, even now, in the banalities of our present time and era, with that self-same moment when the liturgy of Eucharist will be celebrated for the last time within earthly history by the last generation of the earthly saints, at the moment of the Eschaton, when the heavenly liturgy will begin in earnest with all the in-gathering of the total church.

What this means is hard to convey. But it is sensed in the strangely mystical elision of time that happens in the course of the Orthodox liturgy. In the act of praise, some-thing which is essential to the energy of doxology, and above all as this is found in its purest form within the moment of Eucharist, the believer enters the timeless domain of the angels, who as spiritual beings live out of praise as the ontological force of their immortal being. This is why there is only one moment, one *kairos* (or happening of grace), of the celebration of the Eucharist on earth, not many. It is an act that appears to be within time (and surely is so in the normal sense of the word) but is more truly an experience that has moved the believers outside time, into the continuous present, that dominion over time which the Lord's presidency over his church's worship effects and constitutes within history; thereby transcending it. To this extent, the generation of present believers is one with the generation of first believers. As we celebrate the Holy Eucharist early in the twenty-first century of the world's history, a door opens, in an upper room in an inn within a village called Emmaus. The one figure whom time itself serves, and runs backwards and forwards to venerate, stands among us, greeting each and every one of his congregation, as if for the first time, with all the freshness of the resurrectional joy about him. When the faithful receive the mysteries (a word which *par excellence* is used to refer to the gifts of the eucharistic bread and wine) they have entered beyond time and space into a communion with the Lord of history, one which is the prelude and prefigurement of their future union in Paradise.

The reception of the Eucharist is, therefore, one of the great religious events in the life of the Orthodox faithful. It may be something that happens many hundreds of times in the course of a life, but it is a single event into which one feels continually 'initiated', and the depths of which are continually extended, according to the development of the disciple's faith, so that even if one were to receive these gifts every day of one's life, for eight decades, one could not plumb it all. Orthodoxy understands the continual reception of the holy mysteries to be necessary for the normal growth of the sacred charisms that underpin maturity in discipleship.

Early in the second century St Ignatios of Antioch called the Eucharist the 'medicine of immortality' (*pharmakia tes athanasias*). St Cyril of Alexandria described how it was an encapsulation not only of the redemptive Passion and death of the Lord, but also of the manner in which his Incarnation had deified the human race.[95] For St Cyril, as the Incarnation transfigured human flesh with the presence of the indwelling deity, so the deifying gift of the Holy Eucharist utterly changes and transfigures the believer who receives it. It is not merely symbolic bread and wine that reminds us of the presence of the Lord. In the Orthodox Church it is recognized as that very presence in deed and in fact:[96] the glorified body of the Lord, in all his radiant resurrectional power and grace, given in supreme humility to his disciples in the nourishing form of the most homely of all expressions of utter intimacy: bread and wine. Orthodoxy thus believes directly and firmly in what the Catholic tradition has, in the West, called the 'Real Presence'. But it does not care to dwell much on the scholastic theories of 'transubstantiation'. While agreeing with the general point of transubstantiationism as a defence of the real presence of the Lord in the eucharistic mystery,[97] and the reality of the gifts as the true Body of Christ, Orthodoxy is not so sure that the medieval categories of accident and substance are very helpful in illuminating this sacred 'change'.[98] In fact it prefers simply to speak of the transformation as a change that is best left to be understood by the heart,[99] and which is effected by the word of the Lord and the power of the Holy Spirit.[100] It is also not very interested in the niceties of how the glorious body coinheres with the elements of bread and wine that remain, being content to speak of a synthetic union of natures, in which the real bread and wine are, nevertheless, in the Eucharist the Lord's own body in mystical form, just as Christ's own incarnate flesh on earth, was itself 'divine flesh' within the hypostatic union, albeit it remained fully, enduringly, and authentically human.[101]

Orthodoxy sees the Holy Eucharist as a sacrament of reconciliation and healing. Those who are sick are strongly encouraged to attend the Eucharist with greater regularity than before. This is offered by the church as the primary step towards healing, one to be taken even before thinking of calling in a doctor. For St Gregory of Nyssa, the Eucharist is a deifying drug: 'For so the immortal body, when it passes into us who receive it, changes the entire body into its own nature... It is not otherwise possible for our body to become immortal, except that it participates in immortality through that which is itself incorruptible.'[102] The Orthodox believe, and sense, that each reception of the holy mysteries takes them further into the mystery of the Christ-life, heals and deifies them, protects them and their homes from innumerable troubles.

The Holy Eucharist is preserved in all the Orthodox churches,[103] usually on the altar, or near the altar, in a special gilded vessel. In ancient times this vessel was often fashioned in the shape of a silver dove. The main purpose of the reservation

291

was to have the eucharistic gifts available for any of the sick or dying that required them in an emergency, so that the priest would be able to take them day or night. In ancient times the deacons are often recorded as having taken the gifts to the confessors in prison for the faith. In the Orthodox Church there is not the same baroque form of devotion to the Eucharist that one sees in Roman Catholicism's rite of benediction, or exposition of the Blessed Sacrament. The link between the Eucharist and the communal eating together of the people of God is more strictly observed in the Eastern tradition; but during the eucharistic liturgy itself, the holy mysteries are treated with extreme reverence, and worshipped for what they are, the presence of the Lord himself. After the words of institution in the divine liturgy, and after the prayer for the descent of the Holy Spirit upon the gifts, the clergy and faithful bow down in profound reverence (*proskynesis*), and they will equally make three reverences before receiving them. It is not an uncommon sight to see Orthodox laity on their way to the altar to receive the mysteries making full-length prostrations as they progress.

The mysteries are always received under both kinds. The clergy at the altar communicate first. If a bishop presides, all the other clergy receive directly from his hand. If only a priest and deacon celebrate, the priest communicates himself then gives the gifts to the deacon. Then the eucharistic bread is placed inside the chalice that contains the Precious Blood and is distributed to the community by a silver or golden spoon. If the Liturgy of St James is being celebrated, another ancient practice is sometimes observed of placing the eucharistic bread directly into the hands of the faithful, who then receive the chalice separately, from the deacon. In the normal method of communion by intinction, the reception of the Eucharist can be a substantial experience of eating, since leavened bread is always used in the Byzantine liturgy. Sweet wine is also preferred, in assonance with the psalm: 'Taste and see that the Lord is sweet.'[104] I myself remember one child of 2 years of age receiving, from my hands, the mixture of the Holy Eucharist and (in all innocence) closing his eyes and saying, 'Yummy!' It was not exactly the correct liturgical form, but it did express a very proper Christian, and prophetic, response. So one learns even from the mouths of babes.[105] Apart from being a supreme sign of the Lord's own humility (to choose bread and wine as the elements of his abiding presence to his church) the medium of food and drink for this mystical communion was also chosen for the connotation of festival that it intrinsically has (the wedding feast that symbolizes the advent of the Kingdom on earth, and the new wine that goes with it). It is also intrinsic to the sacramental form that the bread and wine should be shared from a single loaf and a common cup.

Those who eat from the same table cannot do so while sustaining resentments and old enmities (even basic human psychology militates against it). To take the gift of food stretched out from another hand necessitates we forgive the enemy and reconcile in the act of common eating. Such was also the Lord's intention in establishing this sacramental form and showing his own gift of communion as a primary act of reconciliation. The Eucharist is *par excellence* the sacrament of reconciliation and healing. In its power of restoration to communion (between God and mankind; and between men and women once divided among themselves), it shines out as the great eschatological sign of the 'Kingdom come'. Even a refusal to accept the hand of communion (witnessed in Judas' darkening of soul as he took the gifts) cannot withstand the energy for communion and reconciliation that shines out incessantly from this mystical gift. The death of the Lord, the symbol of the world's ultimate attempt to refuse reconciliation and peace, becomes subverted in the saving economy of the Passion. His blood is poured out, not fruitlessly, but for the forgiveness of sins. The chalice of suffering is filled to the brim, but it becomes the mystical wine of the new Kingdom, which the Lord will drink with his faithful in the joy of Paradise.

The liturgies used in the ancient church were originally varied and diverse, but slowly came to a standardized set of fewer forms as the local churches more and more adopted the rituals and practices that were in use among the greater metropolitan churches whose rites and ceremonies had become more universally known, and which generally excited admiration. So it was, for example, that ceremonies from the church of the Anastasis[106] in Jerusalem, and the various forms of ritual observed there, always had a very wide circulation among all the churches of the Christian world from an early time. The church of Rome used a vernacular Greek[107] liturgy in its first 400 years of life, only adopting a Latin-language liturgy in the time of Pope Damasus. Its practices, as the leading Christian city of the Latin-speaking world, then eventually displaced several other rival rites[108] to become a common and very widely diffused liturgical inheritance in the West. In the Eastern, Greek-speaking, provinces of the early church, the ritual forms of the Antiochene, Syriac-speaking churches were very influential. The Byzantine rite is, at its heart, a form of the west Syrian liturgy.[109] It has, therefore, a close relation to the Aramaic churches that still remembered the original language of the Lord himself. But by the later fourth century the new capital of the Christian Roman empire at Constantinople had begun to serve as a central vortex, influencing all the other Greek Christian sees in its large ambit, and it spread out among them the Syro-Byzantine rite as a common syntax of international liturgy in the Eastern Christian world.

St John Chrysostom, the archbishop of Constantinople at the very end of the fourth century, arranged slight changes to the prayers comprising the liturgy, and since his time the whole liturgical rite of Byzantium has been commonly attributed to him as its author. He thus became the symbolic 'father' of all the liturgy which had existed (long) before his time, and would adapt after his time.[110] He was not the sole author and originator of the liturgy that bears his name; the true story was one of more complex change and absorption of different liturgical 'families' and customs that tended, as the centuries moved on, towards greater conformity of types in the East, rather than to greater diversity. The Byzantine liturgical rite did not assume its general (and more or less contemporary) shape until after the ninth century, but it has its roots in very ancient soil, with a direct continuity, of course, back to the Lord's own Mystical Supper, and his own command to 'Do this in memory of me.' The final shaping of the Byzantine liturgical rite was the result of several changes in the make up of the Eastern Christian world as it was facing the expanse of Islamic power. After Islam had cut off Palestine from ready communication with the other parts of the Roman Christian world, Mar Saba monastery, near Bethlehem, started to excel as an important centre of monastic liturgical life and development. This, the so-called monastic ritual of the Eastern Church, laid out patterns of prayer services, monastic offices, and so on, that were heavily scriptural in form. The prayers of the desert ascetics were rooted in the Scriptures, and the recitation of the Psalter played a large part in them. Jerusalem liturgical traditions were also predominant, of course. The general character of these monastically designed services was significantly penitential in tone. The services were often long, meant in some cases to last the whole night through, and were very sober in tone and style. The churches of the desert monks were usually very small and poor buildings, designed for the use of single-sex communities of ascetics, devoted to the word of God in a common life of great simplicity and focus.

In the capital city, however, the liturgy was designed to revolve around the state buildings. It was a liturgical style that was built around many state processions, in which the emperor and patriarch played central parts with all their magnificent retinue of attendant clergy, and aristocrats. There were numerous stational liturgies (visits to significant city churches, and holy shrines where relics were kept, each with their own local traditions). In the capital the very liturgical architecture played a significant part too. Justinian's magnificent church of Hagia Sophia[111] was a stage for awe-inspiring ceremonial, far removed from the tiny intimacy of the monastic chapels of the provinces. Professional choirs were brought together, employing some of the finest singers in the known world, and putting to work some of the most famous poets and hymn-writers of the era, who composed extensive paraphrastic songs (*kontakia*, *troparia*, canons), based on the scriptural narratives, but full of detail and rhetorical coloration. Accordingly two types of ritual style grew up in the Eastern Church of the Byzantine era, known now as the monastic and the cathedral *typika*. The liturgical process in general use, after the ninth century, was a form of synthesis of these two types. The different characters can now be seen juxtaposed in Orthodox liturgy, which is a rich weave of Syrian, Palestinian, imperial Greek, and monastic observances. It can be seen in the standard Liturgy of St John Chrysostom: a splendid ceremonial sense of style, allied with a very sober use of a scriptural skeleton of supporting prayers, as it were, and profound patristic theological invocations shaped around the ancient liturgical kernel of the reading of the Word of God, followed by the celebration of thanksgiving for God's wonderful creation, and redemption, as culminating in the Lord's gift of himself for his church.

The monastic style is predominant in the services of the offices of the hours, as might be expected. In the celebration of the mysteries, however, and in the public services of blessing, and the observance of the feasts, especially Pascha, there is a sense of restrained magnificence and awesome ceremony. Even the humblest of parish churches in the poorest of areas glimmers with lights and incense, and the twinkle of golden vestments, and church vessels wrapped in precious cloths, and a sea of candles burning around the icons and altar. The fine synthesis of the sober monastic style of *typikon* together with the ceremony inherent in the cathedral rite gives the Orthodox liturgy a distinct flavour. At first it might appear to someone who is not familiar with it perhaps even unapproachable or forbidding (especially if it is being celebrated in a language one does not know, such as Greek, or Slavonic, or Romanian), but a closer familiarity, such as the Orthodox themselves develop over many years of attending church services, leads one to a deep level of 'belonging' to the rhythms and nuances contained in this most rich of all languages. The ceremonies themselves are profoundly biblical in form and content, and the incessant use of Scripture and intercession makes for a seamless weave between the activity of the clergy and the prayers and chanting of the people, something that is true even when a permanent choir is used to lead the people's prayers.

Today there are four liturgies still serving as the common forms of Orthodox ritual. The first is the Divine Liturgy of St John Chrysostom, which is the commonly used rite, on Sundays and weekdays. The Liturgy of St Basil the Great is also used ten times in the course of the church's year, mainly during the course of Great Lent. It is a more sober liturgy, with much-extended prayers. Most of the different elements of the service, however, are in those parts which the priest often says quietly behind the icon screen, and so most of the faithful would not normally recognize much difference between the two liturgies. In those places where the Anaphora is said aloud, however, there would be a significant difference observable in the great prayer of thanksgiving. The Liturgy of St James, the brother of the Lord, was once the standard eucharistic *typikon* of the Church of Jerusalem. Formerly it was used only there and on the Greek island of Zante. Nowadays it has witnessed a revival among more Orthodox churches. It is used once a year on St James' feast day, 23 October. The fourth is known as the Liturgy of the Pre-sanctified Gifts of St Gregory the Dialogist.[112] This is strictly speaking a liturgical service of Holy Communion, with several elements of vesperal evening prayer, but without the consecration of the mysteries. The gifts that are received, therefore, are consecrated on the previous Sunday's Lenten Liturgy of St Basil, for use in the presanctified liturgy of the weekdays following. The presanctified liturgy is used on the Wednesdays and Fridays of Great Lent, and on the first three days of Great Week, leading up to Pascha.

The structure of the Orthodox liturgy follows the ancient pattern of the early Jewish-Christian communities, which used the forms of the synagogue meeting: reading and reflecting upon the Word of God and then giving God blessings (*berakha*) for his salvific care for his chosen people. From the very beginning, this reading of the Word was conducted in the light of the great covenant-making they knew that God had contracted with them as the New People, in the mystery of the Lord's Passion, death, and resurrection. This is one of the reasons that the Passion account of the Gospels was among the first long, through-written narratives of the evangelical story.[113] From earliest times also, the Passion story was read in the light of the New Passover of the Lord.[114] Jesus' gift of the Eucharist to his church was the covenantal moment in which the scriptural types of Passover and Liberation reached their consummation. This is why, for example, the liturgy of the Word takes place on the road to Emmaus, when Jesus explains all the passages in Scripture that refer to his New Covenant, and why the veil is lifted from their eyes only as the Eucharist is given to them, and they realize his meaning retrospectively from the 'burning' of their hearts.[115] To this day the liturgy of the Word, the service of Scripture readings and reflection (including the homily which ought to be a 'breaking of the word of Scripture' to the people[116]), takes place as the prelude, preparation for, and commentary on the eucharistic celebration which follows after it.

The liturgy thus falls into two major parts: liturgy of the Word, and liturgy of the Eucharist (Synaxis and Anaphora), each being a commentary upon the other. In the earliest times of the church the Synaxis was a separate service to the eucharistic rite, but from the fourth century onwards they have been fused together. The climacteric part of the Synaxis is always the chanting of the Holy Gospel by the deacon or priest. Similarly the climacteric of the Anaphora is the consecration of the mysteries, as summed up in the Epiclesis.[117] It is not possible, however, to single out the 'single significant moment': the whole structure of both the Synaxis and Anaphora is clearly designed to be an ongoing seamless doxology of consecration and thanksgiving. In Orthodoxy there is not the sense, as in parts of Western Catholic theology, that it is the priest's enunciation of the words of institution which effect the consecration at that moment. The Orthodox Church has always insisted that, whatever grace the mystery of ordination confers on the priest, it is not he who consecrates the mysteries, but God himself.[118] In later times this simplicity of arrangement into these two fundamental parts was extended into five sections. Two preliminary, and preparatory, rituals were added to the beginning of the liturgy of the Word, namely the Proskomide (or Prothesis[119]) rite and the Enarxis rite. And then a short ritual of thanksgiving and dismissal was added on to the end of the eucharistic prayer. This gave the eucharistic service its complete, and present-day, form as outlined below.

The eucharistic liturgy

1   Proskomide (or Prothesis: The Offering)

A beautiful preparatory ritual usually quietly performed by the clergy behind the icon screen, preparing the bread and wine for use in the Eucharist. The 'Lamb' (the portion of bread that will be consecrated) is cut from the loaves brought for the day, and numerous prayers are offered to commemorate the Blessed Virgin, the angels, and great saints. Commemorations are also made, by name, of the living and dead whom the parish wishes to pray for. Particles of bread (not to be consecrated) representing the Virgin and the 'nine ranks' of saints are laid alongside the Lamb on the *diskos* to symbolize the gathering of the church around its Lord. Particles are left beside the Lamb also for the names of each of the living and dead who are read out in the diptychs.[120] It is felt, in a concrete way, that these particles mystically symbolize the gathering of all the souls of the living and dead around the throne of the glorious Christ. The Proskomide concludes with the incensing of the prepared gifts, which are laid on a side altar, and with the preparatory incensing of the whole church building (usually referred to as the 'temple').[121]

2   Synaxis (The Gathering)

(a)   Enarxis (The Opening)
  Priestly 'Blessing of the Kingdom'[122]
  Litany of peace
  Antiphon 1 (Ps. 102)
  Little Litany
  Antiphon 2 (Ps. 145, and the hymn 'Only Begotten Son')
  Little Litany
  Antiphon 3 (usually the Beatitudes, with Troparia, i.e. hymns)

(b)   The Little Entrance (in ancient times the beginning of the service, with clergy processing into the church with the book of Gospels)
  Introit (the entrance hymn of the day)
  Trisagion hymn ('Holy God, Holy Mighty, Holy Immortal have mercy on us', sung to a solemn melody)

(c)   Scriptural readings
  Prokeimenon (antiphonal singing of psalm verses)
  The Apostle (readings from the Acts of the Apostles, or an Epistle)
  Alleluia (singing of the Alleluia refrain with intercalated scriptural verses)
  The Gospel (sung by the clergy)
  The homily (often erroneously dislocated to the end of the service[123] or (worse) given as the prelude to communion)

(d) Great Litanies of Intercession (not all of them always said audibly)
      Litany of Fervent Supplication
      Litany for the Departed
      Litany of the Catechumens (and dismissal of catechumens)

3   The Holy Eucharist (The Thanksgiving)

(a) Two Litanies of the Faithful

(b) The Great Entrance. (Solemn processional entrance of the clergy carrying the gifts in the chalice (*poterion*) and paten (*diskos*) which are about to be consecrated, so as to lay them upon the altar in readiness for the great eucharistic prayer. In ancient times this was the 'bringing in' of the gifts to offer from another, and separate, building into the main church. On the way to the church where the faithful were gathered, the penitents would formerly congregate in the city streets, or the *narthex*, to kiss the clergy's vestments, and the cloths surrounding the vessels, because they were debarred from attendance at the Eucharist itself. Nowadays the gifts are usually brought only from the side altar, out through the iconostasis, and back through the royal doors, to be laid on the Holy Table. The choir meanwhile sings the Cherubikon hymn.

(c) Litany of Supplication

(d) The Kiss of Peace (now normally exchanged only among the concelebrating clergy, but once a general act of reconciliation among the congregation)

(e) The common recitation of the Nicene–Constantinopolitan Creed

(f) The Anaphora (the great eucharistic prayer, or Holy Oblation). Its elements are:

    (i)   Call to give thanks

    (ii)   Great Prayer of Thanksgiving for God's saving work. Narrative of the Mystical Supper and Jesus' Words of Institution

    (iii)   The prayer of Anamnesis ('calling to mind' the great victories of Christ's economy of Passion and Resurrection, the priest holds the gifts on high and offers them to God on behalf of all)

    (iv)   The Epiclesis (in a most solemn prayer the priest prays for the descent of the Holy Spirit upon the gifts to consecrate them as the Body and Blood of the Lord)

    (v)   The Great Commemoration of the Saints (all the church is prayed for, past and present, beginning with the patriarchs and prophets, and culminating with the Blessed Virgin the apostles, and evangelists; then prayer is made for all the living and dead)

(g) Litany of Supplication and the Lord's Prayer

(h) The Elevation of the Mysteries, and the Fraction (division) of the Lamb

(j) The communion of the clergy and people

4   Apolysis (Dismissal)

(a) Communion hymns and short service of dismissal, thanksgiving, and final blessing

(b) Distribution of the *antidoron* (meaning 'instead of the gifts': the remainder of the loaves of offering which were not consecrated during the liturgy – as a sign of eucharistic fellowship and *agapé*)

The eucharistic liturgies of the Orthodox Church contain a wealth of the most profound prayers, hymns, and intercessions, and are universally regarded by believers as a major deposit of the highest level of theological wisdom that the Orthodox Church possesses. They came to their literary maturity in a time of high patristic inspiration, and they bear a character of venerable profundity, steeped in a rich conception of prayer as a trinitarian mystery which the entire church (heavenly and earthly) concelebrates as a foretaste of the Kingdom's arrival. The old rule of *Lex orandi lex credendi* (the pattern of worship reveals the essence of the church's faith) is nowhere seen as more aptly true than here. It is not possible to give more than a brief flavour of some of these prayers which carry and reveal the church's conception of what the Eucharist means.

At one moment when the Cherubikon hymn is being sung to a slow and solemn melody, the priest prepares himself to commence the eucharistic prayer proper, and so bends down over the altar and says this prayer quietly:

None of those who are entangled in carnal desires and pleasures is worthy to approach you, or draw near to you, or serve you, O King of Glory; for to serve you is a great and awesome thing, even for the heavenly powers. Nevertheless, on account of your inexpressible and measureless love for mankind, you became man without change or alteration, and were named our High Priest; and as Master of All you have committed to us the sacred ministry of this liturgical and bloodless sacrifice. You alone, O Lord our God, are ruler of all things in heaven and on earth: enthroned upon the Cherubim, Lord of the Seraphim, and King of Israel, the Only Holy One who rests in the holy place. And so I entreat you, who alone are good and ready to listen: look upon me your sinful and unprofitable servant, and purify my soul and heart from an evil conscience. By the power of your Holy Spirit enable me, who am vested with the grace of the priesthood, to stand at this your Holy Table and celebrate the mystery of your holy and most pure Body and your Precious Blood. For I come before you, bending my neck and saying: Do not turn your face away from me, do not reject me from among your children; rather count me, your sinful and unworthy servant, worthy to offer these gifts to you. For it is you who are the one who offers, and is offered; who receives and is distributed, Christ our God, and to you we give glory, together with your Father, who is without beginning, and your all-holy, good, and life-giving Spirit; now and ever, and to the ages of ages. Amen.[124]

The heart of the Anaphora is contained in the following long prayer that unfolds from the Preface to the Trisagion, to the Epiclesis after the words of institution. It reads as follows:

Let us give thanks to the Lord... It is fitting and right to hymn you, to bless you, to praise you, to give you thanks, to worship you in every place of your dominion, for you are God, ineffable, incomprehensible, invisible, inconceivable, ever-existing, ever the same; you and your only begotten Son and your Holy Spirit. You it was who brought us from non-existence into being, and even after we had fallen, you raised us up once more and left nothing undone until you had led us back to heaven and granted us your Kingdom which is to come. For all these things we give you thanks, and to your only begotten Son, and to your Holy Spirit; for all the gifts that we have received, whether known or unknown, whether manifest or secret. We thank you also for this liturgy which you have been pleased to accept from our hands even though there stand around you thousands of Archangels, tens of thousands of Angels: the Cherubim and the Seraphim, six winged, many-eyed, who soar aloft upon their pinions singing the triumphant hymn, shouting, proclaiming, and saying:

[*Choir*] Holy, Holy, Holy, Lord of Hosts, Heaven and Earth are full of your glory. Hosannah in the highest. Blessed is He who comes in the name of the Lord. Hosannah in the highest.

With these blessed powers Master and Lover of Mankind, we also cry aloud and say holy are you, all holy, you and your only begotten Son and your Holy Spirit. Holy are you, and all holy, and magnificent is your glory. You so loved your world that you gave your only begotten Son, that whoever believes in him might not perish, but have eternal life. And when he had come and had fulfilled all the dispensation for us, on that night in which he was given up, or rather gave himself up, for the life of the world, he took bread in his holy, most pure, and blameless hands and, when he had given thanks, and blessed it, and sanctified it, and broken it, he gave it to his holy disciples and apostles saying: 'Take, eat, this is my body, which is broken for you, for the remission of sins.' Likewise, after supper he also took the cup saying: 'Drink of this all of you. This is my blood of the New Covenant, which is shed for you and for many, for the remission of sins.'

And so, remembering this saving commandment, and all those things which have come to pass for us; the Cross, the Tomb, the Resurrection on the third day, the Ascension into heaven, the Sitting at the Right Hand, and the Second and Glorious Coming, [*elevating the gifts over the altar*] we offer you your own of your own, on behalf of all, and for all.

Again we offer to you this spiritual and bloodless worship, and we ask, and pray, and supplicate you: send down your Holy Spirit upon us and upon these gifts here offered ✠ and make this bread the precious Body of your Christ. [Amen]. ✠ And that which is in this cup, the Precious Blood of your Christ. [Amen].

✠ ✠ ✠ Making the change by your Holy Spirit, that they may be, for those who partake of them, for the purification of soul, for the remission of sins, for the communion of your Holy Spirit and the fulfilment of the Kingdom of Heaven, for boldness towards you, and not for condemnation.

Again we offer you this rational worship for those who have fallen asleep in the faith: ancestors, fathers, patriarchs, prophets, apostles, teachers, evangelists, martyrs, confessors, ascetics, and every righteous spirit made perfect in faith; [*the sacred gifts are incensed*] especially for our most holy, most pure, most blessed and glorious Lady Theotokos and Ever-Virgin Mary. [*The Anaphora continues with the commemorations of all the living and the dead*][125]

One of the short prayers said together by priest and people just before the congregation communicates recalls the ancient discipline of the *arcana*, when the mysteries were kept secret from the uninitiated:

Of your Mystical Supper, O Son of God, accept me today as a communicant; for I will not speak of your mysteries to your enemies; nor like Judas will I give you a kiss; but like the thief will I confess you: Remember me O Lord in your Kingdom.[126]

Before the priest calls the faithful to the altar to receive from the chalice, he breaks up the leavened bread, which has now been consecrated, into four parts,[127] according to the way the Lamb has been stamped in the baking process with the letters IC XC NIKA, signifying: 'Jesus Christ has the Victory'. The quadrant marked for Jesus (IC) is placed into the chalice with the Precious Blood with the quiet prayer: 'The fullness of the Holy Spirit'. That marked 'Christ' (XC) is retained for the communion of the clergy, and the remaining two halves (of NI-KA) are reserved for the communion of the laity. Hot water is added to the chalice with the prayer: 'The warmth of faith, full of the Holy Spirit.' The hot water (*zeon*) typifies the energy and fervour of the Holy Spirit within the sacred mysteries.[128] After the clergy have communicated, the particles for the laity are added into the chalice and the priest stands in front of the royal doors issuing the invitation to all those who are prepared: 'With the fear of God, with Faith, and with Love, draw near!' As each communicant draws near they cross their hands over their heart and receive the mysteries under two forms from the spoon[129] held by the priest, who says: 'The Servant of God [*Name*] receives the Precious Body and Blood of our Lord and God and Saviour, Jesus Christ, for the remission of sins, and for the everlasting life.' After communion those who have taken the mysteries give thanks to God and eat some blessed bread that is kept to the side for them, along with some sweet wine to break their fast.[130] After the final prayers and blessings are given, the faithful line up to receive the *antidoron*, or the blessed bread of fellowship,[131] and to kiss the cross held for them by the priest. Most will make a tour of the church at this time, kissing the main icons on the iconostasis, kissing the Cross, and the priest's hands (in so far as he has been the minister of the mysteries of God). Those who have communicated, however, kiss neither icon nor minister that day. They have within them the King of Kings, and will usually receive (and give) congratulations for their glorification after they have taken the mysteries, while the choir are still singing the post-communion hymn around them:

> We have seen the true light.
> We have received the heavenly Spirit.
> We have found the true faith
> In worshipping the undivided Trinity,
> For the Trinity has saved us.[132]

The mystery of *metanoia*

The church is the community of the saints, the holy elect of God. It is also a community of Christians who manifestly fall away from their evangelical calling on a daily basis. One 'ought' to be able to enter any Orthodox church in the world and find a loving and compassionate family, radiant in the graces of Christ. Such is our aspiration, of course, but the reality can differ, perhaps too often, and this itself is a great paradoxical mystery: how the redeemed elect can still shrink back from their baptismal glory. Once, in that total commitment and consecration of the self to God in the baptismal promises to renounce Satan and all his works, the whole person was received and dedicated. The week following baptism[133] was called 'Bright Week', not only from the radiance of the white robes of the newly baptized, but in reference to the spiritual radiance of these new creatures of Christ. Sin, and spiritual coldness in a lesser degree, is an incomprehensibility in the eyes of God, for it is a fading away into nothingness ontologically speaking. Even minor sins are a sickness of non-being that calls the Christian away from the fullness of life in Christ. Such is the strange paradox of post-baptismal sin. And yet, the fact that this paradox still cannot defile the purity of the church as Christ's own body is seen also in the manner in which the sickness can be reversed and healed in the Christian community.

The early church too could not understand this aspect of the defection of the believers. Nevertheless, it struck them with great force in the age of the early persecutions. We today often think of the age of the martyrs as a time of great courage and purity of faith, and so it was; but for the bishops of the third century it also caused momentous problems of understanding the nature of the church as they also saw many 'respectable' believers lapsing from the faith in spectacular ways, even preferring to offer incense and animal sacrifices to the pagan gods, or to the genius of the persecuting emperor, rather than risk their lives or property. One of the first reactions to post-baptismal sin within the community at large, and it can be seen very clearly in Tertullian[134] and later in the Novatianist and Donatist schisms, was to cling rigorously to the theological truth of the church as the body of the pure elect of Christ. From this it was a short step to conclude that sinners in the Christian assembly could not really be Christians at all. Accordingly, if someone lapsed dramatically from their baptismal commitment (the three 'unforgivable' sins of murder, adultery, and apostasy were generally cited as examples of moral lapse from which there was no return to the communion of the church) they were regarded as having ceased to be Christians, root and branch. They were left to God's judgement, but were no longer admitted into Christian fellowship. This position, however, soon struck the Christian majority as being only partly consistent with the concept of the church as the immaculate Bride of Christ, and not even the best way to express the church's purity. For was it not true that the purest of all, the Lord himself, went out of his way to meet with sinners, to comfort them, to reconcile them, not to consign them to the wilderness of anathematization? Was it not true that the great Peter himself, the symbol of the faithful disciple, had apostatized disastrously yet had still been restored by the Lord, and set up once more as the leader of the apostolic band?[135] Was it not true that Jesus' whole ministry of salvation had been summed up as the quest to seek out and bring back what had been lost and wandering?[136] And if so, was it not true that the church's purity was best expressed in the manner in which it was capable of ministering the grace of reconciliation? Its innate power of purity was not to be abandoned so easily on account of the moral lapses of believers among it. This indefectible purity was an article of faith,[137] a theological commitment to the assurance that Christ's reconciling grace would never fail to spring up within his church, so as to keep it immaculate as his chosen bride.

Deeper reflection on the mystery of forgiveness among the elect supplied the understanding that the gift of reconciliation could be administered among itself in a continuing way as part of the gift of apostolic charism. And so the promise of the Lord came more and more to be understood to refer to the mystery of repentance: 'Jesus said to them again, Peace be with you. As the Father has sent me, even so I send you. And when he had said this, he breathed on them, and said to them, Receive the Holy Spirit. If you forgive the sins of any, they are forgiven; if you retain the sins of any, they are retained.'[138] This power of 'judgement',[139] in a sense an anticipation of the great

Judgement of the Lord,[140] was thus conferred among the apostles, and their successors the bishops.

If the earliest ecclesiastical policy of admitting no post-baptismal repentance of the most serious sins[141] served to express the church's deep sense of its necessary purity, the refusal to deal with sinners in the assembly seemed to compromise that purity, not enhance it; to compromise it by not being faithful to the law of Jesus himself, who had configured his church as a communion of the reconciled and the forgiven.[142] And so, by the early third century (and hastened onwards by the problem of those who had lapsed in the times of persecution), the church's leaders instituted a system of public penance.[143] The bishops at large, and despite many protest voices that they had opened the doors to laxity, began to exercise their apostolic charism to dispense this mystery of repentance.[144] From the beginning, the presbyters were involved alongside the bishop who presided over this system, but soon the presbyters came to be the normal ministers of the mystery in the times when the presbytery was divided out into many distinct parishes within a larger diocese. Priests, then, as well as the bishops, celebrate this mystery by virtue of their ordination in the apostolic succession. It has never been a charism expressed by the deacons or monastics, though at one time in the early church it was widely believed that surviving martyrs (or confessors who had been imprisoned or tortured for the faith) might have this charism.[145]

The first manifestation of the church's public system of penance may seem immensely rigorous to us when we read its protocols today; but when it was first employed, in the large city churches of Alexandria and Rome, there were theologians who were appalled that 'standards' had fallen so low to as require an 'economy' such as this. Those who had lapsed from Christian morals in a public way[146] were required to adopt the lifestyle of a penitent. Of this there were several degrees.[147] The ancient churches generally had an outer and an inner porch (*exonarthex, narthex*) with doors that then led on into the main hall of assembly (the nave, or *naos*) where the Eucharist was celebrated. The penitents were instructed to confess their status as sinners[148] to the assembled presbyters of the church, in the sight of all, by asking on their knees for forgiveness. The bishop would bless them and send many of them off to pray thereafter in one of the church porches. This would apply for periods of many years, and in some cases for the rest of someone's life, and they would only receive the Eucharist again on their deathbed.[149] At the moment of the Anaphora, the doors would be shut upon them and upon the catechumens preparing for baptism: a sobering lesson for all concerned. When the period of penance for sins such as apostasy (twelve years' absence from the mysteries) had elapsed, the penitent was brought back into the body of the church and received a laying on of hands from the clergy, and was then restored to the eucharistic fellowship.

The system was so public and rigorous that the main body of the faithful soon began to react against it. By the middle of the fourth century this was very visible in the way that most Christian families would by choice defer baptism for themselves and their children until very late in life. They would, thus, spend most of their Christian vocation in the preliminary condition of catechumens and thus sat at one remove from the more rigorous rules that applied to communicating Christians. At birth they would be dedicated to Christ with the initial catechumenal rites of the signing with the cross, but would then leave it at that. Having never received baptism, of course, none of the other mysteries were available to them either. St Gregory the Theologian in the late fourth century found it necessary to give several homilies in Constantinople urging the faithful to come for baptism, and not spend most of their lives in this suspended status of the catechumen, which he recognized as having assumed the status of a corruption of church discipline.

So it was (and for good pastoral reasons) that the system of public penance became less rigorous in the church as time went on. At the very end of the fourth century Patriarch Nektarios of Constantinople abolished the ecclesiastical office of Grant Penitentiary, and after that point little more is heard of the ancient system, though it continued longer in the Western Church, whose penitential system remained more strict and possibly more 'penal' in character.[150] Another factor that greatly affected the system of penance in the East was the rise of the monastic movement after the fourth century. By the fifth century the ascetical practice of opening the heart to the monastic elder (*higoumenos, pneumatikos*) was established. This involved the younger monks, those who were still struggling with the new standards imposed on them by the radical life of monastic discipleship, opening up to their mentor all the thoughts of their hearts, in other words their secret desires and inmost attitudes. This total projection of the self to the scrutiny of another was part of the renunciation of the self that comprised the monastic life, and served to accelerate a form of 'death of the ego' and the birth of a new sense of openness to a different self, in which honesty before God was given paramount status. This practice of the 'confession of the heart' began to merge, in the wider church, with the ancient system of public penance and, as time passed, came to be more and more a synthesis of the older system of repentance, allied with the monastic practice of the scrutiny of the soul under the guidance of an elder.

There is a spiritual practice still continuing in Orthodoxy today where the faithful may, if they wish, speak out the secrets of their heart to a chosen elder, either male or female,[151] in a manner very similar to sacramental confession. This 'manifestation of thoughts' derives directly from the old monastic custom of the confession of the heart's secrets. The practice also continues extensively in the monastic life, but has now also spread to many devoted layfolk who follow the spiritual guidance of (mainly) monastic guides and mentors. If the elder is not ordained, however, although they will reassure their spiritual disciple about the problems they may have shared and discussed, the last word will be to send the person to the priest at church on the next convenient occasion to confess sacramentally and receive the Holy Eucharist afterwards. Many non-monastic clergy serve in the role of spiritual guides for their parishioners, but it is not exactly the same as this relationship of elder and disciple, and they ought not to be confused (although an elder does not have to be a monastic, simply a Christian who is deeply grounded in the Christian life, endowed with deep wisdom and insight into the advanced paths of the spiritual life, and called to this special ministry by signs from God). All the clergy who are ordained and have been blessed to hear confessions by the bishop are empowered to celebrate the mystery of *metanoia*, but that does not guarantee that all parish confessors can function well as spiritual elders. When the two charisms meet together in a bishop or priest it is a great blessing for the church, and there have been many famous confessors[152] in the Orthodox tradition who have been able to console and reconcile and assist many of the faithful through this ministry. St John of Kronstadt, the late nineteenth-century Russian parish priest, was one such, but happily there are many others still living today, known to their own spiritual children.

303

The sacramental mystery of penance,[153] however much it may owe to monastic practices, is ultimately related to the more fundamental question of the renewal of the baptismal consecration given by Christ as the energy of his own redemption of the world through the mystery of his saving economy, through his death and resurrection. Accordingly the mystery of penance is often called the 'second baptism', or the 'baptism of tears', to demonstrate this connection. The chief celebrant of the mystery is Christ himself, of course. It is not the bishop or priest who forgives anyone's sins, but the Lord himself who does so, in the form of the consoling word of the ordained minister who witnesses the confession of the truly repentant Christian.[154] Witness is a key factor in this mystery. The priest and the person wishing to confess will go apart in the church, usually at the front near the iconostasis, where a Cross and a book of the Gospels will be placed before an icon of the Lord. Both will stand together in front of the icon.[155] The priest will then recite a series of penitential prayers on behalf of the person, always including the Penitential Psalm[156] and culminating in the 'Prayer of Manasseh':

> O God our Saviour, who through your prophet Nathan granted forgiveness of sins to penitent David, and received Manasseh's prayer of repentance; now yourself in your accustomed kindness receive your servant [*Name*] who repents of all the sins (s)he has committed, and overlook all that (s)he has done. You who forgive offences and pass over transgressions. For you O Lord have said: I do not desire the death of a sinner, rather that (s)he should turn from wickedness and live; and also have said that sins should be forgiven even seventy times seven. For as your majesty is incomparable so too your mercy is immeasurable. But if you should mark our iniquity who could ever stand? But you are the God of the penitent, and to you we ascribe glory ✠ to the Father, and to the Son, and to the Holy Spirit, now and ever and to the ages of ages. Amen.

Then (in the Slavonic service books) the priest invites the person to confess their heart's troubles with the following encouragement:

> Behold my child, Christ stands here invisibly to receive your confession. So do not be ashamed, and do not conceal anything from me. Tell without hesitation all that you have done, and thus you shall have pardon from our Lord Jesus Christ. See his holy icon is before us, and I am but a witness, bearing testimony before him of all the things which you have to say to me. But if you conceal anything from me, you shall have the greater sin. So take heed that having come to a physician you do not depart unhealed.

Penitents will then confess the sins and failings that trouble their hearts, and will also take the opportunity to speak of the whole range of their life in the perspective of the problems they have in living out the Gospel spirit. The priests, well aware of their own fallibility, listen with compassion and supportive pastoral care, and offer the best advice for all the problems their parishioners lay before them and suggestions for spiritual practices that might help them make progress. If the priest thinks the occasion demands it, he might lay upon the person an *epitimion*, an admonition, which is something like a penance to be performed in token of the earnestness of the repentance. This might be an instruction to say some extra prayers, or a period of fasting which the person ought to undertake before receiving the Eucharist. It is not always the case that an *epitimion* is given at all. Orthodox confession is not concerned with 'satisfaction' to be made for sin; instead it is entirely focused on the induction of the repentant believer into a more educated and holistic understanding of God's love. It is a joy to return, comparable to the prodigal son who may have expected to receive a stiff dressing-down when he got back to his father, but instead received embraces, new clothes, and a family party.[157] The priest will then usually give the penitent a blessing to receive the Holy Eucharist at the next celebration of the divine liturgy, so as to signal the completion of the reconciliation which this mystery of penance has initiated. In this way the ancient unity of the mysteries of initiation (baptism, chrismation, and Eucharist) is once again signalled. The priest makes a prayer of absolution over the penitent, who now kneels down and accepts the stole of the priest as it is laid over his or her head. In the Slavonic liturgical tradition the priest lays his hand on the penitent's head while saying this solemn prayer of blessing that confers the grace of reconciliation:

> May our Lord and God, Jesus Christ, through the grace and compassion of his love for mankind, forgive you my child [*Name*] all your transgressions. And I, an unworthy priest, through the power given to me by him, do forgive and absolve you from all your sins ✠ in the name of the Father, and of the Son, and of the Holy Spirit. Amen.

This liturgical formula came into the Slavonic books from the liturgical revisions of the great Ukrainian bishop theologian Peter Moghila,[158] and was accepted as a general rule in the Russian Church, and its circle of influence, after the eighteenth century. The Greek ritual has an older, deprecative, formula of absolution that reads as follows:

> May God who pardoned David through the prophet Nathan when he confessed his sins, and also Peter when he wept bitterly for his denial, and also the sinful woman weeping at his feet, and the publican as well as the prodigal son, may this same God, through me a sinner, forgive you all things both in this world and in the world to come, and cause you to stand uncondemned before his awesome Judgement Seat. Have no further care for the sins which you have confessed. Depart in peace. ✠ May Christ our true God through the prayers of his most holy Mother, and of all the saints, have mercy on us and save us, for he is gracious and loves mankind.

The regularity of parishioners making confession is something that differs from country to country and parish to parish within Orthodoxy. Most Orthodox would normally ask to make their confession in times of illness or trouble. The Greek Church perhaps does not celebrate this mystery in the parishes with as much frequency as the Russians do, many of whom will make a weekly confession. Whole parishes are strongly encouraged to make their confession at least at the end of Great Lent, near Pascha time. In times when communion was only received once or twice a year, it was the invariable custom to make a confession immediately before the reception of the Eucharist (at one's name-day, or at Pascha, for example) and to have fasted for many days prior. In recent times, and in places where the custom of more regular reception of communion has become established, it is not always the case that confession precedes every reception of the Eucharist, although this is still the custom that applies in many parts of the Slavonic liturgical tradition. It is a matter that is usually discussed with an individual's priest or spiritual elder, in reference to finding the best pastoral practice in each case. In any event the celebration of the mysteries of *metanoia* and Eucharist remain essentially tied together, as aspects of the same initiation into the profound grace of redemption won for the church by Christ.

The mystery of the great anointing

The mystery of holy anointing (Greek: *euchelaion*, or 'prayer of the oil') is celebrated whenever an Orthodox Christian is seriously ill, mentally or physically. It is a long and solemn ceremony of seven anointings with consecrated olive oil, interspersed with extensive scriptural readings especially the seven Gospels which focus on the healing power of the Lord. It is also known, as the mystery of the holy unction. The ideal form of the celebration is that seven priests are called together,[159] and each one reads one of the seven Gospels and performs one of the seven anointings, all the while praying for the recovery of the sick person. The mystery is the continuation of the ritual of healing mentioned in the Gospel of Mark[160] and more elaborately in the Epistle of St James:

> If any among you is sick, let them call for the presbyters of the church, and let these pray over the sick person, anointing him with oil in the name of the Lord. And the prayer of faith shall save the sick person, and the Lord shall raise them up. If they have committed sins they shall be forgiven them.[161]

This is no less than the continuation of the apostolic charism of healing that was given by the Lord to his missionary disciples, as a sign of the nearness of the Kingdom.[162] His own powerful ministry of healing was a sacrament of the Kingdom.[163] The same Lord has given to his church the role of continuing that eschatological sign of the Kingdom among the 'continuing present' of the world. As it was with the Lord himself,[164] the prayer for healing is not a magical rite. It depends on the grace of the Lord, not upon some inherent power of a separate holiness abiding in his servants. Yet it remains true that Christ has given his enduring gift of healing to the church. The grace of healing can evidently flow through the prayer of a righteous person, and even if the celebrants are themselves less than transparent windows to the Lord's grace, they are still empowered by this mystical rite to give a powerful and indefectible blessing by virtue of the grace of the apostolic succession that derives from their ordination, and through the mystical grace of the sanctified unction. As in all the other mysteries, it is the mercy of the Father, the grace of Christ, and the consoling gift of the Holy Spirit that empowers the rite, and accordingly their power of blessing cannot fail. A dramatic physical healing may not always occur, though it often does; but this is only one of the multitude of ways that this sacrament unfailingly confers the joy of the Lord, for the deep consolation of the sick person.

The celebrating clergy are meant to prepare themselves carefully through prayer and fasting. The sick person too, according to his or her strength, makes a special preparation. On the evening before, or the morning in advance of the healing, the sick person makes a private confession to the leading celebrant priest, and their conscience is quietened and strengthened by the sacrament. The prayers of the anointing ritual constantly stress the link between our sinful state and our sufferings.[165] This is not to imply a simplistic link between our state of sinfulness and our state of health,[166] but rather to admit our human need and our fallibility, of which physical and mental sickness are the clearest of all symbols.

The admission of our need, not least in the form of our sinfulness, is a necessary part of the mystery. It is an elemental part of the issue of *metanoia*, or repentance, to which the mystery of unction is so closely connected. In the pain of the human condition, the Christian is revealed as one who does not stand up to rail against God, but one who humbly confesses weakness, and asks for the compassion of the Supremely Compassionate One. His children do not have to persuade their God to give mercy, yet a healing is a special gift whose 'timing' is a mysterious thing. If the mystery of the unction does not result in the healing of a very sick person it is accepted as a sign that God has other plans, and this sacrament becomes a very important stage in the adaptation of the sick person to their sufferings or (perhaps) to the death that ultimately waits upon each one of us. The anointing is always a gift of the forgiveness of sins, however, and a sign that the suffering of the sick believer has been rendered 'acceptable' in the sight of God. Having become so blessed, and sanctified, may not necessarily make the pain any the less bitter, but can empower the sufferer to see it in a different light, for the valley of the shadow of death thereafter becomes a very different place when the gentle luminosity of God's mercy has shone into it, to light a path that may not have been seen among all the rocks before.

The unction is not a sacrament for the dying, however. The last sacrament of all is meant to be the gift of the Eucharist as *viaticum*: food for the journey. And that is not a sorrowful packing up of our goods, but a joyful setting out on a fresh pilgrimage, with the holy gifts which we shall eat with the Lord as new wine in the Kingdom of God.[167] The mystery of unction is fundamentally a sacrament for the sick, for their healing and recovery, even though sometimes it may be the first stage of their preparation for death.[168] It falls to the pastoral discretion of the priest to counsel and prepare the sick person for this mystery, according to their state and condition, and to talk extensively with them, so that their own heart is open to the visitation of the Lord, and their mind prepared in confidence, trust, and peacefulness. Orthodoxy is immensely compassionate, but it does not shrink from death as from an obscenity. Death is in itself a gift from the Lord, and one that sheds its terrors to the mature Christian drawing near to the end of the road. Such a road, for the friend of the Lord, is not a bleakness of desertion and wilderness, but rather the gloom of a journey made that opens into the twinkling lights of a welcoming village ahead, the Emmaus of a new encounter.[169] In many cases, however, sickness and pain catch us unawares, and often unprepared. The desolating sickness of a person can destroy the harmony and peace of whole households, and so it is that the family and friends of a sick person are meant to gather for the celebration of this mystery along with the priests and deacons, so that it can be communally experienced. This sacrament is a long and repetitive service of prayer and Scripture, that begins to form 'the mind of Christ' in those who participate in it. It is a beautiful and heart-resting experience, whose healing effect moves outwards far beyond the sick person who is at the centre of the anointings to embrace and comfort also those who are wounded by the suffering of their loved one. Those present, and not least the clergy involved, feel the graceful presence and compassion of Christ very immediately indeed.

307

The mystery of unction is shown as an eschatological sacrament also in so far as the sick person is an icon of the Lord, in his communion with his own mystical body. The compassion to the sick shown by the church is one and the same as the active love for Christ that makes the family of the church live in the grace and power of its Lord. This is the mystery spoken of in the Gospel when it describes the eschatological charge of the Last Judgement: 'Lord when did we ever see you sick? . . . Whenever you did it to the least of one of these my brethren, you did it to me.'[170] So it is that we still give by receiving, and receive abundantly by giving.[171]

The prayer of the consecration of the oil expresses a theology of gladness. It reads, in part, as follows:

> O God without beginning and without end, Holy of Holies, who sent your Only-Begotten Son to cure every sickness and every weakness both of body and soul, send down your Holy Spirit and sanctify this oil. Let it be for your servants who are anointed, the complete deliverance from their sins, and the inheritance of the King-dom of heaven. For you are God, great and wonderful, and you keep your covenant and mercy to those who love you . . . May this oil, O Lord, be an oil of gladness, an oil of sanctification, a royal vestment, a powerful breastplate, a protection against every work of the devil, an inviolable seal, joy of heart, and everlasting delight, so that all who are anointed with this oil of regeneration may become mighty against their enemies and shine brightly with the radiance of your Saints, and be without spot or wrinkle, and that they may be received into your eternal rest and win the prize of their high calling. For it belongs to you to have mercy and to save us, O God, our God, and to you we give glory, ✠ To the Father, and to the Son and to the Holy Spirit, now and ever, and to the ages of ages. Amen.

After the pure olive oil has thus been consecrated (with prayers that clearly connect it with the mystery of baptism[172]), the seven priests take turn anointing the sick person, invoking also the help of all the church's great saints who have excelled in healing charism in past ages. These are known in the Orthodox Church as the 'Holy Unmercenaries'.[173] The sick person is anointed eleven times, with a cross on the forehead, the nostrils, the cheeks, the lips, the chest (or upper neck) and both sides of each hand. The anointing and the prayer of healing that accompanies it are the formal elements of the mystery, but they take place in the closest harmony with the recurring sevenfold reading of the Epistles and Gospels that open out the mystery of Christ's healing grace among his faithful. The actual anointing prayer is as follows:

> Holy Father, physician of our souls and bodies, you sent your Only-Begotten Son our Lord Jesus Christ to heal every disease and to deliver us from death, now heal your servants also from the weakness of body and soul which binds them, and give them life through the grace of your Son. This we ask through the prayers of our most holy Lady, the Theotokos and Ever-Virgin Mary, by the might of the precious and life-giving Cross, through the protection of the honourable, heavenly, and bodiless Powers, of the honoured glorious Prophet, Forerunner and Baptist, John, of the holy, glorious and all-praised Apostles, of the holy, glorious and victorious Martyrs, of our venerable and God-bearing fathers, of the holy and healing Unmercenaries, Cosmas and Damian, Cyrus and John, Panteleïmon and Hermolaos, Sampson and Diomedes, Mocios and Acinitos, Thalalaios and Tryphon, of the holy and righteous

Forebears of God, Joachim and Anne, and of all the Saints. For you are the spring of all healing, O God, our God, and to you we give glory, ✠ To the Father, and to the Son and to the Holy Spirit, now and forever, and to the ages of ages. Amen.

This sacramental ritual is repeated in a more generalized form in Great Week,[174] on Wednesday evening. Unction with the blessed oil is offered to all the faithful who attend that liturgy in memory of the Lord's impending death. During the successive readings of the Epistles and Gospels, the whole congregation is anointed on the head and hands in the usual manner, while a refrain is sung in a solemn melody: 'Hear us O Lord, Hear us O Master, Hear us O Holy One.' The link between the death of the Lord, in which his faithful find a source of healing and blessing, is underscored once again in this liturgical connection, and is highly reminiscent of the relation between this mystery of anointing and the baptismal initiation into the life-giving death which is celebrated in that primal sacrament. The church performs this ritual in preparation, as it were, for the burial of the Lord which will take place in the great mysteries of Pascha in a few days' time. The anointing of the whole congregation, Christ's own body, fulfils the Gospel text: 'She has done what she could, she has anointed my body beforehand, as for its burial.'[175]

Sickness is one of the ways in which the disciple enters into the experience of death 'beforehand'. In this consoling mystery, the Lord who himself once suffered bravely shares his mercy, understanding, and compassion with his beloved. On very many occasions that mercy results in the manifest gift of healing, so that we can resume our pilgrimage with fewer burdens, having glimpsed the joy of Christ, and the boundless compassion that actually surrounds us all the time. We merely lose sight of it occasionally.

The mystery of marriage

The Lord revealed the heart of his understanding of marriage on several occasions during his earthly ministry.[176] He changed its significance considerably, from that of the Old Testament 'contract' (which remains the inspiration of civil law to this day) into something greater than that: an entrance into a spiritual profundity of communion that actually mirrors Christ's own love for his church. When he was asked about the Mosaic law of divorce he clearly taught the Pharisees that they were mistaken to set the bond of marriage in the context of contractual 'law', but should rather see it in terms of the divine covenant God made with humankind in the creation:

> And the Pharisees came up to him and tested him by asking, Is it lawful to divorce one's wife for any cause? He answered, Have you not read that he who made them from the beginning made them male and female, and said, For this reason a man shall leave his father and mother and be joined to his wife, and the two shall become one flesh? So they are no longer two but one flesh. What therefore God has joined together, let not man put apart. They said to him, Why then did Moses command one to give a certificate of divorce, and to put her away? He said to them, For your hardness of heart Moses allowed you to divorce your wives, but from the beginning it was not so.[177]

309

Over and against the economies that were necessary for society where hardness of heart was the common order of the day, Christ begins to set a new standard for his church, which itself goes back to the more fundamental creation covenant, which he has come to restore and repristinate in his church. The Mosaic law of contractual divorce is made to give way to a higher 'law of one flesh', that is communion. It is God who bonds a man and a woman in a mystical union that grows out of the union of flesh. This psycho-physical bond is a profound sacrament of the love Christ has for his church. It is as deep as death, and as limitless as God's own compassion. To speak of divorce, fracture, betrayal, and disloyalty in the same breath alongside this mystery is to speak sacrilege in the holy place, and this is why Christ rebukes the Pharisees. In the face of the former limited contract of mutual rights and obligations, the Lord places the image of the contract of God's creation ordinance: a mutuality of love in which the invitation to love is a command to transfigured transcendence. The language of marital purposes, functions, contracts, obligations has been used so heavily in times past (and in secular society especially) to hedge around the mystery of marriage: such terms are not inapplicable (considering the responsibilities to others that the marriage bond itself creates), but they are secondary. The Christian theology of marriage begins in a spiritual mystery of communion that is awesome in its power and significance. It is this alone that can breathe Christ's joy and his life into all the contracts the world can draw up.

In his own teaching the Lord constantly refers to marriage, and the happy festivals that marked a marriage in ancient Palestine, as a fundamental 'type' of the coming Kingdom of God.[178] It is instructive that in reference to this concept of the Kingdom, the most elevated form of his Father's will for the cosmos and his presence within it, the Lord continually chooses to use the symbol of the wedding feast. This takes its force, of course, from the ancient biblical notion that God is the sole bridegroom of Israel. But it is also indicative of how the mystery of marriage is itself one of the great symbolic gates that can open up the manifestation of the glory of the Lord. Like the disciples at Cana (who were already chosen and blessed as apostles, and already following their Master), the initiates of this sacrament can actually 'start to believe' from what they have seen.

At the Cana wedding, we are told that he 'allowed his glory to be seen'[179] and brought belief to life in the hearts of his closest disciples. This marriage served as a symbolic and joyful background against which the new covenant of his merciful advent could be suitably manifested. The mystery of the great outpouring of new wine was the sign of the new covenant in his blood which would bond together God and mankind in a new marriage where God would be the sole husband (the *baal*) of Israel, and would tolerate no other spouse for his elected bride. Marriage is, therefore, a centrally important symbol of the union with God in the new covenant. This is why the apostle calls it a profound mystery of the union of Christ with his church:

Be subject to one another out of reverence for Christ. Wives, be subject to your husbands, as to the Lord. For the husband is the head of the wife as Christ is the head of the church, his body, and is himself its Saviour. As the church is subject to Christ, so let wives also be subject in everything to their husbands. Husbands, love your wives, as Christ loved the church and gave himself up for her, that he might sanctify her, having cleansed her by the washing of water with the word, that he might present the church to himself in splendour, without spot or wrinkle or any such thing, that she might be holy and without blemish. Even so husbands should love their wives as their own bodies. He who loves his wife loves himself. For no man ever hates his own flesh, but nourishes and cherishes it, as Christ does the church, because we are members of his body. 'For this reason a man shall leave his father and mother and be joined to his wife, and the two shall become one flesh.'[180] This mystery is a profound one, and I am saying that it refers to Christ and the church; however, let each one of you love his wife as himself, and let the wife see that she respects her husband.[181]

In this extraordinarily beautiful apostolic text, somewhat unpopular today because people often read it carelessly and erroneously, as a chauvinistic endorsement of patriarchal authority, what is actually said is that husband and wife ought to outdo one another in putting their own self at the service of the other. This is the epitome of all the Christian life: that searching out of the 'mind of Christ' (*phronema Christou*) that seeks a *kenosis* in order to gain the love and communion of the beloved.[182] The wife should reverence her husband as she venerates Christ, while the husband should aspire to love his wife to the degree Christ loved his church. The underlying text, of course, is that in loving the beloved in this way, the married couple love their own flesh: since they have become 'as one flesh' in Christ. They are one flesh in their mutual love, and they are one flesh in their Christian communion together, and with their common Lord. In a uniquely mystical way they are called to fulfil the supreme command of disciples: 'Love one another as I have loved you.' Their mutual love and joy must indeed function to others (as well as themselves) as a living icon of the burning love Christ has for his church, and how that love will be the eschatological bonding of all the disciples, in the kingdom of his joy.

In his text, the apostle is pastorally urging his married disciples to use their love for one another to deepen their evangelical experience, by finding more and more ways to lose themselves in love and service, just as Christ himself loved the church and laid down his life for it. The apostolic words sound a note of warning: for a true marriage of heart and soul inevitably involves a death to the old self. Self-centredness is doomed to be shattered by the demands of familial love. Those who refuse this daily death to the self will find their marriage can turn into a living nightmare. Those who embrace it can find marriage the most authentic arena of Christian maturity and 'revelation'. The death to the old self is, of course, the opening out to the possibility of the birth of newer levels of being, newer depths of life. Just as the glory of the Lord once shone through the marriage feast of Cana, so the true manifestation of the glory of Christ's love can shine out in the mystical passion of devotion and love, and also the wonderful gift of extended relations and kinships, that comes from the outgrowth of the family unity.

The first step in this extension of love is in the new covenant of the engaged couple, but soon it is an issue of the union of families and wider kin groups, and ultimately seen in one of the most mystical events two human people can share, the birth of a new child that has resulted from their love. In turn that child goes on to make more and more new connections of love, until a couple in a family stand at the heart of a vast network of loving bonds that in a miniature form make an icon of the church itself: a family bonded in love, that stands in the service of Christ. It is not always the case that a marriage can result in the birth of children, though in the ordinary sense of fulfilling the Creation ordinance, 'Be fruitful',[183] children will (and ought to be) at the heart of a marriage. Christians who are capable, but who absolutely refuse to entertain the notion of children for the sake of careers or advancing their wealth, have struck at the very essence of what this mystery is meant to symbolize, and have consequently eroded its sacred blessing. Those who are not given the gift of children, for the many causes that may lie behind this, have not voided the blessing of their marriage. For in Orthodoxy marriage does not exist solely for the issuing of children. It is a symbol in itself of the love of Christ; and the mutual support of husband and wife, as they each travel the paths of a world full of sorrows, is an inestimable consolation for themselves, as well as an important icon for the wider community. In such cases of unforeseen childlessness, the Orthodox couple may refer to medically aided fertilization of the type that does not break the marital bond; or they may extend their desire for communion in the philanthropy of adoption.

Whether the married couple remain a small dyad standing at the intersection of larger kin groups, or whether they begin a new home and family of their own, what is at stake in terms of the Gospel is the manner in which this foundation of a new locus of love, a home, becomes a place where the Gospel injunctions are fulfilled: to clothe the naked, to instruct the ignorant, to heal the sorrowing, to feed the hungry. The practising of the fundamental attitudes of Christ on our immediate family is the beginning of our training. The married couple who have fulfilled the blessing of their consecration actually go on together in life to make a home where observers can say: 'Here is a place where indeed the stranger was made welcome, the poor were fed, and the sorrowing were comforted.' It is in this workshop of love that the children of the marriage will also first learn the meaning of the Gospel, from the charity of Christ it engenders all around it.

Children are, in the normal course of events, an integral part of the marriage equation, but they are not the sole rationale for this sacrament. For this reason, although it is a debated point in the writings of theologians, Orthodoxy has never condemned outright the use of artificial methods of birth control. From ancient times it has certainly 'disapproved' of them in its ascetical writings because of a desire never to separate married love from the sources of life-making which it is inherently related to,[184] and also because in ancient thought contraception was seen as an inherent part of a culture of abortion. Some of the early Church Fathers, it has to be said, also wrote with scorn about contraception because the whole debate of their time was set within a pagan philosophy (Stoicism) that was hostile to the very notion of pleasure, a view that contradicts the more joyful ambience of the Scriptures. Some more contemporary Orthodox writers, following these ancient ethicists of the church, have made a formal logical proposition out of the biological 'purpose' of sexuality,[185] and concluded that all sexual activity in marriage ought to be 'life-orientated'. Pressing this also to a logical conclusion, they have argued that all sexual acts should be open to conception, and thus that contraceptive use is not ethically permitted to Orthodox married couples. Others, however, have argued that an ethic of openness to life does not logically require that each and every sexual act needs to be opened to the possibility of conception, and thus that this logic of natural law cannot take precedence over all other ethical considerations in relation to the priestly mystery of sexual love within the sacramental life of the married couple. Each sexual act, clearly, must be open to the expression of mutual love, and in this it finds its ethical goal or *telos*. In the successful creation of a climate of mutual love and trust (in which sexual attraction and mutual delight can be a profoundly constructive force) the marriage thereby becomes the fruitful nurturing ground of openness to life: and the desire to have children together is one that flowers out of long-term responsible choices and planning. The most intimate celebration of charismatic love, using the flesh to bond the heart and spirit too, is ultimately a matter for the two spouses. They may individually or together consult a spiritual adviser about this, as about any other matter of their Christian lives, but the normal practice of Orthodoxy customarily refuses to allow anyone else to intrude in this holy ground.[186] It would, for example, certainly not be expected of the priest-confessor to ask any intrusive questions of his spiritual children in this matter of conjugal privacy.[187]

Contraceptive methods that involve abortifacient means, however, are strictly forbidden. Such an attitude to the planning of life is hostile to the mentality of the life-ethic which marriage is meant to symbolize as part of God's 'creation ordinance'. From the very beginning of its history, all the Christian Fathers have been unanimous that abortion and abortifacient devices are seriously wrong, in so far as they intervene in God's sacred domain. Christians may control the process of fertilization in appropriate ways, including abstinence, but they must not interfere in God's own creative process of the affirmation and the development of life *in utero*. Such an intrusion is sacrilege: the elevation of the human parent or doctor in the place of God. The widespread lack of any sense that the womb is a sacred sanctuary, under God's own protection[188] has led to tragic results outside the church in recent generations. In many countries of the world in the latter part of the twentieth century the unthinkable occurred: abortion became a relatively normal method of birth control, to judge from its staggeringly high incidence. In the Orthodox understanding, the death of a sense of horror at the destruction of the unborn is always a clear sign of the departure of the Holy Spirit from the consciousness.[189] The Lord and Giver of Life, that Holy Spirit of Truth, is most clearly seen as fostering life and all its flourishing. The opposite spirit is a lord of death inspired by constant hatred towards humanity, and a delight in all that harms it physically and spiritually. The issue of Orthodox ethics in relation to abortion will be considered more fully in the following chapter.

Christian reflection on the beauty and holiness of sexual love certainly needs some development. In times past the majority of the theologians of the church have tended to be monastics or ascetics. This has been the case from the fourth century onwards. As a result, the church has had very few theologians who have really celebrated the glory of the married condition rhapsodically, and from the lived inner experience of it. Being predominantly approached from the perspective of celibates, and often denigrated as something defective, or at least much less elevated than the celibate ascetical life, it has not yet been sung about in a full range of theological keys. One of the first of all the Christian heresies was the attempt to impose celibacy on all Christians as a 'higher standard', and these zealots were denounced by the apostle as having followed 'deceitful spirits' to teach the 'doctrine of demons'.[190] They are harsh words. But from the very beginning it was felt to be necessary to protect the glories of the married vocation. And perhaps this is true today. The church still waits for great theologians and poets who can sing the glories of this condition properly. Only in the latter centuries, and perhaps especially when women disciples across the world can command an elevated standard of literary education (which has only relatively recently come to be the case in terms of world history, where education was reserved for men of privilege or from patronized backgrounds) will such works of theology come to be written in a fitting style.

The truth is that it is incorrect to speak of either the ascetical path or the married path as being 'higher'[191] than the other. The ascetical vocation is glorious for those the Lord has called to it. No less glorious and mystical is the path of married love, for those to whom God has appeared within it. Its secrets are hidden from those without. Its profundities are blessed by God with a Creation ordinance to 'be fruitful and multiply'.[192] Of this vocational path many Orthodox theologians have likened the couple's journey towards union in flesh and spirit, with a trope of the *perichoresis* of the Persons of the Holy Trinity, radiating out essential unity in their harmony. The Trinity itself, the goal of all Christian life, is the pattern and aspiration of the mystical unity that the marriage can bear witness to. Such a mystery of union is only possible because of the indwelling Trinity.

Such a level of union is not attainable in the world; it is only achievable by the initiated of God. The mystery of married love has also, more specifically, been described by the apostle as a 'type' of Christ's love for the church: a divine mystery. Again, there could hardly be more elevated praise. Added to these profound *encomia* we can also note that it is also not the case that the ascetical life (however glorious in itself) has been given so clearly as marriage the status of one of the great mysteries of the New Covenant. However, rather than looking to see which is the 'higher' or the 'lower' vocation, it is more correct to follow the truth that knows that the highest vocation of all is the one to which God has led each of us along the freely chosen, yet carefully guided, path of his overarching providence for each one, whether that is dedicated celibacy or consecrated marriage.

Indeed, many marriages, through a mysterious, special, and unusual providence of God, are the arena of sickness and suffering. The joy of children may be denied such a couple. Often they are called on to support one another in extraordinary pain. Such a marriage, that could crush the spirit of most people, can sometimes call out immense courage and love in the partners involved. Then, in a way not normally envisaged, it reaches a new level of fecundity in imitation of Christ. Such a path can be one of the most ascetically elevated in the whole witness of the church. Chastity is a fundamental virtue required of all Christians, in all ages and life conditions. The chastity of the married couple, however, differs in character from that expected of the single person, or that required of the ascetic. Such chastity is, in essence, not reducible to a fear of the flesh, or ought not to be. Nor it is it simply a denial of the natural processes of human desire and attraction: for these fundamental matters constantly direct the psycho-affective life of all, even the dedicated celibates in the church. Chastity is as much a matter of the spirit as it is of the body and the imagination. It is an issue of fidelity; a constant struggle to make all things in a Christian life charged with light and graciousness, not least the powerful forces of the desire for acquisition and the desires of the flesh. How one uses money, and how one approaches the issue of physical pleasure, are, of course, two enduring benchmarks of an individual's authenticity in the life of the Gospel. But the Gospel does not advocate salvation for the dispossessed simply on that basis, nor does it presume that one should be devoid of desire: it is the use to which the fundamental drives of human energy are placed that is in question.[193] Christ, in all things, instructs us with a simple word, a broad invitation which we must then learn to flesh out ourselves from our wit, zeal, and charismatic enthusiasm from day to day: 'Seek first the Kingdom of God, then all other things will be added to you.'[194]

314

In this light marriage is the broad highway where most Christians are called by God. When they are so called, it is to perform once more the priestly task of refining raw matter into the purified gold of spiritual glory. For marriage in the eyes and ways of this world is a simple contractual matter, to mark off sexual and legal relations; something that is entirely in the hand and at the disposal of the men and women who fashion this bond among themselves (which is why its survival rates are so desperate in this day and age of spiritual bankruptcy). However, in the processes of the church it is not like this. Marriage itself is called to become something new: a great mystery, as it rises into the art of being the way in which two Christians form one heart and mind with Christ as their common Lord, and in harmony with Christ as the master of the new household, a new *ecclesiola* (church in miniature) is born; a consecrated family of Christians whose purpose is to bring into concrete, immediate, and intimate existence a place on the face of this earth where the love of Christ is incarnated in all its fullness and range, embodied in all the passionate joy that 'oneness of flesh' signifies. This is only partly concerned with sexual union, it is far more extensive than simple sexual intimacy, and it actually brings to mind the entire range of kin bonding, that runs backwards to countless generations of ancestors and forwards to the new bonds formed by kin as yet unborn: all of whom are reunited in deeper and more complex ways within the overarching mercy of the Lord, who calls his earthly creation onwards in these ever-growing complexities of love and communion.

'There are many mansions in my Father's house', the Lord told his apostles;[195] marriage is the mystery by which means many of those mansions are being fashioned out of the raw matter of history, and through the struggle of kin and families to create a common heritage of Christian civilization across generations. In the Orthodox Church great stress is placed on the celebration of the feast days of Christ's ancestors 'according to the flesh'. Their life stories, their achievements, and their personal histories are caught up into something greater than they could ever have known. So it is with the mystery of marriage: each smaller unit of the new family is part of a greater and more complex hidden family of ancestors. The mutual love of two Christians is part of the very spiritual and moral formation that has been given to them by generations that were mature before they were even born. Born out of love, they in turn learn to love and create new love, and co-create new life. The spiral of human history making its way forwards in a civilizing power, despite each and every setback of war, or poverty, or disease, is seen most clearly revealed in the forward progress of family love and mutual care within the church. Within the mystery of marriage, therefore, the priestly vocation of the Christian is fulfilled, that same priestly task that marks off all discipleship's endeavour: the consecration of human matter into spiritual significance, through the hallowing force of love.

Sexuality is, therefore, an important part of the vocation of married life. In many cases humans sexuality fails and wanes in the face of life and its difficulties, and in the face of relationships and the repeated disappointments they can often bring in their train. The world knows it as 'falling in and out of love'; but in the church things are not meant to be like this,[196] for the endurance of the love that God gives to his initiates is greater than life itself,[197] and will outlast its merely earthly stage.[198] Almost half of all marriages in contemporary Europe, for example, are reported to have reached a state, after twenty years, where mutual sexuality hardly plays any part at all. Our contemporary age prides itself on being one of the most sexually liberated ever.

It prides itself wrongly in this regard, since a perusal of our voluminous literature on the subject of sexuality reveals not a liberated society at all, but one with a deeply wounded and anxious attitude to sexual love. The blame for this has often been laid at the door of the Christian Church, with its (alleged) favouring of the ascetical path and its stern attitude to sexuality. But even when ascetical theologians wrote treatises lauding virginity and 'allowing' marriage, the reality was always that the vast majority of Christians loved, and married, and flourished in their children, regardless of their opinions. It was simply that the ordinary person did not (either in antiquity or today) by preference 'write' about these fundamental realities of life, but lived them out in the 'inmost chamber', as it were. Accordingly, when one only reads the texts of the ascetics one is not quarrying the true sources of a Christian celebration of life. Christianity has always celebrated life, and love, and children. And I might even say that, despite its rhetoric, that was abundantly true throughout history, and remains true to this day.

A new ethos of sexuality divorced from religion, such as is witnessed in the post-modern culture of consumerism, that has apparently elevated cyber-sex as its token, is not (or so it seems to me) in any better position to discover the joyfulness of human sexuality. It is, arguably, in a much worse position. The vast increase of traffic on the internet (that marvel of human communication) regarding sexuality more often than not demonstrates an interest in pornography in preference to human love, and isolated excitement rather than socially enriched experience. If this becomes a pattern for the future (as at present it threatens to be[199]), to the point that every other child's first experience of sexuality will be through the medium of disconnected pornographic imagery, then it is a bleak future that lies ahead of our most curious race. This problem of a sexuality disconnected from community (and from the real world) is also growing at a time when the fertility rate of the human species (never an 'easily reproducing' genus despite our race's success in the last few millennia) is at a historic low point. At a time when male fertility has never been more endangered, and when the environment that nurtures life has become so unbalanced by our own carelessness, the rate of the species' rejection of its own future, in terms of abortion, has never been higher. This is a strangely mysterious paradox of our time. Sexuality has a great power over the immensely curious and imaginative human mind, and a powerful hold over the individual both physically (for the delight it brings can also become addictive) and, above all, emotionally. The deep roots of sexuality in the human psyche and the complete 'rounding out' of human personality and its development have only been clearly understood over the course of the last century, a very recent philosophical development that still needs to be digested in society's behavioural patterns. The relative disconnection of sexual expression from issues of fertilization, brought about by the mass availability of reliable contraceptive methods since the middle of the twentieth century, also brought in its train a massive reorientation of attitudes to sexuality. In most parts of Europe and elsewhere in Western culture today, it is considered normal for sexual experimentation to begin in the early teens, and for a series of sexual relationships to long pre-date any possible marriage. Indeed marriage is now commonly regarded by non-Christians simply as a bourgeois convention that needs to be regulated simply through tax legislation and child-care rules.

In the Orthodox understanding, Christian marriage thus reverts more and more to the appearance it once had of old: a distinctly 'offbeat' approach that brought the secular marriage contract[200] under the eyes of Christ to ask for a specific blessing, and consecration. This decision to present oneself in the church for the blessing of the bishop, so as to consecrate the marriage to Christ, was in its day regarded as an eccentricity of the Christians, and something related to their peculiar belief that their initiation rituals such as baptism, Eucharist (and now *gamos*) actually 'did' something different to the legal contract that was also expected of them by the wider society. This understanding of marriage among Christians as something far different from the secular contract is a perspective that is increasingly being lost (even among the churches), and it needs to be restored among the Christians at an early stage of catechesis. Nevertheless, it is the consecration conferred by the sacrament that makes marriage into a sacred mystery relevant to the path of discipleship. The mystery of marriage, as the church has understood it, gives a very different signal to that discovered in the world, though the world still longs for the ideal of a monogamous and love-filled union even as this slips more and more rapidly from its fingers in a tumult of divorce. The sacred mystery of Christian marriage sings a different song to the anxious (and often violent) subtext of sexuality as the world knows it.

The key issue, of course, is the presence of joy. And joy is wholly a spiritual phenomenon that cannot be counterfeited. It is the spirit of joy that renews a Christian marriage in mutual love and which springs up unfailingly across the years and generations. Without this humble love, and this renovatory 'mind of Christ' at the core of a Christian marriage, the very concept of two human beings staying with one another for decades would be unimaginably boring and suffocating. With it, the love deepens day by day, for those who have the eyes to see, and reveals new layers of the significance of being. The constant renewal of love between two souls in a successful marital bond is one of the greatest of spiritual mysteries in the world. When two Christians achieve this ever-deepening acclimatization, in an atmosphere of mutual respect, cherishing closeness, and joyful fecundity, one knows the presence of God is very near. The life such a relationship issues from its core is not merely physical (the creation of a new family) but spiritual, the formation of a clan of souls in the syntax of love. This priestly work is one of the greatest in the church. It still awaits its poets and theologians to sing of it properly. It also requires immense sensitivity from the bishops and priests of the church to support Christian marriages in an age where so many societal trends seem to erode its very foundations.

Because marriage in the Orthodox understanding is meant to be a most intimate priestly collaboration of two initiated Christians, to bring a powerful focus of new love into being, and ultimately (if God so wills) to bring new life into the world and thus form a new small church around the centre of the kin group, it is not an ideal preparation for this double priestly ministry if one of the couple is not a Christian. Such a bond, while it could certainly signal deep human love, could not function, in the Orthodox understanding, to make the marriage serve as a cultic celebration of Christ's dominion in the immediate life of the family. The two could not be priests if one of them was not an initiate of Christ's mysteries, and if this priesthood could not function the mystery of the marriage could not occur. It is for this reason that the Orthodox Church will not celebrate the marriage of an Orthodox Christian with someone who is not baptized. Marriage is, therefore, a mystery that can only be given after the initial mystical initiation of baptism has taken place. A non-believer, or someone from a religion other than Christianity, should only marry an Orthodox

Christian if they elect to share the spouse's faith. In other words, the mystery can occur only if they choose the spirit, as well as the heart, of their elected Orthodox partner.

In times past the church's law[201] also forbade marriage to be sacramentally solemnized between Orthodox Christians and members of other Christian confessions who were not Orthodox. Today, this stricture has been largely relaxed, although the whole point and purpose of the Christian marriage as the 'formation of the *ecclesiola*' is put into jeopardy by the very notion of a 'mixed marriage'. Such an idea (referring to the marriage of two different denominations of Christian in the Western understanding of that term) has often been described by Western Christians who have lived out their vocation in this way as a liberating and fulfilling Christian experience. But this is largely because in the Western churches there is an extensive understanding among the laity (even if it is not always acknowledged by the clergy of those denominations) that an effective intercommunion exists between those church experiences. Frequently a family will worship one way on a particular Sunday, and then engage fully in the other type of Christian service another week. In Orthodoxy this is not possible, and, to the same extent, a mixed marriage does not normally open out into a full ecclesial experience for the partner who is not chrismated as an Orthodox. It is normally understood that all the children of an Orthodox marriage will be baptized and chrismated as Orthodox from their infancy. And again the 'mixed marriage' is problematic, because it is impossible to initiate a child into the mysteries of the faith in a way that engages its imagination and its love when one partner of the marriage is not initiated into the faith to begin with.

For such reasons the Orthodox clergy try, with careful pastoral advice, to encourage full Orthodox marriages, and will also encourage the non-Orthodox partner to consider entrance into the Orthodox Church as a fully communicant member;[202] this is not mere 'proselytism' but rather part of the very experience of the mystery of marriage that they are seeking to experience in the sacrament – a union of heart, and spirit, and soul, and body. Union with Christ is a profound part of that totality which the couple who have fallen in love are seeking through the mystery of marriage. It is a sadness when it is only considered late in the day, or when the arrangement of flowers at the reception banquet attracts more consideration than the issue of the mutual balance of the spiritual potency and psychic acuity of the bride and groom. Even so, the powerful grace of consecration that the mystery gives to the bride and groom works around them and with them for the long years ahead.

The wedding service in Orthodoxy has two separate parts. Today they are often combined into a preparatory rite and the main marriage service on the same day; but they are quite distinct. The first is the betrothal service. In Byzantine times this was regarded as solemnly as a full marriage, and a subsequent breaking of a betrothal required an ecclesiastical divorce. Its central symbolism is the blessing and exchange of rings, and the biblical recitation of the instances of deep love that formed the creative context for the saving works of God, culminating in the appearance of Christ. It is the duty of the priest to establish that the necessary freedom is present in both the betrothed at this stage, since freedom is the necessary soil out of which this sacramental mystery will grow.

In the Orthodox marriage ritual the bride and groom are 'crowned' to one another. This presses into Christian service the ancient Roman custom of the floral *gamos* crowns. In the Greek liturgical tradition the crowns are made up as two wreaths of white flowers, joined together with a long white ribbon.[203] The usual type is orange blossom, a symbol of perennial bloom. The husband's crown and that of the bride are exchanged over their respective heads, by the *koumbaros*, while the priest makes the sign of the cross over them saying each time: 'The Servant of God –N– is crowned to the Servant of God –N–.' Then, three times the priest solemnly blesses them with these words: 'O Lord our God, crown them with glory and honour.' The Orthodox Church understands the crowning and the triune blessing to be the solemn consecration of the marriage. Without either part a marriage is not believed to have been sacramentalized in the church. Orthodoxy, then, does not approach marriage in the same sense as the Western Church, which has for long been of the opinion that the bride and groom minister the sacrament of matrimony to one another in their exchange of consent. In the Orthodox Church it is clearly understood that the minister of the mystery of marriage is the bishop or the priest, consecrating and effecting it by the grace of the Lord bestowed in the sacred blessing.

After the crowning the couple are given the 'shared chalice', a drink of sweet wine from the same cup to symbolize the joy of their union; they are then led by the priest[204] three times around the wedding-table set up in the centre of the church, on which have previously lain the rings, the Gospel book, the cup of wine, the dish of sweet honey, and the wedding icons.[205] The wedding attendants follow behind holding the crowns over the heads of the bride and groom. During this procession (an ancient symbol of sacred oath-making, which is the equivalent in the Eastern rite to the sacred promises made by the bride and groom) the Canticle of Isaiah[206] is sung by the choir. This is the same solemn hymn which is sung at ordinations in the Orthodox Church, and it is meant to underline the fact that the bride and groom, similarly, are embarking on a new form of priestly ministry,[207] a newly specific form and style of consecrated discipleship. At the end of the wedding ceremony the bride and groom are given a common cup of sweet wine to drink from. It underlines the symbolic link to the wedding at Cana where Christ's glory first shone out. A spoon of honey and chopped walnuts is also sometimes given to symbolize the sweetness of a new love[208] that will never go stale if it is part of the mutual commitment of two disciples to obey the words of God.[209]

While the couple process around the Gospel table a *troparion* is sung to remind them that, like martyrs, they will need to 'lay down their lives' in this new evangelical vocation. The crown is, for the church, also taken to be a symbol of martyrdom.[210] Though the union is one of deep joy, the wedding opens to the bride and groom the necessity of living together in the discipleship of Christ; and that requires the acceptance of the *phronema Christou*, Christ's own mentality,[211] which is one of willingness to accept the death of self for the sake of the loved one. This choice to prefer love over selfishness is the martyrdom that will preserve the marriage as a living spiritual mystery for long years ahead.

The spiritual bond of this union begins a trajectory which begins in the church but will reach into the fullness of the Kingdom of God. For this reason Orthodoxy has no belief corresponding to that sometimes heard in Western wedding rituals: 'Until death do you part'. Marriage is a mystery of the kingdom, and its goal is admittance into the kingdom of the two consecrated souls who have become one flesh in Christ. It may begin in time but it will not end in our chronological age, for the relationship it initiates passes on as a fundamental part of the eschatological joy of the Kingdom, the Lord's own wedding feast. The Lord himself said that the elect in heaven would not be given in marriage since they would be 'as the angels are'.[212] This was to show that the slavishly legal mentality of the Sadducees (who used the concept of the Law to deny the truth of the Resurrection) was fundamentally misguided.[213] What the Lord meant by this saying was that the Sadducees had very little conception of the significance either of marriage, or resurrection, or of the nature of the heavenly metamorphosis of the elect, simply because they did not understand the power of the Scriptures and the power of God's saving grace.

The union created by the mystery of marriage, however, is not cast aside in the Kingdom. This is not the significance of the Lord's words. It is precisely this sacrament of union with Christ, and with all those other elect of Christ's who have also become one with him, that the mystery of marriage symbolizes and effects. Marriage itself will only be superseded because the elect will have passed into an even deeper form of the union it once initiated. It will be superseded because it will be fulfilled, not cast away. Just as the married couple's own physical limitations will be superseded in the Resurrection, without this implying that they cease to be bodies in any sense (the spiritual body is not the same as the body of flesh we now inhabit), so the contract of marriage, once exclusive in nature, will pass away into a metamorphosis of universal union in Christ for the elect. This union will be far deeper and more perfect than even the greatest of human loves on earth have been able to attain. But such a transfigured union will not cast away that earthly experience of sacramental marriage, which it metamorphoses, just as Christ's own glorious body was still his own body, still bearing the marks of the nails in his feet and hands, although it was now for him a body of light, and joy, and gladness. In a similar way the radiant Christian marriage that endured 'into the Kingdom' will be transcended in the time of the Resurrection when it comes into its fullness; but it will not be cast away. It will be taken into a new pitch of wonder in Christ. Neither will the universally profound nature of the union of all the elect with Christ, in the time of the Kingdom, necessitate the dismissal of all the kin and family bonds that have been instrumental in preparing countless souls to enter it. Far from it.

In our present earthly experience marital, and family, love tends to be exclusive, for its protection and nurture. Then, it will have transcended exclusivity, without losing its own character and uniqueness. In short in the Eschaton all that is truest and finest about the love of disciples for one another on earth will be brought to a more glorious perfection. The unity of the one flesh will metamorphose into a unity of the one spirit, since this is the appropriate manner for the angels to be united with one another. This is what Christ meant by saying: 'They shall be as the angels are.' Once again he used marriage as a symbol of the richness of the loving union that character- ized the eschatological condition. But he was speaking to dim minds who regarded marriage as first of all a legal contract, and secondly as predominantly a sexual affair, and this was why his words were a dismissal of their premises. It is a great mistake, nonetheless, to interpret his words as being dismissive of the eternal significance of the sacrament of love, which this mystery is; for a proper exegesis of his saying shows that the Lord himself uses the idea of marriage as the appropriate symbol for the joy of Paradise, transfiguring all the best of what we now know on earth in terms of communion. The 'becoming one flesh' which the Lord himself uses to describe the import of marriage does not simply mean one sexual relationship, but precisely what the church says it does: one flesh in Christ. As in Christ himself, the one flesh of his human nature is indissolubly related to his divinity,[214] so too the two souls joined in marriage are given the potential to become spiritually bonded in a mutual hypostatic relationship which, in Christ, is unique to them. For this reason Orthodoxy forbade a second marriage as a possibility. It eventually relaxed this stringent requirement on the faithful, but did so out of pastoral concern and compassion for the limitations of the faithful who could not always measure up to the standards of the kingdom in their earthly lives. Today it does permit second marriages, but still retains its original position that the one, unique, 'marriage enduring into the Kingdom' is the appropriate symbol of the union of Christ and his church, and a true gateway into the metamorphosed union of that Paradise.[215]

When the church first considered the issue of a second marriage it was not thinking about the issue of remarriage after a marital breakdown; on the contrary, when it forbade second marriages in its earliest canonical legislation it was entirely thinking of the death of one partner, and the subsequent decision of the surviving one to marry again. This the church regarded as a scandal, precisely because the marriage was not (as the secular contract regarded it) merely 'Until death do you part' at all, but rather something that was 'of the Kingdom itself'. The second marriage was thus a refusal of the first, a rejection of the bond of the two disciples' mutually related passage into the kingdom of God, of which the remaining time on earth of the bereaved disciple was an integral part. The early church called the desire for a second marriage (perfectly permissible by the secular law of all periods) bigamy, or digamy. The many references to digamy in the ancient canons of the church testify to the sense of scandal that always attached to it. To this day the canons of the Orthodox Church refuse to permit the higher clergy (that is, priests or deacons, since from the sixth century bishops were already required to be celibate) to contract a second marriage, if a bereavement intervenes in the first. This is not because it is believed that ideally clergy 'ought to be' celibate but because the great mystery of Christian marriage is 'towards the Kingdom', an ultimately eschatological mystery which sings out Christ's love for his church, and thus which is not completed until it reaches its metamorphosis in the kingdom.

The intrusion of a second marriage into a first one interrupted by the death of spouse, therefore, is canonically treated in Orthodoxy in ways symbolically equating it with a divorce. Clergy who are bereaved and who wish to marry again[216] are allowed to do so 'economically' (that is, as a concession) but they are normally[217] not permitted to serve again as priests, though in times past they could continue serving the church in another capacity, such as teacher, clerk, or choirmaster. Lay men and women who are bereaved are in exactly the same situation, canonically speaking. A second marriage is not regarded as a proper Christian response. Nevertheless, economically, a dispensation from the strictly appropriate course of action is allowed. A second marriage is permitted to them, without any canonical impediment being raised as to their future approach to the eucharistic mysteries. Nevertheless the second marriage is celebrated in church with liturgical signs of repentance. It is celebrated without some of the festive elements of the full crowning service, and with penitential prayers inserted, in just the same way as for a marriage that follows after a divorce. In Orthodoxy even a third marriage is allowed in church (this one celebrated with even more marked elements of penance inserted within it); but never a fourth.

321

The church, by the fourth century in the East, had realized that this ideal state of marriage was not one that could easily be 'presumed' to be standard. It was the appropriate condition for Christians to enter into lifelong marriages whose ongoing love and freshness made them a veritable icon of the joy of the Kingdom: but such was not always the case. Marriages withered, and were shattered for a variety of reasons. By the fourth century, just as the penitential system had allowed more exceptions to its primitive rigour, so too did the earlier prohibitions of any form of second marriage begin to give way also. Roman (secular) law had permitted the possibility of divorce and remarriage; and the church was increasingly faced with the pastoral problem of Christians who had divorced under secular law, and were now being refused the right to communicate under church law. St Gregory of Nazianzus, himself a dedicated and large-hearted ascetic celibate, who in the late fourth century was the archbishop of Constantinople, wrote one of the first 'position papers' on the pastoral need to allow leeway for the case of marital breakdown. His eloquent sermon[218] directs that one should always exegete Christ's sayings with regard for the 'mind of the Lawgiver', not simply the apparent meaning of the words.

Having thus set out his principles, he set himself to comment on the Lord's words prohibiting divorce.[219] If the context of the mind of the lawgiver is critical in all attempts to settle legislation, then in the case of the Lord his compassion was perennially at the forefront of all he said and did. In Gregory's estimate, the men and women of his time were 'like fishes swimming in a sea of misery' and Christ's intent as lawgiver would be to show mercy. For this reason above all others, Gregory argues, the church should not insist on the full rigour of the spiritual law of single marriage. If a marriage has foundered publicly and permanently, the church should not 'close its eyes' pretending that it has not. If such a marriage is clearly not the mystery which will 'endure into the Kingdom' an economy could be made to allow disciples another chance to discover the mystery of love. After the time of Gregory this has become the standard canonical treatment of marriage in the Eastern Church: the celebration of the first marriage; an economical allowance for the second marriage; a reluctant permission for the third marriage. The teaching in St Basil the Great's Canonical Epistle is also given much authority in this regard.

Is this granting of ecclesial economy a refusal of allegiance to the Lord's teaching on the indissolubility of marriage? Well, he himself made an exception to the general rule of refusal of divorce, and that was the exceptional case of adultery. Such a wreckage of the essential meaning of marriage as a sacrament of love and sacrament of the unity of the Kingdom has rendered what was a potentially holy thing into a non-existent spiritual bond. Secular attitudes can often speak as if marital sexual infidelity (including the admittance of others into the sexual intimacy of a married couple) was a normal type of strain and stress which a marriage can weather (especially if the unfaithful partner can successfully cover it up). Spiritually speaking this is completely false. The secular contract might endure the infidelity. The spiritual sacrament, however, has certainly withered in a fatal way. The consecration can only be found again through another mystery, that of *metanoia*.

At first the Orthodox Church only allowed divorce and remarriage for the cause of adultery which had *de facto* proved the first union was hardly that which would 'endure into the Kingdom' since it could hardly endure a few years on earth. Eventually, however, and again for pastoral reasons of compassion, it began to allow a few other causes as well.[220] A secular divorce, on its own, is not sufficient to permit a second marriage in church. It is the bishop alone (sometimes through his chancery, and sometimes through delegation to his parish priests) who should review the petition from an Orthodox Christian to secure an ecclesiastical blessing, and who will act in the person of the Lord to give absolution and permission to contract another marriage in church. Marital breakdown is a result of sin and weakness. Adultery or the uncontainable alienation and mutual antipathy of the partners is a direct contradiction of that most particular vocation, and command of discipleship, given to the married couple by the Lord: 'Love one another as I have loved you.'[221] For this reason, however complex or multifaceted a breakdown can be, it has also been a defection from the mind of Christ, and the ecclesiastical divorce is granted as a concession to mercy once the repentance of the believer has been demonstrated. It is in this way that the teaching of the Lord that marriage is a profound symbol of unity is combined with the sad reality that many Christians fall short of this goal, and then need the consolations of the Lord of mercy, who will not close to them the fountain of grace. In each case it is the duty of the local priest to counsel parishioners whose marriages are in difficulties, and try to help them before a breakdown becomes inevitable. Nevertheless there are times when this cannot be remedied, and in those cases the church extends a deep pastoral mercy. It is, indeed, one of the signs of the authenticity of the church that there is never a case in the catalogue of all the failings and sufferings of the earthly disciples (apart from the stubborn denial of Christ) which cannot be healed by the church's pastoral mercy, administered with careful wisdom in the name of the Lord by the ruling bishop, and guided by the canons that are designed to discipline, cure, and lead the church collectively to the standard of Christ's compassion. It is because of its gracious pastoral care that the Orthodox Church, so clear and decisive about its doctrinal and ethical teachings, does not lose sight of the suffering human person in the midst of it all. Orthodoxy is never a fanatical or zealotic religion: its sympathy for the individual is too deeply developed to allow it to be such. In this attitude it has the confidence that it is following the footsteps of Christ himself, who combined truth and justice with boundless mercy.

The mysteries of ordination

The mysteries, so far, have combined a pattern of general initiation (such as baptism, through which gate all Christians must pass) with that of specific invitation to a certain form of lifestyle as disciple (such as marriage). Ordination is another of the specific mysteries that consecrate certain men (in ancient times it embraced women too in one of its degrees) for specific service in the Church of God. Priesthood in the Christian Church is different from all other understandings of priesthood within history. It is not that of the Old Covenant, where certain families were set apart from birth as ancestral priests and Levites (the *kohanim*). The Lord himself was not a priest in the Levitical or Aaronic line: for he did not inherit this gift from an earthly father. He was a priest in a different order of religion. The Scriptures describe him as a priest in the order of Melchisedek.[222] He was the king of Salem (his name means 'King of Righteousness' and his title was 'King of Peace') who brought gifts of bread and wine, and blessed Abraham in the name of 'God the Most High', and to whom Abraham gave a tithe of

323

his goods. The apostolic writer of Hebrews uses this symbol of Levi (still unborn) giving homage to Melchisedek as a sign of the old priesthood acknowledging the superiority of the new priesthood that Jesus, a descendant of Judah, brought along with the New Covenant he instituted.[223] For the author of Hebrews, the High Priest, Jesus, enters a sanctuary not made by human hands, and his own blood is a sacrifice of atonement which needs no repetition, but cleanses the church definitively, for all time. Symbolically (that is, typologically), Jesus is a priest of the order of Melchisedek, appointed to this salvific ministry of reconciliation of mankind with the Most High God, by his Father alone: not from any human law of descent. What is true, however, is that Melchisedek's priesthood is a 'type' and not an antecedent. In other words 'of the order of Melchisedek' does not mean 'in the order of Melchisedek'.

The unique high priesthood of Jesus is only figured by Melchisedek, but does not find its origin there. So, in the Church of Christ there remains the one priesthood of the Lord: this is the source of all the power of reconciliation which Christ himself continually and unfailingly presides over in his ever-active ministry of reconciliation and the bestowal of grace. All grace and life flow from the Father, through the priesthood of Christ, to the church in the energy and grace of the Holy Spirit. There is no place for any intrusion in this system of the transmission of grace. The only power of priesthood in the Church of Christ, therefore, remains that of the Lord. For such reasons, understanding this aspect of the Scriptures correctly, some Christian movements within Protestantism have gone on to conclude (most erroneously in the judgement of Orthodoxy) that there can be no such thing as a specific office of Christian priesthood represented by any human disciples. It is instructive, both historically and theologically, that the widescale rejection of the concept of Christian priesthood in the time of the Reformation also led to an extensive collapse of the sacramental system in those same movements. How closely the two things are connected. This, in a deep sense, shows that an understanding of the mystery of the priesthood reveals in itself a clear window onto the nature of all the mysteries, and their operations of grace.

Christian priesthood is not a sacral phenomenon, distinct from Christ's priesthood, and not a mere 'office' to which certain Christian individuals can be elected, or from which they can be deselected, as a matter of administrative convenience. In the Orthodox understanding, Christian priesthood is a sacred sharing in the charism of the Lord's own high priesthood which he gives to certain elected members of his own flock, so that they can lead it, and teach it, and act as his own ministers of sanctification within it. Their powers of teaching and sanctifying are his power. They offer themselves as ministers of his single grace. Their sanctification and blessing is his holiness and benediction: the reconciliation they mediate is the sole reconciliation which he alone has mediated for the world. The Christian priest, consecrated as a minister of the Lord in his church, is an icon of the Lord's single high priesthood, never separated from it; never understandable in any sense apart from it. It is a most honoured and sacred mystery of grace to be elected into such an exaltation of office; but it is a charism that is always empowered by the priestly grace of Christ himself.

In the Orthodox Church it is the custom for the faithful to greet a bishop or a priest by kissing his hand. This the believers do because they show their profound respect for the hand that has touched the mysteries of the Lord himself, in the celebration of the Eucharist, and the hand that has been given by Christ the power to bless and heal and sanctify. Some of the younger clergy, aware that all that they have in the ministry of priesthood is the grace of the Lord's own holiness, sometimes try to withhold their hand, as if they were saying 'I am not worthy.' This is a mistake. No one believed they were worthy in the first place! The faith of the people that expresses itself in the kissing of their hand is not offered to them: it is offered through them, as living icons, to the hand of the High Priest, the Lord himself. Just as it is a mistake to think that veneration offered to an icon of the Lord is a false worship offered merely to wood and paint (which would be idolatry of the dimmest type), so it is mistake to think that Christian priesthood, as found among Christ's bishops and priests and deacons through this sacred mystery of ordination, is a division or a diminution of Christ's sole high priesthood. It is merely one of the ways in which it is flashed out on the world and among the believers. It is a great gift and deeply loved by the faithful. It is perplexing to the Orthodox why the beauty of the sharing of Christ's priestly ministry among his church has been so decisively rejected among so many parts of Western Christianity which only recognizes the common 'priesthood of all believers'; and from this there follows a large alienation from the Orthodox ethos.

The gift of ordained priesthood is a specific focusing of the gift of priestly grace given to all the baptized in their chrismation at baptism. It is, nevertheless, not reducible to this 'priesthood of all believers'. The sacred chrismation elevates in all the baptized the priestly charism of the disciple: to share in Christ's work of reconciliation, and to take their own part (in living out the Gospel) in the sacred cosmic task of the consecration of matter, and the rendering of history subservient to the claims of the Kingdom. Ordination confers another set of charisms, based upon this overarching gift of baptismal consecration, but which are more specific and more elevated. They are related first and foremost to the offices of sanctifying, leading, and teaching the flock of Christ.

In Orthodoxy there are three degrees of priesthood: that of the deacon (*diakonos*, a word which means the servant or the minister), the priest (*presbyteros*, which means the elder), and the bishop (*episkopos*, which means the overseer or superintendent). The word 'priesthood' is itself an Old English corruption of the Greek *presbyter*. Eventually the church adopted the words for priesthood that had been common parlance in the ancient Hellenistic world (*sacerdos* in the Latin West, after Cyprian; and *hiereus* in the Greek East), but at first the Christian Fathers were anxious to make it clear that the church had a very different sense of 'priests' ministering among it than did the pagan cults. Once that difference was understood and established, however, the wider range of words for priestly office was admitted into patristic literature. Nevertheless it is still important to remember that for Christ's community a new sense of priesthood was initiated by the Lord himself. Christian priesthood has typological antecedents, both in the Melchisedekian and Aaronic priesthoods, but more fundamentally it is something that is wholly new in Christ, and which wholly derives from the Lord. The Christian priest does not manifest a share in the charism of Christ's priesthood as if this could be cut up and divided out. Just as it is with the Eucharist itself, the one bread is 'broken, but never divided, eaten but never consumed',[224] and so too the one high priesthood of Christ empowers the sacred priestly ministry of all those he has called to this intimate and awesome form of obedience and discipleship. The priest exercising the sacred charism of his ordained office is a medium of the priestly power of Christ, a channel of the Lord's own sanctifying grace. Just as there is only one Eucharist in the world despite the great number of eucharistic celebrations experienced daily, so too there is only ultimately the one priesthood of the Lord manifested in the church through the number of disciples called to share in his pastoral work, and given specific charisms to apply for the benefit of the chosen people. The priest, like the Lord himself, is one who is at the service of the people of God. If he is a leader of the people, with a status that is remarkable, it is because he has learned from the Master the charism of being the minister, that is the servant, of all.[225]

Orthodoxy speaks of ordination in two forms. Only the first is specifically and particularly relevant to the mystery of ordination. The key word describing this mystery is *cheirotenia*. This is 'the laying on of hands', which is witnessed in the Scriptures as an apostolic charism of conferring the grace of the Holy Spirit for special ministry,[226] and which harks back to the Lord's own method of conferring grace by the powerful laying on of his hands.[227] This laying on of hands, as performed in the apostolic ministry and by the council of the presbyters,[228] is continued now by the 'laying on of hands' bestowing the sacred chrism in baptism, through the absolution prayer when the penitent receives the laying on of hands for the forgiveness of sins, through the laying on of hands for healing in the mystery of the unction, and lastly in the mystery of ordination when the bishop lays hands upon the head of the person to be consecrated for priestly service as bishop, priest, or deacon. All of these laying on of hands are integral to the greater mysteries. There is also a second term in use: *cheirothesia*. This word also designates the laying on of hands, but for a lesser blessing. It bestows what are known as the 'minor orders' as distinct from the three 'major orders'. Today the minor orders have been restricted to those of subdeacon and lector (reader). In the ancient church there were several others, such as exorcist, fossor (gravedigger), acolyte, porter, and several 'orders' specific to Christian women such as widows and virgins. All of these have now lapsed and been 'restricted' because of changed circumstances. But they show the way for the principle of having specific ministries formally acknowledged by the church by the special 'blessing' and public approval, and commission, of the bishop. These blessings of *cheirothesia* are not ordinations as such, not part of the great mysteries, and are conducted at the offices of the church (Vespers or Matins) not during the course of the eucharistic liturgy.

In the ancient church, and up until the twelfth century, the priestly order of diaconate was accessible to women. They too were ordained at the altar, during the sacred liturgy, with the laying on of hands by the bishop, and thereafter stood vested in their sacred dalmatics and stoles, for the celebration of the eucharistic liturgy with the other clergy. The form of the ordination prayer for female deacons, and the placing of it within in the eucharistic liturgy around the altar itself, are clear signs that we are speaking here of a sacred ordination (*cheirotenia*) not a mere blessing (*cheirothesia*) as some writers have argued.[229] The female diaconate was distinguished from the male diaconate only in that the women deacons did not administer the eucharistic gifts publicly, although they themselves received the gifts along with the other deacons around the altar of the church. They were also required to be celibates.[230] The liturgical witness of women deacons was a great blessing for the church which after the twelfth century (much earlier in the Western Church) faded away. Some have said that this was a providential development. It is hard to see their justification for so surprising a conclusion considering that the ordination ritual for women deacons still exists in the sacred liturgical books of the church, thus clearly testifying to its status as an integral part of the Orthodox tradition; and the abolition of the office came about as a result of the increasing social collapse that affected the Byzantine world after the rise of Islam. It came about, therefore, as a result of the oppressive damage being done to the Christian movement in the wider culture of the medieval East, not as a positive response based on Christian developments. It also has to be confessed that the attitude of the predominantly male monastic movement after the fourth century was hostile to the concept of the deaconess. After the sixth century, when the bishops themselves were co-opted into the celibate ranks of the ascetics, the phenomenon, still seen in the fourth-century golden age of the Fathers, where deaconesses could even be members of the bishop's own family,[231] became more and more a mere memory. Monastics, who themselves were at first not a regular part of the local church organization (living in the wilderness far away from the metropolitan church) soon came to dominate the ranks of clergy, and thereafter pressed for the appointment of more and more celibate clerics by preference.

Monastic pressures first exiled the deaconesses from smaller village churches, and finally from the larger city cathedrals, where even into the Middle Ages aristocratic and powerful Christian women, could still be found gracing the ranks of the major clergy. Recently the Church of Greece decided synodically to allow each of the bishops the option of blessing ascetic female 'deaconesses' to serve in the convents, and to offer the already consecrated eucharistic gifts to ascetic communities which did not have the benefit of clergy. It was a development noted with wide interest, though the synod made it abundantly clear that this was not an ordination (*cheirotenia*) they were engaged in, but a *cheirothesia*. For a 'deaconess' to be appointed in this way, of course, would be the equivalent of the elevation of a new form of minor order designated for women. However significant this movement is, therefore, it has not yet addressed the issue of whether, and how, the ordination of female deacons could be reinstated within the Orthodox Church, and so it is difficult to see, at the present, whether this initiative will be a positive one, or a side-stepping of important questions (the invention of the role of 'neo-deaconess' considered as a blessing for female monastics). It is a question of high importance at a time in Orthodoxy when women's education has brought them to the very forefront of societal life in a manner that once more raises new potentialities for a reinvigoration of the forms of women's ministry within the church, and accordingly will have to be seriously discussed among all levels of the faithful, until a new synodical consensus can be established.

In the Western Church the councils of Epaon (517) and Orléans (533) specifically ruled to abolish the female diaconate, though it survived elsewhere among Latin Christians until the eleventh century. There was no formal synodical rejection of the ministry in the East and there is no impediment, theoretically speaking, to the restoration of this ancient order if (as many Orthodox now think) it could serve an important role in the future for women disciples exercising the specific functions of ordained clergy. In ancient times the male and female deacons supplied different functions within the church, though the ministry of both is specifically characterized by their 'availability' of service to the larger community. In antiquity this was clearly marked by the way the male deacons administered the social welfare of the community, as well as the leading of the public prayers in the nave, and the regular assistance in the distribution of the gifts. Female deacons took special care for the education of women in the church, and assisted at their baptisms, and took predominant charge of the visitation of sick women in their homes, and the distribution of the gifts to them, privately.

An ordination to one of the major orders can only take place individually within Orthodox liturgical practice.[232] That is, no more than one deacon, one priest, and one bishop can be ordained at any single eucharistic liturgy. The ordinations to each of the three major ranks take place at different times in the course of the celebration of the Eucharist, symbolizing different aspects of the ministry of each of the three.[233] While an archimandrite or an archpriest can be delegated to serve as the bishop's representative at the blessing of a minor order, only a bishop in person can ordain a person to one of the three major orders of priesthood. If it is a bishop that is being ordained (the word consecrated is also sometimes used of episcopal ordinations) there must be three ordaining bishops to perform the mystery (or never fewer than two).[234] This is because a bishop's office is essentially collegial, and the ordination by the pre-existing episcopal colleagues of the region signifies their acceptance of the new bishop's doctrinal orthodoxy and impeccable character of life. Ordinations also allow the whole people of God to express their involvement. At a certain stage in the ordination process the candidate is 'presented' to the congregation by the ordaining bishop. It is customary for the people in church to shout out 'Axios!' (He is worthy!), and so, given the people's consent, the service proceeds. The consultation is a remnant of the robust system of the ancient church, wherein if the local congregation did not approve of 'their' candidate, they were unlikely to accept a minister imposed on them by the will of the college of bishops, or the aristocrats. There were many occasions in the early church where a bishop ordained in the capital for a provincial post had to return to the capital crestfallen, since he was ejected by a non-receptive local population. The great Constantinopolitan archbishop Proclus was one such example: he lived in the capital for such a long time prior to his elevation because he had been rejected by the local church for whom he had been first ordained as a bishop.

Bishops, since the sixth century have been required to be celibate. This means that today (although it was not the case in the early patristic age, when many bishops such as St Gregory the Theologian's father, Gregorios the Elder, or St Gregory of Nyssa, or Synesios of Cyrene, were married) bishops can only be selected from among the monastic clergy. The chief scriptural 'qualifications' for a bishop[235] presume that he ought to be married and to have 'proved' himself in the administration of his own family before assuming the guidance of the whole diocese. The prescripts of 1 Timothy now, of course, cannot be fulfilled by the college of bishops, except symbolically. It is not impossible that in a future age the requirements of the Quinisext Council, establishing celibacy as a necessity for bishops, might be changed again, if they were felt to be for the greater good of a church in a new environment. Some Orthodox theologians have recently suggested this should be an item of discussion in a mooted great pan-Orthodox council. If such a council ever meets this matter of discipline may well be discussed. One of the current problems is the relatively constrained nature of the monastic life as now existing within Orthodoxy. As we are not exactly in one of the 'great ages' of monasticism, it might be argued that restricting the supply of bishops to the churches solely from the ranks of the ascetics is a policy that is no longer as brilliantly inspired as it once was. Metropolitan Kallistos once described the situation in the following words:

> Such is the case of monasticism in many parts of the Orthodox Church today that it is not always easy to find suitable candidates for the episcopate, and a few Orthodox have even begun to argue that the limitation of bishops to the monastic clergy is no

longer desirable under modern conditions. Yet surely the true solution is not to change the present rule that bishops must be monks, but to reinvigorate the monastic life itself.[236]

How that reinvigoration might be orchestrated is, of course, a difficult matter to envisage. Also perhaps the point is being missed here, that while monastic bishops have brought inestimable glory to the church in the quality and character of their leadership in the past, as well as in the fire of their dedication and selflessness, one nevertheless has to admit that the charisms of the married leader have also been sadly missing for many centuries. The pastoral benefits of an episcopal father of the flock who had been through the joys and sorrows of married life, and known the complexities, passions, and turmoil of bringing up children and feeling their own lives (in all their diverse joys and sorrows) as a direct extensions of his, is something that one should not underestimate as being of benefit to the people of God. Indeed the election to the Orthodox episcopate of many widower-priests both in the past and in the present, has manifested something of this important charism to the wider family of God.

The spiritual office of the bishop is first and foremost to be the icon of Christ in the local church. He rules the church, with the loving humility of Christ himself. His power over the family of believers is that of the chief servant of the flock. Imaging Christ himself, the bishop is the servant-lord of the people of God. The chief charism of the episcopal priesthood is reflected in a threefold intertwining of activities: the first of these is his call to expound the word of God to the people as a whole.

In ancient times it was the bishop alone who preached on the meaning of the Scriptures to the assembled church. Only in later times when the extent of the community became so large that this was impractical, was the task of preaching the word also delegated to the presbyters. This remains, today, one of the chief functions of the episcopal charism. It means something far more than simply offering homiletics on Sunday, of course. The exposition of the Word of God, springing from profound exegesis of the prophetic and apostolic words of Scripture, means that the bishop is charged with being the leading prophetic interpreter of the community: translating for it, and unravelling for it, how the complexities of day-to-day life can become transparent to the call of God in the present moment. The exegesis of the Scripture in church thus begins the larger exegetical duty of the bishop for his people: to guide them in the byways of modern life along the true Gospel path. This sacred task of preaching the Word also includes the duty of the bishop to ensure the present Orthodoxy of his churches: how in each church true doctrine is continually manifested in accordance with the ancient traditions of the apostles and Fathers. To this extent the bishop has a supervisory role[237] over all the teaching of his clergy and faithful. It would be inconceivable in the Orthodox Church for believers, or clergy, or theologians, to regard themselves as 'independent of' or 'above' this episcopal right; accordingly, there exists, generally speaking, a very close and genuine bond between the bishops and the local clergy and faithful. The bishop, in exercising this charism, watches over the spiritual and intellectual life of his local church.

The synod of bishops, meeting together regularly, exercises the same pastoral role in relation to the individual bishop; ensuring their collegial togetherness (Slavonic: sobornost) or 'catholic' oneness in the faith. The ultimate expression of this sobornost, and its ultimate safeguard in seriously important matters is the General (Ecumenical) Council of the church, whose deliberations were restricted to bishops.[238] Decisions of the bishops assembled together in the ecumenical councils are given a unique status within the church. They were not regarded as a majority vote on obscure matters; on the contrary, the gathering of bishops at such occasions was always seen by the Orthodox as a moment of high inspiration when the hierarchs exercised their priestly and prophetic charism with one mind. When new problems arose they were expected not to have to struggle to find the 'correct' solution, or a new formula to 'save' the faith, but were expected to be able to stand together with a single voice and soul, and express the ancient faith of Christianity in which they had been brought up, and which they themselves had formed in their own churches. This is why, for an ancient ecumenical council, nothing less than a totally unanimous vote was required on all matters of faith.[239]

The second of the threefold charisms of the episcopate is the offering of the gifts in the eucharistic Anaphora. The bishop is the president of the eucharistic offering of all the churches of his diocese. In primitive times when there was only one church building in all the dioceses, this was an easier task to manifest symbolically. The presbyters all gathered around the bishop who made the great prayer of offering in their midst and on behalf of all. Before the great eucharistic prayers were written down, and formalized, they were extemporized. The presiding bishop, therefore, was expected to be able to act prophetically, to sing out the eucharistic praises of all the church, through the great spiritual joy in his own faithful heart. Later, when the presbyters went out separately to preside over the Eucharist in parish churches, the clarity of the symbolism of the single president was somewhat blurred. But the principle remains the same today: no Eucharist in the Orthodox Church takes place apart from the unity of the local bishop. The priest is appointed to this task by his ruling bishop, and both he and the people will always pray for the diocesan bishop, by name, at several parts of the ritual. The bishop's charism of unity is expressed, mystically, above all else in the way he is at the heart of the whole of the local church's joyful celebration of the unifying presence of Christ in the Eucharist.[240]

The third of the three charisms woven together in the episcopal calling is related to the two preceding ones, that is the roles of teaching and sanctification, and consists in the bishop's power, given to him in the apostolic succession, to 'rule' the local church. This charism of the supreme rule over the local church belongs to the bishop alone, and to the presbyters by delegation.[241] This he exercises by supervising and applying the ancient canons of the church's discipline. These, in their own turn, ensure Orthodoxy and purity among the body of believers. Always, the bishop is charged to put into effect this ministry of the discipline of his church in the spirit of the loving Christ, the Good Shepherd, who was willing to walk over the mountains if necessary to find out and welcome back even the one wandering lamb. The supervision of the canons means that a bishop is required to be familiar with them all, and to always seek to deepen the discretion he has from Christ, to know when it is appropriate to enforce them or when he should 'close his eyes'. In this way, guided by pastoral concern and a love for the preservation of the holy tradition, the bishop passes on the guidance of the local church to his eventual successor. It is not enough for a bishop simply to stand as a 'rock of unchanging tradition'. The fight for the ancient tradition of the church in the modern age is not a thing that can be undertaken by someone who chooses the most conservative or reactionary position possible on any question that is posed to him, in any circumstance. Such a philosophy can ensure that little happens under a bishop's watch over his church: but the little that happens may also mean that little happens for the good as well as for the bad. The true bishop's response to the need to preserve the ancient tradition alive and powerful in this conflicted age of the church is something much greater than that simple self-identification with conservatism, and incomparably more elevated as a spiritual path of life. It is nothing short than the call for the bishop to stand before the local church as the one Christian in the community who has pre-eminently fulfilled the common vocation of all to 'be' Christ, for the sake of the other. But this vocation is of awesome responsibility, and inevitably involves a heavy cross. When an Orthodox bishop is ordained, it is customary for the concelebrant bishops to console him (as much as to congratulate him) after the consecration.

The bishop's 'engagement' with his local church is regarded in Orthodoxy as tantamount to a marriage. It is not expected that a bishop will 'leave' his ecclesial charge, but rather that he will live with it and die in it, as a faithful spouse. Today this rule is not always observed in the strict spirit of the canons of Nicaea, and there are bishops who retire, and who are 'promoted' to other sees. But it is still common for an Orthodox bishop to live out the whole of his priestly ministry in faithfulness to one church until death. This makes it all the more pressing, of course, for the selection of bishops to be undertaken with supreme discretion. The charism is such an elevated one, and so difficult to support, that the fulfilment of its manifold aspects requires the loving support and harmony of all the clergy and people. St Gregory the Theologian, in his *Defence of his Flight*,[242] called this shepherding of minds that was at the essence of the governing charism the most difficult of all tasks and the 'vocation of vocations'.

The office of the bishop has since earliest times been recognized by the church as the direct descendant of the apostolic charism of the leadership of the churches of God. The bishop, then, is appointed as leader of the local church in the apostolic succession, and bears special charisms which are proper to him alone in the Christian priesthood. His word and his discretion can dispense a Christian from obligations and duties, or can require them to fulfil them under penalty.[243] The bishop alone has the power and right to ordain others to the priesthood in all its degrees. He alone is in charge of the gathering together (the *synaxis*) for the Holy Eucharist. All the ecclesiastical institutions in the diocese, each parish and religious foundation,[244] look to him as the spiritual head and inspiration. It is an awesomely demanding office, and one that is not always accepted when the holy synod of a church calls a monk to adopt it. The synod has no power to force any of the faithful to become a bishop, and there are several examples of shining candidates who have not had the heart to accept. Those who do take to themselves the love for a whole family of God, and bear the charge of presenting it before God at the altar, and supervising its zeal and its progress. They must always look for any way they can render the communion of the faithful in their diocese more zealous, more dedicated, more transparent to the grace of the Spirit. This task, of course, is made the more possible when they too, by virtue of their high consecration, themselves become ever more transparent to the grace of the loving Christ. Bishops who have achieved this metamorphosis into the humility of Christ are justly loved by the faithful, who regard them, rightly, as living icons of Christ the High Priest.

At his ordination as a bishop the new candidate is specially scrutinized for the character of his doctrine. It is an especial duty of the bishop to see that right doctrine (the Nicene faith of the church) is proclaimed in the churches, and that the Gospel is preached and the mysteries correctly administered. Orthodox bishops are in regular contact with their people, and are always welcome guests in their visitations to the local parishes, which they tend to visit on the occasions of the local feast days, not simply when there is a problem to be addressed. In many parts of the Orthodox world, the bishops are very significant political leaders as well as moral and spiritual guides. A bishop possessed of a powerful charism of his office will often be attended by thousands of people when he goes to an area on visitation, and his words carry weight, unlike in the more secularized West, where the office has tended to fall under some degree of scorn. It is often an experience of very deep and graceful charism to encounter an Orthodox bishop, especially those many who are suffused with the gentleness and joy of Christ.

As for presbyters and deacons, Orthodox canon law stipulates that a priest must not be ordained until he has reached the age of 30, and a deacon not before 25. There are exceptions that can be made to this general rule, but it stands to ensure that a general degree of 'maturity' is witnessed in the local leaders of the Christian community. In antiquity those ages would be the equivalent of now adding at least fifteen years more to each of them. As well as personal spiritual refinement,[245] and the will to serve, the ordained clergy ought above all to demonstrate compassion and a zeal for the work of the Lord; whether that is in the form of administering the active works of a parish or diocese (a typical diaconal charism) or for teaching and guiding disciples in the ways of the Spirit (a typical episcopal and priestly charism). The work of all three orders of the priesthood reaches a synthesis in the Holy Eucharist, the common celebration of which is the focal point around which their other priestly functions revolve: the deacon in the leading of the prayers and litanies, and the assistance of the bishop, the priest in the offering of prayers and blessings and the offering of the great Anaphora in the companionship of the bishop, and the bishop himself in the exegesis of the sacred Scriptures for the benefit of the people of God, and in his teaching and pastoral rule. The three orders together are meant to work as a single harmony.

The deacons at first were the close associates of the bishop, and their office retains many marks of this association. In parishes today they may assist the priest in the celebration of the liturgy (never serving the mysteries alone). They stand in different times in the altar, and without, leading the prayers of the people, and then having care of the sacred vessels containing the eucharistic gifts, and assisting the priest in the distribution of the gifts to the people. To them falls the care of good order inside the churches during times of prayer, and they have an oversight of the minor orders and how they conduct themselves during divine service. In the ancient church their primary works outside the liturgy were the administration of the church's charitable offices. In later times this task was often displaced by the monastics. During the liturgy the deacon wears a broad robe (*sticharion*), often in a cloth of gold, and over it a stole which is the special symbol of his office (*orarion*), which is very long and worn diagonally over the shoulder. Near the time of communion the *orarion* is wrapped around the deacon in a cross-shaped fashion to symbolize that the diaconal office typifies the presence of the angels during the sacred liturgy.

The priest originally served his liturgical function in a college. This collegial character of the priesthood is still seen in the ancient rite of concelebration of the Eucharist
by several priests together, or with the bishop and deacons. In the earliest period of
the church the presbytery served as a council of elders, and occupied the easternmost
ring of benches in the churches, in the apse of the church building behind the Holy
Table. The bishop would preside over the council of elders, and to this day a bishop will
always serve as the president of any celebration of a Eucharist at which he is present
with his clergy. It was the bishop's particular duty to expound the Word of God as
well as to lead the great eucharistic prayer. As the church expanded, the original unity
of the bishop, priest, and deacons, physically manifested in their common prayer, was
disrupted as presbyters were sent out into the country regions, or into the suburbs
as city churches grew too large for one single building to contain all the faithful.
The priest in the provinces or suburbs became then the single president of the
Eucharist, representing the bishop in this office. After the fourth century it also became
more and more common for priests to exegete the sacred Scriptures too. This remains a
sacred function of both bishops and priests, which was meant to demonstrate how the
Scriptures remained prophetically alive and relevant for the day-to-day lives of the
people. It is all too easy for this task of preaching to degenerate into boring homiletics;
but it is essentially a sacred charism that demands a careful and energized prophetic
ministry, and should never be carelessly neglected or underestimated.

In Orthodoxy a priest cannot celebrate the eucharistic mysteries legitimately without delegation from the bishop. This is usually symbolized in the bishop entrusting
the local priest with the signed *antimension*, the altar cloth which authorizes and
makes possible the celebration of the Eucharist under the diocesan bishop's authority.
To this extent the priest's immediate authority to sanctify, and teach, and rule, derives
from the bishop who is, typologically speaking, the 'High Priest' under Christ. The
priesthood of the presbyter, however, does not derive from the bishop, except as
mediated through him in the sacrament of ordination. This is because the priesthood
of all the three ranks derives directly from Christ, and represents the single priestly
charism of the Lord himself ever active in the church as its sole principle of sanctification in the Spirit. The rule manifested in the three orders of priesthood is that of the
whole church taken to a higher pitch of symphony: that there should be one heart and
one mind. A bishop ought not to act like a disconnected monarch in the diocese, but
should consider the council of the presbyters. The presbyters in turn should honour
and support the bishop as the father of the diocese, bearing the apostolic charism of the
leadership of the whole people of God. The deacons ought to work in harmony with the
bishops and priests, be supported by them in their important work, and be respected by
them as co-workers and brethren. In this symphony of body and soul the pattern of
Christ's own authority is manifested, the authority of the Servant Lord. Sadly, in many
cases, the ecclesiastical mentality erects around itself a love for rankings and distinctions,
and in some cases the system of the spiritual symphony of the clergy can degenerate
into something that evokes a parallel army: with officers, superior and inferior.

In times past it was often the case that a much more elevated standard of education
was required of the higher clergy. Village deacons and village priests were often not
very well educated at all. In those cases the bishop would often restrict the right
to preach and hear confessions to the more educated clergy of the towns, those
whom he had licensed to teach. These more educated clergy would travel round the

different parishes over the course of a year. Today the educational standards of Orthodox clergy are once again on the rise after centuries of political setbacks when even the very textbooks necessary for a basic seminary education were systematically denied them. By the grace of God a new era of peace may witness a new generation of educational deepening in the candidates for the priesthood. Orthodoxy, however, has always known that it required in its priests not merely an intelligent capacity for teaching and governance of the parishes, but pre-eminently men of the spirit, who could serve as living icons of the love of the Lord who was in their midst.

Because of their iconic role all the Orthodox clergy are expected to appear in the churches always in the correct clerical dress. In some of the former communist-governed countries of eastern Europe the custom of clergy always wearing clerical dress in ordinary life too has not been universally observed, but in Greece, for example, it would be most unusual for a priest not to wear the *riassa*, or cassock, in public as well as in church. Priests serving in the parishes of the Russian Orthodox tradition also wear a pectoral cross.[246] Other clergy, of different national churches, wear the cross as a sign of distinction, as a gift of the bishop or the local synod. The clergy of the Slavonic tradition who are distinguished in this way for special services are given a golden cross;[247] the ordinary clergy wear a silver cross. Married clergy wear a black *riassa* but can also wear different colours (grey or blue are common), while monastic clergy always wear black. For formal liturgical occasions, the monastic clergy wear over their heads a large cylindrical hat with a long black veil coming out from behind. Married clergy also wear the priest's hat but it has a smaller, cylindrical shape. The Greek parish clergy have a small rim around the top of this, giving rise to the colloquial description of it as a 'stove-pipe hat'. Monastic priests and deacons are known as 'black' clergy, while those that are married are known as the 'white clergy'.

A candidate for the diaconate or priesthood must, if they wish to marry, be married before ordination. After ordination remarriage is not permitted to serving priests. Those who are ordained without being married are generally expected to become monastics before their ordination. There are some celibate clergy who have not taken the monastic habit, although they live celibate lives, but they are not many. It used to be the expectation that parish clergy, priests and deacons, would be married with families of their own living in the parish which they served. The shortage of clergy has for many years made the monastic parish priest a regular factor in Orthodoxy, although the situation is not meant to be the norm. In parishes in Orthodox countries where there are monasteries of monks and nuns within reasonable distance, there is a very close relationship between the parishioners and the monastics. The clergy will often take out large numbers of their parishioners on annual visits (or even more frequently) and both the parochial clergy and the faithful will avail of the monasteries' spiritual elders for advice and spiritual guidance.

The office of the priest, like that of the bishop, is marked above all else by its call to assist Christ in the perfection of his church. It is, in essence, a sanctificatory charism that the priest fulfils. The supreme example of this is the priest's involvement in the sacred blessings which constitute the holy mysteries, most especially the Eucharist, which for most priests is the 'holy ground' of their encounter with the Lord, and the essential locus of their understanding of priestly charism. But Christ's grace of priest-hood flows out in the 'liturgy after the liturgy' just as much, and catches up within it all aspects of the priest's life: his marriage, or his monastic life, his personal development and spiritual refinement: all things are charged with a new light for someone who has been initiated into this great mystery. It is like a source of light shining out from coloured crystal. The thing remains the same, but in this new light it is never seen in the same way again. In many times past, even in anciently established Orthodox countries, the vocation of the priesthood was 'looked down on' as a form of career path. One result of this was that, especially in Russia for example, priests tended to be ordained out of priestly families, and married the daughters of other priestly families. This is no longer as prevalent as it was, though some priestly families within Orthodoxy still run back over several generations. With rising standards of education among the clergy, it can be hoped that their social standing may also improve, though when all is said and done, those who receive the blessing of ordination know that, however much the wider world may despise them, their vocation to be Christ's priests is one of the most luminous life-paths that there can be. In times of crisis in the church (one recalls the dark years of Soviet power, or the period of the civil war in Greece) the priests have always been among the first to give the witness of their life-blood for the sake of Christ and his church. The number of priests killed by Soviet persecutors in the twentieth century puts them in a class that can more than hold up its head alongside that of the martyrs of antiquity. All over the world, in little dusty churches, where the winds whistle through ill-fitting windows, and there may not even be enough money to replace the candles, where the parish house is poor and shabby below even the standards of the rest of the village, the priests of the Orthodox Church have proved to be the faithful stewards of the Gospel: still singing out the words of Christ himself, in all conditions, and across all generations: and they will do so until the very end of time.

The lesser blessings of the church

For many years in the past, the offices of the burial of Christians and the ritual of profession for monks and nuns were themselves described as 'mysteries'. They, like countless other rites of sanctification and consecration that are celebrated in the Orthodox Church on a regular basis, have the character of the mysteries, because they are full of the energizing power of the grace of God. Orthodoxy has never fully wished to draw sharp boundaries in the manner of the Latin Church's definition of 'Seven Sacraments'. After the great mysteries it prefers to talk about other rites of power and grace that have the character of mysteries: lesser mysteries if you will. They are regarded, however, with more force than the corresponding Latin concept of 'sacramentals'. They are seen as authentic channels of grace and holiness. So, for example, the Orthodox faithful will regularly require of their priest a supply of solemnly blessed water so that they can keep it in their houses, to drink in times of oppression or sadness or to wash their children with if they are sick. They will also use blessed oil, and have many blessed icons in their homes, offering incense before them in honour of the Lord, or in veneration of his Holy Mother, or one of the saints, as they pray. In all these means (and countless other rites of blessing that are contained in the Orthodox service books – blessings ranging from benedictions of fire engines and boats, to prayers to banish worms from the crops, and rats from wells) the Orthodox sense the humble presence of the great Lord of grace, serving their needs with intimate closeness. Christ the Lord of All (Pantocrator), for the Orthodox believer, is not a terrifying God who is angry with them most of the time, but a gentle Saviour who is as concerned as they are about the paltry (and yet so important!) needs of the day to day. It was the Lord himself who taught them this attitude: not to be afraid to ask for daily bread,[248] and never to be afraid of their request going unheeded.[249]

The services of prayer

The celebration of the great mysteries and the lesser blessings constitutes a large proportion of the 'services' of the Orthodox Church. The Eucharist is the still centre around which the regular life of the church's worship turns. Baptism is related to it as its gateway. In antiquity the annual baptisms used to be celebrated on the vigil of Pascha night, timed so that the newly baptized could walk in to the eucharistic celebration of the rest of their community and communicate along with them at the vigil feast. Even now, if baptism is not celebrated immediately before a Eucharist, its closeness to that mystery is demonstrated when the newly baptized child, or adult, is immediately given the eucharistic gifts to show the final stage of their initiation. The mystery of *metanoia*, at least in parishes with more than one priest serving, is regularly celebrated on Sundays just before the eucharistic liturgy. Solemn ceremonies of blessings, such as the Great Blessing of Waters on the feast of Theophany,[250] are fused within the eucharistic gathering, ending it with a procession from the blessed font, out of the church and into the landscape to the nearest source of water. In Greece the seas are blessed and the cross thrown into them, as far as he is able, by the celebrating priest (to be retrieved by young divers waiting there for the purpose). In Russia, where the time of year often meant the rivers were frozen over, holes were smashed in the ice so that the life-giving waters could be blessed. In the high summer, on 6 August, the feast of the Lord's Transfiguration on the mountain, the grapes were brought in from the harvest (in Russia it was the apples) and blessed in the church. All of human life was symbolically caught up in the overwhelming transfiguration of the cosmos that was happening through its irradiation in the light of Christ. This blessing of the external gifts of God, of course, was a profound symbol of what was transpiring in the life of the believer, God's priest within the cosmos, who was not only arranging the blessing of all the material things around him, but was himself, and herself, the centre of God's illumination and deification of the creature into the New Being in Christ. After Theophany the faithful generally request the priest to come to their houses and renew the blessing of them that was celebrated when they first took up their residence. The blessing of the house is a beautiful ceremony, involving the anointing of the house wall in all the compass points with blessed oil, scriptural readings, hymns and prayers of sanctification, and the sprinkling of holy waters everywhere. A blessing of a house will normally conclude with a large and convivial party of celebration.

Apart from such services of blessing and celebration there are other prayer services in the Orthodox tradition which are more personal, more sober in tone. If one of the Orthodox is terminally ill, a priest will be called to the house, or hospital, to hear the last confession of the dying Christian (if they are still alert), and to deliver the *viaticum*, the last gift of the Holy Eucharist for the soul's journey to the Lord.[251] When there are clear signs of approaching death the priest will read the Office for the Departing of the Soul, which is attended by all the family and friends who can be near, to bid farewell to their loved one and ask for them the protection of the saints and angels and the compassion of the Holy Mother of God as the soul makes its journey to the presence of its beautiful Lord and Maker. It is full of comforting and inspiring words, that balance the sense of awesome passing with the trustfulness appropriate to a believer in such a merciful Saviour. When one of the faithful dies, the Orthodox tradition is to recite the entire Psalter over the body as it is laid out in a shroud marked with the Cross and instruments of Christ's Passion,[252] in preparation for its reception into the church for burial. This always used to be done in the home of the deceased believer. All the family were involved in the task of preparing a loved one for burial. It is sad that today so many of these important and sacred tasks have been shunned by families who are too anxious to feel they could manage them, and instead are handed over to professionals who have no personal relationship whatsoever with the dead person. The washing of the body with the prescribed prayers, while the priest or deacon read the Psalter over it, was a way in which the church assisted families to grieve from the heart, but always in hope. It was a way of making grief a healing and purgative entrance into a new level of understanding life. With the bypassing of many of these rituals in our insular modern city life, Christians have often made it much harder for themselves to understand the spiritual illumination of the experience of dying, which Christ usually gives to us iconically, through our loved ones, many times before we are expected to celebrate that great mystery ourselves.

There are also many other forms of more personal devotions (though some of them are also occasionally celebrated in church in different parishes) such as the intercessory canons (*parakletikos canon*), to the Blessed Virgin, or to different saints. These are services of prayer used over several days, when a believer has special need of assistance. The most favoured of all prayers in Orthodoxy, one that has been fostered by the monastics for centuries past, is the Jesus Prayer.

On a rosary made of thick woollen rope, having large knots in it (sometimes thirty-three, sometimes a hundred or more), the Orthodox slowly mark off their passage through 'a century' of invocations of the Holy Name. As the fingers are occupied in the slow progression through the rope, the prayer is said very quietly and slowly, in harmony with the slowed breathing: 'Lord Jesus Christ, Son of God, have mercy on me.'[253] The constantly repeated Name of the Lord recalls the advice of Jesus himself[254] when talking about the essence of prayer, and offering to the church the image of the publican 'who went home at rights with God' because all he did was look down on the ground and say 'God have mercy on me a sinner.' Among the Orthodox this humble prayer, repeated like the ambience of a wave at the seashore, is not uttered with any neurotic sense of anxiety or timidity; but rather in the full sense of the distance between the creator and the creature that has been bridged by the loving mercy of the Saviour. The emphasis in the prayer, like the correct stress placed within an accented word, is on the holy name itself. This is the divine name that carries within it the force of the divine presence. Its invocation in the heart of the believer, and over the materiality of the cosmos itself, is a sacred consecration and inherent blessing. It lightens the heart, refreshes the mind, restores the soul. It banishes gloom, despondency, and sin. Those who practise the Jesus prayer can do so, quietly, without making even a sound, and can call down the name of the Lord on themselves and on all those they are with, on the upper deck of a London bus just as well as in the fields and forests. The engagement of the body, as the fingers slip the knots, and as the breathing comes into step with the invocations, as well as the engagement of the mind in the constantly recurring sameness of the prayer (in all its apparent simplicity, like the Lord's Prayer, it is unfathomable in its profundity) allows the believer to become 'quietened'.

Most of our life of prayer, let alone our ordinary world during the course of a day, is conducted in the midst of an immense 'static' hiss. If we are not surrounded by constant noise, we import our own. The refreshment of silence sometimes becomes so abhorrent to us that we will switch on a radio or a television simply to fill the room with noise so that we can avoid having to think or reflect. The Jesus Prayer is an easy way to lead our souls into the peacefulness necessary for true prayer. When the body and mind have been brought to a peaceful and trustful state by the waves breaking over them of the Holy Name, the spirit is allowed the space to become aware. For this reason it is also known as the 'Prayer of the Heart'.[255] The invocation of the Name unfailingly works. Our Saviour is not unaware of us, even though much of the time we may be unaware of him. When we call upon the Beloved he is near to us, and when he knows our heart's desire has risen to him, he becomes present to us. When this takes place the spirit of the believer has been made ready by the Jesus Prayer, so as to be able to recognize the advent of the Lord and the grace of the Holy Spirit of God. From that point onwards prayer cannot be easily spoken about; the believer passes behind the veil of the Temple and 'comes away' into other mysteries of the spirit.[256]

Daily prayers and devotions are collected for the Orthodox from a vast ocean of patristic and scriptural sources. Some small collections have been printed in English[257] and are used in the home prayers of families. Those who have grown up from childhood in Orthodox homes know these prayers (and often large tracts of the Psalms along with them) by heart, having recited them so often that they have become part of their most familiar mental landscape. In the custom of daily prayers an Orthodox believer will customarily pray the Scriptures, especially using the Psalms, and will try to read passages from the Scriptures each day. Several parish calendars set out what are the appropriate readings for each day of the year, and many follow this regular way of praying from the inspired text. The Beautiful Corner[258] of the Orthodox house, which is where the family icons are kept with a shelf in front of them for the votive lamps, and the incense burner, and copies of the prayer books, is the place where devotions normally take place in the mornings and evenings. The lamps are lit, or trimmed, and incense may be offered in honour of the Lord, and the individual or the family prays standing.[259] The basic structure for all home prayers in Orthodoxy (and for most of the other services of prayer too) is the initial prayers that commence devotions, which are known as the Trisagion prayers. They are a sequence of prayers that all Orthodox know by heart and which they always use to 'enter into' the domain of prayer. The sign of the Cross is made very often (and is marked with a cross in the text that follows):

The Trisagion prayers[260]

✠   In the name of the Father, and of the Son, and of the Holy Spirit. Amen.[261]

O Heavenly King, the Paraclete, the Spirit of Truth, who are present everywhere filling all things, Treasury of good things, and Giver of Life, come and dwell in us, cleanse us of every stain, and save our souls, O Good One.

✠ Holy God, Holy Mighty, Holy Immortal, Have mercy on us (*three times*)

✠ Glory to the Father, and to the Son, and to the Holy Spirit, Now, and forever, and to the Ages of Ages, Amen.

All Holy Trinity have mercy on us. Lord forgive us our sins. Master pardon our transgressions. Holy One, visit and heal our infirmities for your name's sake.

Lord have mercy, Lord have mercy, Lord have mercy.

✠ Glory to the Father, and to the Son, and to the Holy Spirit, Now, and forever, and to the Ages of Ages, Amen.

Our Father in Heaven, hallowed be your name. Your kingdom come. Your will be done, on earth as it is in heaven. Give us this day our daily bread, and forgive us our trespasses as we forgive those who trespass against us. And do not lead us into temptation, but deliver us from the evil one. (*If a priest is present*: ✠ For Yours is the Kingdom and the Power and the Glory, of the Father, and of the Son, and of the Holy Spirit, Now, and forever, and to the Ages of Ages.) Amen.

Lord have mercy, Lord have mercy, Lord have mercy,
Lord have mercy, Lord have mercy, Lord have mercy,
Lord have mercy, Lord have mercy, Lord have mercy,
Lord have mercy, Lord have mercy, Lord have mercy.

✠ Glory to the Father, and to the Son, and to the Holy Spirit. Now, and forever, and to the Ages of Ages. Amen.

✠ Come let us worship and bow down before God our King. (*metanie*[262])

✠ Come let us worship and bow down before Christ, our King and God. (*metanie*)

✠ Come let us worship and bow down before Christ himself, our King, and our God. (*metanie*)

The daily offices

The Trisagion prayers also open the more formal services of prayer that originally grew up among the monastic communities and formed the basic structure of the ascetical daily offices of prayer. They still are the skeleton around which the prayer life of the monastic houses of men and women are organized in the Eastern Church.[263] The full cycle of the offices of the hours is said only in the major monasteries or some cathedrals, but elements from the offices are central to Sunday service in all parishes, and on other festival days in the week the services of Matins (Greek: Orthros, that is, 'prayer at dawn') or Vespers (Greek: Hesperinos, or 'prayer at the evening time') may also be celebrated. Matins and Vespers are the main hinge points of the daily offices, but the monastics also consecrated the night hours with Night Prayers (Compline) and Midnight Office, as well as marking the middle of the days with the different offices of Third Hour, Sixth Hour, and Ninth Hour.[264] First Hour, like the other offices, begins with the Trisagion prayers, and then uses Psalms 5, 89, and 100 along with different psaltic verses and hymns to the Virgin Mother of God and other prayers. The final prayer of the different hours reflects the time of day that is appropriate. That of the First Hour, the beginning of the light of day, is as follows: 'O Christ, the True Light which illumines and sanctifies every man coming into the world: Let the light of your countenance be signed upon us, that in it we may behold the light ineffable. Guide our footsteps aright, to the keeping of your commandments; Through the intercessions of Your All-Immaculate Mother, and of all Your Saints. Amen.' The Third Hour (based around Psalms 5, 89, and 100) recalls the descent of the Holy Spirit on the apostles[265] and has within it a solemn invocation for the grace of the Lord of Life:[266]

> O Lord, who at the Third Hour, sent down the Holy Spirit upon your apostles: do not take the same from us, O Good One, but renew Him within us who pray to you. (✠ *metanie*). (Response:) A pure heart create for me, O God. Put a steadfast spirit within me. (*three times*)

The concluding prayer for Third Hour is as follows:

> O Lord, who are worshipped and glorified, at all times and in every hour, both in heaven and on earth; Christ our God, long-suffering and abundant in mercy and compassion; who love the just and show mercy to sinners; who call all mankind to salvation through the promise of good things to come: Lord receive now our prayers at this present hour, and direct our lives in accordance with your commandments. Sanctify our souls, purify our bodies, set right our minds, cleanse our thoughts, and deliver us from all danger, wrath, and distress. Compass us around with your holy angels that, guarded by their hosts, we may attain to the unity of the faith, and to the comprehension of your ineffable glory. For Blessed are You, to the Ages of Ages. Amen.

The office of Compline (based on Psalms 50, 69, and 142) contains many beautiful prayers and overall it sets the tone of peaceful repentance for whatever failings there may have been in the day, and of quiet trust in the mercy and faithfulness of God, and his ever-provident care over each of his faithful. The final prayer to the Theotokos says this:

> O spotless Virgin...by your wondrous conception you united God the Word to mankind, and joined our outcast race to heavenly things. You, the hope of the hopeless, the ready help of those in trouble who have recourse to you, are the refuge for all Christians. Do not despise me who am a sinner, most wretched, who have made myself unprofitable by shameful thoughts and words and deeds. Taking the heartsease of life's pleasures I have bound myself in slavery of mind. But, Mother of the God who loves mankind, you too will take pity on me a sinner and a prodigal, from your own love for mankind, so receive my prayer to you even though it is uttered from unclean lips. From your boldness as a mother intercede with your Son, our Master, that he would open even to such as me, his loving compassion and his goodness; and that overlooking my innumerable sins, he would turn me towards repentance and make me someone who fulfils his commandments well.

The office of Vespers follows Hebraic liturgical tradition, where the onset of evening commences the liturgical festival of the new day. Christians, from earliest times marked the setting of the sun with a sense of expectancy (still noticeable in Mediterranean countries, and unlike the colder northern climes) that a time of rest and fresh beginning had arrived. In the second century a hymn to Christ the 'gladdening light of evening' was already popular, and it is mentioned by the fourth century as a standard practice among Christians to sing this hymn as they lit the first oil lamps of eventide, in their homes:

Jesus Christ, The Gladdening Light of the Immortal Father's holy Glory; the Heavenly, Holy, Blessed One; as the Sun declines we see the light of evening, and sing our hymn to God, the Father, Son, and Holy Spirit. Worthy are you, O Son of God, through each and every moment, that joyful songs should hymn you. You are the Giver of our Life, and so the world gives glory.

The Orthodox monastics of the fourth century developed this simple ritual of evening prayer with the usual structure of psalms and hymns around it. The service begins with the initial (*proemiac*) Psalm 103, read by the church cantor, during which time the celebrant priest comes out from the altar area vested simply in cassock and stole, and quietly says the seven Lychnapsia prayers (prayers of the lamplighting) standing in front of the icon of Christ. Each of these evokes God's blessing of the past day, and of the coming day, upon the people of God. The seventh of the prayers reads as follows:

O Great and Most High God, you who alone have immortality, and dwell in light inaccessible; you who have made all creation in wisdom, and have divided the light from the darkness, and appointed the sun to rule the day, the moon and the stars to rule the night; you who have granted to us sinners even at this present hour to come before you with confession, to offer you our evening praise: May you yourself, Lord and lover of mankind, direct our prayer as incense before you, and accept it as an odour of sweet fragrance. Grant that we may pass this present evening and the coming night in peace. Put on us the armour of light. Deliver us from the terror of the night, and from everything that walks in darkness, and grant that the sleep, which you have appointed for the repose of our weakness, may be free from every imagination of the devil. And Master, who give us every good thing, may we be moved to penitence even upon our beds and call to mind your name in the night, so that enlightened by meditation on your commandments, we may rise up in gladness of soul to glorify your goodness, presenting our prayers and supplications to your tenderness of heart, for our own sins, and for those of all your people; that through the intercessions of the Holy Mother of God, you might look down on them with mercy. For you are a good God, who loves mankind, ✠ And to you we ascribe glory, to the Father, and to the Son, and to the Holy Spirit. Now, and forever, and to the Ages of Ages. Amen.

The basic skeleton of Vespers is the cluster of Psalms 140, 141, 129, and 116.[267] Collectively, and from the opening words, this is known as the 'Lord I Have Cried'. Parish choirs sing this to a lovely and gentle melody. At the second verse of Psalm 140, 'Let my prayer arise like incense before you', the priest in church will make a general censing of the building and icons and people. After the singing of the 'Lord I Have Cried' the priest will make the 'Entrance'[268] carrying either the censer smoking with incense (symbol of the grace of the Holy Spirit) or, on feasts, the Gospel (symbol of the advent of the Word of God in the Incarnation), and then the hymn, 'Gladdening Light' is sung in common.

Towards the end of the service there are two 'evening prayers'. The first is recited by the choir leader:

> Grant, O Lord, to keep us this evening without sin. Blessed are you, O Lord, the God of our fathers, and praised and glorified is your name forever. Amen. Let your mercy be upon us, O Lord, as we have placed all our hope in you. Blessed are you O Lord, teach me your statutes. Blessed are you Master, make me understand your statutes. Blessed are you, Holy One, enlighten me with your statutes. O Lord, your mercy is everlasting; do not despise the work of your hands. All praise belongs to you, and all worship, and all glory; ✠ To the Father, and to the Son, and to the Holy Spirit, Now and forever, and to the Ages of Ages. Amen.

After another litany of intercessions the priest completes the second prayer of evening:

> (*Silently*) O Lord God who bowed the heavens and came down for the salvation of mankind; look upon your servants and your inheritance, for to you, the fearful Judge who yet loves mankind, have your servants inclined and bowed down their heads before you, not waiting for any help from men, but looking to your mercy and confidently expecting your salvation. Guard them at all times, during this present evening, and in the approaching night, from every enemy, from all the powers of the devil that may assault them, and from all vain thoughts and evil imaginations. (*Aloud*) – For Blessed and glorified is the power of your Kingdom ✠ Of the Father, and of the Son, and of the Holy Spirit, Now and Forever, and to the Ages of Ages.

The service ends with the New Testament 'Hymn of Simeon' sung by the choir:

> Now, Master, let your servant depart in peace, according to your promise, for my eyes have seen the salvation which you have prepared before all your people, a light for the revelation of the gentiles, and the glory of your people Israel.

Afterwards there is a final blessing and the people depart home. In the parishes those wishing to make confession before the Sunday liturgy of the next day will often use this time. On feast days the service of Vespers includes the ritual of the blessing of wheat, wine, oil, and bread (known as the *artoklasia*, or the *litiya*), and after such a service the faithful are anointed on the forehead with blessed oil and eat together the bread that has been sprinkled with wine. In the Slavonic liturgical tradition parishes will usually combine Vespers of the Saturday evening with Matins of the Sunday morning in one long service known as the 'Vigil' (a relic of the monastic all-night vigil of prayer that preceded great festivals). Greek custom is to celebrate Vespers on Saturday night separately, and to hold the Matins on the Sunday morning, in the hour immediately preceding the celebration of the Eucharist. In smaller parishes, where the resources of singers may not be so readily available, sometimes the morning liturgy is preceded by the simpler offices[269] of First and Third Hour.

The office of Matins is a long and complex ceremony with a quite different tone to that of the quiet and reflective Vespers. By contrast, it is full of references to the

342

bright light of new day. Sunday Matins is a long song of triumph rejoicing in the resurrection of Christ. The office begins with the preliminaries of Psalms 19 and 20, while the church is incensed, and then the cantor recites the Hexapsalmos.[270] While these are in process, the priest recites quietly the Twelve Prayers of Morning. The fourth of these is as follows:

> Master, Holy and Incomprehensible God, who commanded the light to shine out of darkness, who have refreshed us by the slumber of the night and raised us up to glorify and petition your goodness: As we implore your own tenderness of heart, so receive us now who worship you and return thanks to you in the measure of our strength, and grant us all our petitions which pertain to salvation. Make us children of the light, and of the day, and heirs of your everlasting blessings. Be mindful, Lord, in the multitude of your mercies, of all your people here present with us, and all our brothers and sisters on land, or sea, or in the air, and in every place of your dominion, who are in need of your philanthropy and your help; and grant to all your great mercy, that being preserved in safety of soul and body, we may confidently magnify your wondrous and blessed name; of the Father, and of the Son, and of the Holy Spirit. Now and forever, and to the Ages of Ages. Amen.

The recitation of the psalms in their appointed *kathismata* now follows, interleaved with litanies and hymns, though today in the recitation of Matins in parishes most of the appointed psalms have been extensively cut back, and are generally replaced with different forms of Byzantine hymns, paraphrasing the Scriptures. The priest then chants one of the eleven appointed *eothinon* (the Greek word means 'early morning') Gospels for Matins, and the choir responds to it by singing the hymn of resurrection:

> In that we have beheld the resurrection of Christ, let us worship the holy Lord Jesus, the only sinless one. We adore your Cross, O Christ, and we praise and glorify your holy resurrection; for you are our God, and we own no other beside you, and we call upon your name. Come, you the faithful, let us adore Christ's holy resurrection. For see, through the Cross, joy has come into the world. Let us ever bless the Lord and sing of his resurrection: for by enduring the Cross for our sake, he destroyed death by death.

Further psalms (especially Psalm 50) and hymns (the Idiomela of the Resurrection, and the Glories) and litanies are chanted, and then a long series of Byzantine poems known as the canons follows. These are broken up (around intervening shorter hymns and litanies) into three groups of three sung together, though the perfect nine (symbolizing the unfallen heavenly host) is said to be no longer appropriate since some of the angelic ranks fell into darkness, and accordingly the second canonic division is omitted, leaving eight canons from the nine. The liturgical canons are a vast quarry of beautiful Byzantine poetry that reflects on the great narratives of biblical salvation history in the light of Christ's death and resurrection. In the Greek and Slavonic traditions, which have had special music assigned to the canons from ancient times, they often rise to immense beauty, and can serve to instruct the faithful (as they have done for centuries) in whole vistas of biblical theology. Before the ninth canon is sung the choir interleaves the 'Magnifications' or the Magnificat of the Blessed Virgin. The 'Praises' then follow (Psalms 148 and 149), and after a few more hymns and litanies the priest lifts up a lighted candle and intones in a loud voice the words: 'Glory to You who have shown us the light!', at which point the choir commences the solemn singing of the 'Great Doxology':

> Glory to God in the highest, and on earth peace and good will among men. We praise you, we bless you, we worship you, we glorify you, We give you thanks for your great glory. O Lord our King, Heavenly God, Almighty Father: O Lord, Only Begotten Son, Jesus Christ, and Holy Spirit; O Lord God, Lamb of God, Son of the Father, Who takes away the sin of the world, Have mercy on us, you who take away the sin of the world. You who sit at the right hand of the Father, Receive our prayer, and have mercy on us. For you alone are holy, you alone are the Lord, Jesus Christ, To the glory of God the Father. Amen. Every day I will bless you, and will praise your name forever; Yes, forever and ever. Grant Lord to keep us this day without sin. Blessed are you, Lord, teach me your statutes (*three times*). Lord, you have been our refuge from one generation to the next. I said, Lord have mercy on me, heal my soul for I have sinned against you. Lord, I have fled to you, teach me to do your will, for you are my God. For with you is the source of life, and in your light we shall see light. Continue your mercy to those who know you.

During the singing of the Doxology, the priest once more incenses the church and collects the Gospel book which has been left (after the chanting of the Gospel reading) on the *analogion* in the nave, to return it to the altar in readiness for the eucharistic celebration which will soon follow. If there is not to be a celebration of the Eucharist that day, Matins will continue for a short while longer with a few more litanies of intercession before the final blessing and dismissal from the priest. The offices of Vespers and Matins, each in its own different way centre on the concept of Christ as the light of the world. The gentle light of eventide that cheers and gives hope, or the bright light of morning that makes a new world order. Both services, being as they are the twin hinges of the monastic structure of prayer, are chanted services, full of hymns and poems and litanies and ceremonies. The lesser offices, by contrast, are said in a very sober and 'homely' kind of style. People who visit or share in Orthodox worship would get a very different impression depending on whether they attended one of the main liturgical mysteries, celebrated in all their liturgical splendour, or the great offices (still with much ceremony but overall more simple in character and more solidly based around the repetition of prayers and psalms and biblical hymns), or the lesser offices of prayer, very chaste and humble in spirit.

Since the greater services of Vespers and Matins require a singer and a relatively complex liturgical style, the Orthodox in their homes will not usually pray these rites domestically (though they may take several hymns and elements from them) but instead use a simpler form of morning and evening prayers. These are customarily opened with the Trisagion prayers, and then often combine several prayers and devotions taken from the writings of the great Fathers and saints of the church. A very common morning prayer is as follows:

> Rising from sleep we fall down before you O Blessed God, and to you O Mighty One, we sing the hymn of the angels: Holy, Holy, Holy, are you our God. Through the prayers of the Theotokos, have mercy on us. ✠ Glory to the Father, and to the Son, and to the Holy Spirit. O Lord you have raised me from my bed and from sleep. Now enlighten my understanding and my heart and open my lips that I might sing to you O Holy Trinity: Holy, Holy, Holy are you O God. Through the prayers of the holy

Theotokos have mercy on us. ✠ Now and ever and to the ages of ages. Amen. Suddenly the Judge shall appear, and the deeds of each one will be laid bare. With fear we cry out to you at midnight: Holy, Holy, Holy are you O God. Through the prayers of the Theotokos have mercy on us.

Morning and evening prayers will always customarily end with intercessions for one's family and kin, both living and departed, as well as for all the church, and all God's suffering people. Night prayers are filled with a sense of trusting repentance, and of prayers for 'those who have loved us and hated us', as well as deceased and living kinsfolk. One of the Slavonic ritual's prayers at night-time is the twenty-four invocations attributed to St John Chrysostom, symbolizing an assigned intention for each one of the hours of the preceding day:

O Lord do not deprive me of your heavenly blessings.
O Lord deliver me from everlasting torment.
O Lord if I have sinned in mind or thought, in word or deed, forgive me.
O Lord deliver me from every ignorance and heedlessness, from smallness of soul and flinty hardness of heart.
O Lord deliver me from every temptation.
O Lord enlighten my heart which evil desires have darkened.
O Lord I have sinned, for I am human, but you, who are God, forgive me in your philanthropy for you know the weakness of my soul.
O Lord send down your grace to help me that I may glorify your holy name.
O Lord Jesus Christ, enrol me, who am your servant, in the Book of Life, and grant me a blessed end.
O Lord my God, even if I have done nothing good in your sight, even so grant me to make a beginning in the good according to your grace.
O Lord sprinkle on my heart the dew of your grace.
O Lord of heaven and earth remember me, your sinful servant who is defiled and cold of heart, when you come into your Kingdom. Amen.
O Lord receive me in repentance.
O Lord never leave me.
O Lord do not lead me into temptation.
O Lord grant me thought of the good.
O Lord grant me tears, the remembrance of death, a sense of peace.
O Lord grant me mindfulness to confess my sins.
O Lord grant me charity, humility, and obedience.
O Lord grant me endurance, greatness of soul, and gentleness.
O Lord plant in me the root of all blessings, your fear in my heart.
O Lord grant that I may love you with all my heart and all my soul, and obey your will in all things.
O Lord shelter me from the wicked, from demons, from the passions and unlawful things.
O Lord you know your creation, and all that your will has destined for it, may your will also be fulfilled in me who am a sinner. For you are blessed for evermore. Amen.

From these and an almost infinite other array of prayers and devotions available, the Orthodox person, whether clerical, monastic, or lay, is able to make up a daily rule of prayer which is fitting to his or her lifestyle. The Father Confessor often advises an individual Orthodox what is appropriate for the different lifestyles, occupations, and ages of the faithful. One constant factor for the development of the Christian life of each one, of course, is regular attendance at the mysteries and offices celebrated in the church with the whole community – above all at the regular celebrations of the mysteries of *metanoia* and Eucharist. But in addition to this, the fostering of a lively sense of prayer in the home itself is very important for the mystical maturation of each of the faithful. Each Orthodox household will have its Beautiful Corner where the icons and their glimmering lamps serve as a constant reminder of the gracious presence of the Lord and his saints. In the old customs of Orthodox countries, a house would have small icons near the entrance door. A person calling would, when the door was opened, venerate the icons, even before greeting their friends.

Personal prayers

Most Orthodox have learned an array of personal prayers that are just beneath the surface and come to mind instinctively in any troubles or needs. The most frequent is the sign of the cross. This is the prayer 'In the name of the Father, and of the Son, and of the Holy Spirit', which consecrates any action to the glory of God, and which drives away despondency and fear with the power of a great blessing. While the words are being said the right hand is set into the position where the thumb and the first two fingers are brought together (to symbolize the holy Trinity), and the remaining two fingers are folded over into the palm (to symbolize the two natures of the Incarnate Lord who revealed the Trinity). The fingers thus placed are positioned on the forehead, the middle of the waist, the tip of the right shoulder, then the tip of the left shoulder,[271] to make up the actual sign of the Holy Cross. Many Orthodox will also say this prayer in moments of stress or fear: 'Lord, fence me about with the power of your honourable and life-giving Cross, and save me from every evil thing.' The monogram, written in the form of a cross-in-square IC XC NIKA, with the IC XC on the top line and the NIKA beneath them, is also a prayer in its own right, being the Greek abbreviation of the invocation 'Jesus Christ has the victory [in the Cross]'. One finds the sign (a modern equivalent of the revelation to the Emperor Constantine[272]) all over Orthodox culture, both ecclesiastical and personal.

The vast array of personal prayers, and the way in which so many are memorized and intimately internalized by the Orthodox, is a living characteristic of domestic Orthodox spirituality. Such a practice provides an ethos, an ambience of prayer that encloses the believer, so as to become for each one a grace of sanctification, and even for all others whom a believer may encounter in the course of a normal day, a source of blessing and consolation.

Traditions of Orthodox Prayer and Spirituality

Because Orthodoxy is so biblically and liturgically rooted, and so distinctly communal in character, much of the tone of its spiritual tradition is determined by the mysteries and services of the canonical offices of prayer that take place in the common meetings (*synaxis*) of the church. Yet there is a deep and ancient tradition, or, to be more exact, a series of distinct traditions, of spirituality that have grown up over the centuries in the history of Orthodoxy, and which in most cases have 'run together' in closely woven syntheses, to represent an ethos of Orthodox spirituality that also forms the character of individual religious practice and prayer life, both clerical and lay. Most of these traditions originated in monastic circles but have since spread out from that ambience to become the common property of the laity in their homes and private devotions. There is scope in this chapter to mention only a few of the more notable traditions of Orthodox spirituality, such as the methods of prayer, the Prayer of the Heart, the Jesus Prayer, Hesychasm (see below) generally, and the Orthodox traditions of fasting and feasting.[273]

Methods of prayer

Orthodoxy retains a vital tradition that the method of prayer is important. It matters how one prays. All prayer is good, of course, but luminous prayer is something that has to be performed well. The commonly spread idea in some Christian circles that the outward forms of prayer are irrelevant is not one that is sustained by the early Church Fathers. Several instructions for prayer exist from the ancient church; from them we learn that the most ancient custom of the Christians has been maintained in Orthodoxy, that when one wishes to pray there are certain postures that ought to be adopted as the norm. One should face east, the place of the rising of the sun, and the symbolic 'orientation' to Christ. One should stand as the normal posture of prayer, and pray with upraised hands. A person who is expressing prayer of repentance and sorrow should kneel. Standing implies, therefore, that Christian prayer, normally speaking, should be a confident and joyous thing. St Aphrahat the Syrian put it this way:

> From the moment you start praying, raise your heart upwards, and turn your eyes downward. Come to a focus in your innermost self, and there in that place, pray in secret to your heavenly Father.[274]

The rules about posture of prayer are not rigid, of course, if one feels tired and unable to stand long, it is the best thing to start prayer standing up, and then to sit down and either read from the Psalms or a book of prayers, or just sit in quiet in the presence of God. The most important of all the preparatory steps before prayer begins is again expressed by Aphrahat:

> Before you pray, first forgive all those that have offended you. Then pray. Only then will your prayer rise up into the presence of God. If you do not forgive, your prayer will languish on the earth.[275]

The Orthodox use icons a great deal in their prayer, and these too assist greatly in keeping the wandering mind focused on the presence of God to the one who worships.

The church introduces the Lord's Prayer with this note: 'Grant that we may have the audacity [*parrhesia*] to say, Our Father.' To have courage and confidence before the face of God is a mark, not of presumption, but of faith in the fundamental nature of God as merciful Father, as a gentle Lord, as the nurturing Comforter. Orthodox prayer always, without exception, begins with the making of the sign of the Cross over the individual. If a priest is present it also begins with a blessing. After this the Orthodox will then make a *metanie*. This is a deep bow before the Lord. It can be done in the form of the greater or lesser *metanie*. For the lesser *metanie*, once the right hand has finished making the sign of the Cross, it is brought from the left shoulder at the same time as the worshipper makes a profound waist-level bow, and it sweeps down across the right knee towards the ground so as to touch the ground before the right foot of the worshipper. For the greater *metanie*, after making the sign of the Cross, the hand drops down to the ground in the same way as the worshippers fall to their knees, bow their head, then lower themselves into a full prostration, placing their forehead on the ground, before rising up to kneeling posture, and standing up again while making the sign of the Cross over themselves once more. Monastics often spend many hours of prayer making the *metanies* so as to bring their bodies into the common song of their mind and heart. Laity use them less, but still as a regular part of prayer. If one makes the small *metanie* before venerating an icon the Orthodox will usually make two of them in approaching the icon, then kiss the icon itself, and one more *metanie* departing from it. If one makes a metanie before the Cross, on feasts of the Cross, it is usually a full *metanie* made three times, and the following verse is sung or said on each prostration: 'Before your Cross, we bow down O Master, and your glorious Resurrection we magnify.' If the *metanie* is made before the icon of Christ, the Virgin, or one of the saints, as an act of reverence, the appropriate *troparion* (hymn verse) is also said. The *troparion* used before the icon of Christ is:

We venerate your most pure icon loving Lord, and we ask your pardon for our offences Christ our God. By your own choice you were well pleased to ascend the Cross in the flesh, to deliver those whom you had fashioned from the slavery of the enemy. And so, with thanksgiving we cry out to you: You have filled all things with joy, our Saviour, by coming to save the world.

The common *troparion* before the Virgin's icon is:

As you are the spring of compassion, have pity on us O Theotokos. Look upon a people who have sinned, and show us your power as always; for hoping in you we cry out: 'Hail and Rejoice', as once Gabriel did, the Taxiarch of the Bodiless Powers.

or:

Open to us the gates of your compassion O Blessed Theotokos. In that we have placed our hope in you may we never be confounded. Through you may we be delivered from all our adversaries, for you are the salvation of the race of Christians.

Each service of Orthodox prayer, private or public, begins with the *enarxis* (opening) verses during which three *metanies* are always made:

- ☦ Come let us worship and bow down before God our King.
- ☦ Come let us worship and bow down before Christ, our King and our God.
- ☦ Come let us worship and bow down before Christ himself, our King and our God.

It is important to synthesize the physical acts (bowing down and speaking out words) with the sentiment of the intellectual worship contained within the words: and both (that is the physical reverence and the intellectual prayer) are themselves important only in so far as they serve to bring the human soul into a conscious attentiveness towards God. Orthodox spiritual traditions are generally geared to this threefold understanding of the task of prayer: the harmonizing into a single sounded note of the body, the mind, and the heart (*kardia*). By the latter term, early Greek Christian thought meant the locus of the soul and the arena of prayer: that holy place in the human creature (sometimes called the *nous*, or spiritual intellect) where the awareness of a limited being is raised up to the presence of the Almighty.[276] St Paul speaks of the heart as the synonym for the 'inmost self' the inner person longing for salvation.[277] The evangelical doctrine reaffirms that the heart is the seat of the understanding, the source of human reflection and contemplation[278] as well as the arena of volition and moral decision.[279] It is, for these reasons, the centre of creaturely consciousness to which God turns when he reveals his presence in the world, making it the centre of the divine encounter for humanity. It is the holy place in which the human being knows and relates to God in the deepest seat of religious awareness.[280]

Prayer of the heart

The Orthodox spiritual tradition is heavily influenced by the ascetical writings of the early monastic theologians. These books amount to a veritable library of texts advising on prayer, discussing its processes and its higher mysteries, which is generically called the Paterika, and represents literature from the fourth century through the high Middle Ages. Among the Paterika are famous ascetical texts such as the *Apophthegms of the Fathers*, the *Ladder of Divine Ascent* by St John Klimakos, and the *Spiritual Meadow* of St John Moschos (desert monastic literature), as well as medieval collections such as the *Evergetinos*, compiled out of the Evergetinos monastery (Our Lady the Good Helper) at Constantinople. This Orthodox monastic tradition was itself a great Byzantine synthesis of Alexandrian, Egyptian, Syrian, Cappadocian, and Palestinian streams of spiritual writing, where each 'school' of thought added its own distinctive colour.[281] At a later time the Russian Church added more works on the spiritual life, enriching the literature with its own distinctive voice.[282] And since then so too have most of the other national Orthodox churches, from their own array of saints.

One of the dominant ideas of the Orthodox approach prayer is the concept of the preparation of the heart of the believer to receive the divine presence. The heart is seen, in the biblical manner, as the central locus of divine consciousness in a human being. It is a seat of intelligent awareness, moral sensibility, and spiritual perception. It is akin to the use of the 'soul' in Western Christian literature, but carries a deeper range of resonances, especially those of illumination and mystical perception. The Orthodox saints speak of the heart being moved and warmed by the arrival of the Spirit of God in times of prayer. They advocate that when one begins to pray it should be done, initially, with much fervour and zeal, while the mind is fresh and attentive. This 'push' at the beginning is important in order to rouse the bodily faculties to attention and

349

Figure 6 The homely interior of a Romanian nun's hesychasterion – a hermitage at the convent of Varatec, where small groups of ascetics live together adjacent to the large common-life monastery, and focus on the interior life in a more concentrated way, especially devoting themselves to the 'Prayer of the Heart', the Jesus prayer.
Photograph: John McGuckin

to engage them in the actions needed to begin to align the powers of the mind. So it is, for example, that the various initial prayers and prostrations customary when an Orthodox begins to pray serve to focus the mind and bring about, through all the words and ideas that are being voiced, a simple and deepened sense of the heart to desire the holy presence, which is the goal and end of all prayer.

One of the great spiritual teachers from Sinai in the eighth century, Abba Hesychios, explains the prayer of the heart in this way:

> Attentiveness is the stillness of the heart, unbroken by any thought. In this stillness the heart breathes and invokes, endlessly and without ceasing, only Jesus Christ, who is the Son and God Himself. Through this invocation enfolded continually in Christ, who secretly divines all hearts, the soul does everything it can to keep its sweetness and its inner struggle hidden from the sight of all.[283]

350

One of the great theologians of prayer in the early church, St Makarios the Great, described why the heart was seen as so important a focus:

> The heart itself is only a small vessel, yet dragons lurk there and lions; there are poisonous beasts and all the glitter of evil; there are rough and uneven roads there, and precipices too; but there also are God, and the angels; life is there, and the Kingdom; there too is light, and there the apostles, and heavenly cities, and treasures of grace. All things lie within that little space.[284]

From here the 'prayer of the heart' develops in the hands of great teachers into a practice that is common in Orthodoxy to this day: the Jesus Prayer. For the Orthodox spiritual masters the essence of this form of prayer is 'attentiveness' (*prosoche*): being able to enter the inner sanctum of the human heart, as into a holy place, and being able to quieten the noisy mind and the restless body sufficiently to be able to do that. But then, having entered the holy place, to be aware of the great power of holiness that is within, when the Lord himself comes to speak to the heart that desires him. That moment of prayer does not need words to fill it; it is a stage of communion already transcending words.

The Jesus Prayer

The Jesus Prayer is a precise summarized form of the Prayer of the Heart. It was the culmination of a long monastic tradition that advocated using repeated scriptural phrases (recited over thousands of times in the course of a day) by which means the early monks in the desert tried to contain the tendency of thoughts (*logismoi*) and distractions to 'run away' with them. The monastic *higumen* would set his monks a biblical text to meditate on, in the hope that by the constant repetition it would, as it were, 'enter into the heart' and flower there in understanding and grace. Over the course of time the Byzantine Fathers preferred, above all others, the scriptural invocation taken from Jesus' parable of the tax collector and the pharisee,[285] to which they added the invocation of the Holy Name. In the Old Testament and the early church alike, the uttering of the Holy Name of God was believed to contain an abundance of blessing and power of light within it. So the Orthodox still believe. As the apostle said, merely to acclaim the name of the Lord is to achieve a high spiritual inspiration from God.[286] The Orthodox understand that the power of the Name, working within the inmost heart of the disciple, brings about a majestic purification and assistance, simply by its enunciation, so sacred is its character and so awesome is the holiness evoked by its enunciation.[287] The Jesus Prayer, then, is a matter of setting the heart in quietness and stillness, and quietly and slowly reciting the words (perhaps aloud at first, then maybe silently as time goes on) of the prayer:

Lord Jesus Christ, Son of [the Living] God, have mercy on me [a sinner].

If several people are saying the prayer together, it is recited aloud, by one person only, and the optional words 'a sinner' are not used, since one can only identify oneself as a sinner, but must never presume that anyone else is. The phrase 'have mercy on us' is then substituted. Some newer monasteries have introduced this practice of the recitation of the Jesus Prayer as one of the central acts of common monastic prayer, and it is now expanding as a communal Orthodox prayer service in many parts of the world, though formerly it was exclusively used as a method of private prayer. Orthodox often use the prayer rope (*komboskini, chotki*) to help them focus, a rope rosary of a hundred large knots or more (a century). It is used to count off each invocation in centuries. Some pray the Jesus Prayer for a century or two, others pray through long hours of the night using the *komboskini*. The chief thing is that the invocation is filled with hope and gladness; it is not the point to impress on oneself one's hopeless status as a sinner, but to focus on the beauty of the name of Jesus as Saviour and Son of God, who liberates us from the darkness of despair.

The endless waves of the Holy Name that break over the soul like waves of an ocean bring light and joy to the heart: they lift and scatter despondency and bring about the very salvation we are praying for. Many Orthodox will, at some stage, envisage loved ones in their prayers, and other people in need, and then add in the variation: 'Lord Jesus Christ, Son of God, have mercy on him [her].' Always the prayer needs to be recited quietly, slowly (without hurry or anxiety), and if one's attention begins to wander one is able to make a *metanie*, and begin again with focus on the content of the words. Usually, however, after a few minutes of prayer, the attention of the body is captured by the rosary and the regular rhythm of the words (like a child that has been given some lovely toys to play with), and the mind and heart are left free to sink into the Holy Name itself. It is something that the Jesus Prayer aims for continually, and it has long proven itself to be a wonderful method of prayer for advanced souls and beginners alike.

Some writers have advocated that the best posture for the Jesus Prayer is a kneeling position with the head low down on the knees. Some find this useful; others find it impossible. Some writers have also advocated that the first half of the phrase should be recited with the intake of a breath, and the second half with the exhalation. This only works if the prayer is said *sotto voce*. It also works best if the prayer is said in Greek,[288] since the English translation does not have the same euphonic balance. The point of this was to emphasize the body's attentiveness even more so, by tying the recitation of the words in to the pattern of taking breaths, and so (in a sense) physically 'pulling' the name down into the chest and making it enter the heart. The methods can be of use to some, but they ought not to distract the believer from the fundamental concern which is that the Name of the Lord enters the soul and brings light to it, ultimately liberating it from the tyranny of thoughts and reflections, so that it can sit for an eternal moment of stillness in the presence of its master. The Jesus Prayer is now commonly practised by the laity (as well as the monks) in most Orthodox countries, and has been spread to the West by such spiritual literature as *The Way of the Pilgrim* and other translations of Russian devotional writing as well as the Greek *Philokalia*.[289]

Hesychasm

Orthodox spirituality generally speaks little about methods and practices but talks a lot about the need for spiritual stillness (*hesychia*). This gave rise in the fourteenth century to a great movement of synthesis in the Byzantine world called Hesychasm.

It was not a new phenomenon, more of a grand gathering into order of all the disparate Orthodox traditions of prayer that had gone before; but it did point up new emphases. Chief among them was the need to teach the restless soul some quiet attentiveness before the face of God, and also the ways of discerning the manner in which the holy presence brings light to the soul. The themes of stillness and radiant light are very much to the fore in Hesychast thought, and it takes the mystery of the Transfiguration of Jesus on the mountain as the chief symbol of how the soul is also destined to be transfigured in light.[290] The greatest writers of the Hesychast school are St Symeon the New Theologian,[291] St Gregory of Sinai, and St Gregory Palamas.[292] Their works are now available in English translation, and are conveniently gathered together, in extensive excerpts, in the English translation of the Philokalia, a library of patristic writings on prayer assembled on Mount Athos in the eighteenth century. Not so commonly known outside the boundaries of the Orthodox Church are the numerous writings of Hesychast *startsi*, or elders, who have practised hesychastic prayer in more recent times. Before the devastation of the hermitages by the Soviets, the Valaam and Optina monasteries in Russia were great centres of hesychastic prayer, and the writings of many of the historic elders are now available in English.[293] The treatise of the saintly bishop Ignatius Brianchaninov (1807–67) on the Jesus Prayer has achieved a classic status.[294] There are also renowned practitioners of Hesychasm throughout the contemporary Orthodox world. Some of the writings of Elder Joseph from Mount Athos (d. 1959) are now available in English,[295] and there are a growing number of studies of the history and method of this much-beloved prayer.[296]

Fasting and feasting

Along with its high mystical tradition of prayer, Orthodoxy remains grounded. It encourages all believers to learn vocal prayers by heart. In times of distress or need, it is good to be able to recite prayers known intimately. Most Orthodox have a large range of such prayers that they make use of, and they encourage their children to have a large repertoire too. The calendar is also used in a significant way in directing a personal spiritual life. This is made up of the church's year, day by day and season by season. One part of the calendar is fixed, the festivals of Christmas or Theophany (Epiphany), for example, always occurring on the same dates each year. Another part is a moveable cycle, based around Pascha, which affects the feasts dependent on it such as Ascension and Pentecost. The church's year still follows Byzantine practice and begins in September, thus commencing with autumn and ending with the harvest season. It is in this way more deeply attuned to the natural life-cycle than the secular calendar commencing with New Year's Day on 1 January.

Each day in Orthodoxy is a celebration of a particular saint (often several of them). There are twelve Great Dominical Feasts, celebrating the Lord's ministry (such as the Nativity, or the Transfiguration) and many feasts of the Blessed Theotokos (the Entry to the Temple, the Birthday of the Virgin, the Falling Asleep of the Virgin[297]). Orthodox believers observe their saint's name-day as a big feast. This is customarily the name given to the child on its baptismal day. The name-day has greater significance in the Eastern Church than the 'birth-day', which is the common, more secular, celebration elsewhere. On such feasts there are special meals prepared in the houses and a festival atmosphere in church services. There are also regular seasons of fast in the Orthodox year. The Great Fast extends over the forty days before Pascha and is rigorous. No meat or dairy products are consumed; wine, alcoholic drinks, and oil are left aside; and fish is rarely eaten except on festival days that fall in Great Lent, such as the Annunciation (Evangelismos). Other lesser periods of fast occur around Christmas time, the feast of the apostles Peter and Paul (29 June), and the feast of the Koimesis of the Virgin (August 15). In every ordinary week of the Orthodox year (with the exception of the immediate season after Pascha) Wednesdays and Fridays are observed as fast days (no meat, wine, oil, or dairy).

By the practice of fasting Orthodox are reminded in a direct bodily way of the presence of the Lord. Fasting in Orthodoxy is not done out of a spirit of 'atonement' for sins. It is approached as an act of ascesis of love. *Ascesis* is the ancient word for athletic practice; and the regular practice of fasting in Orthodox parish life (monastics pursue it more rigorously than the laity) becomes a peaceful way of cleansing the mind as well as the body: reminding the flesh that it has to be obedient and in good condition to serve the Lord. The practice of fasting was common in the church from the earliest times, and was always associated with the preparation for prayer. Before approaching the holy eucharistic mysteries each Orthodox (those who are old enough and strong enough) must abstain from all food and drink, at least from midnight of the previous day. Many who prepare for holy communion fast much more than this, and join their fasting with the recitation of the Psalms. The ancient Fathers regarded this as a spiritual method that called down the blessings of God's mercy and forgiveness on the soul; and the great spiritual teachers of the Orthodox Church have always regarded fasting as an essential thing for those who wish to make progress in the ways of the Gospel. Orthodox fasting in the normal manner is not something that harms the health in any way; on the contrary, it makes the person more alert, energized, and peaceful. Anything more than the usual fasting (by which the Orthodox largely mean the restriction of types of food that can be taken) should only be undertaken with the advice of a spiritual guide, so that it is always appropriate, and undertaken for positive reasons and attainable spiritual goals.

THE HOLY ICONS: DOORS TO THE KINGDOM

Sacred art

When people visit an Orthodox Church for the first time, often on holiday in Greece or Russia, they are usually struck by the richness of the church decoration: often a strong contrast with the more sober church style of northern Europe, and offering a distinctly different ambience to the exuberant baroque of Mediterranean Catholicism. There is a difference in tone, between the various national Orthodox churches, with the Greeks (especially on the smaller island churches) being the most restrained of all the different styles; but an overarching character distinguishes the visible style of all the Orthodox churches, and it is largely because of Orthodoxy's particular approach to sacred art. The icon is, in many senses, a touchstone of Orthodox experience. In recent years this has proven to be an attraction to many outside Orthodoxy. Fifty years ago an Eastern Christian icon was a curiosity and a rarity indeed. Now there is a large market in icon reproductions, and hardly a Christian bookstore (of any denomination) that does not hold numerous works on the subject. But sacred art remains something of a smouldering problem in the churches of the West, not least because it was one of the areas of bitter contention fought over between Protestantism and Catholicism in the Reformation era. The great cathedrals of England, with their row upon row of empty stone niches and blank wall spaces, are a mute testament to the great iconoclastic purge that took place in the Reformation period. Holy images were pulled down and set on fire and stone statues were smashed to pieces, in an attempt to stamp out alleged 'idolatry' and false worship. When Western Christians encounter Orthodoxy, therefore, they are often brought up sharply, once again, against the need to assess how they stand in the face of religious representation, and its role in worship.

For the Orthodox the icon is a sacred, sacramental, means of evoking the presence of the Lord (or the Virgin or the saint that it depicts). It is a holy thing charged with a powerful blessing to assist the believer who prays before it, in order to act as a medium of that presence which the believer desires to be in: be it that of Christ, the Virgin, or the saint. Orthodox believers come before an icon and make the sign of the Cross over themselves and bow down in reverence. This is not some form of magical worship of an idol (many Protestants may feel this so deeply because it is an experience of worship utterly alien to them and thus, perhaps, a prejudice hard to get over). The Orthodox are not so dim in their faith as to mistake bowing down before a dumb idol for the veneration of Christ. When the Orthodox come before an icon of Christ, let us say, they bow down before it so that they can express their heart's devotion to the Lord himself. The fundamental theological principle of Orthodox veneration, therefore, is that which St Basil the Great enunciated in the fourth century: 'The honour given to the image passes over directly to the prototype.'[298]

In other words when an Orthodox venerates an icon (they never 'worship' an icon) they bow down not to the image but to Christ himself, who is represented in the image. The reverence of this iconic 'type' of Christ passes directly to the prototype, Christ himself, and thus the reverence of the icon becomes, in that moment of prayer, the direct and actual worship of the Resurrected Lord Jesus. But this transmission of the act of reverence, from the icon to the one it signifies, works for other icons too. So when an Orthodox venerates an icon of the Blessed Theotokos, the reverence is passed directly to her. It becomes an immediate act of veneration to the Virgin. The church understands 'type' in the sense of how a material thing can 'stand for' another thing. The Cross, for example, can 'stand for' Christianity, or for Jesus himself. If one was asked to spit upon the Cross (as were the Japanese martyrs of the twentieth century) it is clear to all, Christians and persecutors alike, that this was no matter of trivial symbols (such that 'it was only a piece of wood and meant nothing at all anyway') but an actual encounter between the believer and the Lord through the symbol of the Cross. For this reason the martyrs chose death rather than to spit on or trample upon the Cross which their persecutors offered to them as a way to save their lives. This is a clear example of how the Christian instinct recognizes the power of 'types' in its experience. There are other 'types' in the Old Testament, according to Christian tradition, where Isaac bearing the wood of his sacrifice, or the water-giving rock in the desert are 'types' of Christ.[299]

In the case of the icon of Christ, the reverence passes into being worship: for Christ is God incarnate, and is given the worship of his church that is due to God alone.

The Virgin, as all the faithful know, is one of the creatures like us, though highest of all the saints. The reverence given to her icon, as a 'type' of her presence, passes through the icon to become a direct reverence of her holy person, a delight in her closeness to Christ, her Lord and ours. The same is true also of icons of the saints. Reverence of their icons passes through to each of the saints depicted in the icon, and becomes a direct veneration of them because they were, and are, Christ's friends. To express this sense of degrees of 'reverence' Orthodoxy elaborated several theological terms to clarify the distinctions. Unfortunately, this refined vocabulary was a casualty of the Reformation era, and post-Reformation thought had a massively restricted set of terms to connote 'worship', thus making it very confused about what the Orthodox were doing in their iconic prayer.

The Orthodox vocabulary of worship

Orthodoxy uses three distinct words to describe the process of worship: *latreia*, *hyperdouleia*, and *douleia*. We can render them as worship/adoration, high reverence, and reverence. Worship and adoration are to be given to God alone. To do otherwise would be idolatry. But Christ himself is to be afforded worship and adoration, just as the Father and the Spirit are in the unity of the Trinity; for Christ is God in the fullest sense of all that that means. The divine worship of *latreia* cannot be given to the icon, considered as an icon. What the believer does before the icon is make an act of *proskynesis* (the word means a bowing down in reverence): but this physical act (bending down in the presence of the icon of the Lord) is the material form of a worship which flowers into *latreia* (adoration) of the divine Christ. English uses the word 'worship' very loosely in this regard. Orthodoxy has actually thought about the matter far more deeply, and elaborated a much clearer theology of prayer and reverence in ancient times. In the English marriage service, for example, the bride and groom are called upon to 'worship one another' with their bodies. Here the term clearly means 'hold in respectful veneration'. At other times English intends to reserve the word worship for the adoration due to God alone: as in the phrase from the Old Testament: 'You shall worship no other God, for the Lord is a jealous God.'[300]

The English translation of the Old Testament, used so heavily by the Reformers, had made worship in this sense the sole translation of 'adoration due to God alone'. The ancient Christian Church, on the other hand, only read the Septuagintal Greek Scriptures (not the Hebrew), where the range of vocabulary for worship, adoration, reverence, veneration, respectful greeting was much more extensive, and graded according to the different contexts of what was being spoken of. If adoration and worship were due to God alone, it was fitting that reverence and respectful behaviour would be attributed to God's prophets, the anointed kings and judges of Israel, and, in the New Testament dispensation, clearly to the apostles and great saints. None of these heroes was given worship or adoration; such a thing would be offensive. When the pagans tried to do this to the apostles Paul and Barnabas they were horrified.[301] But the Orthodox know the basic distinction between adoration and reverence (*latreia* and *douleia*). To Christ, and the Divine Trinity of course, that is to God alone, is given adoration and worship (*latreia*).

356

To the Virgin and saints is given profound reverence (*douleia*) because of their closeness to God, and because of the way they have been assimilated so closely with Christ's glory. To venerate the Virgin and the saints is, the Orthodox believe, another form of giving glory to Christ. But even so, there is a very big difference between veneration and worship/adoration. If Christians of the Reformed tradition could trust that Orthodox know what they mean, and know what they are doing when they venerate icons, much suspicion could be ecumenically avoided. Idolatry is as detested by the Orthodox as it is by the most zealous evangelical. On the other hand, the Orthodox are very puzzled why some Protestant believers think that they honour Christ by refusing to respect his Mother and his saints; puzzled, too, by the way that many people who hate icons and would cast them out of the churches seem to have their own homes filled with pictures (photographs and suchlike) of those whom they love, often gazing upon them reverently and devotedly as things that evoke the presence of their loved ones. The first thing an Orthodox person does before an icon is to bow; the second thing is to kiss the hand of the person depicted in the icon (it is regarded as somewhat sacrilegious and presumptuous to kiss the face). There must be very few people who have pictures of deeply loved ones in their homes who have not, at some time or other, handled the photograph and felt that impulse as entirely a natural one. Perhaps it is something to do with upbringing and culture: be that as it may, Orthodox love the icons of Christ and the Virgin and the saints, and fill their churches and homes with them.

There is not a single home of an Orthodox person which does not have icons in it. The east-facing corner (if geography allows) is usually the place where a corner shelf is made and the family icons are set up, known as the 'Beautiful Corner', and near the corner will be kept the family bible and prayer books. At every wedding the Orthodox guests make sure that the new couple have a gift of an icon of Christ and the Virgin, so as to 'start off' a new home properly. This corner is the place where the family will meet for prayers. Often an incense burner is to be found here. In church priests and deacons will incense the icons and then incense the people of God liturgically as a sign of the blessing of God conveyed upon them. In their homes, the laity will also light a charcoal and place incense upon it so that it rises in the sight of God, in front of the icon of Christ, to accompany their prayer. The priestly prayer at the offering of incense explains the significance of this: 'Incense we offer to you O Christ our God. Receive it upon your heavenly throne, and send down upon us in return, the grace of your all-holy Spirit.' After offering the incense to God the faithful will then take the censer and cense the icons of the Virgin and the saints, and then any of the family who have gathered there in prayer, and lastly the house itself: to call down the blessing of God over all.

Icons and iconoclasm

At two periods in the history of the Byzantine empire there were great controversies over the appropriateness of having icons in the church. Islam had a strong influence on some of the Syrian emperors of the eighth century, and they called for a purge of the Orthodox Church of its icons. This puritanical movement was strongly resisted. St John of Damascus, who wrote during the midst of this controversy (known as the Iconoclastic Crisis), St Germanos of Constantinople, and St Theodore the Studite (who were active slightly later) also produced Orthodox treatises on the theology of icons.

For all of them the veneration of the icon says something about fundamental theo-logical attitudes towards the Incarnation of God in the flesh. For them God made humanity as his 'icon and likeness'. Reverence for human beings is thus a holy thing when they are understood to be icons of God (so it is the Orthodox Church incenses the faithful during the course of the Eucharist, and incenses the dead body during its funeral rituals). But this generic image of God in man is taken to a new pitch in the mystery of the Incarnation. In Christ, God literally became man. And in Christ mankind was mystically caught up into the Godhead by grace. What took place in Christ uniquely, by his assumption of flesh, is the prototype of what is offered to the saved and redeemed believer: communion with the Lord by grace.

From this basic principle of salvation in and through the flesh derives the Orthodox theology of the sacraments or mysteries. This is based on the fundamental principle that God uses materiality as the medium of his salvific power. The iconic representa-tion of Christ is a smaller form of the principle of the Incarnation. The icon materially 'stands for' or typifies, the Lord who came in the flesh to his people. When one considers the icon as a 'sacrament of Christ's presence' in this sense, it is not so powerful a sacrament of presence as the Holy Eucharist,[302] but it is still powerfully graced as a medium of grace. When Orthodox encounter those who (for whatever reason) find their veneration of the icons somewhat offensive, in their own turn they wonder about what kind of sacramental theology their critics have: how they understand the presence of the Lord in the Eucharist; how they understand the grace of the Lord to work through the saints and angels; how they understand the assistance the Blessed Virgin gives to those on earth. It often turns out that those who reject the theology of the icon also reject most of these other things too. For these reasons the Orthodox have always tended to regard the veneration of icons as not a peripheral thing, but a matter central to the health of the Christian.

At the seventh ecumenical council of Nicaea II (787), the veneration of icons was defined as not only a valid expression of faith but a necessary one too: for those who resisted it were seen to be attacking the deeper concept of how the Lord's grace is at work transfiguring the cosmos in and through its essential materiality. There are still many Christians who imagine, perhaps, that God's Spirit works in the world in 'wholly spiritual' ways, but who do not appreciate how the Infinite Spirit of God enters into the very fabric of our material consciousness to accomplish his purposes, for although he is wholly Spirit, we are not, and never shall be (being synthetic creatures of flesh and spirit). Pure spirit, therefore, always acts within the cosmos (as in the Incarnation) in and through the fabric of flesh. Orthodox are not ashamed to want to worship Christ through the material medium of the icon, knowing that the Lord graced the medium of materiality so mystically in his own choice of the incarnate path of redemption.

John of Damascus relates the veneration of the icon directly to the biblical theology of the image. His work on icon veneration is taken as a standard in the Orthodox Church today:

> Some find fault with us for worshipping and honouring the icon of our Saviour and that of our Lady, and those, too, of the rest of the saints and servants of Christ; but they should remember that Scripture says 'in the beginning God created man after his own icon'. On what grounds, then, do we show reverence to each other? Only because we are made after God's image.[303]

A little further on in his argument he speaks of the iconoclasts of his day who have argued that Scripture forbids the making of idols, and commands we never bow down to any graven image. If this is the case surely icon veneration is an anti-scriptural thing? To this he points out that it is necessary to read the Scriptures with some sense of what they mean contextually; not with a foolish literalism. What the Scriptures forbid by false worship is the worship of any other God than the true God. Those who think that the worship of Christ is 'other than the true God' are not in accordance with the Christian faith. Moreover the Scriptures did not forbid the reverencing of material things in the service of the cult of the true God. The book of Leviticus, for example, is full of the commandments of God how the curtain of the Holy of Holies is to be embroidered with icons of the Cherubim, and how the ark of the covenant is to be decorated with graven images of the Cherubim. It is not the use of material images in cult that is being forbidden by the Old Testament, therefore, but the concept of misdirecting the worship of the One True God. The bowing down to idols refers to the worship of alien gods as conducted by the non-Israelite tribes. St John of Damascus argues that all of this was given as a command-ment by God, before the Incarnation took place. In that time and condition, mankind's knowledge of God was defective, he argues, but was utterly clarified and strengthened by the Incarnation, so that the monotheism of Israel was brought to a new pitch in the trinitarian faith of the church. After Christ, therefore, it can be presumed that the spiritual instinct of monotheism alive in the church will no longer be misdirected by icons into a form of native polytheism, which was such a worry to the leaders of the ancient Israelites who lived surrounded by false idols. He puts the argument this way:

> The Greeks sacrificed and the Jews also sacrificed: but the Greeks did it to demons and the Jews to God. So, the sacrifice of the Greeks was rejected and condemned, but the sacrifice of the just was very acceptable to God.... This was why the graven images of the Greeks, as images of false deities, were rejected and forbidden. But in any case who can ever make an imitation of the invisible, incorporeal, uncircum-scribed, formless God? To attempt to give form to the Godhead is the height of folly and impiety. This is why in the Old Testament the use of images was not common. But after God in his tender pity became, in very truth, a man for our salvation (and not in the mere appearance of a man as he was seen by Abraham ... but being truly man) and after he lived on the earth and dwelt among men, worked miracles, suffered, was crucified, rose again and was taken back to Heaven, since all these things actually took place and were seen by men, they were then capable of being depicted for the remembrance and instruction of us who were not alive at that time. In this way though we never saw these things ourselves, we may still obtain the blessing of the Lord by hearing and believing. But since not everyone is literate, and may not have time for reading, the Fathers gave their sanction to depicting these events on icons, to show them as acts of great heroism, in order that the icons could make a concise memorial of them. Often, doubtless when we have been forgetful of the Lord's Passion and then see the icon of Christ's crucifixion, his saving Passion is surely brought back to mind, and we fall down and worship. We do not worship the material, of course, but that which is imaged in it: just as we do not worship the material of which the Gospels are made, nor the material of the Cross, but that which these things typify.[304]

In the day-to-day life of the Orthodox Church his words (however complicated the argument may seem to read) simply depict the ordinary reality of a people's fervent faith in Christ. No Orthodox ever confuses the creature with the Creator, or mixes up Christ and his saints. None confuses the material medium with the spiritual presence it signifies. On the other hand each Orthodox knows that if they wish to be brought into the deeper sense of the embracing presence of the Lord or his saints, they go to stand before the icon and pray there. It is a touching thing to see little children, hardly able to walk, go up to the icons and kiss them. Their theology has gone ahead of that of the learned[305] and they confess the faith perfectly and purely before they have the words or letters to do so.

It would be an oddly 'grey' exercise to attempt a depiction in words of the wonder-fully colourful and dynamic world of Orthodox iconography. It would be far better for a reader to peruse some illustrated books of icons, of which there are now many available,[306] or to use an internet search engine, with the keywords 'Greek and Russian Orthodox icons'. Being married to a very skilled professional iconographer, I have become aware of how often church painters are invited to meetings primarily to 'speak' about icons. In that circumstance my own Preotasa usually says at some stage: 'If I could speak about icons more fluently than I could paint, I would have been a writer, not an artist.' Behind this reluctance for words is the deeper truth that the holy icons are best left uncommented on. They are an apophatic theology that sings louder in silence. Writers (such as myself, however) can never leave well enough alone. So we shall end with a few words of interpretation about an immensely rich subject which contains within it a deep and 'secret' theology of colours and symbols. A little knowl-edge of this can assist the non-Orthodox to begin to see through these 'doors to the Kingdom' and to appreciate how complex the theology they represent really is, and how deeply and biblically Christian it actually is.

Icons are sometimes said to be 'written' not drawn. This is largely a misunderstand-ing of the Greek where the verb *grapho* covers both things equally. The Russian translation lost the dual capacity of signification, and often Russian sources woodenly insist on describing the iconographer as icon-writer. There is a play in the Greek sources, nevertheless, on how the icon circumscribes (draws around) the uncircum-scribable God, for the benefit of circumscribed minds. Because circumscribability was one of the characters of the incarnate deity, this paradox is seen to be an admissible aspect of the Incarnation. But since the Father and the Spirit were never materially incarnated, Orthodox icon theology refuses the admissibility of depicting them. The exception is the depiction of the Trinity known as the Old Testament Trinity, or Hospitality of Abraham, where three angels are used as symbols of the Trinity (as in the typological narrative of the epiphany of God at the Oak of Mamre[307]). One of the most famous and perfect icons of all time, Rublev's Trinity, is an outstanding example of this. Some later iconographers started to make up icons of the Father (as a very old man sitting on a throne), but these represent a decadent stage of iconography, which was at a very low ebb from the seventeenth through to the twentieth centuries.

Orthodox icons are also said to be painted only in egg tempera, an ancient technique where pigment is ground directly into egg yolks mixed with vinegar. It is a medium approximating modern acrylics, though it has a luminous opacity that some love, but which others think can often turn very 'muddy' in the hands of those who are not experts in the medium. Egg tempera painting of icons covered the greatest period of iconography, perhaps the eleventh century through to the sixteenth. But it was not the only way of painting icons. The very first iconic images in Christianity were painted in fresco technique (where the pigment was applied quickly to a wall on which the plaster was still damp). When the wall dried, the paint dried into it and fused with it and would last for centuries if water and fire damage did not intervene. At Voronets in Romania, the beautiful church had frescoes painted inside and outside when it was consecrated in 1547. Centuries of worship using incense and candles have greatly dimmed the inside painting. The outside remains fresh and vibrant to this day, such is the staying power of the fresco. Because of this, fresco panels are among the earliest surviving examples of Christian art. Those that remain from the second and third centuries in Rome and Egypt are mainly funerary art; but they sometimes show archetypal patterns that will still be recognizable in the art of later centuries, such as the theme of the three holy youths in the fiery furnace (a symbol of martyrdom), the procession of the Marys to the tomb, the angel holding the empty grave cloths, or the figure of the Orant (the church at prayer with upraised hands). By the third century the repertoire had grown to include Christ in glory, the Last Supper, the apostles, and several New Testament miracle scenes.[308]

With regard to portable panel paintings (a Greek and Roman technique) the first known Christian examples of icons were done in the ancient equivalent of oils, known as the encaustic wax process. In this style powder pigment is added directly to the panel in a medium of molten wax (kept hot in a small boiler) and fused to the board. It is a difficult technique to master, but it endured a very long time. St Catherine's monastery at Sinai retains some of the oldest examples dating to the sixth and seventh centuries.[309] Among them the so-called Sinai Pantocrator is one of the most electrifying of all ancient icons, although it was somewhat reworked in a later period.[310]

Icons of the Lord

In Orthodox icons the Lord is usually shown in half-length portrait, dressed in imperial robes, holding the book of Gospels open in his left hand,[311] while with his right hand he dispenses blessing to the observer. The Gospel text contains a summative message of the Lord's teaching. Often it is the text: 'Come to me all you who labour and are heavy burdened.'[312] This text frequently accompanies the icons of the Lord's assessment of souls, and is meant to give hope, as one reflects on the mystery of judgement. Another common text is: 'I am the Light of the World; whoever follows me will not walk in darkness.'[313] The fingers of the Lord are fixed in a way that spells out the Greek letters of his name (IC XC): it is still to this day the manner in which priests give a blessing in church, calling down the power of the Holy Name on the believer. The face of Christ in the icons is traditionally desentimentalized. It is not meant to be entirely comfortable, even though it is comforting; and to achieve this the eyes are always depicted as having an intense quality that seems to 'look through' the person who stands before the icon. In some of the older churches in the inner drum of the dome in the centre of the nave, icons of Christ the Judge and Master of All (Pantocrator) were painted which, in Byzantine times, were very fierce indeed. The believer looking up (a painful posture to begin with) would have a very lively sense of Christ's presence as Judge of the World. The frescoes of the Greek monastery at Daphni in Greece are a prime example of this. In the late nineteenth century in both Greece and the Slavonic countries, a certain sentimentalization did come into the iconic features as a result of Westernizing artistic influences, but a modern revival of Orthodox Byzantine-style iconography has returned to more classical models.

As a result of their style, Orthodox icons are often enigmatic and do not give their full range of meaning immediately to the casual observer. Orthodox know that, to understand the message of Christ, long hours of prayer and familiarity are required, and above all an attempt to make one's life conform to the evangelical teachings. It is over the long period, sharing the struggles of a disciple to learn obedience through prayer, that an icon gives up its mystical message slowly. They are not an art form for those who want instant answers and solutions.

Icons of the Virgin

The Virgin is depicted extensively in the iconography of the Orthodox Church, which has a deep and widely practised devotion to her. She is normally shown holding the Christ child on her left shoulder, and often pointing to him with her right hand. This gesture of teaching others the centrality of Christ has led to her title as Hodegitria (the one who shows the way). The Virgin is shown wearing the *maphorion*, the aristocratic head covering from ancient times. On the centre front of her shawl, and on the two shoulders, she wears an eight-pointed star (a symbol of the Eschaton and of perfection). The three stars together symbolize her threefold virginity (before the birth, during the birth, and after the birth), which is a doctrine of Orthodoxy. But always one of the stars is occluded by the body of the child. This is to show that her virginity was perfect and absolute, but that it must not be taken in any way as a diminution of the real humanity of either her or her divine Son. It is one example of how easily, and graciously, iconography (by the symbolic occlusion of one of the stars), is able to make assertions and refinements of doctrine that literal theology would stumble over.

As time progressed so did the number of the variants of the icons of the Theotokos. All of them carry her title in abbreviated form: MP ΘY, the Greek abbreviation for *Meter Theou*, or Mother of God. The proliferation of different styles included icons of the Mother of God the Sweet-Kissing One, which showed a more animated Christ child, and a Virgin who delighted in the baby she carried in her arms. There were also icons of the type known as *vladimirskaya* (from the great original once held in the church at Vladimir) which were icons of the Mother of God of the Passion. In these the Theotokos held the child and looked with great sadness out of the frame, sensing the sorrow that would fall to her, and the suffering that would be the destiny of her Son. To comfort her the prescient child reaches out a tiny hand and puts it round her neck, as if to strengthen this his first and greatest disciple for the trial to come. The Cretan icon of the 'Mother of God of Perpetual Succour' is a Greek icon of this type that was brought into the West and has enjoyed great popularity in Roman Catholic circles since the nineteenth century.

There are also icons of the Virgin of the Sign, which depict the Theotokos standing, or in half-length, with a roundel (*clypeus*) on her breast within which is shown the Christ child with extended arms blessing the world. The Virgin herself is depicted with both hands upraised in prayer of intercession for the world. The icon of the Sign symbolizes the Virgin before the birth of the Saviour when 'she contained in her womb he whom the heavens themselves could not contain' as a Byzantine hymn puts it. Because of this the Greek tradition calls her the Platytera (she who is greater than the heavens). Greek Platytera icons generally show her with the Christ child sitting upon her lap, as she in turn sits upon a throne. Mary herself, in this symbolic icon-set, is the throne on which God takes his rest, as in ancient times he rested upon the Cherubim. In the hymns addressed to Mary in the church she is thus called 'You who are more venerable than the Seraphim and beyond compare more glorious than the Cherubim, for inviolate you gave birth to God the Word.'

The doors that lead into the altar area from the iconostasis in an Orthodox church customarily depict the Annunciation (Evangelismos, or 'Bringing of the Good News', as it is known in Greek). Mary sits, spinning a scarlet curtain for the Temple (a detail taken from the Proto-Evangelium of James) while the angel Gabriel comes to announce the news of the Incarnation. Both Mary and the angel are startled in the style of this famous icon: she because of the sudden arrival of the messenger, and the outstanding message he brings; he because of the great surprise he receives when he 'sees with his bodiless eyes' the Eternal Word taking flesh in the womb of the Virgin, as the great Byzantine hymn of the Akathist puts it.

Another major form of icon in which the Virgin Theotokos features predominantly is that of the *Deisis* or 'Great Intercession' icons. These are formed of a central panel of Christ enthroned in judgement. At either side of the central panel the Virgin and the Baptist stand with hands extended in supplication to the Lord. It is a solemn and ancient tradition of the church that this will be the special role of the Virgin at the Last Judgement, at the Eschaton, when she will be the graceful intercessor for the universal church with her Son and Saviour, who then acts as the Judge of all the World. A magnificent thirteenth-century mosaic example of the *Deisis* survives, though much damaged, in the upper gallery of Hagia Sophia in Istanbul.

Icons of the saints

Each church in the Orthodox world is usually dedicated to a particular saint (though some may be dedicated to the Trinity, the Lord, or the Blessed Theotokos), and often the relics of the saint are to be found in the Holy Table of the altar. When a church is dedicated to a saint the icon of that saint will be the first thing that people entering the church will be faced with, as if the saint himself, or herself, is there to greet those entering in to pray. The iconostasis of the church always displays the icon of the Saviour to the observer's right-hand side of the holy doors, and that of the Virgin to the left. Icons of John the Baptist and the saint of the church are placed adjacent to the two chief icons on the iconostasis.

Over the course of its history Orthodoxy has associated particular functions with various saints: St Tryphon is invoked for assistance in finding lost things. SS Blaise (Vlasy), Spyridon, Florus and Lauros, and Modestus (Medost) are special protectors of animals. Military saints such as George, Demetrios, or Theodore have a special appeal to soldiers, or in times of national trouble. Anastasia, or the 'Holy Unmercenaries'[314] Cosmas and Damian, Panteleimon, or Charalampos, are especially invoked by those suffering illness. For many needs, apart from one's own particular patron saints, the

Orthodox find it natural to appeal to many of Christ's saints for day-to-day assistance. St Nicholas of Myra was one of the most commonly invoked saints of all. He gained the title from centuries from his admirers in Russia (which made him its national patron), of Nikolai Chudotvorets, Nicholas the Worker of Wonders. Saintly bishops and the Fathers in particular are shown in the icons as dressed as for the divine liturgy, and holding the (closed) Gospel book of Christ in their left hand while giving blessing with their right. Ascetic saints are drawn preternaturally tall, a sign of their 'stature' in the eyes of the Lord, and desert ascetics are drawn immensely thin. In the ranks of the saints true equality among the genders is found, for there are as many, if not more, women saints as men; and women in every rank and condition: women apostles, martyrs, confessors, ascetics, prophets, judges, healers, rulers, and servants. It is an extraordinary testimony to the immensity of women's contribution to the ongoing life of Christianity.

Many parts of the Protestant world find this devotion to Christ's blessed ones alien to their faith experience, having set aside the veneration of the saints for so long in their own traditions. The Orthodox, however, do not believe that the veneration of a saint detracts at all from the overwhelming Christian principle that the Lord is the sole source of grace for his church and his world. This focus which the church preserves inviolate, that the Lord is the sole mediator between God and mankind[315] does not, in the Eastern Christian estimation, mean that Christ never shares his grace among the church, and can only act as Mediator in a solitary way. That notion, devoid of the spiritual sense of communion that attends always with the Risen Lord, is hostile to the Gospel spirit. In giving his saints powers of beneficent intercession with the world, Christ expresses his intercessory grace within the world without diminishing it. The saints work powerfully in and through the grace of their one and common Lord. Their activity in the world after their 'glorification' is a mark of the greatness of their compassion and philanthropy while they were earthly saints. The Orthodox believe firmly in the ongoing philanthropy among mankind of the Virgin, the angels, and the saints. Many Orthodox also often pray privately to members of their own families who have departed in Christ, and whom they sense have been blessed and glorified by their holy lives. These also have a special remit of prayer and blessing for their descendants. They are the unofficial saints of the church, of whom there are vast multitudes.

God works in and through multitudes of hierarchies in all that he does for us. He does not educate us at our conversion all in a flash of a moment, but expects us to go on in life learning, and maturing, and growing in wisdom. He teaches us through ranks of different teachers across numbers of years. He rarely heals us in direct miraculous ways, but expects us to avail ourselves of an array of medicines, doctors, and nurturing friends. It would seem ludicrous to imagine that, unless God himself directly heals a wound, we would not accept it as a healing at all. So it is with his bestowal of grace: it comes to us in multitudes of ways, and in day-to-day experience it often comes to us through the hands of the blessed saints of Christ. Sometimes, some imagine that God always sends grace directly to them; that all their prayers are heard directly by God; that God is always immediately attentive to their least need. Such is the spiritual sense of many today, though it seems to the Orthodox to be a solipsistic delusion (*prelest*) much of the time.

While Orthodoxy knows that God sees and blesses all things, it is also filled with a sense that there is a warfare in progress around us, a struggle with hostile spiritual forces that contradict the divine plan at many instances; but also that we are surrounded by great powers that assist and bless us according to the command that God has given them to watch over the earth and to watch over the saints. Into this great angelic mission (those whom God has appointed as intercessors and guides) the saints also are inducted in their glorification. Often on earth they showed the power of Christ's healing grace to others; now after their entrance to glory the church continues to experience their grace, as the mediation of the grace of Christ. Such a thing seems normal and natural to the Orthodox, that God works sometimes upon us directly, but often in and through his saints and angels, as if in a vast extended family of the elect.

The rejection of the saints, and the scorn often shown to the principle of their heavenly intercession, is a thing that troubles the Orthodox greatly about some of the Western traditions, and raises doubts about the notion of spiritual communion that is operative in such a mentality. There is much amusement even in some parts of the Christian world (for we can leave aside the secular world of those who have very little experience of the living mercy of the Christ) as to the notion of the saints' miracles and the holiness and graceful power of their relics. Sometimes this is a barely disguised scorn and ridicule. When Orthodox are visiting churches which contain the relics of the saints they will kneel before the tombs and kiss the relics, or the tombs, with deep reverence on the principle that the grace of God which sanctified the living believer then is now still at work in their sanctified and consecrated remains, and that they too are still alive in the Risen Christ: not mere dumb bones and dusty grave memorials. The Orthodox have a deep love for the saints, and from this a clear expectation that the saints and angels will guide and protect them. They know from innumerable experiences in life that this indeed is the case. For them it is one more sign of the living spiritual vitality of Orthodoxy, and a sign that the church continues to live in the same spiritual communion that led them, in their time, to the glory of the same Master. Accordingly, the Orthodox hold that the graves even of the ordinary faithful are holy places. Many times services of prayer are held there, in the open air,[316] for loved ones departed. The body falls to dust, as God said it would, but love never fails, nor our certainty that the believer lives in the light of the Resurrection of the Saviour.

Notes

1 Orthodoxy requires baptismal immersion, for infants or adults. It has sometimes adapted itself, in some parts and in different eras, to the Western practice of aspersional baptism, but this is not a proper procedure canonically, or theologically (it had originally evolved as an 'economic' form of the baptism of sick people in danger of death), because the element of immersion is a fundamental symbol of entrance into the death and resurrection of Christ (Rom. 6.4–5; Col. 2.12), and thus a basic part of the 'significance' of the sacramental form. Orthodoxy thus acknowledges aspersional baptism but it does not approve of it as a standard practice. From antiquity it has also acknowledged the 'baptism by blood' of those who were martyred before their baptismal ceremony took place.

2 The central prayers of the eucharistic offering, which takes place after the more public initial series of church litanies, and Scripture readings, and recitation of the Creed.

3 The biblical phrase for the revelation of the power of the divine presence. Cf. Exod. 33.22; 1 Kgs 19.11.

4 Matt. 17.26; Mark 4.41; Luke 5.26.

5 Later Western theology has developed the significance of 'mystical' to connote a large element of personal interior knowledge

(as in 'mystics' and 'mystical perception'). In Orthodoxy the word retains its more ancient connotation of having to do with the secret operation of the Divine Lord, especially in the sacramental rites. *Mystagogy*, for example, is a term that means a commentary on the divine liturgy. As one might suspect with a term so closely connected with liturgy (a word which itself means 'the public worship and service of God'), the concept of 'mystical' in the Eastern Church is something that is corporate rather than individualistic; collegial and ecclesial in character rather than personalistic.

6 Luke 2.19, 51.

7 This sense of reverential penitence is also found in the refusal of the Orthodox Church to allow musical instruments in its services, and why the tonal character of the liturgical settings is generally very sober.

8 Exod. 3.5.

9 Bulgakov 1988: 110–11.

10 Dan. 2.47; Wisd. 2.22.

11 Ecclus. 27.16.

12 Matt. 13.11.

13 Rom. 11.25.

14 Rom. 11.28–9.

15 Rom. 16.25.

16 Eph. 1.9, 3.3–4; Col. 2.2–3; 1 Tim. 3.9, 16.

17 Col. 1.26–7.

18 Gregory the Theologian, *Carmina Arcana* 2, On the Son; Cyril of Jerusalem. Catechetical Oration 10.3–4.

19 Just as Christ himself often 'passed by' his contemporaries but was only seen by those who had the 'eyes to see and the ears to hear'.

20 As Metropolitan Kallistos says: 'John of Damascus speaks of two; Dionysios the Areopagite of six; Joasaph, metropolitan of Ephesus (fifteenth century) of ten; and those Byzantine theologians who in fact speak of seven sacraments differ as to the items which they include on their list.' Ware 1987: 282.

21 *Exomologesis*, or 'confession' as it is known, which is closely related to the initiatory mysteries as a form of their renewal. *Exomologesis* is called, to this

extent, a 'second baptism', though the church also knows baptism cannot be repeated. The Fathers, especially St Gregory the Theologian (Oration 39.7), and St John of Damascus (*On the Orthodox Faith*, 4.9) speak of several different 'types' of baptism including the baptism of tears of repentance, and the baptism of blood. The mystery of the seven anointings (of the sick) closely connects the experience of prayer for healing, through the anointing with sacred oil, with the concept of *metanoia* and confession of sins.

22 The Western Church later required children to be of the 'age of reason' before the reception of this mystery, and for similar reasons delayed the chrismation until a later time (designating it as confirmation). The liturgical changes after Vatican II restored the significance of chrismation to the baptism rite, though retaining a separate service of confirmation as well. Orthodoxy has never thought that the reception of the initiations depended on a full comprehension of what was transpiring (otherwise no one would ever be qualified to receive a mystery) and so all the baptized, infant as well as adults, the wise as well as the less learned, are called to the family table of the Lord, where differentiations are offensive to the equality of honour he has given us (Jas. 2.1–5).

23 The bread and wine of the Eucharist, the water and chrism of baptism, and so on.

24 St Basil the Great speaks of the seal as comparable to the marking of the Israelites' houses so that the angel of death would know them to be protected. Exod. 12.13. The idea of the sealing of the servants of God is also found in Ezek. 9.4, and the same notion is evoked in Rev. 7.3.

25 Matt. 9.29.

26 Luke 24.30–2.

27 John 13.30.

28 John 21.15–17.

29 Can a mystery fail to transfer saving grace to an individual? Surely so, though it can never fail 'collectively' in the *sobornost* of the communion of believers as a whole. St Paul speaks of some early believers

'eating and drinking judgement' to themselves (1 Cor. 11.29), because of their perverting of the Holy Eucharist into a counter-sign of grace. They had used the mystery of communion to signify self-centred isolation. But this is always a pathological situation and does not convey the normal vital effect of the holy mysteries. We can distinguish between the 'efficacy' of the mysteries (just as the *Epistle of the Eastern Patriarchs* described them as 'the means which unfailingly act by grace upon those who come to them') and their 'effectiveness', which presumes the freedom of the synergy of the believer's love and faith.

30 Mark 4.11.

31 Luke 17.21.

32 This is the force of the Nicene Creed's profession; 'We believe in one baptism for the forgiveness of sins.'

33 Several of the other repeated sacraments also have some element within them of this 'non-repeatable' character. The Holy Eucharist, for example, is not a regular repetition of the mystery of the Lord's death and resurrection, but rather the one self-same eschatological experience entered into several times in the current of history. The ritual of the mystery of marriage also shows the sense that it is a 'once for all' event, although in economic practice up to three marriages can be solemnized in church. Ordination can be repeated across the different degrees (deacon, priest, bishop) but cannot (if validly conferred) be repeated in the same degree.

34 The priestly prayer at the offering of incense in the divine liturgy shows this sense of sacramentalized conferral of blessing: 'This incense we offer to you, O Christ our God. Accept it on your heavenly throne, and send down on us in return the grace of your Most Holy Spirit.' Liturgy of St John Chrysostom.

35 The remnant of the ancient *agapé* meal after the Eucharist is concluded, when the bread that was blessed but not consecrated at the holy table is given out to those in church.

36 The range of sacraments and their frequency of celebration being heavily cut back in most Protestant parishes.

37 Male proselytes, of course, would be circumcised.

38 St Gregory of Nyssa calls it a purification of the soul which dispenses with the eschatological 'purification of fire' that will be required of the souls of the uninitiated. Catechetical Oration 35.

39 That of the initiation of the resurrection as a new principle of life within mortal humanity. To that extent the mystery of baptism is the gift of resurrectional life, a new form of 'human being', not otherwise experienced in the human race. Cf. Gregory of Nyssa, Catechetical Oration 35: 'The great resurrection has its beginnings, and its causes, here in baptism...and without this washing of regeneration the resurrection of a human person is not possible.'

40 John 1.26. 'Among you stands one whom you do not know.'

41 John 1.29–33.

42 John 1.37–46.

43 Matt. 28.19–20.

44 John 3.3–6.

45 Mark 16.16.

46 The apostle calls baptism the 'washing of regeneration' (Titus 3.5). St John of Damascus connects the baptismal rebirth with the whole mystery of the believer's deification in Christ: 'For it was fitting that not only the first-fruits of our nature should partake in the higher good but every person who wished it, and that a second birth should take place and that the nourishment should be new and suitable to the birth and thus the measure of perfection be attained. Through his own birth, that is, his incarnation and baptism and passion and resurrection, he delivered our nature from the sin of our first parent and from death and corruption, and so became the first-fruits of the resurrection. He made himself the way and image and pattern, in order that we, too, by following in his footsteps, might become by adoption what he is himself by nature, the children and heirs of God and joint heirs with him. He gave us

therefore, as I said, a second birth in order that, just as we who are born of Adam are in his image and are the heirs of the curse and of corruption, so also being born of Christ we may now be in his likeness and heirs of his incorruption and blessing and glory.' *On the Orthodox Faith*, 4.13.

47 Exod. 14.13–15.19. The Pharaoh and his chariots were always taken in patristic literature as types of the demons surrounding the Prince of this World.

48 Eph. 3.19, 4.13; Col. 2.10.

49 Matt. 7.13–14.

50 Acts 2.37–8.

51 *Candidatus* means 'vested in white' and derives from those seeking baptism who were liturgically required to wear white robes for the week after their immersion and chrismation.

52 Through counselling that will culminate in confession if it is an adult who is being received into Orthodoxy by chrismation (for example if they had been baptized previously according to the trinitarian rites of sacramental churches, such as Western Catholicism, or Anglicanism).

53 To show their disdain for the Evil One. Nowadays the adult sponsors of a baby do this; or adult catechumens do it for themselves (encouraged to spit merely a little! – the *denunciation* needs to be enthusiastic, not the actual spitting).

54 Only a bishop or priest can chrismate, however. And if the sick person recovers, the final rites (most especially chrismation) are supplied in church at a later time.

55 Bulgakov 1988: 112.

56 *Nouna* and *koumbara* in the feminine.

57 It is absolutely important, therefore, that Orthodox adults do not sponsor the baptism of friends of similar age, whom they may later wish to marry (and certainly not of non-Orthodox fiancés or fiancées whom they may bring to the church). Usually the baptizing priest has the discretion to advise, and intervene, in these matters.

58 See for example Gregory of Nazianzus Oration 40.

59 2 Cor. 11.2.

60 Isa. 61.3; Ps. 45.7; Heb. 1.9.

61 An adult will choose a new name, of a saint, or angel, by which they will ever after be known in church. Those baptized as infants will celebrate their baptismal saint as their festal name-day, their spiritual birthday, in preference to their calendrical natal day, which latter custom is regarded in the church as a residual pagan influence.

62 Orthodox infant baptisms are usually performed on older children than the typical Western infant baptism. If the child is very small the priest will cover the baby's face with his hand so that water will not enter the lungs. The immersions are done very quickly, and are not harmful in any way.

63 Known as the *photikia* (garments of light), these are sacred vestments and are either kept safely for life, or must be consumed by fire.

64 1 Pet. 2.9; Rev. 1.5, 5.9–10.

65 In contemporary Orthodox practice the patriarch of an autocephalous church, or the chief metropolitan bishop, consecrates chrism for the whole church of his region, often on Thursday of the Great Week of Pascha. If possible the consecration ritual is performed by several bishops together.

66 Exod. 28.41, 29.7; 1 Sam. 16.12–13; 1 Kgs 1.39.

67 Acts 8.14–16, 19.2–6.

68 Canon 6 of the Council of Carthage, forbidding presbyters to sanctify this element by their blessing.

69 The sacred chrism is otherwise used only for the consecration of an altar and the walls in a new church, and for the anointing of an Orthodox monarch when he or she accedes to the throne.

70 Chrismation, along with the renunciation of ideas alien to the apostolic tradition, is also used to effect the reconciliation of a Christian from another confession with the Orthodox Church. After a preparatory confession, and the ritual of chrismation, the person entering the Orthodox Church is given communion in the Holy Eucharist, to complete and perfect their union with Christ in the church.

71 1 John 2.27.

72 Matt. 6.10.

73 The mark of a vow and a consecration.

74 Gal. 3.27; Rom. 6.3.

75 Eph. 5.25–6.

76 Orthodoxy habitually calls baptism 'illumination' (*photismos*).

77 1 Cor. 6.11; Rom. 6.4.

78 The biblical word for breathing, as well as the name of the Holy Spirit.

79 John 3.5.

80 Who, even though with many falls and setbacks, remains true to the Lord their life long, and grows in union with him, organically related to the mystical life of the church.

81 Matt. 24.12–13.

82 This, of course, is why the mysteries of marriage, and ordination, are also extensions of the great mystery of baptism into the all-consuming life and death of the Lord.

83 Josh. 24.15.

84 Cf. John Chrysostom. Homily 17, *On the Letter to the Hebrews*, 3; Theodoret of Cyrus, *Interpretation of the 14 Epistles of St Paul*, On Hebrews, 8.4.

85 St Gregory the Theologian writes, after an illness, to a bishop friend: 'I have at last recovered from a troubling sickness, and so I hasten to write to you since you have been responsible for my return to health. For the word of a priest who speaks wisely of the Lord can call the sick back to health. Now do something even greater for me: release me from the great burden of my sins as you take hold of the resurrection sacrifice....Do not hesitate to pray for me, and be my ambassador, when by your word you draw down the Word himself, and when, with a stroke that draws no blood you sever the body and blood of the Lord, using your voice as the sword.' Epistle 171.

86 Even including the sin-sacrifices of expiation, though these did have (obviously) more of a character of lamentation and aversion to them.

87 The liturgy itself expresses it succinctly, as the priest elevates the gifts immediately after the words of institution saying: 'Your own of your own, we offer you, in all things, and for all things.'

88 'And so it says: "And Christ also was once offered." (Heb. 9.28). By whom was he offered? By himself clearly. Here the author shows that Christ is not only a priest, but also the victim and the sacrifice. Then he gives us the reasons he was offered: "Offered once so as to bear the sins of many." Why does he say "many", and not "all"? It was because not all believed. He, for his part, did indeed die for all, so as to save all; since his death was equivalent to the death of all.' John Chrysostom, Homily 17, *On the Letter to the Hebrews*.

89 Which the Lord himself criticized in the Judaic cult of sacrifice. See McGuckin 1986a, 1988.

90 See Augustine, *On the City of God*, 10.5.6.

91 *PG* 115.140–8.

92 Orthodoxy calls it this in preference to the Western term 'Last Supper'.

93 The question that used to be asked in the older catechism books of Western Catholicism, 'Which sections of the Mass are essential to attend so as to fulfil a Sunday obligation?', has no meaning to an Orthodox. The Western understanding that the 'words of institution' confect the sacramental mystery is not accepted by Orthodoxy, which sees the subsequent Epiclesis as consecratory, but also understands the whole Anaphora (and some Orthodox theologians would say the entire liturgy from the commencement) to be consecratory too. See Ware 1987: 290.

94 St John of Damascus: 'We describe it as participation [*metousia*] since through it we partake of the divinity of Jesus. We also call it communion [*koinonia*], and it is an actual communion, because through it we have communion with Christ and share in his flesh and his divinity. Indeed, we also have communion, and are united, with one another through it. For since we partake of one bread, we all become one body of Christ and one blood, and members one of another, being of one body with the Christ.' *On the Orthodox Faith*, 4.13.

95 'We do not receive the holy flesh and precious blood of Christ, as if it were common flesh (God forbid!), nor as the

flesh of a mere man, sanctified and linked with the Word in a unity of standing, or as enjoying a divine indwelling. No, we receive it as truly life-giving; as the flesh that belongs to the Word himself. Since he is God, he is in his own nature Life, and when he became one with the flesh which is his own, he rendered this too as life-giving.' Epistle 17, *Third Letter to Nestorius*.

96 St John of Damascus puts it simply: 'The bread and the wine are not merely figures of the body and blood of Christ. God forbid we should think this! but are the very deified body of the Lord itself. For the Lord has said, 'This is my body,' not, 'this is a figure of my body': and he said, 'My blood,' not, 'a figure of' my blood.' *On the Orthodox Faith*, 4.13.

97 The Latin term (mainly the notion of the Presence it represented) was endorsed by some of the Eastern patriarchs in their dialogue with Protestantism, especially at the Council of Jerusalem in 1672 which approved the term 'transubstantiation', while carefully adding that this did not constitute an explanation of the mystery.

98 The liturgy itself speaks simply of the 'alteration' of the elements at the consecration (*metaballo*).

99 As St John of Damascus says: 'The body which is born of the holy Virgin is in truth body united with divinity, not that the body which was received up into the heavens descends, but that the bread itself and the wine are changed into God's body and blood. But if you enquire how this happens, it is enough for you to learn that it was through the Holy Spirit, just as the Lord took on himself flesh that subsisted in him and was born of the holy Mother of God through the Spirit. And we know nothing further save that the Word of God is true and energizes and is omnipotent, but the manner of this cannot be searched out.' *On the Orthodox Faith*, 4.13.

100 St John of Damascus puts it as follows: 'For just as God made all that he did make by the energy of the Holy Spirit, so also in this case the energy of the Spirit performs things that are above nature and which we cannot possibly comprehend except by faith alone. Remember how the holy Virgin said: 'How shall this be since I am innocent of man?' And the archangel Gabriel answered her: 'The Holy Spirit shall come upon you, and the power of the Most High shall overshadow you.' And now, you might ask, how did the bread become Christ's body and the wine and water become Christ's blood? And I will answer you, that it is because the Holy Spirit is present and does those things which surpass reason and thought.' *On the Orthodox Faith*, 4.13.

101 Again St John of Damascus puts it succinctly: 'Isaiah saw a coal (Isa. 6.6.), but coal is not plain wood, rather wood suffused with fire. In like manner also the bread of the communion is not plain bread but bread united with divinity. But a body which is united with divinity is not one nature, but has one nature belonging to the body and another belonging to the divinity that is united to it, so that the compound is not one nature but two.' *On the Orthodox Faith*, 4.13. See also, Theodoret of Cyrus, *Eranistes*, 2.

102 Catechetical Oration 37.

103 With the exception of small cemetery chapels, or such like.

104 Ps. 34.8. Also Canticles 2.3.

105 Ps. 8.1–2.

106 Known in the West as the church of the Holy Sepulchre, but to Orthodoxy as the church of the Resurrection.

107 Rome was largely a Greek-speaking community for its first three centuries.

108 Such as the Gallican, Mozarabic, Ambrosian, or Sarum.

109 Before its great rise to prominence as an imperial capital, Byzantium was part of the circle of influence of the Syrian Church with its patriarchate at Antioch.

110 The same is true for the other liturgies, of SS Basil and Gregory. Both of these Fathers of the Church were responsible for liturgical 'developments' and improvements in their own lifetimes, but became the symbolic 'authors' of the whole

liturgies that attached to them, even though these continued to adapt and change for centuries later, and had existed in substance long before them. The Divine Liturgy of St John Chrysostom shows many elements in it that one would date from the sixth century, and some later from the ninth. Both historically and theologically there is a running and living line of tradition, from the institution of liturgy by Jesus among the apostles, to the present era of the Orthodox Church. Orthodoxy has rarely found its liturgy a controversial matter (excepting some divisive issues over the Old Believer schism in Russia), and its attitude to it has long been one of familiarity and loving protection. It has to be admitted, however, that the earlier centuries of the church were much more creative in terms of their different liturgical traditions. For synoptic studies of the Orthodox liturgy see Oakley 1958; Wybrew 1989; Taft 1992.

111 It can still be visited, and is still magnificent, even though in a now denuded condition, in Istanbul (the ancient Constantinople). In the time of the glory of the empire the great churches of St Irene, Polyeuctes, and Holy Apostles rivalled it in majesty, if not in size.

112 Known in the West as Pope Gregory the Great. The form of this liturgy is attributed to the pope who once served in Constantinople as a delegate of his papal predecessor. It has elements in common with the Latin liturgy of Good Friday, which is also a communion service without the consecration of the gifts.

113 The Gospels show that the general pattern of putting together the Gospel account was around strings of short stories and sayings of the Lord. The Passion narrative is unusual for its length and focus around a relatively short number of days in the ministry: the great drama of the covenantal death of the Messiah, of which the Eucharist is the synopsis.

114 A fact which can be seen abundantly in the earliest patristic accounts of Pascha; such as that by the second-century Asian bishop, Melito of Sardis, in his *On the Pascha*. See Stewart-Sykes 1998.

115 Luke 24.25–32.

116 Its proper place is after the reading of the Gospel, and ought to be the continuation of the bishop's prophetic charism, in the early church, of interpreting Scripture in the light of the Lord's mystery of salvation. All too often this task of kerygmatic preaching (a solemn and integral part of the ancient liturgy) is either neglected or reduced to 'chats' from the priest.

117 St John of Damascus describes the Epiclesis (the invocation of the Holy Spirit to consecrate the gifts) as the common work of the economy, completing the Son's ploughing with life-giving dew: 'And the overshadowing power of the Holy Spirit becomes through the invocation, the rain to this new tillage.' *On the Orthodox Faith*, 4.13.

118 St John Chrysostom says: 'He who graced the table [of the Mystical Supper] is the same as he who now graces the table in our churches. It is not man who makes the gift of the oblation to become the body and blood of Christ, but Christ himself who was crucified for us. The priest stands to fulfil the original pattern, and speaks those words, but the power and the grace come from God.... His own statement "This is my body", uttered once, is the command which completes the sacrifice at every table in the churches, from that time onwards, until this present, and even until the Second Coming.' *On the Betrayal of Judas*, 1.6; id., Homily 82, *On Matthew*; St Ambrose, *Homily on Psalm 38*, 25; id., *On the Duties of Ministers*, 1.238.

119 A word which connotes the 'Shewbread' of the Old Testament, which is taken as a type of the Eucharist.

120 The Orthodox will usually come to the liturgy with these lists of their family diptychs and offer them to the priest with a small loaf, or *prosphoron*, who then commemorates them by name.

121 Some scholars think that, at one time, the Proskomide was performed just

before the Great Entrance. When a bishop now celebrates the Eucharist, the Proskomide is performed before the beginning of the service, but is left incomplete, so that the bishop himself completes it, just before the procession of the Great Entrance begins. In Greek practice the Proskomide is performed during Matins (Orthros) of Sunday morning, and in Slavonic practice during the recitation of the lesser hours before the beginning of the liturgy.

122 Used to open the mysteries of baptism, Eucharist, and matrimony: The bishop or priest stands at the altar and intones: 'Blessed is the Kingdom of the Father, and of the Son, and of the Holy Spirit', while making the sign of the Cross with the Gospel book over the altar cloth (*antimension*).

123 But in the sacred liturgy the homily ought not to be the priest's 'thought for the day' but an interpretation of the sacred Scriptures that have been read, and an application of them to the present condition of the parish.

124 Liturgy of St John Chrysostom, prayer of the cherubic hymn.

125 Liturgy of St John Chrysostom, eucharistic Anaphora.

126 Liturgy of St John Chrysostom, pre-communion prayers.

127 During the prayer: 'The Lamb of God is broken and distributed: broken but never divided; ever eaten but never consumed, sanctifying those who partake of it.' Liturgy of St John Chrysostom, prayer of the Fraction.

128 Water was always added to wine in antiquity, and in preparatory rituals of both the Eastern and Western liturgical rites water is added before the consecration. It was a Byzantine table custom, however, to add hot water immediately before consuming wine, and perhaps this is the origin of the *zeon* rite only found in the Eastern liturgies, although it is a point that is still obscure to liturgists. Other later Byzantine liturgical commentators attach slightly different symbolic associations to it. St Germanos

of Constantinople in the eighth century meditates on how it evokes the flowing out of water and blood from the side of the Lord, and Simeon of Thessaloniki, at the end of the fourteenth century, interprets it as a sign that even when the Lord's body was dead it was not devoid of the warmth of the divinity. Nicholas Cabasilas in the middle of the same century explains that it is a symbol of the warmth of the Spirit sent after the Ascension, which actually corresponds to the liturgical prayer that accompanies the action.

129 In earlier centuries the gift of the eucharistic bread was placed into the hands of the believers, who also then drank from the chalice offered to them by the clergy. When congregations became larger, intinction became the standard mode of distributing the Eucharist in the East. St Cyril of Jerusalem, in his fourth-century *Catechetical Lectures*, advised his congregation to touch their eyes and brow and nostrils and lips with the holy gifts before they consumed them, so as to sanctify themselves inside and outside. And he said to do the same with the moisture from their lips after taking the chalice. This practice endured for a long time. St John of Damascus in the eighth century still speaks of it: 'Let us pay homage to it in all purity both of soul and body: for it is twofold. Let us draw near to it with an ardent desire, and with our hands held in the form of the cross let us receive the body of the Crucified One: and let us apply our eyes and lips and brows and partake of the divine coal, in order that the fire of the longing, that is in us, with the additional heat derived from the coal may utterly consume our sins and illumine our hearts, and that we may be inflamed and deified by the participation in the divine fire.' *On the Orthodox Faith*, 4.13.

130 Those who communicate must fast from at least midnight before the liturgy, and must prepare by special prayer services on the evening and the following morning.

131 This (*agapé*) used to be for those who had not communicated, but now even

the communicants eat of it to break their fast after receiving the Eucharist.

132 Liturgy of St John Chrysostom, communion hymn.

133 Which used to be performed predominantly at Pascha, and so now the term has transferred to the week after Pascha in the liturgical calendar.

134 In a spirit of great indignation he called the book of the *Shepherd of Hermas* 'that shepherd of adulterers' because it advocated the need for some system of post-baptismal penance in the church.

135 Matt. 26.33–5, 26.58–75; John 21.15–19.

136 Luke 15.1–32.

137 As in the Nicene Creed: 'And we believe . . . in the forgiveness of sins.'

138 John 20.21–3.

139 Also seen in patristic times to have been conferred by the Lord on the apostles generically by the promise to Peter of the power of the keys of the kingdom. Cf. Matt. 16.18. Origen, *Commentary on Matthew*, 12.14.

140 Reflecting Paul's statement to the church (1 Cor. 5.12–6.5) that they ought to exercise judgement on one another since they will be appointed as judges of the (fallen) angels in the Eschaton.

141 By the third century the presbyter Origen described the practice of his Palestinian Church as follows: 'In more serious offences the opportunity for penance is granted only once. But as regards more common sins, which we frequently commit, these can always be remitted by penance, and are redeemed continually in the church.' He described the process of penitential forgiveness, apart from that received in baptism and martyrdom, as following from acts of mercy (alms), or the forgiveness of others who have offended us, the bringing in of converts to the faith, the outpouring of great love towards God (Luke 7.47; 1 Pet. 4.8), and finally the ascetical way of lifelong mourning for sins.

142 The great fourth-century theologian St Gregory of Nazianzus left behind a powerful sermon condemning the tendency of rigorists to wish to restrict the experience (and practice) of forgiveness and reconciliation in Christ's Church. Oration 39.18–19.

143 Cf. Origen, *Against Celsus*, 3.51.

144 Origen, *Commentary on Matthew*, 12.14.

145 The application of this among the confessors of the African Church in the time of St Cyprian, and at Rome in the time of Pope Stephen, caused such social disruption in the churches that it was quickly restricted to the clergy after that time. Tertullian was highly critical of it in *On Modesty*, 22, after he had become a Montanist sectarian, but in his Catholic days when he wrote *To the Martyrs*, 1, he spoke of it with favour.

146 For many centuries, clergy themselves were not permitted to avail themselves of this system of penance as it more or less required a permanent state of being sidelined in the Christian community, which was contrary to the essential role and function of the bishop, priest, or deacon. Public lapses among the clergy were dealt with by deposition from office.

147 Canon 11 of Nicaea I enumerated them as: Weepers (in the *exonarthex*), Hearers (with the catechumens in the *narthex*), Prostrators (who prayed in the nave up to the liturgy of the faithful), and Standers (who prayed in the nave with the faithful for all the liturgy but did not communicate). The degree of penance, and its duration, reflected the severity of the original lapse. The Nicene canon, speaking of Christians who lapsed without threat to life (simply to protect their property, that is) in the following terms: 'They shall be dealt with mercifully. As many as were communicants, if they heartily repent, shall pass three years among the hearers; for seven years they shall be Prostrators; and for two years they shall communicate with the people in prayers, but without oblation.'

148 It was always sins on the grand scale that were meant by this (that is, notoriety as public sinners).

149 Canon 13 of Nicaea I insisted that a dying Christian could never be deprived of the mysteries.

150 The early medieval Irish ascetics, revising the penitential system, also greatly emphasized the penal aspect.

151 Greek: *geron, gerontissa*; Slavonic: *starets, starissa*.

152 Confessors in the modern sense (not the ancient sense of a surviving martyr) that is the Pater Pneumatikos whom the bishop has blessed to hear confessions. Not all priests in the Orthodox Church have this facility. It is given according to the bishop's discretion, who thus retains a primacy over the celebration of the mystery of reconciliation in the diocese.

153 Sensitively discussed in Chryssavgis 1990.

154 The repentant confession of the heart, and the word of absolution, are the matter and form of the mystery, in the analytic sense.

155 Or sometimes both will sit together.

156 Ps. 51.

157 Luke 15.22–4.

158 Its form was influenced by the Western Catholic ritual books and the absolution there, which was in the indicative tense.

159 In necessity it can be performed by a smaller number, and even by one.

160 Mark 6.13.

161 Jas. 5.14–15.

162 Matt. 10.7–8; Mark 16.17–18; Luke 10.8–9; Acts 5.15–16, 19.11–12.

163 Matt. 4.23–4, 8.16–17; Luke 4.18–21.

164 Mark 6.4–6.

165 'Physician and Helper of those in pain, Deliverer and Saviour of those in sickness, Master and Lord, give healing to your sick servants. Have mercy and compassion on those who have often stumbled, and deliver them from their falls, O Christ, that they may glorify your divine power.' Or again: 'By your divine presence, O Christ, raise up my soul, which has been grievously paralysed by every sort of sin and wicked deed, just as once you raised the paralysed man. For so rescued I shall cry out to you: O merciful Christ, glory to your power!' Chants from the Liturgy of the Unction.

166 Though the New Testament constantly implies a close relation between the Lord's healing miracles in the Gospels and his exorcism of oppressive powers that hurt and afflict human life.

167 Luke 22.16–18.

168 If an anointed person dies shortly after receiving this mystery, the consecrated oil remaining from it is traditionally poured in the form of a cross over their shroud by the priest celebrating their funeral rite.

169 'They constrained him, saying: Stay with us, for it is very late in the day, and the light is now spent.' Luke 24.29.

170 Matt. 25.39–40.

171 Matt. 10.8.

172 Designating it as the 'oil of regeneration'.

173 Meaning those who gave healing 'freely'.

174 Or Holy Week. The Great Wednesday service of anointing is not performed in all churches of the Slavic rite.

175 Mark 14.8.

176 There is now a growing literature on the Orthodox understanding of marriage: see, for example, Chryssavgis 1996; Evdokimov 1985; Meyendorff 1975. *St Vladimir's Seminary Quarterly*, 8/1 (1964) represented papers from a symposium dedicated to the subject. See also Rondet 1960; Ritzer 1970; Raes 1958.

177 Matt. 19.3–8.

178 Among others: Matt. 22.1–14, 25.1; Luke 12.35–6.

179 John 2.11. It is a phrase in the evangelist John which deliberately evokes the manifestation of God's glory when he made the first covenant with Israel at Sinai, as in Deut. 5.24 (LXX).

180 Gen. 2.18–24.

181 Eph. 5.21–33.

182 Phil. 2.5–11.

183 Gen. 1.22.

184 In ancient times contraceptive devices were generally abortifacient (and often part of the sex trade presided over by 'specialists' in brothels), which is why they were thus severely penalized in the disciplinary canons.

185 The so-called 'natural law' argument which prevails in contemporary Roman Catholic sexual ethics.

186 There is a good discussion of the issues in Evdokimov 1985: 174–80.

187 Medieval attempts to regulate marital life through the control of the confessional scrutinies have long since lapsed, showing a finer understanding of the charismatic responsibility of the spouses. See Evdokimov 1985: 175, citing Father Palachovsky, 'Le Péché dans la théologie orthodoxe', in *Théologie du péché* (Paris: Desclée, 1960), 507–8.

188 Pss. 22.9, 71.6, 139.13; Jer. 1.5.

189 It is a 'hard saying', perhaps, but Orthodoxy would regard this loss of sensitivity to the sacred rights of the unborn as a sign both in the individual and in the collective mentality that a serious departure from the grace of the Spirit has taken place. For such reasons, aspects of Protestant ethics which argue for the right of human beings to initiate abortion are seen as major lapses from Christian truth.

190 1 Tim. 4.1–3.

191 This often emerges from a woodenly decontextualized exegesis of 1 Cor. 7.38, but here St Paul is speaking about the expectation of an imminent end to the world, and in this light advises his congregations not to worry too much about wedding settlements, and to care instead for the impending judgement. He is not giving a relative reflection on the merits of virginity or marriage as such. The Fathers who exegeted him in this way were ascetics themselves, concerned with the glorification of the virginal life in a Hellenistic context which broadly despised it. Now the balance needs alteration, for often the ascetical writers give the impression that marriage is an inferior vocation fitting only for those who are 'not able to take up the challenges of celibacy'. Which is a deeply distorted view.

192 Gen. 1.27–8.

193 The rich man will find it impossible to enter the Kingdom of God (if it were not for God's mercy being more powerful than impossibility); but it is not the man who throws away the talent who is praised, but rather the one who makes it

bear fruit (Matt. 25.20), and the one who dispenses it (Luke 19.5–10).

194 Matt. 6.33.

195 John 14.2.

196 Mark 10.43.

197 Ps. 63.3.

198 Canticles 8.6.

199 A 2006 survey of Spanish television habits among children (where a putative 'watershed' cut-off of 9 p.m. for bedtime is not at all socially applicable) revealed that 40 per cent of the current viewing material of the under-12s was of sexually explicit material, more or less completely unsupervised by parents.

200 For surely the 'living together' is exactly synonymous with the secular, pre- or post-Christian, concept of marriage, regardless of what 'form' (or lack of it) the secular mentality attaches to signal it, and it is increasingly regarded as such by state law.

201 See, for example, canon 14 of the Council of Chalcedon (451), or canon 71 of the Quinisext Council.

202 Taking the apostle's words in 1 Cor. 7.12–17 as a guide, though they were designed to cover the cases where conversion to Christianity of one of the partners came after a prior secular marriage.

203 In the Slavonic ritual the crowns (more directly reminiscent of royal crowns) are made of metal. Greek couples will keep their wedding crowns as a blessed and sacred thing in their home, for their whole married life.

204 He holds the book of Gospels during this procession, and often the friends in church throw sugared almonds over the couple.

205 It is customary for the family to present icons of Christ and the Blessed Virgin for the newly married couple to set up in their new home, as the establishment of their *ecclesiola*.

206 'Rejoice Isaiah! A Virgin is with child and shall bear a Son, Emmanuel. He is both God and man, and Orient is his name. Magnifying him, we call the Virgin blessed. You holy martyrs who fought the good fight and have received

207 your crowns; intercede with the Lord that he may have mercy on our souls. Glory to you O Christ our God, boast of the apostles, and joy of the martyrs, whose preaching was the consubstantial trinity.'

207 It is equally symbolic, in the ordination ritual, that there is an association with marriage in the sense that the new priest should regard his parish in the light of the beloved of Christ to whom he must give his sincere love and fidelity. The link with priesthood is explicitly clarified in the prayer of marriage preceding the crowning: 'Blessed are You O Lord our God, priest of mystical and undefiled marriage . . . .'.

208 S. of S. 4.10.

209 Ps. 119.103; Sirach 23.27.

210 In the holy icons a crown (as well as a palm, and a cross) is the invariable sign of a martyr.

211 Phil. 2.5, 4.7.

212 Matt. 22.30.

213 Matt. 22.29: 'You are wrong, because you know neither the Scriptures nor the power of God.'

214 In Orthodox understanding it was not flesh inhabited by divinity but, quite startlingly and paradoxically, the very flesh of God himself, and intrinsically life-giving.

215 Some Orthodox writers have expressed this in the following way: that Orthodoxy does not so much permit two or three marriages, but rather allows two or even three 'attempts' at the one unique marriage Christ spoke about that will prove to be 'of the Kingdom'. See Calivas 1984: 51.

216 The reasons may not simply be the wish for companionship, for sometimes younger clergy are left as widowers with the heavy charge of young children to love and care for.

217 There have been a few recent exceptions made to this standard rule.

218 Oration 37.

219 Matt. 5.32, 19.3–11; Mark 10.2–12; Luke 16.18; 1 Cor. 7.10–11.

220 Abandonment, insanity, prolonged absence from the spousal home.

221 John 13.34–5.

222 Gen. 14.18; Ps. 110.4; Heb. 5.5–10, 6.20–10.23.

223 Heb. 8.13.

224 Liturgy of St John Chrysostom, communion prayers.

225 Mark 10.42–5.

226 Acts 5.12, 6.6, 8.17, 13.3, 14.3, 19.6, 28.8; 1 Tim. 4.14, 5.22; 2 Tim. 1.6; Heb. 6.2.

227 Mark 8.23–5; Luke 4.40, 13.13.

228 1 Tim. 4.14.

229 The claim of some Orthodox theologians that female diaconate was not an ordination has been highly coloured by the desire to argue (in the aftermath of the ordination of women in the Anglican Church) that women can never be admitted to the 'priesthood'. It has never been known in the history of Orthodoxy that women have been ordained as presbyters or bishops, but the refusal to admit the clear historical and theological evidence of their ordination as deacons (and thus their admittance to the order of priesthood at the level of diaconate) seems a problematical emblem of how historical custom (the rejection of women from the ranks of clergy in a society that had lost a sense of their importance in the church) may sometimes overshadow the demands of sacred tradition. For the evidence that female diaconate was an 'ordination' in the strict sense see Theodorou 1989; Fitzgerald 1998; Eutychiadis 2004.

230 *Apostolic Constitutions*, 6.17; Council of Chalcedon, canon 15; See also *novel* 6 of the civil law of Justinian.

231 St Gregory of Nyssa's wife served as a deaconess; so too did the close friend of St John Chrysostom, Olympias.

232 Unlike the Roman rite, where multiple ordinations can occur at one single Mass.

233 Bishops are ordained before the Scripture readings, and the eucharistic prayer (Anaphora) to show their ministry revolves around the exposition of the divine word, and the offering of the gifts. Priests are ordained immediately after the Great Entrance and before the Anaphora, to

show that their ministry revolves around the offering of the gifts (the ministry of the word is by delegation from the bishop), and deacons are ordained after the consecration of the gifts and before holy communion, to show their ministry is concerned with the non-consecratory assistance of the liturgy and the administration of communion.

234 Canon 4 of the Council of Nicaea.

235 1 Tim. 3.2–7.

236 Ware 1987: 298–9.

237 The ancient meaning of the word *episcopos*, or overseer.

238 Though, in antiquity, always with the participation of significant laity, and open to advice from learned presbyters and ascetics.

239 If there were ever dissenters these were regarded as having lapsed from the catholic unity of Orthodoxy, and the council invariably deposed them from episcopal office as one of its final actions.

240 See Zizioulas 2001.

241 The ruling bishop, that is, the diocesan bishop, is the highest authority for the church, though subject to the supervisory discipline of the synod, and ultimately a General Council. The authority of a metropolitan archbishop, or patriarch, who will customarily be the senior 'ranking' bishop in an Orthodox country, does not and cannot intrude into this ruling charism of the diocesan bishop, and represents only a supervisory preeminence, not a jurisdictional superiority. Thus, in Orthodoxy, there cannot be anything comparable to the way that, in Roman Catholicism for example, a senior patriarch (such as the pope) is actually considered 'superior' to any other bishop of the church. Orthodoxy knows an order of precedence, but all bishops are the co-equals of each other: subject, of course, to the common tradition and ultimately to the common Gospel and to the single Lord who rules the Universal Church.

242 Written to explain why he had panicked and temporarily ran away from the local church after his ordination in fourth-century Cappadocia.

243 The ultimate discipline inflicted by the bishop being excommunication from the sacred gifts at the eucharistic celebration: a serious sign of disempowerment among the children of God. Of course, in earlier times, the bishop was also possessed of extensive legal and secular powers, and even the non-pious had to mark his judgements!

244 With the exception of monasteries that are directly governed by a patriarchal mandate.

245 The priest's power of sanctification and blessing is given by Christ, and as it comes from the Lord it flows out incessantly over the people of God; but the individual priest is nevertheless called by the experience of this great energy of the Lord's nearness to rise to a profound intimacy with the Lord, through a zealous life of prayer and dedication. The priestly charism ought above all else to be nurtured in the fire of a loving heart where Christ is truly Lord and Master. There is nothing in the world so sad as a priest who has grown lukewarm in his love for Christ, or become lackadaisical in his religious duties.

246 For them too the wearing of the cross originated as a sign of clerical distinction, but then it was awarded to all Russian clergy by the tsar.

247 And are called *stavrophor*: Cross-bearers.

248 Matt. 6.11, 7.9–11; John 21.9–12.

249 Matt. 7.7–11.

250 6 January, known in the West as Epiphany. The prayers of the Blessing of Waters in the church on that day synopsize how the whole creation (in memory of Christ's entrance into the waters of Jordan, to sanctify them) is rendered transparent to the deifying power of God. All the sacraments have this same *telos* and character.

251 The Latin word means 'with you on the way'.

252 It has been an ancient custom of the Orthodox to make a pilgrimage to Jerusalem if possible at least once in a lifetime, and among the items carefully brought back home were water from the Jordan river and a shroud from Jerusalem

that was laid over the Stone of Anoint-
ment (just inside the main entrance door)
in the church of the Anastasis (Holy
Sepulchre).

253 There can be variations, such as: 'Lord
Jesus Christ, Son of the living God, have
mercy on me a sinner.' If it is prayed in a
group it should end with 'Have mercy
on us'.

254 Luke 18.13–14.

255 Further, see McGuckin 1999a.

256 Canticles 2.10; Mark 6.31.

257 See, for example, the *Manual of Eastern
Orthodox Prayers*, which was originally
published under the guidance of Nicholas
Zernov, for the Fellowship of SS Alban
and Sergius, by the SPCK Press, London,
1945. It has recently been reissued by
St Vladimir's Seminary Press (New York,
1983), with a foreword by the late Father
Alexander Schmemann.

258 From the Russian synonym it is also
known as the Red Corner.

259 The ancient custom of the church is that
prayer is always made standing. Exceptions can be made, of course. Prayer that
is extended for a long time may need to
be made in a half-kneeling position, or
even when sitting down. Kneeling posture
for prayer in Orthodoxy is the customary
position for prayers of penitence. The
canons of the church forbid Christians
from kneeling on Sunday as it is a day of
spiritual rejoicing. The normal posture is
to stand upright with the hands upraised,
and the palms facing away from the body
in supplication.

260 So named from the prayer of the 'thrice
holy' which comes immediately after the
invocation of the Paraclete.

261 If a priest begins these prayer he offers a
blessing such as the following: 'Blessed is
our God, always, now and ever and to
the ages of Ages. Amen.'

262 That is a profound bow to the ground
from the waist down.

263 And in Western Catholic monasticism
too of course, though here the divine
office has taken a different literary
form, though built around the same
core of the Psalter.

264 The 'hours' follow the ancient Roman
system of marking the first hour as the
hour after sunrise. Third hour would
approximate, then, to 9 a.m. Sixth hour
would be at noon. Orthros was celebrated
at sunrise, and Vespers at the moment
when it first became necessary to light
the lamps of evening. The hymn that
Christians sang, from ancient times,
when they lit the lamps in the homes
and their churches, is still a central part
of the rite of Vespers, and is known as the
'Gladsome Light'. Vespers always began
the new liturgical day.

265 Acts 2.15.

266 In the Slavonic eucharistic ritual it is
used three times as the preparatory
prayer for the priests immediately before
the Epiclesis.

267 In Orthodox practice the Psalter is divided
up into twenty *kathismata* (sittings).
Monastics will recite the whole 150 psalms
each week in the course of the various
offices. On Saturday-night Vespers, the
beginning of the Sunday festival, it is the
time to begin again with the first *kathisma*,
opening the Psalter with Psalm 1. Each of
the other offices during the week will have
its own appointed *kathisma* depending on
which day it is. In parishes the psalms are
often extensively abbreviated by the choir.

268 From the altar area into the main body
of the church, to stand before the royal
doors of the icon screen.

269 Being simply recited, these do not
require cantors trained in church singing and in the use of the complex liturgical books.

270 The cluster of the six psalms: 3, 37, 62,
87, 102, and 142.

271 The Western Church reverses this order,
and tends to use only two fingers outstretched from the hand to make the
holy sign.

272 The Fathers Lactantius and Eusebios
record that on the eve of a critical battle
outside Rome, to throw down the last of
the persecuting emperors, Constantine
was given the revelation that Christ
would give him success. A cross of light
appeared in the sky and he understood

the words: 'In this sign conquer [*En touto Nika*].'

273 For more see McGuckin 2001b; Ware 1979; Behr-Sigel 1992; Chryssavgis 2004.

274 *Demonstration on Prayer*, 4.13.

275 Ibid. St John Klimakos also said: 'When you are ready to stand in the presence of the Lord, let your soul wear a garment woven from the cloth of forgiveness.' *The Ladder of Divine Ascent*, 28.4.

276 Further see McGuckin 1999a.

277 Rom. 7.22.

278 Mark 7.21; Matt. 12.34; John 12.40; Luke 1.51, 2.35, 9.47, 24.25, 38; Acts 7.23, 8.22; Heb. 4.12.

279 John 13.2; 1 Cor. 4.5, 7.37; 2 Cor. 9.7; Acts 5.3, 11.23; Col. 4.8; Eph. 6.22; Rev. 17.17.

280 Matt. 13.15, 19, 18.35; Mark 7.21, 12.30; Luke 8.15, 16.15; Acts 16.14, 15.9; Rom. 2.15, 5.5, 8.27, 10.9; 1 Thess. 2.4; Gal. 4.6; 2 Cor. 1.22; Heb. 8.10, 10.16, 22; 2 Pet. 1.19; Rev. 2.23.

281 For more see McGuckin 2006a: 90–105.

282 See Igumen *Chariton* (of Valamo) 1966; Fedotov 1948, 1975; Behr-Sigel 1992.

283 Hesychios of Sinai, *On Watchfulness and Holiness*, 5: Philokalia, vol. 1, p. 163.

284 *Fifty Spiritual Homilies*, 43.7.

285 Luke 18.13.

286 1 Cor. 12.3.

287 See Hausherr 1978.

288 *Kyrie Isou Christe, Yie theou / eleison me [ton hamartolon]*.

289 See French 1965; Palmer, Sherrard, and Ware 1979; Kadloubovsky and Palmer 1967.

290 See McGuckin 1987.

291 Though he was a precursor of the movement. See McGuckin 2005b; Krivocheine 1986.

292 Meyendorff 1964, 1998.

293 In the 'Little Russian Philokalia' series, published by St Herman and St Xenia Presses, California, and St Nectarios Press, Seattle.

294 Brianchaninov 1965.

295 Joseph the Elder 1999.

296 See especially Ware 1974; McGuckin 2001b, 2002b; Behr-Sigel 1992.

297 Known in the West as the Assumption, 15 August.

298 *On the Holy Spirit*, 18.

299 Gen. 22.6; 1 Cor. 10.4.

300 Exod. 34.14.

301 Acts 14.14–18.

302 The Eucharist 'is' the Presence of the Lord, the icon is the type of the presence.

303 *On the Orthodox Faith*, 3.16.

304 Ibid.

305 Ps. 8.1–2.

306 See Coomler 1995; Onasch 1997; Sendler 1988; Talbot-Rice 1963; Temple 2004; Weitzmann 1978; Weitzmann, Chatzidakis, and Radojcic 1980.

307 Gen. 18.1–3. The three 'Lords' addressed as one Lord were taken by the Fathers as a type of the Trinity.

308 See Van der Meer and Mohrmann 1958: 33–57.

309 See Weitzmann 1976.

310 See McGuckin 1999b.

311 Or 'closed', in the form of a scroll, if the Christ is shown as a child with the Virgin, or depicted as the Pre-Existent Wisdom. In these cases the Gospel book is not opened because it has not as yet been symbolically proclaimed to the world.

312 Matt. 11.28.

313 John 8.12.

314 So called (*anargyroi*) because they were once doctors who gave their services to the poor free of charge.

315 1 Tim. 2.5.

316 Orthodoxy strictly forbids the cremation of the faithful as sacrilegious. The priests and deacons will not celebrate the funeral liturgy in crematoria, but will conduct services for the dying person and the bereaved family in the churches, the homes, or the cemeteries.

Chapter 6

'The God-Beloved Emperor': Orthodoxy's Political Imagination

Although the Orthodox Church is not tied to the thought patterns of any nation, society, or culture in the history of humankind, being universal and ready to adapt its witness, as appropriate, to any time or era, it is clear, nevertheless, that it has been deeply marked by the structures and thought patterns of one of its most formative periods, when it was expanding rapidly during the Greek Christian empire of the Byzantines. This, the age of the Fathers, when the ecumenical councils were legislating, and international structures of church organization were first being tested and approved, has left a deep impression on the imagination of the Orthodox world. Many scholars have said that Byzantium still lives on in the imagination, and in the very fabric of the Orthodox world and its ceremonial sense of order. One of the ways this might be so is in the political imagination of Orthodoxy.

CAESARO-PAPIST CARICATURES

Older studies of the Byzantine empire used to dismiss its political structures as hopelessly hierarchical, stultified, and resistant to innovation. More recent, and more substantially founded, research has now demonstrated the extent that this prejudice was based on cliché and *odium theologicum*.[1] One of the things for which the Orthodox Church was criticized heavily in these older studies was the manner in which it elevated a theory of political theocracy, designated 'Caesaro-Papism'. Western Catholic writings saw this as a lamentable departure from its own papal theory which had elevated the Bishop of Rome as the true iconic inspiration of all politics; the priest-king who would ensure the church's domination over secular political lords. In their turn, Protestant writings lamented this as a departure from an allegedly 'truer' biblical model of the church which held it aloof from all political subservience. From the Protestant viewpoint the Orthodox Church's heavy dependence on state support and imperial patronage in its heyday (first in Byzantium and then in other countries such as Russia and Serbia under the tsars) was a sell-out of the church's mission to establish a separate prophetic counter-culture to the secular world of politics. It was, to them, an even

380

more corrupt form of the papal priest-king theory which they had fought against so vigorously in the time of the Reformation. Neither side of Western Christianity, therefore, found there to be much in the Orthodox viewpoint that could commend it to them. In any case, by the time this had come into their purview, the political structures of most of Orthodoxy lay in ruins, subjugated under the Ottoman sultanate. Only Russia was a free and great Orthodox power: and Europe was terrified by the image of absolutism that the tsars represented. This was not a view that relaxed as the tsars fell to Soviet autocrats who were just as bad. Even into very recent times political and social critics have raised the question: 'Does Europe really end where the borders of Orthodoxy begin?'[2]

Caesaro-Papism in the older texts meant that the Orthodox bishops, and the wider church culture, had more or less abdicated political governance to the 'caesar' (tsar), that is, the emperor, whom the church had acclaimed (at least once he became Christian) as the 'God-beloved autocrat'. The very terms sounded alarming: the concept of Caesar married to the pope was hardly likely to endear itself to Protestant sensibilities: and the notion of Caesar lording it over the pope contradicted the heart of the Catholic vision of church polity. Had Orthodoxy managed to get the worst of both worlds, and did it merit the censure of both parts of Western Christendom on this matter? Well, it is worth a closer look. Caesaro-Papism, of course, is not a term one finds anywhere in Orthodoxy. It is a caricaturing concept injected into the debate by hostile critics in the modern era, so perhaps we can dispense with it, listen to what the Orthodox sources had to say about political power in Christian antiquity, and deduce what that might mean for a larger Orthodox understanding of how political power might be seen to stand in relation to the church's vision for the struggle for the Kingdom of God to be manifested more and more perfectly on the face of the earth (since the two trajectories are obviously not to taken as synonymous).

If we begin by dismantling 'Caesaro-Papism' to its two constituent bogeys – autocratic imperial dominion and papal monarchy – it immediately strikes one how inappropriate such a term is to cover an Orthodox Church that rejects episcopal monarchies of all sorts, in favour of collegial consensus and harmony of spirit. No bishop in the Orthodox Church is allowed anything like the extension of power afforded by the monarchical principle inherent in the Papacy. What about the deep respect Orthodoxy always afforded to the emperor as 'autocrat' of the Romans? Well, although the word today sends shivers down our spines, *autokratia* in the Greek sense meant something very different on the ground during the Byzantine empire to what 'autocracy' now connotes in English.

Byzantine Models of Godly Rule

The emperor rarely died in his bed. If nothing else, this has to tell us that 'autocracy' in this world was a radically limited notion. In a time when the ballot box was unknown in the whole Christian world, political power was a question of the efficient wielding of military power and the judicious balancing of the numerous factions that constituted Byzantine society: the working classes, the merchants, the aristocratic power-brokers, the monks, and the hierarchical clergy. If the emperor did not manage this balance well, he was not emperor for long. In some cases (not many) the imperial rule was

381

sidelined or taken over wholesale by patriarchs who were much better equipped to govern; but usually the power of an unsuitable ruler passed to a more capable challenger from the ranks of the generals. Byzantium, although it enshrined the principle of God's election and protection of the imperial ruler, never pressed this to an absolute degree. For example, it never wholly endorsed the principle of primogeniture, preferring the ancient notion of imperial ascent as an 'acclamation' by the people. The Byzantine coronation ritual reflected this to the very end, with the emperor-to-be being raised on a shield by his troops (an echo of the battlefield 'acclamations'[3] which often marked the assumption of the purple by the pre-Christian emperors).

In its theological consciousness Byzantium was deeply aware that the emperor was a 'type' of King David. As such he was like God's anointed prophet-king. But equally, like King David, he was seen to have inherited a throne and a dominion that was based upon the will of God. David had received the crown while Saul still ruled, though God had withdrawn his divine favour and thus his validation from the latter. When God chooses a king, so the Byzantines learned from their scripture, God can also 'unchoose' him. Although it is true, therefore, that Byzantine religious philosophy afforded the emperor the role of prophetic priest-king, its model was the Davidic one that heavily underlined the 'tentative' nature of this sacred role; not its absolute force.

On both counts, then, Caesaro-Papism will hardly do to explain the Orthodox position today. Both in terms of the sacral priestly nature of the exercise of power in society, and in terms of the theory of regal dominion, Orthodoxy did not abrogate its sense of the strict limits of power in a Christian culture, despite the flowery rhetoric it addressed to the ruler from time to time. In such an unstable era, and so volatile a political context, the rhetoric needed to be robust, but the practice of the Byzantine Christians shows, time and time again, that they gave the highest of all mandates to the sense of equity in governance, and security of administration. As far as the church was concerned it never lost its commitment to the principle that the emperor ruled under the eye of God; and only as an icon, or type, of Christ's loving dominion of his world. If the emperor departed from the 'Charter' of Christ (the Gospel and the church canons) his rule was never sanctioned by the church leaders, and both he and those clergy who were his sycophants, invariably came to grief. Many people today look to the Byzantine model for evidence of governance theory, some in a hostile way, and others (especially the Orthodox in eastern European countries struggling to rebuild themselves) searching for positive models. It is a good thing to do so, for we can learn much from history. But it is vitally important to be honest and authentic in one's use of patterns from antiquity. It is not enough to adopt the pro-autocracy court rhetoric (the emperor's voice is the voice of God and so on) without giving equal space to the more sage voices of the Byzantine theologians who insisted that it was only the earthly 'type' of the voice of God when it conformed to the message of God: a very different matter indeed.

It is no use either to pine for a lost world of Byzantine splendour and order, without realizing that this did not emerge from the monarchy as such. In classical Byzantine periods the figure of the monarch was always balanced by the two other immensely strong factions of the educated aristocracy (who formed the backbone of the higher offices of the army and church) and the working poor (who on innumerable occasions would replace the ballot box with the ancient Roman system of 'voting for the disenfranchised', the riot, by which means the masses brought down administrations that had oppressed them. Both these factors, the old aristocracy and the city poor (to dignify them with a political collective) were as important at any stage in Byzantine history as the emperor and his court. Romantics among some of the Orthodox believe that 'monarchy' was just that. They have mistaken the simple symbols for the more complex underlying reality. Despite the romantics, the church is not a religious system that is committed to monarchical principles; and it is not a system that believes authority and power, which are in the image of God, are thereby blessed to be 'autocratic' (at least in the modern sense of what that means). Autocracy, in our modern sense, is endorsed nowhere in the religious tradition. The Creation ordinances of God show how much he has elevated human will and enhanced human freedom. The conciliar and canonical principles of church government show how much the church has always sought to protect the legitimate liberty of the Christians. Christianity is not an enemy of human freedom. Although there have been many instances in the past where ecclesiastical authorities have seemed to be in league with the most repressive and reactionary forces in society, the church has never lacked monastics and simpler leaders (those still in touch with the cry of the poor) who have pointed out the freedoms the Gospel has enshrined for all men and women.

It is a sad reality, however, that the present condition of the Orthodox, and the governments under which they labour, have had such broken icons of governance for so many years past. In trying to reassemble some coherent meaning out of those broken fragments of the Byzantine polity it is critically important in this generation that Orthodox should not be led astray by naive romanticism about the Byzantine polity. It is no use, for example, advocating the restoration of 'strong centralized autocratic rulers' (either episcopal or lay) without some very lively awareness of how Byzantium in its ancient wisdom diffused and defused those central powers to which it also gave its solemn reverence. A strong emperor was always powerfully modified by the voices of the aristocracy. They in their turn depended on the good will of the masses, and extended significant philanthropy to ensure a societal balance.

In modern terms this means a healthy distribution of power between the various 'houses' of the body politic. In many parts of the Western world the statutes of governance of the Orthodox Church are turning this way. Enlightened hierarchs realize that their leadership is not threatened, but enhanced, by being open to the voice of an educated laity. They are also realizing, as the laity become often more educated than the clergy who guide them, that their days of being the solitary voices of sense in the church are (thankfully) now passing away. The episcopacy had, for centuries of Orthodox collapse, to carry the burden of governance of Christian polity more or less alone. The Christian aristocracy of the East was in the dust. The educated men and women of the universities were few and far between. Now this is passing away and more extended voices are once more being heard. It will fall to the wit and wisdom of the episcopate to recognize that this is not a threat to them, but a restoration of what a healthy church should be in a thriving state. It will be, perhaps, the greatest challenge of the episcopal governance of the church for many centuries that it can negotiate this 'widening out' of the voice of the people of God successfully, though it will still take many generations before a more deeply educated Orthodox laity can emerge world-wide. And who knows how a new Orthodox 'aristocracy' can re-emerge, other than an aristocracy of rich patrons (which leaves a lot to be desired)?

So, if we clear away the false mirage of Caesaro-Papism, what could be said about the original Byzantine polity that could assist our thoughts in considering models of governance in the wider Orthodox world today? The first thing to note is that we should strongly query the presumption that there ever was a single Eastern Christian religious political theory, such a one that could be stood in opposition to, or alongside, Catholic medieval or early modern Protestant theories of church–state relations. Such a macro-theory would be very dubious, not least for the anachronism involved in looking at Byzantine theory from the vantage point of the conflict of early modern Western ecclesial politics. I would go further and argue that, while there are distinctively classic Byzantine ideas of the relations of church and state, nevertheless there never was a single, coherent Byzantine political theology. And this for two reasons: first because the fundamental authorities of 'Christian law' (the Gospels, the wider Scriptures, and the later conciliar canons) themselves did not enshrine a coherent theory of the relation of the Kingdom of God to the kingdoms of the earth, nor did they permit a single model to be elevated from the several they each suggested at different periods; and secondly because the significant Byzantine theorists were too much concerned with *ad hoc* solutions to occasional and locally contextualized controversies to allow them to develop an authoritative macro-theory.

THE AMBIGUITY OF SCRIPTURAL PARADIGMS OF POWER

It is impossible to elevate a coherent political theology on the basis of biblical evidence, or at least on the basis of the evidence objectively considered, without processing that data in a highly selective manner which tends to become a prejudgement of the issue. The Byzantine biblical commentators were honest enough to recognize that, even if subsequent Christian theorists of many periods, including our own, have not been. The Fathers, however, knew that there was a problem in taking scriptural texts in an unmediated way for political guidance in the here and now. It is clear, for example, that the Old Testament canonizes a quasi-divine kingship in the case of the Davidic dynasty. But the origins of the sacral kingship in the Scripture are both ascribed to God as beneficial grace for Israel,[4] and to the petty-mindedness of men who stand in opposition to the peculiar covenant that set up God himself as the sole, and jealous, King of his elect nation.[5] If the Davidic king was a messianic sign, however, such a symbol was fulfilled in the person of Jesus the glorified and eternally regnant Christ, as far as any early Christian theory of kingship was concerned. This means that any Davidic idea of kingship has to be subordinated in Christian theory to the principles of the Gospel.

The Lord's own ideas on kingly power themselves range across a wide spectrum. At times he seems highly affirmative. Did he not conceptualize the entire relation of God to the world in terms of kingly dominion?[6] On other occasions he demonstrates a sardonic detachment that can be seen in the saying: 'Render to Caesar what is Caesar's, and to God what is God's'; or in the castigation of Herod Antipas as 'a fox'; or the weary reply to Pilate: 'My Kingdom is not of this world'.[7] He often seems to be deliberately ambivalent, as in the second part of that same Johannine saying: 'Yet if my kingdom *were* of this world, my disciples would have fought to prevent me falling into your hands.' Even the most positive aspect of Jesus' attitude to kingship, the choice of the idea as the primary analogy of his preaching, tends to exclude any but God (or later his Christ) from the active role as king. In other words a theocratic concept of kingship is an exclusion, not an affirmation, of the idea of a centralized kingship in terms of recommended political theory.

Wherever we place our finger on Jesus' statements about, or analogies of, kingship the same ambivalence is present. His kingdom is certainly not 'of' this world, but there is a 'yet' added on as if to suggest how disciples 'might' behave if it were to be established more visibly 'in' this world. Kingly and state authority are flouted in the cause of the Lord's achievement of the goals of the Kingdom in his own ministry, and yet his recorded political statements also advocate obedience and submission. One must 'render to Caesar'. Pilate is told the true source of his power: not from Tiberius, but from God himself who has validated the dominion of Rome's legal representatives: 'You would have no power over me if it had not been given to you from above.'[8] The earliest disciples maintained the same ambivalence of their Master. The apostle Paul advocated obedience to the civil leaders as if to God himself. This text was so popular among Byzantine officialdom that sometimes one finds it inscribed in mosaic on the floor of the medieval revenue bureaux:

> Let every person be subject to the governing authorities. For there is no authority except from God, and those that exist have been instituted by God. Therefore he who resists the authorities resists what God has appointed, and those who resist will incur judgment. For rulers are not a terror to good conduct, but to bad. Would you have no fear of him who is in authority? Then do what is good, and you will receive his approval, for he is God's servant for your good. But if you do wrong, be afraid, for he does not bear the sword in vain; he is the servant of God to execute his wrath on the wrongdoer. Therefore one must be subject, not only to avoid God's wrath but also for the sake of conscience. For the same reason you also pay taxes, for the authorities are ministers of God, attending to this very thing.[9]

St Paul clearly had little conception, when he wrote this, that the age of imperial persecution against the church was to come so quickly. Yet he died, unjustly, under the same sword of governance he seems to laud as always just. After the Great Persecution all Christians took his words, not literally, but as indicative of a good ideal if, and only if, the rulers were righteous. If they executed justice, they were seen as God's agents. If they executed evil, they were seen (according to Jesus' deeper insight and more realistic word) as subjects of the 'powers of evil'.[10]

Other writers than Paul, suffering a sharper edge of religious oppression, saw in the imperial cult the single clearest example of world apostasy and denounced the Caesars as the 'dragon' enslaved to the Beast. Even though Paul gained a wider hearing than the Apocalypse in the Eastern Church (the latter is never cited in the liturgical texts of the Orthodox world), the negative reservations of the prophet of Patmos were not forgotten. On other occasions too, the apostle, as the monks never tired of reminding the bureaucrats among the bishops, had firmly reminded the church that: 'Here we have no abiding politeia.'[11]

Jesus' words on the kingdom as not of this world certainly set a severe limit on the tendency to identify the spread of the Byzantine domains with the spread of the kingdom on earth. Any temptation to resurrect the old theodicy so as to claim the 'New Israel' of the Byzantines as the Kingdom realized once more on earth was fundamentally rejected from the outset of Christianity. The church never wholly flattened its apocalyptic landscapes. Despite the Byzantines' understanding of themselves as the New Elect People, the force of the Gospels in forbidding an identification of this world and God's Kingdom remained strong. The monastic movement, more distanced from the sycophantic tendencies of some of the court bishops, also served to keep the apocalyptic 'distance' alive. It was the supreme apocalyptic kingship of Christ that was ultimately enshrined in the Scriptures, and this led to a polarity in the enduring Christian theology of earthly kingship.

The Christian emperor might well be a 'type' of God's power on earth, and even divinely validated, but his rule was subject to God's law, and subject too to the canons of the church (however much he might occasionally affirm his elevation above Roman law). If the king deviated from this kind of rule his own dominion was rendered fragile. It is these two biblical principles above all others – first, that the king is subject to divine law, and second, that the Kingdom of God is not synonymous or coterminous with the kingdom of the people of God on earth – that prevent Byzantine political theory from falling into the mould of ancient Greek theories of divine kingship. They remain perennially valid, and also prevent Orthodoxy from ever validating any principle of absolute governance of any earthly ruler. Orthodoxy regards it as a grave problem for the church that the Western half so badly developed its political theology that it forgot the strict limits of monarchical authority demanded by the Gospels and the *koinonia* of the church, and then, in addition, rolled its concept of priest and emperor so much together that it developed an overwhelming model of absolutist monarchy in the Papacy.

There were strands in ancient Greek and Roman kingship theory that had already elevated the emperor as *nomos empsychos*, the living personal embodiment of Law. This was in accordance with the absolutist tendencies of the move from principate to imperium in late antiquity, where the emperor was defined as *fons et origo legum* (the source and origin of law). But the Christian bishops are careful to distance themselves from this principle, which is not endorsed by the Scriptures. For all his fulsome rhetoric, Eusebios, Constantine's panegyrist, never attributes this title to the ruler. In this he was faithful to his mentor Origen, who had decisively argued that it was a title reserved for Christ alone.[12] And St Gregory the Theologian expresses the more sophisticated Byzantine balance more exactly when he reminded Theodosius the Great that even as emperor he was under the law, and not the Law itself.

In a study of Byzantine political theory which had a large influence (but was fundamentally flawed), F. Dvornik[13] cites Gregory the Theologian as one among other significant figures who endorsed pagan kingship theory. He based this assessment on a mistaken exegesis of Gregory's citation of the ideal of Theodosius 'being like a god' to his people. But here Gregory was not citing Aristotle at all, but rather the Psalms; and he knew exactly what the Scripture meant, and how much it 'challenged' the absolutist tendencies of any ruler.[14] To make his ironic point clear to any careful Christian reader Gregory added to the psalm the other dominant Byzantine political motif of Proverbs 21.1:

> Emperors respect your purple. For my oration lays down laws that also bind our legislators. Know how much has been committed to your conscience and what a mysterious thing your kingly power is. The whole world lies in your hands, however small the crown or weak the body. What is above you belongs to God; what is below you belongs also to you. If I may express it in this way: be as gods to your subjects (Ps. 81.1, 6). The king's heart is in the hands of God (Prov. 21.1). It is there your strength should lie, not in your gold or your armies.[15]

The whole thrust of this is to reject the theory of *nomos empsychos* and to remind the monarch that his typological *mimesis* of God, and his validation from God, are entirely conditional. He stands under judgement, and this is particularly brought out by the two biblical phrases Gregory has selected. The image of God holding the heart of the king is double-edged, signifying support as well as the ability to terminate that life in a moment. This, of course, is also the gist of Gregory's contrasts of imperial glory, and human frailty, a suitable reminder to a conqueror who only a year or so before was lying on his deathbed in Thessalonike. The psalm text equally makes clear that the king's power is sustained by God only in so far as he exercises that God-given power correctly; that is, as the same psalm goes on, when he 'does justice for the weak and the orphan, and defends the poor and the needy'.[16]

Figure 7   The relics of St Gregory the Theologian (Gregory of Nazianzus), a major father from the fourth century. His relics were kept in the 'Red Church' in Nazianzus, Turkey, until the Middle Ages, when they were taken to Constantinople. Brought by the invading Crusaders to Rome, they rested there after the thirteenth century, and then, from the sixteenth century onwards, in St Peter's. Most recently they were returned to the patriarch of Constantinople (where the saint had been archbishop in 380) by the late Pope John Paul II, as a gesture of ecumenical rapprochement between the Orthodox and Catholics. *Photograph: © Mustafa Ozer/AFP/Getty Images*

387

Dvornik's thesis that Byzantine religion more or less 'sold out' to absolutist pagan kingship theories systematically elevates unfortunately contextualized, or simply erroneous, exegeses of patristic sources to come to its false conclusion.[17] It needs to be set aside now, so as to allow a less clichéd study of the actual evidence to emerge. If this is done, a simultaneously simpler yet more diffuse picture emerges. The Byzantine tradition, as such, never adopted a single theoretical attitude to the monarchy, but developed instead a set of responses that arose from a common set of stimuli and authoritative evidences, responses that varied according to the manner in which the emperors of any given period intersected more or less vigorously with the monks, the remaining city populations, and the hierarchs on matters of religious controversy. The actual 'Byzantine' Christian theology of kingship, therefore, emerges as less a coherent theory than a series of rhetorical tropes that could be applied.

Now some of these were indeed continuations of ancient kingship theory, though now shorn of many of its presuppositions, such as the concept that monarchy stabilized earthly order as a politically blessed *mimesis* of monotheistic rule. Many Christian writers found this a helpful analogy in a polytheistic environment, though never to the extent that they simply absorbed the Hellenistic theology that the king was an earthly mirror of the divine will for his subjects, such that the affairs of this earthly dominion ran parallel with those determined in heaven. The biblical notion of the apostate king, along with Jesus' sceptical teachings about the powers of this world, conspired to prevent this. What the scriptural body of evidence did allow, however, came out among the Byzantines as three descriptive 'marks' of good political theology; a particularly Eastern Christian refiguring of ancient kingship theory. I take these three marks to be the ascription of a priestly status to the Christian king, some view of that office as ideally apostolic (though this in itself was a complex issue), and lastly the aspiration that there would be an attempt at *symphonia*[18] (harmony) between the earthly ruler's policies and the values of God's Kingdom (as was also the central aspiration of the Lord's Prayer[19]) and thus a corresponding ideal *symphonia* between the church and the state in a Christian imperium. Let us consider those three aspects more closely.

THE CONCEPT OF THE PRIESTLY KING

The Byzantine consideration of the office of emperor in quasi-priestly terms follows from Psalm 109, which first described the messianic role as a priesthood, while being quite aware, of course, that the King of Israel was not a priest in the commonly meant sense of Aaron or the sons of Levi. It is assigned to the mysterious priesthood of Melchizedek. The psalm reads:

> A prince from the day of your birth on the holy mountains ... The Lord has sworn an oath ... you are a priest for ever, a priest like Melchizedek of old.

Since the Epistle to the Hebrews had already assigned this text as a Christological type,[20] the priestly kingship was assigned primarily to Christ, but in this charism the Christian emperor was thought to have a certain share. This was expressed by traditions that invested the emperor with ceremonial duties in Orthodox ritual. His priesthood was, therefore, defined *kat' oikonomian*: by economy. It is an important distinction in Eastern Christian canon law. What does not touch the substance of the faith may be subjected to adaptation according to local necessity.

In the case of the emperor, it would seem, a particular claim had already been lodged by Constantine, and affirmed by the court bishops of his circle, for some continuance in the Christian world of his traditional (pagan) roles as *pontifex maximus*. The manner in which these were affirmed by later Byzantine tradition, however, reflect how they limited and trimmed back the priestly prerogatives of the emperor, thus denying them in substance, by affirming them economically. The Christian emperor had the right to take communion behind the iconostasis where only clergy communicated. This he did, however, after all the clergy, even the youngest of them, had communicated. He therefore took communion as the most privileged of all the laity, one who could enter and communicate in the holy of holies from the hand of the high priest, the bishop. He did not communicate himself, but received from the hand of the bishop. The bishop alone had command of the celebration and distribution of the mysteries. The emperor, by virtue of this highest of his liturgical privileges, which was to approach the altar (though never to pray the priestly intercessions there), was iconically given honour as having a priesthood *kat' oikonomian*.[21] It was never suggested, nor ever understood by anyone in the Byzantine world, that this was a *de facto* priesthood.[22] And the exercise of priestly functions was never attempted by the emperors.

The incensing rituals conducted by the ruler at court, as described by Constantine VII Porphyrogennitos,[23] and claimed as part of the imperial priestly privilege, have to be contextualized in the post-iconoclastic environment where the censing of the icons had been appropriated widely among the monks and laity too. The same can be said of the manner in which emperors were occasionally expected to preach to the congregation in the multitude of church services they attended. All of these special liturgical roles were evidently privileges *kat' oikonomian*. Neither church nor emperor in Byzantine times ever came close to confusing the respective roles of priesthood and imperium. Bishops and priests and deacons were incapable, by canon law, of exercising arms, or spilling blood. Priests were also forbidden (and still are) the exercise of secular judgements over the laity. To have enjoyed a priestly office would have been to debar the emperor from his most important state functions, and to have strayed into secular power would have canonically rendered a priest unfit to celebrate. These canons have always been most strictly interpreted, and still hold today in Eastern canon law.

But apart from a ceremonial affirmation of the emperor's liturgical privileges, the Byzantine theological tradition means one thing above all others by its affirmation of the 'imperial priesthood', and that is the emperor's defence of Orthodoxy, as interpreted by synodical judgements of bishops. This is the manner in which it appears in the acclamations of the Council of Chalcedon.[24] The same idea is found in the correspondence between Pope Leo and the emperors Marcian and Leo,[25] and also between Pope Vigilius and Emperor Justinian.[26] Priestly charism is attributed as an aspect of character. This is how the priesthood is attributed to the emperor by the historian Socrates, who (most unrealistically) describes Theodosius as the 'most gentle' of all men on earth.[27] The emperor always has a 'priestly soul', or a 'priestly character'. The emperor is not a priest. The idea was obvious to the subtle Byzantines, perhaps not so to numerous subsequent commentators, who have concluded either that Orthodoxy is unable to think itself free of 'state establishment', or that it somehow 'needs' the figure of a monarchical tsar to advance a viable political theory. Neither is true.

DOMINION AS APOSTOLIC CHARISM

Although Constantine's mausoleum was built by his son it was to the symbolic design of the father. Attached to the church of the Holy Apostles[28] in Constantinople, it was a circular structure made up of twelve porphyry tombs, to symbolize the twelve apostles, with a central magnificent tomb in the middle to house Constantine himself. The clergy of the day interpreted this as Constantine's admission to the rank of thirteenth apostle. To this day his title in the Orthodox Church is that of Isapostolos (Equal to the Apostles). Being the thirteenth was a charism that had already been afforded to (several) others, such as Paul, and Barnabas, and Apollos, as an honorary nomenclature. By the time of St John Chrysostom the issue of an imperial apostolicity is clearly canonized in Orthodox tradition; but it is reserved primarily for Constantine alone. Later Christian emperors saw themselves in the line of his spiritual succession, and often made arrangements to be buried in the 'vestibule' of the Holy Apostles church. This custom of public dynastic burial claims was probably intended by the emperors as a way of asserting their right to be seen as sacral rulers; but it was interestingly interpreted by Chrysostom, and 'absorbed' by the church's tradition as an indication of how the new Christian dynasties had become the humble servants of the fishermen:

> Those who wear the diadem in Constantinople, consider it a great thing to be buried in the vestibule, not adjacent to the apostles. It is a matter of honour for the emperors thus to be the doorkeepers of the fishermen. It is their glory in death, not a source of shame, and a glory they wish for their children too.[29]

Chrysostom was very intent on this programme of keeping the sacral role of the court in its proper place, already sensing the manner in which it would impinge on his own right to preach the Gospel. He would soon die as a martyr, asserting that right fearlessly.

Some have read the words of the historian Sozomen in a way that suggests the Byzantine Church had no difficulty seeing the emperors as sacral equivalents to bishops. Sozomen says: 'Bishops were also buried [in the Holy Apostles church], since the priestly dignity is of the same honour as the imperial dignity; or rather in holy places it takes precedence.'[30] But this is a false interpretation of what he means. In any case his remarks were not at all accurate. No bishops of Constantinople were ever associated with the imperial burial place. What he is talking about is more likely to be a cryptic reference to the return of the relics of St John Chrysostom to the church of the Holy Apostles in January 438, ordered by Theodosius II and widely seen as an imperial 'climb-down'.[31] This gives Sozomen the excuse to dress up his argument that the priestly dignity exceeds the imperial, for it had been a recurring theme of Chrysostom's own subversive writing that the priestly dignity was superior to that of the civic leaders.[32] Byzantine political theory, therefore, as exemplified in some of the leading theologians of the era, does admit a certain sacrality in the role of the emperor considered as God's anointed ruler. But it is certainly not an uncritical or a wholly subservient theory that hands over its own ideas of self-determination to an absolute autocracy. On the contrary, it has precise notions about what were 'appropriate' spheres of operation for clergy and rulers. It wished to prevent the indiscriminate merging of roles, and wished to emphasize with vigour that the state power had to be validated by conforming to the Gospel. To convey this sense of appropriate distinction alongside close affinity (for it also abhorred the idea that power in the state should be exercised in a secular way, that is, divorced from any religious context at all, a notion it saw as worse than paganism) it coined the notion of *symphonia*: harmonious correlation.

Patristic Ideas on *Symphonia*

To a large extent the idea of *symphonia* was always an aspiration to be aimed for, not an elaborated political theory; but this does not mean that it was not the subject of a considerable amount of thought in the early Byzantine period. St Gregory of Nyssa expressed the classical basis of the belief (based on the biblical idea of God's unfailing protection of his covenant people) in the form: if the emperor followed the will of God and the people preserved faith then God would bless the affairs of the earthly dominion with his protection and favour. A *symphonia* of earth and heaven would result, especially seen in the protection of the Christian imperium from its many enemies.[33]

Chrysostom also tried to describe *symphonia* in terms of a clear delineation between the proper roles of church and state. It is, however, an attempt to distinguish the affairs of the body and the soul, which Chrysostom knew well enough was a syzygy that could only be notionally, never really, distinguished. Chrysostom's experience of church–state relations was far from being a happy one. This is why he regularly uses the example of the King Ozias, who was afflicted with leprosy for his impertinence in offering priestly incense to God.[34] He describes the two limits concisely in his *Oration to the Antiochenes*:

> Therefore, stay within your proper domain. The government and the priesthood each have their own boundaries, even though the priesthood is the greater of the two. A king should not be judged merely on the appearance, or valued merely from the gold and jewels in his costume. His domain is the administration of earthly affairs, whereas the jurisdiction of the priesthood is a power derived from above.... Bodies are under the care of the king, souls under the care of the priest. The king remits earthly debts, the priest remits the debts of guilt.... One uses earthly weapons, the other uses spiritual weapons, and it is the latter which bears greater power. This is why the king bends his head to the hand of the priest, and why, in the Old Testament, kings were always anointed by priests.[35]

Athanasios, also using the cautionary tale of Ozias, had himself tried to plead for the same kind of 'space' in his *History of the Arians*, from an equally unhappy context.

In 358 when Athanasios wrote, he had been radically disillusioned by the role the Emperor Constantius II had played in church politics. He tried to draw a clear line between church and state, and cites the case of Bishop Hosius of Cordoba (Constantine's personal ecclesiastical adviser) to make his position clear:

> Do not interfere with church affairs, or give instructions in ecclesiastical matters. Rather take instruction from the bishops. God has given the imperium to you. To us he has commended the church. If a man took away your imperium he would be offending against the providence of God. Just so, you yourself should be aware that if you subject the church to your own will you will be committing a great wrong. It is written: Render to Caesar what is Caesar's, and to God what is God's. Just as we bishops are not allowed to rule the world, you have no power to swing the censer.[36]

The idea of *symphonia* can also be clearly discerned in the Byzantine understanding of the role of the emperor in the governance of church affairs through the ecumenical councils. This was a friction point of church governance: the exercise of imperial authority in matters which usually did relate to substantial matters of the faith. Constantine began the dialectic himself with his intervention in the Donatist affair, and his intervention over Bishop Alexander's condemnation of Arius. His summoning of Nicaea, of course, is the same thing on a larger scale.

The church had long been accustomed to settling local and regional issues by synodical process. After Constantine first handed over the Donatist issue for papal judgement, we can see the Roman Church being careful to preserve synodical form, and not make the bishop of the capital simply 'stand in for' the emperor on religious questions. A certain collapse of the synodical system as it was racked over the Arian crisis of the fourth century (with numerous conflicting synods taking place), and the attempts of the Constantinian dynasty to impose a common state-recognized orthodoxy around homoiousianism, led soon enough to the settling down of the Byzantine theory of *symphonia* into a doctrine that the emperor had the right to summon a council that affected the international church, and had the duty to ratify and impose its findings afterwards. He had no right, however, to interfere in the proceedings of the council or press the bishops towards his own views. Such, at least, was the theory.

It is difficult to see any pattern emerging from Theodosius I, who was imposing a state Orthodoxy in the Nicene cause. His personal promulgation of the standard of the 'faith of Peter and Damasus' (the current patriarchs of Alexandria and Rome) to be observed in the East, at first sight demonstrates a continuance of the programme of his predecessor Constantius, that is the advocacy of an imperially led religious policy. And yet when Theodosius advanced this he did so knowing it was the form of 'Orthodoxy' recognized at three of the major sees, and was now bringing the fourth, Constantinople, into alignment with the international synodical *symphonia*. It is difficult to read his actions solely as an imposition of 'imperial state orthodoxy' such as Constantius had imposed so heavy-handedly. Certainly his convocation of the second ecumenical council shows him anxious to determine Eastern affairs through synodical process, and in 381 his limited interventions in the council demonstrated that, under the umbrella of reconciliation, he was willing to tolerate a wide range of opinions. At the end of the proceedings in 381 the conciliar bishops themselves appealed to Theodosius to ratify their work directly.

By the time of Ephesus (431) all the episcopal protagonists at Rome, Alexandria, Antioch, and Constantinople clearly wanted to use regional synods independently of the court. It was only when the court determined that an international (not national) synodical process was in order that the ecumenical status of Ephesus was assured. It was then that the procedure of Theodosius II's dynasty was established, and thereafter became the 'gold standard' for subsequent regimes: emperors summoned and ratified the councils, they did not participate in their decrees. This was the privilege of the bishops alone. Theodosius II stated that principle in his *Sacra* letter read as the prelude to the council of 431:

> The stability of the state depends on the religion through which we honour God. The two are closely linked, as each depends on the other and thrives as the other flourishes. Since God has handed us the reins of government, and made us the link of piety and righteousness for all our subjects, we shall preserve the association between the two and watch over the interests of both God and men.[37]

This principle of non-interference was often much honoured 'in the breach', of course, but by its regular reiteration of the Theodosian 'ideal', Byzantium rehearsed its creed, even if it did not always observe such an idealistic *symphonia* in practice.

Justinian, who had a much more 'hands on' policy of church interference than any of his recent predecessors, states exactly the same principle in his letter convoking the Council of Constantinople II in 553:[38] it was the duty of the priests to define the faith, and the task of the emperors to carry out the conciliar decrees as state religious policy. In the legal preface to his sixth Novel (the Byzantine term for a newly issued imperial law), issued in March 535, he promulgated his definition of the respective spheres of governing power (*basileia*) and priestly authority (*sacerdotium*).

> The greatest gifts that God's heavenly philanthropy ever gave to men are the *sacerdotium* and the *basileia*; of which the former serves divine affairs, and the latter presides and watches over human affairs, and both proceed from one and the same principle, and regulate human life. So, nothing should be so much the care of the emperor as the saintliness of the priests since these constantly pray to God on his behalf. If the priesthood is in all ways blameless and acceptable to God, and the *basileia* rules justly and properly over the state entrusted to it, good harmony will result, which will bestow all that is beneficial on the human race.[39]

This depiction of *symphonia* has often been seized on as an example of how Justinian so pressed the boundaries as to almost revert to Hellenistic kingship theory. It has often been elevated as a mantra for 'Caesaro-Papist' readings. In fact, this is not a text where Justinian imposes any new or intensified theology at all. It is simply a learned biblical allusion (frequently not recognized by less learned commentators, it has to be said) to Psalm 131 (especially verses 8–12), which defines the Christian understanding of political *symphonia*. The king is blessed by God. He ensures the holiness of the priests who in turn pray for the welfare of his kingdom, so that his throne shall endure, but only as long as his sons: 'keep the covenant, and observe the laws which I have commanded'. Here in the hands of one of the most vigorous of the emperors is simply a restatement of the classical Byzantine doctrine of *symphonia*: the biblical doctrine of the conditional blessing from God upon the administration of the court based upon covenant fidelity. Justinian used this argument of harmony to justify his imperial role in the oversight of correct doctrine in the churches. But the harmony would only be possible, he goes on to say in the same preface to the sixth Novel:

> If the holy canons are observed which the rightly praised and venerable apostles, the eyewitnesses and ministers of God's word, have transmitted to us, and the holy fathers have preserved and interpreted.

A little earlier than this, in the time of Emperor Anastasius, Pope Gelasius had tried to argue a more separatist vision of the spheres of church and state. It was a draft of an argument that would grow and grow into the Western Church's 'Two Swords' theory.[40] The pope had been heavily criticized by the emperor for not keeping the court informed of his election (at the time of the Acacian schism). To justify his actions in retrospect, Gelasius tried to elaborate a theory that would keep the church and state spheres more distinct than the East seemed to want them. *Potestas* (jurisdictional power) might belong to the state; but *auctoritas* (moral power) belonged to the church. Gelasius wrote as follows:

> There are two things, August Emperor, by which this world is ruled: the sacred authority of the pontiffs and the royal power. Of these two the priests carry the heavier weight, as they must render an account to the Lord's judgement seat even for kings. Most merciful son, you know well enough that you surpass all mankind in your dignity, yet even so you must bend your head in submission to the ministers of divine things, and from them receive the pledge of your salvation. In receiving the heavenly sacraments, which it is their office to dispense, you must depend on their judgement and not desire to submit them to your will. In matters concerning public life, the ministers of religions understand that the imperial power has been given to you from above and they themselves will obey your laws.[41]

In Justinian's decree of May 535 he wanted to go on record to nip this naive separatism in the bud. If it were allowed to go ahead it could only result (as proved to be the case) in a model of Christian society where priests were given the right to dominion, or where the laity divorced themselves from ecclesiastical concerns: both prospects (either hieratic or secular government) were seen to be very bad ideas indeed. Justinian pressed on instead with a firmer definition of how the notion of *symphonia* understood the exercise of the two powers:

> The priesthood and the imperium do not differ very greatly. Nor are sacred things so very different from those of public and common interest.[42]

His distinction was not carelessly used. Here we have the fruit of a long reflection by the best legal minds, on the shibboleth that Gelasius had raised. *Potestas* was what mattered most to the Roman mind. The Senate could bear *auctoritas*. Moral prestige lay with it, but it was *potestas* that signified effective power. In Roman law only the holder of *potestas* effected religious legislation on the advice of those who held the *auctoritas*. The bishops, of course, claimed for themselves canonical *potestas* in religious affairs within the church. But in so far as these came within the public domain (and very little did not after the increasing Christianization of the empire) the emperor had to validate all large-scale matters of public concern. This gave to the Eastern Church a definite commitment to the concept of a Christian civilization, manifested in both law and culture. It did not mean a priestocracy, however, but an attempt to achieve the unattainable ideal of a Christian civilization through a balanced harmony of civic and ecclesiastic mutual respect. This has remained an ideal of the Orthodox Church to this day.

NEW POLITIES IN THE AFTERMATH OF BYZANTIUM

Byzantium has fallen. And relatively recently too: not with the death of the last anointed tsar in 1918, but with the likes of the Politburo chairmen who ran on such a ghastly and secularized mockery for another seventy years of what they thought the 'Autocrat of the Romans' was supposed to be for his people. The Orthodox do not expect another *Basileus* to arise, but neither are they entirely convinced that modern democracy has to run along the secularized lines sketched out for it by Western theorists who have so unconsciously 'bought into' the more divided political religious philosophy of Western Christendom: that there ought to be 'Two Swords', and that the state and church ought to be strictly segregated. The Orthodox generally believe that the union Christ brings (the communion of heart and soul established in his grace) is meant to run on into a vision of greater union and harmony for the families of mankind. The church is not merely a 'spiritual matter'; it is a sacrament of union, and accordingly an ideal form of how patterns of political harmony ought to be structured in society. But having affirmed such a profoundly religious vision of society, Orthodoxy needs also to underline its political 'reservations'.

The heart of the enduring Orthodox political theology is expressed in the concept of *symphonia*. This has two particular aspects that are worth repeating. The first is the manner in which *symphonia* as an ideal evokes the biblical doctrine of the 'conditional' blessing from God upon his people for their political stability, a conditionality in some sense based upon covenant fidelity, but a blessing that regularly renews itself after numerous failures in the socio-political and moral dimensions of life, simply in the graciousness of 'restoration'. In fact the Byzantines, by this concept of *symphonia*, remained fundamentally faithful to the biblical witness that salvation is first and foremost understood in terms of gracious restoration and renewal of a people. The second, and this is something that particularly distinguishes Byzantine thought, gains its force from an important distinction in Roman law: that between *auctoritas* (such as the Senate possessed) and *potestas* (such as the effective ruler possessed). *Auctoritas* amounts to substantial influence over another's sphere of action. *Potestas* is the ability to perform definitively that which is constitutive of your own proper sphere of action. This, simply put is the political principle of 'To each one, his own proper sphere of governance. Between them all a moderate system of listening and balance.' This is a distinct form of the 'principle of subsidiarity' which did much in the late twentieth century to elucidate and enliven reflection about transnational legislation in the counsels of the European Union. The Byzantine principle of *symphonia* which configures the principle in much wider contexts of civilization-building, might well have a role to play yet in reconstituting political systems in eastern Europe. Its new application in a large range of political matrices can be surprisingly effective. Only liberal atheists find it intolerable.

In most states that still comprise the thought-world of eastern Europe, Byzantine cultural paradigms run deep. An authentic understanding of the root tradition in these Orthodox societies would be a great benefit. It would prevent nationalists from traducing Byzantine religious political theory and remaking it into a sacrilege of autocratic chauvinism; and it would serve as a counter-measure to those who wish to advance a model society purged of religious commitments or culture. Both foundational ideas behind Byzantine dominion theory – the religious notion of accountability and the political concept of *symphonia* – stand to offer a great deal to modern theorists considering the relation of Orthodoxy to democracy today, especially in the light of the extensive damage done to human and political systems in the aftermath of the bankruptcy of totalitarianism in eastern Europe.

The symphony that should exist between church and state is a relative and fragile thing. No matter how godly the Christian emperor might appear, at the end of the day, as the monks knew from their constant recitation of the Psalter, they were advised to 'put no trust in princes, nor in the leaders of the people'.[43] The sacrality of the emperor, and the apostolic status of Constantine as model for subsequent emperors, were both put forward as 'economic' theological positions. Like the theory of *symphonia* itself, they were in the nature of dialectics. The Byzantine political theology never lost sight of its biblical underpinnings, though many subsequent commentators have not recognized the amount of exegesis underlying its rhetoric and have, in consequence, overstated that rhetoric and often falsified the picture by creating an anachronistic Caesaro-Papist caricature, or models of unmitigated absolutism that do no justice to the more complex evidence.

In the final analysis the emperor is dead. In the systems that replace him, the Orthodox tradition brings a set of much experience, and deep memories. It is not committed to absolutist monarchies at all, as some of its critics have accused it; but it does have a deep and enduring commitment to the concept of state government as having much to do with establishing the moral and religious sensibility of a people, or, put another way, of the spiritual responsibility of the state for the building of an enduring and elevated human culture. Many modern states have abrogated this duty and now stand with much hand-wringing over the sight of the breakdowns of polity that result on every level. Too late they have realized that the neglect of sacred values leads back and downwards to a human society that becomes unrestrainedly brutish, not onwards and upwards to freedom and joy. Orthodoxy will never compel men and women into an absolutist theocratic vision of government. The Orthodox in recent centuries have had to fight too long and too hard to secure their freedom ever to wish to deprive others of theirs. But equally, Orthodoxy will never abrogate its responsibility to the state in which it lives, to be a major force advocating the preservation and advancement of religious polity, namely the culture of Christ. As Eastern Orthodox lands come ever more directly into the body politic of the European Union, this dialogue with partners singing new strands of song will become more and more evident.

Notes

1 Part of a long-standing historical tendency to dismiss the Christian East as 'backward' compared to the innovations and vitality of the West. It was helped by the fact that from the Renaissance, when these historiographies started to be written, Orthodoxy was recumbent under Islamic power and could not 'answer back'. For more see McGuckin 2005c.

2 This is more than a geographical question, meaning rather: do the traditions of free thought come to an end under the Eastern Orthodox world-view, rooted in allegedly absolutist paradigms of government and obedience, and so apparently contrary to Western cultures of dissidence? See Huntington 1997.

3 That of Constantine the Great being the precedent for Byzantium. His acclamation was led by the oddly named British King Crocus in what is now the undercrypt at York Minster, and was then the Roman garrison headquarters.

4 Deut. 17.15; 1 Sam. 15.1; Ps. 2.7.

5 1 Sam. 8.5–7, 12.17.

6 *Basileia tou Theou.*

7 Matt. 22.21; Luke 13.32; John 18.36.

8 John 19.11; see 1 Sam. 12.14.

9 Rom. 13.1–6.

10 Luke 22.53.

11 Heb. 13.14.

12 With the exception of Clement of Alexandria (and a few claims to the effect in the *Novellae* of Emperor Justinian), the reservation of the title of *nomos empsychos* for Christ was the tradition observed by Greek patristic thought as a whole.

13 Dvornik, *Early Christian and Byzantine Political Philosophy* (1966).

14 While pagan theory argued that the king was 'a god for his people' and thus merited the worship and total obedience of his followers, Ps. 81.6–7 teaches something quite different. It runs like this in context: 'I have said to you that you are gods, all of you sons of the Most High, and yet you shall die like men, fall like any of the princes.'

15 Oration 36.11. Gregory delivered this speech as his farewell to the court and capital, after resigning from the presidency of the Council of Constantinople in 381.

16 Ps. 81.3–4.

17 See McGuckin 2003.

18 A typological *mimesis* in the Christian sense, that is, not a mirroring in the Hellenistic manner.

19 'Let your Kingdom come! Let your will be done on earth as it is in heaven.'

20 Heb. 5.5–6, 6.20, and following.

21 In the Byzantine *Book of Ceremonies* of Constantine Porphyrogennitos, the imperial liturgical privileges are listed as the incensing of the altar, kissing the altar and relics and sacred vessels, reading the Gospel, giving the congregation a blessing at solemn services, receiving communion in the sanctuary, and preaching. Cf. Dvornik 1966: 645.

22 This 'economic' nature of the ascription of priestly honours is often overemphasized by readers with little understanding of Orthodox ritual process or rhetorical style.

23 In his tenth-century treatise *Book of Ceremonies.*

24 'To Marcian, the new Constantine, the new Paul, the new David: many years to the Emperor David. . . . Many years to the Priest-Emperor. You have built churches, conqueror of battles, you have destroyed heretics. May your empire be eternal.' Acclamations after Session VI of the Council of Chalcedon.

25 Leo writes to Marcian in a letter of 453, commending him on his defence of Orthodoxy through his support of the Romans at Chalcedon: 'You have the priestly palm as well as the imperial crown' (Mansi 1759–1927: vol. 6, p. 219, Epistle 111.3; Schwartz 1914–84: 64, Epistle 58). He wrote to Bishop Julian that the continuing vigilance of Marcian and Pulcheria against Monophysite resistance was a sign of 'the sublimity of their royal

greatness, and their sacerdotal holiness' (Epistle to Bishop Julian, Mansi 1759–1927: vol. 6, p. 235, Epistle 117.2); cf. Dvornik 1966: 773. Subsequently, the pope wrote to Emperor Leo I that his imperial policies to suppress heresy would be his 'association with the apostles and prophets', and that 'The Lord has given you the royal power not merely to rule the world, but mainly to protect the church' (Mansi 1759–1927: vol. 6, p. 325, Epistle 156; cf. Dvornik 1966: 773).

26 Vigilius says to the emperor: 'Not least is it to our satisfaction to see that God in his mercy has designed to give to you not only an imperial but a priestly soul as well. When the pontiffs offer sacrifice according to ancient tradition, it is so that the Lord may deign to unify the catholic faith throughout the world. This your piety has effected with all possible strength when you imposed in all the provinces the inviolate maintenance of that faith which was defined at the most venerable synods of Nicaea, Constantinople, Ephesus 1 and Chalcedon' (Mansi 1759–1927: vol. 9, p. 35; Pope Vigilius, Epistle 4; cf. Dvornik 1966: 822).

27 'Theodosius was like the true priests of God . . . in fact he surpassed in gentleness all true and genuine priests. What was written about Moses [that he was the meekest man on earth: Num. 12.13] can be said about the Emperor Theodosius, that he is the gentlest of all men in this world. It is owing to his gentleness that God has brought all his enemies under his power without a battle.' Socrates, *Church History*, 7.42.

28 Demolished by Mehmet II in 1453 to be the site for his Victory Mosque (Fatih Jamii).

29 *Against the Jews and Pagans*, 9; also in Homily 26.5, *On Second Corinthians*.

30 *Church History*, 2.34.

31 Ibid. 5.36; Dvornik 1966: 761.

32 He means the prefects and magistrates. It is an easy step, later, to extend it to the emperors. 'There is a form of leadership more sublime than civil authority, and what is it? It is the leadership that prevails in the church which Paul speaks about when he says: Obey your superiors and be subject to them for they are on the watch as men who must give an account of your souls (Heb. 13.17). And this leadership excels the civil authority as much as heaven excels earth, and is even more noble still. For its first important care is not the punishment of crime but its prevention. And if a crime is committed the spiritual leadership is not concerned with expunging the criminal, but rather his guilt.' Homily 15.4, *On Second Corinthians*.

33 Gregory of Nyssa, *Funeral Oration for the Empress Flacilla*.

34 2 Chron. 26.16–18. Chrysostom, Homily 4, *On Osias*, 'I Saw the Lord' (*PG* 56.126); also Homily 21, *Eclogue on Imperial Rule*.

35 Homily 3, *To the People of Antioch*.

36 *History of the Arians*, 44.

37 See McGuckin 1994b: 51–4.

38 *PG* 86.1035.

39 *Corpus Iuris Civilis*, vol. 3: *Novellae*, ed. R. Schoell and W. Kroll (Berlin, 1928), 35f.

40 Dvornik 1966: 807 sees in Gelasius' desire to distinguish the two spheres (and in the pope's implicit claims to spiritual *potestas* as well (in the binding and loosing) the real beginning of the end of the old Byzantine compromise theories of state–church relations, and the start of a new medieval mindset. This is seen emerging in Gelasius' treatise on the power of binding and loosing (*De anathematis vinculo*: *PL* 59.108f.). The idea of separation of the two powers is even more underlined in the letters exchanged between Pope Symmachus and Anastasius: 'You administer human affairs, the pontiff dispenses to you divine things. I would not say that the priestly honours are greater than the imperial, but certainly they are equal.' Pope Symmachus, Letter 10 (*PL* 62.68). This is well on the way to the position of the medieval popes as princes rationalizing their stand-off before the emperors of Byzantium.

41 Gelasius, Letter 8, *To the Emperor Anastasius*.

42 *Novellae* 7.2.1, p. 53.

43 Ps. 118.9, 146.3.

Chapter 7

Orthodoxy and the Contemporary World

The Orthodox Church has had a long pilgrim's journey through history so far. It is still in transit, and cannot yet put down its pilgrim staff, or do other than live in society as a community on the move. To do otherwise would be to forget its obedience to the Lord's commands and the apostolic encouragement it has received. It cannot forget the words of the Lord:

> If the world hates you, know that it has hated me before it hated you. If you were of the world, the world would love its own; but because you are not of the world, but I chose you out of the world, therefore the world hates you.[1]

Nor does it forget the words of the apostle: 'Here we have no abiding city, but we seek the city that is to come.'[2] Because of its long involvement in the world, and its accumulated store of experience, however, there is little in the human condition that it has not already met, considered, and passed a comment on, as to how human affairs can be bettered in the light of the Gospel. For these reasons it is natural for the church instinctively to look to precedence to establish any authoritative stance on significant matters of faith or ethics. Its holy tradition (*paradosis*) is one of its chief inspirations, and its perennial guide in all discussion in the present moment about Christianity's involvement in the present world order, or its resistance of the present world order, since both attitudes are abundantly necessary, and the discernment necessary to see which one is appropriate at any given instance is of the utmost importance.

THE POOR AT THE RICH MAN'S GATE

But the present era has also been a time which Christianity has met altogether new conditions. The speed of societal change in the last two centuries has exceeded all that human history has ever known before. The rate of change continues at a bewildering pace. The world has been introduced to inequalities of staggering proportions. Space has been colonized, but in some villages of the majority world that is not part of the rich elite today the standard of life continues at the old, slow rhythm in conditions that are a only short step up from the medieval. In some locations diseases flourish that could be eradicated with minimal medical attention, while other parts of the world invest millions in inane frivolities, in a globalized consumerism that exhausts the human spirit and leaves it morally impoverished. Many decades have passed since the world was more than capable of feeding itself to abundance. The continuing existence of famine in the world today is predominantly a moral choice of our race in this era: a moral choice that has not been the case in prior generations. It is a choice that is frequently voiced in terms of percentages of national budgets that could 'feasibly' be allocated to humanitarian relief; but it is a moral choice of the populace nonetheless, that has collaborated in making such unequal political and economic structures effective in oppressing the weak and justifying lifestyles of excess. What is more, no previous generation really 'knew' the scenarios of suffering across the world. This generation, with its powerful access to global media, cannot offer such an excuse for its inaction. But the invisible poor are not simply those overseas. Once a human being has decided it is best to render the poor invisible, they can be stepped over in the local high street. It is a knack that is easily learned.

In times past, therefore, the church advocated strongly for 'those who had' to assist those who had not. It pleaded with the rich (those who had too much) to be generous patrons of the poor. It even softened the harsh words of the Lord to the rich[3] in the hope of encouraging them to learn generosity, and in this benefaction to find salvation. Accordingly, although Orthodox thought has a rich and longstanding tradition of advocacy for the poor,[4] such that one of the early titles of a bishop was *Philoptochos*,[5] it has tended to approach the concept of charitable aid from the premodern conditions of economic philosophy, and the understanding that local economies were predominantly based on agricultural exchange. The far greater complexity of the newly globalized world economies will, increasingly, require the Orthodox world leaders to increase their advocacy for a more just systematic redistribution of world resources. This will not, *de facto*, remove the church's advocacy of the right to personal possession, and freedom in the charism of sharing with the poor, but it will require a greater stress on the concept (already familiar to Orthodoxy) of 'sins known and unknown, those committed in ignorance or knowledge'; for the continuing oppression of the poor, by virtue of the rich world's desire for lifestyles of excess, is a 'systemic sin' that has seduced whole nations. Orthodoxy in the years to come needs to give a far stronger voice to the education of its own people and the education of the un-churched in relation to the duties of a Christian towards the needy. It may also be the case that the stress on the 'local' involvement with the poor will give way to a wider sense of the global village, as more and more parishes adopt other 'majority world' villages to assist them in basic infrastructure-building. In both cases (whether the poor are on the next block, or whether they are half a world away) the involvement of dialogue is crucially important. It is not just one's money that is required (a cheque in the post or a regular bank draft) but one's hand and heart. This dialogue of love is important exactly because it is two-way. It does not simply work from the benefactor 'down' to a patronized recipient. Such is not the way God sees the relationship. It is a rapid process of two-way learning that assists all involved in a clarification of ways of living.

The Orthodox traditions of fasting will be a useful tool in this process. For fasting, such an integral part of Orthodox daily life, but so demeaned by so many parts of contemporary Christianity, is a way of touching, in the body and the living nerve, the need to re-educate our desires to consume. Fasting (meant as a spiritual way of rejoicing in the Lord) is an occasion to say: 'Not needful.' It is a way to simplify the accumulative clutter that is an instinct of our lesser, hypothalamic, brain. For centuries monastic lifestyle has advocated this practice as a fundamental part of 'staying awake' in the Lord. Today, the church needs to advocate it all the more urgently, and restore the original practice of the ancient Christians, that the money saved by the many periods of fasting could be sent to the assistance of the poor. This is not only an 'individual' programme; it ought to be a communal activity of every church, so that from that platform it can be advocated as a distinctively Christian way of seeking to redress the balance. This is nothing new in the history of Christianity; but the pressing need for its renewal and reappropriation in the church to hasten to meet the needs of the hungry and dying is something new, and the world leaders of Orthodoxy will be increasingly assessed in terms of their fidelity to this vocation and duty. It is a pressing duty of the leadership of every priest at local level.

Global consumerism and the plight of the world's hungry are inextricably connected. In times past Christian hierarchs stressed the need for accumulating enough of the goods of this world to ensure one's family had the basic essentials. This striving together, by the labour of one's hands or one's intelligence, to provide a stable lifestyle that would move from the securing of basic needs to encourage the acquisition of higher goals was seen as part of the Creation ordinance: that human beings needed to work, not only to gather sufficient to live, but also to advance in wisdom and understanding and societal care. Again in earlier times, the hierarchs of the church advocated that those who had enough must also help those near them who, for a multitude of reasons, did not have the basics. The emphasis in Orthodox thought was on the immediate care of the local poor and suffering. The care for the poor was a Gospel command of a very high order. The poor were the body of Christ, and the believer's attitude to them was a fundamental part of their salvation. Alluding to the Lord's own words,[6] Mother Maria Skobotsova,[7] an ascetic in Paris during the Second World War, answered her critics who had censured her for being involved with street refugees although she was a consecrated nun by saying:

> At the Last Judgment I will not be asked whether I satisfactorily practised asceticism, nor how many prostrations and bows I have made before the holy table. I will be asked whether I fed the hungry, clothed the naked, visited the sick and the prisoner in jail. That is all I will be asked.

This command of the Gospel remains central to the lived experience of the church. A parish that does not have a programme of assistance specifically focused on the poor is a threadbare family indeed. An individual Orthodox who does not wish to make their heart and purse available to the suffering is someone who has not yet drawn close to the Lord; though the mercy of the Lord may still have time to enlighten them. It is very hard indeed to free our hearts from the stifling embrace of the desire for acquisition, and to remain free to seek the Kingdom of God where the Lord is, with his poor.

The Grace of Peace and the Curse of War

Another of Orthodoxy's 'new conditions' is the manner in which war is conducted in the contemporary world. War is nothing new to the church. Despite the voices that are often ready to invest it with the trappings of 'glory', it remains what it has always been, one of the curses of the human race, dragging after it the shambling train of death, orphans, widows, disease, destruction of the environment and of cities, rape, forced prostitution, and all manner of human wickedness and misery. The voices that glorify war are not illumined ones, and never have been. It may have been the case, some of the time, that wars have been fought by the just, and for a 'just cause' (by which the church understands the legitimate defence of one's home or nation, or the protection and rescue of the weak from insupportable oppression). But the majority of wars have not been fought on these terms at all. And even in those that have, the corruptions of war have led to many instances of the just finally acting as badly as the wicked, and losing sight of their goal. War is a curse; and even when the situation of war seemed unavoidable, and might be said to be for reasonable and defensible goals, the Orthodox Church has never endorsed it with anything comparable to the theory of the 'just war' that has played such a large part in the consciousness of Western Christianity. Even a military engagement that has been conducted on strictly 'just causes' (have there ever been any?) is a matter of lamentation. Those who seek to justify military action as God-given, God-blessed, or God-pleasing are bewildered indeed, and seem to take their theological justifications from a decontextualized and fundamentalist reading of the Old Testament. Those who believe they can find glorification of righteous war in the teachings of Jesus have made some serious mistakes in their interpretation of the New Testament.

Christianity was, and remains at heart, an apocalyptic religion, and it is no accident that its numerous biblical references to war and violent destruction are generally apocalyptic ciphers, symbols that stand for something else, references to the 'Eschaton' (the image of how the world will be rolled up and assessed once universal justice is imposed by God on his recalcitrant and rebellious creation). Biblical descriptions of violence and war, in most of Christianity's classical exposition of its biblical heritage, rather than being straightforward depictions of the life and values of the existing world order are thus eschatological allegories. To confound the two orders[8] (taking war images of the apocalyptic dimension for instances of how the world here ought to be managed[9]) is a gross distortion of the ancient literature. This has become an increasing problem since the medieval period, as allegorist readings of Scripture have been progressively replaced (especially in Protestantism) by wholesale historicist and literalist readings of the ancient texts.[10]

Many Protestant theologies of war are heavily based on such readings of the Old Testament which prove to be greatly injurious to the health of the church (and mankind). This is not to say that Eastern Christians have not been guilty of their own misreadings of evidence, at various historical moments, or that they have no blood on their hands, for that would be to deny the brutal facts of a church that has progressively been driven westwards, despite its own will, by a series of military disasters, for the last thousand years. But Christian reflection in the Eastern Church has, I would suggest, generally been more careful than in the West, to remind itself of the apocalyptic and mysterious nature of the church's place within history and on the world stage, and it has stubbornly clung to a less congratulatory theory of the morality of war (despite its advocacy of 'Christian imperium'), because it sensed that such a view was more in tune with the principles of the Gospels.

The Fathers of the Church, following the general example set by St Basil the Great in his influential canons, argued that a Christian who is faithful to the Gospel must sometimes take up arms to fight. His argument is illustrative of a much wider attitude in the Orthodox tradition. Basil's canons[11] (ethical judgements as from a ruling bishop to his flock) on morality and practical issues became highly influential in the universal church because of his role as one of the major monastic theorists of early Christianity. His canonical epistles were transmitted wherever monasticism went: in the Eastern Church of antiquity (because monasticism was the substructure of the spread of the Christian movement) that more or less meant his canonical views became the standard paradigm of all of Orthodoxy's theoretical approach to the morality of war and violence, even though the writings were local and occasional in origin. Basil's ninety-two canonical epistles were adapted by various ecumenical councils of the church that followed his time. His writing is appealed to in canon 1 of the fourth ecumenical council, which took place at Chalcedon (451), and in canon 1 of the seventh ecumenical council, Nicaea II (787), and it is cited verbatim in canon 2 of the sixth ecumenical council, at Constantinople (681), which paraphrases much else from his canonical epistles. By such affirmations his canons entered the Pandects of Canon Law of the Byzantine Church, and they remain authoritative to this day.

St Basil has several things to say about violence and war in his diocese. It was a border territory of the empire, and his administration had known several incursions by 'barbarian' forces. Canon 13 considers war:

> Our fathers did not consider killings committed in the course of wars to be classifiable as murders at all, on the score, it seems to me, of allowing a pardon to men fighting in defence of sobriety and piety. Perhaps, though, it might be advisable to refuse them communion for three years, on the ground that their hands are not clean.[12]

The balance and sense of discretion is remarkable in this little comment, one that bears much weight in terms of Eastern Orthodox understandings of the morality of war. The 'Fathers' in question refers to Athanasios of Alexandria, the great Nicene Orthodox authority of the fourth-century church. Athanasios' defence of the Nicene Creed, and the divine status of Christ, had won him immense posthumous prestige by the end of the fourth century, and his works were being collated and disseminated (in his own lifetime his reputation had been highly conflicted, his person exiled numerous times, and his writings proscribed by imperial censors). St Basil seems to wish to add a cautionary note that not everything a 'Father' has to say is equally momentous, or universally authoritative. In his *Epistle to Amun*, Athanasios had apparently come out quite straightforwardly about the legitimacy of killing in time of war, saying:

> Although one is not supposed to kill, the killing of the enemy in time of war is both a lawful and praiseworthy thing. This is why we consider individuals who have distinguished themselves in war as being worthy of great honours, and indeed public

monuments are set up to celebrate their achievements. It is evident, therefore, that at one particular time, and under one set of circumstances, an act is not permissible, but when time and circumstances are right, it is both allowed and condoned.[13]

This saying was being circulated and given authority as a 'patristic witness' simply because it had come from Athanasios. In fact the original letter had nothing whatsoever to do with war. The very example of the 'war hero' is a sardonic reference *ad hominem* since the letter was addressed to an aged leader of the Egyptian monks who described themselves as *asketes*, that is, those who laboured and 'fought' for the virtuous life. The military image is entirely incidental, and Athanasios in context merely uses it to illustrate his chief point in the letter, which is to discuss the query Amun had sent on to him as archbishop: 'Did nocturnal emissions count as sins for desert celibates?' Athanasios replies to the effect that, with human sexuality, as with all sorts of other things, the context of the activity determines what is moral, not some absolute standard which is superimposed on moral discussion from the outset. Many ancients, Christian and pagan, regarded sexual activity as inherently defiling and here Athanasios decidedly took leave of them. His argument, therefore, is falsely attributed when (as is often the case) it is read out of context as an apparent justification of killing in time of war. He is not actually condoning the practice at all, merely using the rhetorical example of current opinion to show Amun that contextual variability is very important in making moral judgements.

In his turn St Basil, wishes to make it abundantly clear for his Christian audience that such a literalist reading, if applied to the church's tradition on war, is simplistic, and that is it is just plain wrong-headedness to conclude that the issue ceases to be problematic if one is able to dig up a justificatory 'proof text' from Scripture or patristic tradition (as some seem to have been doing already with these words of Athanasios). Consequently, he sets out a nuanced and corrective exegesis of what the church's canon law *should really be* in terms of fighting in time of hostilities.

One of the ways he does this is to attribute this aphorism of Athanasios to indeterminate 'Fathers', who can then be legitimately corrected by taking a stricter view than they appeared to allow. He also carefully sets his own context: what he speaks about is the canonical regulation of war in which a Christian can engage and be 'amerced';[14] all other armed conflicts are implicitly excluded as not being appropriate to Christian morality. St Basil's text on war needs, therefore, to be understood in terms of an 'economic' reflection on the ancient canons that forbade the shedding of blood in blanket terms. This tension between the ideal standard (no bloodshed) and the complexities of the context in which a local church finds itself thrown in times of conflict and war, is witnessed in several other ancient laws, such as canon 14 of Hippolytus (also from the fourth century).[15] The reasons St Basil gives for suggesting that killing in time of hostilities could be distinguished from voluntary murder pure and simple (for which the canonical penalty was a lifelong ban from admission to the churches and from the sacraments) are set out as the 'defence of sobriety and piety'. This is code language for the defence of Christian borders from the ravages of pagan marauders.

The difficulty St Basil had to deal with was not war on the large scale, but local tribal insurgents who were mounting attacks on Roman border towns, with extensive rapinage. In such circumstances the Caesarean bishop has little patience for those who do not feel they can fight because of religious scruples. His sentiment is more that a passive non-involvement betrays the Christian family (especially its weaker members) to the ravages of men without heart or conscience to restrain them. The implication of his argument, then, is that the provocation to fighting that Christians ought at some stage to accept (to defend the honour and safety of the weak) will be inherently a limited and adequate response, mainly because the honour and tradition of the Christian faith (piety and sobriety) in the hearts and minds of the warriors, will restrict the bloodshed to a necessary minimum. His 'economic' solution nevertheless makes it abundantly clear that the absolute standard of Christian morality turns away from war as an unmitigated evil. This is why we can note that the primary reason St Basil gives that previous 'Fathers' had distinguished killing in time of war, from the case of simple murder, was 'on the score of allowing a pardon'. There was no distinction made here in terms of the qualitative horror of the deed itself, but rather in terms of the way in which the deed could be 'cleansed' by the church's system of penance.

But, we may ask today, is it logical to expect a Christian of his diocese to engage in the defence of the homeland, while simultaneously penalizing him if he spills blood in the process? Well, one needs to contextualize the debarment from the sacrament in the generic fourth-century practice of the reception of the Eucharist, which did not expect regular communication to begin with (ritual preparation was extensive and involved fasting and almsgiving and prayer), and where a sizeable majority of adult Christians in a given church would not have yet been initiated by means of baptism, and were thus not bound to keep all the canons of the church. By his regulation and by the ritual exclusion of the illumined warrior from the sacrament (the returning 'victor' presumably would have received many other public honours and the gratitude of the local folk), St Basil is making sure at least one public sign is given to the entire community that the Gospel standard has no place for war, violence, and organized death. He is trying to sustain an eschatological balance: that war is not part of the Kingdom of God (signified in the eucharistic ritual as arriving in the present) but is part of the bloody and greed-driven reality of world affairs which is the 'Kingdom Not Arrived'. By moving in and out of eucharistic reception Basil's faithful Christian (returning from his duty with blood on his hands) is now in the modality of expressing his dedication to the values of peace and innocence, by means of the lamentation and repentance for life that has been taken, albeit the blood of the violent. St Basil's arrangement that the returning 'noble warrior' should stand inside the church (not in the outer porch where the other public sinners were allocated spaces), but refrain from communion, makes the statement that a truly honourable termination of war, for a Christian, has to be an honourable repentance.

Several commentators (not least many of the later Western Church Fathers) have regarded this as 'fudge', but it seems to me to express, in a finely tuned 'economic' way, the tension in the basic Christian message that there is an unresolvable shortfall between the ideal and the real in an apocalyptically charged religion. What this Basilian canon does most effectively is to set a 'No Entry' sign to any potential theory of just war within Orthodox Christian theology,[16] and should constitute a decided refusal of post-war church-sponsored self-congratulation for victory. All violence, local, individual, or nationally sanctioned, is here stated to be an expression of *hubris* that is inconsistent with the values of the Kingdom of God, and while in many circumstances that violence may be 'necessary' or 'unavoidable' (St Basil states the only legitimate reasons as the defence of the weak and innocent) it is never 'justifiable'. Even for the best motives in the world, the shedding of blood remains a defilement, such that the true Christian, afterwards, would wish to undergo the kathartic experience of temporary return to the lifestyle of penance, that is 'be penitent'. Basil's restriction of the time of penance to three years (seemingly harsh to us moderns) was actually a commonly recognized sign of merciful leniency in the ancient rule book of the early church.[17]

This ancient set of canons may seem quaintly archaic to many readers today, but they serve as interesting 'boundary markers' since because of them the medieval Eastern Church under the Byzantine emperors never erected a theology of holy war, or just war, despite the many temptations to do so as the borders of Byzantium were systematically eroded by Islamic forces. As a result Eastern Orthodoxy does not have to work hard at demolishing such bad medieval structures before it can address the present crisis of war and peace. For things have changed. All ancient theories of war (whether those of St Basil, or the just war notions of St Thomas Aquinas) were conceived in a context where war was limited. It was limited by season, by combatants (mostly a male affair between professional warriors), and by the inherent limitations of weapons. When cannon and crossbow first made their appearance they caused moral shock waves throughout medieval Europe, as they were regarded as so destructive that they tipped the balance of this principle of war limitation. They had indeed, and technology after that era would carry on moving modern warfare into a wholly different category of moral engagement. Today the concept of non-combatant is so eroded that it has more or less ceased to function. Cities and whole populations are destroyed by air attack, or remotely controlled missiles, and it is thought that a subsequent apology for the unavoidable deaths of non-combatants is sufficient.

Innocence died at Dresden and Hiroshima in more ways than one. The greatest of all ends to the limitation theory was the invention of humanity's nuclear arsenal. War theory has since then been dominated by the concept of playing face-down poker[18] with bigger and bigger missiles among a small community of 'Powers' while the rest of the world is encouraged to continue their battles with conventional weapons. But even that theory (thoroughly defective though it appeared in the light of day) has now started to fray irremediably, with politically unstable nations managing to climb up to the nuclear table without an invitation. With nuclear arms in Israel (undoubtedly) on the borders of India and Pakistan, probably in North Korea, and possibly coming soon to Iran, can anyone in the whole world be at ease that we have advanced so little in our theory and practice of war in the last sixty years of the nuclear age that we have been forced, of late, to reinstitute war crimes tribunals for the addressing of genocide?

What appeared to be the archaic and non-systematic approach of the Orthodox Church to war, that it was inherently defiling, even for the righteous who were caught up into its madness by default, needs to be a message restated loud and clear by Orthodox leaders, especially the hierarchical leaders of national churches who so often will be called upon to endorse the latest 'nationalism' of whatever temporary politician is in power.[19] It is a frightening thing to hear senior hierarchs come out with statements (as in the old Soviet days) about the need for the church to 'stand loyally as one with national patriotism'. Our allegiance is to Christ, not to local politicians or to mass sentiment so easily played upon by political manipulators. 'Patriotism' is not a Gospel value. Mercy, and courage, and defence of the weak, and a desire for the peace of the world; all of these things are Gospel values. But in this present age, where war can no longer be limited, or its results foreseen, any belligerence is madness. A riot in a Gaza camp is capable of unbalancing the world. In any case, with the extensive development of economic aid as the most powerful political tool of manipulation, declarations of war are hardly necessary any longer, except in the more and more frequent cases where corrupt governments wish to distract from their home agenda and shore up their obvious deficiencies. Orthodox leaders of the future will be required more and more to become commentators on this complex political scene, and the education of future leaders will require a serious focus on such issues. In the interim it is not a bad thing to return to the basics.

War is a curse on the human race. It arises only from evil, and causes only wickedness. The Orthodox Church can never legitimately endorse it.[20] In some cases it falls as a duty upon some of the righteous to be involved with it, in order to effect a good end (the protection of the weak, or the pursuit of the unjust) through the best means possible. Orthodoxy would never expect all to be summoned to fight: such would be an unjustifiable compulsion of conscience. St Martin of Tours is a prime example of a courageous warrior who became an objector of conscience, and demonstrated the holy courage involved in this form of peace witness. The appalling abandonment of values that normally takes place in war, however – the indiscriminate killing of civilians, saturation bombing, the land-mining of extensive territories – can never be justified morally, and since these things have now become standard military procedure, one is forced to conclude that no righteous person can safely entrust their confidence in any leadership structure of the modern military world (in the sense of blindly giving over their moral awareness to the hierarchy of command). Obedience to orders no longer works as a moral excuse (as the Nuremberg war trials established), and thus it is a very difficult matter for the righteous who are caught up, in various ways, in army life, especially in times of war. For them the advice of their clergy and chaplains is very necessary indeed. They are, as the war situation will readily reveal to them, in a situation that has very dim edges, and needs to be approached 'economically': doing the best one can in a situation, with an overall view to the greater good (clinging to the 'noble aim') that must exclude immoral means. As in the ancient times, when membership of the Roman army often meant martyrdom for the Christian, a righteous believer's requirement to follow military orders will more and more place them in situations where they will be forced to balance the morality of the order against their baptismal consecration. No righteous servant of God can ever be found assenting to war crimes, in any capacity, no matter how apparently 'venerable' the authority commanding them.

There are some voices in the church that would not assent to this, and which still hold to the concept of the 'virtue of war', pointing to the few examples of Orthodox soldier saints and warriors. My answer is that most of the soldier saints of the church went voluntarily to their deaths, as passion-bearers,[21] or martyrs; and some of them were actually martyred for refusing to obey their military superiors. Few indeed (if any) are those who died in the struggle as military heroes. But, freely admitting that there are those who go to war as the righteous, if they return as the righteous vindicators, their nobility has only been enhanced by their spiritual attitude of conquering not only an 'enemy', but the very chaos and wickedness they have been forced to be part of, all around them. It is precisely these great heroes whose virtue has been

407

tested, and proven true, who would be the first to teach us the wickedness of war, and the need for our leaders to be forced to keep to the path of truth and peace, not least by the refusal to indulge in clichés and lies. I myself learned these lessons from virtuous Christian warriors, my father, and my grandfather before him. They knew, from their bitter experience of war, that the advocacy of peace is Christ's path. His church ought to be at the forefront of it, forming the conscience of its own people and of nations beyond.

FREEDOM IN AN UNFREE WORLD

Orthodoxy knows much about the human tendency to absolutism. It has suffered from it profoundly during the course of the twentieth century. In recent times, large parts of the Orthodox world, most notably Russia and Romania, have been liberated from dull tyrannies and are on the brink of emerging with new-found confidence. The world will be waiting for their reflections on freedom with great attentiveness; though aware that a long endurance of tyranny is rarely the best preparation for the psychology of freedom. The leaders of the Orthodox world have also a deep investment in monastic practices of obedience and conformity. How they will speak to a world which urgently needs models of Christian freedom explained to it, so that it can avoid the extremes of totalitarianism and antinomian hedonism, is an important matter.[22]

Freedom is another of those things which are important but which are not entirely self-explanatory in the Orthodox tradition. The apostles and Fathers who spoke on the theme in the past usually did so from specific contexts that no longer apply. In addition there is something in the concept of freedom that is perennially elusive. Nevertheless, it is not only an extremely important issue for Christian civilization in the present (and future), but an issue that is of great spiritual significance for the health of the Orthodox community. Many commentators have highlighted, when discussing the day-to-day ethos of Orthodoxy, how much it values personal freedom, and how openly, with regard for individual choice, the structures of the church are organized in comparison, say, with Roman Catholic church laws, or Protestant ideas of religious polity and organization. Orthodox monasticism, compared to the ordered Benedictinism of the West, certainly appears to value individual freedoms much more highly. There is also a high premium laid on individual insight and personal choice in the elaboration of the sense of life-vocation in the Orthodox Church. At the same time, however, Orthodoxy is full of regulations; and the concept of obedience to church leaders is strongly inculcated. How do these things reconcile with one another? Is Orthodoxy a communion of the spiritually free? Or is it a church where authoritarian attitudes still loom large? To unweave the opposing images of freedom and control, that Orthodoxy often presents to the observer, one needs to go back to deep sources to understand the nature of religious liberty and responsibility; this is true now, in the aftermath of collapsing totalitarianism, and the struggle to fashion new democratic polities in eastern Europe, more than ever before.

Freedom is Christ's gift to his people. Those who are spiritually alive in him have a greater charism of freedom than those whose Christ-life is still relatively undeveloped. The latter have a greater need than the former of spiritual guidance, and the support of a community that will assist their processes of discernment; though we ought to remember, always, that 'one does not need to seek permission to do the good'. This is why Jesus, in the Gospel accounts, appears as so powerfully free a human being, bewildering all around him with his charism of freedom. Allied with this freedom is his majestic sense of purpose, or vocation. He was free to act because he knew what was required of him by the Father. Our own freedom only comes hand in hand with our admission into our sense of vocation in life. So many people, sadly, lack a developed personhood, because they are solipsistically deficient in regard to altruistic mission.

Similarly, St Paul manifested the apostolic charism very decisively in his own life when he insisted on his 'freedom'. He felt his mission to the gentiles was being hindered by the church leaders in Jerusalem who tried to insist on the circumcision of all Christians. Against them he wrote: 'The law of the Spirit of life in Christ Jesus has set me free from the law of sin and death.'[23] And: 'For freedom Christ has set us free; stand fast therefore, and do not submit again to a yoke of slavery.'[24] His vision of liberty in Christ was such that he saw the whole material creation sharing in the 'glorious freedom of the sons of God'.[25] For St Paul, the freedom sensed in the new life given by the Lord was subject only to that intrinsic invitation of Christ to all believers, to be servants of the other.[26] What the apostle manifests here, it seems to me, is that in the spiritual life there is a 'default' value of a tendency to freedom. When this is not operative it is a sign of lack of development. Christ wishes to illumine his faithful: to that extent he also wishes to set them free. The perfection of that freedom will not result in chaos or disorder, because of the love of service that marks the true disciple of the Saviour; but equally, his service does not produce timid conformists, but rather courageous martyrs, evangelists, and apostles.

St Maximos the Confessor theorized extensively about this question of the freedom of the individual conscience in his important distinction between natural will and gnomic will. Natural will was comparable to that which Adam had in the paradisal Garden, when he walked hand in hand with God and innocently and instinctively chose the good as an immortal being. Gnomic will occurred after the Fall. Gnomic will was a deducted choice. One could no longer, as a fallen creature, instinctively choose the divine, the right. One had to deduce it, and often even then had to force oneself to follow such a choice. Gnomic will was that principle of volition now rooted in every human being. In the person of the Lord, Maximos argued, there was no gnomic will, only natural will. He was always attuned to the divine, fully and completely. But he still truly worked through a human will: one that made all of Christ's human choices instinctively one with the divine will. Thus, although Jesus had two wills, one divine (as the Logos of God ruling the cosmos) and the human (manifested, for example, in the fearful decision in the Garden of Gethsemane to accept the cup of suffering) there was nevertheless a permanent and absolute unity: the Lord never for a moment deviated from the choice for good, because his human life was so radically in communion with the life of God. Maximos' powerful theological conclusion was that in this pattern the Incarnate Logos gave to humanity the potential for the redemption of will: the redefinition of human freedom as perfect communion with God. The ecumenical council of Constantinople III in 681 endorsed this theology of the will of Christ, and incidentally thus gave a further impetus to the notion of human freedom as a divine quality. It has not been much elaborated in modern theological thought but it is surely one of the most important implications of late patristic theology and philosophy.

409

What this means is that, in Orthodoxy, the will is seen as fundamentally graced with the charism of freedom. In Catholicism and Protestantism, following Augustine's more pessimistic premises, human will tends to be seen as more fundamentally broken and degenerate. Athanasios the Great describes the fallen human condition as a mirror clouded with verdigris.[27] The human soul does not function properly in reflecting the glory of God, because of rebellion and self-interest; but it is not utterly corrupted. The mirror needs cleaning[28] and the presence of Christ in the flesh, the life-giving principle of the incarnational grace, is that cleansing power. The essential functionality of the soul as the mirror of the image of God in the human life is not destroyed by sin, only disoriented. Since will, or volitionality, is the soul's primary function, the Fathers taught that its deep healing was part and parcel of Christ's gift of new life to the world.

The Greek patristic tradition, however, is fully in harmony with Augustine when it comes to the stress placed on the grace of God as necessary for the advancement into pure freedom. But it also insists that grace leads the will of the believer to take a step to the light, and that each step towards the service of God is met by God's generosity. The Lord, in Orthodox ascetical theology, is never to be outdone in generosity, and his gift of grace is not meant to be given to the soul as overriding motion to a passive paralytic, but so as to educate us into freedom and action. While Orthodoxy affirms the prevenience of God in all good, therefore, it distances itself from the terms of the Augustinian theology of grace by insisting that God's grace expects the increasing co-operation of the enlightened soul. Our co-operation with the grace of the Spirit is not independent of the gift of God, but this does not mean that God does not accept it as our gift of praise, as the very constituent energy of our Christ-life. Each time a believer moves towards the Christ-mind, the capacity for that *phronema* is increased within them. Freedom is that state when self-interest, and timidity in the face of doing right, can be more and more instinctively overcome for the pursuit of the good. The will of the saints is thus strengthened day by day, and the truth of the person is cumulatively manifested as the false ego falls before the image of Christ in the body of believers. This implies of course, that not only are we *not* free when we think we have the right to pure self-determination (whether or not that set of choices helps anyone outside our ego) but that we do not even enter our true self until we have learned to strip away the false ego of desire and the will to acquire.[29] The true self is the *phronema Christou*, our mystical assimilation to the Lord, which will be perfected only when our natural will is harmonized with his.

Truth quintessentially sets a person free: 'If the Son makes you free, then you shall indeed be free.'[30] It was this truth that Dostoevsky was meditating on when he penned his famous parable of the Grand Inquisitor in his *Brothers Karamazov*.[31] In the parable, told by Ivan to his brother Alyosha, the Cardinal Grand Inquisitor of Seville, having arrested Christ, who has returned among his people, accuses him of having led humanity to greater suffering by having encouraged them to develop their spiritual freedom. 'Instead of taking over men's freedom', Jesus has increased it, 'and forever burdened the kingdom of the human soul with its torments'. The Inquisitor contrasts this irresponsible sense of invitation to freedom with the controlled order that the medieval church, with its strict legislation (and inquisitions) has brought to society, to a humanity that, essentially, does not want to be free. Throughout the accusations (which mirror the three temptations of the Lord in the Gospel of Matthew[32]) Jesus remains silent. But at the end he stands up and kisses 'the aged and bloodless lips' of the Grand Inquisitor. He releases Jesus, warning him not to appear in public again, who then departs silently along the darkened streets. The parable is as powerful for what it does not say as for what it does. The narrator, Ivan, poses before his religious brother as an atheist, and at the end of his story asks him if he will accept or reject him now that he knows his position. Alyosha answers only with a kiss on his brother's lips, to which Ivan good-naturedly replies: 'But you are plagiarizing my poem!' The sense of how much the spiritual freedom of Christ costs is as much to the fore here as the temptation to seek to stifle it with regulations.

A NEW STATUS FOR WOMEN

Despite some ancient writers in the church who appear to have thought it,[33] women are not inferior to men; they are not 'vessels of defilement', and they are not defective parts of humanity. They are, and always have been, the substrate of the church on earth, its vital leaven, the most extensive class of believers above all others (even considering the marvellous apostolic efforts of the monastics) who have nurtured the faith across the centuries, training new generations in Christianity by leading them there in love and wonderment rather than by more formal paths of theology or academies. For St Paul one of the wonderful things about the new life brought in the process of the acceptance of the Gospel was the clattering fall of the ancient prejudices (race, slavery, class, and gender). He sums it up in an important challenge to the Christians of his day (one which still resounds to us): 'Anyone who is in Christ, is a new creation. The old has passed away. Look, for the New has come.'[34] And in terms of what that meant in particular for his own community he went on: 'For as many of you as were baptized into Christ have put on Christ. Now there is neither Jew nor Greek, there is neither slave nor free, there is neither male nor female; for you are all one in Christ Jesus.'[35] Old ways of thinking, where gender and power imbalances made women and slaves subject to masters, and where race differences were thought to make for distinctions of the elect and non-elect, are all left in ruins, despoiled by the Cross of Christ, as far as the apostle is concerned; not, of course, as far as the 'thinking of men' may be concerned, for it is an ongoing struggle to allow the prejudices of society to be reformed by the Gospel mentality, and often habituated practice is clung to when any justification for it is long past.

This word of the apostle is a macro-level reflection on the status of gender within the church. Those who point to other apostolic ordinances that seem to contradict this fundamental reflection on the effect of the Resurrection on the world[36] often do not seem to appreciate how 'economic' those latter texts are compared to the fundamental character of the earlier apostolic call for new orientation. In 1 Corinthians and in 1 Timothy the ordinances given for women not to teach, to be subservient to their husbands, and to find their salvation in childbearing, are economically positioned within the context of Hellenistic churches where women were almost invariably uneducated. It is a significant falsification of the exegesis of sacred texts when they are read (without an eye to their function) as permanent archetypes instead of temporary rules of discipline, something which is certainly at issue in these loci.

St Gregory the Theologian explicitly criticized the thinking of those who appealed to 1 Timothy to argue that women disciples must always be subordinate 'because Eve

411

sinned before Adam'. He made a caustic comment on those in the fourth century who were using this text to justify a heavier canonical penalty on erring women than on erring men. Why, he asks, does the law of Christian Romans punish the female adulteress with severe penalties, but a man who commits adultery has no penalty under the law? Obviously, the law was made by men, St Gregory says, and he goes on: 'I do not accept this law. I cannot approve this custom. Such a law cannot reflect the God who is equitably even-handed to all.'[37] What possible justification could be brought forward for this uneven treatment of women in a Christian context of legislation?, he asks his audience. St Gregory raises some of the arguments he has heard advanced. Is woman not the cause of the Fall? Well, he replies, Eve sinned, but Adam did no better, and have such thinkers not considered that Christ redeemed both Adam and Eve since those days, so how can such texts apply as paradigms of Christian behaviour? But, is not Christ honoured primarily as a male, that is, one coming 'from the seed of David'? Certainly, Gregory says, this is a title of Christ, but it celebrates his ancestry purely from his mother's side, no male was involved. In contrast to all these weak biblical citations, the Theologian argues, one ought to consider the apostolic revelation that the husband in a marriage ought to reverence his wife as he would reverence Christ himself. It is only the woman who is called the icon of the Word of God in this case.[38] In such arguments St Gregory foresaw, and rebuked, those who would try to defend unequal treatment by a fundamentalist, decontextualized mis-reading of sacred texts. There are many who advance the old disciplinary texts, such as those in 1 Timothy 2.11–15, to oppose the reality of the great advancement of women disciples, even presenting the Orthodox Church as 'closed' to any concept of women's leadership. Some even seem to love to search the ancient canons to find and elevate any archaic rule that serves to restrict women's freedom in church. At the same time they are often very ready to apply every 'economy' of the Scriptures and the old canons to themselves, for their own advantage.

Choosing to find innumerable inconvenient canons 'obsolete', but canons that restrict women to be 'perennial', they stand in the same place as those whom St Basil also rebuked as elevating proof texts from the Fathers to justify indefensible positions on war and violence. In his thirty-seventh Oration, St Gregory argued powerfully that, when it comes to any important discussion of theological principle in the church, the wider context of Christ's mercy can be the only context in which new ideas are debated his hierarchical perception, courage, and leadership, remain a model for Orthodoxy today faced with its new environments.

Contextual interpretation is very important here, and it is an area where fundamentalist obscurantism can be not only deceptive, but very damaging. For women disciples, the Christian past is a difficult territory; for in the past women were largely 'transparent' to history. They were not the educated class that created and disseminated literature, and so did not have an impact on the Hellenistic patterns of thinking that were the overwhelming context of early Christian thought about women and their role in the family and society. In that intellectual universe women were of the 'private' domain, while men were of the 'public' domain. The home, and domestic interiority, were seen as 'female' by the ancient Greek mind, and the open space of the *agora*, together with association in public, and 'discourse' (*logos*), was seen as a male phenomenon. Textuality was thus part of the male domain, and textuality, of course, became the primary historical record. It is clear enough that wealthy women in antiquity were educated, and textual; but it was never a common thing then for women to be educated, at least not in the higher levels of a rhetorical school in one of the great cities. This leads inevitably to the great problem of the 'textual invisibility' of women in the records of Graeco-Roman society, and especially in the annals of Christianity in the early period. Women are spoken of, extensively so, but always from the male perspective. The stage dramas of ancient Greek literature summarize the problem exactly: the characters who present the views of women are using words entirely supplied to them by male authors, for the exclusive benefit of male viewers, and are themselves (as the law required) male actors impersonating females.

In the early church, women were disadvantaged by this ubiquitous Greek invisibility. Women were married young, in their mid teens, to considerably older men, who enjoyed extensive authority over them, socially as well as financially. Their families made the decision of marriage for them, and with a life ahead of childbirth and domestic labour, without sophisticated medicines, the death rate was high. It would not be unusual for a woman to be regarded as being in advanced old age by her late forties. As women played no great part in the formation of the great patristic textual tradition (being closed out of the major leadership offices of bishop and priest in antiquity, and those who served as deaconesses being predominantly ascetics) they have largely been passed over in secular as well as church history, up to the present century. In fact, many of those same conditions disadvantaging women have endured up to the present in many less developed societies across the world. In many parts of the world even today, women are the dominant force in progressive economies, but have little access to the corridors of power. In the majority world, women still have to struggle to access educational and labour resources. But in the West the situation has changed dramatically. In educational environments, especially the humanities, women students are now beginning to outnumber men. In future generations their impact in every sphere will be increasingly marked: and that will include the life of the church, where they will begin, ever more visibly, to feature as Christian teachers, theologians, and community leaders.

The mid to late twentieth century has already witnessed a remarkable flowering of women's studies, not least in the domain of early church life. The significant presence of women apostles in the earliest generations of Christianity has been reclaimed for the record by many notable biblical scholars,[39] and decades of scholarship by skilled women patristic theologians and historians of late antiquity has only recently begun to make a mark, excavating the dust of the 'Greek silence', to reveal a fuller picture of the impact women had on early Christianity from the post-biblical age to the early Middle Ages.[40] As a result of that pioneering work, it has become clear that asceticism was used by many early Christian women as a channel for self-development that allowed them new vistas of opportunity.[41] To many moderns, the path of virginity might look like a narrowing of prospects, but the liberation from the ancient contexts of marriage, and the capacity to determine one's own financial and social identity, were nurtured imaginatively by important female ascetics in the church, several of whom were also respected teachers[42] and deaconesses, such as the Ammas: Macrina, Syncletica, Melania, and Olympias. But it is a contemporary Orthodox woman theologian who has one of the best of all synopses of the patristic understanding of gender: 'In the image of its creator, humanity is one in the distinction of persons, at the same time equal in dignity and yet ineffably different, capable of communicating, called to

413

commune with respect to the otherness of the other person, the mysterious, indescribable, inexplicable otherness, coloured by sex but not reducible to sexual difference.'[43]

The extraordinary flowering of Christian women's intellectual, social, and apostolic life, because of the new opportunities that contemporary society has opened up in many parts of the more developed world, is something wonderful to which the Orthodox Church must pay increasing attention. Now is the generation within Orthodoxy which must witness and develop this dialogue. We have already seen, when discussing the female diaconate, that this is an ordained ministry that has been 'withdrawn' from the wider Orthodox experience for the last 800 years. The reasons for the lapsing of the order are obscure, but are related to the ever-increasing monasticization of the Eastern Church in a time when it was suffering from political decline. In the present era when the church is enjoying a New Spring, and at a time when women's educational qualification has never been so advanced, and the range of skills they can bring to the service of the church is inestimable, it is surely time to advance the reinstitution of a canonically ordained female diaconate as an important and timely symbol.

Chiefly important in this discussion of new possibilities and potentials will be the voice of women faithful of the Orthodox Church themselves – young women and old, the single, mothers, and monastics – all of whom will bring their own rich experience of Orthodox Christian life to illuminate the issue of discussing the future role of women in Orthodox pastoral, liturgical, and apostolic avenues. The dialogue has already started, not least with a significant gathering of women Orthodox theologians at the Romanian convent of Agapia (1976), where important topics were broached. This was followed by meetings of Orthodox women theologians at the inter-Orthodox consultation on Rhodes (1988),[44] at Crete (1989), at Damascus (1996), and at Constantinople (1997).[45] The Rhodes meeting issued a communiqué which spells out the programme for the future, as well as the problem:

> Owing to human weakness and sinfulness, Christian communities have not always and in all places been able to suppress effectively ideas, manners and customs, historical developments and social conditions which have resulted in practical discrimination against women.[46]

For some, the widespread allusion to Levitical rules about blood and ritual cleanness in regard to Orthodox women and liturgical presence has become just such a sign of the inability in some quarters to distinguish between outmoded and defective 'traditions' in Orthodoxy and the Orthodox tradition itself, wherein the Spirit of God breathes grace and renewal at every instance.

When Levitical cleanliness traditions were first mentioned in relation to Christian liturgical laws they were rejected as hostile to the Gospel spirit.[47] Afterwards they crept in to church practice.[48] To regard Leviticus now as a guide to Gospel reflections is a very odd way to proceed, to say the least. We ought to follow, rather, the urging of St Gregory the Theologian, that we must not work from micro-arguments to macro-principles, but from archetypal truths to economic occasions to manifest them. Such canons that seem to enshrine[49] a view of woman as defiled or defiling, based on Levitical, or Hellenistic misogynistic, notions of women's 'impurity' fade away before the power of the Risen Lord who has brought a new life of liberty equally to his sons and daughters in the church. Other 'traditions' that are not essential to the holy tradition, such as the practice of the priest taking a newly baptized infant boy into and around the altar, but only taking an infant girl up to the royal doors, have also reached a state where they now speak a contradictory symbolic message to Orthodox parents (whatever truth they were once intended to depict) and now must surely be revised to reaffirm the sacred equality of all the baptized: 'For *as many as have been baptized* into Christ, have put on Christ.'[50]

This is a controversial area of dialogue for contemporary Orthodox. Some of the voices of Orthodoxy in eastern Europe (wrongly) think that it is solely a matter of interest for the Orthodox of the affluent West, who are under the influence of Protestant forms of feminism. The theologian Elizabeth Behr-Sigel has spoken extensively about the need to learn 'to speak the truth in love'[51] among the various families of Orthodoxy; not all of whom are at 'the same place', and cannot always be presumed to share the same cultural contexts, even when there is a unity of faith and a common spirit. This is bound to be an area of considerable difficulty, given that Orthodoxy is led at the highest level by monastic hierarchs, whose upbringing and training have, to a large degree, inevitably separated them from womankind. This is exactly why it calls for courage and openness of heart to be able to listen to one another in love, and why the informed voice of Orthodox women theologians and ascetics is all the more important in this present generation and the next.[52]

BIOLOGICAL AND OTHER NEW ETHICAL ENVIRONMENTS

From ancient times the Orthodox Church has had a care for the physical welfare of its people, and was one of the great forces in the ancient world that instigated and inspired the formation of a society-wide system of health care. The monastics of the Eastern Church are the first examples of Christians who organized hospitals, leprosaria, orphanages, and old people's homes.[53] St Gregory of Nazianzus' Oration 14, *For the Poor*, was one of the first times that a major Greek rhetorician laid it out to his society that the strong had a duty to help the poor precisely because they were the poor. Before that time, the concept of a duty of assistance to the suffering sick was regarded as ridiculous. Those whom the gods had cursed deserved their fate. St Gregory, by insisting that the icon of God is in the soul of each person, and is not dimmed or taken away because a person suffers, gave to the world a powerful articulation of a Christian philosophy of philanthropy. Since his time the church has been in the vanguard of the systematic advancement of care systems. In recent generations the Orthodox world has not been able to sustain this mission as clearly or evidently in some parts of its territories as it once did in the times of the Christian empire. In several places recently, not least Soviet Russia, the clergy were explicitly forbidden by state law from having any involvement with the hospital system, and in the long years of Ottoman oppression it was very difficult to sustain the necessary resources for these labours of charity.

In more recent times the state system of developed countries has taken it upon itself, more and more, to deliver supportive welfare for its citizens (a philosophy it learned from the Christian culture that underpinned it), and there has even been a certain corresponding sense that social welfare systems are a secular phenomenon.

Nevertheless, the church remains committed to the work of the care of the sick, the orphan, and the aged, as something that is central to its mission of mercy, and its witness to the Kingdom of God. It can fulfil this task in collaboration with all people, or agencies, of good will; or it can operate on its own initiative, according to the most suitable circumstances.

The present age has seen astounding advances in medical science. Biotechnology has revolutionized the whole provision of health care today. It has brought with it a new range of medical-ethical problems too, as issues are now being considered that could not possibly have applied in any other age. Orthodoxy has a deep and rich set of ethical reflections and guidelines, some of which are contained in the patristic pastoral writings, and some of which are synopsized in the ancient canons which give bishops guidance as to how to assess ethical disciplinary cases. In each case the Orthodox Church proceeds from fundamental principles of the observance of the Gospel commands, and understands ethics to be the practical manner in which a Christian applies those principles in day-to-day life.[54] In matters of controversial decision, the Orthodox accept the spiritual guidance of the bishop as an instance of his high-priestly charism to teach and lead the local church. In significant ethical matters affecting society as a whole (such as new legislation that has a bearing on ethical choices) the bishops synodically gather to offer a collective teaching in unanimity for the guidance of the church.

Orthodoxy's overriding principle, or ethical 'compass setting', is an ethic of love that celebrates human life and dignity and resists, in this age as in every prior age, the forces of secular humanism that regard man as the measure and master of his own destiny. Orthodoxy sees a human life as God-endowed in every stage of its being: from conception to death, and beyond death. The protection of the rights of the unborn and the dying are high on the agenda of Orthodox ethics, especially in the present era when they seem to be so low on the agenda of so many others. Both abortion and euthanasia are seen as great offences against the divine order. Both positions are taken by the church for the same reason: that the human being is the icon of God. In life and in death, his redeemed and consecrated saints are sacred and under his direct providence as concerns the time of their appearance in history (conception and birth) and their departure from earthly history (their summons before God). For a human being to intervene negatively in the life process and set a term to what God has reserved for himself is seen as a great sacrilege; and the belief that any human being has the right to terminate the life of another, is seen as hubris, and a sin. Bioethical issues of medical fertility assistance are generally seen by Orthodoxy as blessed extensions of God's creative care for his people, except where these scientific outreaches have their feet planted in death (the use of aborted cell tissue, for example).

The end of life is an area where some have argued, generally out of good-hearted motives, that the poor quality of life or the issues of excessive pain argue that euthanasia is the proper course as a 'mercy killing'. But the arguments over pain are paradoxical in an age when pain control has reached its highest efficiency in human history. Orthodoxy does not regard the endless quest to keep life sustained in a failing body (another factor that has not appeared in previous generations) as a particularly good end. It believes that the constant 'prolongation' of life in hospital environments can be a cause of suffering in and of itself. Failing health and great sickness may be a sign that we need more of the healing arts than before. Equally they may be a sign that

416

God is sending the message to an individual that it is time to come home. Orthodox believers struggle to acquire the wisdom to know the difference. If one still lacks the spiritual wisdom and courage to face death in advanced age, it is necessary to rely on a supportive spiritual community to provide the enveloping sense of prayer, wise counselling, and loving encouragement, to help the aged and dying discern this important part of life-learning under the eyes of God.

Each one of us, from the moment that we are born, is in the process of travelling to God through the gate of death. To be surprised by this at the end is a testimony to the degree of illusion we have allowed to master the human consciousness. But death aversion is the philosophy of the age. No one washes their dead any more in Western cultures. No one in the family digs graves any more, and few physically throw dirt over their loved ones, and the result is a great naivety, or a deeply irreligious fear, on the subject of death and dying.

By contrast, the Orthodox funeral service leaves the lid of the coffin open as the person is buried, and the worshippers come into the church to give the 'farewell kiss'. The relentless flight from death seems, to the Orthodox, part of modern humanity's spiritual sickness, and a desire to flee the face of God by pretending to one's fragile consciousness that one is an immortal god: an illusion doomed to disappointment. Orthodoxy does not, therefore, expect that medicine should be used to prolong life at any cost, 'beyond the normal expectation', an issue that is decided by the person in question or, if incapacitated, by their loved ones. It is important therefore, that these end-of-life issues should have been talked about in the family, and that the subject of death should not have been avoided as a taboo. In complex cases of medical ethics the guidance of the priest, as well as his pastoral support, is always close at hand; and if he does not have an immediate answer he refers to the guidance of the bishop who, in the Orthodox Church, always remains closely involved in the pastoral care of his people.

At the other end of the life-scale are equally pressing problems facing the church in the contemporary world. Abortion has, in some countries of recent times, been used almost as a contraceptive method of choice. This is a failing of great proportions for our human generation, and witnesses (if one takes a distant perspective) a strange loathing of the self and the race that underlies such an extensive rejection by a species of its own progeny. Some Protestant Christian groups have argued recently that abortion is a morally acceptable thing, necessary for the cause of the advancement of the rights of womankind. Orthodoxy regards this as specious reasoning. The right of the unborn to life is one of the main areas in which the church is called upon to defend the rights of the poor and the defenceless against the predations of the powerful. In doing so in the case of abortion, however, the church has to recognize that in many cases (certainly not all) the motive to seek abortion comes from the poor themselves in the face of a feeling of being overwhelmed in their poverty.

The Orthodox defence of the rights of the unborn, therefore, has to advance hand in hand with the advocacy of liberational, educational, and support programmes for those whose lives are a constant struggle. Today many abortions take place outside the context of marriage or a loving home. To ground its ethics and compassion in the soil of reality, the Orthodox Church increasingly has to take the initiative to institute systems of support (moral as well as financial and physical) for those who are pressed towards an option of abortion after they have made personal and relational mistakes. Such an elaboration of church-sponsored systems of care is an important element of

Orthodoxy's ethic of life and needs to be advanced more systematically at every parish, as well as national ecclesial, level.

The child, in Orthodox theology, is not the property of the parents. It is given to the parents by God so that they can 'learn to be as a god' for it in its time of need, and so fulfil their destined *mimesis* of the love of the Father over the cosmos. The rejection of the child, deliberately, from the womb is a dereliction of that invitation from God, and a great sacrilege committed against the sacredness of a new life sent into this world. Orthodoxy utterly rejects those who claim, in the name of Christianity, that there is divided opinion on the 'real humanity' of the foetus within Christian tradition. From antiquity the voice of the church has been expressed unanimously in its saints and Fathers that abortion is a great sacrilege. Yet, because it is an area that few human consciences approach easily, or without deep (and often heart-wrenching) regret afterwards, the Orthodox Church also does not stand in condemnation over individual women who have sought out abortions. Orthodoxy condemns the philosophy and practice root and branch. It condemns those who advocate and broker abortion as a business or as a 'positive social value', holding them (if they are Orthodox Christian) as excommunicate. Those who are outside its communion who systematically advocate the normality, or rightness, of abortion (especially under alleged evangelical terms) it resists as having lost a fundamental spiritual connection with the springs of Christian ethical consciousness. For individual believers who have undergone terminations, however, the Orthodox Church does not have words of condemnation on a personal level, but tries to offer consolation and reconciliation. It calls them back compassionately to communion after repentance (since abortion excludes any Orthodox believer from admission to the mystery of the Eucharist).

Several Orthodox churches have special services of prayer for the reconciliation and comforting of believers who have been led astray and had abortions in circumstances that overwhelmed them; for God's mercy heals and restores in every circumstance, and human fallibility can never dim the radiance of God's 'remaking of all things new'.[55] The mystery of *metanoia* has been the path towards healing of many mothers who have themselves been deeply wounded by the event, the mistake, of abortion. There is at present a short service of prayers for Orthodox mothers who have lost children, to which the Romanian episcopate in America has added a pastorally sensitive separate service of reconciliation and consolation for mothers who have lost their children through abortion. The Orthodox believe that, as always, the correct procedure among Christians is to be adamant on what is right and wrong, and to declare it; yet also for the church to be immensely compassionate towards those who (for the multitude of different circumstances that afflict us all) are not always able to preserve the true standard in their lives.

Some Orthodox ethicists have reflected recently on the very new scientific knowledge available to us from the advances in cell research, and have concluded that the process of life itself cannot be said to have begun formally until the splitting of the female egg into a syzygy;[56] an event which takes place only a day or so after fertilization following on sexual intercourse. This being the case they have concluded that the immediate 'stopping' of the process of the development of the syzygy is not an equivalent to abortion, but a final and extraordinary stage of contraception. Heavy doses of oestrogen taken at this time will cause the womb to reject the egg. Orthodox theologians who have recently made this distinction, have advanced the argument, thinking especially of the aftermath of cases of rape, incest, and sexual violence against minors, and that in such cases the so-called 'morning-after pill' would not be intrinsically and inalienably wrong. After the stage of the syzygy, however, it is arbitrary to make any distinction in the overall life-process that will lead the human foetus (in God's normal providence) into the fullness of human life, and interruption of its development is not in the same category at all, but has passed from contraception to being abortion proper.

In the contemporary ethical environment of massively secularized Western societies, one that is reverting rapidly to a pagan consciousness, the church recognizes it has a difficult role: to stand firm for the great truths it has been delivered, while offering consolation for believers who have been led adrift by the false ethical and theological environments all around them. This is why the church advocates regular immersion in the divine liturgy, the spiritual life, and the reception of the mysteries, and an ongoing education in Christian culture, as necessary for an active and effective life as a Christian today. Once, a deeply formed Christian society provided these contextual supports at every corner; now it is to be generally presumed that the societal 'mind' is more likely to be that of the hostile powers than that of the Lord who loves and fosters life. Ordinary Christians are called to extraordinary levels of reflection in this day and age, just in the task of staying faithful.

Issues related to genetic engineering also raise new ethical questions that are still the subject of widespread discussion, within and outside church circles. Orthodoxy does not stand opposed to any of these new developments in principle, and rejoices in the advances made for the betterment of human life on earth, as a sign of the blessing of God on the labours of so many dedicated scientists. It insists, however, that all these advances should be discussed philosophically and ethically (not merely scientifically) to understand whether they really do represent progress for the benefit of the race, and on what terms. The use of stem cells taken from the aborted foetus is simply a case of a wicked means applied to a good end, that cannot be used to justify the result. Approaching stem cells as if they were a commodity encourages (and indeed springs from) the widespread attitude, in a consciousness alien to Christ, that human life is cheap and mechanical, and can be moved around in a body-parts mentality under the direction of medical high priests who often regard religious issues as merely medieval mumbo-jumbo. Stem cell research can be conducted from cells present in the placental remains: a blessed and deeply symbolic way of approaching a source of new healing; and one that avoids covering it with the mantle of sacrilege from its outset. Medical innovations, critical for the religious and cultural health of a society, not merely for its physical well-being, must be considered and arbitrated by a wider and deeper range of authoritative voices than solely doctors or hospital administrators. Whether they wish to or not, governments cannot shuffle out of their moral responsibilities in these critical areas, or pretend that they can be resolved by appeal to a political 'consensus' when the very problem consists in the creation of an informed conscience. In that ongoing debate it is going to be of more and more importance to have Orthodox bishops and theologians skilled in these matters who will contribute their voices persuasively.

The many new environments that modern science presents raise multitudes of other ethical questions. Orthodoxy has not faced many of those questions before; but it is not bamboozled, or rendered dumb and anxious in the face of what response it may have

419

to make. Those who are immersed in the Gospel of Christ are soon formed into the *phronema Christou*, and having this mind of the Lord can see how all complexities, sorrows, problems, and joys in life can be woven into a pattern of obedience to the Saviour. Where we refuse to admit obedience to the Lord into life we make for ourselves, unerringly, greater sorrows and deeper troubles; but in such cases all the Orthodox know that there is a road always open to us, however dark our self-made cul-de-sacs have become, and that is the road of *metanoia*. *Metanoia* is the admission in honesty that we have gone astray from the communion of Christ and his church, and an honest admission that we need the Lord's restoration. For those who accept this *metanoia*, Christ's forgiveness is found to be more ready and generous than anything else in this world.

SEXUAL ETHICS AND PASTORAL CARE

Orthodoxy understands sexuality to be a God-given power that develops and deepens human communion by spiritual and physical love, and the mutual opening out to the other that intimacy fosters. The sexual drive of attraction to intimacy naturally moves in a more complex cycle, as a process of mutating that communion of two persons outwards from spiritual union, to biological diversification, the 'openness' to new life that develops the double bond of the lovers into the extended bond of a new family. For these reasons, and representing both aspects in its dimensions (communion and creativity), human sexuality is understood by Orthodoxy to be God-blessed when it is within the context of deep mutual love and open to the transmission of new life. In other words the church understands human sexuality to be raised to the standard of divine blessing in the context of marriage. Sexual love is given by God to the world as a Creation blessing. It is something beyond and outside the Church of Christ; but the Orthodox understand it in a new way, for it is a universal blessing on the race which has been taken to a new and wonderful level by the grace of Christ that fulfilled its ancient aspirations for communion, and refashioned it as one of the ways that the saints have to discover spiritual communion. In Christ, sexuality can be transfigured to the level of sacramental communion. This is the blessing that is spoken of and celebrated in the Orthodox Church's wonderfully joyous wedding service. It is this fire of love that the Orthodox Church looks to with wonderment as a standard of sanctification for the majority of its believers on earth.

Some of the faithful find their sexual joy and fulfilment in the difficult path of chaste celibacy, undertaken with gladness in the cause of serving the Lord in the monastic life. Sexual identity in the case of celibates is refined and shared as gracious mutual affection. Through the strict disciplining of erotic physical desire, the innate sexual powers are directed towards the intensification of a life that is emotionally stabilized in Christ; a life of prayer, self-denial, and the drive to communion with others in an altruistic missionary sense. For most Christians, however, the natural sexual drives lead a person through a growing experience of maturation, and ever-growing complexity of patterns of external relationship: from the self-referential desires for satisfaction of infantilism, through the years of learning to be aware of the needs of others in adolescence, to the growing conceptualization of the fulfilment of self-identity in communion with another in emotional and spiritual maturity. The sexual drive naturally propels human beings along this spiritual path of ascent. It is, however, a very powerful drive, and can as easily propel the human experience into addictive and unhappy behaviours as it can lead it to the transcendent fulfilment of love.

One of the common lies of the modern era is that everyone everywhere is having glorious sexual experiences devoid of the last vestiges of Christian sex-hating Puritanism. Almost any magazine sells this illusion of sex. Statistics show a more worrying side of the reality, however: that male fertility in the species has been steadily declining by large percentages over the last fifty years. We may think this is not so significant, given the fears we have of a world population explosion, but it is important to remember that humans, like gorillas, pandas, and elephants, are a species that has relatively great difficulty in reproduction, and a small imbalance in fertility rates can lead to precipitately bad results very quickly. At a time when the media suggest sexual liberation has brought unrestricted sexual freedoms and happiness, the reality is that the sexual life is a source of deep unease for many human beings. For many it has become a life-threatening terror. For many others, caught up in the commercial exploitation of our insatiable human curiosity, it has led to lives blighted by exploitation.

The reason sexuality can become a problem (that is, become a source of dissonance within the human being rather than a force of joy and wholeness) is that humans are meant to experience sexuality in a way very different from any other animal on the face of the earth. Human sexuality begins in the procreative process common to all biological species, but ends (because humankind is in the image of God) in a mystery of love and spiritual fulfilment. If sexuality is divorced from the rhythms inherent in this spiritual path it does not offer a road of blissful enjoyment of pleasure; on the contrary it offers a stony track to dissatisfaction and alienation from the roots of our being. The problem is, of course, that it is an urgent loud voice sounding in one's ears after the age of puberty, and in contemporary society where unethical media are often the most available voices of guidance, it is now often the case that young men and women first learn about sexual identity from the least qualified, most dubious, sources. The fundamental spiritual law in Christ's Church, relating to any approach to sexuality, is that the believer allows the Lord to enter in and transfigure the sexual power, from being merely an innate biological drive into becoming a vehicle for love, and ultimately a vehicle for spiritual communion.

The learning involved in sexual ethics is a learning that is truly embodied. One needs a context: supportive and wise voices, and powerful role models. In an age such as this, and in an ecclesiastical environment where the topic is too often avoided like a taboo, it is difficult to find a context where human sexual development can be properly and powerfully harmonized with the path of spiritual development; where sexual joy and chastity can be discussed as two concomitant spiritual powers that need harmony in any balanced life, let alone the higher mysteries of the Christ-life. This call to give guidance is one of the highest 'priestly' tasks of the married couple in the family home. This important educational process in ways of living is a testament to the spiritual maturity and common love of Christians living together. It is a process that cannot be left to school or state, or adolescent peer group. The Orthodox Church, knowing how significant it is to learn, and re-learn, sexual ethics as one grows and changes life condition, encourages all the faithful to have a spiritual guide, a *starets* or *starissa*, or at least a priestly confessor, who can be relied on to be a wise and safe guide. Parents should be involved in helping the young to choose such a spiritual counsellor carefully, one who will often be a mature Christian of their own gender, since the role of spiritual father or mother is not restricted to the clergy. The guide can offer a powerful support and encouraging counsel for matters that the adolescent believer may not wish to discuss with their parents. These soul-guides, as the ancient Irish Church used to call them, are very important resources for the Orthodox of all ages as they navigate the realities of their ethical lives, especially in matters relating to sexual behaviour.

Chastity within marriage is an ongoing aspect of the chastity expected of all believers while single, except that it takes a different form from celibate chastity. In an Orthodox marriage the chastity of the couple is the manner in which their sexual powers are constantly nurtured in reference to one another, and for the purpose of sustaining the flame of mutual interest and delight across the years of living together. Such marital chastity excludes all others in order to include all others within the greater power of the stable bond of love such exclusivity produces. This type of chastity is not simply a matter of 'not' committing adultery or extramarital flirtation, a negative set of injunctions; rather, it is a spiritual attitude that feeds from the bodily and spiritual delights of sharing an intimate life with a beloved person. Sadly, little has been written on this beautiful song of love from within the church, mainly because the vast majority of Christian authors and poets throughout history have been single ascetics. But the song of Christian lovers is a hymn to the glory of God that delights even the angels. But when sexual delight in the other fails, it is often a symptom that many other levels of delight (both spiritual and physical) have also begun to fail. Men and women can learn to love again; but the catastrophic level of the collapse of marriages in the twenty-first century suggests that it is a widespread spiritual problem that causes untold levels of suffering. On the other hand, when a God-blessed Christian marriage shines in a darkening world, it offers an ineffable witness of how human affection can be taken to ever new heights by Christ, sustained across the years in an unfailing spring, and bringing the couple and countless others, rejoicing, into the very Kingdom of God.

The church's pastoral care attempts to give the deepest level of sympathetic support and encouragement to Christian families. Every effort should be undertaken by the clergy to help married couples in difficulties; but if a marriage falters and falls, the Orthodox Church extends compassionate care to find the best solution in what St Gregory the Theologian once called 'the sea of human sorrows'. Up to three marriages, sacramentally solemnized, are permitted by the Orthodox Church, though it always teaches and propagates that the ideal view, and the perfect fulfilment of the Christian ideal for the sexual bond, is a single marriage lived out in the joy of Christ.

It would be naive to suggest, however, that, even within the Church of Christ, all believers are either virginally celibate or chastely married. There are many, both married and single, whose sexual relations are ecclesiastically 'irregular' in the sense that they are unable to live stably in accordance with the church's prescripts on sexual behaviour. The majority in secular society may reject any concept of the church having any right to suggest 'rules' for personal behaviour, sexual or otherwise; a context of societal life that is once more very much like the ethos of ancient paganism that surrounded the church in its earliest centuries when it first drew up rules for guiding the sexual lives of believers. The discipline of the Orthodox Church, however, provides for a regular pattern of 'striving and repentance' through its sacraments of *metanoia* and Eucharist. Living penitently is not, in the Orthodox conception, a miserable psychic life of self-loathing for endless failures, but rather a peaceful and joyful attitude of honesty before a gentle God who at one and the same moment calls out to the disciple to transcend, yet offers immense healing for our inability or unwillingness to respond.

The canonical discipline of the church does not mean that all who are not living up to its standards are required to withdraw from the church. The church is not a hothouse of exotic virtuous blooms, but a refuge for sinners who wish to become more faithful to Christ day by day, and year by year. There is no other kind of Christian than this. Nor does it mean that the Holy Eucharist is only for the utterly pious, or should be restricted to pre-adolescent children or old folk. If so, the greatest power of renovation for sinners on the course of our pilgrimage would have been removed from us all. It means, rather, that each Orthodox Christian must approach the Eucharist with joy, but penitently, submitting their lives to the blessing, as well as the judgement, of our merciful God, and dedicating himself or herself to the ongoing attempt to attain a higher standard of discipleship than they know themselves to be in at the present moment. God sees the effort; God sees the heart. His grace remedies all our failings and incapacities most wonderfully and most mercifully. In short, Christian life in general is a matter of endlessly repeated efforts for the ideal, and a willingness to admit error and aim for a higher standard under the aegis of a Lord whose compassion is great.

And yet it is important not to allow delusions to enter the Christian life, and also to avoid the equally destructive problem of guilt arising from the vanity of not being able to claim a perfection of Christian fidelity at any given time in life. Christ's disciples, in all times, are those who know how to turn again to the Lord in regular and trusting *metanoia*, rather than those who pride themselves on never having fallen at all. Single Christian life is a difficult path, especially in a world where virginity is commonly ridiculed, and chastity is regarded as mentally unbalanced. It is a labour of asceticism, and the church encourages all believers to the form of chastity appropriate to their life condition, while at the same time offering its consolation and reconciliation for those who fall from the standard.

There are also some Christians whose mature sexuality does not demonstrate any heterosexual drive towards marriage. When the Orthodox Church affirms its ancient and unbroken teaching that all God-blessed sexual relationships should take place within heterosexual marriage, considering all other forms of sexual liaison as canonically irregular, and as lapses from the standard of God-blessed creative communion, such men and women feel bereft by this teaching, and are often dismayed that their deepest sexual affinities find no resonance within it. In ancient times almost all the ethical reflection that the church conducted on the subject of homosexuality was based on the premise that such men and women freely elected their sexual preference, and grounded, or established, themselves within it as life developed, by force of habituation. That view no longer commands the universal agreement of scholars as it once did when the church drew up its canonical discipline and advice on this subject. Scientific studies now suggest that as many as one in ten human beings may find themselves in this life condition. Christians among them have often grown up from early school years ridiculed, isolated, persecuted for their difference, because of deep-seated instincts they have not chosen and are often unable to comprehend. The Orthodox Church is drawn, in the imitation of the Christ, to offer consolation and grace to all the children of God on their pilgrimage to the Kingdom, and finds homophobia and all forms of prejudice, verbal or otherwise, to run counter to the charity and purposes of the Lord.

Such Christians may not feel called to monasticism or to marriage, and yet do not wish to face the world alone. Although they can often be tempted to desolation, and feelings of hopelessness, they are the children of a merciful God who will not abandon them. Their affective development and their path towards security of affection within the world and to stable relationships with supportive friends is a matter of great care and concern to the Lord, and ought to be also to the wider church community. The Orthodox Church believes that it is especially appropriate for them to have the regular help and advice, the consolation and encouragement, of a spiritual father or mother, to whom they can open their heart, and hear in return words of grace. The deepening of friendship, affection, and love between Christ's saints, and its transcendent unfolding into bonds of a depth that surpass what the world can imagine, is a gift to all believers. Such a mystery of love is not a prerogative of the married only, for: 'When Christ dwells in our hearts we are rooted and grounded in love.'[57]

Among all the believers there are many who, in the course of their life's journey, may find themselves in an ecclesiastically irregular position because of the power of the human sexual drive. While Orthodoxy may condemn the sin, it does not condemn the sinner, and tries never to lose sight of the overwhelming good news of Christ's mercy which, through the infinite turns and byways of human life, psychology, and action, draws the soul that loves the Lord always onward to the safe harbour of his compassion. The church is their home, and remains so always. All Orthodox Christians, wherever they are and in whatever condition they find themselves, struggle daily with the ascetic task of integrating their sexual drive into the pattern of discipleship and the values of the Kingdom of God. But the same is true of the need to integrate the relentless will to acquire, or the insatiable will for power. Poverty, Chastity, and Obedience have always been a significantly related triad in Christian spirituality. It is a life-long calling and process, not something that any person can think they have 'solved' at any stage. The obedient disciple, whatever life condition he or she finds themselves in, is called to transcendence. Such is the unalterable rule of the spiritual life. Doing the best one can, in the circumstances one has, is the simple beginning of that path for everyone. Those who have set their compass on Christ will never ultimately be set adrift, however great the difficulties that life sets along the way: whether in the pulse of the body, the heart's aching core, or the conflicting of our brightest dreams and hopes for human intimacy. Christ's love does not scorn, or turn out, or crush down. The church, following its merciful Master, always holds up to all, in every condition, that which is both the challenge and the consolation: 'All that the Father gives me will come to me; and whoever comes to me I will not cast out.'[58]

ECUMENISM AND THE REUNION OF THE CHURCHES

In recent history Orthodoxy has no longer been a matter of Christian experience in a wholly 'Eastern' setting. The currents of global immigration and population shifts have brought very many Orthodox into contexts of living out a Christian witness in close proximity to other Christians of the Latin or Protestant traditions. As we have already seen in the discussion on the nature of the church, those who take the most severe line in Orthodox ecclesiological reflection have reasoned that since the church is by definition Orthodox all those Christians of other traditions are *de facto* heterodox. The argument goes on that heterodoxy is ineluctably heretical, and the Scriptures command the faithful not to have any dealings with heretics. Accordingly ecumenism (one of the more interesting internal Christian movements of the twentieth century) is regarded by this school of thought as a pan-heresy that must not be dabbled in by any who are true Orthodox. In the same vein, applying ancient canons of the church from different contexts to the modern environment, it is argued that no Orthodox should even pray with any of the heterodox. This is a view that is regularly heard in Orthodox circles, but it is not a view that (despite its desire to do so) can claim the high ground of Orthodox belief. It has a linear, almost wooden logic as its rhetorical selling point, but it fails to take in several major elements to its narrow parameters.

First of these is the presumption that Christians of good faith who belong now to the Latin and Protestant churches are themselves to be classed as heretics because they espouse positions taught by their churches which differ from Orthodoxy. The term 'heretic', however, was always used by the ancient church of those who, with an obtuse spiritual power, knowingly and energetically deviated from the Christian tradition. The ancient canons of the church have always been careful to distinguish those who wish to reach out to Orthodoxy from other communions, and does not use that charged word for them. Countless men and women of good faith have been formed within their religious traditions of birth for centuries since the Latin Church was no longer considered to be in the communion of the Orthodox churches. It is the narrowest and least charitable of all views to categorize them all, indiscriminately, as 'heretics'.

Second is the presumption that Orthodoxy is so weak that it cannot engage in honest dialogue with Christians of separated communions without either compromising its core beliefs, or being led astray. The view presumes that the Orthodox faithful either do not know and love their tradition, or are incapable of being charitably attentive to others who disagree with them. The dialogue of love which is at the heart of the best of modern ecumenism is an important part of Christians learning to have good will for one another. Those who argue that all who are not Orthodox are not even Christian are like the philosopher whose hat fell down over his eyes and who promptly defined the world as solely black and woollen. The reality of divided Christianity in the modern world is one of the greatest missionary tasks that the Lord has given to the Orthodox. Speaking the truth in love within this divided family is an unavoidable duty of the Church of Christ. But to speak the truth in love requires charity, and grace, more than it does self-righteous zealotry.

The patriarchate of Constantinople, and other major Orthodox leaders of the twentieth century, have offered a very different vision than those among the Orthodox who fear ecumenism and seem to scorn their separated brothers and sisters so much. The patriarchate of Constantinople has regularly addressed the need for the Orthodox to speak to Christian brothers and sisters in other communions with respect and openness. Documents emanating from the patriarchate over the space of almost a century now have accumulated to a wise and authoritative source of eirenical guidance for the Orthodox engaged in ecumenical efforts.[59] The 'dialogue of love' that is represented by the best aspects of modern ecumenism is something that Orthodox of good will should welcome. It does not involve the Orthodox Church in having to deny its ancient teachings, or masquerade as something other than it is, or even to depart

425

from its canons of discipleship, except in those ways in which Orthodox regularly excuse slight digressions from those canons: that is, for reasons of charity. It is basic to all the Orthodox, however, that while a profound lack of unity exists among the Christian communions, and for as long as there are serious divisions among them on core matters of creed and practice, no Christian of any other communion can be admitted to the sacramental life of the Orthodox Church as part of this dialogue of love. Intercommunion is not a means to such union; the Orthodox see it as the goal of the union yet to be discovered.

While the ecumenical dialogue of love is a very good thing, and the general principle it has advocated of fraternal collaboration in such Christian endeavours as are susceptible of common effort is also a useful strategy for modern Christian action, there are, nevertheless, some aspects of the ecumenical movement which seem to be very 'off course' for most of the Orthodox. In some of the recent meetings of the World Council of Churches there has been a growing friction between many of the Orthodox delegates and representatives of liberal Protestant traditions. Some of this has been caused by synthetic prayer services which have been regarded by the Orthodox as having significantly departed not only from the Orthodox canons, but even from mainstream Christian values.[60] Just as it is true that many aspects of the modern European civilization can no longer be regarded as even vestigially Christian, so it has also come to a pass, sadly, where even some of those movements which call themselves 'Christian' have adopted so many novelties, and distorted positions (false 'gospels of prosperity' or secularized gospels of self-fulfilment) that the Orthodox now need to know from close study of the traditions, and first-hand engagement with the leaders of such movements, who actually are the protagonists with whom ecumenism claims to be speaking.

In this new environment there are some things in the ecumenical movement that Orthodoxy does not, and will not, endorse, or ever wish to be part of. The WCC, for example, will never be regarded by the Orthodox as a 'super-church', nor as a body that can claim to speak for essential Christianity by virtue of its majority votes. But the issue of Orthodoxy speaking the truth in charity to great Christian communions, such as that of the Latins, with whom it has shared so much in history, or to those Protestant communions that reverence the Scriptures and the catholic tradition of truth, is surely a different matter. Ecumenical partners in all such dialogues need to know that the Orthodox regard themselves as the fulfilment and embodiment of God's Ekklesia on the earth. But far from closing a discussion about Christianity in the modern world, that profession surely starts one; and not one in which Orthodoxy believes that all everyone else has to do is listen. But the overall agenda that lies behind positive Orthodox understandings of ecumenism is a readiness to explain the Orthodox faith to others, and learn together how Christian divisions might be overcome. The dialogue is important. The witness aspect is essential.

Religious Pluralism in the Global Village

The Orthodox Church is no stranger to the issue that has recently come to effect much of Western Christianity, that of living in a pluralist environment where many world faiths meet together in close proximity. Orthodoxy has lived, from its very beginning,

426

in a very diverse multi-faith environment. It has advocated tolerance as a basic religious right, and been glad for the times it received it across centuries of often being a minority presence in Islamic societies. When the church was itself being persecuted by the machinery of state religion and polytheist mob violence, in its earliest generations, it learned how important it was to allow the rule of law and charitable relationship with neighbours to overcome the tendency to absolutist rigidity that religious bigotry always brings into society. When the church rose out of persecution and became itself the dominant state religion, under the Byzantine emperors, it may at times have endorsed state policies that reduced the civic rights of dissident religious believers, but it did not endorse any forcible programme of 'conversions'. Religious coercion remains a wicked thing that brings no honour to God, and sows the seeds of violence on earth. Today Orthodoxy actively seeks to encourage world peace, and calls for men and women of all religious traditions to live together in harmony: respecting one another's difference, and never advocating violence in the name of the God of Peace.

To foster that harmony of peace among social groups, it is absolutely important to respect the other. One does not have to advocate the support of other religious systems, or detach oneself from judgements about their respective claims, but respect for the sincerity of the other is necessary in a world where frictions between the great religions can increasingly lead to a level of violence that seems to be willingly fostered by pseudo-religious bigots. In the domain of modern inter-faith dialogue some Western Christian theorists have adopted a syncretic pluralist approach based around the premise (or cliché) that all religions are the same and that they are all equally valid paths to the same God. Orthodoxy rejects both statements. It sees the revelation of the ineffable Father, in Christ the Word Incarnate, through the efficacy of the Holy Spirit, as the perfection and consummation of all truth, and thus the fulfilment of all the religious aspirations of the human race. But it is also aware that the plan of God for the salvation of the entire world in Christ does not proceed mechanically. The message of the Gospel has been heard across the globe; but it is an invitation that has to be freely accepted, and can never be forced on another.

The church believes that it has a duty to witness to the message of Christ to a world deeply loved by God, in ways that are characterized by an open heart and a charitable rhetoric, but also in a way that never dilutes its proclamation of Christ as the centre of all the religious aspirations of humankind: 'The Way the Truth and the Life.'[61] The apostolic injunction is treated seriously: 'Guard the truth that has been entrusted to you by the Holy Spirit who dwells within us.'[62] But the same apostle also set out the command that inter-religious dialogue has to be undertaken with sensitivity, discretion, and respect.[63] It is not in accordance with that instruction to designate all those who are non-Christians as 'under a curse of damnation' as parts of Protestant fundamentalism often does. Orthodoxy adheres to the dogmatic position that the church is the great ark of salvation. But those who are outside that ark are not *de facto* the damned (no creature on earth has the right to conclude that about another living soul); they are, rather, in the hands of the God of Salvation and, strictly speaking, Orthodoxy does not know what their standing is: God alone knows it. Yet the church certainly has a deep and ancient sense that men and women who have tried to live justly, honestly, and mercifully will be recognized by God as having kept the vestiges of the divine image which he himself wove into the fabric of the human race at the Creation.

Several of the early Fathers, such as Justin Martyr[64] and Clement of Alexandria, thought that the Divine Logos had a universal presence in the souls of the righteous pagan before the time of the Gospel. They described this common level of divine awareness in all humans as the *Logos Spermatikos*: seeds of the Divine Wisdom in the human soul. St John Chrysostom also taught that God gave a salvific law that worked as a *pro-paideusis* for those outside the church: for the Jews it was the written Torah, for the pagans it was the natural law of conscience's higher instincts inscribed into their hearts.[65] Not all mankind is within the boundaries of the church; but all humanity was made in the divine image; and in that mystery lies the confidence of the Orthodox that God does not overlook those who try to live well but who have not yet found the joy of Christ.

The Orthodox have a responsibility to engage in a charitable inter-religious debate, not least because it has a God-given mission to the church to sow the seeds of unity among humankind, since it is the communion of the God of all unity. Orthodoxy senses a deep distinction to be made, in the first place, between, first, religions such as Judaism and Islam,[66] which reverence the sacred Scriptures and are so deeply influenced by the holy prophets; second, monotheistic faiths that have a metaphysic of communion and an uplifting ethic; and, finally, polytheistic faiths or those religions where ethical transcendence is not a high systemic priority. In other words, in accordance with the teaching of the Fathers of the Church, Orthodoxy adopts an economical attitude to world religions, weighing them in accordance with its own understanding of the truth given in Christ. Judaism stands in a unique relation to the church of the Messiah.

The apostle describes how the final consummation of the life of the church on earth will include the return of Israel to the communion. He describes the Lord himself as 'A Servant to the Circumcision',[67] by which he meant the people of Israel. In his Epistle to the Romans, St Paul teaches the profound mystery that God's promises to Israel have not been superseded or abrogated by the wonderful inclusion of the gentiles in Christ's salvation; that is, he has not rejected the People of Israel because they have not adopted the Gospel, but for a time they have been resistant so that through the mercy shown to the gentile Christians they too will finally come into mercy. It is a text[68] that sets out a charter for Christianity's continuing (and often troubled) relations with Judaism. It is a relationship that should be characterized by deep mutual respect, and a reverent sense among Orthodox Christians that the Jewish people were once the foundation of the Covenant mystery, and that they still remain invested within it. This is an apostolic doctrine, and those Orthodox, or other, Christians who regard the Jewish people and their faith as utterly alien to the church are very misguided.

In relation to Islam, St John of Damascus, having carefully considered the new religion as it presented itself to his first-hand experience (he was a political courtier of the caliph before becoming a monk) concluded that it was, in essence, a 'new heresy'. This has often been taken in a negative sense, by those who think that Orthodoxy's first theological assessment of Islam was wholly misguided. In the positive sense, few have perhaps understood that St John, a great theological authority for the Orthodox Church, was suggesting that, although there are many things in Islam which, of course, Orthodoxy will not accept, overall it lies somewhere within the family of Christianity, not without it: in the category of dissidence, rather than in the category of 'new religion' as such. This is a patristic view which he offered in a time when, although he and his nation had suffered at the hands of Islamic armies, he still had hope that a dialogue could bear fruit in love. Over many centuries Orthodoxy has regularly engaged in serious and eirenical religious dialogue with Islam.[69] Little of that exchange is known to the wider world since, until recently, Western Christianity showed little interest in the matter. Signs of that 'exchange of the reverence of God' can still be seen in many parts of the world where the Orthodox live side by side with Muslims. Sometimes they even share the same holy places, coming together in prayer to venerate the Blessed Mother of God, or local saints held in honour by both communities. These moments of shared devotion rarely seize the media headlines, which seem to be reserved for incidents of political or inter-religious violence.

Polytheistic religions, or those that do not admit the existence of a deity at all, are at a much greater distance from Christianity. In the times of the early Roman empire, as much of a pluralistic world as ours today, the Fathers affirmed that the mind and heart of men and women who were not Christians, but who worshipped the gods in their traditional faiths, could be elevated to the One God in discrete stages. Removal of the self from the worship of false gods was the primary step of enlightenment, and the cessation of animal or incense sacrifices was a strict requirement of those the church welcomed as serious seekers of the truth. The second stage was the alignment of the ethical standard of the individual, however and wherever it had been formed, to the ethical norms of the Gospel. These were both believed to be the necessary preparations for bringing a soul into the state where the teaching of the Gospel could be heard for what it is, the message of the offer of life in God. The final stage, the 'heart's hearing of the Gospel' however, is a matter of divine invitation. It is the task of the church to proclaim the Gospel, and strive to witness it in love. It is the work of the Spirit of God to move the hearts and minds of non-believers to Christ.

Orthodoxy has thus been said to be highly exclusivist in its approach to religions other than Christianity. This is true in the sense that the Orthodox profess that Christ is the sole salvation of the world and the single mediator between the Father and the cosmos. It is not accurate in so far as it does not follow that all the Orthodox believe that all who profess a religion other than Christianity will be 'outside salvation' because of that simple and basic fact. While some Orthodox do make that deduction, it is only because they have not asked themselves fundamental questions about God's providence for the whole world, and not merely for his church. Scripture speaks quite clearly: 'God Our Saviour desires all human beings to be saved and to come to the knowledge of the truth.' The apostle Peter also spoke quite plainly about God's providential care of the entire human race when he said: 'Truly I have perceived that God shows no partiality, but in every nation anyone who fears him and does what is right is acceptable to him.'[70] The early Fathers, pondering on this mystery, envisaged a theology of salvation that included the concept of how the Divine Logos worked within other religious systems to render the best elements of them into a *pro-paideusis* of the truth he revealed (in his own incarnation into history) most fully in the church.

As with St Paul at Athens,[71] there is a real sense in Orthodoxy that men and women of good will who are historically and culturally bound up in their native religions can still be apprehending the Divine Logos whom the church knows and serves as the sole gateway to God. This affirms for the church the value of eirenical dialogue with men and women of other religions, that at one and the same time does not obviate the duty to preach the Gospel of Christ, nor reduce that dialogue to a thinly disguised apologetics. The dialogue of love is very significant today in a world where religion is too often used by rigid and narrowly bigoted mentalities to advocate the path of anger and violence. Orthodoxy's mission, as a communion of love, is to call all mankind to the love and peace of God, and remind all human beings of their common dignity as bearers of the divine image, and their universal invitation to become the sons and daughters of God the Father. In fulfilling that mission the church will find that its most powerful argument for the beauty of Christ over the entire cosmos will be its own ongoing struggle to be more faithfully conformed to him who has mercy on all the world of his own making.

Evangelism in a New Millennium

The need to renew the zeal of the church in the proclamation of the Gospel to the world has never been more urgent than in recent generations when secularism and apathy have eroded much of Europe's roots of Christian civilization. The church has always understood the need to evangelize alongside the need to advance the ongoing catechesis of its members. Both tasks have been greatly hindered in traditional Orthodox lands for many centuries past by hostile governments. So many Christian Orthodox institutions have been destroyed, and suffocated, that a great labour now remains for world Orthodoxy coming out into the light of day. The future rebuilding of an ecclesial structure throughout eastern Europe will not only or simply be a matter of rebuilding the churches and monasteries knocked down by the communists, for Orthodoxy will also be able, though with difficulty and through many sacrifices in years ahead, also to begin rebuilding its schools and universities, as well as new parishes in urban centres that have not seen church planting before.

In the times of the Byzantine empire Orthodoxy was a generously evangelistic faith. The Eastern Orthodox culture spread from Constantinople to the highlands of Persia and even to the Chinese borders; south to the hill country of Ethiopia and the Nubian kingdoms where Sudan now lies; through Arabia, and Syria; westwards through the great land mass of Asia Minor; north to the vast and snowy lands of the Slavs. At no time was the ancient Orthodox Church immobile in its evangelical efforts. But more recent centuries have seen it dwindled and reduced in freedom. Even so, where it remained free to act, especially in sixteenth-century Romania under the voivodes, or Russia after the eighteenth century, the evangelical outreach of Orthodoxy was always seen as an integral part of Christian life. Many Western Christians have complained of the 'inward-looking' nature of the Orthodox Church, perhaps being naively oblivious of its sufferings in early modern history, or ignorant of its great heritage in evangelism. Today as the shackles of oppression are being progressively cast off, its missionary zeal will reawaken.

Orthodoxy has sometimes been disturbed by the sight, of late, of missionaries from Western Christian origins coming into eastern Europe to bring 'evangelism', seemingly unaware that the evangelization of a Christian country is actually 'proselytism'. Orthodox are very careful not to proselytize in the countries of the West where they live. They do not see the conversion of Protestant or Catholic Christians to Orthodoxy as an honest form of 'evangelism', which should rather refer to the conversion of men and women to their first knowledge of Christ. Nevertheless, where other Christians are led to the family of the Orthodox they are welcomed in God's providence. The

Figure 8 The monastery church at Rohia, northern Romania. The new (unfinished) church building is a sign of the extensive rebuilding that is going on all over eastern Europe as the Orthodox Church emerges from the long winter of communist oppression. Rohia is known as the 'Athos of Transylvania'. Under the inspired leadership of its local bishops, Justinian and Justin, it is a centre of monastic revival in the Romanian Church. *Photograph: John McGuckin*

experience of visiting Western evangelists who wish to bring the divisions of Reformation theology into the heartland of the Orthodox, and have often used more than preaching zeal to accomplish their purposes, is something that is not warmly welcomed by the Orthodox hierarchs; but ultimately it will be properly addressed, not by complaints about the defective ecclesiology of others, or by appeals to the state authorities, but rather by a radical renewal of the zeal of the local Orthodox churches to preach in public the wonderful message of the Gospel that has been committed to them. Orthodoxy has been called 'the world's best-kept secret'. The time is coming when it will, after long years of silence, be able to give that secret out more widely.

It is to be hoped that the Orthodox world's song of the glory of its Lord will be, for the Western Christian brothers and sisters who hear it, a consolation and an encouragement for them to renew their own understanding of the essential Christian

431

tradition; and for those who have not yet heard the Song of the Lord at all, a chance to find the power and beauty of Christ and to be created anew by them. The world may often seem dark, and faith may indeed seem to many to have grown cold,[72] but the Orthodox Church has an irrepressible instinct when signs of dusk draw near: to light the lamps of eventide and sing the ancient song:

> Jesus Christ,
> The Gladsome light
> Of the Immortal Father's holy glory;
> The Heavenly, Holy, Blessed One.

> The Sun grows dim
> We see the light of eventide
> And sing our hymn to God:
> The Father, Son, and Holy Spirit.

> Worthy are you,
> O Son of God,
> Through each and every moment,
> That joyful songs should hymn you.

> You are the Giver of our Life.
> And so the world gives glory.[73]

Notes

1 John 15.18–19.

2 Heb. 13.14.

3 'How hard it is for those who are wealthy to enter the Kingdom of God.' Mark 10.23.

4 Among numerous examples one could take the Homilies of St Gregory the Theologian (esp. Oration 14, *On the Poor*), or the many of St John Chrysostom on this theme. See Avila 1983; Holman 2001; Phan 1984; Queré-Jaulmes 1962; Ramsay 1991; Shewring 1948.

5 'Lover of the Poor.' See de Vinne 1995.

6 Matt. 25.37–45.

7 She is now canonized as a saint of the church. See Plekon 2002.

8 What the ancient sources described as the 'two ages': this age of turmoil that stands within the historical record and permits brutal oppression as the ultimate symbol of 'the Beast', that is evil personified, and the other age, which is the transcendent 'Kingdom of God' when peace will be established by the definitive ending of violent powers hostile to the good, and the comforting of the poor.

9 It is a major category mistake, therefore, for fundamentalist Christians to apply apocalyptically matrixed scriptural references to 'war in the heavens spilling out on earth', as authoritative 'justifications' from the Bible for Christians to engage in violent conflict for political ends. The essence of biblical, apocalyptic, doctrine is that the two ages must never be conflated or confused. The 'next age' cannot be ushered in by political victories gained in 'this age'. By this means Christianity, in its foundational vision, undercut the principles that continue to inspire Judaism and Islam with their (essentially) non-apocalyptic understandings of the spreading of the Kingdom of God on earth in recognizable borders, and militarily if necessary.

10 As if, for example, the biblical narratives of the Pentateuch where God commands Moses and Joshua to slaughter the Canaanite inhabitants in the process of seizing the 'Promised Land' were to be read literally, as both vindicating war for

'righteous reasons' and validating the forced appropriation of territories after conflict. Orthodoxy does not read Scripture in this way.

11 The Canonical Epistles of St Basil, otherwise known as the Ninety-Two Canons. They can be found in English translation in the *Pedalion*. Cummings 1957: 772–864.

12 Basil, Epistle 188.13; Cummings 1957: 801.

13 Athanasios, Epistle 48, *To Amun*; the full text is in *St Athanasius, Select Works and Letters*, trans. A. Robertson, Nicene and Post-Nicene Fathers of the Church, vol. 4 (1891; repr. Grand Rapids: Eerdmans, 1980), 556–7.

14 That is, find canonical forgiveness for the act of shedding blood, which is canonically prohibited.

15 'A Christian should not volunteer to become a soldier, unless he is compelled to do this by someone in authority. He can have a sword, but he should not be commanded to shed blood. If it can be shown that he has shed blood he should stay away from the mysteries (sacraments) at least until he has been purified through tears and lamentation.' *Canons of Hippolytus*, 14.74; text in Swift 1983: 93. See also *Apostolic Tradition*, 16.

16 As developed especially (out of Cicero) by Ambrose of Milan, *On Duties*, 1.176, and Augustine, Epistle 183.15 and *Against Faustus*, 22.69–76; and see Swift 1983: 110–49. But Ambrose (*On Duties*, 1.35.175) specifically commands his priests to have no involvement (inciting or approving) whatsoever in the practice of war or judicial punishments: 'Interest in matters of war', he says, 'seems to me to be alien to our role as priests.'

17 Ordinary murder was given a twenty-year debarment from the church's sacraments, as well as all accruing civic penalties: Basil, canon 56, *Pedalion* (Cummings 1957: 827); manslaughter received a ten-year debarment: Basil, canon 57, *Pedalion* (Cummings 1957: 828).

18 Even the anti-proliferation treaties of recent decades have not altered this in substance. The stockpile is still more than enough to incinerate civilization. All it did was to put an end to excess spending on silos, so that other, newer weaponry could be developed instead, all of which is capable of delivering nuclear warheads more efficiently.

19 For a collection of recent hierarchical statements about war see Webster 1995.

20 Though it will readily give its blessing to those who are drafted into war, the blessing of the righteous soldier being an important distinction from the wholesale 'blessing of armies' or endorsement of war. The Orthodox Peace Fellowship, with its journal *In Communio*, is one of the leading English-language sources for Orthodox attitudes to peace studies.

21 Princes Boris and Gleb, the sons of Prince Vladimir, chose to allow their brother to assume sole rule in the civil war following their father's death, and submitted without resistance to their execution, as they believed their Christian faith made it incumbent on them to do. Though they had a moral right to self-defence, they waived it in order to avoid the suffering of many others. They have since become known as 'passion-bearers' because of this.

22 For a deep consideration of the issue see Yannaras 1984.

23 Rom. 8.2.

24 Gal. 5.1.

25 Rom. 8.21.

26 Gal. 5.13; 1 Cor. 9.1, 19.

27 *Against the Gentiles*, 8.2, 34.1–3; *On the Incarnation*, 7.4, 11.3–4, 12.1–6, and 14.1–2.

28 He is thinking about ancient mirrors of copper and silver that needed regular polishing in order to shine.

29 See. Phil. 2.4–7.

30 John 8.32, 36.

31 *Brothers Karamazov*, pt. II, bk. 5, ch. 5.

32 Matt. 4.1–10.

33 See Ruether 1974.

34 2 Cor. 5.17.

35 Gal. 3.27–8.

36 1 Cor. 14.33–4; 1 Tim. 2.11–15.

37 Gregory, Oration 37.6.

38 Ibid. 37.7.

39 See Laporte 1982; Clark 1983, 1986; Stanton 1988; Lang 1989.

40 Clark 1993; Cloke 1995; Harrison 1994.

41 Elm 1994.

42 Kadel 1982; McNamara 1984.

43 Elizabeth Behr-Sigel, 'Women in the Orthodox Church', in Plekon 2001: 115–26.

44 A consultation sponsored by the ecumenical patriarchate, where the issue of ordained ministry for women was broached, and a unanimous resolution from the delegates was recorded that the female diaconate ought to be widely restored.

45 See Behr-Sigel's synopsis in Plekon 2001: 121.

46 Papers of the consultation at Rhodes, 1988.

47 The Apostolic Constitutions dismiss the concept of bodily flux rendering a Christian defiled as a lamentable reversion to Judaism.

48 It is often noted that the Council of Laodicea (canon 44) prohibits lay women from entering the altar; it is less often noted that the same canon says that laymen are also prohibited (see also canon 69 of the Quinisext Council). Those who (regularly) aver to Laodicea's canons to support the prohibition on Orthodox from admitting heretics to the churches, or to insist that the Orthodox are not allowed even to offer prayers in the company of heretics (regularly used to gainsay the ecumenical movement) do not refer so often to the same council's canons, forbidding clerics from entering any tavern or wine shop, and prohibiting any Christian from taking rest on a Saturday, which must remain a 'working day'. The decontextualized citation of 'proofs' is a curious phenomenon when examined.

49 Language about 'cleansing' a woman from defilement, as seen in the churching ritual, for example, is actually predominantly based upon a Hebraic concept of 'defilement by contact with the sacred', a positive and powerful notion of being rendered so 'sacrally charged' that a certain dissociation from normal life is presumed necessary. But it is a concept that is so difficult to convey through the negative surface language implying that childbirth and sexuality 'defile', that the ritual itself stands in need of an extensive pastoral retranslation.

50 Gal. 3.27.

51 See, for example, Plekon 2001: 16–17.

52 See, for example, Behr-Sigel in Plekon 2001.

53 See Constantelos 1968.

54 Leading Orthodox ethicists writing in English include Harakas 1973, 1980, 1983a, 1983b, 1990, 1992; Breck 1998, 2005; Woodill 1998; Yannaras 1984. The Armenian theologian Vigen Guroian (1987, 1994) offers a magisterial consideration of the problem of ethics in a new environment.

55 Rev. 21.5.

56 The breaking of the single cell into a twofold form which then continues in ever-increasing complexities of division as the foetus develops into a living human being.

57 Eph. 3.17.

58 John 6.37.

59 See Patelos 1978; also Zernov 1961.

60 The invocation of spirits at one 'open-faith' ceremony at a general meeting of the WCC in Canberra prompted the most severe protests from the patriarchs of Georgia and Jerusalem, and their withdrawal of trust from what they saw as the new ethos of the WCC as a pluralistic version of Christianity. Stricter guidelines for common worship were subsequently agreed on in the WCC.

61 John 14.6.

62 2 Tim. 1.14.

63 2 Tim. 2.24–5. 'And the Lord's servant must not be quarrelsome but kindly to every one, an apt teacher, forbearing, correcting opponents with gentleness. God may perhaps grant that they will turn and come to know the truth.'

64 Justin Martyr, *The First Apology*, 36; *The Second Apology*, 8, 10, and 13.

65 John Chrysostom, Homily 7.4, *On the Letter to the Romans*.

66 See Papademetriou 1990; Yiannoulatos 1996.

67 Rom. 15.8.

68 Rom. 11.28–31. 'As regards the gospel they may be enemies of God, for your sake; but as regards election they are beloved for the sake of their forefathers. For the gifts and the call of God are irrevocable. Just as you yourselves were once disobedient to God but have now received mercy because of their disobedience, so too they have now been disobedient in order that through the mercy shown to you they also may receive mercy.'

69 See Ziakas 2000.

70 Acts 10.34–5.

71 Acts 17.23: 'For as I passed along, and observed the objects of your worship, I found also an altar with this inscription, "To an unknown god." What therefore you worship as unknown, this I proclaim to you.'

72 Luke 18.8.

73 Orthodox vesperal hymn, Phos Hilaron.

Glossary of Orthodox Terminology

aer Greek term for the cloth (Slavonic: *vozdukh*) which is the largest of three veils coverings the chalice and paten during the liturgy (one for each vessel, and the *aer* covering both together). It has a symbolic connotation of the shroud of Christ. During the recitation of the Creed, during the divine liturgy, the priest shakes the *aer* to signify the earthquake that accompanies the mystery of the Lord's Resurrection. It also signifies the descent of the Holy Spirit.

agiasmos Greek term for sanctification. Normally used to designate holy water (Slavonic: *sviataia voda*) that is used in churches and homes to bless objects, or which is drunk in domestic healing rituals.

Akathistos (Slavonic: Akafist), literally 'not sitting down': in other words a processional hymn, of Byzantine origination. Today the most famous of all Akathistoi, and usually what is meant by this term, is the great early seventh-century hymn to the Blessed Virgin. It has twenty-four stanzas saluting the Virgin as the 'Unwedded Bride', and so is also known as the Chairetismoi (salutations). Progressive quarters of the whole hymn are sung in church on each Friday of Great Lent, and on the last Friday of Lent the whole composition is sung to commemorate her miracle of saving the city of Constantinople in 626.

altar (Greek: *hieron*; Slavonic: *prestol*).The easternmost area in an Orthodox church that corresponds to the Western 'sanctuary', behind the icon screen and in which the Holy Table is found.

ambon Greek term for the raised platform or podium on the north side of the solea, in front of the iconostasis, from where the priest or deacon chants the Gospel, and delivers the homily. It corresponds to the Western pulpit.

analogion (Slavonic: *analoy*) A wooden stand in church. It can carry the book of Scriptures, or an icon.

Anaphora The central prayer of the eucharistic rite beginning with the Preface and Trisagion Hymn (Holy, Holy, Holy), and culminating in the offering of the sacred mysteries, the Epiclesis, and the solemn prayers for all the church.

Anastasis The Resurrection of Christ as an event within, and transcending, history; and also signifying the principle of Christ's abiding energy and rule of his heavenly and earthly church (the Resurrection presence).

antidoron The word means 'instead of the gifts', and describes the blessed bread that has been taken out of the loaves of eucharistic offering, but not consecrated. In the course of the liturgy this will be held over the chalice, to be blessed, and distributed to all the faithful (those who did not communicate) at the end of the liturgy as a sign of blessing and fellowship in Christ.

It is a surviving remnant of the ritual of *agapé* that once was performed in tandem with the Eucharist in the ancient church (an element which can also be seen in the *litiya* ritual of festal Vespers).

antimension   (Slavonic: *antimins*) The altar cloth. Square of consecrated fabric, often printed silk, with scenes of the Passion and Deposition from the Cross. Inside the *antimins* (the word means 'instead of the altar' and signifies that this can be regarded in some cases as a 'portable altar') are sewn relics of the saints, and at its foot is the signature of the ruling bishop of the diocese who has given this altar-cloth for the authorized celebration of the Eucharist under his priestly presidency.

antiphon   Greek term (meaning alternating voices) for a short scriptural refrain sung in the Synaxis ritual. It also refers to three of the main hymns taken from Scripture that make up the Enarxis (initial) service that begins the eucharistic liturgy. In Byzantine times the great churches would have two choirs responding to one another antiphonally.

apodosis   (Slavonic: *otdanive*). Term for 'putting away'. It signifies the 'octave' and occurs on the eighth day after a feast (though it can then last more than a day). It concludes a liturgical festal 'season'. The 'eighth day' is an ancient eschatological symbol of the New Age. The *apodosis* of Pascha occurs only after forty days, and takes place on the vigil of the Ascension.

apolysis   Greek term for a dismissal rite.

Apolytikion   From the root of 'dismissal', a liturgical hymn in honour of a saint or the Blessed Virgin, on their feast day, sung at the end of services, and still occupying this place in Vespers.

archimandrite   From the Greek for 'head of the sheepfold'. Originally the title of a leading monastic abbot, it has tended to become an honorary rank in the church for senior monastic priests.

artoklasia   *See* **litiya**

asteriskos   (Slavonic: *zvezditsa*). Term for 'little star'. One of the sacred eucharistic vessels made of two arched bands of metal that are bound with a central rivet, allowing them to swivel closed or open. When opened they form a cage that is laid over the Lamb on the *diskos* in the Proskomedia ritual, so as to prevent the *aer* disturbing the particles. The *asteriskos* is removed during the course of the Anaphora.

autocephalous   An Orthodox church that is self-governing, with its own patriarch or metropolitan archbishop, and national synod.

autonomous   An Orthodox church which, while not being autocephalous in itself, is allowed predominantly to govern its own affairs through the appointment of a leading hierarch by the patriarch of the founding church.

canon   Greek word for 'rule', 'standard', or 'measure'. It is used in the church in several fashions. First to signify the canon of Sacred Scripture, the list of books regarded as inspired writings. Secondly, it is a term for a long hymnic form, such as is still used in the structure of Orthros, or Matins. Thirdly it is a term that is commonly used to describe the disciplinary regulations attached to the episcopal synods or ecumenical councils (or sometimes the patristic writings on disciplinary matters, such as the canons of St Basil). These rules, or canons, have been gathered together over the centuries to form the rule book to guide the church's discipline. They are regarded as very authoritative, but not infallible in so far as they applied to particular historical circumstances, and need adaptation to changes of conditions. They can be altered by other ecumenical councils if these are ever held again in the future. In the meantime the canons are applied according to the discretion of the ruling bishop in a diocese, or the episcopal synod.

censer   (Greek: *thymiato*; Slavonic: *kadillo*). The equivalent of the Western thurible. A metal lidded bowl, hung on chains for the burning of incense during the liturgy. The chains have twelve bells attached, symbolic of the preaching of the apostles.

Cherubikon   The hymn of the Cherubim. In ancient times this was sung by the choir of imperial eunuchs in Hagia Sophia cathedral. Today it is the solemn chant that takes place during the liturgical 'Great Entrance'. Its text is: 'We who mystically represent the Cherubim, and sing the thrice-holy hymn to the life-creating Trinity, now lay aside all earthly care, as we receive the King of All, invisibly escorted by angelic hosts. Alleluia, Alleluia, Alleluia.'

Compline   (Greek: Apodeipnon; Slavonic: Velikoye povecheriye). The office of night prayer. It can be combined with Vespers to make up the 'All Night Vigil' (Olonychtia).

crowns   (Greek: *stephana*; Slavonic: *ventzy*). Crowns woven of white blossoms to symbolize undying love. They are worn by the couple during the marriage service to symbolize the royal union of bride and groom. In Russian ritual the crowns are usually made of metal.

diskos   The sacred vessel which holds the eucharistic bread during the liturgy. It corresponds to the Western-rite paten, but it has a deeper dish, and is raised up on a metallic foot. It is sometimes engraved with scenes of the Nativity.

doxology   From the Greek *doxa* (glory): the act of giving glory to God, especially in prayer. Doxological theology, the praise of the earthly and heavenly church, is the highest form of theological utterance, though not all of it is suitable for the ears of the uninitiated, and so other forms of discourse are also prevalent in ecclesiastical discourse.

eagle   (Greek: *dikephalos*; Slavonic: *orletz*). A small round woven rug with an eagle depicted flying over a city. It can also be a mosaic roundel permanently set into the church floor. It is placed in the altar area or the solea of the church to designate the place where the bishop stands. It is a mark of his jurisdiction over a city church.

Ekklesia   The Church (Greek term derived from the Scriptures). Its root meaning is from the term 'to be called out' or gathered. It was the Greek rendering of the Hebrew *kahal*. The church is thus the in-gathering of God's servants, the New Israel, the Elect People with whom he has made a covenant through the mystery of Jesus.

Epiclesis   The prayer of 'Calling Down': the solemn invocation of the Holy Spirit to descend and consecrate the eucharistic gifts, said by the presiding celebrant of the liturgy after the words of Institution have been sung over the gifts of bread and wine. The prayer is: 'We offer you this spiritual and bloodless worship, and pray you, and ask you, and supplicate you, to send down your Holy Spirit upon us, and upon these gifts here set forth, and make this bread the precious body of your Christ; and that which is in this cup, the precious blood of your Christ, making the change by your Holy Spirit. Amen, Amen, Amen.'

epinoia   The 'aspect' of Christ by which he adapts his saving presence to the needs of different parts of his creation in their different stages of spiritual perception. The multitude of the titles of the One Lord reflect his many aspects (*epinoiai*) as Saviour.

epitrachelion   Greek term for the distinctive vestment or stole of the priest (Slavonic: *epitra-khil*). Worn around his neck and fastened together in the middle with pomegranate-shaped buttons, it is always worn when the priest exercises his sacred ministry, even if other vestments are not.

eulogia   Greek term for blessings given by a bishop or priest (Slavonic: *blagoslovenije*). Sometimes meaning a blessing in the form of a 'permission', by one's confessor or spiritual elder, to do something or embark on a certain vocational path. Also used by extension to refer to the *antidoron* given out at the end of the Eucharist, or to icon cards or pious mementos distributed at church gatherings.

Evangelismos   The feast of the 'evangelizing' of the Blessed Virgin (the bringing to her of Good News). It corresponds to the Western feast of Annunciation (25 March).

exomologesis   Greek term for the sacrament of confession before a priest (Slavonic: *ispoved*). Penitent and priest stand together before an icon of Christ and after saying prayers and hearing the statement of sorrow from the penitent the priest gives encouragement and advice and administers the prayer of absolution.

Great Entrance   The procession bearing the chalice (*poterion*) and paten (*diskos*) to the altar for the eucharistic Anaphora. It moves from the side altar through the side doors of the iconostasis and back through the royal doors where the clergy either lay down the gifts on the Holy Table, or hand them to the presiding bishop who stands in the royal doors waiting for them. It corresponds in form to the offertory procession in the Western rites.

higumen   (Slavonic: *nastoyastel*). Head of a monastic community.

Holy Table   (Greek: *Hagia Trapeza*; Slavonic: *Prestol*). The eucharistic table, corresponding to the 'altar' of the Western Church. Inside the Holy Table are always found the relics of the saints. The Holy Table is consecrated with profound ceremonies when the church is founded, and after that point is only touched by the ordained clergy. All the ordained who come into the altar area prostrate full length three times and kiss the Holy Table before doing any other task. The Holy Table is also seen as the throne of God on earth, the divine presence especially occupying the 'High Place' immediately behind and above the easternmost face. Whoever walks here must mark themselves with the sign of the Cross as they do so. From ancient times no 'dead thing' was allowed to touch the altar, and so today almost all Gospels, permanently laid on the Holy Table in all Orthodox churches, are covered in brass or gilt, not in leather.

iconostasis   Large screen, usually carrying many icons, which divides off the altar from the temple nave. Behind the iconostasis will be found the Holy Table, and a side altar to the north wall, where the Prothesis rite is celebrated, as well as a sacristy (*diakonikon*) to the south wall where the vestments and service books are kept.

kamilavki   (Slavonic: *kamilavka*). The black cylindrical hat worn by priests. Clergy who are monks also wear a black veil attached to this (*epanokalynafkon*).

kenosis   Self-emptying in loving service (based on Phil. 2.7). Also used by the Fathers as a synopsis of the humility of the Word of God in assuming the limitations of a genuine human life in the Incarnation.

Koimesis   The 'Falling Asleep' (or Dormition) of the Blessed Virgin Mary. Major feast day on 15 August. Known in the West as the Assumption.

Lamb, the   (Greek: *Amnos*; Slavonic: *Agnetz*).The central square of bread, normally a two inch cube taken from a stamped loaf offered for the eucharistic ritual. It bears upon it the Greek Letters IC XC NIKA (Jesus Christ Victorious). This is prepared during the Proskomedia ritual and laid upon the paten before the service begins. It is this Lamb which alone is consecrated as the eucharistic gift. After the consecration the Lamb is divided into fragments for the communion of the clergy and faithful.

lance   (Greek: *lonche*; Slavonic: *kopije*). Triangular-ended knife used by the priest to cut the Lamb in the liturgical preparatory rites (Proskomide). It symbolizes the lance used against Jesus on the Cross.

Lent   Periods of fasting and abstinence in the Church in preparation for great feasts. The longest and strictest Lent is that in advance of Pascha; there are other shorter Lents preceding Nativity, the Koimesis of the Virgin, and the Feast of the Apostles. Most Wednesdays and Fridays are also observed as fast days in the Orthodox Church calendar.

litiya   Slavonic term for the ritual of the blessing of bread and wine and wheat and oil, which occurs on special feasts and is celebrated in the course of Vespers. The Greek term is *artoklasia* (the breaking of the bread). The faithful will eat the blessed bread soaked in the wine afterwards, and will be anointed on the forehead with the blessed oil.

liturgy   The word in the Greek Old Testament (LXX) for public worship of God. It is used in the church to signify the solemn services celebrating the mysteries: predominantly the Eucharist, but also the other great mysteries such as baptism and confession. Other church services, such as the recitation of the hours, are not liturgical in this strict sense.

mandias   The long, coloured cloak worn by a bishop when he officiates outside the divine liturgy; symbolizing his ascetic dedication and his right to teach in the Christian assembly.

439

mystery (Greek: *mysterion*; Slavonic: *tainstvo*). A sacrament or sacramental ritual. Also a biblical concept for the mystical presence of Christ in his Church, and the Christ-life into which the Christian grows.

narthex The porch of a church. In ancient times it was used as a gathering place for the catechumens and penitents who were not allowed to attend the actual celebration of the Eucharist. Some large churches also have an outer porch or *exonarthex*.

noetic creation *See* **nous**

nous *Nous* (adj. 'noetic') is the Greek Christian term for the spiritual element of creation. The *nous* in a human being can best be translated as 'spiritual intellect'. The other two constitutive parts of humanity, for ancient Christian anthropology, are the *psyche* (the soul or the emotive part of the spiritual being) and the *sarx* (the material and bodily aspect of a person). The Fathers understood humans to be partly noetic and partly material, with the soul moderating the other respective spheres of action. They understood the angelic order to contain wholly noetic beings, and they are often called the noetic creation.

omophorion The distinctive broad stole of a bishop, worn over the shoulders, outside the liturgical vestments while he is celebrating the liturgy. In a wider sense being 'under the omophorion' signifies attachment (especially of clergy) to the jurisdictional authority of a particular bishop, or patriarch.

orarion The long stole of the deacon, worn around the neck and over the right shoulder. It is held aloft each time the deacon prays on behalf of the people.

Orthodoxy Sunday First Sunday of Lent commemorating the restoration of icons to the Church, and the downfall of the iconoclastic heresy.

Orthros Greek term for the service of 'Day-Dawn' or Matins (Slavonic: Utrenia). Celebrated in most monasteries daily, it is usually celebrated in parishes following Greek liturgical custom on the Sunday morning immediately preceding the eucharistic liturgy; in Russian-rite parishes, it is combined with Vespers on the Saturday evening before (Vigil Service).

Panagia Title of the Blessed Virgin, meaning the 'All Holy One'. Also a word denoting the icon a bishop wears on his chest (*enkolpion*) as a sign of office, since this normally depicts the Theotokos.

Panikhida (Greek: Mnemosyno, or Trisagion). The memorial service that is celebrated at the graveside or in church. Memorials take place on the third, ninth, and fortieth days after a death; then after six months, and annually thereafter according to the family's arrangements.

Pantocrator Greek term for the 'Lord Who Rules over All'. A title of the Son of God. Also in art contexts it signifies the icon of the Lord in the central dome of a church, where he gives his blessing out as Lord and Judge of the cosmos.

paradosis Greek term for 'tradition', especially the handing on to successive generations of the evangelical tradition given to the church by the Spirit of God.

Pascha The great feast of feasts: the Lord's Passover, or Resurrection. Generally known in the English-speaking West as Easter (according to some from the name of the pagan goddess of spring, Yeostre, whose festival the Christian missionaries were trying to displace). Latin Mediterranean countries witness alongside the Orthodox, the more ancient, and more appropriate, Christian designation of the feast as Pascha. It is celebrated according to Orthodox usage on the Sunday following the first full moon after the spring equinox.

patriarchate An autonomous and autocephalous ecclesiastical jurisdiction in the Orthodox Church of great antiquity or national importance, that is headed by a patriarch. In ancient times there were five patriarchates in Orthodoxy (Rome, Constantinople, Alexandria, Antioch, and Jerusalem). Today there are the four remaining Eastern patriarchates, together with the four more recent patriarchates of Russia, Bulgaria, Serbia, and Romania.

phelonion (Slavonic: *felon*).The liturgical overgarment which with the stole (*epitrachelion*) is proper to the priest. It is comparable to the chasuble of the Latin rite, but with the front cut away beneath the waist level, and the back hem reaching down to the heels. It is usually of radiant cloth, often cloth of gold, but reflecting the liturgical season too, and generally in sober colours for Lent or for funeral services. There will be embroidered on the back either a cross or an icon of the Lord which the priest kisses before wearing it.

photikia   Greek term for garments of light (Slavonic: *krizhma*), the white garments worn by the newly baptized. They are meant to be kept safe as sacred vestments, and if they have to be disposed of, must be consumed by fire.

phronema   The mind, or mind-set, of the Christian following from assimilation to Christ. Based on 1 Cor. 2.16.

pogrebeniye   Slavonic term for the funeral ritual (Greek: *taphe*).

poterion   Greek term for the eucharistic chalice. It is generally larger than the normal chalice used in the Western eucharistic rites, as it is used to communicate all the faithful with communion under both species.

preotasa   Priest's wife (Romanian). (Greek: *presbytera*; Slavonic: *matoushka*).

presanctified   Liturgy of Holy Communion without the consecration of the gifts, attributed to Pope Gregory the Dialogist (so named because he was the author of 'Dialogues') or Pope Gregory the Great as he is known in the Latin tradition. It is celebrated on the Wednesdays and Fridays of Great Lent, and on the first three days of Great Week leading up to Pascha.

Proskomide   Service of preparation (also known as the Oblation or Prothesis from the name of the table (placed to the north of the Holy Table), on which it is celebrated before the Eucharist begins. During this ritual the Lamb is made ready on the sacred vessels and the intercessory prayers of the people are gathered together.

raso   (Greek: *anteri*; Slavonic: *podryasnik*). The cassock or long garment (usually black or grey) worn by the clergy. An outer, coat-like garment with wide sleeves and open front is also worn on occasions on top of this (Greek: *exoraso*; Slavonic: *ryassa*).

royal doors   (Slavonic: *tsarkije vrata*). Sometimes referred to as 'beautiful gate'. Predominantly meaning today the main entrance into the altar through the centre of the iconostasis. The royal doors carry the icons of the Evangelismos (Annunciation) and the four evangelists. They are normally kept closed, and only opened during the progress of the Great Mysteries. When the Eucharist is being celebrated only the bishop or priest will pass through the royal doors which are seen as the gateway to heaven. Their opening, during the course of the liturgy, is a symbol of how the gate to paradise has been laid open by the presence of Christ in the mystery.

sacristy   (Greek: *skevophylakion*; Slavonic: *riznitsa*). Place in the south side of the altar area of an Orthodox church where the vestments and sacred vessels are kept.

sakkos   The dalmatic-shaped vestment which a bishop wears on top of other liturgical vestments. It denotes his right to rule, and derives from the imperial garments of the ancient Byzantines.

salos   (Slavonic: *iurodivyi*). The Fool for Christ. The ascetic (especially of earlier ages in Orthodoxy) whose radical dissociation from social conventions served to highlight their role as prophetic commentators. The Holy Fool Nicholas of Pskov once presented to the fearsome Tsar Ivan the Terrible, instead of the bread and salt he was expecting on a Lenten visit to one of his Russian cities, a plate of meat dripping with blood. The disgusted tsar saw in his own hands a prophetic synopsis of his cruelty that no one else had the courage to tell him. There is a more homely account of the Iurodivyi Grisha in Tolstoy's part-autobiographical memoir 'Childhood'.

sobornost   Slavonic word for the collective communion (Greek: *koinonia*), especially the inner spirit of the church as a familial union, with a common consciousness.

sticharion   Greek word for the long white garment (though it can also be of other colours) which the priest wears over the cassock as the first level of liturgical vestment (Slavonic: *podriznik*). Because it was always white in the Latin rite it came to be known in the West as the alb.

Synaxis   The intial part of the eucharistic liturgy that includes the preparatory litanies and scriptural readings. It derives from the Greek word for 'assembly'.

tabernacle (Greek: *artophorion*; Slavonic: *darochranitelnitsa*). A receptacle (often elaborately figured in the shape of a church with towers) used to reserve the eucharistic gifts in the altar, for use in the communion of the sick, or in the liturgy of the presanctified.

temple (Greek: *naos*; Slavonic: *khram*). Normal word in use among the Orthodox for the church building.

theologoumenon A theological position or theory that cannot command universal assent in the Orthodox Church, though which may be rooted in legitimate attitudes to aspects of church history or pious traditions.

Theotokos Title of the Blessed Virgin signifying 'Mother of God', since her child was truly God. The title was defined as necessary to true faith in Jesus at the Council of Ephesus in 431.

Triodion Liturgical period between the Sunday of the publican and pharisee and 'cheese-fare Sunday' preceding Lent. It is also the word (meaning 'Three Odes') that designates the liturgical book that contains the different hymns and prayers for the moveable feasts leading up to Pascha.

Trisagion Literally 'Thrice Holy'. It designates the solemn hymn sung in every Orthodox prayer service and liturgy: 'Holy God, Holy Mighty, Holy Immortal have mercy on us.' *See also* Panikhida.

typikon (Slavonic: *sluzhebnik*). Rule of liturgical procedure; or the rule which a monastic house observes. Also the book of liturgical instructions which outlines how each service ought to be conducted.

typology The concept of 'type' is that in which one thing serves as a symbolic door to another. Type meant a 'seal' in antiquity (such as a signet ring) which left an impression on a soft substance. It 'typed' its character and form onto something else. Usually the type was a reverse image, which left its impression in the wax (or the struck coin) the correct way round. The Scriptures and Fathers often approach the Old Testament texts as 'types' of the coming of Christ. Abraham's acceptance of the sacrifice of his son Isaac is seen as a type of the Passion of Jesus; the rock that gave the Israelites water in the desert is seen as another type of Christ (1 Cor. 10.4). So, the 'obscurities' of the Old Testament narratives are often mined for their typological relevance to the story of salvation in Christ. The early church understands the Christ story as the 'correct presentation' (the image the right way round) of the figurative narrative the older texts suggested more obscurely, though nonetheless in accurate symbolical form. Modern Western biblical exegesis has largely ejected typological understanding from its approach to the Bible, but Orthodoxy retains the ancient usage. It is not only a prophetic manner of interpreting Scripture (which has the authority of Jesus' own usage, and that of the apostles and Fathers) but it is also a profoundly Christian appropriation of the Scriptures which insists that their meaning is not reducible to the historical-chronological (i.e. first meaning taking priority of sense) and this because the Scriptures are first and foremost *eschatological* mysteries which give meaning to history, not simply taking meaning out of history.

Vespers (Greek: Hesperinos; Slavonic: Vechernia).The formal evening prayer of the Orthodox Church.

zeon The hot water that is added to the chalice in the course of the eucharistic liturgy before the communion of the people. It signifies the 'living warmth' of the Spirit's grace, and in some Byzantine writers commemorates the water that flowed from the side of the Lord when he was pierced by a spear.

Select Bibliography

Alfeyev, H., *The Spiritual World of St. Isaac the Syrian*. Kalamazoo: Cistercian Publications, 2000.

—— *Orthodox Witness Today*. Geneva: World Council of Churches Publications, 2005.

Armstrong, A. H. and E. J. B. Fry, *Rediscovering Eastern Christendom: Essays in Commemoration of Dom Bede Winslow*. London: Darton, Longman & Todd, 1963.

Arseniev, N., *Mysticism and the Eastern Church*. London: Student Christian Movement, 1926.

Attwater, D., *The Christian Churches of the East*, vol. 2: *The Churches Not in Communion with Rome*. Milwaukee, Wisc.: Bruce, 1962.

Avila, C., *Ownership: Early Christian Teaching*. New York: Orbis, 1983.

Badcock, F. J., *The History of the Creeds*. London: Society for the Promotion of Christian Knowledge, 1930.

Baddeley, O. and E. Brunner (eds.), *The Monastery of Saint Catherine*. London: St Catherine Foundation, 1996.

Barrett, D. B., G. T. Kurian, and T. M. Johnson (eds.), *World Christian Encyclopedia*, 2nd edn., vol. 1. New York: Oxford University Press, 2001.

Baynes, N. H. and H. Moss, *Byzantium: An Introduction to East Roman Civilization*. Oxford: Clarendon Press, 1961.

Beck, H. G., *Kirche und theologische Literatur im byzantinischen Reich*. Munich: Beck, 1959.

Behr, J., *The Nicene Faith*, vols. 1 and 2. Crestwood, NY: St Vladimir's Seminary Press, 2004.

Behr-Sigel, E., *The Place of the Heart: An Introduction to Orthodox Spirituality*. Torrance, Calif.: Oakwood Publications, 1992.

Bentley-Hart, D., *The Beauty of the Infinite: The Aesthetics of Christian Faith*. Cambridge: Eerdmans, 2003.

Benz, E., *The Eastern Orthodox Church: Its Thought and Life*. Chicago: Aldine, 1963.

Berthold, G. C., 'Maximus the Confessor and the Filioque Controversy', *Studia Patristica*, 18 (1985), 113–18.

Bettenson, H., *The Early Christian Fathers*. London: Oxford University Press, 1963.

—— *The Later Christian Fathers*. London: Oxford University Press, 1970.

Binns, J., *An Introduction to the Christian Orthodox Churches*. Cambridge: Cambridge University Press, 2002.

Birkbeck, W. J., *Russia and the English Church*. London, 1895.

Blane, A. (ed.), *The Ecumenical World of Orthodox Civilization*, vol. 3: *Russia and Orthodoxy. Essays in Honour of Georges Florovsky*. Paris: Mouton, 1974.

Bogolepov, A., *Toward and American Orthodox Church (The Establishment of an Autocephalous Church)*. Crestwood, NY: St Vladimir's Seminary Press, 2001.

Bolshakov, S., *The Foreign Missions of the Russian Orthodox Church*. London, 1943.

Bouteneff, P., *Sweeter than Honey: Orthodox Thinking on Dogma and Truth*. Crestwood, NY: St Vladimir's Seminary Press, 2006.

Bouteneff, V. (trans.), *Father Arseny: Priest, Prisoner, Spiritual Father*. Crestwood, NY: St Vladimir's Seminary Press, 2004.

Bratsiotis, P. B., 'The Fundamental Principles and Main Characteristics of the Orthodox Church', in K. Bridston (ed.), *Orthodoxy: A Faith and Order Dialogue*, Faith and Order Paper No. 30. Geneva: World Council of Churches, Oikoumene Press, 1960, pp. 7–16.

Breck, J., *The Power of the Word in the Worshiping Church*. Crestwood, NY: St Vladimir's Seminary Press, 1986.

—— *The Sacred Gift of Life: Orthodox Christianity and Bio-Ethics*. Crestwood, NY: St Vladimir's Seminary Press, 1998.

—— *Scripture in Tradition: The Bible and its Interpretation in the Orthodox Church*. Crestwood, NY: St Vladimir's Seminary Press, 2001.

Breck, J. and L. Breck, *Stages on Life's Way: Orthodox Thinking on Bio-Ethics*. Crestwood, NY: St Vladimir's Seminary Press, 2005.

Brianchaninov, I., *On the Prayer of Jesus*, trans. L. Moore. London: J. M. Watkins Press, 1965.

Bridston, K. (ed.), *Orthodoxy: A Faith and Order Dialogue*, Faith and Order Paper No. 30. Geneva: World Council of Churches, Oikoumene Press, 1960.

Bulgakov, S., *The Orthodox Church*. London: Centenary Press, 1935; repr. Crestwood, NY: St Vladimir's Seminary Press, 1988.

Burghardt, C., *The Image of God in Man According to St. Cyril of Alexandria*. Washington: Catholic University Press, 1957.

Burns, J. P. and G. Fagin, *The Holy Spirit*, Message of the Fathers of the Church, vol. 3. Wilmington, Del.: Michael Glazier Press, 1988.

Calivas, A. C., 'The Sacramental Life of the Orthodox Church', in F. K. Litsas (ed.), *A Companion to the Greek Orthodox Church*. New York: Greek Orthodox Archdiocese of North America Communications Department, 1984, pp. 31–52, 277–86.

Charanis, P., 'Church–State Relations in the Byzantine Empire as Reflected in the Role of the Patriarch in the Coronation of the Byzantine Emperor', in A. Blane (ed.), *The Ecumenical World of Orthodox Civilization*, vol. 3: *Russia and Orthodoxy. Essays in Honour of Georges Florovsky*. Paris: Mouton, 1974, pp. 78–90.

Chariton (Igumen Chariton of Valamo), *The Art of Prayer: An Orthodox Anthology*, trans. E. Kadloubovsky and E. M. Palmer. London: Faber & Faber, 1966.

Chryssavgis, J., *Repentance and Confession in the Orthodox Church*. Brookline, Mass.: Holy Cross Press, 1990, repr. 1996.

—— *Love, Sexuality, and the Sacrament of Marriage*. Brookline, Mass.: Holy Cross Press, 1996.

—— *Beyond the Shattered Image*. Minnesota: Light and Life Publishing, 1999.

—— *Light through Darkness: The Orthodox Tradition*. London: Darton, Longman & Todd, 2004.

Clark, E. A., *Women in the Early Church*, Message of the Fathers of the Church, vol. 1. Wilmington, Del.: Michael Glazier Press, 1983.

—— *Ascetic Piety and Women's Faith*. Lewiston, NY: Mellen Press, 1986.

Clark, G., *Women in Late Antiquity: Pagan and Christian Lifestyles*. Oxford: Oxford University Press, 1993.

Clément, O., *L'Église Orthodoxe*. Paris: Presses Universitaires de France, 1985.

Cloke, G., *This Female Man of God: Women and Spiritual Power in the Patristic Age, 350–450*. London: Routledge, 1995.

Coniaris, A., *Introducing the Orthodox Church: Its Faith and Life*. Minneapolis: Light and Life Publishing, 1982.

Constantelos, D. J., *The Greek Orthodox Church: Faith, History, Practice*. New York: Seabury Press, 1967.

—— *Byzantine Philanthropy and Social Welfare*. New Brunswick: Rutgers University Press, 1968.

—— (ed.), *Orthodox Theology and Diakonia: Trends and Prospects*. Brookline, Mass.: Hellenic College Press, 1981.

Coomler, D., *The Icon Handbook: A Guide to Understanding Icons and the Liturgy, Symbols, and Practices of the Russian Orthodox Church*. Springfield, Ill.: Templegate, 1995.

Cummings, D. (trans.), *The Pedalion or Rudder of the Orthodox Catholic Church: The Compilation of the Holy Canons by Saints Nicodemus and Agapius*. Chicago: Orthodox Christian Educational Society, 1957; repr. New York, 1983.

Dalmais, H. I., *The Eastern Liturgies*. New York: Hawthorn Press, 1960.

Dalrymple, W., *From the Holy Mountain: A Journey in the Shadow of Byzantium*. New York: Holt & Co., 1998.

Davis, L. D., *The First Seven Ecumenical Councils: Their History and Theology*. Wilmington, Del.: M. Glazier Press, 1987.

de la Taille, P. In *Orientalia Christiana*, 5, 21 Feb. 1926.

de Vinne, M. J., 'The Advocacy of Empty Bellies: Episcopal Representations of the Poor in the Late Empire', Ph.D. dissertation, Stanford University, 1995.

Dearmer, P., R. Burne, W. J. Birkbeck, and H. Frynes-Clinton, *The Russian Church: Lectures on its History, Constitution, Doctrine and Ceremonial*. London: Society for the Promotion of Christian Knowledge, 1917.

Demetrakopoulos, G. H., *Dictionary of Orthodox Theology: A Summary of the Beliefs, Practices and History of the Eastern Orthodox Church*. New York: Philosophical Library, 1964.

Dragas, G. D., *Ecclesiasticus: Introducing Eastern Orthodoxy*. Rollinsford, NH: Orthodox Research Institute, 2004.

Dvornik, F., *The Photian Schism: History and Legend*. Cambridge: Cambridge University Press, 1948.

—— *Early Christian and Byzantine Political Philosophy*, 2 vols. Dumbarton Oaks Studies IX. Cambridge, Mass.: Harvard University Press, 1966.

Elm, S., *Virgins of God: The Making of Asceticism in Late Antiquity*. Oxford: Oxford University Press, 1994.

Eno, R. B., *Teaching Authority in the Early Church*. Message of the Fathers of the Church, vol. 14. Wilmington, Del.: Michael Glazier Press, 1984.

Eutychiadis, P., 'Building an Orthodox Contextual and Liberative Social Ethic', doctoral dissertation, Union Theological Seminary, 2004 (UMI Dissertation Services No. 3124307).

Evdokimov, P., *Les Ages de la vie spirituelle*. Paris: Desclée de Brouwer, 1980.

—— *The Sacrament of Love*. Crestwood, NY: St Vladimir's Seminary Press, 1985.

—— *The Art of the Icon: A Theology of Beauty*. Torrance, Calif.: Oakwood Publications, 1990.

Every, G., *The Byzantine Patriarchate*. London: Society for the Promotion of Christian Knowledge, 1962.

—— *Misunderstandings Between East and West*. Richmond: John Knox Press, 1966.

Farrell, J. P., *St. Photios: The Mystagogy of the Holy Spirit*. Brookline, Mass.: Holy Cross Greek Orthodox Press, 1987.

Fedotov, G. P., *A Treasury of Russian Spirituality*. New York: Sheed & Ward, 1948.

—— *The Russian Religious Mind*. Belmont, Mass.: Nordland, 1975.

Fitzgerald, K. K., *Women Deacons in the Orthodox Church: Called to Holiness and Ministry*. Boston: Holy Cross Press, 1998.

Fitzgerald, T. and P. Bouteneff, *Turn to God, Rejoice in Hope: Orthodox Reflections on the Way to Harare*. Report of the WCC Pre-Assembly Meeting. Geneva: Oikoumene Press, 1998.

Florovsky, G., *Ways of Russian Theology*. Paris, 1937.

—— 'The Ethos of the Orthodox Church', in K. Bridston (ed.), *Orthodoxy: A Faith and Order Dialogue*. Faith and Order Paper No. 30. Geneva: World Council of Churches, Oikoumene Press, 1960, pp. 36–72.

—— *Collected Works*, vol. 1: *Bible, Church, Tradition: An Eastern Orthodox View*. Belmont, Mass.: Nordland, 1972.

—— 'The Elements of Liturgy', in C. G. Patelos, *The Orthodox Church in the Ecumenical Movement: Documents and Statements 1902–1975*. Geneva: World Council of Churches, Oikoumene Press, 1978, pp. 172–82.

Frangopoulos, A., *Our Orthodox Christian Faith*. Athens: Sotir Press, 1985.

French, R. M., *The Eastern Orthodox Church*. London: Hutchinson University Library, 1951.

—— (trans.), *The Way of a Pilgrim and The Pilgrim Continues his Way*. New York: Seabury Press, 1965.

Gaith, J., *La Conception de la liberté chez Grégoire de Nysse*. Paris: Vrin, 1953.

Galtier, P., *Le Saint Esprit en nous d'après les pères grecs*, Rome: Analecta Gregoriana 37, 1946.

Gavin, F., *Some Aspects of Contemporary Greek Orthodox Thought*. Milwaukee: Morehouse Publishing, 1923.

Geanokoplos, D. J., *Byzantium: Church, Society, and Civilization Seen through Contemporary Eyes*. Chicago: University of Chicago Press, 1984 (florilegium of ancient texts).

Gill, J., *The Council of Florence*. Cambridge, Mass.: Harvard University Press, 1959.

Gillét, L. [a monk of the Eastern Church], *Orthodox Spirituality*. London: Society for the Promotion of Christian Knowledge, 1945.

Glubokovsky, N. N., *Orthodoxy in its Essence* (Russian); English digest in *The Constructive Quarterly*, 1/2 (1913).

Gouillard, J., *Le Synodikon de l'Orthodoxie: Édition et commentaire*, Travaux et Mémoires II. Paris: Centre francais d'études byzantines, 1967.

Gross, J., *La Divinisation du chrétien d'après les pères grecs*. Paris: Gabalda, 1938; published in English translation as *The Divinization of the Christian According to the Greek Fathers*, trans. P. Onica. Anaheim, Calif.: A & C Press, 2002.

Guroian, V., *Incarnate Love: Essays in Orthodox Ethics*. Notre Dame, Ind.: University of Notre Dame Press, 1987.

—— *Ethics after Christendom: Toward an Ecclesial Christian Ethic*. Grand Rapids: Eerdmans, 1994.

Hapgood, I. F., *Service Book of the Holy Orthodox Catholic Apostolic Church*. New York: Association Press, 1922.

Harakas, S., 'Creed and Confession in the Orthodox Church', in J. Meyendorff and J. McLelland (eds.), *The New Man: An Orthodox and Reformed Dialogue*. New York: Agora Books, 1973, pp. 40–62.

—— *For the Health of Body and Soul: An Eastern Orthodox Introduction to Bioethics*. Brookline, Mass.: Holy Cross Press, 1980.

—— (a) *Let Mercy Abound: Social Concern in the Greek Orthodox Church*. Brookline, Mass.: Holy Cross Press, 1983.

—— (b) *Toward Transfigured Life: The Theoria of Eastern Orthodox Ethics*. Minneapolis: Light and Life Publishing, 1983.

—— *Health and Medicine in the Eastern Orthodox Tradition: Faith, Liturgy, and Wholeness*. New York: Crossroad Press, 1990.

—— *Living the Faith: The Praxis of Eastern Orthodox Ethics*. Minneapolis: Light and Life Publishing, 1992.

Harrison, V., 'The Feminine Man in Late Antique Ascetic Piety', *Union Theological Seminary Quarterly Review*, 48/3–4 (1994), 49–71.

446

Haugh, R., *Photius and the Carolingians: The Trinitarian Controversy*. Belmont, Mass.: Nordland, 1975.

Hauser, A. and D. F. Watson (eds.), *A History of Biblical Interpretation*, vol. 1: *The Ancient Period*. Grand Rapids: Eerdmans, 2003.

Hausherr, I., *The Name of Jesus*. Kalamazoo: Cistercian Publications, 1978.

Henry, P., *Les Églises de la Moldavie du nord: Des origines à la fin du XVIè siècle. Architecture et peinture*. Paris: E. Leroux, 1930.

Holman, S. R., *The Hungry Are Dying: Beggars and Bishops in Roman Cappadocia*. Oxford: Oxford University Press, 2001.

Huntington, S. P., *The Clash of Civilisations and the Remaking of World Order*. New York: Touchstone, 1997.

Hussey, J. *The Byzantine World*. London: Hutchinson University Library, 1951.

—— *Church and Learning in the Byzantine Empire. 867–1185*. New York: Russell & Russell, 1963.

Janin, R., *Les Églises orientales et les rites orientaux*. Paris: Letouzey, 1955.

Joanta, S., *Romania: Its Hesychast Culture and Tradition*. California: St Xenia Skete Press, 1992.

Joseph the Elder, *Monastic Wisdom: The Letters of Elder Joseph the Hesychast*. Florence, Ariz.: St Antony's Greek Monastery, 1999.

Jugie, M., *Theologia dogmatica Christianorum orientalium ab Ecclesia catholica dissidentium*, vols. 1–4. Paris: Letouzey, 1926–35.

—— *L'Unité de l'Église*, vol. 1: *Rencontres avec l'Occident Chrétien*. Chauny: Éditions Baticle, 1946.

Kadel, A., *Matrology: A Bibliography of Writings by Christian Women from the 1st to 15th Centuries*. New York: Continuum Press, 1982.

Kadloubovsky, E. and G. Palmer, *Writings from the Philokalia on the Prayer of the Heart*. London: Faber & Faber, 1967.

Karakatsanis, A. (curator), *Treasures of Mount Athos*. Thessaloniki: Museum of Byzantine Culture, 1997.

Kidd, B. J., *The Churches of Eastern Christendom from AD 451 to the Present Time*. London: Faith Press, 1927.

King, A. A., *The Rites of Eastern Christendom*. Rome: Catholic Book Agency, 1947.

Kontzevitch, I. M., *The Acquisition of the Holy Spirit in Ancient Russia*. St Platina, Calif.: Herman of Alaska Brotherhood, 1988.

Kovalevsky, P., *L'Unité de l'Église*, vol. 2: *Exposition de la Foi Catholique Orthodoxe*. Nancy: Humblot, 1943.

Kowalczyk, J., *An Orthodox View of Abortion*. Minneapolis: Light and Life Publishing, 1979.

Krivocheine, B., *In the Light of Christ. St. Symeon the New Theologian: Life, Spiritualiy, Doctrine*. Crestwood, NY: St Vladimir's Seminary Press, 1986.

Lang, J., *Ministers of Grace: Women in the Early Church*. Slough: St Paul, 1989.

Laporte, J., *The Role of Women in Early Christianity*. Lewiston, NY: Mellen, 1982.

LeGuillou, M. J., *The Spirit of Eastern Orthodoxy*. New York: Hawthorn Books, 1962.

Line, J., *The Doctrine of the Christian Ministry*. London: Lutterworth Press, 1959.

Litsas, F. K. (ed.), *A Companion to the Greek Orthodox Church*. New York: Greek Orthodox Archdiocese of North America, Communications Department, 1984.

Lossky, V., *The Mystical Theology of the Eastern Church*. London: James Clarke, 1957.

—— *The Vision of God*. London: Faith Press, 1963.

—— *In the Image and Likeness of God*, 2nd edn. London: Faith Press, 1975.

—— *Orthodox Theology: An Introduction*. Crestwood, NY: St Vladimir's Seminary Press, 1978.

Louth, A., *Greek East and Latin West: The Church AD 681–1071*. Crestwood, NY: St Vladimir's Seminary Press, 2007.

McGuckin, J. A. (a) 'The Sign of the Prophet: The Significance of Meals in the Doctrine of Jesus', *Scripture Bulletin*, 16/2 (1986), 35–40.

—— (b) *St. Gregory Nazianzen: Selected Poems*. Oxford: SLG Press, 1986.

—— *The Transfiguration of Christ in Scripture and Tradition.* Lewiston, NY: Mellen, 1987.

—— 'Sacrifice and Atonement: An Investigation into the Attitude of Jesus of Nazareth Towards Cultic Sacrifice', in *Remembering for the Future*, vol. 1. Oxford: Pergamon Press, 1988, pp. 648–61.

—— 'The Concept of Orthodoxy in Ancient Christianity', *Patristic and Byzantine Review*, 8/1 (1989), 5–23.

—— (a) 'Perceiving Light from Light in Light: The Trinitarian Theology of St. Gregory the Theologian', *Greek Orthodox Theological Review*, 39/1–2 (1994) [commemorative volume for St Gregory's sixteenth centenary], 7–32.

—— (b) *St. Cyril of Alexandria and the Christological Controversy: Its History, Theology, and Texts.* Leiden: Brill, 1994; repr. Crestwood, NY: St Vladimir's Seminary Press, 2004.

—— 'The Vision of God in St. Gregory Nazianzen', *Studia Patristica*, 32 (1996), 145–52.

—— 'Eschaton and Kerygma: The Future of the Past in the Present Kairos. The Concept of Living Tradition in Orthodox Theology', *St Vladimir's Theological Quarterly*, 42/3–4 (1998), 225–71.

—— (a) 'The Prayer of the Heart in Patristic and Early Byzantine Tradition', in. P. Allen, W. Mayer, and L. Cross (eds.), *Prayer and Spirituality in the Early Church*, vol. 2. Queensland: Catholic University of Australia Press, 1999, pp. 69–108.

—— (b) 'The Enigma of the Christ Icon Panel at St. Catherine's at Sinai: A Call for Reappraisal', *Union Theological Seminary Quarterly Review*, 52/3–4 (1999), 29–47.

—— (a) *St. Gregory of Nazianzus: An Intellectual Biography.* New York: SVS Press, 2001.

—— (b) *Standing In God's Holy Fire: The Spiritual Tradition of Byzantium.* London: Darton, Longman & Todd/New York: Orbis-Maryknoll, 2001.

—— (a) 'Il lungo cammino verso Calcedonia [The Long Road to Chalcedon]: The Unfolding Nexus of Christological Definition from Origen to Dioscorus', in A. Ducay (ed.), *Il Concilio di Calcedonia 1550 anni dopo.* Rome: Libreria Editrice Vaticana, 2002, pp. 13–41.

—— (b) *The Book of Mystical Chapters: Meditations on the Soul's Ascent from the Desert Fathers and Other Early Christian Contemplatives.* Boston: Shambhala Press, 2002.

—— 'Biblical Hermeneutics in Patristic Perspective: The Tradition of Orthodoxy', in T. Stylianopoulos (ed.), *Sacred Text and Interpretation: Perspectives in Orthodox Biblical Studies. Papers in Honor of Prof. Savas Agourides* (Brookline, Mass.: Holy Cross Press, 2005) (= *Greek Orthodox Theological Review*, 47/1–4 (2004), 293–324).

—— 'The Legacy of the Thirteenth Apostle: Origins of the East-Christian Conceptions of Church–State Relation', *St. Vladimir's Theological Quarterly*, 47/3–4 (2003), 251–88.

—— (a) *The Westminster Handbook to Patristic Theology.* Louisville, Ky.: Westminster John Knox Press, 2004.

—— (b) *The Westminster Handbook to Origen.* Louisville, Ky.: Westminster John Knox Press, 2004.

—— (a) 'Origen and the Mystery of the Pre-existent Church', *International Journal for the Study of the Church*, 6/3 (2005), 207–22.

—— (b) 'A Neglected Masterpiece of the Christian Mystical Tradition: The Hymns of Divine Eros by the Byzantine Poet Symeon the New Theologian (949–1022)', *Spiritus*, 5 (2005), 182–202.

—— (c) 'Orthodoxy and Western Christianity: The Original European Culture War?', in V. Hotchkiss and P. Henry (eds.), *Orthodoxy and Western Culture. Festschrift for Jaroslav Pelikan at 80.* Crestwood, NY: St Vladimir's Seminary Press, 2005, pp. 85–107.

—— (a) 'Christian Spirituality in Byzantium and the East (600–1700)', in A. Holder (ed.), *The Blackwell Companion to Christian Spirituality.* Oxford: Blackwell, 2006, pp. 90–105.

—— (b) 'Non-Violence and Peace Traditions in Early and Eastern Christianity', in K. K. Kuriakose (ed.), *Religion, Terrorism and Globalization: Non-Violence – A New Agenda.* New York: Nova Science Press, 2006.

—— (c) 'Deification in Greek Patristic Thought: The Cappadocian Fathers' Strategic Adaptation of a Tradition', in M. Christensen and J. Wittung (eds.), *Partakers of the Divine Nature: The History and Development of Deification in the Christian Tradition.* Madison, NJ: Farleigh Dickinson University Press, 2006.

McNamara, J. A., 'Muffled Voices: The Lives of Consecrated Women in the 4th C', in J. A. Nichols and L. T. Shank (eds.), *Medieval Religious Women: Distant Echoes.* Kalamazoo: Cistercian Publications, 1984, pp. 11–29.

Mansi, G. D., et al., *Sacrorum conciliorum nova et amplissima collectio*, 53 vols. Florence, 1759–1927.

Mascall, E. L. (ed.), *The Mother of God.* London: Dacre Press, 1949.

Mother Mary and K. Ware (trans.), *The Festal Menaion.* London: Faber & Faber, 1969.

—— *The Lenten Triodion.* London: Faber & Faber, 1978.

Meyendorff, J., *The Orthodox Church: Its Past and its Role in the World Today.* London: Darton, Longman & Todd, 1962.

—— *A Study of Gregory Palamas.* London: Faith Press, 1964.

—— *Orthodoxy and Catholicity.* New York: Sheed & Ward, 1966.

—— *Christ in Eastern Christian Thought.* Washington, DC: Corpus Books, 1969.

—— (a) *Byzantine Theology.* New York: Fordham University Press, 1974.

—— (b) 'Free Will in St. Maximus', in A. Blane (ed.), *The Ecumenical World of Orthodox Civilization*, vol. 3: *Russia and Orthodoxy. Essays in Honour of Georges Florovsky.* Paris: Mouton, 1974, pp. 71–5.

—— *Marriage: An Orthodox Perspective.* New York: St Vladimir's Seminary Press, 1975.

—— *Living Tradition: Orthodox Witness in the Contemporary World.* Crestwood, NY: St Vladimir's Seminary Press, 1978.

—— *Byzantium and the Rise of Russia.* Cambridge: Cambridge University Press, 1981.

—— *Imperial Unity and Christian Divisions.* Crestwood, NY: St Vladimir's Seminary Press, 1989.

—— *St. Gregory Palamas and Orthodox Spirituality.* Crestwood, NY: St Vladimir's Seminary Press, 1998.

Meyendorff, J. and J. McLelland, *The New Man: An Orthodox and Reformed Dialogue.* New York: Agora Books., 1973.

Moore, L., *Sacred Tradition in the Orthodox Church.* Minneapolis: Light and Life Publishing, 1984.

Motovilov, N., 'Conversation of St Seraphim on the Aim of Christian Life', in *A Wonderful Revelation to the World.* New York: Orthodox Press for the Jordanville Seminary, 1953, pp. 23–5.

Newman, J. H., 'On St. Cyril's Formula: Mia Physis Sesarkomene', in *Tracts Theological and Ecclesiastical.* London, 1874, pp. 283–336.

Nissiotis, N. A., 'An Orthodox View of Modern Trends in Evangelism', in A. Blane (ed.), *The Ecumenical World of Orthodox Civilization*, vol. 3: *Russia and Orthodoxy. Essays in Honour of Georges Florovsky.* Paris: Mouton, 1974, pp. 181–92.

Norris, F. W., *Faith Gives Fullness to Reasoning: The Five Theological Orations of Gregory Nazianzen*, with introd. and commentary by F. W. Norris, trans. L. Wickham and F. Williams. Leiden: Brill, 1991.

Oakley, A., *The Orthodox Liturgy.* London: Mowbray, 1958.

Obolensky, D., *Byzantine Commonwealth: Eastern Europe 500–1453.* London: Weidenfeld & Nicolson, 1971.

Onasch, K. and A. M. Schnieper, *Icons: The Fascination and the Reality.* New York: Riverside Books, 1997.

Pacini, A. (ed.), *L'Ortodossia nella nuova Europa: dinamiche storiche e prospettive.* Rome: Fondazione Giovanni Agnelli, 2003.

449

Palmer, G., P. Sherrard, and K. Ware (trans.), *The Philokalia. The Complete Text: Compiled by St. Nikodimos of the Holy Mountain and St. Makarios of Corinth.* London, Faber & Faber, 1979.

Palmer, P. F., *Mary in the Documents of the Church.* Westminster, Md.: Newman Press, 1952.

Panagopoulos, J., *He Hermeneia Tes Agias Graphes Sten Ekklesia Ton Pateron,* vol. 1. Athens: Akritas Press, 1994.

Papademetriou. G., *Essays on Orthodox Christian–Jewish Relations.* Bristol, Ind.: Wyndham Hall Press, 1990.

Papadopoulos, G., 'The Revelatory Character of the NT and Holy Tradition in the Orthodox Church', in A. J. Philippou (ed.) *The Orthodox Ethos.* Oxford: Stoudion Publications, 1964, pp. 98–111.

Papastephanou, E., *Belief and Practice in the Orthodox Church.* New York: Minos Press, 1965.

Paraskevas, J. E. and F. Reinstein, *The Eastern Orthodox Church: A Brief History.* Washington, DC: El Greco Press, 1969.

Patelos, C. G., *The Orthodox Church in the Ecumenical Movement: Documents and Statements 1902–1975.* Geneva: World Council of Churches, Oikoumene Press, 1978.

Pelikan, J., *The Christian Tradition: A History of the Development of Doctrine,* vol. 1: *The Emergence of the Catholic Tradition.* Chicago: University of Chicago Press, 1971.

—— *The Christian Tradition: A History of the Development of Doctrine, vol. 2: The Spirit of Eastern Christendom (600–1700).* Chicago: University of Chicago Press, 1974.

—— *Mary through the Centuries: Her Place in the History of Culture.* New Haven: Yale University Press, 1996.

Pentiuc, E., 'A Christological Interpretation of the Old Testament: A Critical Review', *Greek Orthodox Theological Review,* 47/1–4 (2002), 37–54.

Percival, H. R., *The Seven Ecumenical Councils of the Undivided Church,* vol. 14: *The Nicene and Post Nicene Fathers.* Oxford: James Parker and Sons, 1900.

Phan, P. (ed.), *Social Thought.* Message of the Fathers of the Church, vol. 20. Wilmington, Del.: Michael Glazier Press, 1984.

—— *Grace and the Human Condition.* Message of the Fathers of the Church, vol. 15. Wilmington, Del.: Michael Glazier Press, 1988.

Plekon, M., *Living Icons.* Notre Dame, Ind.: University of Notre Dame Press, 2002.

Plekon, M. and S. E. Hinlicky, *Discerning the Signs of the Times: The Vision of Elisabeth Behr-Sigel.* Crestwood, NY: St Vladimir's Seminary Press, 2001.

Pomazansky, M., *Orthodox Dogmatic Theology.* Platina, Calif.: St Herman of Alaska Brotherhood Press, 1997.

Popovitch, J., *Philosophie orthodoxe de la vérité: Dogmatique de l'Église Orthodoxe.* Paris: Age d'Homme, 1997.

Prestige, G. L., *God in Patristic Thought.* London: Society for the Promotion of Christian Knowledge, 1952.

Queré-Jaulmes, F., *Riches et pauvres dans l'Église ancienne.* Paris: Grasset, 1962.

Raes, A., *Le Mariage dans les Églises d'Orient.* Chevetogne: Monastery of the Holy Cross, 1958.

Ramsay, B., 'Christian Attitudes to Poverty and Wealth', in I. Hazlitt (ed.), *Early Christianity.* London: Routledge, 1991, pp. 260f.

Ritzer, K., *Le Mariage dans dans les Églises chrétiennes du Ier au XIIème siècle.* Paris: Beauchesne, 1970.

Rogers, G., *Apostolic Succession.* Mount Hermon, Calif.: Conciliar Press, 1989.

Romanides, J. S., *To Propatorikon Hamartima* [The Ancestral Sin]. Athens: Zoe, 1957.

—— 'St. Cyril's "One Physis or Hypostasis of God the Logos Incarnate" ', *Greek Orthodox Theological Review,* 10 (1964–5), 82–107.

—— *Franks, Romans, Feudalism and Doctrine: An Interplay Between Theology and Society.* Brookline, Mass.: Holy Cross Press, 1981.

Rondet, H., *Introduction à l'étude de la théologie du mariage.* Paris: Le Puy, 1960.

450

Roques, R., *L'Univers dionysien: Structure hierarchique du monde selon le pseudo-Denys*. Paris: Aubier, 1954.

Ruether, R., 'Misogynism and Virginal Feminism in the Fathers of the Church', in R. Ruether (ed.), *Religion and Sexism: Images of Woman in the Jewish and Christian Traditions*. New York: Simon & Schuster, 1974.

Runciman, S., *The Eastern Schism*. Oxford: Clarendon Press, 1956.

—— *Byzantine Civilisation*. London: Edward Arnold, 1959.

—— *The Great Church in Captivity*. Cambridge: Cambridge University Press, 1968.

Russell, N., *The Doctrine of Deification in the Greek Patristic Tradition*. Oxford: Oxford University Press, 2004.

Salaville, A., *An Introduction in the Study of Eastern Liturgies*. London: Sands & Co., 1938.

Schmemann, A., *Sacraments and Orthodoxy*. New York: Herder & Herder, 1965.

—— *Introduction to Liturgical Theology*. London: Faith Press, 1966.

Schwartz, E., *Acta Conciliorum Oecumenicorum*, 8 vols. Berlin: De Gruyter, 1914–84.

Sendler, E., *The Icon: Image of the Invisible*. Torrance, Calif.: Oakwood Publications, 1988.

Sheerin, D. J., *The Eucharist*. Message of the Fathers of the Church, vol. 15. Wilmington, Del.: Michael Glazier Press, 1986.

Sherrard, P., *The Greek East and the Latin West*. London: Oxford University Press, 1959.

—— *Athos: The Holy Mountain*. Photographs by Takis Zervoulakos. New York: Woodstock, 1985.

Shewring, W., *Rich and Poor in Christian Tradition*. London: Burnes, Oates & Washbourne, 1948.

Shlenov, V. and L. Petrushina, *Pravoslavie i Ekologii*. Otdel religioznogo obrazovanii i katekhizatsii. Moscow: Moskovskii Patriarkhat, 1999.

Simonetti, M., *Biblical Interpretation in the Early Church*. Edinburgh: T. & T. Clark, 1994.

Solovyov, V., *The Meaning of Love*. New York: Lindisfarne Press, 1985.

Staniloae, D. *The Experience of God: Revelation and the Knowledge of the Triune God*. Orthodox Dogmatic Theology, vol. 1. Brookline, Mass.: Holy Cross Press, repr. 1998.

—— *The Experience of God: The World: Creation and Deification*. Orthodox Dogmatic Theology, vol. 2. Brookline, Mass.: Holy Cross Press, 2005.

Stanton, G. N., *Women in the Earliest Churches*. Cambridge: Cambridge University Press, 1988.

Stebbing, N., *Bearers of the Spirit: Spiritual Fatherhood in Romanian Orthodoxy*. Kalamazoo: Cistercian Publications, 2003.

Stewart-Sykes, A., *The Lamb's High Feast: Melito, Peri Pascha and the Quarto-Deciman Paschal Liturgy at Sardis*. Leiden: Brill, 1998.

Stylianopoulos, T., *The New Testament: An Orthodox Perspective*, vol. 1: *Scripture, Tradition, Hermeneutics*. Brookline, Mass.: Holy Cross Press, 1997.

—— *Christ in Our Midst*. Brookline, Mass.: Department of Religious Education, Greek Orthodox Archdiocese of America, 1976.

Swift, L. J., *The Early Fathers on War and Military Service*. Message of the Fathers of the Church, vol. 19. Wilmington. Del.: Michael Glazier Press, 1983.

Taft, R., *The Byzantine Rite: A Short History*. Collegeville. Minn.: Liturgical Press, 1992.

Talbot-Rice, D., *Art of the Byzantine Era*. London: Thames & Hudson, 1963.

Tanner, N. P., *Decrees of the Ecumenical Councils*. London: Sheed & Ward, 1990.

—— *The Councils of the Church: A Short History*. New York: Crossroad, 2001.

Temple, R., *Icons: Divine Beauty*. London: Saqui Books, 2004.

Theodorou, E., 'L'Institution des diaconesses dans l'Eglise Orthodoxe', *Contacts*, 146 (1989), 2.

Thunberg, L., *Microcosm and Mediator: The Theological Anthropology of Maximus the Confessor*. Lund: Gleerup, 1965.

Trakatellis, D., *Hoi Pateres Hermenevoun: Apopseis Paterikes Biblikes Hermeneias*. Athens: Apostolike Diakonia, 1996.

451

Tsirpanlis, C. N., *Introduction to Eastern Patristic Thought and Orthodox Theology.* Collegeville, Minn.: Liturgical Press, 1991.

Van der Meer, F. and C. Mohrmann, *Atlas of the Early Christian World.* Edinburgh: Nelson & Sons, 1958.

Vischer, L., *Spirit of God: Spirit of Christ: Ecumenical Reflections on the Filioque Controversy* London and Geneva: World Council of Churches, 1981.

Visser 'T Hooft, W., *Anglo-Catholicism and Orthodoxy: A Protestant View.* London: Student Christian Movement, 1933.

Ware, K., *The Power of the Name: The Jesus Prayer in Orthodox Spirituality.* Oxford: SLG Press, 1974.

—— *The Orthodox Way.* London: Mowbray, 1979.

Ware, T. [Bishop Kallistos], *The Orthodox Church.* London: Penguin Books, 1987.

Webster, A. F. C., *The Price of Prophecy: Orthodox Churches on Peace, Freedom, and Security.* Grand Rapids: Eerdmans, 1995.

Weitzmann, K., *The Monastery of Saint Catherine's at Sinai: The Icons.* Princeton, NJ: Princeton University Press, 1976.

—— *The Icon: Holy Images – The Sixth to the Fourteenth Centuries.* New York: Braziller, 1978.

Weitzmann, K., M. Chatzidakis, and S. Radojcic. *Icons.* New York: Alpine Fine Arts, 1980.

Wellesz, E., *A History of Byzantine Music and Hymnography.* Oxford: Clarendon Press, 1961.

Wheeler, E. P., *Dorotheus of Gaza: Discourses and Sayings.* Kalamazoo: Cistercian Publications, 1977.

Woodill, J., *The Fellowship of Life: Virtue Ethics and Orthodox Christianity.* Washington, DC: Georgetown University Press, 1998.

Woodward, G. R., *The Most Holy Mother of God in the Songs of the Eastern Church.* London: Faith Press, 1919.

Wybrew, H., *Orthodox Liturgy: The Development of the Eucharistic Liturgy in the Byzantine Rite.* London: Society for the Promotion of Christian Knowledge, 1989.

Yannaras, C., *The Freedom of Morality.* Crestwood, NY: St Vladimir's Seminary Press, 1984.

—— *Elements of Faith: An Introduction to Orthodox Theology.* Edinburgh: T. & T. Clark, 1991.

Yarnold, E., *The Awe-Inspiring Rites of Initiation: Baptismal Homilies of the Fourth Century.* Slough: St Paul Publications, 1972.

Yiannoulatos, A., 'Byzantine and Contemporary Greek Orthodox Approaches to Islam', *Journal of Ecumenical Studies,* 33/4 (1996), 512–28.

—— *Facing the World: Orthodox Christian Essays on Global Concerns.* Crestwood, NY: St Vladimir's Seminary Press, 2003.

Zankov, S., *The Eastern Orthodox Church.* Milwaukee: Morehouse Publishing, 1929.

Zernov, N., (a) *Orthodox Encounter: The Christian East and the Ecumenical Movement.* London: James Clarke, 1961.

—— (b) *Eastern Christendom.* New York: Weidenfeld & Nicolson, 1961.

Ziakas, G., 'The Ecumenical Patriarchate of Constantinople and the Dialogue with Islam', in *Phanari: 400 Years.* Istanbul: Publication of the Ecumenical Patriarchate, 2000, pp. 575–713 (Greek text); pp. 714–25 (English text).

Zizioulas, J., 'The Eucharistic Community and the Catholicity of the Church', in J. Meyendorff and J. McLelland (eds.), *The New Man: An Orthodox and Reformed Dialogue.* New York: Agora Books, 1973, pp. 107–31.

—— *Being as Communion: Studies in Personhood and the Church.* London: Darton, Longman & Todd, 1985.

—— *Eucharist, Bishop, Church: The Unity of the Church in the Eucharist and the Bishop, during the First Three Centuries,* trans E. Theokritoff. Brookline, Mass.: Holy Cross Press, 2001.

Index

Page numbers in bold denote entries in the Glossary.